C000219360

CHOICE, NOT FATE

≡ CHOICE, NOT FATE ≡

The life and times of Trevor Manuel

PIPPA GREEN

PENGUIN BOOKS

PENGUIN BOOKS

Published by the Penguin Group
Penguin Books (South Africa) (Pty) Ltd, 24 Sturdee Avenue, Rosebank, Johannesburg 2196,
    South Africa
Penguin Group (USA) Inc, 375 Hudson Street, New York, New York 10014, USA
Penguin Group (Canada), 90 Eglinton Avenue East, Suite 700, Toronto, Ontario,
Canada M4P 2Y3 (a division of Pearson Penguin Canada Inc)
Penguin Books Ltd, 80 Strand, London WC2R 0RL, England
Penguin Ireland, 25 St Stephen's Green, Dublin 2, Ireland (a division of Penguin Books Ltd)
Penguin Group (Australia), 250 Camberwell Road, Camberwell, Victoria 3124, Australia
(a division of Pearson Australia Group Pty Ltd)
Penguin Books India Pvt Ltd, 11 Community Centre, Panchsheel Park, New Delhi – 110 017,
    India
Penguin Group (NZ), 67 Apollo Drive, Mairangi Bay, Auckland 1310, New Zealand
(a division of Pearson New Zealand Ltd)

Penguin Books (South Africa) (Pty) Ltd, Registered Offices:
24 Sturdee Avenue, Rosebank, Johannesburg 2196, South Africa

www.penguinbooks.co.za

First published by Penguin Books (South Africa) (Pty) Ltd 2008

ISBN 978 0 143 02533 7

Typeset by CJH Design in 10/15 pt Zapf Calligraphic
Cover designed by Flame Design, Cape Town
Printed and bound by Paarl Print, Cape Town

In memory of my mother Molly

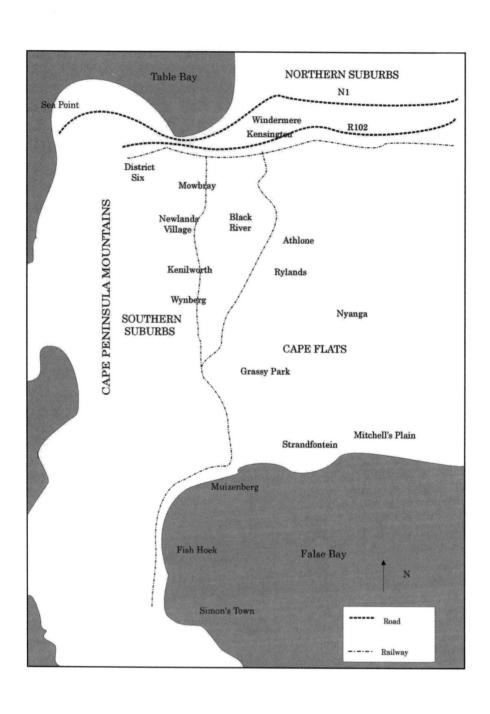

Contents

Acronyms and Abbreviations

ANC	African National Congress
APDUSA	African People's Democratic Union of Southern Africa
APO	African People's Organisation
ASA	African Students' Association
ASUSA	African Students' Union of South Africa
AZAPO	Azanian People's Organisation
BEE	Black Economic Empowerment
CAAA	Comprehensive Anti-Apartheid Act (United States)
CAC	Coloured Advisory Council
CAD	Coloured Affairs Department
CAHAC	The Cape Areas Housing Action Committee
CLOWU	Clothing Workers' Union
Codesa	Convention for a Democratic South Africa
COSAS	Congress of South African Students
COSATU	Congress of South African Trade Unions
CPC	(South African) Coloured People's Congress
CRC	Coloured Representative Council
DBAC	Disorderly Bills Action Committee
DCC	Duty Credit Certificate
DEP	Department of Economic Planning
DHAC	Durban Housing Action Committee
DIP	(ANC) Department of Information and Publicity
DRC	Dutch Reformed Church
EPG	(Commonwealth) Eminent Persons Group
FCWU	Food and Canning Workers' Union
FOSATU	Federation of South African Trade Unions
GATT	General Agreement on Tariffs and Trade

GDP	Gross Domestic Product
GEAR	Growth, Employment and Redistribution Plan
GEIS	Generalised Export Incentive Scheme
GWU	General Workers' Union
HPAE	High Performing Asian Economies
ICU	Industrial and Commercial Workers' Union
IFP	Inkatha Freedom Party
IMF	International Monetary Fund
JSE	Johannesburg Stock Exchange
KAGRO	Kensington Action Group
MDM	Mass Democratic Movement
MIDP	Motor Industries Development Plan
MK	Umkhonto we Sizwe
MWASA	Metal Workers' Union of South Africa
NEC	National Executive Committee (of the ANC)
NEDLAC	National Economic Development and Labour Council
NEF	National Economic Forum
NEUM	Non-European Unity Movement
NGK	Nederduitse Gereformeerde Kerk
NGO	Non-governmental Organisation
NIC	Natal Indian Congress
NLL	National Liberation League
NP	National Party
NPA	National Prosecuting Authority
NWC	National Working Committee (of the ANC)
OAU	Organisation of African Unity
PAC	Pan Africanist Congress
PEBCO	Post Elizabeth Civic Organisation

RDP	Reconstruction and Development Programme
SAAWU	South African Allied Workers' Union
SACC	South African Council of Churches
SACP	South African Communist Party
SACTU	South African Congress of Trade Unions
SACTWU	South African Clothing and Textile Workers' Union
SACU	Southern African Customs Union
SAIC	South African Indian Council
SARS	South African Revenue Service
SASO	South African Students' Organisation
SBDC	Small Business Development Corporation
SRC	Students' Representative Council
TEPA	Teachers and Educational Professional Association
TIC	Transvaal Indian Congress
TLSA	Teachers' League of South Africa
TRAC	Train Apartheid Resistance Committee
TRC	Truth and Reconciliation Commission
TUCSA	Trade Union Council of South Africa
UBJ	Union of Black Journalists
UCT	University of Cape Town
Unisa	University of South Africa
URC	Umbrella Rentals Committee
UWC	University of the Western Cape
WARC	World Alliance of Reformed Churches
WASA	The Black Writers' Association of South Africa
WCCA	Western Cape Civic Association
WEF	World Economic Forum
Wits	University of the Witwatersrand
YCW	Young Christian Workers

Acknowledgements

T HIS BOOK HAS BEEN more than three years in the making. It could not have happened without the support and help of a wide circle of people.

Non-fiction writing, by its nature, is an expensive and sometimes lonely business. A narration has to be guided by facts and figures, found and checked. That can be time consuming and costly. So I am especially grateful to those who believed enough in this project to support it both morally and financially.

I am deeply indebted to the Wits Institute of Social and Economic Research (WISER) which not only gave me financial and office support during the first difficult six months of this project, but also provided a collegial and intellectually stimulating home to work from. I especially valued the intellectual insight and collegiality of WISER director Debbie Posel, Jonathan Hyslop, who made me think about biography, and of Achille Mbembe and Sarah Nuttall as well as Najibha Deshmukh, who helped make my sojourn at WISER congenial and productive. The Academic and Non-Fiction Authors' Association of South Africa – a worthy cause in South Africa – also helped support this project with a grant for which I am deeply grateful. Non-fiction writing is still poorly supported in South Africa, and my hope is that ANFASA's collective pens will grow in influence and strength.

I am also grateful to Vincent Maphai of Billiton, Michael Spicer, formerly of Anglo American, Morakile Shuenyane of Total, and Rudolf Gouws of Rand Merchant Bank for supporting requests to their public affairs or foundation funds to help fund this project, and to Dick Foxton for advice on how to raise funds.

Dines Giwala and Jakes Gerwel, through South African Airways, helped me fund some of the necessary research trips to Cape Town. I am also grateful for Dines's advice and support at various stages through this project.

There were people who were generous with their time and knowledge. Sean Field of the Centre for Popular Memory at the University of Cape Town helped me gain access to the fascinating oral history interviews that record the tragedy of the forced removals of Cape Town and readily shared his expert knowledge of the subject. The librarians and staff of the Mayibuye

Archives at the University of the Western Cape, the African Studies Library and the Centre for Popular Memory at the University of Cape Town, and the Historical Papers collection at the William Cullen Library at the University of the Witwatersrand, similarly went out of their way to help me locate documents and sources.

I was also fortunate enough to be appointed a visiting professor to the Council of Humanities at Princeton University while I was in the middle of this research. Although the course I taught there had little to do with the book, I nevertheless had access to Princeton's extraordinary library and I benefited from the collegiality and encouragement of the Council's executive director Carol Rigolot and all the staff at the Council. Cornell West, one of the foremost academics and thinkers in the United States, also made helpful suggestions about the reading I should do to understand the stamp that slavery leaves in history.

My research assistant Gerard Ralphs dug up a plethora of interesting documents that have formed a backbone for the historical research of this project. I thank him for his assiduousness and reliability at every step of this project, and for playing the central role in compiling the family tree.

Special thanks to Benny Gool, who generously allowed me to use his photographs. To any reporter who worked in Cape Town in the 1980s and 90s, Benny was a familiar sight, bold and unnerved by the constant physical danger in which he worked. The value of his work outlasts those years and has helped a country come to terms with its past.

My editor Pam Thornley corrected errors, asked the right questions and was a constant source of support and encouragement. Her extraordinary calm, rationality and efficiency kept me going in the last difficult weeks. Thanks also to Alison Lowry and her team at Penguin for their professionalism and belief in and support of this book. That, too, sustained me.

A special tribute needs to be paid to the team at the Treasury. The senior officials I interviewed – and badgered – were unfailingly helpful and maintained, for most of the time, a depth of courtesy that was more than I could have hoped for. I would especially like to thank Lesetja Kganyago, Andrew Donaldson, Kuben Naidoo, Ismail Momoniat, Thoraya Pandy, and Phakamani Hadebe. The ministerial staff were similarly gracious and helpful: Gavin Meeth, Ashford Smith, Reg Moodley, Shahid Khan, Dumisa Jele, and especially the incomparable Patti Smith – to all of them I owe a deep gratitude for the way they eased my path through the bureaucratic corridors of power in Cape

Town and Pretoria, and provided permits, freshly brewed coffee, friendship and insights. Pravin Gordhan from the South African Revenue Service, and Pali Lehola from Statistics South Africa – the outriders of the Treasury – were invaluable and generous with their assistance.

Ian Goldin and Bill Nasson kindly provided me with copies of their written work – in Goldin's case his important book, and in Nasson's an article, both cited in the references at the end of this text. I also thank Ian Goldin for his insistence that I focus on Manuel's international role more carefully. Adam Kahane also sent me a copy of his book on the Mont Fleur scenarios which explained much more than I could have about that extraordinary period in South Africa's history. Martin Nicol, Sean Field and Richard Goode kindly provided me with copies of their theses which were invaluable as sources. Aziz Bardien gave me access to his father's security police file, for which I am most grateful, and David Manuel gave me his handwritten notes on the Manuel family tree. Bruce Scott of the Harvard Business School also helped by clarifying and expanding on some of the notes and articles he has given to his classes over the years, and Robert Edgar of Howard University in Washington helped me to source important information about the presence of freed African-American slaves in Cape Town. Pieter-Dirk Uys kindly provided me with relevant parts of his script of *Evita for President* (2007). Fred Robertson arranged my visit to Rex Trueform and was also a valuable source of information on the last days of District Six.

I am grateful to my friends who hosted me while I was researching this book: Martin Nicol and Marianne Thamm in Cape Town, and Jennifer Davis and Bill Kovach in Washington DC. They never failed to stimulate and engage me about history, politics, journalism and writing. John Allen gave me valuable advice and help about constructing a narrative that is not near its end. James Barkhuizen helped me track down Essie Esterhuyse – the former security police officer who developed a relationship with Manuel that rose above political difference – and helped me translate some of the more arcane Afrikaans phrasing I came across in my research.

Trevor Manuel's family – his sisters, Beryl Tungcheun, Pam Barron and Renecia Clayton, his cousins, Dawn and Ursula von Söhnen, David Manuel and Christine Amansure – gave generously of their time and memories and hospitality, as did Lynne Matthews. His mother Philma and Sylmore Poggenpoel outdid themselves with a generosity and warmth that was beyond any call of duty. When my mother died suddenly in the winter of

2006, Mrs Manuel even took the time to come to her funeral. Maria Ramos gave me her time and insights, but more than that, she frequently provided gracious hospitality on the occasions when I was in her home. I am of course deeply grateful to her and all the others I interviewed or corresponded with, for their time and insights and memories. They are listed at the back of this book. There are no substitutes for living human memory. That they shared their stories and insights with me was a gift of lasting value.

Murray Michell played a key role in this project almost from the start. He was source, sounding board, and analyst, a role that continued long after I had completed a series of formal interviews with him.

Trevor Manuel, the subject of this biography, was generous beyond expectation with his time and insights for this book. He always made time for interviews, even in the midst of schedules that would have flayed most mortals, he took time to check facts and dates, and never once did he try to impose his own views on this work. He showed respect for my editorial independence in particular and for the value of independent research in general. He allowed me into his family, his circle of friends, his colleagues and comrades, his life. I thank him for allowing me to retrace his extraordinary journey with him.

I am also grateful to him for allowing me to attend several Budget rehearsals at his house or in his office, and for the Treasury team's slightly bemused but gracious acceptance of my presence. I was allowed to record and report freely on their interactions while they drafted the speeches for each Budget that I attended.

Finally, I must thank my own family: my father Michael, for urging me each week to switch off my cellphone and get on with it; my late mother Molly, who entreated me never to write anything boring – I hope I have not failed her entirely; my son Matthew for his forbearance with my snappiness and solitude at various phases of this project; but especially Alan, my husband, who read early drafts of my manuscript, criticised them robustly, and was usually right. Even through my worst moods or moments of despair, his love and support were unstinting.

Copyright acknowledgements

Grateful acknowledgement is made to the following for permission to reproduce copyright material: East African Educational Publishers Ltd, Nairobi, for the extract from Jorge Rebelo's 'Poem' from *When Bullets Began to Flower*, edited and translated by Margaret Dickinson (1972).

Every effort has been made to trace copyright holders or their assigns. The author and publisher apologise for any inadvertent infringement of copyright and, if this is drawn to their attention, will be pleased to make the necessary correction in subsequent editions.

Copyright of the pictorial images is held by the individuals credited in the picture captions. The author and publisher thank them for permission to use their images. The assistance and generosity of Benny Gool/Oryx Archive is particularly appreciated.

Introduction

> *Men make their own history, but they do not make it as they please; they do not*
> *make it under self-selected circumstances, but under circumstances existing*
> *already, given and transmitted from the past. The tradition of all dead*
> *generations weighs like a nightmare on the brains of the living.*
>
> Karl Marx, *The 18th Brumaire of Louis Bonaparte*, 1852

> *Only a fool wants everyone to like them.*
> *Only a fool wants to please everyone.*
>
> Ben Okri, *In Arcadia*, 2002

IN THE LATE ANTARCTIC SUMMER OF 2000, part of an ice shelf broke off the continent forming a large iceberg which floated off into the southern oceans. The shelf was about 17 kilometres long, and carried on it six large fuel tanks from the South African base on Antarctica. The tanks had been put there, as they usually were, about two kilometres from the edge, to await the arrival of a refuelling ship. Then they were supposed to be hauled back to the South African base by caterpillar across the icy wastes to a point further inland. When the refuelling ship arrived it spotted the bright orange tanks on the now drifting iceberg and tried to retrieve them. But the iceberg was higher than the ship itself – some 35 metres above the water. A German ship in the area tried to help, so did a Russian vessel. South African and Russian helicopters tried to lift the tanks with winches but they were too heavy and the iceberg, propelled as it was by strong winds and currents, moved too fast.

In the tabling of the legislation that allows for spending adjustments, Trevor Manuel had to explain this to Parliament. Large as they were – empty, they weighed about eight and half tons each – the tanks cost just over R1 million to replace, a drop in the ocean of budget expenditure. They were also sealed, reducing the risk of pollution.

Yet there were important lessons to be drawn from the incident. One was the reality of global warming: that same summer when the ice shelf broke off, there were devastating floods in southern Africa. They cost an extra R250 million for the repair of damaged infrastructure and for disaster relief.

There was a more philosophical lesson too. It was about what we can control, and what we can foresee. While we can predict the broad effects of global warming, it is harder to pinpoint exactly where or when the ice shelf may break off, or the floods may hit. 'The world doesn't conform to our wishes, or even our best-made plans,' Manuel told a university audience the day after he'd reported to Parliament on the fuel tank incident. 'The world is not of our own making. But just because that is so, does not mean that we just fold our hands and accept there's nothing you can do about it.'[1]

The world is not of our own making. Certainly, for Manuel, the world he was born into circumscribed his choices. Reared in a working-class coloured family in Cape Town at a time when a triumphant apartheid government tore apart the city – and his family – his choices were limited.

The questions of biography are twofold: one is how a life intersects with history to allow the subject, the human being, to grasp the historical moment. The other is harder to unravel because it is more interior. It is about changes in a personal life that force self-reflection, and possibly self-transformation.

This book deals mainly with the first question. If we do not make history in circumstances of our own choosing, as Marx said, how do we change those circumstances? What role do individuals play in forcing that change?

The South African resistance movement against apartheid has long had an ambivalent relationship with the role individual leaders have played: on the one hand they have tried to minimise the role played by individuals by emphasising the 'collective'. This is so deeply entrenched that some of the older African National Congress leaders rarely use the word 'I' in their discourse. Some use 'one' as the personal pronoun, as in 'One wrote that paper.' Nelson Mandela famously uses the word 'we', wonderfully inclusive but sometimes confusing, as when he backed the quest of the South African rugby team to retain the Springbok as its emblem in the interests of nation-building. 'We were all alone,' he said of the disagreement it provoked among his comrades.

On the other hand, many of the freedom songs of the struggle exalted individual leaders – Mandela, Oliver Tambo, Chris Hani, Joe Slovo. The more

---

[1] Manuel, T A: 'Economic Policy in a Changing Global and Local Environment'. Notes for a speech to the Department of Management at the University of the Western Cape, 13 October 2000.

apparently dangerous the apartheid government branded a leader, the more rousing the songs about them.

There can be little doubt though that the quality of leadership plays a critical role in the outcomes of history. P W Botha and F W de Klerk, for instance, were faced with much the same array of historical forces in the late 1980s. How they dealt with those forces made the crucial difference. Likewise, the leaders of the resistance movement, both internal and external, were faced with a bewildering set of choices at the same time. They opted for a particular path and, more importantly, took a constituency with them, wounded and angry as they were.

The second question about biography deals with the 'interior life' of a subject. What is it in a life that becomes a pivotal moment? As Mark Gevisser writes in his compelling biography of Thabo Mbeki, no biographer can truly 'know' his or her subject.[2] The anxieties and disappointments and hopes that cripple or drive each of us in our journeys of lived experience are hard to penetrate, sometimes even by ourselves.

Perhaps the point is not that there are unique moments of suffering in a life – although there are indeed those – but how they are dealt with that determines a path. We can track with more certainty how people act against the backdrop of historical circumstance – whether, to paraphrase Manuel, they unfold their hands and how they do so. How do they grasp a historical moment to craft a new one?

Imposing a narrative structure on any life is, necessarily, an arbitrary exercise of judgement on the part of the writer. Even to find a starting point is difficult, because it is not necessarily birth that heralds a beginning (although it is a good focal point). And when the subject is very much alive and engaged in public life, as Manuel is, an end point is impossible. So there are no parameters, and no obvious patterns to telling a tale. 'The instability of human knowledge is one of our few certainties,' wrote Janet Malcolm in her biography of Gertrude Stein and Alice B. Toklas.[3] 'Almost everything we know we know incompletely at best. And almost nothing we are told remains the same when retold.'

Within those limitations, I have tried in this narrative to tell a story of the way a man journeyed through a rough terrain. The anti-apartheid struggle, in

---

[2] Gevisser, Mark: *The Dream Deferred: Thabo Mbeki*, Jonathan Ball, 2007, pxiii.
[3] Malcolm, Janet: *Two Lives: Gertrude and Alice*, Yale University Press, 2007, p186.

its last years, was dangerous but also exhilarating. The years of reconstruction after the 1994 democratic elections were potentially as treacherous, although the dangers were hidden. As I write in 2008, they still are. The decisions leaders made then, or now, can have profound repercussions for the future of an entire country.

History is the backdrop against which people act, against which they are measured. The exigencies of today become the history of tomorrow, by which we measure courage, wisdom, correctness, however unfairly. The anti-apartheid struggle was complex and multilayered. I have painted the backdrop of this history in the Western Cape in some detail, hoping the reader will understand why: the events that forged the Western Cape with its peculiar location in South Africa shaped Manuel and his generation. Not to understand that, is like trying to explain the rupture of the Antarctic ice shelf without any reference to climate change. The difference with Manuel is that he was one of the few who escaped the clutches and pitfalls of a history that divided and impoverished so many people in that lovely but rough south-western corner of Africa.

Many of the people I interviewed for this book, especially those who grew up with Manuel in Cape Town, cannot pinpoint the first time they met him (except his mother who knows the day and hour). Nor can I. But he began to loom large in my peripheral vision in the late 1970s. I had come of age in the same city, and in the same political milieu, back to back as it were; he, a trainee civil engineer by day and a political activist the rest of the time; myself a student, later a reporter on a daily newspaper. I had scant appreciation of the circumstances he'd grown up in, even though reporting opened my eyes to a world beyond myself: black workers and their attempts to organise, the sprawling settlement of Crossroads, the courage of the internal resistance activists, and the terrifying climax of the long fight back against apartheid. I began to understand that world long before I knew more than the most superficial details of Manuel's life. But his consistent role in both the resistance and post-apartheid reconstruction intrigued me. This book tries to tell a story of that world and how Manuel moved in it.

In 2000, when I returned from a year at Harvard on the Nieman fellowship, the newspaper I worked for seconded me to Manuel's department for nine months. I became aware then of the pivotal role that Manuel's Treasury played in government – today, a point that is mentioned more frequently as a criticism than as an endorsement. It was the crossroads of government, and unlike the image of the Department of Finance officials of old as somewhat grey automatons, the Treasury officials now comprised a vibrant, energetic group who engaged Manuel robustly while they crafted fiscal policy for a new country and a new moment in history.

It was a fascinating interlude, but the work I loved was journalism which, with all its deficiencies, allows the space to reflect a nation back to itself and encourages a healthy irreverence which is surely good for democracy. Yet the debates in Treasury, and the intensity, the humour and rancour that accompanied them, stayed with me. How does a new democratic government make choices in a world that, increasingly, was not of its own making? And who was this man, this loud but articulate revolutionary I had known throughout the 1980s in the fractious Cape, who now stood at the crossroads of governance?

In 2002 I asked Manuel if I could write his biography. He was surprised but not averse to the idea. His mother Philma was even more surprised. 'Is he important enough for a book?' she asked.

It was only in 2005 that I could start work on it. Until then Manuel and I met a few times and spoke in a dialogue that was something more than a conversation, but less than an interview. In those talks, he began to reflect on the turning points of his own life. When we began a structured series of interviews in mid-2005, the story of the early part of his life came out in a fluent narrative. As history ran into the present, his recollections became less of a narration and more reflective. By mid-2008, the African National Congress, the organisation in which he had invested his life's energy and faith and hope, was in a state of internal turmoil. In a country such as South Africa, still vulnerable and developing, this has implications beyond merely a scrap between politicians. The country still faces huge and pressing problems, the worst being unemployment and the concomitant poverty that goes with it. It is the 'intractable difficulty', Manuel told me at the time.

Yet more energy was being spent in scoring political points than in dealing with problems so big they could threaten the core of the country.

In our last formal interview in July 2008, as I was finishing this book, he reflected on government and governance, and on the role of ordinary people in change. He had recently returned from India where his counterpart there told him of how salaries for the top civil servants in India (the equivalent of directors-general in South Africa) had gone up so much since the early

1990s, that now they could afford to drive a 'small family car'. In 1993, they could afford only bicycles. In South Africa, in contrast, even middle-rank civil servants can and do drive high-end German cars.

I sensed that he rued the loss of the values of service in the heart of a movement that led South Africa to freedom. He mourned the loss of a civil society that could stand on its feet. Left behind in this transition, he said, 'has been this failure to communicate the fact that change is a process that actually involves people themselves. This idea that you've got this kind of victim syndrome, crime happens, people can't do anything about it . . . societies aren't built like that. Our whole struggle against apartheid was largely premised on the idea that we had to do something for ourselves. We actually did amazing things. And now we pretend that we don't know how.'

Manuel's story is the story of the many people who intersected with his life who did some of 'those amazing things'. A biographer, as Malcolm reminds us, often treats 'minor characters . . . less tenderly than major characters', using them to advance a narrative, then 'carelessly (dropping) them when they have performed their function'. I, too, may be guilty of that transgression, yet not I hope of the ultimate one that Malcolm pinpoints: in order to write a life, not lives, the writer 'must cultivate a kind of narcissism on behalf of his subject that blinds him to the humanity of anyone else'.[4]

But political life in South Africa was so connected, particularly towards the end of apartheid, it is impossible to imagine any leader standing on his own. There were hosts of courageous people who took a stand on one of the great moral issues of our time. I have interviewed nearly a hundred people for this book, most of them on the record. I hope I have not treated them with less humanity, because all of their stories are indeed remarkable. The story of Manuel's personal and political struggle is deeply reflected in their own. He is not only a product of historical circumstance, but a product of his relationships, political, professional and personal.

There are times, such as these when I write, when the weight of the present obscures both a past and a future. Some of those who played central roles in both Manuel's life and in the resistance movement have fallen dramatically out of favour with a new leadership in the African National Congress in 2008. History is often forgotten in a maelstrom – or opportunistic – moment at hand. Humanity is eschewed, not so much by biographers, but by the newly

[4] Malcolm, Janet: op cit, p205.

powerful who dictate a new discourse.

Perhaps this is why we tell the stories of our past and those who have led us out of it. This is why we focus on choices taken by human beings rather than on a predetermined march of history – or the relentless flow of severed ice shelves in a strong current. It is to try to capture the humanity in others, to help us find our own.

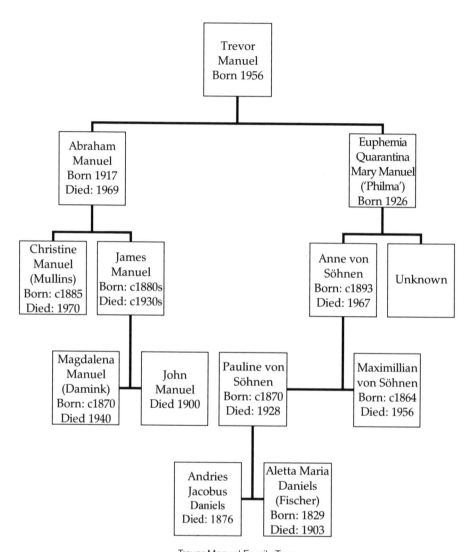

Trevor Manuel Family Tree

≡ PART ONE: Origins ≡

CHAPTER 1

Shattered Cape

E AST OF DEVIL'S PEAK, beyond the long shadows it casts, Voortrekker Road
strikes a determined trajectory away from the city's heart. Past corner
cafés and small factories, past the Maitland Cemetery and beyond, it marches
its way to the townships on the Cape Flats. Kensington lies just north of
the cemetery. An ordered, modest, mainly working-class suburb, it spreads
itself on low-lying ground much of which was once under water in the wet
Cape winters. It is one of the oldest coloured areas in Cape Town, running
seamlessly into Factreton, a slightly poorer area on its eastern flank, and
almost as smoothly, on the other side, into Maitland, a white working-class
area.

Not as far-flung as the newer black[1] suburbs on the sandy Cape Flats,
nor as dire in circumstance, Kensington nonetheless bears its own scars of
upheaval, forced removal and neglect.

But on that late summer's night in 1956 when Trevor Andrew Manuel drew
his first breath in the front bedroom of a semi-detached house in Kensington,
the claws of apartheid were only beginning to flex.

3

ON 31 JANUARY THAT YEAR, Manuel's parents, Abraham and Philma, had lived in their house in Seventh Street for less than two years. Their two elder children, daughters Beryl and Pam, had been born in the rented house around the corner in Second Street – Beryl in 1951, and Pam in 1954. Philma, a garment worker, and Abraham, a municipal worker, had saved assiduously since their marriage in 1950 and bought the house for the equivalent of R5 200.

'In those days,' said Pam Barron, Manuel's sister, 'newly-weds lived in one room. But my mother didn't want that. So she waited until they could afford to rent, then buy.' It seemed fitting that their first – and only – son should be born in the house they had worked so hard to buy.

More than 50 years later Philma Manuel was still living in the three-bedroomed house. In structure it is indistinguishable from its neighbours, but today it is painted a bright corn-yellow which cheerfully contrasts with the generously large pink and red rose bushes in the tiny front garden.

A long, narrow semi, it has three bedrooms, a lounge, a kitchen. When Manuel was born, in the only bedroom that captured the sun, the bathroom was in the yard. Today it is inside, off the kitchen, one of the few visible nods to modernity.

Today the house is also much emptier. When Manuel was a boy, he shared it with his parents, three sisters – the youngest, Renecia, was born in 1959 – and two grandmothers. Today Mrs Manuel shares the house with long-time companion Sylmore Poggenpoel, who has spent most of his adult life as a seaman and officer. It is he who has carved the ornate wooden door leading from the flower-filled garden in front of the house to the side alley and backyard. Philma Manuel was almost 80 when I first met her. Hospitable and plain-spoken, she showed few signs of her age or the hardships that have punctuated her life. Deeply religious, God and hard work have been her cornerstones. Throughout the later years of apartheid when her son spent much of his time in prison or in hiding, she prayed through the days and nights. 'It was terrible but in a way I kept my faith. My faith has kept us strong, so many people always praying.'

PHILMA MANUEL WAS BORN Euphemia Quarantina Mary von Söhnen, the only child of Anne von Söhnen, in the nearby Cape winelands town of Stellenbosch in 1926. Her mother was born into a well-established Stellenbosch family in a large house in Andringa Street, a street lined with oak trees that cuts through the centre of this old Cape Dutch town.

Anne's father Maximillian and his sons ran a successful plumbing and welding business from their house and were well known in the district.

Anne herself worked almost her whole life, first in a canning factory in the rural Boland, then later in Cape Town in a dry-cleaning business. 'I can't tell you what my father did,' Mrs Manuel said, 'because I never knew my father.'

If giving birth to an illegitimate child was a blight on the respectable Von Söhnen name, they never showed it to Philma. Although she went to live in the inner-city Cape Town suburb of Woodstock to attend school when she was a child, and was cared for by a foster mother, she and Anne spent many weekends together in their family home in Stellenbosch.

The contrast must have been marked for the young girl. She left the large, gardened house spanning two erfs in the picturesque town of Stellenbosch to live in one of Cape Town's oldest and densest inner-city areas. The suburb of Woodstock spreads like a large footprint from the slopes of Devil's Peak, where District Six once flourished, to the city centre and down to Table Bay. It was a suburb that briefly prospered in a property boom in the early part of the twentieth century, partly because of its proximity to the city, the mountain, and the harbour, but just as quickly collapsed.[2] And then it continued as it began, a haven for newly arrived immigrants and working-class people of all colours, attracted by the magnet of new industries, shops, and jobs in Cape Town soon after the First World War.

Philma Manuel went to the local school, Wesley Practising and Secondary, until she was 15. Because her mother was single and working, Philma was brought up in Albert Road in lower Woodstock by Fredericka Brown, effectively her foster mother, whose children were by then grown up. Even after her own mother came to live in Woodstock, Ma Brown remained Philma Manuel's second mother, and her children's third grandmother. It was her own mother Anne, and Ma Brown, who eventually shared the Kensington house with her, her husband and her children in later years.

When she was 15, Philma von Söhnen felt her mother needed her help and left school. The principal said he was sorry. She was a clever girl, he told her, and might have made a good teacher some day.

But it was not something that she dwelled on. 'I don't think I was that way inclined.'

More pressing was the need for a job, and in those days she did what scores of other young working-class girls of her generation did in Cape Town.

She walked from her tenement house in Woodstock up to Queen Victoria Road where she turned towards the imposing building of Rex Trueform in Salt River. Rex, as it is ubiquitously known in the Cape, boasted it was the largest clothing manufacturer in the southern hemisphere. Then, in 1940, it was only eight years old, having begun as a small workshop in Plein Street in Cape Town. It was run by Bernard Shub, a name that was later to become synonymous with clothing manufacture in Cape Town, and a young immigrant, Philip Dibowitz, who doubled up as a cutter. In today's terms the young factory would be described as 'niche', manufacturing trousers under a brand name, 'while concentrating on style and finish'.[3]

But the war, with its concomitant demands for military clothing, and the factory's expansion into jacket manufacture, accelerated demand to the extent that it had to move from its old premises in Plein Street to the shiny new building in Salt River. It prided itself on being the most modern clothing factory in South Africa, not only in design but also in industrial relations. 'This factory will stand as a model to industrialists and is all that a factory should be,' said Senator A J P Fourie the then minister of commerce and industries, at the opening ceremony in 1932. Rex Trueform, boasted a Cape Town city publication in 1963, was 'pioneering an industrial revolution in South Africa and one of the results today is that the clothing industry in this country has a reputation as being one of the most enlightened anywhere in its practical working conditions. The founders were certain that better labour facilities would produce better garments. Light, well-ventilated working rooms, canteens and rest-rooms, health and first-aid facilities provided an environment under which the rapidly increasing staff could put their best into their work.'[4]

The young Philma von Söhnen did not much care whether Rex Trueform pioneered the industrial revolution. For her Rex was just the obvious place to work. It was an industry that, for reasons less than altruistic, relied heavily on partly educated young coloured women. By the late 1930s it employed 4 000 workers, mainly coloured women, in 30 factories.[5] Girls as young as 12 or 13 were employed for as little as two shillings and sixpence a week.[6] The clothing industry was a staple part of making a living for the coloured community on the Cape Flats. And notwithstanding the company's boast about modern industrial relations, the unionist Solly Sachs (father of Constitutional Court judge Albie Sachs) who organised Afrikaner garment workers in the then Transvaal, considered the wages and conditions of work in Cape Town as 'probably the worst in the country'.

The industry goes to the heart of many of the conflicts that were to define the experience of racial discrimination, particularly for coloured people, in the Western Cape. From the mid-1920s, garment manufacturers in the Transvaal were afraid that the Cape's ability to employ coloured labour at lower wage rates than those negotiated by Sachs's union would undercut their competitiveness. This concern was fully shared by Sachs, who was later banned as a communist. He personally inspired and led repeated organising campaigns in Cape Town from 1929 to 1955 to ensure geographical divisions would not undercut his ability to bargain. Sachs tried spectacularly hard to organise one united national union for garment workers. He also failed spectacularly. In the 1960s Transvaal wages fell to Cape levels and the white workers were replaced by blacks.

Sachs had not reckoned on equally energetic employers in the Cape who saw their best defence not in fighting an established national trade union, but in setting up what was effectively their own bosses' union under the protection of the labour laws. No one quite reckoned on what can only be described as the militant subservience of the Cape union. Johanna Cornelius, one of Sachs's comrades from the Transvaal union, found this out the hard way. At a meeting in the Woodstock town hall in 1954 called to vote for unity between the two unions, she was met 'noisily with boos and cat-calls. Fights broke out around her. Her hair was pulled by supporters of the Cape union, she was kicked and almost had her coat torn off her back.'[7]

Three decades later, underground ANC activists in the Western Cape, comrades of Philma's son Trevor, renewed Solly Sachs's quest to challenge the reformist Western Cape Garment Workers' Union and tried to spawn a rival, more militant clothing union in the Cape. It, too, faltered and flailed, but not before one or two spectacular strikes. 'The garment industry is the heart of the Cape Flats,' one of those activists told me much later. 'Not to understand that is not to understand Cape Town politics.'

POLITICS WAS FAR FROM Philma von Söhnen's mind as she stood outside the Rex Trueform gate on that autumn afternoon in 1940. When the foreman came out the huddle of girls eyed him anxiously. 'I'll take you ... and *you*,' he said pointing at Philma.

'He just looked at all of us and said: you, come here. He took two of us that morning and I was one of the lucky ones.' Rex's boasts about its modern industrial policies obviously didn't extend to its recruitment practices.

Nearly 70 years later, she laughs about the arbitrary selection process. Did the two fortunate new employees look like harder workers? Were they prettier? Better dressed?

Philma didn't care. She was in and there she stayed for the next 18 years. After Trevor was born she found work at a factory nearer her marital home. All told, she worked 36 years in the industry, taking home when she left in 1976 a wage of R21 a week.

She began work as a machinist and quickly trained herself. 'You were shown first, you know, then just followed on ...'

She was paid about fifteen shillings a week, although she remembers it in rands. 'Don't laugh! It was R1,50 a week. And you worked overtime till 9pm on a night like tonight. Raining! You'd get two biscuits and a cup of black tea, and you worked till 9pm.'

There wasn't much choice in the matter. If there were orders the women worked, and there was a lot of work in those days: army clothes, jackets, gents' suits – Man About Town, a prized label in the Cape.

'We worked on conveyor belts. It wasn't like that always. You'd get your work and you'd pull out what you must do and as soon as the belt reaches the second person you'd have to have that back in there. You know, we used to turn out 40 garments an hour.'

Philma von Söhnen began her days in the factory working on the inside canvas of jackets. Soon she was doing the seams, and not much later the backs. 'I was an all-rounder.'

Her bosses? Strict but good bosses. The 'Cape' union, which became a closed shop after it won its battle against the radicals from the north – did she join? 'You had to!'

But she was happy. Those 18 years at Rex were among the happiest of her life.

It is a measure of both her values and of her time and place in history that she would not have dreamed of complaining. 'Everybody was like one family. There was no apartheid in those days.'

Indeed, apartheid crept so insidiously on Cape Town that it took a whole generation to notice it. But a deep awareness of colour, not just black and white but all the shades between, stamped the consciousness of the coloured community.

Philma von Söhnen met her husband, Abraham James Manuel, at a dance in Woodstock soon after the war, and the couple married in 1950.

ABRAHAM MANUEL, OR AWIE, as he was known, was the second youngest child
of nine born and raised on the slopes of Devil's Peak in District Six. His father,
James Manuel, had been brought up in the same house at 44 Eckhard Street.
Abraham's parents were, in the words of his older sister Hester Seale, 'very,
very strict'. Auntie Hessie, as Trevor was later to call her, recalled how her
mother taught her to scrub the kitchen floor. She was 14. 'She had a cushion.
She gave me bucket of water. Show me how I must scrub. I must put the cloth
around the wood. I must do it. I was finished and said I was finished.'

'Finished, Hester, so quick,' said her mother. 'I must first come and see.
And you never asked me for a second bucket of water ...'

'She came and said, I'm very sorry, that is not the way I showed you. You'll
have to do it over again ... Now another bucket of water and back on your
knees.'

Hester's tears had no effect. 'Crying, and the tears were running, but it's
not affecting her,' she remembered.

'You've got to do as I told you because, you must understand, mommy
doesn't know how long mommy will be alive with you,' her mother told
her.[8]

As it happened, 'mommy' – Christine Mullins who married James Manuel
in the early years of the twentieth century – was alive for about 50 more years.
But her husband James died before any of his grandchildren knew him.

This was the family that reared Abraham Manuel: affectionate, close, but
disciplinarian.

Thrifty, too. Christine Manuel insisted on cooking a proper meal for lunch
and dinner. No sandwiches for the children who returned from school.
Cooking a pot of food was better value. As Hester recalled: 'We always had
a stew ... Lots of people go for fish and chips, buying sausages and things.
Not my mommy. A pot of food. We always used to say to mommy, when you
going to change it?'

'I don't have enough money,' Christine Manuel would reply. 'You know
what? It costs a lot to fry. And (then) 9 o'clock you say you're hungry again.'

'A half slice of bread each with dinner,' Hester remembered. 'You got the
second half if you finished that.'

'I don't want anything to go into the bin,' her mother would say. 'You can
have more, but not to be wasted.'

HESTER'S YOUNGER BROTHER ABRAHAM, Trevor's father, was born in 1917. Partly because of the age gap between them (about eight years), Hester does not remember much of his childhood, but soon after he left school he went to work for the City Council.

His job was skilled but relatively unrewarded. He copied plans on to sepia or linen from the original drawn on 'expensive paper with what was called Indian Ink', said Manuel.

Abraham Manuel had been working at least 15 years by the time he and Philma were married in 1950. Marriage presented its own set of difficulties. Where to live was one of them. The District, as it was universally known, was already overcrowded. Even before apartheid was entrenched, no new houses were being built. The Manuel family home already had a married daughter and her family in it. So Philma and Abraham waited until they could find a proper house together. When they did, it was a three-bedroomed rental in Second Avenue, Kensington. In the space of a year they married, moved, and had their first child, Beryl. Three years later Pam was born and the family moved to the house in Seventh Street that Abraham Manuel had saved so long to buy.

ABRAHAM MANUEL BOUGHT THE house from Hilda Waynick Elkin, the daughter of a prosperous landowning Jewish family who owned many of the cottages and tenement buildings in this rapidly expanding area. Seventh Street runs east-west, parallel to Voortrekker Road. It commands a dominant, if distant, view of Cape Town's famous Table Mountain. It was then, and is now, treeless, although many of its residents have planted bursts of colourful plants in their postage stamp front gardens. The backyards almost always housed toilets and washing lines. Its houses are close set and mainly semi-detached, the homes of Cape Town's working people like Philma and Abraham. Just around the corner were long tenement buildings – terraced row houses, each one featuring six rooms leading off a single passage, one family per room. It was a quintessentially urban, working-class area reminiscent of many such areas in cities around the world.

With one difference.

South Africa's urban development was, even before the onset of apartheid, defined increasingly in terms of colour. As the suburbs closer to the city grew 'whiter', the existing coloured areas of District Six and Woodstock grew more crowded. Coloured people moved further away from the city centre. Areas such as Kensington, on the immediate periphery of the city, were quickly settled.

There was another factor, too, one that eventually bedevilled the most careful social engineering policies of the apartheid government: African people migrating from the squeezed and pressured rural areas had also begun to make the area their home.

New migrants to the city began to settle in Windermere, on the eastern periphery of Kensington, in the 1920s and 30s. Attracted by Cape Town's growing economy, people of all colours came in search of a better life. Either because they could not find homes in the inner-city areas, or perhaps because they liked the relative wilderness of Windermere and Kensington, many chose to come here where they could keep cattle and goats and perhaps even grow a few vegetables.

The name Windermere was gleaned, in typical colonial fashion, from England's Lake Windermere because of the large vlei in the middle of the area, later to disappear when Cape Town's main highway north, the N1, was built. But it was starkly different from its Cumbrian namesake that Wordsworth gazed on. In 1923 there were about 2000 people living there, according to a Divisional Census.[9] But during the war, as a result of both increased poverty in rural areas and more job opportunities in Cape Town, more African people began to settle in the area. By 1943, the African population in Windermere was estimated at 19000.[10] By the early 1950s, the total population of the area had grown to about 30000.

It was essentially then a mixed area: many families had intermarried and coloured people and Africans lived, not only next door to each other, but in the same households. Even in Mtsheko, the main African section of Windermere, there were several coloured families. In Mtsheko, two huge stockades or 'kraals' of inward facing shacks dominated the area, called Timberyard and Strongyard. 'Of course the Bantus and the coloured lived together,' said one former (coloured) resident, unwittingly using the dated pejorative. 'It was one row of shanties. As the shanties, then a coloured lives here and here lives a Bantu, rows, rows houses ... it was people and chicken and animals in one kraal. You could say the people lived with animals. This was now Timberyard, this was Strongyard ...'[11]

Contrary to the ideological myths later propagated by the apartheid government that Africans were newcomers to the Cape, many families who ended up living in Windermere had in fact settled in Cape Town much earlier. There had been a large African settlement in Ndabeni, for example, just to the south of Kensington, but many African families were moved from there to the newly established township of Langa.

'This was a whole wilderness,' remembered an old resident, recalling the green spaces, the ubiquitous goats and chickens. Despite the sometimes romantic bucolic memories, it was a difficult place to settle. Only 50 feet above sea level, the whole area was prone to flooding in the wet Cape winters. An elderly man who lived in 12th Avenue, about six blocks east of the Manuels' home, said that in winter 'it was nearly like a small sea. Here where we now sit was a whole river, there from Voortrekker Road, from there down to Graaf's bush'.[12]

A newspaper reporter wrote in the winter of 1944 that practically every byway 'is under water for some part of its length. Residents said that a few days ago the water in some streets was to waist high. There was a lake 75 yards long and two feet deep for its full width down one street. Some parallel streets were linked by lakes, with houses and shanties marooned between them. Children had been swimming in some of the streets and ducks, pigs and goats were splashing about. Some houses were completely surrounded by water which came right up to the front entrance.'[13]

Added to this was an appalling lack of sanitation. As much as there was plenty of water around in winter, hardly any of it was potable. There were few standpipes and a crude bucket latrine system, so it was not surprising that in the 1940s there were two serious outbreaks of disease, one of typhus, the other of tuberculosis.

In the mid-1940s, before the formal onset of apartheid in 1948, the authorities fixed on the view that this was a diseased slum and even then suggested that the solution lay in separating Africans from coloureds. The Cape Town City Council argued that 'no half measures can be tolerated here. Conditions are too bad. It is essential to separate natives from coloured people. There are more mixed abodes here than anywhere in the country ... Unwanted natives must be repatriated; remainder must go to Langa.'[14]

Liberal whites, apparently concerned about the living conditions of people, added to this discourse: 'I have visited this area and the conditions of overcrowding and filth exceed anything I have seen in the worst country locations,' Donald Molteno, a liberal member of Parliament, testified to the Cape Flats Committee of Inquiry in 1942.[15]

12

Not all of those in Kensington/Windermere lived in such dire conditions. Many African families moved into houses in Kensington (which unlike Windermere was under Cape Town City Council jurisdiction so had better servicing). 'Staying in Kensington was a pleasure because, number one, a person can do what you feel like doing ...' said one African man who was forcibly removed to the Langa township.[16]

But mostly Africans could not do what they felt like doing. Before 1937 Africans had been allowed to purchase land and property in Cape Town, but the Native Urban Areas Amendment Act made this almost impossible. Almost immediately after the National Party won its election victory in 1948 and instituted the policy of apartheid, conditions deteriorated for both African and coloured communities, but more sharply and more frighteningly for Africans. Pass laws were introduced, and with that came the terrifying raids in the night or early morning. A web of unequal relationships that can only survive in an oppressive society emerged. For instance, Africans were not allowed to buy liquor. Many in Windermere had made a living from running shebeens or illegal taverns. Now they had to get their coloured neighbours to buy liquor for them. Called 'mailers', it was a relationship that opened the way to exploitation, inequality and dishonesty. As one former 'mailer' told Sean Field, a Cape Town historian who has written extensively about the area, many 'mailers' would pour a little brandy out of each bottle, keep it for themselves, and fill the remaining quarts with water.

Then, in the early 1950s, the onslaught began in earnest. African families in Windermere started being rounded up, arrested for pass offences, and moved, many to the 'bachelor quarters' – grim single-sex hostels – in Langa and Nyanga, a new African township further east on the dunes of the Cape Flats. Women were 'repatriated' to rural reserves. The terror of pass raids – the almost unfettered power of the police to swoop on any African – is vividly recalled by one old resident of Windermere who was moved to Langa: 'If you forgot your pass it was either you had to outrun the police or you got arrested ... the van would just sort of appear from nowhere, and before it is stationary the police are off and you would run. You know, it was so pathetic that sometimes a person would run and after he would discover that "I got my pass on me" ... So it was, I won't be able to paint a fairer picture, it was such a nightmare thing. It was such a nightmare thing.'[17]

As African people were steadily moved out of Windermere, so the City Council built houses on the old site and called it Factreton. Many families were mixed – coloured women had married African men or vice versa – and were torn apart with no regard for their future. One visionary coloured man in the area who saw what was coming helped several Africans reclassify as coloured and was jailed for several years for his efforts.

It was a brutality that, once begun, steadily tried to destroy every human bond that had existed across racial lines.

STRANGELY, IT DID NOT altogether succeed. By the time Trevor Manuel was born in Kensington in 1956, most Africans had been removed from Windermere and the slums so decried by the city authorities had largely been cleared. Factreton was being built where shacks had once stood and in 1951 the government declared both Kensington and Factreton as coloured areas.

But Manuel's earliest memories are of several African families still living in houses in the area east of Fifth Avenue which, like the other avenues, cuts across the streets that run parallel to Voortrekker Road, Kensington's outer boundary. The further east you go, the poorer the area. The Manuels' house was just on the western side of Fifth Avenue. 'My immediate neighbourhood was predominantly coloured so my first friends would have been in the immediate neighbourhood,' he recalled.

His mother, too, remembers African families living 'on the other side of the avenue … we were all one.' And there was a township 'lower down … by Twelfth Avenue … Then one day you would just see that those people are not here any more.'

Philma Manuel had left her job at Rex Trueform soon after Trevor was born. She worked first for a manager at Rex who had left to start his own factory, but that went 'belly-up', so she went to work at Gold Knit in Maitland. She was to work there for the next 18 years.

The work was hard and conditions rough. According to Beryl Tungcheun, her oldest daughter, who left school before matriculating to work there as a wage clerk, it was an 'extremely *verkramp* (conservative) place … like an army camp. If you were working you couldn't look up. Especially for mommy-them on the machines. I used to sit in an office above them at one stage and I used to watch them and it used to be terrible watching these women feeding (the material) through the machines. And you *dare* not look up.'

But the Manuel household was full and happy in those early years. Here was a working family intent on seeing that their children had better opportunities than the generation before. Trevor, the only boy, was a much loved child. His

14

mother remembers his 'golden curls'. A 'pretty child', remembers his cousin Christine Amansure, 'the prettiest'. Mrs Amansure is the daughter of Lena Brown (born Manuel), his father's older sister. She is nearly 20 years older than Manuel, and remembers that, as a small boy, 'he was very smart, always doing his best'.

'He had bandy legs,' remembers his slightly more trenchant older sister Pam Barron.

Except for his father, Trevor grew up in a household of women and girls: his mother, three sisters, and his two grandmothers: his maternal grandmother Anne von Söhnen and Fredericka Brown, the woman who had brought up Philma Manuel in Woodstock. The three girls shared a room with Ma Brown, as they called her. He shared a bedroom with his grandmother Anne whom the children called Mama. His parents had the front bedroom. Being the only boy made a difference. His grandmother Anne, then working at the dry-cleaning firm Nannuci in the city, always made an effort to give him toys that the girls never got. 'He had a bicycle, that none of us were allowed to have. I had to learn to ride on his bicycle,' said Pam.

And his father took a special interest in his son – taking him to the soccer field to practise, taking a keen interest in his school work.

Philma Manuel was more of a 'friend' to her children. Their father Abraham was, as his own mother had been, a strict disciplinarian. Pam remembers an incident in junior school when her term-end report showed she came sixth in class. 'He gave me one shot. He said, "Manuels don't come sixth. Manuels come top." '

Pam changed schools the next year, from the local primary in Windermere to Wesley in Salt River where her mother had gone. It was a significant transition for the girl: new school, now a bus ride rather than walk away, different language, from Afrikaans to English. But 'I was back on top. Find my feet. Manuels only came at the top.'

Trevor, two years younger than Pam, started at her primary school, Windermere Prep, three weeks before his fifth birthday in 1961. The school was then only a few years old. Fifty years later, in 2005, to celebrate its anniversary, and the success of probably its most famous pupil, the school enlarged the photograph of the register of the young Trevor's first day at school. It reflected his birthdate as 31 January 1954 which, if true, would have made him three weeks older than Pam. The fudging of the year was to ensure that he didn't sit around at home. Nursery schools and crèches were unheard of in Kensington. His parents both worked, his grandmother worked.

It was not unusual that parents in the area would try to get their children into school sooner rather than later. So in order to verify a child's ability to cope, the school system devised a rather crude test. If the child could put his arm over his head and touch the ear on the opposite side, he was deemed ready for school. 'If your arm didn't touch your ear then they wouldn't let you into school because all the parents lied because they wanted their children to get into school,' said Manuel.

Trevor passed the arm-to-ear test and was admitted.

The legacy of Windermere and its racial mix lingered in the school. In that first year nearly half the children in Trevor's class were Xhosa-speaking. In fact the classrooms were so full that Sub A and Sub B (as Grades 1 and 2 were then called) were platooned into a double shift. One week, a group of children would start classes at 8am, the next at 12.30pm. The five-year-old knew from classroom conversations that his African classmates were being moved.

That year, too, South Africa, under the apartheid government, cut its ties with the Commonwealth and became a republic. It was the start of apartheid's apogee. In the next decade the economy would boom, Afrikaner businesses would flourish, and the white working class would be absorbed into protected, skilled employment in the state or parastatal sector.

But for the community in Kensington and Windermere – both coloured and African – it was the start of more than two decades of steady impoverishment and the heartache of upheaval.

Trevor had no idea what the Republic Day celebrations meant. The school gave him and his sister Pam miniature South African flags – the orange, white and blue – and medals, which they proudly took home. He and Pam stood on their little veranda showing their father the flags and the medals. Across Fifth Avenue, just two blocks east of their house, they saw a large white government truck. Government workers were moving furniture on to it. The furniture belonged to one of the last African families in Kensington. The family had told Abraham Manuel they were being moved to Nyanga West (later renamed Guguletu). Their father promptly burned the flags and threw away the medals. 'We couldn't be seen to be identifying with the Republic. People were being moved right there. (My father) wasn't a member of a political party then but it was just a wrong thing to do, you see,' said his son many years later.

If such empathy was not unusual among the coloured community, it certainly was not consistent. The year before, when 30 000 Africans from Langa township staged a huge protest march to Caledon Square, the central police station in Cape Town, as part of nationwide strikes and protests against the ever-tightening pass laws, Pam remembers being struck by the fear of her teachers. They told their pupils to 'run like hell' because the 'blacks living in the kraals at the bottom of Kensington are going to march and kill us'.

Yet the year the Republic was proclaimed, in 1961, 'tens of thousands of coloured men and women stayed away from work. For the first time, coloureds demonstrated a more solid response than Africans to a campaign of mass resistance.'[18]

If the community teetered then on a cusp between fear and resistance, it was amply demonstrated by Abraham Manuel's response to what his children had been told at school. He distilled Pam's fear (about the march) and Trevor's pride (about the medals) into shame, by pointing out the sight of their neighbours being herded on to trucks and moved. 'It wasn't high politics,' recalled Trevor. But it was simply wrong that their neighbours should be treated so.

By the next year Windermere Prep had become considerably less congested, and early in Trevor's third year the shift system stopped completely. The African children were gone.

CHAPTER 2

People of the world

THE SOUTH AFRICAN SATIRIST Pieter-Dirk Uys has a skit about Manuel that refers directly to his changeable countenance. 'Trevor,' he says, dressed as a 'bergie',* rolling the 'r' and stretching out the first syllable.

'My *ou* pal Trev! I'm always so proud when he makes his budget speech. I go down St George's Mall and find a shop that has a TV on in the window. And there is *ou* Trevor on teevee presenting his budget in Parliament with such confidence, like he's doing Sun City singing: "I did it My Way!" He's gone through so many changes from the old struggle days, has *ou* Trevor. First he looked like a coloured, then a Greek, then a hippie, then a Jew. Now a bleddie banker! Jissus! Trevor the banker?!'[1]

Tall like his father was – more than 1,8 metres – but more muscled and less lanky, Trevor Manuel has a skin of unburnished brass, an aquiline nose, and alert blue-green eyes. He does indeed look as though he could hail from almost any corner of the world.

---

* A Cape Town term for a vagrant.

But in South Africa, under apartheid, he, like others whose looks defied glib definition, was classified 'coloured'.[2]

Coloured identity has long been a matter of dispute, and of pain. The race classification laws of apartheid divided communities and families, stripped away dignity and wrecked lives. It is an identity that has been the subject of derision, not only by whites and some Africans in the Western Cape,[3] but even by coloured people themselves. Coloured intellectuals who belonged to the Non-European Unity Movement, a Trotskyist group, established their dominance over left-wing discourse in the Cape in the apartheid era by using inverted commas around the word 'coloured' to express a distaste for, yet a reluctant acceptance of, the term. The inverted commas were accepted in almost every political circle to the left of the apartheid government. In conversation, there was hardly a mention of the term 'coloured' without it being prefaced by the word 'so-called', Sometimes, in writing, people even put 'so-called' in inverted commas.[4]

To a large extent, it served to hide history rather than to illuminate it, to avoid a prickly question rather than confront it.

Who are the coloured people?

To understand the peculiar dynamic of race relations in Cape Town between whites, coloureds and Africans, to glean from those relations the moments of hope and long decades of bitterness, we need to confront an ugly part of South African history that has been overshadowed in the larger discourse of oppression and freedom.

The Cape Town academic and writer, Mohamed Adhikari, begins his book *Not White Enough, Not Black Enough*[5] with a well-worn South African joke that starts with Jan van Riebeeck, the leader of the first party of Dutch settlers who arrived in the Cape in 1652. 'The joke begins by describing a scenario that provokes a Coloured person into hurling racial insults at an African ... The African then counters this tirade with the punchline: "God made the white man, God made the black man, God made the Indian, the Chinese and the Jew – but Jan van Riebeeck, he made the Coloured man." '

The idea that miscegenation between whites and indigenous people created those later defined as coloured runs deep in South African lore, both black and white, and from the right to the left. The historian J S Marais wrote in the 1930s that 'this philosophy of blood and race leads to a passionate aversion to miscegenation ... which is the primary article of faith of the South African nation.'[6] Nelson Mandela told Neville Alexander, a fellow political prisoner on Robben Island, that coloured people were the progeny of a white and black union,[7] and even Kenny Jordaan, a left-wing coloured intellectual and member of the Trotskyist Fourth International Organization, wrote in 1952 that Van Riebeeck was indeed 'the father of the Coloured people'.[8]

But the real history is more layered, more complex, more painful, and goes to the heart of both the oppression and marginalisation of the coloured people in the Western Cape.

IT MUST BEGIN SOON after Van Riebeeck arrived but not with miscegenation between the settlers and the indigenous Khoi people (although there was some intermarriage between the Dutch and the Khoi; one of Van Riebeeck's commanders was the first known settler to marry a Khoi woman, Krotoa, who was Van Riebeeck's interpreter).

It begins in 1658 with a shipload of 174 Angolan slaves, who had been pirated from the Portuguese, and later that year with a Dutch slave trader en route from Guinea to the East Indies who also left a cargo of human beings at the Cape. Thus, as the historian George M Fredrickson points out, in 1659, 'the colony suddenly had 226 slaves and less than 140 whites ... The Cape colony was virtually born as a multi-racial slave society.'[9]

In the next 150 years, some 67000 slaves would be imported into the Cape. And crucially, unlike many of the other infamous slave societies of the time such as the American South, for almost the entire period of slavery, 'slaves outnumbered the Burgher residents of the Cape'.[10] In Stellenbosch, for instance, in 1827, out of a population of 16325, 8465 were slaves, many working in the vineyards and farms there.

They came from across the world: from the west coast of Africa, and the east; from the East Indies, from Indonesia, from Malaya, from Ceylon, the Coromandel Coast, from China, from India, and from Bengal. More than a quarter came from Africa, one third from India and another third from the East Indies. Of the African slaves, more than half came from East Africa and Madagascar, and about 5 per cent from West Africa and Angola.[11]

Slavery was not simply a minor indulgence of Cape colonial society, a way of plugging the labour gaps left by the stubbornly independent indigenous Khoi people. Slavery was central to the economic development and subsequent social relations of the Cape. Proportionately, it was one of the biggest slave societies of the world.

Mortality was high, mainly because of disease and malnutrition; there were also runaways, sometimes shielded by the indigenous Khoi but often not.[12] As a result there was a constant need for replenishment, and the Dutch East India Company which ran the colony built special slave ships that would sail regularly for Madagascar where traders would barter with Malagasy royalty for slaves.

The trade was so fervent and so regular partly because there was a massively disproportionate number of males to females in the slave population. So the number of children born to slaves was not enough to replenish the labour the colonists needed. It was an imbalance that mirrored for a time the unequal male/female ratios among the settler population.[13]

In contrast to the vast plantation slavery of the Carolinas or Jamaica, Cape slaves were scattered throughout households. By the mid-eighteenth century, one half of all free burghers owned at least one slave. Even free blacks in the Cape, sometimes themselves manumitted slaves, were slave owners. Only seven people owned more than 50 slaves. There was therefore a wide dispersal of slaves around the Cape.

Add to that the cultural heterogeneity – they came from around the world – and it becomes easier to understand that the echo left by slave culture in the Cape has been muted. True, there were two rebellions, the first organised with the help of two Irishmen on a farm near Malmesbury, about 80 kilometres north of Cape Town, in 1808; the other an uprising in 1825 on a farm owned by Willem van der Merwe at the foot of the Koue Bokkeveld mountains a little further north. Both were defeated and in both cases the leaders were executed. More than a century before that, a free black, Sante from Cape Verde, and a slave called Michiel burnt down buildings in Cape Town as a form of protest.[14] There were arson attacks too, throughout the eighteenth century. Again the leaders were punished in the cruellest ways – one was reportedly roasted alive in 1714. The arson attacks did, though, have an enduring effect on the architecture of Cape Town. By order of the VOC (or Dutch East India Company), houses in the city were then built with flat roofs instead of eaves, and with the shutters on the inside rather than the outside of the house.

But while rebels were singled out as examples and executed 'in the most horrid of ways',[15] the daily lives of Cape slaves were different from those in the plantations of the American South in many significant ways. One was that they were mostly, at least in Cape Town, household slaves and enjoyed greater protection from routine physical abuse than slaves on the large plantations of the New World.[16] Secondly, because they were household slaves, a certain intimacy developed between them and their masters.

This is apparent in every corner of Cape culture today, particularly domestic culture. Many of the Afrikaans words used for domestic goods are derived from the Eastern languages the slaves brought with them: *baadjie* (jacket), *koejawel* (guava), *bredie* (stew), *blatjang* (chutney), *piesang* (banana) and, interestingly, *sjambok* (whip), are some of them.

The first Afrikaans book, written in 1856 – 22 years after the emancipation of the slaves – was written in Arabic script by a freed political prisoner, an Imam from Indonesia, who had become a teacher and mentor to several freed slaves in Cape Town. The second book, written in 1869, was by A Effendi, a prominent Islamic leader and teacher in the Cape.[17] And as Islam became a religious haven for many slaves and former slaves, Afrikaans, not Dutch or Arabic, became the language most often used in the mosque.

There was also far more social mobility and racial mixing between the slaves and burghers of the Cape than there was in the plantation slave societies. Perhaps because of the intimacy forced on them, many owners married (and freed) their slaves. The third slave to be freed in the Cape, at the end of the seventeenth century, was Angela of Bengal who eventually made a lively business selling vegetables to ships passing through the Cape. She married a burgher, Arnoldus Willemsz Basson, beginning the Basson lineage, now a well-known Afrikaans surname in South Africa. She owned slaves herself and was also a landowner of note, as was her daughter, Anna de Koningh.[18]

Even Simon van der Stel, who was to become a hero of Afrikaner nationalism two centuries later and whose name the town of Stellenbosch still bears, was the grandson of a freed slave woman, possibly of Indian origin.[19] Had he lived in the town he founded after 1940, he would have been classified coloured and moved out, as indeed Philma Manuel's family was to be.

Generally, few slaves were freed under the Dutch – a total of only 1075 in the last 80 years of Dutch rule. In the 38 years of British rule before emancipation, 2312 slaves were freed.[20]

The key legacy of slavery in the Cape was threefold. Firstly, there was the possibility of mobility. Unlike the American South, where racial discrimination was based on the 'one drop of blood rule', displaying what Fredrickson[21] calls the southern whites' obsessive concern with 'race purity' at the start of the twentieth century, the lighter-skinned descendants of slaves and burghers in the Cape were often accepted as white.

It led Maurice Evans, an early South African segregationist, to declaim in horror when he visited Cape Town in the early twentieth century: 'The toleration of colour and social admixture … (it) is evident in the streets, the tramways, in the railroad stations, public offices and places of entertainment … As a rule, whites and Coloureds keep apart and do not mix but there are a great many exceptions. Young white men will be seen walking with well-dressed coloured girls, and an older European may often be seen with coloured wife and children of varying shades, taking the air and gazing in shop windows. The doors of a bioscope are open and the crowd waiting admission and jostling each other as they get tickets including representatives of each colour … and if he enters the overcrowded room, he will find no distinctions made, all and any colour occupy the same seats, cheek by jowl, and sometimes on each other's knees …'[22]

The second effect was felt after emancipation, and it was to do with the creation of a group of people called 'coloured' that had not hitherto existed as a discrete group.

The British, who then ruled the Cape, outlawed slavery in 1834 but, partly to placate farmers in the outlying areas, they allowed for a four-year apprenticeship period afterwards. On the eve of emancipation, there were 35 745 slaves in the Cape.[23] The vast majority lived in the city itself or in the more arable districts of Stellenbosch and Worcester. Some of the city slaves had acquired artisanal skills but most of the slaves on farms were simply field labourers or domestic servants. In the city, many freed slaves moved out of their masters' homes to the new inner-city slums – District One (now the flourishing and expensive De Waterkant area at the foot of Lion's Head), Bo-Kaap, and later Woodstock and District Six. In fact, residing in a master's house was seen to bear such a mark of slavery's shame that by the 1850s the white residents were complaining that they could not get live-in servants.

People were freed without land or capital. Many of those who had worked on farms were forced to remain, working for clothes, alcohol and food – pretty close to their original condition of slavery. There was no prospect of any peasant class developing, despite some mission stations establishing freehold land for some former slaves in areas north of Cape Town. Unlike the rest of the country, where colonialists had wrested land from reasonably successful, and free, agriculturalists, there was no such thing in the Cape.

Emancipation, combined with Ordinance 50 of 1828 which allowed more freedom of movement to the indigenous Khoi, partly to solve the looming labour crisis on farms caused by the end of slavery, created for the first time what came to be known as the 'coloured people'.

Before then, people had been known as Mozambiquans, or Malays, or Khoikhoi (Hottentot was the derogatory and more widely used term). And then came freedom, when a large group of former slaves and indigenous people were faced with the ardours of making a living on the worst of terms.

Jakes Gerwel, an accomplished academic who headed Nelson Mandela's office in the new government and who turned the coloured University of the Western Cape into an anti-apartheid fortress, has studied this phenomenon. He told me: 'The whole concept of coloured first really surfaced after the emancipation of slaves, if that's the word to use, and Ordinance 50 of 1828 that created this category of Khoi ... (and) ... freed them too. Emancipation and freedom. Which was very ironic because it destroyed them. That's where the concept "coloured" came from ...'

The third effect of slavery was the obliteration of the ancestral roots of many of those classified as coloured in the Western Cape. As in many slave societies, pasts and families became merged or suppressed and forgotten. Names given to slaves were often invented and paternalistic, such as naming them after the months of the year in which they were sold. Hence many Cape Town coloured families bear the surnames September, October, April and so on.

One such is Reg September, one of the first militant coloured members of the African National Congress, who spent most of his adult life in exile. He was to become a key figure – albeit fleetingly – in Trevor Manuel's life many years after he fled the country. When I spoke to him in Cape Town he was 82 and struggling, as he has all his life, to come to grips with the legacy of racial identity in the Western Cape. In his view, if the history of the coloured people was better known, better taught, more spoken about, it would change for the better the often prickly relations between Africans and coloureds in the Western Cape. The forebears of those later classified as 'coloured' by the apartheid government were the first to experience the harshness of colonial rule, and the first to resist it.

September was keen to start a centre for the study of slavery and its legacy, perhaps partly because his name bears a direct link with slaves. He was excited to find, in a collection of papers on slave trials, the names of three Septembers who had taken part in rebellions. But there is no real proof that they were direct ancestors of his: they may just have arrived at the Cape in the same month.

Genealogy, he admitted, is a 'wall you run into'. Take the name Manuel: it could be a slave name or an immigrant name.

These days some of the guesswork can be taken out of genealogy thanks to mitochondrial DNA testing which can trace, within limits, a person's ancestry. There is evidence in the Manuel family, a family member told me, that their matrilineal ancestry goes back to the roots of indigenous African people, while their father's ancestry has traces of Eurasian. The archival evidence, where it exists, supports this conclusion. Manuel's maternal grandmother's family tracks back to the indigenous people of the Northern Cape; likewise his father's mother's family can be traced back a few generations to the indigenous people of the Atlantic west coast. There is less evidence about his father's paternal forebears. But the point is this: while it became fashionable in post-apartheid South Africa to somehow differentiate between the descendants of African agricultural societies and those who had been classified as coloured, the extant evidence does not support this. Even those who were descendants of slaves, rather than of indigenous people, were almost as likely to have had ancestors from other parts of Africa, as they were to have them from Asia. Cape history, and the history of its people, is intimately connected with the history of Africa. At one point many in the media took up a refrain that Manuel's political career was, of necessity, limited because he was not an 'African'. Scientifically, and historically, that argument is almost entirely without substance.

FAMILY LEGEND AMONG THE older members of the Manuel family is that Trevor Manuel's great-grandfather John Manuel emigrated from Portugal in the mid-nineteenth century.[24] But there is no certainty about this.

What we do know is that he married Magdalena Damink, a dark-skinned indigenous woman from Saldanha Bay who outlived him by a few decades and lived in the District Six house with her son James and his growing family.

John Manuel may have been an immigrant. But Manuel was also a common slave name. In 1699, for instance, a freed slave, Manuel of Angola, along with Antonie of Angola and Louis of Bengal, was granted 57 morgen of land in the Jonkershoek Valley. (They also all owned slaves.) The farm was then called Schoongezicht. The freed slaves were eventually bought out by a Dutch settler, Isaq Shriijver, and when the farm was sold in the early twentieth century to a British woman she changed the name to Lanzerac.[25] It is now the site of a luxury hotel and restaurant that nestles in the valleys around Stellenbosch. Perhaps the Manuels came originally from Angola. Perhaps they came from the Philippines when a number of Filipino fishermen settled in Kalk Bay from the mid-1800s onwards, with Spanish and Portuguese surnames such as De la Cruz, Menigo and Gomez that persist in Cape Town's coloured community today. Or perhaps they came from Portugal.

What we do know for certain is that James Manuel, Trevor Manuel's grandfather, was born in Cape Town, probably in the early 1880s, and brought up in the house at 44 Eckhard Street in District Six. He married Christine Mullins, who came from the Atlantic west coast. Her mother's family name was Vraagom, which is a common indigenous name in the Saldanha Bay area.

James and Christine Manuel had nine children – five boys and four girls born, according to Hester Seale, the eldest daughter, about two years apart. She was born in 1909; the oldest, Johnny, in about 1904; and the youngest, Maria, in 1919. Trevor's father Abraham was born in 1917.

They grew up in the heart of District Six, James Manuel working at B Lawrence, a large retail store in Buitenkant Street in the city.

'He had quite a job there,' said Hester. 'They used to sell groceries and things. He was a supervisor, and a packer ... he ordered the boys around.'

When the retail store closed down, he became a salesman. It is difficult to confirm exactly when he died but it appears that Hester was in her early twenties.

The Manuel house was sixth in a row of nine terraced houses, all painted green. There were three big rooms, a kitchen, a tiny yard in the back and a large veranda in the front. When they were growing up, the three girls shared a room with their granny, Magdalena (Damink) Manuel, the four older boys had one room, and James and Christine shared the room that was used as a living room with the two babies, Abraham and Maria. No bathroom, but a toilet in the backyard. A double burner wood stove in the kitchen and a large table made that room the centre of family life. Although the Manuels were strict on the protocol of saying grace at table and not being too rowdy, it was the place where school and work and the day's business were discussed. It was also the place where the family bathed in front of the wood stove in a galvanised iron bath. There were carpets in the room where the parents slept and a mat for the boys. Hester dreamt of having a carpet.

26

It could not have been an easy life, especially for Christine Manuel who cooked daily for 12 people, who washed and darned her family's clothes and who ironed with a large iron heated on the wood stove and then cooled on a sandbag. There was no such thing as last-minute ironing. 'That Saturday night you had to iron your dress for Sunday,' said Hester. 'Even if it's creased, you're not going to get an iron tomorrow morning.' Kitty Manuel, as Christine was known, hardly left the house. She never worked, 'or walked around or went to bioscope'.

The chores, the mealtimes, the prayers and the routines were a kind of strict order the Manuels imposed on their large family at a time of considerable uncertainty in the country and in District Six itself. The Manuel children grew up at a time when gangs were beginning to form on the streets, a time when the Depression left many people in Cape Town, but especially coloured people, unemployed or in lower paying jobs as the 'civilised labour' policy took hold.[26] 'If your daddy comes home,' Kitty Manuel once warned the older boys who had gone to a nearby field to play football with 'Europeans', 'and he asks for you, you better be there.'

Although there was still a racial fluidity in Cape Town in the years before the Second World War, from the 1930s onwards there was far more social consciousness about race, underpinned by real economic hardships imposed on coloured working-class people. In 1922, for example, when Hester would have been about 13, and Abraham Manuel just five, the Apprenticeship Act set minimum educational standards for artisans which many coloured artisans were hard-pressed to meet, most having been to inferior schools.[27] The white labour policy also meant a marked decline in coloureds in the public service in Cape Town. From 1924-1932 the number of coloured public service employees dropped from 44 per cent of the total to 30 per cent, while the proportion of white employees rose in the same period from 44 to 68 per cent.[28] In manufacturing, a similar story: the proportion of coloureds dropped from half to about 40 per cent in that period. By the end of the Depression, the only coloured craftsmen left were 'clinging to the building trades'. The only industry that increased during that period was the clothing industry – it almost doubled in size despite the Depression, and young coloured women began to flood into the industry.

All of this exacerbated poverty and uncertainty in coloured households. In 1937 the Willcocks Commission of Inquiry into the socio-economic conditions of the coloured population found that the infant mortality rate for coloured babies was twice that of whites, and that government spent twice as much on white children's education as it did on that of coloured children.[29]

It was a time when the permeability of the colour bar was the only hope for many coloured families. It made perfect economic sense, if you could, to reclassify as a 'European'. The Manuel family, like thousands of others, were aware of this possibility and discussed their options.

But, like many, the family itself varied in hue. James Manuel was tall, with blue eyes and light hair. 'Oh, he passed for European,' said Hester. 'And (his) other sisters, all, sisters and brothers.' But Kitty Manuel was a short, slight woman with darker skin and dark hair. 'Beautiful long hair. She was a lovely woman.'

Some of James Manuel's siblings registered as 'European'. At that time, before the cruder, crueller rigours of apartheid's racial testing, they judged you on 'face value', as Hester put it. If you looked white, you were white. But the Manuel family – many of the children in young adulthood now in the late 1930s – discussed it and decided not to go and register for a 'European card'. 'Come on Hester,' someone told her. 'You can get a better pension.'

'I said "pension"? We honoured my mommy. She was too lovely. To turn around now! Why should we? God will provide. So none of us went. We didn't worry. We all stuck together.' Even though, as she said, her 'daddy's side was white' and her 'mommy's side coloured'.

In later years one of Abraham and Hester's sisters did reclassify as white, one after she married a white man. There was scarcely a family who was immune from the crude indignities, and subsequent pain, of dividing themselves racially.

Reg September, who grew up in the 1930s and 40s in Kenilworth, a suburb in the desirable southern part of the Peninsula which became white under apartheid, recalls painful family outings. His mother was fair, his father a 'copperish' colour. After train apartheid was introduced in the 1950s his father, Nicholas September, urged his mother Florrie to travel in the first-class, whites-only compartment of the train, while he and the children travelled at the back in the coloured section. And September's sister, who was also light-skinned, would entertain white colleagues at her home when she started work. If Nicholas, her father, happened to walk into the house during these visits he would pretend to be the gardener (he was actually a builder) so as not to embarrass her. September is still aghast: 'Can you believe it? When you know what we did to our own people?'

It is not surprising that Hester was Trevor Manuel's favourite aunt whom he visited regularly until she died in 1995, soon after he became a cabinet minister. ('Ooh! She was so proud of him,' recalled his sister Beryl, who was with Hester when she died.) Manuel inherited many of Hester's traits. She was forthright, outspoken, loyal. In the face of the most devastating forced removal the Cape had seen up till then – of District Six – she simply refused to move to one of the grim townships on the Cape Flats set aside for coloureds. She took up residence in the city and spent her last days in a flat above the Methodist Church in Buitenkant Street, ironically where the District Six Museum is now. She took after her father in looks. Skin a light creamy coffee, and long slate-black hair. Her family remembers her as a beautiful woman: 'A fox, an absolute fox,' says Manuel's sister Pam.

She could indeed have 'passed' but she never tried. In fact she prided herself on her 'colouredness'. She married Ernest Seale, a man of African origin whose ancestors had been among a small group of freed African-American slaves who came to the Cape at the end of the nineteenth century.[30] Ernest Seale worked at a large department store called Pickles, long since closed down. 'She always had on her best,' said Pam. 'Very classy.'

Hester had begun work in a sweet and box-making factory, Buchanan's, when she was about 18, soon after her father died. She spent 41 years there and was a respected supervisor for most of that time. She supervised 'girls' making boxes for candy. The only other coloured supervisor was Benny Kies, the father of Ben Kies who was later to become the head of one of the most influential organisations in coloured politics, the Teachers' League of South Africa. Mr Benny, as Hester called him, supervised the candy makers.

She had started as a girl in pigtails, and although she enjoyed the work and was proud of what she did, she was never satisfied with her pay. Twice she threatened to leave. And then one day, after she was married, she had an altercation with one of the white bosses. She told him that she earned such a little and she gave 'everything' to her work. She had told him off in front of 'her girls'.

As she recounted the story later, the Sunday after that fight Mr Benny brought the general manager, a Mr Saunders, to see her. 'I was pale as a sheet when I opened the door,' she recalled. They tried to placate her. 'To think you're a coloured girl, and you're so gifted,' said Mr Benny. And then he added: 'Hester, there isn't another person in the factory that had the guts to speak to Mr Cooper like that.'

29

'So I said, yes, Mr Benny. I'm not scared of a white man. I said my daddy's also a white man.'

It was a peculiar type of confidence and pride that refused to be bent by the circumstance of race discrimination then being so steadily sharpened.

TREVOR MANUEL'S MATERNAL FOREBEARS, the Von Söhnens, showed a similar robustness in navigating a world whose circumference seemed to tighten around them. Unlike the Manuels, they were slightly more well-to-do and owned property.

Maximillian von Söhnen was born in Prussia in 1864. He arrived in the Cape on a naval ship from Germany, probably in the 1880s. He worked as a welder and boilermaker on the ship and was also a skilled plumber. Somehow, he made his way to Stellenbosch, the winelands town about 80 kilometres from Cape Town, met Pauline Daniels, married her and settled there.

In his pictures he looks the archetypical Prussian: pale, with fierce blue eyes and a moustache.

Pauline Daniels was a midwife who came from what must have been a fairly well-to-do indigenous family in the Northern Cape.

The centre of family life for the Von Söhnens for the next 80 years would become a large property – 'fifty-eight square roods, forty-eight feet' – in the tree-lined Andringa Street, the very centre of the picturesque town of Stellenbosch that spreads itself through the verdant valleys under the Hottentots Holland Mountains. It was bought by Pauline's father in 1888 for 50 pounds. Eight years later, in 1896, it was 'passed in favour' to Maximillian von Söhnen. In 1932, Maximillian's fourth-born child Leonard bought the house from his father for 600 pounds.

It was here that Von Söhnen senior, who became a naturalised citizen of the Cape (and later of the Union of South Africa) in 1899, started his plumbing business which was to last through two generations. And it was here, in this large, sprawling house, blessed with a rose garden and orchard, that Philma Manuel's mother, Anne von Söhnen was born and raised.

Anne was the second of six children born to Maximillian and Pauline von Söhnen. She was born in 1893. (There was also an adopted son, Eduard, who died of tuberculosis in 1939.) Her younger brother Leonard, who inherited both the house and the business, was born seven years later in 1900 and became the effective head of the Von Söhnen family and guardian of its name after Maximillian died in 1956.

Andringa Street in the heart of Stellenbosch is redolent (*deurdrenk*) with a history 'both sweet and sour', as Stellenbosch academic Hermann Giliomee, writes. 'It was a busy shopping street (as indeed it still is) with banks, furniture shops, a printing shop, and electrical shop. Further north, towards the mountain, was Seritsky's news agency, where white and brown gathered in big numbers every Saturday to buy the last edition of the *Cape Argus* with the sports results.'[31]

The street also seemed to be a centre for civil engagement. At various times, General Jan Smuts, South Africa's wartime prime minister, J B M Hertzog, leader of the Afrikaner Nationalist Party, and Dr A Abdurahman, the best-known coloured political leader in the first half of the twentieth century, 'addressed brown voters' from the Temperance Hall there. Later the building was to become the Stellenbosch Onderlinge Vereniging (SOV) hall, of which Maximillian von Söhnen was an active member.

On the northern end of the street, near the Gaiety Bioscope and behind the little Dutch Reformed Church, was the Von Söhnen house.

Dawn von Söhnen, the oldest daughter of Leonard, who grew up in the house, remembers it as 'fairly big' – four bedrooms, a huge dining hall, a sitting room, a games room. Outside were old stables that had been converted for the family business: plumbing and welding. There was also a shoemaking business and a little barber shop on the premises, and in the early part of the century it housed a classroom for children from the school run by the nearby church.

Many accounts of local of Stellenbosch history describe Maximillian, and later his son Leonard, as 'respected' and 'loved' in the community. They were plumbers for a wide range of people including Giliomee's brother and the Rupert family, icons of early Afrikaner business who owned wineries and the tobacco company Rembrandt van Rijn. 'We used to go to Fleur de Cap (the Rupert wine farm) with my father,' said Dawn. 'Sometimes he would take us with just for the ride.'

Von Söhnen senior was also famous for the fish horns he made. In the days before apartheid wrecked the community, Stellenbosch got its fresh fish from fishermen who rode up in carts from the Strand about 20 kilometres away on the coast. Von Söhnen made the tin horns for the fish carts, 'first the mouthpiece then the horn to be soldered together'. 'When the coloured population heard the sound of the fish horn they would cry, "The Fish is blowing!" and converge on the cart, as did the whites. The horn was audible

31

from a distance, giving everybody enough time to leave his house and buy fresh fish as the cart went by.'[32]

If there is one thing that the Von Söhnens, father and son, were even more famous for than their plumbing and welding abilities it was their inability to issue accounts. 'It was well known,' Giliomee wrote of the older Von Söhnen, 'that he did outstanding work but never sent an account ...'[33]

His son Leonard inherited this trait. An elderly white man in Stellenbosch, Willem Lubbe, remembers the regular work Von Söhnen did for his family and how he never sent an account. Lubbe's father would ask him: 'Man, when am I getting the account?' and Von Söhnen would reply, 'Sir, I haven't yet put it together but it will come.'

'But it never came and I can remember a month before my father's death he asked Von Söhnen to come as though there was work at the house for him, and when he arrived said, "But no, I have no work for you, but I want to pay you," and again came the answer that he would send an account.' But his father, wise to Von Söhnen's forgetful generosity, gave him a cheque for R1 000 (this was in the late 1960s), saying: 'Von Söhnen, if it is too little, then come and get more money, if it is too much, then please keep it.'[34]

'He was very bad at that,' said his daughter Dawn. 'He was a poor administrator. At the time I suppose he just did his work and when he needed the money would call in the bills.' It helped that he had a contract with the local hospital and he must have finally called in his payments because until his death he employed four or five people in the business. He also sent his daughters to university and helped relatives pay for their children's education.

Relations between the races in the small town were sometimes tense even before apartheid and even in this close-knit community. In 1940 white students from Stellenbosch University, enraged by the South African government's decision to support the Allied forces in the War, and by an order compelling them to hand in their arms, took out their anger on those they perceived to be its nearest and most vulnerable supporters. These were the coloured residents of Andringa Street. There was some rationale for the bullying too: at least one quarter of voters in Stellenbosch were coloured at that time.[35]

On a winter's evening at the end of July, between 200 and 300 students armed themselves – in defiance of the ban – with sticks and other crude weapons and went to the coloured section of Andringa Street looking for trouble. 'Respectable coloured people sitting in their houses were beaten, furniture and wireless sets broken, windows smashed and other damage done by a crowd of students,' reported a local newspaper.[36]

There had been a similar clash between white right-wing students and coloured people earlier that day in Adderley Street, Cape Town's main street, sparked by a government call for a minute's silence in the city in support of the troops. The white students had come off worst. Cissie Gool, the daughter of Dr Abdurahman and then the leader of the Non-European United Front of South Africa, described the attack on Andringa Street as a consequence of their routing in Adderley Street, an attempt 'to wreak their vengeance out on somebody ... their desire for revenge, combined with their hatred of the Coloured race led to the mass attack'.[37]

Throughout the rampage, the two Von Söhnen men, father and son, were reputed to have sat stoically on their veranda, glowering at the hooligans. Somehow, even in the midst of a rampage, they were too respected and respectable to become victims.

Years later, as apartheid was in its death throes, Trevor Manuel wreaked a kind of inter-generational revenge against Stellenbosch students who were foolish enough to display similar conduct.

But in 1940 the 'white riot' of Andringa Street was only a foretaste of the bitterness to come.

By the time Maximillian von Söhnen died in 1956, Leonard had taken over the business completely. Old man Von Söhnen was buried with his wife Pauline, who had died in 1927 when their grandchild Philma was just a baby. The old man, who had spoken to his family all their lives in 'broken Afrikaans with a German accent', had gone to his room to lie down. When one of his children looked in on him, he said simply: '*Dis klaar,*' and died. He was 92.

Philma's mother Anne had grown up in the substantial shade cast by this family. Yet even though the business had prospered, she still had to earn a living. For women in those days, particularly coloured women, the options were few, but yet better than in any other part of the country. Women in the Cape were a far higher proportion of the workforce than elsewhere in South Africa. Anne must have started work in her late teens, possibly in the second decade of the twentieth century. The post-First World War period gave a 'major fillip' to industrial growth in the Cape.[38] Trade boomed and the food and canning industry, whose nucleus was in the arable south-west of the Cape, became one of the leading industries in the region. In 1916/1917, at the time Anne must have started work, it employed nearly a quarter of the region's industrial workforce. She began work at a fruit farm (Rhodes fruit farm) and later moved to a winery.

After she gave birth to her only daughter Philma in 1926 she continued working in the industry. Her family remembers that she became an active member of the Food and Canning Workers' Union (FCWU) after it was founded in 1940. In sharp contrast to the servile Garment Workers' Union, which her daughter Philma was forced to join, from the outset the FCWU was visionary in the sense that it refused to divide its members racially. The racial division of trade unions between coloured and African workers was later to become a serious obstacle to black unity in the Western Cape. And the FCWU was militant. One of its founders was Ray Alexander, a young Jewish Lithuanian immigrant who was also a Communist Party stalwart. Two decades later, when apartheid had strangled almost every avenue of resistance, she went into exile with her husband Jack Simons, also a member of the Communist Party. The union's non-racialism and its militancy sparked hostile reaction among the conservative farmer-industrialists in the rural Cape. In the early years of the Second World War, a junior manager at a fruit packing firm in Montagu, a little town north-east of Cape Town, had told a union deputation 'we're not going to sit down and discuss things with Joodse, Hotnots and Kaffirs'. Union leaders asked the senior managers if they 'were prepared to co-operate and support this Nazi outlook',[39] and managed to shame the firm into some type of cooperation.

But Anne von Söhnen kept the extent of her involvement in the union quiet. Her family only had a vague idea of it. In the same way, when her only daughter Philma was born, she gave no clue about who the father was or her relationship with him. And after Philma was born, she seemed to focus only on her work. Both Philma and her grandchildren remember her as an independent, hard-working woman. 'She was out of this house at ten past five every morning,' recalled Philma Manuel.

Forthright, also. One day, walking in the streets of Salt River with Manuel's sister Pam, Anne tripped in a pothole and fell. Gerry Ferry, a blacksmith who became something of a populist mayor of Cape Town in the 1960s, lived in Woodstock, unusual for a white mayor but in keeping with the kind of 'man of the people' mantle he wore around his shoulders. It was early evening. Without hesitation she limped around the corner to his house and banged on his door. He was in bed but invited the woman and girl in. 'She gave him a

34

ticking off because there were potholes in the road and she fell,' said Pam.

The Von Söhnen family mirrored the Manuels, as it did so many others in the Cape, in that it was a world in one household. Anne von Söhnen was dark-skinned, as were her brothers Jack and Peter. Leonard and the two sisters, Pearl (Hedwig) and Lettie, took after their German father – fair-skinned with light eyes. One sibling was reclassified white after she married a white man.

Pam remembers her fairer cousins well, and the illicit trips they sometimes took to whites-only beaches on whites-only buses. Her mother, and her grandmother, would have disapproved, she said, not so much because it was against the law but because it was a core denial of who you were.

And while the white cousins visited their coloured relatives, the same courtesies often could not be returned. 'The saddest of all is that they came to your funerals, but you could never go theirs,' said Pam. 'They were buried alone.'

CHAPTER 3

History unhooked

WHEN TREVOR MANUEL WAS seven, he left Windermere Primary and started classes at Wesley Practising and Secondary School in Salt River. It was the same school his mother had attended growing up in Woodstock. His sister Pam started a year earlier, 'the minute we could travel by bus'.

It was not only that his mother had attended the same school that made Wesley more desirable for the Manuels. It was considered better somehow – a school where the medium of instruction was English, rather than Afrikaans, and where, although it went only to Standard 8 (Grade 10 today), it funnelled students into a Teachers' Training College or into two of the three best coloured schools in town, Harold Cressy and Trafalgar, both nearby.[1]

For Trevor Manuel the boy, Cape Town of the mid-1960s was a world which now had well-defined racial limits. To get to Salt River he caught the bus that went up Voortrekker Road towards the mountain and the city. He could sit anywhere he liked on that bus as it passed through predominantly coloured areas to pick up and drop off its passengers. But as soon as he boarded a bus that went down the spine of the Peninsula, in and out of white areas, or to the

Atlantic coastal suburb of Sea Point, he had to sit on the segregated top deck or at the back if the bus was empty.

Sometimes at the Woodstock stop the Manuel children would see their cousin Max, the son of their grandmother's sister Pearl. He would nod at them as they boarded, but would take a seat in the downstairs section, while they would troop upstairs. Max was classified white, because his mother, who had married a white man, had been reclassified.

Train apartheid, in contrast to the buses, was by then firmly entrenched. It had been introduced to Cape Town in 1949 by the new apartheid government which ran the railways. Coloureds sat in second-class coaches, and Africans in third-class on austere benches facing inwards. Buses, under the purview of the Cape Town City Council, had reflected that body's ambivalent attitude towards apartheid for some time into the 1960s.

Every morning, Trevor and his two older sisters took the bus into Salt River with their father who went on to the city to his job at the Council. The boy's life became centred around the area where both of his parents had grown up and where the working class of Cape Town had first clustered and emerged. He changed his boys' cub troop from Kensington to Salt River; he visited his father's family in District Six, just up the hill, more frequently, and if he went to movies it was at the large cinema known as the Palace in the lower Main Road, Salt River.

He also began to speak English at school and to encounter a generation of teachers who believed that strict rote learning was a way out of the historical trap afflicting coloured people. One such was Lesley Jacobs, a man who was for a time married to one of his father's sisters. They learnt multiplication tables and poetry off by heart. 'This stuff was drummed into you day in and day out,' remembered Manuel. 'And if you knew nothing else you knew those two things. My sisters and I, we can say the same poems with the same intonation ... This man was a lunatic.'

Lunatic perhaps, but he gave the Manuel children a taste of learning without let-up, of a framework they could not step out of. Their schools, so carefully picked out by their parents in a world of few choices, were chosen precisely for this reason.

It was a time when race classification was in full force. Although there had been a dilemma in the ruling National Party (NP) about precisely what to do about those who became 'coloured' people,[2] any prevarication was settled in 1956 with the ascendancy to power of the conservative Transvaal faction of the National Party led by J G Strijdom, apartheid prime minister of South Africa from 1954 to 1958. A hardliner, he pushed to a conclusion his predecessor D F Malan's attempts to remove coloureds completely from the voters' roll – a qualified franchise in the Cape had been in place and protected by the constitution since 1909. His faction of apartheid's ruling party had consolidated their victory over the slightly more subtle Cape Nationalists who, as Hermann Giliomee described them, were 'kleurling verlig maar swart verkramp' (enlightened about coloureds, but conservative about blacks).[3]

As Ian Goldin writes, coloured identity became an 'ideological battleground of great intensity within the National Party'.[4] The divide was not really surprising; the majority of coloured people in the Western Cape shared the same language as their Afrikaner counterparts and in many ways the same culture and the same lineage.

The outcome of the battle was that both coloureds and blacks in the Western Cape got the worst of both worlds. Coloured people, who until then had a limited and unequal franchise, were removed from the voters' roll completely and, in huge upheavals, from the homes and communities they had lived in for generations. For Africans, it meant stricter influx control laws and a plummet in the standard of living as the Western Cape was declared, as a kind of sop to the Cape Nationalists, a 'coloured labour preference area'. Known as the Eiselen line (after NP ideologue W W Eiselen), it declared anything west of an imaginary line drawn southwards down the country from Port Elizabeth as a coloured labour preference area. This meant that all Africans, with the exception of a few whose families had lived there for generations, could come to the Western Cape to work only on sufferance and in the lowest paid, most unskilled jobs. They lived in single-sex migrant worker hostels in the African townships. Unlike the Transvaal, there was almost no African middle class, and less commonality between Africans and coloured people than there had been in the pre-apartheid days.

Coloured people were now almost totally relegated to unskilled and semi-skilled work; further, the 'efforts to promote racial identities were associated with a massive programme of legislation'.[5] And whatever racial fluidity there had been before was gone. For the first time 'coloureds' were defined in law as a separate race.

After H F Verwoerd came to power in 1958, he 'took a very, very tough line over any sort of toenadering or verbroedering met die kleurlinge' (togetherness

38

or brotherhood with the Coloureds), remembers Giliomee, a member of the Cape National Party at the time. 'You can't have different policies, because if you *do* keep coloureds in Parliament (Verwoerd argued), then the Africans will continue to hope to be represented in Parliament as well.'

Of course to make it all work, you had to know who was who and that was not always easy in Cape Town, given its mixed and fluid history. Undeterred, the National Party government under Verwoerd tightened up the Population Registration Act so that acceptance as a white was no longer on 'face value', as Manuel's aunt Hester Seale had described it a decade or so earlier. The Act was amended and tightened 15 times between 1956 and 1986, and coloureds themselves were divided into seven subcategories.[6] Race became determined by 'general acceptance' and not only appearance.

It led to a situation worthy of Kafka where, as in *The Metamorphosis*, the punishment precedes the crime. Informers were paid to tattle on neighbours whom they thought might not be white; it led to vendettas, break-up of families, illness, suicides and emigration.

One victim was well-known welterweight boxer, Ronnie van der Walt, who was reclassified from white to coloured in 1967. 'Van der Walt had attended a "whites-only" school and boxed on the more lucrative "whites-only" circuit. However, a letter was sent to the Cape Boxing Control Board querying his race on the day he was due to fight in a tournament at Green Point Stadium. Van der Walt's name was taken off the bill. He lodged an appeal with the Race Classification Board and began to prepare a case to prove his "white" descent. However, the family feared that if he were to fight the case his wife's coloured ancestry would be traced. It was a catch-22. If her origins were revealed, he would have been convicted of contravening the Immorality Act for living with a woman classified "coloured".'[7]

Van der Walt, like many other victims of race classification with some means, did not wait for his appeal to be heard: he left the country, his boxing career finished.

The Mixed Marriages Act and the Immorality Act, designed to prohibit the kind of mixed families that Manuel's forebears had grown up in, sent a deliberate message to those who thought they might flout racism through marriage: 'The door is being closed to them,' said H J Erasmus, an NP legislator defending the Mixed Marriages Act. 'They are being given the opportunity in their own ranks to aspire to a higher status for themselves.'[8]

A crude ugliness developed in South African society: one famous manifestation of this was the 'pencil test', whereby a pencil was put in the hair of someone whose race 'purity' was in doubt. If it stuck in natural curls, it was a sign of African or coloured ancestry. As in most societies where race determines social status, there developed a warped sense of hierarchy based on appearance in the underclass itself.

At that time Abraham Manuel was involved in the administration of soccer and darts. There was a plethora of teams around Cape Town, many bearing the names of the white suburbs where they had once lived. So, for instance, a soccer team based in Bonteheuwel, a grim Cape Flats coloured township, was called the 'Sea Point Swifts', after their origins on the Atlantic coast. But within those teams there were also sharp prejudices against 'Malays', against people with darker skins, against those with short, curly hair. 'In the Cape District football union, which was based in Wynberg (a mixed suburb in the southern Peninsula), if you were Muslim, Malay, you couldn't play there, if you had short hair you couldn't play there,' Manuel recalled his father explaining to him. 'So there was within the coloured community their own kind of pencil test mentality.' In some instances, the constitution of the clubs specifically prohibited 'Malays' – Muslims – from joining.[9]

It's a legacy that still permeates the country but in its unspoken subtlety, particularly in Cape Town, it is barely apparent to outsiders. When he came back from exile in the 1990s, Reg September started a branch of the African National Congress in Wynberg, near the suburb where he had grown up. He fell into conversation in the street one day with a Muslim woman and told her about an ANC house meeting he planned to host in the area.

'Am I allowed to come?' she asked.

'Of course you are,' he replied. He didn't ask her why she had asked the question. He knew.

This detailed racial pecking order in societies defined by race is not a phenomenon unique to South Africa. C L R James, the renowned West Indian cricket writer and historian, and one-time cricketer, recounts in his book *Beyond a Boundary*, that Maple, the cricket club in Trinidad that he joined after nursing serious doubts 'was the club of the brown-skinned middle class … Class did not matter to them as much as colour. They had founded themselves on the principle that they didn't want any dark people in their club. A lawyer or a doctor with a distinctly dark skin would have been blackballed, though light-skinned department-store clerks of uncertain income and still more uncertain lineage were admitted as a matter of course.'[10]

James, despite his dark skin, was eventually let into Maple mainly because many of his friends played there. But he found in Trinidad similar patterns after emancipation as pertained in Cape Town: 'Between the brown-skinned middle class and the black there is a continual rivalry, distrust and ill-feeling, which, skilfully played upon by the European peoples, poisons the life of the community.'

In the South Africa of the 1960s this 'poison' towards the darker-skinned was more contemptuous, more aggressive. And it was enshrined in law. Only sometimes would merit take precedence over colour. So Manuel remembers his father telling him of how a District Six club accepted a darker-skinned player called Vince Belgiums only because 'he was a very good soccer player … and he was going to bring fame to them'.

What had once been a discriminatory but fluid society in the Western Cape was transformed into a rigid racial hierarchy and what had been, at best, a putative 'race' descended from indigenous people, slaves, and sometimes colonists, was reinvented as a distinct racial category.

The heavy hand of complete segregation made its presence felt more acutely in Manuel's generation and space than in any other in South Africa. For Africans in the north of the country, segregation was not as new – it was old and established and discriminatory laws had long been applied. And in the Cape, the generation that Manuel's parents belonged to was still somewhat protected by the fluidity of the colour line.

But now, in the 1960s, the hurt was immediate and apparent, particularly for children. Cheryl Carolus, who was to become a close friend and comrade of Manuel's a decade later, describes the impression it made on her as a small child.

Darker-skinned than Manuel – her grandfather was Xhosa – there was no way that she or her family could float past the colour bar. In the early 1960s she remembers her family going on an outing to Clovelly, a pristine beach edged on False Bay in the southern Peninsula. It was not a traditional 'coloured' beach – it was better. That's why her parents, a printer's assistant and a nurse aide, opted to take her and her sisters there one Sunday.

'It was a big thing, just going on the bus even out of the township where you were … You save up to go to the beach so it wasn't like something you did every weekend.' This particular weekend, her family had cooked roast chicken on Saturday evening, prepared cream crackers with cheese. On Sunday they packed their lunch, pots and all, into a large suitcase.

They had caught the bus to the train station in Mowbray from their home in Athlone on the Cape Flats, taken the hour-long train journey down the line through white and coloured suburbs, past the ageing, shabby charm of Muizenberg, the seaside resort, past the 'traditional' coloured beach of Kalk Bay, a fishing harbour, before alighting at Clovelly.

At the beach, after they had unpacked the food, spread out towels and blankets, and settled the Carolus baby in the suitcase to sleep, two white men walked towards them and called her father over. From a distance, she saw 'it was quite a heated thing between them.

'Then he came back and very abruptly told us we had to go. Now firstly we'd just arrived and we were just about to have this fabulous time.

'Secondly, you know how kids smell blood. And there wasn't a logical explanation at all for this thing, and we wanted to know why. And he was very abrupt about this thing, very forceful that we had to pack up.'

It was how apartheid worked, Carolus observed many years later: black men had to police their own families, and make them believe 'they shouldn't even aspire towards these things'.

It may explain why Abraham Manuel always expressed more open resentment to apartheid than did his wife Philma. Certainly he felt its immediacy when his family house was torn down in Eckhard Street in District Six, and his mother moved to Heideveld with her granddaughter Christine Amansure, the daughter of Abraham's older sister Lena Brown. Lena worked at the box-making factory with Aunt Hester, and Christine, born in 1936, had spent almost every afternoon after school in the District Six house with her grandmother.

Heideveld is far from the shadow of Devil's Peak, the mountain which Hester Manuel and her siblings climbed as soon as they were old enough. About 25 kilometres from the city, it is located on the windblown, sandy Cape Flats. On its eastern side runs a railway line that borders the African township of Guguletu, which by then housed many of Trevor Manuel's childhood neighbours from Kensington.

There is barely a coloured family in the Western Cape who has not been affected by the Group Areas Act. The generation that is now in middle adulthood had parents and grandparents who were moved; friends, cousins, aunts and uncles once lived in the leafy mountain suburbs of Newlands, Claremont, the Atlantic coastal area of Sea Point, in Wynberg and Kenilworth above the railway line that came to delineate clusters of colour and class in the southern Peninsula as much as it provided a transport system. Most of all, the large coloured working class, many on the cusp of something better gleaned through education and hard work, lived in District Six.

Residential segregation was not unique to apartheid. When the first segregation bills, known as the 'Hertzog bills' were introduced in 1926, they tried to segregate Africans from coloureds in the Cape.

Ten years later, coloured people vigorously fought off attempts at residential segregation. In 1936, about one third of Cape Town's suburbs were racially mixed, although more and more segregated coloured housing schemes, such as Kensington, were being built. In 1938, General Jan Smuts, then prime minister of the Union of South Africa, publicly declared his support for residential segregation between coloured and white.

As in all South African history there are layers of deep irony in this: often seen as a saviour by the coloured elite and middle classes in the earlier part of the century, and as a world statesman during the Second World War, Smuts nevertheless threw in his lot with a growing band of voluble white segregationists who emerged in the 1930s. The intellectual politician had, like so many Capetonians, taken solace in mountain walks, and Trevor's Aunt Hester had once bumped into him on one of her first trips up the mountain. So excited was she at the meeting that she asked if she could take a picture of him.

'All right, but you'd better hurry up,' he responded gruffly. There is no sense of acrimony in her account of this.

The National Party of D F Malan, who was to become apartheid's first prime minister, rallied around a petition in 1939 calling for complete social, political and residential segregation. The threat of residential segregation provoked huge ire among coloured political organisations who took up the campaign even more energetically than the campaign for an equal franchise. In Kimberley and Cape Town, where the majority of coloured people lived, thousands turned out on the streets at Days of Prayer and Days of Protest to object to the proposals.[11]

Smuts's government attempted a clumsy compromise, proposing a 'Servitude Scheme' whereby residents could keep an area uni-racial if 75 per cent of them put racial restrictions into their title deeds; in effect, restricting new owners to a particular racial group. This proposal went by the misnomer of 'voluntary segregation'.

Smuts back-pedalled on some of these moves as the Second World War

43

loomed large, probably because he needed the loyalty of coloured servicemen in the war effort.

In District Six, though, the largest coloured working-class area in the city of Cape Town, the Servitude Scheme was academic. The vast majority of residents there rented their houses.[12]

'Very few of the properties in District Six belonged to the coloured people, it was mostly the Indians and Europeans that owned property there,' said Sergeant Willem Nel of the Police Special Unit who worked in District Six in the late 1940s. 'Some of these flats in Vredehoek (a nearby white suburb) were built from money made in District Six by landlords and shopkeepers. That's why white people complained … about the destruction of District Six, it was because they were making money there.'[13]

Certainly District Six had a mean and grim side.[14] And certainly it was beset by poverty in many parts. Sergeant Nel recounted how he would often see extended families of '40 to 50 people sitting in the rain out on the pavement (after failing to pay rent). I've bought food out of my pocket for the children.'[15] In 1946 more than half the coloured children in the District were found to be suffering from malnutrition, and nearly three quarters of the black children.[16] Towards the end of the Second World War interest rates rose; in 1951, a Rents Board put a ceiling on rentals. Landlords stopped buying rental properties and the result in the inner-city areas was even more serious overcrowding.

And yet there is barely a person who grew up in the District who has bad memories of it.

Fred Robertson, who became a close friend of Trevor Manuel in adulthood, was born and raised in St Philips Street, around the corner from the Manuel family home. He was one of the earliest pioneers in black business, establishing his own insurance and financial services firm towards the end of apartheid.

He was one of nine children, two boys and seven girls, and it was only when I asked him how big the house was that he thought, for the first time, that it may have been crowded. 'It was probably a 40 to 50 square metre house. Two bedrooms and a kitchen. A small back room and a shed in the yard.' Where did he sleep? 'Behind my mother's back.' The seven sisters slept sardine-like on mattresses on the floor in one bedroom.

But, as in the Manuel family home, in the kitchen there was 'this Dover coal stove, where the family gathered in winter … Everybody would sit. There would be a pot with water on. Somebody would go to the butcher and buy bones because that was all we could afford … Crayfish *toppies* (the shells after the meat had been removed for white people), we throw in there and whatever. But while that fire's going, the father, even if he's unemployed, and the mother, could keep that family going.'

It is the warmth he remembers: of the stove, of the community, the loud streets. 'Which is not something you have in the shanties, not in the scheme houses, so there's no warmth, no physical warmth, which is what we had.'

Scores of old residents remember the pots of food on the stove: if someone had lost his job, the children would take the family a plate of food. Most people eschewed pork because their Muslim neighbours wouldn't have eaten it, and they may well have dropped in.

Unusually, Fred Robertson's father owned the house. Frederick Anthony Robertson, born in 1917, the same year as Abraham Manuel, organised 'coon troops' in the summer and darts tournaments in the off-season. A lively relic of the days of slavery and emancipation, the coons, garishly attired bands of minstrels that originated in the streets of District Six, have slipped in and out of political correctness in the long, tortured history of the country. But that they were a central part of life in the District cannot be ignored.

As a child, Fred knew the Manuel family but only met Trevor later in adult life. He sold bowls of fruit at their door, fruit gleaned from the remains of a local hawker's barrel, and newspapers too. 'And when it comes down to Christmas, we would go knock on doors and go wish Merry Christmas even to people we don't know.'

It was a buzzing yet ordered community. Hanover Street, the main thoroughfare in District Six, could overwhelm an outsider. *Cape Times* journalist Brian Barrow described it on a Saturday, any Saturday, morning: 'a river of people, cars, barrows, buses, horse-drawn carts and small boys racing down the slopes in soap box carts ... messengers, fah-fee runners, cripples, skollies, loafers, dope-peddlers, men and women with haunting faces – oriental, Arabic, Semitic, European, Hottentot African, people whose faces were the faces of Malaya, India, Ceylon, Mauritius, Mozambique, Africa, Western and Eastern Europe, all blending with each other but each somehow retaining a shadow of its origins.'[17] (This was written in the days before the word 'Hottentot' was considered a pejorative.)

Fruit hawkers, fishmongers, butchers, barber shops, tailors, milliners and general dealers lined Hanover Street. Many shops were run by white people, some by Indians. But there was an unforgettable sense of community and energy that struck outsiders and is revered by insiders to this day.

It may have been this early connection with the Manuel family that sparked Trevor Manuel's affection for Robertson. Fred spoke like his Aunt Hester, a peculiarly local and fluid mix of Afrikaans and English, a District Six patois that is unique to the area. Only with his Aunt Hester, when she was still alive, and with Robertson does Manuel talk like that, or even use Afrikaans in that way.

It seemed then that an invincible thread bound the community. But it was not strong enough to withstand the Group Areas Act, which consolidated the years of white prejudice and fear about the District.

District Six was declared a white area in 1966, 16 years after the Group Areas Act was enacted. In the next 15 years, some 60 000 people were moved out of the District, among them Abraham Manuel's mother and her daughters' families, and Fred Robertson and his family. The destruction of the community happened almost imperceptibly, little by little.

First, says Robertson, 'they brought the freeway in. So in doing that they obviously got a lot of liberals on their side from Wynberg, Newlands, Rondebosch. So then the houses along the highway had to go, they destroyed those.'

In fact, the Eastern Boulevard, now the main highway that carries traffic from the Cape Flats and southern suburbs to the city, had been mooted 20 years earlier in mid-1940. And in the minds of planners it was always connected with the destruction of District Six. Mr E Beaudouin, then chief architect to the French government, was engaged by the Cape Town City Council to replan the city. In mid-1940 he wrote a report (kept under wraps at the time) advocating 'slum clearance' of District Six, the Malay Quarter (now Bo-Kaap) and the Docks area (where several Africans lived). 'The replanning of District Six will present an opportune occasion for [the extension of a freeway towards the Cape Flats]'.[18]

'It is a healthy site and commands a magnificent outlook,' wrote the City Engineer in the same year. 'Today it is a blot in a beautiful city and a disgrace to civilised conceptions of how human beings should live.'[19]

THE FIRST BATCH OF PEOPLE to move out were offered houses in Vanguard Estate, east of the city on the plains of the Cape Flats. Then in Bonteheuwel, further east, a rougher suburb where gangs quickly developed and ruled the streets.

When Trevor's grandmother Kitty Manuel moved out Fred was about 14 years old.

46

'When people moved out, you noticed, and yet you didn't notice ... because someone always remained behind ... It was like an onion you were peeling off.'

Kitty Manuel moved to Heideveld in 1967 with her granddaughter Christine Amansure who was by then married with four children.

The Manuel daughters, all now married, gathered at the house in Eckhard Street and asked the old lady what she was going to do. 'When we got the letter (from the Group Areas board),' recalled Mrs Amansure, 'I was working at that time, and I came home and I said to my gran, I said well, we better move or what do we want to do? And she said to me, no, your husband asked me already, I'm going with you. That's why she went along with us and she stayed with me ... My granny wasn't a person who would put herself out with things, she was a very gentle old lady.'

It may have been something of a puzzle to the younger generation that there was not more resistance to the obliteration of District Six, especially when there had been such massive protests against residential segregation before the war. It may have been something of a puzzle even to the Manuel family of Abraham's generation that the mother who had raised them – strict, thrifty, unbending – would seem so apparently unirked by such upheaval.

After all, the razing of District Six wiped out not only a community of some 60 000 people but an entire legacy of culture and literature. Like its counterpart in Johannesburg, Sophiatown, also a vibrant cross-cultural bed, it gave life to some of the best talent of the time: among those who grew up there were the novelists Alex La Guma and Richard Rive, and Trevor Jones, composer of movie scores who made it big in Hollywood.

But the two decades of apartheid rule that preceded the first removals had, by then, 'just knocked people into subservience', guessed Pam Barron, Trevor's sister.

For Christine Amansure and her grandmother Kitty Manuel it became simply a practical matter. When they got 'the letter' declaring District Six a white area, they knew right away they wouldn't win if they fought it. And anyway the houses were a bit cramped and the neighbourhood around them was disintegrating. They could get a three-bedroomed house at the edge of Heideveld, a nice house, said Mrs Amansure, although the kitchen was nothing like the Eckhard Street one. They moved sooner rather than later to avoid being packed off to a township that was even less attractive.

For Fred Robertson the move was more traumatic. His family moved in

1971, four years after the Manuels, when he was in the middle of his final year at high school. He attended Trafalgar, a school that, with Harold Cressy, had originally been built for coloured children who lived around the dense inner-city areas. Both schools, along with Livingstone in Lansdowne, were considered the best coloured schools at the time.

Now, no longer a walk away, he had to take the train every morning from Retreat, a coloured suburb in the south where he moved in with a married sister. Then he went to live with a friend in Walmer Estate, a small middle-class coloured suburb on the slopes above Woodstock that had escaped 'the Group'. 'I squatted there for a few days a week, but your whole life was in transition. You lived out of your school bag.'

He is much less sanguine about the consequences than Christine Amansure who took in her grandmother from the family home. 'It was a *huge* mission to go and visit a relative. It destroyed soccer clubs, rugby clubs. It threw people together who were from all over and … it put gangsters in with decent people and made gangsters of everyone. It ripped out the heart of the community, and with ripping out that heart it denuded the community of all the intellectuality that resided there.'

Between 1957 and 1980, some 150 000 coloured people in the Western Cape had been moved out of their homes under the Group Areas Act.[20] The old city, writes Pinnock 'was destroyed and built to a different rhythm'. By the end of the 1960s 'the working class in Cape Town were like a routed, scattered army dotted in confusion about the land of their birth'.[21]

In the mid-1960s, too, similar clouds began gathering over Philma Manuel's family home in Stellenbosch. Leonard von Söhnen, known far and wide as the best plumber in the area, and the most honest, took note when the authorities built the coloured township of Cloetesville on a slope up the mountain. 'He predicted that something was going to happen,' said his daughter Dawn von Söhnen. Cloetesville was the poorer of the two coloured townships built near the town – the other was Ida's Valley. Those who rented houses in the middle of Stellenbosch were the first to be moved. Hermann Giliomee, then a lecturer at Stellenbosch University and a supporter of the National Party, remembers questioning an official who was carting the furniture of a coloured family on to a truck.

'Is this the right thing to do?' asked Giliomee.

'*Ja, meneer, die mense wil trek*' ('Yes, sir, the people *want* to move'), the official replied. And Giliomee felt uncomfortable but accepted it.

The Von Söhnens had owned their house for three generations. The clouds loomed, but in the 1960s, at any rate, kept at bay.

FOR THE YOUNG TREVOR MANUEL 1967, the year that his grandmother lost the family home in District Six, went by in a kind of blur. 'What dims my memory,' he recalls, 'is that we were engaged in two other battles.'

The battles were at home with his two maternal grandmothers.

Each year at Christmas Anne von Söhnen would spend about a month in her family home in Stellenbosch. During the Christmas holidays of 1966, she returned early because she'd taken seriously ill. Early in 1967 she had an exploratory operation. The diagnosis was stomach cancer. It was an exhausting illness, not only for Anne von Söhnen but for the family. She bled. She was incontinent. Worse, she lost the independence she had valued throughout her life. One night her daughter Philma would stay up to nurse her, the next it would be Pam, then only 13 and starting high school.

In the same period, Philma Manuel's foster mother, Fredericka Brown, developed a tiny sore that turned gangrenous. She was diagnosed with diabetes. She went in and out of diabetic comas, in and out of Groote Schuur Hospital. When she came home she, too, would need nursing day and night. Philma Manuel had to give up her job at Gold Knit, the garment factory where she worked, for about six months. Sick leave, compassionate leave, most leave, was unheard of in the garment industry. The family, already short of Anne von Söhnen's salary, now lost Philma's too. 'But God was good to me,' she said. 'And there were always people bringing me things.'

Somehow the Manuels scraped by. They were always fed, said Pam, and on weekends their father knew where to buy cheap fruit. But there were no outings, and there was barely enough for bus fare to get to school. There were never any new clothes. Pam didn't own a swimsuit – which was OK because her grandmother believed you got germs from municipal swimming pools, but she was embarrassed when her friends invited her to go with them to swim. She always wore handmade clothes, made from waste fabric her mother brought from work. When she'd coveted a duffle coat, then considered high fashion among her peers, she'd found a weekend job as a packer in a Kensington supermarket called Punkies. Her father, angered that she would be distracted from her schoolwork, refused to talk to her for several days. But Pam stuck it out and each week put 'lay-by' money aside at Ackermans, a large department store in downtown Cape Town, until she could afford the coat.

In many ways Pam, two years older than Trevor, set the pace for him. Of all his sisters he has always been closest to her, and he bears a lot of her traits: stubborn, and born with the natural sense of confidence she inherited from her father. She may have worn funny clothes sometimes, but her classmates looked up to her as she was always top of the class and, importantly, the Manuels spoke English. Kensington was predominantly Afrikaans-speaking and 'English-speaking people were considered a cut above'. And Manuels, as her father had reminded her in junior school, always 'came top'.

Language, like skin colour, established social status among coloured people in Cape Town. Perhaps because Afrikaans was the language of slaves; perhaps because the better schools taught in English; perhaps because knowledge of English allowed for more worldly horizons. For these reasons, English-speaking children who excelled at school were not lightly dismissed.

Anne von Söhnen died in July of 1967; Fredericka Brown died ten weeks later in September. The two women who had anchored Philma Manuel's life were gone. The stress of looking after them both and their loss took their toll on the steady woman. Her children think she teetered on the edge of a breakdown through much of that year.

And then came District Six. 'In the middle of that all,' said Manuel, 'you kind of wiped out your eyes and this house that your father had been born and raised in was GONE. It's really kind of just unhooking things, unhooking history in a peculiar kind of way.'

Before, Trevor used to hop on to a bus to Woodstock and walk up to District Six or take the trackless tram from town to Hanover Street, but visiting his paternal grandmother now became an ordeal. He had to take a bus to Salt River, then walk up to the Main Road and take another bus to Mowbray, and then a third out to Heideveld on the Cape Flats. 'It took for ever. There were no train links to speak of, no taxi links and if you didn't have a car that was all you could do.' Trevor went with his father to visit his grandmother on her first Christmas in Heideveld. The man and boy left their Kensington house at 7am, and got back at 1pm just in time for lunch, having spent but half an hour there. In fact, it can only be 10 kilometres between Kensington and Heideveld but the radial and inflexible bus routes reinforced the effect of the Group Areas Act, making family contact difficult.

So visits to his Manuel grandmother tapered off and District Six became no more than a passing and occasional topic of conversation at the dinner table.

In 1968 Trevor began high school at Wesley, following his mother and sister Pam. Early in his second year there his father told him there were going to be 'coloured' elections for the newly established Coloured Representative Council (CRC) in September that year.

It had been nearly 13 years since coloured people were finally and resolutely removed from the voters' roll by the Strijdom government.[22]

The Labour Party, which was to contest the 1969 elections, was set up in 1966 by Richard van der Ross (who was later to become rector of the University of the Western Cape designated for coloureds). Among those leaders responsible for its launch were those linked to the South African Coloured People's Congress (an ANC-aligned organisation which had been driven underground in the 1960s) and the Teachers and Educational Professional Association (TEPA), an older and more conservative version of the left-wing, Trotskyist Teachers' League of South Africa (TLSA).

It was a 'hodge podge' of a party, as Manuel described it many years later, in a way doomed to failure by the acid mix of anti-apartheid politics in the Cape and the heavy hand of the apartheid government.

On its right was a party that unashamedly supported separate development – the Federal Party, led by Tom Swartz, 'real Uncle Toms', as Manuel described them. On its left was the Unity Movement, led largely by the coloured middle class, teachers and professionals who were 'purer than driven snow', in Manuel's words, and who refused to participate in most broad fronts, least of all government-created structures. But for many of the broad band of coloured centrists in Cape Town, hard hit by apartheid, the Labour Party represented a vestige of hope.

'A Vote for Labour is a Vote Against Apartheid', was its slogan.

Many of its supporters were ex-servicemen who had fought in the Second World War, and felt utterly betrayed by apartheid. Jakes Gerwel, who was on his way to becoming a leading anti-apartheid campaigner, said many saw the Labour Party as a 'possibility to mobilise, not necessarily to do something but to stem something'. There was an ambivalence about the Labour Party then: the newly emerging black consciousness groups at the University of the Western Cape, where Gerwel was a student at the time, flirted with it.

For Abraham Manuel, the Labour Party and the forthcoming elections for the CRC presented a possibility to *do* something about the tide of apartheid that threatened to swamp him and his family. He decided to throw in his lot with them.

'Get a buddy to come along,' he told his son. 'It's important that we go out and talk to people in our area.'

The buddy Trevor chose was Brian Williams, who lived (as he still does) in Acre Street at the northern boundary of Kensington, adjacent to what is now the N1 freeway.

Both Brian and Trevor, then aged 14 and 13, began going door-to-door with Abraham Manuel every evening. 'I want you to talk to people,' Trevor's father told the two boys. 'I want you to tell them it's about *your* future. And if there are difficult questions, I'll answer.'

Throughout the wet winter nights of August and early September, the trio would walk through the streets of Kensington, knocking on people's doors and talking to them about the issues that concerned them. Abraham Manuel wore his long trench coat and a hat, cheery, optimistic, and determined to visit every household in his neighbourhood. Often the two boys would do the talking.

'That was partly what astounded people,' recalls Williams, who later became a trade unionist far to the left of the politics that eventually consumed Manuel. 'They thought: these kids are able in a very simple and logical way to explain why they should vote for a certain party and why that vote should be a rejection of apartheid. And so we developed *huisbesoek,* the idea of house visits, canvassing, trying to convince people ...'

At times they came across Unity Movement sentiment among people who told them that a vote in the CRC election, even for the Labour Party, was a vote *for*, not against, the apartheid system. 'Even at the beginning we tried to argue that we have a chance to say something and that by voting for the Labour Party you are voting against the National Party. You are saying something. So even if you are not going to change the status quo, it would be an expression, a formal expression of unhappiness,' said Williams.

Abraham Manuel was 'nowhere near leadership', recalled his son, 'not even local leadership', and the candidate was a 'fool' (an epithet Manuel still uses to describe those whom he holds most in contempt). He remained unconvinced about whether voting for the Labour Party was wrong under the circumstances. But it left him with a far more important lesson, and one that was to stamp all of his future political activism: 'It allowed me to understand the value of talking to people in their own homes ... I thought it was exceedingly educational. You could hear what people's issues were, you could reflect and you could really do grassroots level kind of politics.'

As the election, set down for 24 September, neared, the *huisbesoek* got more intense. Now they were going back to visit the 'doubters', those whose minds may have been swayed. On the chilly, late winter evening of 11 September Trevor and Brian canvassed with Abraham Manuel, and at about 9pm returned to their respective homes in Kensington. Trevor and his father sat down, listened to the news on the radio, drank tea together, and went to bed.

The next morning before dawn Trevor awoke to his mother's screams at his bedroom door: 'Come quickly, your daddy's dead.'

'I just woke up,' she recalled many years later, 'and there was a dead man next to me. Trevor was very upset. He was on the bed on top of his father.'

Pam, the most composed, washed the corpse, and comforted her mother and brother. Her mother screamed so loudly that 'the neighbours on both sides could hear'.

At age 52, Abraham Manuel had had a heart attack during the night.

For 13-year-old Trevor the incident was both earth-shattering and life-changing. 'I can't explain the shock, the trauma, the horror of that.' Nearly four decades later his voice chokes as he recalls it. 'I mean, we generally hadn't been tight, tight, tight, close. But now a period arises, we collaborate every single day, we go out and do this stuff together and suddenly this guy has a heart attack in his sleep and he's just not *there* any more.'

His sisters recall the occasion – and its effect on Trevor – with startling clarity. 'He had a tough time at school' after the death, his sister Beryl told me. 'He couldn't concentrate for a long time. He was actually very badly thrown by my father's death and it took him a while to come out of it.'

Abraham Manuel was the kind of father, according to Renecia Clayton, the youngest Manuel sister, who would play regularly with his children on the streets of Kensington: ball games, marbles and the like. Every July he would take three weeks' leave to be with his children for their long mid-winter holiday.

At around the same time there were other issues that stamped themselves on Trevor's consciousness. A bare three weeks later Imam Abdullah Haroun, a political activist who had been detained in May of that year, became the nineteenth person to die at the hands of the police in solitary confinement since 1964. He had been held just up the road from the Manuel family home in the Maitland police station. Some 30 000 people attended the young Muslim leader's funeral – he had been the Imam of the Claremont mosque – despite the ambivalence with which the official Muslim mouthpieces in Cape Town reacted to his detention and then death.[23]

For Trevor, his father's death ran together in a kind of blur with the other big events of the year: the year that Imam Haroun was killed; the year a man walked on the moon, the year an earthquake in Tulbagh, more than 100 kilometres away, sent tremors through the ground in Cape Town.

The year Abraham Manuel died.

Suddenly, too, the realisation that his mother, at age 43, had four children to feed, clothe and educate on her garment worker's wages. Life chances changed and dimmed as the family contemplated the need for extra income.

Asked later how she coped, Philma Manuel said her only prayer at the time was that she could bring up her children to be 'decent', a meaningful hope in an environment that was fast turning dangerous with disaffected gangsters.

But there was another lesson too for the young Manuel, one that stayed with him as he built his activist and later his political career: start with what people care about. Start talking to them about their homes, their wages, the buses, their children's schools, before you start with points of high principle. That is how you build organisations.

It was a philosophy that was to become the backbone of the first successful anti-apartheid political organisation in Cape Town in more than three decades – the United Democratic Front, born in the 1980s.

Three days before Haroun was killed, 13 days after his father had died, the elections for the Coloured Representative Council took place. Trevor and Brian went to the polling stations wearing Labour Party rosettes; 'hoppers', they rode in older campaigners' cars to houses urging the doubtful, the lazy, the immobile to come to the polls to vote. 'I did it because in my own mind it was what my father wanted me to do,' said Manuel. His mother had broken her coccyx that day. Running after Trevor's younger sister Renecia, who wanted to skip school to go with him to the polls, Philma slipped on the wet veranda in the rain and came crashing down on her back. She was in intense pain, and fed up with her youngest daughter. 'But even in her understanding, this is what I had to go do: to deliver victory for the Labour Party because in the last months of his life that was my father's *life.*'

The Labour Party won a resounding victory. Nearly half of the 637 587 eligible voters cast their votes, more than ever before or since.[24]

But in terms of the law, the government could appoint 20 of the 40 representatives to the Council.

Although the Labour Party won nearly two thirds of the seats on the CRC, and although the leader of the pro-government Federal Party, Tom Swartz, lost his election deposit, Swartz became chairman of the CRC and his party claimed the majority. The Labour Party, despite its victory at the polls, became a weak and increasingly discredited opposition.

'That was the last fling for participatory politics,' Jakes Gerwel told me. 'Because when they (the coloured electorate) saw what happened, they saw there was no point in participating ... The Nats (National Party government) were quite stupid now when you think about it because some semblance of democracy may have served their cause to contain things.'

It seemed then that the left-wing Trotskyite organisations in Cape Town – particularly the Unity Movement – were entirely correct. Participation in the system was waste of time, at best, a distraction, and subversion of the real struggle at worst.

For the young Trevor Manuel it was another example of history unhooked: an election won, then lost, a political leader murdered in the local police station, a city divided, and him, a boy left to face adolescence without a father.

Top left: Maximillian von Söhnen, Trevor Manuel's great-grandfather, who came to the Cape from Prussia in the 1880s (courtesy Dawn and Ursula von Söhnen)

Top right: Magdalena Manuel (born Damink), Manuel's paternal great-grandmother who came from the Cape West Coast (courtesy David Manuel)

Left: Pauline von Söhnen (born Daniels), Manuel's maternal great-grandmother who came from the Northern Cape (courtesy Dawn and Ursula von Söhnen)

Below: Abraham Manuel's family who lived in District Six. Abraham is centre back; his older brother Johnny is next to him. Sisters Hester and Lena are in front, far left and third from the left, respectively. Their mother Kitty Manuel (born Mullins) is far right (courtesy Trevor Manuel)

Top left: Trevor Manuel, aged about two, 1958 (courtesy Trevor Manuel)

Top right: The Manuel family in 1958 before the birth of their youngest child Renecia. Philma and Abraham Manuel stand behind Beryl, Trevor and Pam (courtesy Trevor Manuel)

Below: A prize-giving event for a darts competition in District Six in the late 1950s. Abraham Manuel and Frederick Anthony Robertson (Fred Robertson's father) are fifth and sixth from the left respectively (courtesy Trevor Manuel)

Left: Trevor with his older sisters Beryl and Pam, about 1958 (courtesy Manuel family)

Below: Trevor and his father meet Santa, about 1957 (courtesy Manuel family)

Below: The Manuel family at an organised walk. Trevor is fourth from the left (number 267); next to him are his sisters Pam and Renecia. His mother Philma is on the far right, Beryl is behind her and his father Abraham (in the hat) is at the back (courtesy Pam Barron)

Above: Trevor at high school, about 1971 (courtesy Trevor Manuel)

Below left: Trevor with his first-born niece, Tania Tungcheun, 1972 (courtesy Beryl Tungcheun)

Belolw right: Trevor Manuel hiking in the Outeniqua mountains, about 1980 (courtesy Trevor Manuel)

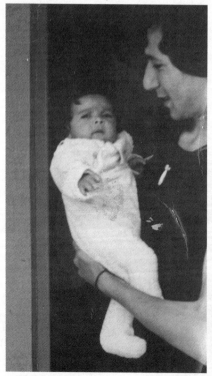

Top: Taufie Bardien with his taxi, Kensington,
in the 1960s
(courtesy Aziz Bardien)

Right: Shaun Viljoen and Trevor Manuel, 1975
(courtesy Trevor Manuel)

Below: At Langebaan, where the Viljoen family
had a house, 1976 (courtesy Trevor Manuel)

Left: Trevor Manuel with Joe Adams at an early meeting of the Cape Areas Housing Action Committee, about 1980

Above: In Crossroads at the launch of the Million Signatures Campaign in 1983 with Mosiuoa 'Terror' Lekota and Popo Molefe

Below: A UDF meeting in 1984. Allan Boesak had his head bowed as the others sang the Internationale

Bottom: Manuel, in shorts, at the meeting of the election candidate Peter Marais in mid-1984. He and his comrades broke up the meeting and were charged with public violence

Top: 6 August 1989, outside Huxley Joshua's house, Hazendal. The Defiance Campaign: Manuel is warned by a security policeman that he is breaking his banning order after attending the church service that launched the Campaign (courtesy Benny Gool/Oryx Archive)

Above: Manuel with Oscar Mpetha in Worcester, 1984

Right: A UDF press conference, 1984

Mom,

We've severely limited this year on the number of cards we can send. Please explain this and convey my best wishes to Aunt Aleas, Mrs de Bruin, Mrs Brown, Melanie, Rowland, Fr Stubbs & everybody else.

Mom

Life is hardly a rose-strewn highway ~ but never despair.

Warmest Greetings for Xmas and the New Year.

Love, Gratitude and Strength

Trevor

Right now,
Pain seems like the only reward
for a lifetime of toil
to rear your only son.

Courage, Faith and Fortitude.
The dividends will yet be yielded.

Manuel taught himself calligraphy in jail. This is a Christmas card he crafted for his mother while in Emergency detention (courtesy Philma Manuel)

≡ PART TWO: An Education ≡

1970-1975

CHAPTER 4

'Let us live for our children'

MONEY IN THE MANUEL household trickled to a thin stream after Abraham Manuel's death. Fortunately the Manuel parents had paid the last instalment on their house shortly before Abraham's death, according to Renecia, the youngest daughter; still there was little cash in hand at the end of the month. Whereas Pam had once worked weekends at the Kensington supermarket for money for her duffle coat, now she had to work for money for bus fare to school.

Trevor, who turned 14 in 1970, soon joined her. He worked first at Punkies, then at Pick 'n Pay, today an international operation, then a pioneer in the supermarket business in Cape Town. 'Fridays, Saturdays, end of the month, where possible the fifteenth of the month when the army got paid. I worked at Pick 'n Pay for 24 cents an hour through my schooldays. I don't remember it ever changing.'

The money he earned paid his bus fare from Kensington to Salt River; it also allowed him to party, a leisure activity that he has never shown himself, then or since, averse to.

But it was a tough year – his 'hardest', he said many years later. 'I'm adolescent, I'm 14, I don't have a father figure. Woodstock (in the United States, not Cape Town) is happening, there's stuff around you in the township. I think that was a particularly difficult year for me.'

His weekend work meant he had to give up his sports on Saturday, as well as the cub troop he attended. It was a loss for the teenager because not only did he enjoy the games, but he liked the sociability of both.

He struggled with his school work too. After an auspicious start in primary school – he not only passed the arm-to-ear test but wrote the best essay in his class in Standard 1, according to Aziz Bardien, a contemporary – his work slipped steadily in high school. Combined with the trauma of his father's death was a bout of mumps at the end of his Standard 7 (Grade 9) year. Unable to write his end-of-year exams he was nonetheless pushed through to the next grade.

His mother wanted him to go to Harold Cressy in Standard 6 (the year before his father died), but he didn't pass the fairly stringent entrance tests. She was insistent for a number of reasons. Wesley only went as far as Standard 8, and Cressy had an excellent reputation, particularly in science and maths.

It was a time when the effects of apartheid were being acutely felt in Cape Town, particularly in the schools. In 1963, the government passed the Coloured Persons Education Act,[1] segregating schools completely. The Group Areas Act had a devastating effect on schools, scattering teachers and pupils around the Peninsula and resulting in shortages of teachers in the new areas where they were needed most.[2] By the end of the 1970s, expenditure on coloured pupils by the government was about one fifth of what it was on whites (and on African scholars about one twelfth).[3] Ironically, though, high school enrolment increased for all race groups during the 1960s and 70s, even for the most disadvantaged. For coloureds (the vast majority of whom lived in the Western Cape), high school enrolment grew from 25 000 in 1960 to 57 520 in 1970.[4]

But more education did not equate to either better education or better jobs. The Theron Commission into the circumstances of coloured people reported that, in the 1970s, only 3,6 per cent of economically active coloureds filled higher level management, professional or technical positions. One third lived below the subsistence level, and the government's education policy effectively trapped most people 'in the ranks of the labouring poor'.[5]

But education, however poor or unequal, was still the best chance out of a dead-end street and, surprisingly, there were still a handful of coloured schools in Cape Town that offered excellent education.

One was Harold Cressy. Situated in Roeland Street, on the upper slopes of the city close to where District Six had been, it was in the top ten of the 'feeder schools' for the prestigious (and largely whites only) University of Cape Town (UCT), a cut above even some of the elite white schools at the time. Under certain restricted circumstances, coloured and African students could attend the university.

The school is named after the first coloured man to have graduated from the University of Cape Town (then known as the South African College) in 1909. Later, he became one of the founders of what became a central organisation in coloured political life in the Cape, the Teachers' League of South Africa (TLSA). Cressy, described by his contemporaries as a brilliant scholar, was himself a victim of discrimination when he was barred from taking up a teaching bursary because the South African Rhodes and Victoria Colleges refused him entry on the grounds of his colour.[6] He went on to become the first principal of Livingstone High School in the southern suburb of Claremont, also seen as a centre of educational excellence since its inception in 1910.

Cressy, like many others of the coloured middle class of his generation, saw education as the salvation of the community and fought a continual battle against increasing discrimination.[7]

'Let us live for our children' was a key slogan of the Teachers' League. In fact the League produced unusually good teachers in an era when apartheid education tried to undermine every facet of excellence in black schools. Many of the prescribed textbooks gave teachers of the League wonderful teaching material, if only in their repudiation. Nothing was neutral. Even English grammar textbooks contained such sentences as 'All the Bantu who had been drinking beer began to fight one another', as American author William Finnegan discovered.[8]

Finnegan, who taught for a year at Grassy Park High, a more poorly equipped school than Cressy, and who recorded his experiences in an evocative book, *Crossing the Line*, found many of the standard textbooks to be full of such 'racist mischief'.

But Cressy was different, in large part because of the political tradition of the teachers who taught there. One was Helen Kies, widow of the TLSA leader Ben Kies who was banned for life from teaching in 1956 because of the role he played in opposing apartheid education.

Mrs Kies taught Latin and English at Cressy and revelled in being able to repudiate a syllabus that was replete in racism. 'Our main lesson was: We are One Human Race; there are no Superior and no Inferior Races,' she told author Alan Weider.[9]

She remembered Manuel at school. But she did not have much to say about him, partly because he did not do Latin, partly because he was not a star pupil at the time, and probably mostly because of the politics he adopted in later years.

I visited her at her home high up in Bo-Kaap on Signal Hill with a commanding view of the city and mountain. At 80, she was still intellectually sharp, and warm and hospitable to me in spite of her reputation for being somewhat icy. In conversation her formidable knowledge of education, both in its practice and its history, was clear, and in her analysis of the present she showed the superior intellectual skills that made her such a powerful teacher. She must indeed have been a tower at Cressy, as many of her former students testify. But she did not let me interview her. Instead she provided me with reams of literature about the history of the Unity Movement (of which the Teachers' League was a vital part) and the Teachers' League. Her hospitality belied the tales of her intolerance that persist among older coloured ANC activists in the Western Cape, remnants of a long enmity. But those tales are there. Reg September said she turned her back on him at a function soon after he returned from exile; and she refused to attend a presidential function to bestow a posthumous award on her husband.

Nonetheless, the teachers at Harold Cressy, her among them, were legendary for the quality, no-nonsense, politically provocative education they provided. After his failed first try, Trevor managed to get into Cressy in 1971, following his sister Pam. He was now in Standard 9 (Grade 11), the penultimate year before matriculation.

He still worked weekends at the supermarket, partied Saturday nights, and on Sundays would 'chill' with friends. His school work floundered. As a result he failed maths and physics that year and was kept down.

'I was quite distraught about it,' he recalled.

'He *cried*,' said Pam.

'The teachers told my mom that he had a lot of potential but he was just not interested,' said his eldest sister Beryl. 'And then they failed him, *deliberately* failed him Standard 9. And … that pulled him right … he had to sit up and take note.'

Somehow his pride withstood the failure. After all, he'd started school a year young, he reckoned. So in 1972 he started Standard 9 a second time.

When he walked into the Standard 9 classroom at Harold Cressy that year, Shaun Viljoen, a studious boy who came from a middle-class family in Athlone, made for his usual place in the front row. 'I was a student who always used to do very well, to the irritation of other students,' he said.

But a shout from a seat in the back corner of the classroom made him look up: 'Come and sit here!' It was Trevor Manuel.

'I didn't know him well then,' said Viljoen. But something made him move to the back row anyway. 'That's how our friendship started. My academic results took a huge dip in the next two years but what I learned about life from him was huge.'

It seemed then that Manuel's three years without a father, having to work to make ends meet in his household, had roughened his edges. He was 'naughty', said Viljoen, the word a euphemism for more serious mischief-making. The well-built teenager was renowned for disrupting classes with chatter, flirting relentlessly with girls, sneaking off to the toilets to smoke, and once even stabbing a fellow pupil with his pencil.

The contrast between him and Shaun, who became one of his closest friends in that period, could not have been greater. Viljoen, now a lecturer and author based at Stellenbosch University, was withdrawn and studious. Manuel was gregarious and voluble. Viljoen came from what he described as a 'home ownership' family in Athlone, his family house situated on the 'right' side of the divisive railway line. His father was a clerk at the City Council and a leading member of the Unity Movement and Teachers' League.

The Viljoens' house in Athlone would often be used for Teachers' League fund-raisers and the cream of Cape Town's intellectual elite in the coloured community, such as Helen Kies, would gather there.

Manuel, on the other hand, came from a working-class family in Kensington, far on the wrong side of the tracks. Neither of his parents had gone to university – his mother hadn't even finished high school, nor did two of his sisters. Politics was rarely discussed in their house, other than at the time when he canvassed for the Labour Party with his father in the months before he died. The instincts he gleaned from his parents were moral, rather than political.

Yet in the years following his father's death, Manuel developed a marked ability to communicate with what Viljoen called 'ordinary *ouens*' (fellows) about political matters. He spoke easily, for instance, with bikers (he was to acquire one himself), with the girls in the school, with people in the street. He was popular with girls. Popular with boys. Popular.

It may have started in the days when he walked from house to house with his father asking the people of Kensington what their concerns were. Or it may have come from the past two years of packing at tills in the supermarket. Or from his dedicated partying. Whatever the reason, his gregariousness stood in sharp contrast to Viljoen's diffident thoughtfulness.

The latter came from a very protected home. Manuel's background was different, as was his easy loquaciousness and a kind of reckless courage that he carried with him way into his political career. 'There was something about him that attracted me: his popularity – as though it rubbed off on me by association. He initially befriended me, what it was I don't know. In retrospect I don't know what he got out of the relationship,' he said.

What Manuel got out of the relationship was an intellectual nutrition that he thirsted for, brain food that he had not found before.

Partly, he found what he was looking for at Harold Cressy itself. The teachers were, almost all of them, dedicated to providing a critical anti-apartheid education. It began with teachers such as Helen Kies. Unusually for a woman, and a coloured woman at that, she had graduated in maths from the University of Cape Town. She had been aware there that despite her obvious intellectual grasp of the subject, she had not been treated with anything like the same respect as the white or male students.

Far too intelligent to be cowed by the new apartheid rules in education, she helped organise campaigns against the persistent attempt by the education authorities to inculcate a sense of inferiority in black students. One such was a so-called 'intelligence test', a racist device to show that 'Bantu' or 'coloured' intelligence was inferior to white intelligence.

'The Teachers' League immediately set about sabotaging their intentions. We organised schools and parents and pupils to refuse to take part in this nonsense. Parents wrote letters to schools to say that their children should not be involved. We told the pupils that if the education officials tried to force them to do the tests they should fill the papers with nonsense. Except at schools where there were stooge principals, they had to abandon their "separate" intelligence effort.'[10]

Another teacher who stood out was Peter Meyer. An 'avowed atheist', he

64

was nonetheless the religious instruction teacher in Manuel's class. Religious instruction was used as a period to discuss politics. This rebellious atmosphere permeated the whole school: at break they sang freedom songs – 'we shall brothers be – that kind of thing', said Pam – and the school refused to fly the South African flag. There were even, by some quirk or oversight, one or two African teachers who'd survived the apartheid red tape.

The school organised trips – to Kimberley, to Swaziland, even Mozambique, where Shaun got gravely ill with malaria and Trevor nursed him through the nights. It staged plays: both Trevor and Shaun acted in *Romeo and Juliet* and *Oliver Twist*. They read provocative books such as Felix Greene's *The Enemy: What every American should know about Imperialism*. In short, the school did everything that apartheid education was designed to prevent: it nurtured, not quelled, dreams; it sparked, not suppressed, thought; it encouraged excellence rather than mediocrity; and no one, absolutely no one there, was made to feel inferior because of the colour of their skin.

Although there were frequently bitter relations between the Teachers' League and Unity Movement on the one hand, and many of the mass political movements, especially the African National Congress-aligned organisations, on the other, one cannot underplay the enormous influence the Teachers' League had on a generation that was later to lead the rebellion against apartheid in the Western Cape.

'This school has a mission to teach you history which will liberate you,' the Cape Town historian and writer Bill Nasson was told at his school, Livingstone High, another Unity Movement stronghold. 'We are here to make sure that you aren't contaminated by the *Herrenvolk* poison contained in your textbook. We as the oppressed cannot afford colonised minds. Our history, our liberation are inseparable.'[11]

Within that paradigm 'there was space to think, room to think', said Manuel. 'A *need* to understand politics.'

Out of school, through his friendship with Shaun, there were intellectual opportunities unheard of among the Kensington working class. A valuable, if peculiar part of the Unity Movement were the 'Fellowship' centres that were dotted around Cape Town. One was at the Athenaeum in Newlands, next to the railway line (ironically where Fred Robertson's business office now stands – being a one-time enthusiastic follower of the Unity Movement did not save him from capitalist entrepreneurship). There Manuel saw movies by Fellini, Charlie Chaplin, Bertolucci; listened to music by Victor Jara, the

Chilean musician who was tortured and murdered after the US-backed coup in Chile in 1973 when the elected leader Salvador Allende was toppled; and heard poems by Pablo Neruda, Jara's compatriot who fled into exile after the coup. It was, said Manuel, 'stuff that ordinary kids wouldn't be exposed to … a great part of the education. That was more important to me than the politics could ever offer.'

WHEN BLACK CONSCIOUSNESS BEGAN to emerge at the apartheid-designated black universities in the early 1970s, it struck an immediate chord with Manuel, despite the dominant Unity Movement ethos at the school.

The militancy and angry rhetoric of black consciousness ideology, reflected in its slogans and poetry and music, resonated among a whole generation of young black students whose dreams were truncated by systematic racial discrimination.

But the reason it resonated in the Western Cape was more complex. In large part it was because of the dilemmas and denials about coloured identity that had plagued the generation before Manuel's. The racist hierarchy in the coloured community itself, such as manifested in the sports clubs his father had worked in, and the desperate and sad attempts at reclassification which had affected his own family, always sat uncomfortably with him. 'The reason I found comfort in black consciousness is that I could accept my surroundings, accept the disadvantage, accept that I was black. I didn't need to straighten my hair, didn't need to pretend that I was white, I didn't need to do any of those things because I could find comfort and pride in something I thought part of my family was struggling with.'

For Manuel, it was a critical transition. From the discourse of hurt, so apparent in the loss of his grandmother's house in District Six, the loss of the election for his father's Labour Party in 1969 despite its victory, the steady impoverishment of his family, his language became one of anger.

In one religious studies lesson Mr Meyer suggested the class discuss the recent black consciousness protests at the coloured University of the Western Cape – there had been a walk-out off the campus in 1973. He asked his class: 'What would you do if there's a fire burning around you?'

Shaun Viljoen, sitting next to Manuel, put up his hand and answered, quite logically he thought: 'Put it out, Sir.'

But Manuel understood something else. Uncalled on, he jumped out from behind his desk, put his fist in the air and shouted: 'We should stand by it until we are victors!'

It was as though the teenage boy had seen the political moment and grasped it as no other student in the class had done.

But hard economic issues focused him. He had wanted to study law after school. His mother wouldn't hear of it. 'She said politics would dominate my life.'

'Trevor, please, you'll end up on Robben Island,' she said.

Anyway, a more compelling factor then was household income – or lack of it. Even a bursary wouldn't have helped. The Manuel family could not afford passengers. Manuel had to find something that would allow him to earn and learn at the same time.

He thought perhaps he'd be a chartered accountant – he'd heard that a firm would take you on as an articled clerk and pay you R40 a month while you trained. Or he could perhaps pursue his dream another way and work in a law firm, earning while he studied. In his matric year he went for a few interviews at the offices of chartered accountants. He did not know anyone who worked at a law firm. He went through the telephone directory and wrote letters to lawyers asking for an interview.

No one replied.

The value of connections, which many middle-class youngsters take for granted, was brought harshly home to him. 'I didn't know anybody. Being a poor kid in a township, not knowing anybody, not having any connections, not having anybody to take you by the hand, not having the financial resources to get into a tertiary education, being left to your own devices … that for me was a *huge* education.'

That he passed matric at all was unusual in his family. Beryl, his oldest sister, was a 'maths boffin', one of the brightest, said Pam. Beryl left school in Standard 8 (Grade 10), 'went to work in a bloody shop', and got married at 20. (Today her daughter Heidi is a maths teacher at a prestigious Jewish day school in Johannesburg and the author of maths textbooks.) His youngest sister, Renecia, left school in Standard 7 (Grade 9) and went to work first in a garment factory and then became a salary clerk in a furniture store until she was medically boarded in 1991.

Pam matriculated and went to work for the City Council, where she was told she could do a 'housing manager's' diploma, angry for years afterwards that she missed the opportunity of a university education.

Driven partly by that anger, she completed a two-year housing diploma in just eight months, with straight As in her exams, except for building construction, 'because they lost the coloured papers!' So everyone, including her, was given an average mark, a C.

Her anger – mainly at the daughter of a (white) city councillor who'd been awarded a bursary – drove her to excel. Three years after she'd started she was appointed a housing manager, the youngest up to that time.

For her brother Trevor, matric was a moment of reckoning. What was he to do? His enquiries at chartered accountant and law firms had reached a dead end. His mother and two other sisters, Beryl and Renecia, were by then working at Gold Knit, the clothing factory in Maitland. Philma Manuel found him a job there too. She had higher hopes of the job than her son.

The manager, she believed, wanted to train Trevor 'from the bottom' to be a manager. 'That's what he told me. But Trevor was in dispatch where he had to lick labels to put on to the parcels.' Eventually he told her: 'Mommy, I didn't study for this.'

'I was just very clear,' he said years later. 'I said to my mother this is a dead end and I didn't want to end up in a dead end. Because I could see the other men, especially in that factory: it was sex with as many women as possible, and as much booze as possible, and no prospect of *life*.'

So he continued to scour the papers daily, and one day he saw a tiny advertisement by the large construction firm, Murray & Stewart (later to become Murray & Roberts), looking for civil engineering technicians. It was one of the jobs he'd applied for in his matric year – Murray & Stewart had even come to his school looking for recruits but they hadn't taken him. 'I could never work out why.'

This time he was luckier. He got an interview. The man who interviewed him was an Afrikaner called Montgomery. ('No first name,' he told me. 'Just *meneer*' (sir)). 'OK, you can start in two weeks,' Montgomery told him. 'Go to Foreshore Freeways and you can start out as a costing clerk.'

Foreshore Freeways was a large construction site near the docks at the edge of the main highway out of the city. It was a foot in the door, thought Manuel, hoping that being a clerk would be just a stage.

After a few months he asked Mr Montgomery 'nicely' whether he could train as a civil engineering technician. 'No, don't worry, you're a good clerk,' replied his boss.

Eventually when he was moved to another building site, still as a costing clerk, he began to 'badger' Mr Montgomery. 'I badgered him and badgered him – I knew that being a clerk was a bloody dead end – until he put me in touch with the man who was in charge of the technicians, who was the man I should have seen in the beginning.'

Almost a year after he'd joined the firm, Manuel began to train as a civil engineer.

Working on a construction site flung him into a world far removed from the intellectual and political discussions he had enjoyed at school. A white Zambian, gruff and rude, became his mentor.

Abusive perhaps, but he was 'exceedingly thorough and a master craftsman'. 'He used to swear at me and tell me how fucking useless I am,' said Manuel. 'And he'd make me sit till 8pm writing figures because he said I needed to learn how to write so that other people could read it. He badgered me ... but I emerged from that with a very clear understanding both of the world and of the craft of survey.'

He enjoyed his work. But he was struck by the conditions endured by the African workers on the construction site. Mostly migrants from the Transkei, the impoverished 'homeland' in the Eastern Cape, he began to talk to them about their experiences, learned some Xhosa and even spent a holiday in one of their villages in the Transkei.

His friend Shaun Viljoen had gone to UCT to do an arts degree, but the two young men still kept in touch. It was a confusing time for Manuel politically. Shaun had been recruited into the ranks of the Teachers' League, as was expected of him. For Manuel, black consciousness held more appeal. It had been attractive to him at first because it had given 'colouredness' a sense of pride rather than of shame.

Now it had allowed a means to connect with those outside of his world – particularly African workers.

But the Teachers' League (and its ally, the Unity Movement) had spurned black consciousness. Although far from non-racial in its composition, it nonetheless regarded the principle as a 'holy cow', as Viljoen put it. Black consciousness was anathema because 'it used colour in a way that it (the Unity Movement) felt was retrogressive and fudging the issues of class oppression and exploitation'. It even brought out a booklet condemning black consciousness as a 'reactionary tendency'.

Manuel and Viljoen began to move apart politically.

But their friendship continued, as did frenetic partying. There was also a group of young civil engineers at M&S who knew how to have 'a lot of nice times'. 'There was a kind of lust for living the way we combined politicking with partying. A lust for life. The partying was part of the resistance to the diminution of the spirit,' said Viljoen.

It was not only his social life that was hectic. Manuel still went to the fellowship clubs. He began to read prodigiously along with his peer group who were now at university: Karl Marx, Paulo Freire, Lenin: *What is to be Done?*

What was to be done was tough because while his university student friends could wake when the sun was up, he had to be up at 5.30am for work. Those early mornings on the construction site were rough when you'd been grappling with dialectical materialism and the negation of the negation in the early hours.

He bought a motorbike, and was suddenly mobile. Through a friend at work, he joined the Young Christian Workers, a left-wing Christian group that was doing community work in many of the coloured and African areas.

Around this time his old Kensington friend Brian Williams, who was now apprenticed to be an electrician, told him there was going to be a bus boycott. 'Why?' Manuel asked.

'The fares are increasing,' replied Williams, and then suggested they go to a meeting called by the party they'd canvassed for only six years before. Now, though, the idea was not to support the Labour Party but to subvert them. 'We can't allow these chaps to run this thing,' said Williams.

So he and Williams and a few of their friends went and 'pummelled' the Labour Party with questions.

There were about 400 people there – transport was an increasingly emotive issue in Cape Town as hundreds of thousands of people had been moved away from the city. Manuel, Williams and a few radical University of the Western Cape (UWC) students were elected on to a local committee. 'Young Turks', they now had their first real mandate which took them into other areas to organise around the transport grievances.

As it happened, the bus boycott that year fizzled out, but a skeletal political network remained, called KAGRO, the Kensington Action Group, which met once a week to focus on community projects and to continue a reading programme to better get to grips with how exactly to run the revolution.

What kind of revolution it would be was still rather vague in their minds.

And certainly, for Manuel, his thought processes were interrupted by a serious setback. He had been working on a bridge near Cape Town's foreshore. He'd climbed on to the scaffolding to help a fellow worker measure for any deflection; his feet slipped from under him and he came crashing down on to the pavement on his head.

'It was touch and go,' said his mother. She was at work when she heard about the accident. 'I rushed out. I said to my supervisor, "I've got to go." It seemed like I could have walked next to the bus just to push it further, it seemed so slow.' When she got to the hospital, 'the world was already there' – friends from work, his neighbourhood, his community groups, his reading groups.

It was a first indication to Philma Manuel of just how widespread his connections were.

When Manuel was discharged after a month in hospital he began his first block of instruction at the Peninsula Technikon (Pentech), as promised to him by his employers.

It was also at this point that he began to tread a particular political path with more confidence. His school had sparked his interest in politics; he was of the generation that was beginning to express outrage against apartheid. He was attracted by the anger and romanticism of revolution. But he had started out on several paths, some of which had converged, and others which had simply petered out.

Now he began to see certain pointers that had been submerged for a long time in Cape politics.

CHAPTER 5

The politics of withdrawal

T HE STRUGGLE AGAINST APARTHEID in South Africa occupied a distinct place
in international consciousness for years partly because of its moral
simplicity.

In the Western Cape, however, anti-apartheid politics has always been
treated slightly derisively by other parts of the country, and as a slight mystery
in other parts of the world.

Sophisticated left-wing discourse on the one hand, coupled with deep
divisions on the other, left up-country activists scratching their heads about
the efficacy of 'armchair politicians' – revolutionaries who spoke the purest
language but who, in most instances, couldn't pull off a single decent street
campaign.

That is, until the 1980s; until Trevor Manuel's generation turned the streets
of Cape Town into a battleground that tested apartheid's forces as never
before.

We will come to that. But to understand the decisive break that Manuel
and his generation made with its own past, it's necessary to find the threads

that bound Cape Town politics in a stultifying discord.

Jakes Gerwel gave the phenomenon a name: the politics of withdrawal. It goes back to the days of slavery, he told me, to the disparate peoples who became 'coloured' after the emancipation of slaves, and Ordinance 50 which freed up the movement of the indigenous Khoi people. The fluidity of being coloured also truncated political organisation: in the early part of the century, the most articulate leaders of the coloured community were often 'lost' as they became 'white'.[1]

It was only after the onset of apartheid, when the coloured community became much more precisely defined in law, that a generation arose who unequivocally threw in their lot with African people.

For more than a hundred years there have been organisations within the coloured community that fought for equality. Only a few had reached out to Africans. Many faltered and failed and fought each other. Still others struggled with the basic question of identity: who were they as a people?

One of the earliest organisations was set up in Kimberley at the end of the nineteenth century by coloured alluvial diamond diggers, known as the Afrikaner Bond. It was, argues Ian Goldin in his book *Making Race*, an early manifestation of 'coloured' ethnic identity – the diamond diggers saw themselves as 'coloured Afrikaners' distinct from whites and Africans.[2]

In Cape Town in the early twentieth century a man called John Tobin initiated what became known as the 'Stone meetings', community meetings at the top of Clifton Street in District Six, where each Sunday the community would gather to 'debate political issues, current affairs and labour matters'.[3]

'Africa for the Africans, white or black,' was one of their slogans.

But only at the time of the Union of South Africa – the unification of the British colonies of the Cape and Natal with the Boer Republics of the Orange Free State and Transvaal – did an organisation with a distinct coloured identity emerge. This was the African People's Organisation (the APO), led for 35 years, often with great aplomb, by a man who came to embody the aspirations of a coloured middle class increasingly short-changed. Dr Abdullah Abdurahman, a doctor who lived in Woodstock, just below District Six, founded the APO on one main issue – the protection of coloured rights in the Cape colony.

He was the first black man to be elected to the Cape Town City Council (for District Six), a seat he held for 26 years until his death in 1940.

The coloured franchise, such as it was, excluded the vast majority: in 1904, barely 4 per cent of the coloured people in the Western Cape were registered voters, compared with about 21 per cent of whites.[4] Most of the enfranchised coloureds were concentrated in certain constituencies, District Six and Stellenbosch among them. Even fewer Africans in the Cape qualified for the vote and four whites represented those who did in the Cape Parliament.

Nonetheless, the coloured franchise was a symbol of huge hope and aspiration for the coloured middle classes for whom equality would mean the final shaking off of the legacy of slavery.

Before Union, a report of the Native Affairs Commission set up to devise a 'uniform native policy' for all four territories that would form the Union of South Africa defined 'Native' as 'an aboriginal inhabitant of South Africa ... to include half-castes and their descendants by Natives'.

It must have struck an ominous note for Abdurahman. Added to his woes were signs of early division among coloured organisations. John Tobin and F S Z Perregrino, a West African immigrant to the Cape who founded the Coloured People's Vigilante Council and preached Pan Africanism, were opposed to lobbying in London, the seat of colonial power, to extend the franchise. But the APO responded by saying that both Tobin and Perregrino had 'betrayed' the coloured people, and appealed to the British government to 'act in accordance with the liberal principles embodied in the Cape constitution of 1854'.

But to no avail. As Gavin Lewis writes: 'Having decided the union of the South African colonies and not black rights was the priority, British parliamentarians determined to approve the draft act ... They assuaged their conscience with pious and meaningless expressions of hope that the white colonists would deal fairly with their black subjects.'[5]

The APO organised a large protest meeting in 1909, as the constitution for Union was being drafted. Held in the Cape Town City Hall, it attracted more than 3 000 people.[6] But the Union of South Africa came into being with scant regard for existing or future coloured or African rights. It represented 'the triumph', said the APO, 'of the narrow illiberal spirit over the Cape liberal ideal'. For coloured people in Cape Town, particularly the aspirant middle class, it was an occasion of 'humiliation rather than exultation'.[7] In 1913, a year after the founding of the South African National Native Congress (which became the African National Congress (ANC)), the TLSA was established by Harold Cressy and another teacher, H J Gordon, both of whom were members of the APO.

Education was increasingly seen as the path to upliftment. The APO leader, Abdurahman, was himself evidence of this. Born in Wellington in the Cape countryside in 1872, he had studied medicine in Scotland (and was married to a Scottish woman), and was a practising medic. He had become 'both to himself and to the rest of the coloured community ... (a)... living example of the power of education to uplift the coloureds'.[8] This was even more remarkable because his grandparents were manumitted slaves.

Yet the colour bar still took precedence over good education. Abdurahman's daughters – one of whom, Cissie Gool, went on to take over leadership of the APO – were both refused entry into white private school despite excellent academic results.

For the majority of coloured pupils, simply surviving in reasonably good health was a challenge. Dr A H Gool (Cissie Gool's husband) told the inaugural conference of the TLSA that '80 per cent of coloured schoolchildren in the Cape suffered either tooth decay or infestation with lice, 30 per cent suffered defective eyesight or hearing, malnutrition, anaemia or mental deficiencies' – evidence of the growth of a neglected underclass.

Yet the APO, for all its eloquence and good intentions, never made significant inroads into the ranks of the coloured working class. Many coloured workers joined artisans' unions and some (about 10 000) joined the African-dominated Industrial and Commercial Workers' Union (ICU) in the mid-1930s. There were other unions that were fine examples of coloured and African unity, notably the Food and Canning Workers' Union. But, by and large, whatever unity there was among workers did not translate easily into political organisations until the 1980s.

A recurring theme in Cape Town's political history is the way that coloured people have been played off against Africans, and then just as quickly kicked in the teeth. And so in the 1920s African workers were dismissed from the docks and replaced by coloured workers, and in 1923 the Native Urban Areas Act exempted coloured people from carrying passes while extending them to more African men (these laws were not as draconian as the pass laws imposed under apartheid, but their aim was the same: to control African labour in the cities and white agricultural areas).

A package of bills passed by the Hertzog government in the 1920s and 30s disenfranchised Africans in the Cape more completely than the Act of Union had done, introduced tighter residential segregation for Africans, but also protected the small coloured franchise that still existed. A legislator responsible for piloting the bills through Parliament said: 'It is not safe for the Europeans themselves to force the Coloured people into the hands of the natives.'[9]

Yet, at the same time, coloured people got poorer. The 'Civilised Labour Policy' – as the job colour bar was odiously named – meant that there was practically no upward mobility for coloured people at work. Between 1924 and 1934 the percentage of coloureds in employment declined from 44 to 30 per cent.[10] In manufacturing they dropped from being half the workforce in 1924 to about 43 per cent in 1932.[11] In 1937 the Willcocks Commission reported that: 'Coloured youth had great difficulty in obtaining work and that even when work was found it was generally in blind alley occupations.'[12] By 1940, 53 per cent of coloured households lived below the poverty line, compared with 6 per cent of white households – the main cause being the economic colour bar.[13]

In the late 1930s, when it was clear that the reasoned and polite submissions of the APO were not gaining ground, politics began to take on a more radical form. First the National Liberation League (NLL) was formed by Jimmy La Guma and Johnny Gomas; also active in the NLL were Cissie Gool and her brother-in-law Goolam Gool, although the latter two were later to divide markedly over politics. Then the Teachers' League was taken over by a new set of Young Turks including Ben Kies, who later married Helen Kies, the legendary Cressy teacher, and I B Tabata, who was married to one of Goolam Gool's sisters.

That the group was so interconnected by ties of family and marriage was no accident: it reflected the fact that as radical as the new rhetoric was, the resistance movements in Cape Town still had a small, middle-class, professional base.

IN 1937, THE NEW ERA FELLOWSHIPS were founded – part of a breakaway from the old-guard Communist Party of South Africa which was, in the view of many of the Cape socialists, uncomfortably close to the Soviet Union and its undemocratic policies. These fellowships survived well into the 1980s and played a key role in stimulating political debate among the generation that eventually led the Cape Town rebellion against apartheid. But the New Era Fellowships were at heart elitist, establishing forums where, as they put it, matters 'could be discussed by the more advanced members of the community for the benefit of the less mature'.[14]

Reg September was just coming of political age in this period. A pupil at

Trafalgar, he had joined the NLL and was active in opposing the Servitude Bill, which would have imposed residential segregation in the 1930s.

He was part of the newly radicalised generation. He was shocked, for instance, when his own mother, whom he adored, was subserviently grateful to R S Stuttaford, the minister in the Smuts government responsible for the Servitude Bill, for a paltry donation to a church bazaar stall she ran. Stuttaford brought a few dozen bottles of fruit cordial to her stall: 'And my mother thought the world of him because (of the donation). And how he could dare pull the wool over my mother's eyes like that? It was totally improper, quite unacceptable to me.'

The most radical intellectual break with the past came during the Second World War. The Non-European Unity Movement (NEUM) was formed in 1943, an organisation that grew out of the Fellowships and the newly radicalised Teachers' League. Its policy was simple, and informed to a significant degree by the anti-fascist movement in Europe during the war. Strict non-collaboration. The term used to denote collaborators – quislings – was derived from Vidkun Quisling, the head of the Norwegian government which collaborated with the Nazis. Its founding document was the Ten Point Programme, a document that parallels the ANC's Freedom Charter in many respects, albeit less poetically. It calls for, among other things, a universal franchise, the right to work, compulsory and free education, housing and health for all, freedom of movement and expression, racial and gender equality, and a redistribution of land.

The new body had an immediate political target. The government, in a major segregationist step, had set up the Coloured Affairs Department (CAD). The anti-CAD activists, as they became known, began to dominate all aspects of Cape politics. 'For some four years,' wrote Neville Alexander, a teacher, academic and socialist who broke with the Unity Movement and was later jailed for 12 years for his political activities, 'these young activists consisting largely of teachers, students, a few doctors and lawyers and a sprinkling of semi-skilled workers and artisans penetrated virtually every kind of organisation of the people, including sports bodies, church groups, cultural societies, student organisations, trade unions, benefit societies, coon carnival and Christmas choir bands ... The mainstay of this movement was the Teachers' League of SA which from 1937 onward, had been put on a "new road" of anti-collaboration by the young men and women who entered it from the NEF (the New Era Fellowship) and made life impossible for the conservative reformist leaders.'[15]

The TLSA was adamant about non-collaboration in the 1940s and well into the 1950s, 60s and even 90s. As far as 'quislings' were concerned, their dictum was: 'Don't have any social or personal intercourse with them. Don't greet them. Don't have any conversation with them ... don't meet them, even if it's necessary to cross to the other side of the street.'[16]

The APO faded to nothingness after Dr Abdurahman's death in 1940, although a massive crowd of about 30 000 turned up for his funeral. It was more a measure of respect for the man than a reflection of the strength of the APO at that stage. Yet between 1943 and 1948 'a mass movement flourished in the Western Cape as it had never done before'.[17] And the Teachers' League reached out to scores of coloured schools, even in remote rural areas.

It was, confirms Reg September, the most powerful coloured organisation at the time. 'Take into account the fact that the teachers are the *meneer* (sir); wherever they work, they're the *meneer*. And they've got all the facilities at their disposal, many of them had telephones, many had motor cars. And we didn't have those things,' he told me.

Jakes Gerwel, who came from the Eastern Cape – where the ANC occupied the hegemonic place in resistance politics – was struck when he first came to Cape Town in the 1960s to discover just how influential the Teachers' League was.

'They really represented, in my view, armchair politicians, but they had tremendous influence. That always astounded me; how a relatively small group of people would have such an influence: they almost had a political/ moral hold over people. You had to almost justify yourself and your own actions with reference to them,' he said.[18]

It was precisely this influence that the government feared when it banned Ben Kies from teaching. The security police articulated it clearly. In a secret report to the minister of justice in 1961 they describe the TLSA as '(exercising) the most influence on the youth and ... succeeding to raise an embittered young coloured generation' (*oefen die meeste invloed uit op die jeug en slaag daarin om 'n verbitterde jong kleurlinggeslag groot te maak*).[19]

Virginia Engel has similar memories of the government's anxiety about the Teachers' League. Engel was to become one of the Cape's leading trade unionists, as well as an underground ANC activist in the 1970s and 80s, and one of Manuel's comrades. A little older than Manuel, she had attended Livingstone High, where the Teachers' League dominated. A number of her teachers at both primary and high school were banished to rural areas because their influence on city children was considered dangerous. At high school, she experienced the removal of African children, as Manuel had done in primary school. Her school refused to expel the handful of African children who remained at the school. 'So the police came into the school grounds and fetched these children.'[20]

WHATEVER THEIR INFLUENCE IN the coloured schools, the Unity Movement and TLSA were hamstrung by two key social factors. The first was that as much as TLSA leader Ben Kies believed that coloured teachers had sprung from the 'loins of the working class', it never developed a mass base. The second factor was its distance from Africans in the Western Cape, a distance that was reinforced by incidents such as the forcible eviction of African schoolchildren from the coloured schools.

Added to that was the fact that its initially effective use of the boycott as a weapon grew over time into a principled refusal to participate in almost anything. For instance, the Unity Movement refused to participate in the Train Apartheid Resistance Committee (TRAC) in 1948, leading to bitter squabbles with the Communist Party which had backed the initiative. The Unity Movement withdrew at the last moment because 'only 450 people had volunteered instead of the thousands expected'.[21]

'We are not prepared to send into action the few volunteers whose self-sacrifice would not make any impact on the train-apartheid issue ...' they wrote to the Communist Party.

The train apartheid incident was, as Neville Alexander put it, 'a dismissive but tragically erroneous policy to what it called ad hoc campaigns'.[22]

It repudiated Mahatma Gandhi's campaign of passive resistance sparked by the 'Ghetto Acts' (which proposed residential segregation for Indians) on the grounds that it was 'riddled with reformist Gandhism'. When radical Indian leaders sought closer ties with the ANC by signing what became known as the Doctors' Pact of 1947 (between A B Xuma, Yusuf Dadoo and G M Naicker, presidents of the ANC, the Transvaal Indian Congress and Natal Indian Congress respectively, and all doctors), the Unity Movement eschewed the new alliance. By the time the National Party had come to power in 1948, NEUM 'had repudiated every leading black political organisation in the union'.[23]

'Non-collaboration,' wrote Alexander, 'came to mean abstaining from any struggle that did not somehow immediately challenge the "fundamentals" of South African society.'[24]

For those, like Reg September, looking for political activity with some return, or for those coloured people who simply hoped for more decent treatment, the war offered a glimmer of hope. Many coloured men signed up for service, only to be bitterly disappointed in the late 1940s when their remaining rights were stripped away.

Reg September had already had his share of political disappointment by 1948. He had become somewhat trapped in the ongoing political battle between the then pro-Soviet Communist Party and the anti-Soviet Trotskyites of the Unity Movement, although he admired leaders in both camps. Nor was he able to take solace in what a teacher at Trafalgar, seeing that he was troubled, had said: 'Don't worry, Reggie, my boy. The day we have a strong Teachers' League in SA our troubles are over.'

But September had, by then, realised 'the frailty of the teachers', and he couldn't glean much comfort from this reassurance.

But the incident that convinced September that the politics of the Unity Movement was a dead end was when bus apartheid was introduced in Cape Town in the mid-1950s. He and Alex La Guma (son of Jimmy La Guma and a well-known writer who went into exile soon after) went to see Ben Kies in his Walmer Estate home. 'I remember standing on his doorstep and saying we've come to talk to you about the threat of bus apartheid in Cape Town. And he came back very sharply and said, since when are we interested in Communist Party stunts? And I said to him, since when are you *not* interested in the threat of bus apartheid?'

Kies invited them inside and they talked for some time about possible protest action. 'He (Kies) said, 'Look, teachers are on holiday at the moment, I'll get in touch with you when they get back.' And that was the first and last time I ever heard from him.'[25]

September had by then found an alternative political home. In key ways, he and a few of his comrades were the path-breakers for Trevor Manuel in later years. September was a founding member of the South African Coloured People's Congress, part of the broad ANC alliance, established in 1953. The ANC was then organised racially – with an Indian branch (the Transvaal Indian Congress and the Natal Indian Congress), and a white branch (the Congress of Democrats). The South African Communist Party, which had been part of the alliance and which had a non-racial membership, was banned by the government in 1950.

September saw his task as organising coloured anti-apartheid supporters behind the main liberation movement in the country, the ANC. It was essential to link up with African people, he told me half a century later. When I asked him why, the elderly man looked at me as if I were a simpleton: 'Oh my darling,' he replied. 'The whole strength of the movement for the struggle for power and for equality in our country was centred in Johannesburg, and that was black, and unless you recognised that you'd be in the wilderness for the rest of your life.'

Yet it was a massive break with tradition in the Cape.

Since Emancipation, Gerwel told me, the politics of withdrawal was 'one strong trend in the politics of coloured communities. And the Unity Movement represented the radicalised version of that: the politics of withdrawal.'

The discourse of resistance moved from pleading and petitioning under the APO to hurt and anger under the Unity Movement.

Nowhere is this more evident than in a booklet the Unity Movement published to commemorate its 50 years of existence. Entitled '50th Year of Struggle', it drew a 'harrumph' from September when he saw it. He shook his head and read the title aloud: '50th Year of Struggle'. He paused, then said: 'Struggle? *Struggle?* Shame!'

It came out soon after South Africa's first democratic elections in 1994, which saw hundreds of thousands of people queuing to vote for three days. In it, the president of the Unity Movement, Mr R O Dudley (a respected teacher and deputy principal of Livingstone High for nearly 40 years), described the new South African government as a new form of 'World Imperialism. It is imperialism that paid for and bought over the collaborators who have been in government since April 1994. But now they are part of government, the collaborators are paid out of taxes they collect from workers and others they now help to oppress.'[26]

Like some extreme religious sect that sees a diabolical global conspiracy in every corner, the Unity Movement, as September had suspected 40 years earlier, was truly in the wilderness.

The question, though, is why September and his comrades made such a decisive break with that tradition – my question about why he'd thrown in his lot with the organisation of the African majority was a serious one, even if he thought the answer was obvious. The question is also why Manuel, and so many of his generation, followed the example set by September, then a tiny minority in the coloured community. Why was the rebellion of the 1980s a rupture with the traditions many of them had schooled in, not a continuum?

In Manuel's case, at least, part of that answer lies with one of September's comrades at the time. He was one of the few in that group with a car. It was his car they used to visit Teachers' League leaders in their vain attempts to get them to support the campaign against bus apartheid. Unlike September, he did not go into exile. He remained in the country and became an effective prisoner in his own home for 15 years.

He was a man who became a giant in the young Trevor Manuel's life. His name was Taufie Bardien.

CHAPTER 6

Lessons from Taufie

MOEGAMAT TAUFIEQ BARDIEN was a towering, handsome man, over six feet tall. A taxi driver, he drove 'big American cars' – a Valiant, a Studebaker, and later a De Soto. He had a garage with a pit for working on cars at the back of his house, unusual in Kensington where he lived.

If there was one thing that Taufie Bardien loved it was cars. But if there was something he loved more, it was politics. His family remembers him spending hours tinkering with his car – he was a self-taught mechanic. But politics, said his son Aziz, 'consumed him: he lived, ate and breathed politics all his adult life'.

From Trevor Manuel's childhood home in Kensington, Bardien's house was just a short walk: turn right on Fifth Avenue, walk two blocks up and jump over the corrugated iron fence straight into his garage. His house was at 99 Fifth Street, on the corner Fifth Avenue. Bardien had lived there all his married life. His wife Soda had lived there even longer, since the age of seven. Her parents owned the two halves of the semi, numbers 101 and 99. When she married Bardien in 1949, 'I just put my leg over the wall and I was in my bridal home.'

Aziz Bardien had been at primary school in Windermere with Manuel. A neighbourhood pal, Manuel often used to visit the house as a child. To have not only a garage in Kensington, but a pit to work on cars, was 'really something'. Bardien also had a map of South Africa on his wall and he would regale his children and Manuel with tales of how he'd once fitted an extra petrol tank on to his Studebaker so that he could make non-stop trips to what was then Bechuanaland to take people into exile.

Bardien was born in Woodstock in 1923. His father, a tailor, was a 'quiet man, very simple', and his mother came from a large family in Paarl called Domingo. Her family had roots in the French Huguenots who had emigrated to South Africa in the late seventeenth century to escape religious persecution. Her father, Bardien's grandfather, had converted to Islam.[1]

Bardien had little formal schooling. He had run away from home at age 16 to join the Cape Coloured Corps (almost always pronounced 'corpse' in the Cape), and was conscripted to go and fight in Alexandria during the Second World War. When he came back, he met Soda Hashim who was then working in a factory in Roeland Street, just down the road from Harold Cressy. He opened her eyes with his worldliness. 'He couldn't help telling me about Egypt, the museum there! It's everything you can think of!'

Soon after the war, he began driving taxis in Cape Town. One of Soda Bardien's brothers taught at Livingstone High, 'and of course ... Livingstone High *was* the Unity Movement ...' And so Bardien became, for a while, 'totally, totally Unity Movement'.[2]

The influence and language of the Unity Movement lasted long after he'd become a member of the ANC-aligned Coloured People's Congress. His son Aziz remembers how he would refer to 'the *herrenvolk*', a euphemism for Afrikaner nationalism, in line with the Unity Movement's refusal to acknowledge race. 'Politics was our dinner, bed and breakfast at the time. And he was always railing at the state for its unfairness.'

Soon after he met Reg September and two other coloured activists, George Peake and Barney Desai, in the mid-1950s, Bardien joined the South African Coloured People's Congress.[3]

Throughout the 1950s he was an enthusiastic organiser in the movement that opposed the apartheid body, the Coloured Affairs Department (CAD). The anti-CAD movement, as it was known, originated in the Unity Movement. But Bardien was restless, just as Reg September was, and decided that success in combating apartheid lay in finding common cause with Africans.

At an anti-CAD meeting in Cape Town in 1959 he told about 300 people, both coloured and African, that 'Coloured and Native Affairs (departments) are the same. They are departments of oppression.' Eighteen months earlier he had urged a boycott of the elections to the Coloured Advisory Council (the CAC, which was to operate under the auspices of CAD). He told a meeting: *'So wil die herrenvolk ons ook vir altyd hou as draers van water en kappers van hout ... As u gaan stem dan gaan u vir hulle die teken gee om voort te gaan met julle onderdrukking.'* (In this way the *herrenvolk* also wants to keep us as drawers of water and hewers of wood ... If you go to vote, then it will be a sign for them to continue with your oppression.) Both these remarks are recorded in a security police report in 1961 urging the minister of justice to ban him. They were especially concerned by a South African Coloured People's Congress meeting he addressed in 1961 attended by 'about 500 people, most of them natives'.[4]

Bardien said: 'The *herrenvolk* of this country realise that oppression of us will be of no use in the future ... I can assure you the so-called Coloured people are with you in this struggle for liberation in this country ... That is the only way we get liberation in this country – to have one liberatory movement of all (the) people ... It is for us to fight with a capital F. Long live the struggle, and long live the names of the freedom fighters, including Patrice Lumumba.'[5]

It was the appeal to unity across the apartheid colour bar that most worried the security police. So they had kept Taufie Bardien on their radar screen for several years by the time the big crackdown came in 1960. That year, when tens of thousands of Africans marched from Langa, led by 23-year-old Philip Kgosana, Bardien joined the throngs outside Caledon Square as they demanded an end to the pass laws. It was 30 March, nine days after police had opened fire on a peaceful protest of Africans in Sharpeville, an African township in the southern Transvaal, about 1 300 kilometres north of Cape Town. Kgosana, a newly arrived and dirt-poor university student, was an admirer of Robert Sobukwe, the Pan Africanist Congress leader later imprisoned for many years on Robben Island, even after he had completed his sentence. Everyone who witnessed that march from Langa to Cape Town remembers Kgosana's youthfulness, and particularly the fact that he wore short pants that day. Many years later, from his exile in Sri Lanka, he wrote to *New York Times* correspondent Joe Lelyveld to say there was 'no magic about the shorts except that … at the time I did not have many clothes to wear'.[6]

Despite his boyish clothes, Kgosana led the huge crowd from Langa along De Waal Drive, which wound along the mountainside above District Six, a distance of about 12 kilometres, to Cape Town's police headquarters at Caledon Square.

This was the march that Pam Barron's teachers had feared. They had sent her and the other coloured children home in a panic. But it was a remarkably peaceful event. The thousands who gathered outside Caledon Square – who may well have stormed that citadel had they been so commanded – turned around and went home on the promise that the authorities would negotiate with Kgosana about the hated pass laws.

For not the first or last time, the promise was betrayed. Kgosana was arrested. Saracens were sent into Langa, and scores of people were jailed.

A State of Emergency was declared, and hundreds more were detained. One of them was Taufie Bardien. Held for 90 days, he was released with a restriction order confining him to his home at night and at weekends and prohibiting him from attending political or social gatherings until the end of the Emergency. It was a foretaste of what was to come.

By now Bardien had rattled the security police to the core.

His speeches, they wrote to the minister of justice in 1961, especially those calling for unity between Africans and coloureds, 'is of such a nature that the security of the state is put in danger'. As he was holding meetings throughout the country 'a restriction order … is extremely desirable' (*uiters gewens*).[7]

All these reports were secret. Under the apartheid security laws, which became increasingly stringent, neither the minister of justice nor the police had to give any reasons for prohibiting a person from engaging in public life or social gatherings. On 21 October 1961 Bardien received his first banning order. By then five of his six children had been born. The oldest, Noor, was 11. Aziz was only seven.

Among the restrictions were the following: he was not allowed to receive any visitors at home, except his mother and mother-in-law (who lived next door); he could not go to a factory; he could not go to any African area; he could not be quoted or publish anything.

On 22 October 1961 Bardien wrote a letter to Justice Minister B J Vorster (who was to become prime minister after the assassination of H F Verwoerd): 'It is a well known fact that I and many others banned by you and your government are totally and uncompromisingly opposed to your policy of nazifying South Africa for your own ends … the ban on me will in no way deter all democratically minded people from striving to build a non-racial democratic government of the people, for all the people, by all the people in a new South Africa, free from fear, racialism, oppression and exploitation of man by man.'[8]

It was a defiant, angry letter full of warnings and ultimatums. The government was vindictive in return. In 1962 he was charged with breaking his banning order to attend a meeting of the Road Transportation Board – a body that licensed and regulated all taxis. 'Bardien on Anti-Red Act Charge' reported the *Argus*, somewhat dramatically.[9] He was acquitted, but not before a lengthy trial that took him away from his taxi-driving business.

In 1962 Bardien was caught trying to smuggle George Peake, his CPC comrade, out of the country while he (Peake) was out on bail and facing a sabotage charge (he'd tried to blow up a post office, according to the police). Two years later Bardien and three others were charged with trying to help five suspected saboteurs awaiting trial in Pollsmoor prison to escape. He was acquitted because, said the security police, 'it appeared that the subject (Bardien) has such a great influence among the Coloureds that they usually water down their evidence so much that a conviction is impossible'.[10]

In 1965 the police finally managed to nail him: for breaking his banning order and possessing banned literature. He was sentenced to 90 days and released in February 1966. In a lengthy memo to the minister, the police complained that his restrictions had done absolutely nothing to 'stop his left-leaning activities' *(sy linksgesinde bedrywighede aktief voortgesit)*. He drove his taxi 'all over the Peninsula' to attend meetings. Now was the time, they urged, not only to reissue a five-year banning order but to tighten the restrictions. He must not be allowed to drive around 'the whole Peninsula' but should be permitted to take fares only in the magisterial district of Cape Town, which included the city and Kensington, and excluded almost all of the new outlying coloured areas. He must be in his house every night, and most of the weekends (he was allowed to work Saturday mornings); he must report to the police station weekly, and as before he may not have visitors or attend social or political gatherings.

As Taufie Bardien emerged from jail, he was served with a house arrest order that was to last 10 more years.

Now Bardien could no longer take fares to coloured areas; he couldn't take sailors or passengers to the harbour; he couldn't take fares at night. He couldn't work after 3pm on a Saturday.

Aziz Bardien was 12 years old when the first house arrest order was served on his father. He had a special job in the family. It was to listen to the radio on Saturday afternoons. When the announcer said it was five minutes to three, he would open the garage gate. At 3pm exactly his father would drive his big American car in, and Aziz would bolt the gates. Five minutes late could have meant another spell in jail.

Bardien's earnings plummeted. Soda Bardien went out to work as a seamstress for R12 a week. It was not enough money to support six children. Bardien made plea after plea to the security police to allow him to run his taxi business throughout the Peninsula. Most coloureds no longer lived in the city, he said. Most of them were being moved out under the Group Areas Act. In terms of taxi apartheid, he was not allowed to pick up whites. In fact he had lost his taxi licence briefly in 1969 for picking up passengers of other races. 'I beg you to … be allowed to take taxi fares in the Cape Peninsula,' he wrote to a magistrate. 'I find that I cannot earn enough to feed my family and pay my accounts. No one can convince me that the Minister's Order on me is meant to leave me destitute. My earnings is already halved (sic) by my 12-hours house arrest, and your kind permission is requested to allow me to operate my one taxi for fares in the Peninsula which will help me to live and feed my children. I beg this please.'[11]

The police opposed the request. 'Instead of discontinuing his subversive activities he … made extensive use of his taxi service to … further the aims of the Coloured People's Congress … It is clear that Bardien … has only himself to blame for the predicament in which he finds himself.'

Appeals met with a steely response. Amnesty International wrote to the government on his behalf. The sole anti-apartheid legislator in the white Parliament, Helen Suzman, wrote several letters asking for his restrictions to be eased. But in the end Bardien was reduced to charity.

'If it wasn't for Amnesty International sending us food parcels, the family would not have survived,' said Aziz Bardien.

By then three of Taufie Bardien's closest comrades were gone. Reg September, who was banned in 1961, went into hiding after he was charged in 1963 for breaking his banning order. He travelled to Johannesburg, then caught a train to the Swazi border, walked across, and a year later came back through the country to go west to Botswana. It was a dangerous trip but he found, to his astonishment and delight, help from quite ordinary black people on every leg of his journey. Barney Desai stowed away on a ship to Tanzania. (He later left the ANC with Bennie Bunsie in protest over what he saw as its rigidly racial structures of organisation and joined the PAC.) George Peake was in jail.

'All of them, *all* of them, they all left,' said Soda Bardien more than 40 years later. 'We couldn't go. He was his mother's only son, I felt I couldn't do that to her. And I didn't like any other country. I was a Muslim – I couldn't see myself raising my children in Britain with my religious concerns.'

Mrs Bardien, a small, precise woman, was 82 when I met her. She still had a well of energy. She was an active member of her local ANC branch. She cooked every day – dozens of pies for neighbours and family, orange preserves, tomato preserves, scones. It was as though those years of a hard married life had honed a kind of resigned indefatigability in her.

A religious Muslim, she had family ties in Saudi Arabia – her grandmother's first marriage was to an Arabian. When her husband died, her grandmother had returned to South Africa with her son. Her in-laws did not allow her to bring her daughter because they disapproved of the way women lived in non-Muslim countries. The son, Haji Hashim, was Soda Bardien's father. I asked her whether a Muslim country had not been an option for exile. She thought for a moment and then said firmly: 'The culture's not the issue. Being Muslim, you know what to expect. But South Africa is the most beautiful country in the world.'

So Taufie and Soda Bardien battled it out under extraordinary conditions. Almost every aspect of Bardien's life was open to the security police. For matters that in most families would be private moments of grief or pride, he had to apply for official permission: permission to visit his dying mother in Wynberg: granted; to go to her funeral: approved as long as he reported at the police station on his return; to attend his daughter's graduation ceremony at the University of Cape Town: refused.

TREVOR MANUEL BEGAN TO VISIT TAUFIE BARDIEN without his peers present when he was in his teens. Bardien had just begun his third five-year banning order and his second house arrest order. Manuel was intrigued by this man, by his map on the wall, by his cars, by his stories, but particularly by the copy of the Freedom Charter that Bardien showed him.

The Freedom Charter, a wide-ranging document that addressed democratic rights and economic welfare was drawn up by the ANC-sponsored 'Congress of the People' in Kliptown outside Soweto in 1955. Although the document itself was never banned, it was so closely associated with the ANC that it became a kind of contraband in apartheid South Africa.

Moreover, the decade of suppression that followed the banning of the ANC had obliterated a sense of the past. ANC and PAC leaders, including Nelson Mandela, were in jail. Others were in exile. In Cape Town, apart from the Unity Movement, which hid behind reams of theory, it was as if there had been no history. Reg September had left. La Guma was gone, so was Desai. Peake was in jail. Bardien was the only connection with a political past that had once dared to dream differently, and he too was largely silenced.

Trevor Manuel's curiosity grew to captivation. At every opportunity, he'd leap over the steel garage gate, being careful not to be seen. One never knew which neighbour would report to the security police, and Bardien was breaking his restriction order simply by talking to Manuel.

But it did not deter either the man or the boy. Trevor was 'a *fine* young person', recalled Soda Bardien, and he would spend hours in Taufie's garage.

Bardien possessed a well of courage that was evident particularly in his younger days. He was never afraid to stand up to the security police. When they came to his door one day on the pretext of giving him a parking ticket (his car was parked on the wrong side of the road, although it was the only car in the street), he tore it up in front of them; when they came to search his house in the dead of night looking for banned literature, he forbade them from turning on the lights in the room where his children slept. They had to search by torchlight. He'd been trained in the military, he spoke fluent Afrikaans, and he engaged his tormentors as equals.

In many ways, his robust egalitarianism when dealing with the security police was echoed by Manuel later in life when he found himself in similar situations. But age and experience had taught Bardien how to temper his anger. Nearly 15 years of living a life in the shadows had taught him about risk-taking.

One day in 1974, when Manuel was 18 and Bardien was entering the final stretch of his house arrest order, they chatted about an impending sports tour to South Africa by the British Lions. In defiance of the international sports boycott, it was expected to be heavily protected by the police because rugby was *the* sport of the political rulers.

'All right,' Bardien said to Manuel that day. 'You say you are committed. Now about this Lions Tour: there's only one place they can play in Cape Town and that's the Newlands Rugby Ground.'

The suburb of Newlands nestles in foliage high on the slopes of the mountain. The city's main cricket and rugby stadiums lie at its eastern end like shimmering green carpets. Newlands was once a racially mixed area, but by now was solidly white and middle class.

'What I want you to do is to take action,' Bardien said. 'Are you ready?'

'Sure,' said Manuel, itching for it.

'Here's what I want you to do: I will arrange with the watchman at the City Council depot on Keurboom Road in Newlands (just down the road from the stadium) to turn a blind eye. You go steal a bulldozer; go to Newlands Thursday night. You can churn up the entire ground and they won't be able to play the test match. That's the biggest protest you can make.'

As a chaser, Bardien suggested he explode a pamphlet bomb off the roof of the OK Bazaars, a discount department store, in Adderley Street in the city.

Manuel was open-mouthed.

'I don't want you to give me an answer now,' said Bardien. 'I want you to go think about it and we can talk tomorrow.'

Manuel did not sleep that night. How, he fretted, was he to manage this heavy vehicle? He couldn't even drive a car then, let alone a bulldozer. And if he got caught ...?

The next day Bardien asked Manuel if he'd thought about his proposal. The young man hummed and hawed. 'I don't want you to beat about the bush,' said Bardien tersely. 'Can you do it or can't you do it?'

'I don't know that I can,' replied Manuel, pausing between every word.

To his surprise, Bardien was not disappointed.

'Now we're talking,' he said. 'Part of what we need to understand is that in politics there's risk, but you've got to be able to calculate the risk. The risk must not be impossible. The risk must not set you up for definitely being caught. These are issues you must be able to talk about, work through. And you have to trust those you're working with.'

Trust, comradeship, calculating risks – it was these lessons that Manuel took with him into a political struggle that was to become even more treacherous than the one Bardien faced.

Shortly before his house arrest order expired in 1976, the security police offered Bardien an all expenses paid trip to Mecca, with his wife, if he reported back on the activities of his old friends Reg September and Barney Desai. 'Of course he flatly refused,' said Aziz, 'although he wanted to go to

Mecca.' Apart from his stint in Egypt during the war, and a few illicit trips to Botswana, he'd never been out of the country. But to Aziz it showed the arrogance and ignorance of the authorities that they thought they could use his religion as a temptation to traduce his political comrades.

The last house arrest order had been particularly tough for Bardien. He had written to the minister of justice in 1971 when his restrictions were reimposed for another five-year period, protesting that he had done 'absolutely nothing to justify these further bannings'. This letter, though, was different from the angry, defiant one he had written to Vorster 10 years earlier. This time there was a sort of tongue-in-cheek pliancy. 'During the past year,' he wrote, 'I have come to accept that taxi apartheid is here to stay ... (and have) decided not only to accept it *passively* but to work for it *actively*.' In fact such was his commitment to its success that he even proposed that white taxi signs be kept green and non-white taxi signs be altered to yellow. 'This would enable the public to see immediately which is white and which is non-white.'

Again he remonstrated that he had to refuse 'at least 1 000 fares' during the previous 10 years to areas where he was forbidden to go and had to 'battle day in and day out to avoid starvation for me and my family'.

Yet he had to endure another five-year house arrest order.

In February 1976 Colonel M J van Zyl of the security police wrote a brief note to the justice secretary, entitled: 'Restriction: M T Bardien'. It said that the minister of justice had decided not to renew the house arrest order of the 'above-named. He has given notice that he will not be further involved with politics as he has learned his lesson (... *nie verder met die politiek gaan bemooi nie omdat hy sy les geleer het).*

Bardien never had a chance to prove the police wrong. Less than a month later, he collapsed and died. His family only discovered afterwards that he had been a diabetic. He was 53 and had spent more than half his adult life in jail or under crippling restrictions.

Philma Manuel came home from work that March evening and saw her son's suit hanging outside his wardrobe. 'Where have you been?' she asked.

'Mommy,' he said, 'I've been to a funeral. Today we buried a gentleman.'

THIRTY YEARS LATER, in 2006, Soda Bardien, aged 83, died after a sudden and serious illness. She had been so active and alive when I met her just a year before, that her age had not struck me. When she reflected on her life with Taufie and without him, she impressed upon me the unusualness of his defiance in their own community. 'People were so afraid, man, oh my God! The poor coloured people were so afraid. You hardly found coloured people who were politically interested. They were so scared! Their jobs and their homes were important.'

In stark contradiction to Mao Tse Tung's dictum that a guerrilla must be as a 'fish in the sea' amongst the people, Taufie Bardien was like a fish out of water. But Mrs Bardien had quietly, without any fanfare, picked up some of his political responsibilities when he died. The day we met, she'd just returned from a local ANC branch meeting.

She asked to see Manuel a few days before she died. When he saw her, she spoke to him of her illness – she had cancer – in a matter of fact way, of her age, of her religion and what it had meant to her. And she spoke of her community, which she had been immersed in from childhood, and which she loved but which was still 'afraid to commit to becoming truly South African and African ...' She meant of course that the gulf of race had not yet been bridged despite her husband's efforts and her own.

She had spoken too of the need for the ANC leadership in the Western Cape to 'bury its egos' in the interests of the people of the Cape. It was a pertinent point made at a time when the Western Cape ANC had been torn asunder by divisions, some of them racial.

At her funeral, Manuel, in a suit and with a fez on his head, his amber curls now gone, stood on the veranda of the little house in Fifth Street and recounted this conversation to the crowd of neighbours, family and friends who had come to mourn her.

'The conversation reminded for me the reason why, in this very house some 32 years ago, Uncle Taufie so easily convinced me to make life choices for the struggle, and why the only rational choice would have to be in the African National Congress. Convincing me was so easy because Uncle Taufie and Aunt Soda led lives that were worth trying to emulate.'

How fortunate, he said, to have 'among our people such real treasures, such unassuming giants'.

There were no cameras there, no press, and few other potentates, except for the then premier of the Western Cape, Ebrahim Rasool, and Reg September, now slightly bent and grey. But it was a moment that Manuel used to reach back to his roots, and to drive home a point about a political future. Homeboy and politician, neighbour and statesman, trouble-stirrer and peacemaker. It was a combination that had driven his political career since the day his mentor Taufie Bardien had died 30 years before.

The politics of engagement

I F TAUFIE BARDIEN WAS 'the start of it all', as his mother later reflected, then Manuel's own energy drove his activities after he left school. Bardien had 'talked me through' the Freedom Charter clause by clause, he said, and there 'was a kind of log-in about where politically I needed to be'.

The year before Bardien's death Manuel had been a founding member of the neighbourhood civic group, the Kensington Action Group (KAGRO). It petered out and died in a couple of years but in its short life it spearheaded a bus boycott and left a network of politicised youth in touch with one another.

In 1974, his first year out of school, he had begun seriously to question the Unity Movement wisdoms he had imbibed at school. Bardien had hastened his path away from an ideology that seemed to trap one in inactivity. Through a workmate at Murray & Stewart he had linked up with the radical Christian group, the Young Christian Workers (YCW). Begun in Brussels as a platform for young workers' rights in 1925, the YCW has since spread around the world. In South Africa, it had taken a robust position against apartheid mainly because of its work amongst black youth.

See. Judge. Act. That was the dictum the local priest taught at YCW. You see injustice, judge it for what it is, then act on it.

It was here that Manuel met Daphne Williams (now King), a young teacher from Athlone, who could match him in exuberance and energy and outmatch him in loquaciousness. She was attracted to Manuel from the start, and he to her. Both were energetic, and actively looking for a path to channel their disgust at a political system that by now was firmly etched into every facet of South African life. He was 18, she 22. She had spent most of her life in Athlone, studying and teaching in what was then one of the better-off coloured areas. She had been struck by truckloads of African men who would pass daily, morning and evening, on a nearby arterial road. She asked an African woman who worked in the area who they were, and was told they were migrant workers who came from the Eastern Cape.

'Where are their families?' asked Daphne.

'Back in the Eastern Cape,' the woman replied. 'They are not allowed to come here.'

'We must change that,' she'd said.

So she had joined YCW and 'did all this see, judge, act stuff', and there met Manuel who impressed her by having a real job on a real construction site and working with real migrant workers.

'Trevor and I were the big mouths,' she recalled later. 'He was very sincere. A very nice person. We both knew something was wrong with society but we didn't know what. We knew something had to be done but we couldn't put our finger on it.'

So began Manuel's first serious relationship that was as political as it was romantic. He and Daphne gave each other succour as they learned – he, just out of school, with his 'fiery black consciousness ideas', Daphne with her more socialist but equally fiery 'YCW ideas'. 'So the combination was quite electric,' she said.

Shaun Viljoen, Manuel's old school friend, searching too for some truth other than the Teachers' League, which had already recruited him, also joined the YCW as did two other young men, Yousuf Gabru and Yusuf Adam. Gabru had also known Taufie Bardien, and was a friend of his oldest son Noor. A little older than the rest, he had spent time in England and had returned with reams of Marxist literature. So the five formed a reading group.

It was at YCW that the local priest suggested that Daphne and Manuel visit a little office in Mowbray where two young women were training people to teach adult literacy.

By then, the third decade of Bantu Education, literacy levels among both coloured and African adults, but particularly the latter, were dismally low. Migrant workers were unable to read their pay slips, or street signs, or newspapers. It was a crippling disempowerment added to the many that Africans already suffered, particularly in the Western Cape with its strict influx control laws and job colour bar.

The two young women, both of whom became trade unionists and both of whom were later banned, were Pat Horn and Judy Favish. Both were white. They taught a revolutionary type of adult literacy adopted from the Latin American pedagogue Paulo Freire. 'The whole idea behind it is teaching people to read and write through words that reflect themes and problems in their lives so it's based on generating a discussion about that particular word,' explained Judy Favish, who became an educationist at the University of Cape Town in the post-apartheid era. 'Most of the Freirean methods use these generative codes with pictures, so you would start off with a discussion about that picture … try to get people to reflect on why the problem was the way it was, and then try to lead the discussion to what people could do about it.'

A favourite word for those teaching in isiXhosa, the predominant African language of the Cape, was ABASEBENZI, meaning workers. It broke easily into syllables but, more than that, it provided fabulous opportunities for talking about the working-class struggle.

For the generation of romantic revolutionaries, both white and coloured, that was being born, literacy lessons enabled them to reach out to the poor in squatter camps, migrant workers in hostels, township dwellers and cleaners in blocks of flats. Favish and Horn trained scores of people in Freirean pedagogy and soon Manuel, Daphne Williams and a host of other youngsters and students had made inroads into hostels, squatter camps and factories.

David Lewis, then an economics student at the University of Cape Town, was one of the literacy teachers. He shared a house with Favish at the time, where Manuel and Daphne were regular visitors. Lewis, also white, came from the Western Transvaal. He was to emerge as one of the key leaders of an African trade union in the late 1970s. (He was later to be appointed chair of the Competitions Tribunal.) Lewis has always tinged his commitment to the struggle in South Africa with a slightly humorous scepticism about its adherents. So, in recollection, he was somewhat trenchant about whether this group of avid activists, himself included, actually taught many people to read and write in a way that changed their lives. 'These groups were incredibly erratic and rudimentary,' he said. But yet those young people who went out to teach needed a considerable dash of courage. They would go to squatter camps, to townships, and to migrant workers' hostels well after dark. Some of the areas were rough with gangsters; in others, if the police caught you, it may have meant a spell in jail (it was illegal for whites or coloureds to go into African areas without a permit).

For Manuel the experience was another of those bends in a political path that led him away from the traditions of Cape coloured politics. First of all, and most importantly, he was *doing* something, not sitting in a discussion group. Secondly, because he was doing it with white students and unionists, as well as with African workers, he began to rethink the black consciousness politics he had adopted in his final year at school.

Black consciousness had been critical in terms of developing his own sense of self-worth. The first time he had read the words of Steve Biko, the black consciousness leader who was killed by the police in jail, he had been strangely excited. Biko had defined black as African, Coloured and Indian. 'You suddenly found a place. If you were prepared to identify yourself as part of the oppressed, you were therefore part of the solution. You didn't need to pretend. You see, all of this stuff you were growing up with was so bizarre. People straightening their hair, people wanting to be who they weren't. You needed a statement that could say to black people: hold on, what's all this shit?'

But having found his own sense of self, it did not translate easily into racism against others, even against whites among whom were clearly the purveyors of misery for Africans and coloured people. Indeed it was two white women who equipped him with the skills to teach migrant workers who lived in the single-sex hostels in the African township of Guguletu. He eventually had to move the lessons to the coloured area of Heideveld, just across the railway line from Guguletu, because he was picked up too frequently by the police in the township.

'He was unusual in our experience,' recalled Lewis, 'because he came from the "right school" (Cressy) and would have followed a predictable political path to oblivion from there. But clearly that was never his chosen path. He never advanced along Unity Movement lines like other people who were at Cressy did.' Neither was he pure black consciousness nor, according to Lewis, 'an orthodox ANC type from the Reg September school'.

There were other enigmas about him. Unusually for a coloured person, he could speak a little isiXhosa, picked up from his work on the construction site. That impressed the literacy teachers no end. And, most importantly, he had a job, and not just any job but one on a construction site. For young students and activists, starry-eyed with the revolutionary potential of the proletariat but chasms away from it in their own lives, this was a badge of honour. 'I didn't know anybody who even had a *job*!' said Lewis. 'But here he was, a working person, and that made him quite strange.'

But it was the energy of this 19-year-old that struck Lewis and the rest of the literacy group most forcefully.

'The Unity Movement stuff was so powerfully characterised by its inactivism that even if you'd read the same books and listened to the same masters at Cressy or Trafalgar, someone of Trevor's personality would have been enormously dissatisfied in terms of the conclusions it led to about who you could engage with and who you couldn't engage with,' said Lewis. 'And that was always my recollection of him. A hell of an activist orientated character, very charming but really wanting to *do* things.'

If there was any sign that Manuel was not just going to accept what fate dished out to him, it happened soon after he started work on the construction site.

It was 1975 and he had just turned 19. That year, on the long South African Easter weekend, he and his friends planned to go camping in one of the several magnificent mountain ranges that ring the Western Cape. It had become an annual event by then.

On the Thursday afternoon before Good Friday Manuel's group, which included Brian Williams and two of his brothers, his girlfriend, Daphne and Leslie Rutgers, who was a bricklayer, boarded a train at the local station near Maitland. Their plan was to go to Paarl Rock, a mountain near the small town of Paarl about 70 kilometres north-east of Cape Town.

Manuel and his friends were in the black section of the train, third class, and because it was full, they stood near a doorway. Their rucksacks were packed with food and camping equipment, including an axe with which to chop wood. A few stations down the line, a group of about 15 young men boarded the train, 'very merry', with a guitar and a bottle of brandy. They were already inebriated.

As the train clattered along, the young men turned into a pack of predators.

They rolled through the compartment and began to rob and abuse the other passengers. 'Everyone's crying, screaming and being smacked and stabbed by these gangsters and they are methodically making their way up to us,' said Brian Williams.

Brian's brother Davie was bending down at the moment the gangsters passed them, apparently trying to repack his rucksack. One of the ruffians stood on his hand with deliberate aggression. 'You're standing on my hand,' said Davie Williams. 'Well, fuck out of my way,' replied the gangster.

At that moment, Williams arose from his squatting position and faced down his aggressor. His brothers rallied behind him. The rest of the gang, armed with knives and pangas, converged on the small camping party. Manuel and the Williams brothers took off their leather belts and together they began to lay into their opponents. As for Rutgers the bricklayer, he was a stocky young man, preternaturally strong. One gangster stabbed him in the hand. Like an enraged bull, he doubled up, put his head against the man's waist, and using him like a battering ram, ploughed a furrow into all the others. 'Like a rhino,' remembered Daphne.

Bleeding now from the whips of the belt buckles, the predators were undeterred. 'They kept coming,' said Manuel. 'Quite a few of them were hit on the face and the head with these buckles and they're bleeding ... not a pretty sight in the train.'

Perhaps by accident, perhaps not, Davie Williams's axe fell out of his rucksack. He picked it up and chopped at the hand of a knife-wielding man coming towards him. 'They scattered,' said Daphne.

But not before Manuel, who had on his workman's steel-rimmed boots, had kicked one of their attackers 'into kingdom come', as Daphne said.

Everyone who was there that day remembers Manuel's steel-rimmed boots. Unlike Philip Kgosana, who had protested years after he led the Langa march that there was no magic about his short pants, it seemed on that day in the train that there was some magic about the boots.

When I asked Manuel about the boots three decades later he let out a slow, deep roar of a laugh that rumbled up from his belly and rolled in his chest. 'Yes, there was that too,' he said. 'I was very proud of the fact that I was a construction worker. I was reasonably fit and I could jump and kick quite high.'

As the train pulled into the next station, the gangsters, including the axed man, leapt off as the rest of the passengers cheered the ignominious departure of the pack, now 'scampering and whimpering' on the platform.

The floors of the train were slippery with blood, the camping party was covered in it, and the railway police were waiting on the platform. Davie Williams had the presence of mind to throw the axe out of the window just before the train pulled in to the stop.

The police immediately arrested them, beginning by cuffing Brian Williams. Manuel tried to intervene and 'play the paralegal', but a railways cop 'just grabbed me by my throat and lifted me off the ground. And I was a strong lad.' The railways police had a reputation for being particularly rough even in the lexicon of South African constabulary.

Taken aback, adrenalin flowing, Manuel said to the cop: 'You won't get away with this.'

At that point, he felt a fist under his chin, and 'for the only time in my life' was 'floored ... flat, sprawled'.

But despite the added injury, the campers were buoyed by their victory. Apart from Rutgers's hand and Manuel's chin, both of which needed stitches, they were all right. The gangsters, on the other hand, were not. They departed in ambulances, but not before laying charges of assault against Manuel's party.

The police were perplexed by the whole event. For a start, all the assailants had jobs – they were electricians, bricklayers, trainee engineers. Daphne was a *teacher*. The police were aghast. *'Juffrou? En jy gaan so aan innie trein?'* they exclaimed. (Miss? And you carry on like this in the train?)

Secondly, the campers all spoke English. In the class hierarchy that had established itself by then on the Cape Flats, gangsters only spoke Afrikaans. You can't be a *gangster*, they figured, and speak English.

The other passengers came to their defence and explained what had happened. After charging them, the police let them go on their way to the camping site. They even retrieved Davie Williams's axe from the railway line and gave it to him. Their concern about what their respectable families might think if they were charged with assault did not dampen the campers' enthusiasm for reliving their triumph. 'We told the story over and over,' said Brian Williams. 'Do you remember *that*? And do you remember *this*? And did you see how I hit this guy with a belt? And did you see his *head*?'

The next week, when the police discovered that the axe victim was actually out on bail for a charge of murder, they dropped charges.

It was a seminal moment for the campers. Gangsters ran a reign of terror against most people on the Cape Flats. New, unsafe residential areas, public transport that was unprotected and unfriendly, and the disparate communities created by apartheid made ordinary people easy prey. Gangs were to become a strong factor later obstructing political organisation in the coloured areas.

That was still to be. For now, though, a group of teenagers had taken on a gang who'd outnumbered them, and won. It was an early lesson for the young Manuel about when to take risks, when to stand up for oneself, when to fight back and how. 'We had the courage to take on the enemy,' said Daphne 30 years later. 'After that the government was nothing!'

≡ PART THREE: Building ≡

1976-1985

CHAPTER 8

'Like tides, like stars'

JUNE 16, 1976 WAS A PIVOT IN SOUTH AFRICA. It turned history.
When school pupils in Soweto took to the streets that day to protest against Bantu Education, it not only changed the apartheid government for ever but also alerted black youth to the necessity of solid organisation. Partly planned, the immediate spark for the protests was the imposition of Afrikaans – for most a third language – as the medium of instruction in schools. In the winter of 1976, without the right textbooks, students were suddenly confronted with the prospect of writing their exams in Afrikaans. The arrogance of apartheid's civil servants exacerbated their anger. The local school circuit inspector, Mr Thys de Beer, told a Soweto school board: 'If you want to learn English, then go to England ... The voters have ordered that you must learn this way.'[1] The new language rule ignited embers that smouldered over inferior education. Overlooked in the subsequent bedlam was that a month later the order was overturned, with the same Mr de Beer declaring: 'I'm just a public servant, personally I couldn't care less: let them have all their schooling in English if that is what they want.'[2]

But by then there was a far more fundamental object of the protests than simply the language of instruction. It took two months for the uprising to reach Cape Town: it began with a march of African schoolchildren to the Guguletu police station on 11 August 1976. After attacking the children with a volley of tear gas, police arrested 19 pupils. This became the impetus for a much larger protest to demand the release of detainees. Demonstrations on the predominantly white and coloured campuses of the University of Cape Town and the University of the Western Cape were also broken up by police. By the end of that first week 27 people were dead and hundreds injured.

Surprising at the time was the ferocity with which the protests hit the windblown areas on the Cape Flats that had housed the thousands of coloured people evicted from their original homes. The first child to be killed in the Cape Town uprising was Christopher Truter, a 15-year-old, shot in the back of the head. Bonteheuwel was sealed off by the police in late August (many such townships were designed to allow police to block one or two access roads and isolate the area), and not even ambulances were allowed in. Gangs exacerbated the violence and many coloured areas became fierce battlegrounds.

'In 1976 my school was gutted completely,' recalled Ebrahim Patel who was to become one of the key student leaders of the period. Only 14 then, Patel was born in District Six but had gone to school at Parkwood High in a coloured area of the southern Peninsula after his family was forcefully removed from the District.

For young working people like Manuel and Daphne, 1976 was both a frustration and an opportunity. A frustration because the protests centred largely around schools and campuses and excluded those outside of them. But an opportunity because it allowed these two young activists to actually *do* something.

Reading groups were abandoned as Manuel and Williams, together with Shaun Viljoen, Yousuf Gabru and Yusuf Adam, decided to help scores of arrested youths to get out of jail. They worked closely with Dullah Omar, a human rights lawyer. Viljoen's family knew Omar through their common membership of the Unity Movement – Omar was a leader in a civic association and had Unity Movement ties, but he struck the young activists as committed to a cause way beyond the narrowing confines of Unity Movement ideology. Another young lawyer with whom they worked, who had also emerged from the Unity Movement, was Siraj Desai. (Omar was later to become the first minister of justice in the Mandela government and then minister of transport. He died in 2004. Desai is a High Court judge on the Cape bench.)

The young activists wrote scores of letters at night, by hand, on behalf of the parents of detained pupils, giving lawyers like Omar and Desai authority to represent them. At that time hundreds of schoolchildren had been arrested and charged with public violence, an offence that could carry a penalty of five years or more. Conviction and sentencing could be done in a day with no legal representation. But now parents could produce lawyers' letters, and often lawyers themselves, in court. They would apply for bail. So instead of the speedy convictions the police had hoped for, cases often dragged on for months. Several of the accused were acquitted, including three youths charged with burning down a library in Kewtown, a working-class suburb near Athlone.

'There was no political movement that was guiding us,' recalled Daphne. In fact some Unity Movement adherents had even tried to persuade them to drop their crusade. 'They said, "You know, Daphne, you cannot defend everyone who gets picked up." And I said, "You know what, don't dictate to me. I'm doing the defending here. Because I'm not going to knock on someone's door and say, Is your son a *skollie* (a gangster) or is he a student?"'

'There was no political organisation,' confirmed Viljoen. The five set about raising money for bail and fines. 'Yousuf (Gabru) would come with wads of notes and we'd go off to different courts and as the youngsters came up we'd say, here's the bail.'

For Viljoen, Manuel was the driving factor. Viljoen did what he did for friendship because 'it was not the sort of thing I would have done as a Unity Movement member'.

IT WAS AN EARLY SIGN of the loyalty that Manuel demanded. He and Viljoen were rapidly growing apart politically. Indeed, Viljoen had been formally recruited into the Teachers' League while studying for his teacher's diploma, and he was still strongly connected to the Unity Movement. Two years earlier, he'd taken Manuel to visit Ben Kies, the formidable intellectual leader of the Teachers' League (although by then he had long been banned from teaching or taking part in its activities). Manuel walked into Kies's lounge in Bo-Kaap with its majestic views and froze. The size of the room, Table Mountain bearing down through the picture window, the wing armchair in which Kies was sitting would have been enough to overwhelm him. But the conversation was even more daunting.

'I don't know what to say to somebody like that … He's saying to me: "Speak up, young man." And I'm shitting in my pants, you can't have a conversation, what do you say to this man? Because they write in the *Educational Journal* (the official journal of the Teachers' League) and they write about Greek mythology and they apply Greek mythology to SA. I can't have a *conversation* with him!'

It must have been one of the few times in his life that Manuel was silenced by awe. It is a measure of the huge esteem in which Kies was held in Cape Town that he could so completely overwhelm such a confident youngster.

Yet Manuel had few doubts afterwards about the political path he'd found. It drove him and Viljoen apart ideologically but, strangely, in fractious, factional Cape Town, their friendship survived.

Viljoen himself was changed enough by his friendship with Manuel to opt to teach in a working-class school in Heideveld rather than Livingstone, the middle-class Unity Movement stronghold that the Teachers' League had earmarked for him. Five years after their fund-raising activities for the students of '76, Viljoen, who in later life became an author and academic at Stellenbosch University, wrote a poem for Manuel that articulated the conflict he felt between his personal loyalties and the political ones. There was a 'great gulf' between them, he wrote:

Foolish to imagine that things will change.
Yet, your presence
Like tides like stars
Persists in my blood
And persists.
I wonder how much of me
Remains in you?

When Viljoen's father died a decade later, Manuel turned up at his house with a huge pot of biriyani. 'His gesture was amazing,' said Viljoen. He had written the poem to mark the 'irrecoverable loss' of a personal lodestar because of a difference in politics. And yet here Manuel was on his doorstep again, bringing food and friendship.

1976 WAS FORMATIVE IN other ways too. If a breeze of change came from the student uprising of 1976, then a gust came from the rapidly emerging black trade union movement in the 1970s.

'For more than a decade,' wrote former labour reporter Steven Friedman, 'African workers had been seen but rarely heard: only a few small unions, most of them tightly controlled by registered unionists, remained to carry the flames of African unionism and workers were silent as their bargaining power and living standards wilted under new assaults.'[3]

When 2000 workers in Durban refused to work on the morning of 9 January 1973, demanding a pay rise, it caused a stir. The workers won a small increase (not near the R30 minimum a week that they had demanded) and went back to work.

But it sparked a wave borne of the misery of making ends meet in a country where black workers were almost completely without a voice. In 1973, the average take home pay of an African worker in Durban was R13 a week – well below the Poverty Datum Line (low by any standards) for Africans of R18 a week. By early February the strikes had spread not only through the city of Durban but to other small towns in the province of Natal. By mid-February, some 30 000 workers were on strike.[4]

African unions were revived in the early 1970s, mainly in Durban and Johannesburg, by disaffected unionists from the Trade Union Council of South Africa (TUCSA), a conservative body that organised white and coloured workers. In the Cape, it was the federation to which the staid Garment Workers' Union belonged.

But the dissident TUCSA unionists, led by a woman called Harriet Bolton, campaigned vigorously for the rights of African workers to join trade unions, particularly as they were flooding into manufacturing industry. She sought help on the university campuses and found it in the newly established Wages and Economic Commissions which were researching black wages, Friedman reported. Black students on their segregated campuses also began to play a role in organising unions, and groups such as the Young Christian Workers (YCW) harnessed resources.[5]

At about the same time in Cape Town, a group of African trade unionists who had once worked for the South African Congress of Trade Unions (SACTU, which was aligned to the ANC in the 1950s) began to re-establish worker organisation.

One of these was Zora Mehlomakulu, who had been a young trade unionist in the 1960s. Others were people with stronger links to the ANC and SACTU in the past: 'Rev' Sikolakhe Marawu (a lay preacher, later an ordained minister, who was known universally as 'Rev'), Wilson Sidina, Alpheus Ndude and Storey Mazwembe. The latter two worked in the literacy movement, trained, as was Manuel, by Judy Favish and Pat Horn.

This group of African unionists set up a Workers' Advice Bureau in Athlone (in an old building where the Labour Party had given them an office when the Group Areas Act made finding one impossible). Mehlomakulu was the Advice Bureau's anchor. Calm, reasoned, she grew into a fine negotiator who could hold her own with the most troubled workers or intransigent bosses. Those who knew her remember that she held her ground while knitting furiously. 'Beautiful, majestic Zora,' as the Cape Town journalist and political activist Zubeida Jaffer once described her.[6] And indeed she was. There is hardly a unionist or activist from the Western Cape who came of age in the 1970s and 80s whom she did not touch. She died suddenly of an asthma attack in 2001.

The Advice Bureau volunteers at first did not talk openly of forming a union then – such talk would have attracted the wrath of the state. African workers were particularly vulnerable in the Western Cape because of the coloured labour preference policy and harsh influx control laws. Most were migrants who could be sent back to the 'homelands' the moment they lost a job.

Under these conditions it was too difficult to build industrial unions, as had begun to happen in the north of the country. A general union, thought the early organisers, would give more protection to workers and, anyway, fitted in with an idealism at the time. 'Building organisation amongst workers was seen very much as building a socialist movement and (it) should transcend notions of industrial boundaries,' explained Favish. 'So there was a conscious decision not to organise industrial unions, but to organise workers' committees.' More practically, the decision to organise a general rather than industrial union exploited the small legal space available, as it was only workers' committees who asked employers for recognition, rather than formal trade unions.

In the next three years, the Western Province General Workers' Union emerged out of the Advice Bureau. It later became the General Workers' Union as it expanded nationally to organise stevedores in every port. By the early 1980s it wielded considerable clout not only among African workers in Cape Town, but among dockworkers around the country.

But in those early days the volunteers simply gave practical advice to workers who faced a plethora of problems – from not understanding deductions on their payslips to being 'endorsed out' of Cape Town once their contracts had come to an end. They also began to teach literacy to workers at the Advice Bureau. If it was slightly ironic that the donor of their offices was the Labour Party, there was a crueller irony in the sponsor for the literacy project. It was Craig Williamson, who had masqueraded as a radical student activist in Cape Town and Johannesburg for several years before supposedly going into exile. He then went to work for the International University Exchange Fund in Geneva, through which he supported anti-apartheid projects in the country. The literacy project in the Advice Bureau was initially started with funds from the IUEF.

Williamson was later exposed as a high-up police spy, a major in South Africa's feared security police.

Perhaps it was not surprising, then, that in 1976, a year after the Advice Bureau had been set up, Storey Mazwembe, who was also an underground ANC activist, was killed by police after being detained. And at the end of that year Judy Favish, Pat Horn, and several others who had been involved in the Wages Commission, were banned and prohibited from carrying on their work.

WHEN SHE HAD FIRST MET THEM, Favish was excited by her contact with Manuel and Daphne Williams. She thought it was the key to establishing contacts with coloured workers, particularly those who formed part of the vast and underpaid army of workers in the garment industry who were trapped in a closed-shop 'sweetheart' union. Manuel taught literacy to a few groups of garment workers and Favish herself ended up teaching a group in Maitland, Manuel's neighbouring suburb. 'It was hardly a hotbed of revolution,' she admitted later. 'There were two old mamas who really weren't interested in revolution at all. But they used to come faithfully because I think they felt sorry for me rather than because they were learning something.'

The banning of Favish and the other literacy teachers or student union activists that year shocked Manuel and Williams. It was a sign of how determined the state was to suppress even the most tangential groups who reached into the black working class, even if it was just to teach them to read. The effects were immediate. The little literacy office in Mowbray closed down, Shaun Viljoen found a safe place in Athlone where they could store the teaching codes and pictures, and the two key trainers, Favish and Horn, were prohibited from teaching. The literacy group struggled on for another year or so, run by a group of friends who had been trained to teach, before it petered out.

The Advice Bureau – despite the huge shock of Mazwembe's death – weathered the storm a little better. Student activists from the Wages Commission stepped in and helped fund Zora Mehlomakulu to run the office – at the princely salary of R75 a month.[7]

Daphne and Manuel were shaken by the bannings and Mazwembe's death. 'They told us that the time wasn't right … to continue with that sort of activity (literacy classes). Because of the fear of repression one would inevitably end up being more and more reformist. My sense was that they withdrew and read and studied and re-emerged,' said Favish.

After Favish was banned, Manuel and Daphne were frequent visitors to the Woodstock house she shared with David Lewis. 'I remember really enjoying his company because we would talk about politics,' said Lewis. There was both an intensity about him but also an irreverence for political ideologies that Lewis enjoyed. 'I remember him in a way that he's still able to be today, to be sarcastic and scornful of pretty much any standard political grouping.'

But Manuel was still intent on *doing* something. Perhaps a year into Favish's banning he arrived on her doorstep and said he wanted to be part of the Advice Bureau. 'The impression I got from him was that he had genuinely done a lot of thinking about where he wanted to make his mark and he really wanted to get involved in the trade union movement.'

Favish (illegally because of her banning order) consulted the Advice Bureau, run now by a core of African unionists who had re-emerged from the 1960s, and a new generation of mainly white activists who had come out of the Wages Commission at the University of Cape Town.

The discussion went 'round and round', she said. 'Some of us argued strongly that he should (become part of the union), and others argued strongly against it.' The pro faction, which Favish supported, pointed out that he was a good, dynamic organiser. Also, importantly, that he was coloured in an environment where the majority of the working class was coloured.

The anti faction held against him what they assumed was his Unity Movement background and the fact that he and Daphne had withdrawn from the literacy campaign after the government clampdown of 1976. 'There was a fear that he might withdraw again,' said Favish. 'In the meantime he would have learned a whole lot of things that were going on and might get people into trouble. So, basically, how reliable and trustworthy could he be? It was hard because people liked Trevor very much as a person.'

In the end the decision was no. Favish had the unenviable task of conveying the message to him, something which she says, years later, she is still embarrassed about. She had put it diplomatically, she said, saying that perhaps the union could keep him 'in reserve ... but there's a real concern that more people shouldn't come in at this point'. But he 'was very upset, very angry'.

Manuel, three decades on, was quite phlegmatic about this incident, shrugging it off as just another cut in the eristic anti-apartheid politics that consumed Cape Town. Only on one point is he firm: the Unity Movement was a 'sojourn', not home. They were his friends, and gave him intellectual solace but his political heart was never there.

There is a difficult irony in the Advice Bureau's rejection of Manuel, and one that sums up the bitterness of politics in the Western Cape in the late 1970s. Here he was, a genuine working-class boy, whose single mother supported her family on a garment worker's wages, forced to work rather than study, who came from the majority coloured population of Cape Town, being told by a group where white intellectuals played a major role that he was not good enough for them. There is another irony, too, only apparent in hindsight. Then his links with the Unity Movement, to the left of the union and ANC mainstream, earned him opprobrium. In his later years as finance minister, the left wing of the ANC and the union movement would take him on for being too conservative.

The truth is, as Lewis told me, Manuel was not easy to slot into any ideological cubbyhole. Neither then, nor later. In the fractious atmosphere of Western Cape resistance politics, this may have been the key to his subsequent success.

CHAPTER 9

A new mission

Manuel, Viljoen and their friends saw in 1977 at a party at Dullah Omar's house in Rylands Estate near Athlone, where they celebrated the release from detention of several students and activists.

It was a moment of joy for Manuel, as was the prospect of the unbroken year's study that lay ahead. As part of his civil engineering training at Murray & Stewart he studied at Peninsula Technikon (Pentech) in blocks: one block in 1975, one in 1976, and a whole year in 1977.

It was also an opportunity for intensified activism: he was elected on to the Students' Representative Council (SRC).

The new year also brought an important change in his personal life.

A few years before, through his friend Brian Williams, he had met Lynne Matthews, who lived two doors away from Williams's Acre Road house in Kensington. She and Brian were good friends, and initially she had met Manuel at a party when they were in matric. 'I knew him in Kensington,' she recalled. 'He was something of a Casanova. *Everybody* in Kensington knew who Trevor Manuel was and everybody spoke about him.'

She'd danced with him at the party and found him to be 'so forward ... and I just, bloody hell, you know, who the hell do you think you *are*?' After that he hadn't asked her to dance again, but they remained in the same broad circle.

Matthews is a tall, big-boned, elegant woman with strong Indian features and a forthright manner. She was born in Durban in 1953 to a father who was classified Indian and a mother who was coloured. Her parents had divorced when she was a small child. She stayed with her father for a few years, but she 'didn't fit in with the Indian community', and came to Cape Town when she was 12 where her mother Myrtle had remarried a man called Leslie Christian. Christian, another of the countless victims of the Group Areas Act, had moved to Kensington after being evicted from his home in Rondebosch, the neighbouring suburb to Newlands. Lynne had gone to the local high school in Kensington where she had met Brian, Trevor's friend.

Her mother, like Manuel's, was a clothing worker and was involved in local charities in Kensington, an involvement that the teenaged Lynne disapproved of. She thought, as did many young radicals of her generation, that charities were a balm that changed nothing.

When they both served on the Pentech SRC, she and Manuel renewed their acquaintance for a period. Lynne was studying to be a teacher.

It had been a battle to establish the SRC at all and she had played a leading role. The issue that drove the student body from words to action was a forced removal taking place on the doorstep of the campus.

Unibel was a large 'squatter camp' sandwiched between the University of the Western Cape (UWC) and Pentech. It housed mainly Africans who had come to Cape Town in defiance of the draconian pass laws to look for work. The execution of these laws was profoundly politicising for many of the young coloured students at both the University and the Technikon. Many were immersed in the black consciousness philosophy that swept the black campuses in the 1970s, and here was a chance to reach out to their African brothers and sisters in a gesture of solidarity.

Jakes Gerwel, who had graduated from UWC a few years earlier, gone to study in the Netherlands and returned as a lecturer, lived near the university in a suburb called Belhar, a short walk from the sprawling shanties in Unibel.

It was there that Gerwel remembers seeing 'young Afrikaner men, policemen or Bantu authorities, hiding behind the bushes, chasing the poor (African) women and catching them'.

It was a 'most demeaning thing', he said. 'That was the time when influx control was being exercised so cruelly. Those squatter camps were a reflection of what was happening in the Western Cape at the time.' The solidarity shown by coloured students gave the lie to what the government of the day tried to pass off as conventional wisdom that coloured people supported the coloured labour preference policy. That was 'not exactly true', Gerwel told me.

Almost daily the Bantu Affairs authorities, backed by police, would go to Unibel either to demolish shacks or arrest people without passes. It was finally and irrevocably devastated in 1978, but in the face of huge protests, not least those initiated by coloured students at the UWC and at Pentech.

Lynne and Trevor became friends in 1977 after a public argument in a student meeting about what to do about Unibel.[1] 'Trevor was right in the front and I was right at the back and we got up and opposed each other because Trevor was far more politically astute than I was at that stage, and he was far more radical,' said Matthews. 'He wanted us to prevent the squatters from being evicted. I wanted to organise relief for the squatters like food and blankets. I'll never forget him getting up and saying: We can't just put ointment on the sore. We need to prevent the sore.'

Matthews persisted in her argument for pragmatism. She may have disapproved of her mother's commitment to charities but now she argued that the squatters had immediate needs: food, clothing, blankets.

'That was the kind of relationship we had, that's how it actually started.'

Soon Manuel was visiting her in the hostel where she boarded, often bearing books. One of the first he brought her was *The Ragged Trousered Philanthropists* by Robert Tressell.[2] The book was a classic of working class hero literature that despaired of any justice under capitalism.

As Manuel's visits became more regular, Matthews discovered that he had a girlfriend already – Daphne Williams. In her forthright way she confronted him and said: 'You can't see both of us.'

At that point, anyway, Daphne had begun to show interest in someone else – Hedley King, an activist in Cape Town whom she later married. Manuel made his choice and he and Matthews began a more serious relationship.

MATTHEWS WAS AS POLITICAL as Manuel, but she preferred a 'backroom role', she told me. After she left Pentech she began teaching at Kensington High in 1977 and she and Manuel were part of group who launched a newsletter in the area – *Kenfacts*.

116

The newsletter was roneo'd, makeshift and amateurish. But it addressed issues that were of concern in the area, such as rentals, and a planned upgrading that made local residents nervous that it was a precursor to being removed in terms of the Group Areas Act, sandwiched as they were between the two white areas of Maitland to the east and Goodwood to the north.

There was a civic group in the area already. It was a staid body run by what Manuel recalls were 'old men', many of whom were the Labour Party stalwarts of his youth. The newsletters made them nervous. Nonetheless Manuel, Matthews and their group were taken into the civic – they attended almost every meeting – as a kind of a task group in early 1979. The group, which included Jonathan de Vries, then a pupil but later to become a prominent student leader, and a textile worker called Wilf Rhodes, effectively stamped their own agenda on the civic. They raised issues of local concern that always tracked back to the core injustice of apartheid. Rhodes was the oldest member of the group – the rest were in their twenties, or in De Vries's case still at school. They took up concrete grievances of residents in Factreton, Kensington's poorer neighbour, lobbying the City Council to hand over houses to tenants, some of whom had lived there since 1947.

Rentals were becoming a hot issue on the Cape Flats as people got pro-gressively poorer. By 1980, 97 per cent of African households in Cape Town and 74 per cent of coloured households had incomes below the Poverty Datum Line of R310,29 and R314,68 respectively (even PDLs were racially segregated in the days of apartheid).[3] To make matters worse, 'large numbers' of Cape Town families paid more than the government's own stipulated 25 per cent of income on rental in 1980 – nearly half in the case of coloured families, particularly in the new housing estates set up as catchments for those spewed out of their homes by the Group Areas Act.

Simply to provide adequate accommodation the housing stock in coloured areas needed to be doubled, and in African areas tripled.[4] Added to the burden of rentals were increased transport costs – more than 10 per cent of most black households' income went on transport. So the picture was of masses of Cape Town's people getting poorer, and having to spend more of their dwindling income on inferior houses and transport.

Into this frame walked young activists who saw their families and neighbours battling to get through each month.

In some ways it was a classic case of 'entrism' – in much the same way as the Unity Movement had infiltrated sports clubs and cultural societies to

117

ensure their point of view. So this generation of activists entered the extant and staid civics and radicalised them from within.

This new generation of young coloured activists was located deep inside the working-class areas: their neighbours and families, nervous as they may have been about confronting authority, felt the pain of apartheid keenly. The activists were also systematic. In Manuel's lounge, they drew up a large map of Kensington and Factreton, all the streets and houses marked. Drawn from a municipal map of 1960 it was a good enough guide. It was dotted with coloured stickers: orange for 'Trevor and Dennis and Rose', yellow for 'Dantjies and Lynne'; green for 'De Kock and Shireen', and pink for 'Davey and Joe'. And then a note in neat handwriting: 'The following areas must be canvassed on Tuesday, and meeting should be arranged for the 5th, 7th or 8th of May.'

This was in 1980. It was the fruit of two years of footwork in the area – walking the streets and visiting people in their homes.

'I'd read about the M-Plan,' said Manuel referring to Nelson Mandela's plan for mobilisation for a Defiance Campaign where supporters were organised street by street and house by house. 'I'd read about how you formed street committees. And here was this settled area where people had been living since 1945, and we decided to do exactly the same thing. So we went street by street, held house meetings, which were exceedingly well attended, distributed cartoons and pamphlets. This was a first.'

The Kensington group averaged three house meetings a night, dividing themselves up into groups. 'It was systematic, every night ... We needed to demonstrate that this thing could work.'

It was not easy, least of all because of the political differences in the group. Shireen (of the green sticker) was Shireen Pundit and she held to a line that was more 'workerist', according to Manuel. Workerists were suspicious of alliances that crossed class boundaries, even if those classes experienced similar levels of oppression and discrimination. It was a theme that was to run through anti-apartheid organisation in the 1980s. It became a particular gulf later when the civic movement tried to get the trade unions into the broad alliance of the United Democratic Front (UDF). By the time of the launch of the UDF, even Manuel's childhood friend Brian Williams, who had become a trade unionist, was disdainful: 'It was a pop fizz kind of thing. It wasn't sufficiently rooted ... because *everyone* could come along. You could exploit your workers during the day and at night you could wear your UDF badge.'

But most people in Cape Town's coloured townships were on the other side of the exploitation equation by then. Even if they once had been well-to-do, apartheid laws steadily undermined their incomes.

It was at exactly this time that Manuel's mother's family, the Von Söhnens, fell victim to this trend. After nearly three generations of making a respectable living in the middle of Stellenbosch, their large, comfortable house was simply expropriated by the government department euphemistically called Community Development. In a cold, bureaucratic notice served on Leonard von Söhnen in 1971, the government declared that the house that had been in his family since 1896 was no longer his. He was, said the notice 'entirely dispossessed and disentitled to the said land, and that by virtue of these presents the said COMMUNITY DEVELOPMENT BOARD, or its assigns, now is and hereafter shall be entitled thereto conformably to local custom the State, however, reserving its rights' [sic].

Whatever that might mean, in plain language it meant the Von Söhnens had to move.

But Von Söhnen stayed put. No, he told officials, he was not going to move. As government officials – the 'Group' – made increasingly frequent visits to his house, at times threatening, at others cajoling, he stayed on. He took the government to court but lost and was forced to sell. The houses were demolished around him, but still he stayed. Eventually, according to his daughter Dawn von Söhnen, Piet Koornhof, then the minister of the equally euphemistically named Department of Co-operation and Development, which oversaw hundreds of thousands of forced removals, paid them a visit.[5] By then the neighbourhood around them had crumbled. *'Verskoon die toestand van my huis, meneer,'* Von Söhnen told him, *'maar ek* wil *nie trek nie.'* ('Excuse the state of my house, sir, but I do *not* want to move.')

Apparently sympathetic, Koornhof suggested that one way out of the impasse would be for the Von Söhnens to reclassify as white. 'I don't want to be reclassified,' Von Söhnen replied. 'Because then I'll be like you people and you are just bullies.'

Von Söhnen swore he would leave the house only in a coffin, and he was true to his word. He died in 1977, as old as the century, and his family carried his coffin out of the house to the burial ground. A few months later his daughters packed up and moved up the hill to the coloured area of Ida's Valley.

Manuel noted the misfortune that had befallen his mother's family but did not dwell on it. It was, after all, the same fate suffered by hundreds of thousands of people by then and he came across them every day in his civic work. The question was how to drive the work forward, how to connect the dots between personal loss and the political work that was beginning to consume increasing chunks of his time.

Success, Manuel realised, was predicated on making alliances that mattered. His first political principle, learnt on the streets with his father, was speaking to local people in his neighbourhood about what concerned them. In Cape Town, the constant challenge was the racial question – how to reach out to those who suffered greater oppression but of whom many of the coloured civics' potential constituents were afraid.

In 1979 a heaven-sent opportunity presented itself to do precisely this: to expand alliances across class and race.

It began in a milling and pasta factory in Bellville South, which the Food and Canning Workers' Union (FCWU) had been organising for a year. It was one of the only unions in Cape Town that organised both coloured and African workers.

The union, which had been led by exiled SACP member Ray Alexander in the 1940s and 50s, had collapsed into a somnolent and sometimes corrupt bureaucracy by the early 70s. It was revived when an administrative secretary who had worked for Alexander approached a young white labour researcher to ask him to take over as general secretary in 1976. Jan Theron was the son of M E Theron, a Cape judge who had led a delegation of three judges, including Michael Corbett, to Robben Island in 1971 to meet the imprisoned Nelson Mandela and investigate conditions there. At the time, the prisoners were suffering dreadfully at the hands of an abusive, tyrannical warder, Piet Badenhorst. In his autobiography Mandela describes the meeting of himself, the three judges and Badenhorst as a turning point. Badenhorst was removed on the recommendation of the judges, and conditions impoved.[6]

Theron, a law graduate like his father, had played an active role in student politics in the late 1960s. Although proud of his father's intervention on Robben Island, he was disillusioned with the notion of becoming a lawyer in apartheid South Africa. After a stint overseas he decided that organising workers would be an effective means not only of improving the grim conditions black workers suffered, but of undermining apartheid itself. So he jumped at the offer of becoming general secretary of the FCWU in 1976. He pored over old union minutes and documents to understand the history of the once militant union. Then he set about reviving the past. There were still vestiges of memory left in the country towns of the Western Cape: Paarl, Worcester, Ceres and Wolsely, and in the fishing towns of the Cape West Coast. Its members were mainly coloured, but where there were African workers, Theron organised them too. Soon he was asked to be general secretary of the African Food and Canning Workers Union, a 'parallel' union formed to keep within the limits of apartheid law. But unlike the parallel unions of the conservative and large Trade Union Council of South Africa (TUCSA), the two 'branches' of the union effectively worked as one.

It was not an easy task. There were still racial and political tensions: Theron had dismissed the secretary of the Paarl branch, for instance, after she had written a letter to an Afrikaans Sunday newspaper defending the coloured labour preference policy. In many towns, coloured and African women vied for jobs in the canning factories, and one factory in Ashton, one of the only two major canning companies, refused to employ Africans at all.

Theron sought out organisers who had worked under Alexander. In Paarl, he found Lizzie Abrahams, a formidable woman who had been a canning worker and union organiser, and persuaded her to return to the union. The countryside branches revived, capturing a flavour of the union's heyday when it was an affiliate of the ANC-aligned South African Congress of Trade Unions (SACTU).

But in Cape Town, where the union had its head office, there was not a single factory organised, and not a single member by 1978.

Until Fatti's & Moni's.

By then, Theron had tracked down Oscar Mpetha, an old unionist and ANC member who had served a stint on Robben Island. Then working at Walls Ice Cream factory as a security guard, he had opened the union conference the year before dressed in his security guard uniform.

Mpetha plugged away at F&M, trying to persuade workers that their only chance of success against the employers was if African and coloured workers united. Unlike the factories in the Boland, this one had a majority of African (mainly migrant) workers.

'There was some interest, but no definite takers,' recalled Theron. But then something happened which 'was a kind of a lucky break, one of those things where the organiser either takes the break and knows what to do with it or

121

loses the factory'.

Some months before, a worker had broken his spine in an accident at the factory. Most of the African workers were from the same rural area in the Ciskei and knew the man was at home, incapacitated, with no money from Workmen's Compensation. 'Oscar had a lot of chutzpah and went to the pay office and basically demanded the cheque for this guy. It turned out they were sitting with it and he (Mpetha) got it. And that swung it for the African workers,' said Theron. 'As often happened in those times, especially with migrant workers, when there's a decision, everyone's in.'

Soon the coloured workers were in too, remarkable in a city where for so long workers had been racially divided. The workers asked management to recognise the union, and also demanded a minimum wage. However, Fatti's & Moni's said it would deal with the registered union – the coloured workers – but not with the unregistered union representing the African workers.

The strike that followed reverberated throughout the Western Cape. It was such a landmark in the march that led to the great resistance movements of the 1980s that it is sometimes difficult to remember the tiny figures that were at the core of the dispute. Eighty workers on strike for recognition. A demand for a R40 a week minimum wage.

The dispute began on 23 April 1979 when Anthony Terblanche, a manager at Fatti's & Moni's dismissed five coloured workers, whose names were on a petition supporting the wage demand. The next day another five workers, who had asked why their colleagues had been dismissed, were also fired. Theron's appeals that they were breadwinners and should be reinstated met with a blank lack of empathy. They should have thought of that when they signed the petition, replied Terblanche, a man whom the press conjured up as a 'sjambok-wielding boer', said Theron, but in fact was a 'quite weedy accountant type of fellow with a limp handshake, but quite nasty'.

The company, by firing coloured workers only, was sending out a clear message: don't mess with the union or with African workers. 'They thought the coloured workers would fold,' Theron told me. But they didn't.

The managers called in the Department of Labour which threatened to fine the workers R200 (at that time nearly two months' wages) if they went on strike. When its officials asked the coloured and African workers to stand on different sides of the room, the workers declared they were going on strike.[7] They were immediately dismissed.

Perhaps it was the innate justice of the cause; perhaps it was the name and tradition of the union itself, or perhaps it was the moving interracial solidarity of the workers. It was probably a combination of all these things. But it took only a few weeks for the workers' cause to grip the imagination of the community.

Theron knew that time was a factor. 'The rule of thumb is that three weeks after a strike has started, if they've got production going and they're managing without you, you've lost. After about three weeks, that's what happened.' But nobody was ready to give up. The workers met daily, and the union raised money to pay them a paltry R15 a week. Then Theron got a phone call that was to prove a turning point. A representative from the Western Cape Traders' Association, which represented small businesses in the coloured areas, told him that Fatti's & Moni's had its own bakery, Good Hope. 'We didn't even know that,' Theron said later. The traders offered to take the bread off their shelves. 'They were thrilled with the idea and we were thrilled with the idea, because they were talking about *bread*, which is a mass consumer item.' The problem was that few coloured traders stocked Good Hope bread, but it was sold in large quantities in the African townships. So began a long process of negotiations with the African traders. But when the boycott there began, almost two months into the strike, its effect was instantaneous. 'The very next day Fatti's & Moni's sent people to talk to Mr (Thomas) Mandla, the chair of the African Traders' Association, and Mr Mandla said don't talk to me, go set up a meeting with the union. The traders turned it.'

At the same time students on the coloured and white campuses and colleges declared they were boycotting Fatti's & Moni's pasta products in support of the workers.

In the following weeks, the sports unions allied to the South African Council on Sport which supported the Unity Movement, the fledgling civic groups such as Manuel's in Kensington-Factreton, and teachers' bodies announced they were supporting the boycott. Even the Labour Party, generally now ostracised by the predominantly black anti-apartheid organisations, declared its support for the strikers.

It was an extraordinary show of solidarity against an arrogance that characterised much of the white business community accustomed to cheap labour and tough legislation to keep it in line.

Students such as Ebrahim Patel, then in his final year of high school, used some strong-arm showmanship in the supermarkets. He and his comrades would go to Pick n Pay, then the biggest supermarket in Cape Town, load a trolley with Fatti's & Moni's pasta, allow the till checker to ring it all up and then 'grandly declare that the workers of this factory are on strike, this pasta's being made by scab labour and I refuse to pay for this'.

The fierceness of the boycott took management by surprise. Yet they ploughed on. Three months after the boycott started, management declared that the casual labour they had employed to replace the striking workers 'were more efficient and productive'.[8]

Four months into the strike, some workers collapsed in the face of destitution and accepted the company's compromise offer of jobs in Good Hope bakery, but the majority held out and the boycott spread to the Transvaal.

By the end of July it was clear that the company was hurting. Its profits almost halved from January-July 1979 compared with the same period the previous year, despite sales gimmicks like giving away free T-shirts with sales of their flour.[9] By August it had agreed that a South African Council of Churches mediator should help resolve the dispute.

THE STRIKE AND BOYCOTT deserve a central place in Western Cape history for several reasons: it spelled out a new form of cooperation between workers and the community; it politicised Cape Town, and the eventual victory pumped courage into not only the union but the fledgling community organisations.

But there is another reason, too: it threw up the divisions and fissures in the anti-apartheid movement that later became critical in the formation of the UDF. These fissures were reflected even within the union.

For one thing, a conservative backlash was brewing in some factories in the Boland, stoked by the security police who issued letters on union letterheads claiming that organisers had stolen money. There were workers who were suspicious of joining forces with African workers, and suspicious of the 'radicals' in the community who spearheaded the boycott. At the time, Theron told me, 'I was engaged in a desperate battle for my own political survival in the union. And the survival of the union.' This bred in him a caution, believing that workers needed to protect their organisations from what he saw as adventurists in the student and community organisations.

Then there were organisers such as Virginia Engel, who had been at the union for about a year at the time of the F&M strike. She, like Manuel, had been schooled in the politics of the Unity Movement, the radical church groups, and black consciousness. She joined the union when a job came up, because 'the motivating force in my life was striving for justice, and it didn't matter in which way you were going to do it. You were looking for a home that would further that cause.' She knew 'nothing' about unions: 'I didn't know the first thing. I just knew that unions were there, they wanted to improve the lot of the workers who were suffering tremendously and you could make a contribution there.'

She, like Theron, had sought out Oscar Mpetha when he was still serving a banning order after being released from Robben Island. He was reluctant to get involved in a leadership position again. 'At that point he was very tired and he had just got a job,' said Engel.

But Engel battled to communicate with migrant African workers, and the workers had pressed her to find someone who could speak isiXhosa. 'We twisted (Mpetha's) arm and he went with us to address the workers.'

Mpetha's links to the ANC gave the union a more political tinge. A few years after Mpetha became an organiser he was cruelly harassed by the authorities for his role in the Western Cape resistance.

Engel joined an underground 'discussion' group comprising people who described themselves as 'Charterists' – shorthand for those who subscribed to the principles of the Freedom Charter and, by implication, the ANC. She did not tell Theron because she thought he would disapprove. Yet she was also sympathetic to his concerns of preserving the fragile interracial unity they were building.

And there was another official who was key in pushing for closer links between the unions and a political movement, although he worked in the backroom department of the union's medical aid fund. His name was Johnny Issel.

Issel was already something of a giant in Western Cape politics and was, for a crucial period, a mentor to Manuel. He was born in Worcester in 1946, but left there during his last year of school when his mother, who had remarried, moved to Benoni. He scraped through high school and became a factory worker on the East Rand. A few years later he went back to school, wrote his matric exams a second time, getting a university pass. In 1970, at the age of 24, he enrolled at the University of the Western Cape. Being older than the average student, and more politically aware, he 'began to look for ways to organise a group'. By 1972, he had become secretary of the SRC, having polled the highest number of votes in the election, and that same year was elected local chair of the South African Students' Organisation, SASO, the most predominant and eloquent of the young black consciousness groupings.

In 1973, soon after he had enrolled to do an honours degree, Issel was expelled from the University because of his role in leading the walk-off from campus, the same protests that inspired the young Manuel as a high school student. Later that year he was served with the first of several banning orders that were to punctuate his life until 1990.

In spite of his banning order, Issel was a driving force behind resistance politics in the Western Cape for much of the 1980s. At the time of the Fatti's & Moni's strike, he was vocal in his view that it was essential for organised workers to join forces with community organisations.[10]

The union itself, under Jan Theron, was militant when it came to worker organisation and non-racial unity but cautious when it came to open political alignments with non-union organisations. 'I agreed with the position Jan took then,' Engel told me. 'We were essentially a coloured union at the time but we had to strengthen the other union, the African Food and Canning Workers' Union. The two were separate on paper but we had to bring our people together and that was our key task. We felt it was premature to just overtly expose the strategy and to expose workers who were not prepared for the political position we were taking.'

The Fatti's & Moni's strike was a turning point, though, not only for Engel and the union but for the type of organisation that was later to sweep the Cape Flats in the 1980s. 'I felt that we were standing still in terms of strategy,' she said. 'That we had reached a point of organisation that the workers were prepared to link up with organisations where they lived, and that is why they needed to shift.'

These tensions – between an overtly political position on the one hand, and a more focused union one on the other – were brought into sharp relief at the time of the boycott. The union itself didn't call the boycott. Activists on the outside suggested it and had stickers printed that said 'Don't Buy Fatti's & Moni's'. Theron objected because he thought it was an injunction that might fall foul of the apartheid law.

Ferdie Engel, a friend of Virginia (but no relation), who worked a day job in a shop, devoted himself to the boycott. In response to Theron's objections about the original stickers, he had them reprinted. This time they read: 'I don't buy Fatti's & Moni's.' He lobbied the coloured and Indian traders in the Western Cape Traders' Association, the churches, and sports organisations. He drove his grey Beetle Volkswagen after Fatti's & Moni's trucks delivering goods in the coloured areas, and then he'd confront the shopkeeper. 'Do you know the Traders' Association supports this boycott?' More often than not, the chastened shopkeeper would refuse the delivery.

As the campaign gathered momentum it captured the imagination not only of Cape Town but of the whole country. It spanned class and race and isolated the company and the government which tried to help them. The fact that African and coloured workers had stood together, the fact that small businesses in the separate Group Areas, as well as churches, students, the infant civics, and even some white households could unite around this one small issue of justice, was immensely empowering.

But the striking workers suffered tremendously. The union gave them a meal a day in addition to R15 a week, but it was barely enough to stem starvation.

Sometimes community and church groups donated funds. Unbeknown to many at the time, Allan Boesak, then a cleric at UWC, gave R3 000 to the union. 'He came out of the blue,' said Virginia Engel. It was a lot of money in those days. Years later, after he was convicted embezzling funds, some of his old comrades, such as Engel, bemoaned the fact that he did not defend his case in a more political and less legalistic way.

On 8 November 1979, nearly six months after the strike started, Fatti's & Moni's signed an agreement with the union, reinstating all the remaining 56 workers, increasing their pay, and agreeing to recognise both the Food and Canning and the African Food and Canning Workers' Unions which would operate as one. It was, said Jan Theron at the time, 'a great victory for the workers and union ... It is also a victory for workers everywhere and for organisations that were prepared to support the workers' cause.'[11]

In the end, said Theron, the strike was decided by PR people, acutely aware of the company's now shoddy image. Fatti's & Moni's went through three PR people in the course of the strike. The third told them: You cannot win this. You have to settle.

It was also an awkward time for the government because the Wiehahn Commission of Inquiry into Labour Legislation, which it had appointed in 1977, released its report recommending that African workers be allowed to join registered trade unions – a critical concession after a long period when Africans were prohibited from joining unions.

Whatever sense dawned on the PR people at Fatti's & Moni's, it was precipitated by the wave of organisation in support of the strikers. For

Ebrahim Patel there was an enduring message for his generation: 'The one thing we learned out of 1976 was the importance of organisation. 1976 was a huge amount of energy, incredible courage and yet it was just seemingly destroyed in its aftermath by the state. So what we learned out of that is that if we are going to make any progress we've got to find something that builds permanent organisation rather than simply have heroic defiance against the state.'

The long campaign had infused the nascent civic organisations in Cape Town with a sense of power and purpose. The strike itself had shown that unity between African and coloured workers was an ideal that could be realised. The cooperation between a multi-class (and multi-race) community with a trade union was unprecedented in South Africa since the 1960s repression.

In the wake of the strike, the search for new leadership and political direction became more urgent.

There were no 'elders' at the time, complained Ebrahim Patel. During the strike the students had asked Mr Richard Dudley, the legendary leader of the Teachers' League and a renowned teacher at Livingstone High, to speak to them. He refused. 'We saw at first hand fear,' Patel told me. 'Fear from elders, fear from people who were political activists in their own way but whose political activism had been pursued in the comfort of their sitting rooms and their cultural clubs. At the moment when African workers were battling to get recognition and coloured workers were ... trying to help them, the layer that could have given leadership, resources, assistance and logistics ... just found endless excuses why it was inappropriate to come and speak at that meeting ... There would be endless intellectual explanations of why the moment wasn't right, why it was adventurism, why it was this or that, and yet you strip away all the rhetoric, all the clever explanations, all the pseudoscientific analyses and what it comes down to, actually, is it's too dangerous to do that.' There was no courage to confront the state.

For this generation, it was the final schism with the Unity Movement which in many respects had brought them up.

MANUEL FOUND HIS OWN WAY partly by accident, partly spurred by the same sense of dissatisfaction.

A month after the victory at Fatti's & Moni's he went to Botswana, making a meandering journey there through Durban, and then Benoni and finally Mafikeng near the Botswana border. He picked up a couple of friends on the way, one from Durban and one from Benoni.

Their trip was nearly derailed in Mafikeng, which had become Mmabatho, the capital of the newly declared independent black state of Bophuthatswana, the second such rural 'homeland' to be declared an 'independent state' by the apartheid government. The little town was full of the new-found pomp of shallow statehood with police and soldiers conspicuous on the streets.

The main petrol station was outside a hotel and casino (forbidden in white South Africa but one of the main revenue earners for the Bantustans). On Sundays it opened at midday, enough time to keep Saturday night stragglers inside the casino. While Manuel and his friends waited for the pumps to open, a soldier in uniform – 'a coloured guy wearing a stocking on his head to straighten his hair' – sauntered up to them and began asking them questions. Manuel, by his own account, was 'quite bolshie' and told him to 'fuck off'.

'Do you know who you are talking to?' asked the soldier. 'I'm a captain in the army of the Bophuthatswana Republic.'

'Army of what republic?' responded Manuel. 'Don't talk rubbish to me, you little toy soldier.'

At that point the soldier grabbed him and beckoned a military vehicle coming down the road. 'Sergeant, sergeant!' he shouted.

Just when Manuel thought his trip might end in a police station in Mmabatho, a large woman stormed towards them. She faced the soldier and shrieked: *'Robert, jy soek altyd moeilikheid met die mense!'* ('You're always looking for trouble with people!') And smacked him twice through the face. Tshwa! Tshwa! Chastened, Robert the toy soldier slunk off, and Manuel felt foolish at his earlier fear. 'I mean, why didn't I just punch the guy? Punch his lights out? Here this woman came along and just smacked him, really smacked him.'

They crossed the border without further interference. Manuel's friends from Benoni had organised them accommodation in the students' residences in the local university in Gaborone. 'Then somebody picked up our track and said don't you want to meet some people?'

It was always at the back of his mind that he had gone to Botswana looking for the ANC, which had an important exile base there. But to ask to meet anyone would have attracted suspicion. So he kept his mouth shut and waited until word came through that two people wanted to meet them. They were taken to a house and there, waiting for them, was Reg September, now in his sixteenth year of exile, and Shaheed Rajie, who in later years was to work in the National Treasury under Manuel.

The two were interested in Manuel because of his Western Cape links and his involvement in the civic organisations. Manuel decided then and there that this was his future. He wanted to stay, to join the ANC in exile. 'No, no, no,' replied September. 'Go back.'

'He was impressed that I was a civil engineer, a technician, as he called it, and they could do with those skills. But it was very, very important that I went back. And so I did, but I went back with a mission.' His mission was to set up a network that could recruit people for the movement but at the same time he should remain involved in public politics.

When he returned to Cape Town, he took Lynne for a long drive on his motorbike to a little beach called Maiden's Cove on the Atlantic side of the Peninsula. There he told her that he might not be able to have a serious relationship with her because his political life was his priority. 'Fine,' said Lynne. 'If that's how it's got to be, I don't have a problem with it.'

'He was quite taken aback by that,' she recalled. 'This dilemma he had with his political life ... (it was) one hundred per cent commitment and he couldn't do anything that was going to distract him from that.'

'I wanted to make that choice because I didn't want to be saddled in a relationship if I wanted to be a soldier,' Manuel said later.

In the Easter of 1980 he returned to Botswana, this time in secret. Not even his mother knew. He flew this time. No long drives, risking arguments with soldiers and policemen in dusty little towns along the way. It was an altogether more serious mission.

In the four months between his two visits, the political landscape in Cape Town had shifted considerably. A community newspaper had been established, for the first time linking the disparate communities scattered by the Group Areas Act, the civics had taken root, and the youth had a new militancy with a skeletal inter-school organisation in place.

Manuel arrived in Gaborone at night and stayed in a little motel. The next day he walked the streets trying to make the connection. There had been one telephone conversation which had mentioned a bookshop near the main hotel. The first night the connection failed. On the second day, Manuel walked again to the bookshop and a man rode past on a bicycle and said: *'Is jy van die Kaap?'* ('Are you from the Cape?')

'Ja,' replied Manuel.

'Jou uncle het my gestuur' ('Your uncle sent me'), said the cyclist and led him to where Reg September was waiting.

He reported back on developments in the Cape, and again asked to stay in exile, more determined than ever now to become an armed cadre. No, said September, go back. 'That was so much more important,' reflected September later. 'You see it's easy enough to establish an armed wing outside the country, but getting those people back into the country was a king, king, king-sized job. Especially when you imagine that Cape Town is a thousand miles away from the border.'

'I was sent to go bloody organise when I wanted to be a soldier. They say go and do this stuff and make a noise in the streets and print newspapers and do what you're doing,' said Manuel.

It is perhaps only of academic interest to reflect on the turns that a life can take at certain points, but here was a second time in Manuel's then short political career that his choice was rejected. First, it was the union movement that said no to him. Then the option of exile was closed off. Many years later Manuel conceded that being a 'foot soldier' in Umkhonto we Sizwe would have meant a different learning curve. 'I'm shaped by circumstance,' he said. He went back to a situation where, at age 24, he had to learn to run meetings, to work with older, more conservative people, and to manage the often fratricidal politics of the Western Cape. 'Here I was working with people who were tenants in Factreton. They'd been in these houses, some of them for the second generation ... People had come from the war ... You can't just walk in there and (say): "Now, comrades!"'

In other words, it was a political path that forced one to listen and to negotiate. September may have seen in Manuel strengths the young man did not yet see in himself. 'He obviously had financial orientation and political trust, such a valuable characteristic ... (and) the ease with which we could communicate, he was such a good communicator and worked to find a common approach to things.'

September's impression had not changed from the first time he had met him in Gaborone the previous Christmas: 'Good God, I thought he was a prize!' Manuel may have wanted to be a soldier but the ANC had dispatched him to a different front line.

CHAPTER 10

A network of networks

WHEN REG SEPTEMBER LEFT the country secretly, three years after the ANC was declared an illegal organisation, he was amazed at just how rooted the networks around the country still were.

He had left after being arrested (and released on bail) for having broken his banning order in 1963. He went into hiding but in Cape Town the ANC's roots had been smothered. He was unproductive, he said, and 'a bit of an encumbrance'. And so his comrades decided he should leave the country. He shaved off part of his hair, got on a train to Johannesburg where he stayed for a while with Ahmed Kathrada until the latter was arrested as part of the crackdown on the Rivonia group which included Nelson Mandela and Walter Sisulu. 'From there we had to close up shop very quickly.' Then he went Durban on the understanding that he was to board a ship. But Barney Desai, his old CPC comrade, had used the same ship to get to Dar es Salaam and spoken to the media there so the plan fell through.

Instead, he caught a train to the Swazi border. A fellow passenger on the train, asked why he looked so worried. 'I revealed who I was to him.'

The man, whom he had never seen before, advised him to get off at the station before Golela, the border post, and gave him directions to his brother's house.

'He will take you home and look after you until you are ready to go.'

'And that's what happened,' said September, still struck by either the careful planning or fortuitous kindness of a stranger. The brother of his fellow passenger drove him to a point near the Golela border post, and pointed him in the right direction. 'It was pitch dark but I was able to identify a path.' When he came across a house with a light on he knocked at the door, explained his position and the owners let him sleep there for the night. The next day they contacted a local ANC man in Golela who took him to the capital, Mbabane.

A year later, he had to make a similar tortuous journey through the country to go west to Botswana, this time with his wife, Hettie McCleod. He stayed in the Indian township in Benoni from where they took a taxi to the Botswana border. Again, he walked across the border, directed by a local man. This time he was not so lucky in finding a house and they slept under the bushes. They awoke to find themselves near a house. The owners brought them something to drink and skins to sit on while they sent a boy to fetch a donkey cart. They went by cart to another village where a car picked them up and took them to Lobatse where they were met by Maulvi Cachalia.[1]

What amazed September then was the level of organisation at various points along the way. The donkey cart had been specially arranged, as had the car that eventually took them to Lobatse. He still does not know whether the man on the train to Swaziland was an ANC operative or just a sympathetic soul, but he trusted him. 'You *must* be able to do that.'

Nearly five years after being driven underground, the ANC was still operative in strategic corners of the country. There is a strong body of scholarly opinion that believes the ANC was absent or silent from 1960 till 1976, but there were quiet networks and unspoken support that could be activated at crucial times.[2]

The ANC never disappeared. Manuel and his own internal political network discovered this in the 1970s when they began organising politically. But it operated on a number of different levels – through its supporters in legal political organisations, through clandestine groups who were part of the legal bodies, and through deeper underground structures.

By the end of the 1970s several overlapping networks were operating in Cape Town, some of them connected, some quite distinct. It is impossible to understand these in the formal, almost romantic sense of 'underground' work. Many of those in 'core groups', as they were sometimes called, were people who moved openly in the world of resistance politics: the trade unions, the civics, the churches, and eventually in the UDF. One such person was Virginia Engel of the FCWU. Engel had never left the country, never been formally recruited, but during the Fatti's & Moni's strike became part of a regular discussion group that included Ferdie Engel, her husband Desmond, and Johnny Issel. The group was joined by Marcus Solomon who was released from Robben Island after serving eight years, and his wife Theresa Solomon.[3]

Issel linked into several such groups. 'Somehow when people write history there are many things that get lost, like, for instance, within that core group the decision to form the United Women's Organisation was made,' said Virginia Engel. 'And the Fatti's & Moni's strategy was endorsed. Those were the people with whom I could bounce off ideas and then go back to the union and follow a particular strategy.' The United Women's Organisation was the first openly affiliated 'Charterist' organisation to emerge in Cape Town in 1981.

Issel, for his part, saw himself as a driving force. There were no links with the outside for him, he told me. But organising such groups seemed the right thing to do at the time. He'd read Lenin's *What is to be Done?* soon after he came out of detention in 1976 and realised that black consciousness was a dead end. 'Generally, what was felt by people is that we had to beef up our communities,' he said.

The existence of the group was a tight secret, not least from Virginia Engel's own boss Jan Theron, the disciplined, hard-working unionist who, with his then wife Athalie Crawford, had rebuilt the FCWU into a formidable force. He, like many other unionists at the time, was committed to a worker primacy. Workers must run the union: there must be no hidden agendas. Any kind of political adventurism was to be regarded with great caution as it would have given the government an excuse to smash the union.

'I was like a two-faced person,' Engel admits. 'Because beyond that group I didn't talk politics to a whole range of people.' Most activists thought she was a unionist. She never assumed a prominent role in the UDF even though one of the early meetings to discuss its formation had been held in her house. Engel's formal contact with the ANC was 'zilch ... (but) I knew it was the ANC.'

There was another, overlapping 'core group' consisting of Manuel, Cheryl Carolus, Goolam Aboobaker, and four older activists from the African townships who had roots in the Congress movement: Christmas Tinto, Zoli Malindi, Wilson Sidina (also a trade unionist in the Western Province General Workers Union) and Mildred Lesiea. Issel interlinked with both groups. These were just two groups of a range of networks being established around Cape Town. Another coalesced around Hedley King, who was later to marry Daphne Williams, Manuel's old paramour, and there was another that linked more closely to Umkhonto we Sizwe (MK), the military wing of the ANC. But, said Manuel, his group 'had some sort of status in the ANC as well' and thus became known, somewhat disparagingly, as the High Command by activists who felt excluded from what would become a driving seat of organisation.

There were also tactical differences between the groups. Issel, for instance, emphasised an upfront, defiant revolutionary mass movement more strongly than Hedley King. King was supported by Jonathan de Vries, who had met Manuel and Lynne Matthews in Kensington where he lived. Six years younger than Manuel, De Vries was also a product of Harold Cressy, 'a fantastic school', he told me, to which he was 'deeply indebted'. King and De Vries were keener to establish more deeply rooted organisations that would be protected from the police. In later years the differences would lead to open fights: between Manuel and De Vries (Cheryl Carolus once physically pulled them apart when they pounced on each other), between King and Issel (for a long time in Cape Town those who coalesced around either activist were known as 'Isselites' or 'Hedleyites'), and eventually between Manuel and Issel.

But in those early days, despite some jostling, all were bound in a common purpose and by a common trust of the type that September had experienced when he left the country and that Bardien had spoken of to Manuel when he was a teenager.

THERE WERE OTHER LEVELS of the ANC's presence too. One was a more tightly organised underground structure. Key in this was an art student who was to become a close friend of Manuel's, although they never operated in the same 'group'. Murray Michell graduated from Michaelis, the UCT art school in 1979. Young, white, on the edge of the arty counter-culture that swept through Cape Town's disaffected young white community at the time, his boyish good looks, lopsided grin and lackadaisical manner hid a more serious purpose. He was recruited to the ANC in 1979 by former student activists who had fled the country. He had dabbled in student and civic politics until then – teaching community activists how to produce silk-screen banners, for instance, in coloured townships on the Cape Flats. He had become a fairly accomplished photographer in his time at Michaelis but when it came to the end of the year, he had not produced much work. The faculty was split down the middle about whether to fail him or pass him *cum laude*. The latter group won because he convincingly explained to them that because art is 'fundamentally political ... the philosophical position is that you're less concerned about the product and more concerned about the making of it ...' Or something like that.

But underneath the banter that got him through his degree, he was set on a path that was to take him to the top of the ANC's Western Cape command by the end of the turbulent 1980s. For Michell, the political act with most 'meaning and relevance' had to be 'revolution', and one could either be 'individualistic' and 'voluntaristic' (an oblique if unspoken critique of Issel's style) or one 'could subjugate the personal to organised forces ... and that was the route I took'.

His first assignment in 1979 was to get the Freedom Charter translated into Afrikaans and distributed around the Western Cape. The assignment had been discussed in Lusaka, the ANC's headquarters in exile. Unbeknown to him then, the suggestion had come from Reg September, who had seen in the Western Cape an untapped potential for resistance and organisation.

Around this time, Michell became a close friend of Manuel's. He had met him through his silk-screening workshops in the coloured townships in the late 1970s. 'He was an activist,' recalled Michell. 'I didn't really know where he came from; I didn't know his status. I didn't know how central he was to things. But he has a presence and the first instant I met him in someone's lounge in Observatory ... I realised through his presence that he was clearly a player.'

Observatory was one of Cape Town's inner-city areas. Adjoining Woodstock, it was a traditional white working-class suburb but had increasingly attracted students who found large communal houses there to share. Night after night, Manuel and Michell would sit in the lounge of his shared Observatory house until the early hours, drinking cheap instant coffee and discussing politics. 'He basically gave me a crash course in Western Cape politics ... I needed to understand how all of this stuff fits together. We'd have this long engagement in understanding the links, the broken links between the early 1960s and the present. Where were the Congress forces? Who were they? Who were the Unity Movement forces ... On reflection I thought we were doing an analysis of who's who and where they are, and this was very dangerous stuff unless there was total trust.'

Throughout that period, for more than decade, Manuel did not know exactly what Michell was doing, nor did Michell know what Manuel was doing. But they were close enough to each other to know they were in the same network of networks, as it were. 'He would know, I would know ... we would spend hours together ... I would operate on the basis that I had an instruction, therefore that was the line, Trevor would probably get a different instruction, but you'd say, hold it, my views and his views are co-terminous.' Which meant the instructions were similar and coordinated. This may have been fortuitous. Jeremy Cronin, a political prisoner released into the turbulence of the mid-80s in Cape Town, and who later went into exile, said internal activists often connected to difference people in the ANC. 'The famous Lusaka,' he sighed. 'Everyone used to say "Lusaka says, Lusaka says". And I later discovered that well, this one's connecting with Mac Maharaj, this one's connecting with X, Y and Z. A lot of the factions we had back here were really just different personalities sitting in Lusaka. There was no such thing as "the centre".'

Even within one 'discussion group' there would be tensions. In each one, one or two people would report directly either to the ANC in exile, or a local contact, such as Michell. It made for both complex and often fragile structures and relationships at a time when fragility could least be afforded. The 'reporters' in the group were accountable to the group but also acted on instructions from the ANC. Sometimes, however honourable their intentions, if other members of their group discovered that they were reporting elsewhere, they might – and often did – feel manipulated.

The stakes were high. Long jail terms even for just being a member of the ANC were now common. Torture was routine and death a possibility. Towards the end of the 1980s, when military cells in the Western Cape were broken by the police, there was a constant shifting of command structures and of people, and concomitant resentment.

These different levels at which the ANC operated were replicated throughout the country.

As MICHELL WAS GETTING the Freedom Charter translated into Afrikaans for its twenty-fifth anniversary in June 1980, so a group of people in Durban were distributing it in English. Durban buzzed, not only in the wake of the huge strikes of 1973 but with the conscious revival of the Natal Indian Congress (NIC), which had been part of the Congress movement in the 1950s but never banned.

In 1974, a young man who had recently completed a pharmacy degree at the Salisbury College, which became the Indian University of Durban Westville, joined the executive of the NIC as a representative of the youth. Pravin Gordhan was then just 25. A second generation South African – his father immigrated from India in the 1920s – he cut his teeth in student politics in the early 1970s. Those who met him at the time were in awe of his intelligence – 'smarter than all of us, I've rarely encountered a brain like that,' said De Vries. Certainly he was a strategist, a thinker and a doer. Reading groups proliferated, as they did in Cape Town. 'Here's Marx now, he says the masses make history. And then you read (Amilcar) Cabral and he talks about class suicide. And then you read about the role of intellectuals and activists. Now how do you do all this, is the question we were asking. And then you begin to read Lenin and the importance of organising. None of us took it at a theoretical level. Ultimately it was about how do you, as a group of activists, connect to the masses? How do you mobilise around issues that (will) activate people in a climate of absolute fear ... that was the key,' Gordhan told me.

As his counterparts in Cape Town did, Gordhan had a 'triple identity': a place in the ANC underground (and later the Communist Party), one in the overtly political but legal NIC, and the third in local community organisation where the constituents were hard done by but nervous of politics.

Gordhan was later to become a key operative in one of the ANC's most critical operations, Operation Vula, which was set up to re-establish the ANC as the central resistance organisation in the country. So was Michell. This added a fourth dimension to their political identity. And Manuel was in all of the loops, if not active in the last.

THE SAME PATTERNS EMERGED in Johannesburg and the Eastern Cape: layers of ANC involvement and leadership work, and activists who led a marbled existence between the legal anti-apartheid organisations and the underground. Here, though, the police prised open the connection in the early 1980s, and an enormous crackdown resulted in widespread detentions, at least one death, excruciating and crippling torture of some activists, and a long jail term for a young woman who was later to play a key role in the implementation of post-apartheid economic policy.

She was Barbara Hogan. Hogan was recruited into the ANC by an old student comrade, Jeanette Curtis, who had left the country for Botswana and married Marius Schoon, a former political prisoner.[4] Hogan emerged from a generation of white leftist students who had embraced Marxism. For a while she worked for the Federation of South African Trade Unions (FOSATU), the first federation of mainly black industrial unions. Like the newly emerged unions in Cape Town, they were militant on the shop floor but feared political involvement would invite a state crackdown. 'There was an enormously hostile attitude towards any politicisation of the trade union movement,' she said.

Despite this, Hogan grew sympathetic to the ANC partly through linking up with old black activists – Indian and African – who had survived the state crackdown in the 1960s. She was attracted by their non-racialism and their openness to socialism, both of which contrasted with the predominant black consciousness movement popular among intellectual young blacks at the time. Her recruitment – like Michell's, it happened inside the country – had particular tasks attached to it. She was charged with setting up consumer boycotts to support union struggles, of mobilising the white leftists against apartheid and setting up networks around the region. She first worked through a Swazi link and then was transferred to handlers in Botswana, a decision that proved fatal.

'I felt their networks were pretty loose – porous,' she recalled later. They turned out to be worse than porous: one of the messengers used to smuggle messages between the local networks and the Botswana command was Karl Edwards, a police spy who had masqueraded as a white student leftist for several years. Hogan's main task was sending reports on the political situation out of the country in code. She did not join the military wing – in fact she declined to do so when asked. In early 1982 she got a message from an ANC courier to say she must leave the country immediately. The envelope in which she had sent her last coded report had been slashed open, and now the organisation was convinced her network had been smashed.

But she could not leave the country, either legally or illegally. Within a day of receiving the message at least six cars followed her wherever she went. She sent messages to Botswana via two other networks, one an MK cell. Her

ANC contacts replied that they were concerned about the leaks and that she should send a list of all those she either knew or suspected were working with the ANC.

'Don't bother to put it in code,' said the contact. 'I can get it out of the country in 24 hours and then we'll set up a safe house for you.' She sent out the list with a courier who turned out to be a double agent.

'And so all the people on my list were arrested – those people I *thought* might be ANC and those who I *knew* were.'

One of those on the 'possible' list was a young Johannesburg doctor who worked for the Food and Canning Workers Union in the Transvaal, Neil Aggett. (Jan Theron, a close friend of Aggett and his union colleague, said years later that Aggett was not active in the ANC at the time and that his interrogation was related to a discussion group he had belonged to several years earlier.)

Before she could leave the country, before she could even move to a 'safe house', Hogan was detained along with most of the people on the list. This was in the last months of 1981. The detentions went further than Johannesburg to the Eastern Cape and Durban. Gordhan was one of those picked up by the police. In all, nearly 70 people were detained at one point.

'The police thought they'd hit a major underground ANC network,' recalled Hogan. 'But they hadn't. They had hit an ANC nerve but they couldn't establish the links … people were defining themselves as ANC but they weren't necessarily linked to the ANC.'

Still the price was high. Aggett, whom Hogan had briefly encountered in John Vorster Square, the security police headquarters, had given her a cheery smile and 'big salute' when he saw her – the clenched fist sign of the resistance. 'That was the last time I saw him.' A few days later she discovered that Aggett had died in a police cell there. Suicide, the police called it. But few of his friends or family believed it, least of all Hogan: '*Who* have you fucking killed?' she asked her interrogators as they drove her between police stations and she spotted a newspaper poster proclaiming: 'Detainee's Death Causes Furore'.

The subsequent inquest found that Aggett had committed suicide; nobody applied under the Truth and Reconciliation Commission for amnesty for his death. Hardly anyone detained in that crackdown believed he killed himself. Many were viciously tortured by the same policemen responsible for Aggett's interrogation. Thozamile Gqwetha, an Eastern Cape trade unionist who had also worked in the broad ANC networks, was so badly tortured he ended up in hospital barely able to lift his head from his chest.

Gqwetha was one of five others charged with Hogan with furthering the aims of the ANC. In the end only she was convicted – there was simply not enough evidence to stick to the others. All she had done was to send coded political reports out of the country. Her lawyer thought she'd get no more than five years, but the judge said he had to make an example of her to discourage whites from supporting the ANC. Ten years, he said, would serve as just such an example. Hogan had already been in jail a year, mostly in solitary confinement. Because she was the only white woman political prisoner at the time she was to spend another year alone in prison before she got company.

Hogan and Gordhan were both to become key colleagues of Manuel's in the implementation of economic policy in the post-apartheid era. But then they were part of a countrywide network, comrades who hardly knew each other. Each, in their city, was part of the layered networks of ANC supporters that flourished around the country. Hogan in a sense was simply unlucky because she had done nothing that Gordhan had not done in Durban or Manuel had not done in Cape Town. But it was a sign of the price they might all have to pay.

DURBAN WAS PERHAPS THE most advanced in terms of an ANC presence in the mid-1970s. Joel Netshitenzhe, one of the ANC's leading intellectuals and later a close aide to President Thabo Mbeki, arrived in Durban in 1975 to study medicine at the segregated university for black students. Born in 1956 in Sibasa, a village in the Venda-speaking area of the Northern Transvaal, he had had an unlikely first encounter with the ANC, courtesy of the security police. They had brought to his school a member of one of the first MK units who had waged a campaign against the Rhodesian forces in Wankie in the late 1960s. The soldier was captured and 'turned', becoming an early 'askari', as they were later known. The askari told the teenage pupils about how rotten life was in an ANC camp – how they mixed stones with the rice – and how awful Russia was. But instead of putting the youngsters off, it intrigued them.

When Netshitenzhe arrived in Durban he found a vibrant political culture – not the ANC, but black consciousness. He became secretary of the local SASO branch. But his politics shifted in early 1976 just before the Soweto uprisings changed the consciousness of the nation for ever. That year trade

141

unionist Joseph Mdluli was killed in detention. Like Aggett, who came after him, like Storey Mazwembe in the same year, Mdluli was targeted because he was a link between the banned ANC and the emerging union movement. Netshitenzhe attended his funeral and made contact with older ANC members. At that stage the first batch of political prisoners jailed in the 1960s had begun to come off Robben Island. Later that year another ANC activist, Mapetla Mohapi was killed in detention in the Eastern Cape. When Netshitenzhe and his fellow students attended his funeral in Matatiele, a village right up against the Maluti mountains in the north-eastern Cape, he not only met key players in the black consciousness movement, such as Steve Biko, but saw, for the first time, copies of the Freedom Charter.

He began to think, along with many of his generation, that black consciousness was not a replacement for the ANC or PAC. Listening to the ANC's Radio Freedom broadcasts on crackly shortwave radios also helped clarify his thoughts, particularly on puzzles such as the brewing civil war in Angola after the collapse of Portuguese colonialism.

Netshitenzhe left the country via Lesotho after he was charged with several other students for demonstrating in support of the Soweto students. He went for military training in Angola and then moved to ANC headquarters in Lusaka, working first for Radio Freedom and then for the ANC newspaper *Mayibuye*. Even then, as a 22-year-old, he was critically involved in the key political debates of the time, one of which was how to link up with activists inside the country. By 1979, rapid-fire organisation – among students, in civics and in the unions – changed the fabric of the organisation. A committee was set up to drive the revival of Congress activities in the country, and exiles began to make contact with local activists.

When the Fatti's & Moni's strike began, for instance, the ANC set up links with some of the players through Ray Alexander, the unionist who had been in exile for more than a decade and who had founded the FCWU.

Increasingly, as September had done with Manuel, the ANC began to ask activists who wanted to leave the country whether they couldn't be more useful inside. By the early 1980s, said Netshitenzhe, the 'underground structures (in the country) had been revived at a political level: being in touch with people, getting reports, advising people how to engage in mass action.' People in Political Motion, the ANC called it at the time. It was essential to maintain 'a veneer of legality' so that activists could openly mobilise people 'but at the same time as the revolt was intensifying, the separation between the legal and illegal was narrowing all the time'.

It was these circumstances, both internal and external, that Manuel walked into on his second trip to Botswana in 1980. A would-be soldier sent back to organise a movement in the streets, he had no doubt by then 'in whose name I was doing stuff'.

The 'stuff' was to come in concerted and rapid waves after 1980 and was to test him politically, and emotionally, in ways that he had not imagined.

CHAPTER 11

What was to be done?

I F THERE WAS EVER A CHALLENGE for young revolutionaries in Cape Town at the beginning of the 1980s it was that the climate for revolution was lukewarm, at best.

That hundreds of thousands had been pushed around, lost their homes, and seen their paltry incomes swallowed by spiralling rentals was enough to spark discontent but not rebellion. Not yet. The climate see-sawed between defiance and despair throughout the Cape Flats.

As the Kensington civic group grew stronger, Manuel began to move further afield, helping other civics establish a similar presence: Hanover Park, Bonteheuwel, Valhalla Park – names that evoke the dumping grounds for a generation who suffered the brunt of removals.

But they were not simple communities to organise. The main reason was fear. It was fear not only of the government, but of the several criminal gangs now rooted in the dislocated urban communities. Their potential to disrupt political and civic organisation could be profound.

Manuel discovered this in early 1980 when he went to a meeting at

Bloemhof Flats. Bloemhof Flats was sandwiched between what were then the remains of District Six and the city centre. They were well-built solid flats underneath the mountain, a last outpost, but now people were being given eviction notices.

There seemed to be no alternative but to move. The question was where to? If you cooperated with the Group Areas officials, if your neighbours had nice things to say about you, your chances of being assigned a more decent new area were stronger.

At one of the last community meetings at Bloemhof, residents told Manuel how Group Areas officials decided their futures. Clipboard in hand, they would knock on people's doors and enquire of them what their neighbours were like. If the adults were 'good people' but their sons prone to hanging out with 'naughty boys', they would be moved to an area where all the boys were considered 'naughty'. If the children were considered better behaved they would be assigned a house in a better, safer area.

The effect was that 'naughty boys' were clustered together from an array of different communities. 'So the ghetto is established full of gangsters,' said Manuel. It seemed absurd that relatively junior white civil servants could determine a family's fate with a few notes on their clipboards, but this was how many of the removals worked.

One such area which became a buzzing proto-ghetto was Valhalla Park. North-east of the city, it was one of the most windblown and forsaken areas in the Cape Flats.

In 1980, Manuel got a message from residents in Valhalla Park telling him that rentals were about to increase by an astonishing 30 per cent. He drove to the area – hardly anyone there had a phone – and visited a woman named Livonia who told him things were 'very bad', and she would get a group of residents to attend a house meeting to talk to him.

In the next few weeks residents flocked to house meetings. Houses, poorly constructed as they were, burst at the seams with the disgruntled, the desperate and the defiant. One evening, after a run of success in mobilising people, Manuel arrived at a house to be told by the same Livonia that things in the area had got 'even worse'.

'Colin sent his men to my house,' she told him. 'And they said we must stop with these fucking meetings.'

Colin was Colin Stansfield, the founder of a notorious Cape Flats gang called The Firm. He preyed on the vulnerable – pensioners for instance – by using their houses to store liquor and drugs. He ran illegal taverns in the neighbourhood where working men spent their paltry wages. In return, he paid school fees for the children of those who cooperated with him, or gave them the occasional gift. It was rule by a mixture of fear and patronage, something that became common in that decade in Cape Town as the white authorities abandoned people to local lawlessness.

Most residents agreed that Colin was a problem.

A few months after Manuel had begun organising in the area, a lay preacher was shot dead while preaching in a house. Manuel read the story in the local newspaper. When he went to Valhalla Park again a few days later, Livonia was surprised to see him. 'Why are you here?' she asked. 'Colin's chaps were here and they asked whether it was *you* they shot.'

Six years after the incident when Manuel and his friends had faced down gangsters on the train to Paarl, there was a ring of prophecy about Daphne Williams's words: if they could take on the gangsters, the government was 'nothing'.

Manuel's memory is this: 'People said there's the enemy out there: it's apartheid. But there's also *this* – a different kind of enemy: it's destroying our family life.'

There was one particularly poignant case in Valhalla Park that showed just how difficult organisation in the area was. After the civic organisation was established there, a Mr Alexander who worked for the City Council, and who had just moved into a new house was persuaded to take up the reins of chairmanship. He had lived in District Six a few years earlier. His spirit had taken a huge knock with the move, but now here was a turn for the better. He had been assigned a duplex, which gave his family more space, and the civic had given his life some purpose. His wife thanked Manuel for giving her husband the opportunity of leadership. He had stopped drinking, which had been a cause of great misery to his family. He had taken on this responsibility. Life was getting better at home. 'There was just this big sense of achievement, he's the chairman of something, it's a big issue in his life,' said Manuel.

One Sunday evening, soon after he'd moved into his new house, Manuel went to visit him and found him drunk. 'And then I worked through with the family what had happened. They had moved to this larger house, and on the Friday night the house was set upon by thugs. Colin's chaps.'

The family ran upstairs and locked themselves into a bedroom. But the doors of the house were so thin that the thugs simply slashed them open, demanded the family's pay packets and then proceeded to move the furniture out of the lounge downstairs, much of it newly acquired.

There was no hope of protection. Not from the police. Not from the civic. Alexander told Manuel that he now did not see the point of going to civic meetings when in fact it made their lives worse. That was why he was drinking again.

'I don't know whether we could actually pick him up and help him and carry him through successfully,' Manuel reflected later. 'But you had those kinds of setbacks in those areas.'

Stansfield ruled the area with relative impunity until 1994 when, ironically, 'he appropriated the (democratic) victory as his own. He hired the local football fields in the ghetto of his childhood, Valhalla Park, erected a giant marquee, bought thousands of litres of beer and truckloads of meat, and invited every resident of the ghetto to attend. He threw the biggest party in Valhalla Park's history.'[1]

But it was the post-apartheid government that exacted some justice. In 2001 he was convicted of tax evasion and sentenced to six years in jail. He started serving his sentence a year later when his appeals had failed, but the following year he was diagnosed with lung cancer and released on compassionate grounds.[2] He died a few months later.

This climate of fear was replicated in dozens of the new coloured areas in the Cape Flats. Broken, dissipated people were afraid of the government, afraid of gangsters, afraid that if they spoke out their fate would be even worse than the one that had already befallen them. The group of activists who had emerged in Cape Town – many of them with roots in the University of the Western Cape – found that the black consciousness philosophy that had sustained them as students did not equip them to deal with these challenges.

IN 1976, WHILE THE 20-YEAR-OLD MANUEL focused on a new job and organised practical support for those arrested in the 1976 student uprising, Johnny Issel discussed history in Victor Verster prison with his fellow detainees. 'This is our 1906,' a fellow detainee told Issel, referring to the first failed revolution in Russia which preceded the Bolshevik revolution of 1917. The year 1917 signified to Issel 'the complete transfer of power' to the people. The question was how to achieve this in South Africa.

And then this miracle revolutionary manual fell into his hands: Lenin's

What is to Be Done? Yusuf Adam, who worked with Manuel and Daphne supporting the 1976 detainees, had also given them the book. Issel was enthusiastic about it: 'I got into this book because the title was so attracting me, you know. Because the question then is, *what the hell is to be done?* That is the question. That is what I'm struggling with in prison.'

Issel was a tour de force in Cape Town in the 1970s and 80s. Tall, dark, charismatic, and courageous to a point of foolhardiness, he did not allow a revolutionary spirit to wane for an instant. Banned and detained several times, and in hiding for much of the latter part of the 1980s, it was as though nothing could deter his buoyant spirit.

He believed fervently that apartheid would be vanquished by insurrection. How was that to be done? Through organising communities. 'But it was not easy to be among communities because the people were shit scared and people don't want to be involved in politics.'

So what was to be done? For Issel, two things that were to significantly shape Manuel's politics. The first was to start a newspaper. *Iskra* was the original model, Lenin's brainchild that spread the word of revolution in pre-1917 Russia.

As it happened, the time was ripe. In 1977, after the huge clampdown on the black press and journalists, including the Union of Black Journalists (UBJ), black journalists were looking for a vehicle to channel their anger. WASA, the Black Writers' Association of South Africa, was born out of the suppressed UBJ, which had been a haven for black journalists. Many worked on the mainly white newspapers. Frustrated and marginalised, they coalesced in an organisation that reflected the spirit of separatist black resistance at the time.

Two of its Cape Town members were Rashid Seria and Moegsien Williams, both schooled in black consciousness politics at UWC. Both worked on the *Argus*, the afternoon newspaper in Cape Town; Seria had already won awards for his journalism and Williams was then a rookie reporter whom Seria took under his wing. Their 'dream and ambition', Williams said, was to start a 'truly anti-apartheid newspaper'. Seria, regarded as a 'hothead and radical' in the newsroom, by his own description, tried to get the views of black organisations into his own newspaper. 'But lots of organisations couldn't get their stories in the newspaper and that caused a lot of tensions on the newsroom floor.'

In 1979 the two journalists approached Issel with the idea. Although Issel had already moved away from black consciousness politics (as indeed both Williams and Seria were to), there was an immediate union of minds. The idea resonated with Issel's reading of Lenin. Moreover the two journalists knew him and trusted him. 'They were BC guys like me,' Issel said. 'I come from them. I'm like a family member, you know.'

The apartheid government gave their cause impetus by detaining Zwelakhe Sisulu, then a political reporter in Johannesburg and president of the UBJ. He was also the son of two of the most prominent ANC leaders in the country, Walter, jailed on Robben Island with Mandela, and Albertina, banned and restricted to her house in Soweto. His detention attracted international attention and sympathy for the cause of black journalists. Seria, a masterful fund-raiser, was promised money by the German government for the project. Williams went to Pretoria to collect it – hard cash which he brought back in an attaché case. It was the seed money they needed.

But the newspaper born of this union was quite different from either the black consciousness paper envisaged by Seria and Williams, or Lenin's party tool. There is little doubt that the product was shaped in no small part by the role that Manuel and others had assumed in communities around the Cape Flats. 'We saw media as a tool to help organise communities and to help organise politically,' Seria told me. 'But we had to tone down the politics when we came out with a community newspaper.'

Grassroots was launched with Issel as its full-time organiser in early 1980. Its creators may have been inspired by *Iskra* but in reality it was far more modest. It was aimed at uniting the disparate communities scattered by the Group Areas Act. So a rent issue in Macassar, far on the eastern outskirts of Cape Town, would strike a resonance in Bonteheuwel or Heideveld closer to town.

'A paper for YOU that fills the void' declared the editorial in the first edition of *Grassroots*. It was a newspaper that rooted itself in local community affairs with a view to building a worldlier view. 'We hope by informing Guguletu what is happening with Ocean View and Schotsche Kloof (also known as Bo-Kaap) what is taking place in Scottsdene ... we will fulfil (the) important task ... of co-ordination ...' It was significant too that the places named were both African and coloured communities, a conscious attempt by organisers to link them.

'We had to try to communicate with people and try to break the culture of silence,' Manuel told a class of journalism students at Princeton in New Jersey more than 25 years later. 'People had been pummelled into submission ... Thinking back, it was so elementary, then.'

149

Apart from two or three staffers, *Grassroots* relied on volunteers – civic activists such as Manuel, a few left-wing journalists from the local press, and students who knew about layout or silk-screening or photography. Every Saturday morning the volunteers would meet in a little office on the third floor of a building in Cape Town, near the Grand Parade. Sitting on a wooden floor they would identify stories, volunteer to report them and plan the next edition. It was as much a forum for community activists as activist journalists. Occasionally there would be clashes about the truth as the more political members of the group would try to censor stories unfavourable to the 'struggle'. For instance, reporters from the local newspapers and *Grassroots* might disagree about the size of a crowd in, say, a rent protest. 'Let's call it 100,' a *Grassroots* reporter once said to a daily journalist who had counted no more than 35 people, some still in their pyjamas, at an early morning picket.

But it would be wrong to understand its purpose as a newspaper in the conventional sense. It was primarily an organising tool, a means to get into communities and to reflect those communities back to themselves. When volunteers went to distribute *Grassroots*, they went door-to-door in the old style of Manuel's father in Kensington in the Labour Party days of 1969. It was a way to get into houses, to get into communities, to talk to people about their problems and to urge them to organise. 'The gap it filled was a social and political gap that would historically far exceed its power as a newspaper,' said Manuel. Young people from the Cape Flats learned basic skills in newspaper production; they learned how to report and write up community stories, how to take photographs, how to use a light box to lay out a page.

The stories initially centred around the economic hardships people suffered: rents, rising bus fares, wages. *Grassroots*, wrote Mohamed Adhikari, strove 'to achieve attainable goals through community action and thereby raise the consciousness of people politically and induct them into the broader struggle for democracy and a socialist future'.[3]

It ducked the stringent laws on press registration by coming out only ten times a year. More than that was considered a regular publication which needed to be registered with the government, but with ten editions 'you could come in just below the radar screens', as Manuel said.

So *Grassroots* was the first answer to the question: What is to be done?

The second was at Issel's urging, too. Marcus Solomon, who was in Issel's 'core group', had planted another Leninist seed in Issel's head. Solomon was not an ANC supporter. He had gone to jail as part of the Yu Chi Chan club, led by Neville Alexander, a Cape Town intellectual of unusual sharpness who had emerged, but broken, from the Unity Movement. They, and two other colleagues, Fikile Bam and Elizabeth van der Heyden, had been sentenced to between eight and ten years after being convicted of 'conspiracy to commit sabotage'.

Issel was suspicious of Alexander because of what he thought were his 'anti-ANC views' and, by association, of Solomon, but he thought the latter was 'a very sweet person ... a hell of a nice guy'. Certainly Solomon, long schooled in political debates, sparked robust thought in the 'core discussion group' which he had joined with Issel and Virginia Engel. Solomon told Issel that when the revolution was able to provide 'full-time revolutionaries, it really shows a level of progress'. The thought preyed on Issel's mind.

But who could those full-time revolutionaries be? For Issel the answer was obvious. He was already one, working full-time for *Grassroots*. But at the end of 1980 he was detained and then issued with a banning order so severe 'I could not teach my own wife to drive a car'.[4]

The other obvious full-time activist for Issel was Trevor Manuel.

Manuel had already begun to establish a network of civic organisations. This culminated in an organisation called CAHAC (the Cape Areas Housing Action Committee) in 1980. He worked in communities after his day job as a civil engineer. 'We realised that Trevor has outstanding abilities and Trevor can really be the one,' said Issel. 'But how do you get somebody like that? I mean, Trevor has really got a straight job and all of that ...'

Indeed Manuel had been promoted in 1980 at the construction firm where he worked. He had moved to the design office in the firm's headquarters. Now he worked with a draughtsman who would draw up his designs. Now he wore a collar and tie to work; he had an office with his name on the door. He was going places. But 'my life in this cushy job' lasted only until the end of April 1981. 'It was Johnny who basically said, yeah you've worked at Murray & Roberts very long, and I'm sure you're loyal to them and they're loyal to you but the struggle needs you, comrade, so you better pack up there and be a full-time activist.'

It didn't take much persuasion, admitted Manuel. So on 1 May 1981, Manuel marked his first day without a formal job since leaving school.

THE DECISION TO BECOME a full-time activist had come at the end of a year that seemed injected with political dynamite. 1980 had seen a bus boycott – in part spurred by focused reporting in *Grassroots* on bus fares, a consumer boycott in support of striking red meat workers, a student boycott and the growth of a militant student committee, and the establishment of CAHAC in response to the imposition of steep rent increases.

All of these apparently disparate disputes had one thing in common: they were cries from people for a voice in their own affairs. They were cries for democracy, even as they tackled small issues, many of which did not make the local, let alone the national press.

Most telling perhaps was the meat strike and the subsequent red meat boycott. It was a boycott that spurred the Cape Flats communities, as the Fatti's & Moni's boycott had done the year before. But it was more ambitious and harder to pull off because the workers on the factory floor were still divided along racial lines.

The meat strike was sparked by the simplest of demands: that the democratically elected workers' committee be recognised by employers. The committee had been organised by the General Workers Union (GWU). David Lewis, who had worked with Manuel in the literacy group, was now the general secretary. Under him the small, unregistered union organised dockworkers around the country, metal workers in Cape Town and now meat workers. Almost all its members were African migrants, the poorest and most vulnerable workers in the Cape. Unlike the FCWU, it had a fragile relationship with coloured workers, a fact that was to weaken it considerably in its prolonged battle with the meat employers and the government.

Yet, ironically, the union's relationship with the coloured community was sufficiently strong to ensure that the meat bosses' eventual victory over the union was politically costly.

The strike began in March 1980 with a small victory. Workers at Karoo Meat Exchange walked off their jobs after a fellow worker was dismissed without consulting the workers' committee. The GWU had organised the committee in an environment where African trade unions were being granted limited rights. Although the Wiehahn Commission had recommended that industrial trade unions for Africans be officially registered, the GWU was deeply suspicious of this move. Partly, it was because most of their members were unskilled migrants who moved from job to job. So only a general union could have maintained steady membership. But mainly it was due to a fear that the control of the union would be wrested from workers' hands in the bureaucratic process of registration.[5]

The Karoo meat workers faced down their bosses for a week. Workers at 11 other meat companies who had also organised committees said they would not work for the companies until their colleagues were reinstated. The workers and the union won this round: the workers were reinstated and the committee was officially recognised at the factory. 'The days when management could take decisions affecting workers without consultation are now over,' said the union.[6]

But they were not. Two months later, at another meat factory, the same battle ensued. About a hundred workers at Table Bay Cold Storage refused to work when the company refused to recognise their committee. The company said it would talk to a 'liaison committee' which was to be composed of equal numbers of representatives from management and workers. No, replied the workers. We want our own elected committee.

Management dug in its heels. The workers downed tools and when they arrived at work the next day they were locked out. Ten days later every African worker in the meat industry in Cape Town – 800 in all – came out on strike. The government stepped into the fray, quickly and harshly, in support of the employers. Armed riot police monitored their meetings. The union warned that the 'meat bosses', as they became ubiquitously known in Cape Town, '(had) embarked on a path designed to bring them into confrontation with the entire black community'.[7]

In the first few days of the strike, supplies of red meat dwindled. But then as supply grew, demand fell dramatically. The workers called on the community to boycott red meat. At first the call went to the small black-owned butcheries in the African townships: 'The black butchers must realise that the place from where they are buying their meat is where their brothers are suffering,' said the workers.[8]

Butchers soon changed their wares to chicken and eggs.

The boycott spread rapidly to coloured communities now organised by civic organisations such as Manuel's. It spread to the black and coloured schools and the university campuses.

An inter-schools committee, the Committee of 81 (so called because it originally represented 81 schools) had been initiated by students spurred in large part by the leadership of Ebrahim Patel and Jonathan de Vries. For them, the red meat boycott, like Fatti's & Moni's, was a building block towards 'permanent organisation'.

The Committee of 81 worked hard to overcome the racial divisions between coloureds and Africans. During the year's tumultuous school boycott, which coincided with the meat strike and the bus boycott, the director of Coloured Education offered to make some concessions on coloured education to defuse an explosive situation. But the offer was rejected by the students who refused to consider a racially divisive settlement.[9] 'The boycott has deliberately been made a Coloured issue by the ruling class newspapers and television,' said a Committee of 81 Manifesto. 'To attempt to solve the problem of Coloured education is not enough. In spite of the deliberate tribalism fed into our brains we realise that our inequalities spring from the same root causes and that we are not Bantus, Coloureds or Indians but human beings.'[10]

The newly born civic organisations on the Cape Flats were forged in the fires of the student boycott, which gave rise to student-parent committees, and the red meat boycott. Organising support, particularly for the meat workers, was a remarkable test of leadership for the newly emerging generation of leaders such as Trevor Manuel in the largely coloured Cape Flats communities. The fact that, as Lewis put it many years later, they could persuade 'the rank and file to identify with this group of African workers and to identify with what … the unions were trying to do' was a significant test of their own strength and a sign of a fresh political path. 'They showed they were genuine members of the community to the extent that all people would give them an ear.'

The boycott took immediate hold in the black community of Cape Town: 'The red meat shelves of most Cape Flats butcheries were bare and a number of butcheries were closed yesterday,' reported the *Cape Times*, two weeks after the workers had gone on strike.[11] More than 180 butchers on the Cape Flats had resolved not to sell red meat until the dispute was settled.

Yet despite this, despite strike funds collected throughout Cape Town and even, eventually, despite the intervention of enlightened white businessmen, despite the churches and huge sections of the community coming out in support of the 800 workers, despite support from international trade unions, the workers lost.

One reason was the harsh way the government intervened. It used the influx control laws to expel 43 contract workers from Cape Town. Africans charged under the pass laws appeared in special 'commissioner's courts' in the townships. These essentially brutal laws had by now become so banal by their routine nature that apart from some liberal and church groups, which assiduously monitored their effects, the shattering of lives went by largely unrecorded.[12]

The meat strike changed all that. When one of the striking workers, Fumabitile Maguzu, was charged with breaking the pass laws, the court was packed with unionists, supporters and journalists. Maguzu told the Commissioner about the strike and their subsequent dismissal. 'Our employer told us to take off our overalls and go home on 7 May. But when we came back the following day the gates were locked.' The union's lawyer, Lee Bozalek, pleaded with the Commissioner to see the situation from the workers' point of view. It was an appeal in vain. When the employer asked a worker to 'take off his overalls', said the Commissioner, Mr W Fourie, it indicated dismissal. 'When you arrived the next day and found the gates locked that showed he does not need you.'[13]

The publicity given to the case was a sharp eye-opener for most of Cape Town's community to the everyday hardships that African migrant workers suffered. That month, too, the security police detained five key union officials, including David Lewis and Zora Mehlomakulu. It was unusual then for union officials to be detained only for their union work. But wage demands were one thing. This was more dangerous. The government stood like a bulwark before the meat employers because the demand – simple at first glance – was deeply dangerous to the system.

In August the workers, exhausted, impoverished and defeated, called off the strike. Two weeks later, the union officials were released. In a bitter letter to the *Cape Times*, Lewis attacked the hypocrisy of an industrial relations adviser to the meat employers who had written an article three weeks earlier advising employers to adopt a 'more conciliatory ... attitude towards strikes'.

'Please forgive the lateness of response,' wrote Lewis. 'Unfortunately until very recently I and four of my colleagues were detained in prison in Cape Town, an important institution in the industrial relations system adopted by the meat employers.'[14]

The clampdown by the government was one reason for the workers' defeat. There was another reason, too, ironic in the light of the massive support from the civic organisations in the coloured community and amongst students and scholars. This was the fact that the union could never persuade the coloured workers in the meat industry to stop work in support of their African colleagues. This division between coloured and African workers, commented the union in the aftermath of the strike, 'was an ideological victory for the state and bosses. The creation of the divisions between the African and Coloured workers is one of the pillars of oppression in Cape

Town working-class society, and not even the magnificent, selfless support extended by the Coloured community to the workers and their union could disguise the fact that the workers and their union had not been able to break down these absolutely critical divisions.'[15]

A quarter of a century later, Lewis reflected on this defeat. Many of the struggles of that decade were 'unwinnable', he said. 'You have to see them in hindsight as massive demonstrations, massively elaborate demonstrations ... the process of any organisation is not remembered for the outcomes of any single action but for how that all added up into massive demonstrations against the illegitimacy of the government. That is what it was.'

THAT WAS WHAT IT WAS. When Trevor Manuel and Wilf Rhodes became leaders of CAHAC a month after the lost meat strike, their aim was, like the meat strikers, both the immediate struggle at hand, and a more distant dream.

CAHAC was born in September 1980 in the highly charged atmosphere created in the wake of the meat strike, the bus boycott and a schools boycott. CAHAC's birth was spurred in May by a local government announcement of a rents increase for Cape Flats tenants living in City and Divisional Council houses. The announcement came at a time of economic downturn when about half of all Cape Town households lived on an average income of R50 a month. Even Eulalie Stott, a city councillor who chaired the housing committee, conceded that rentals were already beyond what people in the lowest income brackets could afford.[16]

Manuel, with some of the civic and student leaders, called a meeting of eight civic groups which by then were running as residents' organisations. The Umbrella Rentals Committee (URC) was formed to fight the rent increases. The government did two things: it persuaded the local authorities to drop the proposed rent increases – this was after all an incendiary climate – and then banned all meetings of the URC. But in September of that year the URC regrouped under the banner of CAHAC. Wilf Rhodes, Manuel's comrade in the Kensington civic, 'a humble man of solid intellect', was elected chair and Manuel became general secretary.

This was not an easy time to run such organisations. In the early days, there was scant foreign support. Many of the activists, most of whom came from working-class backgrounds, reached into their own pockets to help fund CAHAC, or ran modest fund-raisers – raffles and dances – to fill its coffers. In 1983, three years after its formation, CAHAC recorded an income of R1 863.55.[17]

MANUEL WAS 24 WHEN he became secretary of CAHAC. His main political experience until then had been in the local civic in Kensington, a more stable area than the rest of the Cape Flats and where he had grown up. He had had scant experience in youth organisations or student politics apart from his brief tenure on the Technikon SRC during one of his studying 'blocks' there. 'I had to learn to run meetings, learn to work with older people, learn to manage politics,' he said.

It was an experience that was to indelibly stamp Manuel's politics. Unlike the youth organisations, or the ANC in exile itself, where the approach was explicitly political, here one had first to address people's basic problems and then carry them towards political involvement. 'The approach you take in working with older, conservative people like that (is about) developing approaches that allow you to act *politically*. And how you would take those who've made the commitment of their time on important occasions like June 16 and talk to them about the politics of it, and introduce people to the Freedom Charter ... and to the world of *Grassroots*, and allow them to be shocked by – hey! – meeting white people and Africans and stuff outside their experience.'

It was an approach that required empathy with people who'd been victims of apartheid and still cowered. It was also an approach that demanded that the leaders make linkages between the high rents and bus fares and the lousy houses on the one hand, and the lack of political freedom on the other hand. It was a hard ask.

The CAHAC leaders did not shy from the linkages, though, and in many cases some activists on the left, particularly some of the union leaders, were in later years to accuse them of being too political at the expense of their constituency. At CAHAC's first AGM in July 1982, more than a year after its inception, the chair, Wilf Rhodes, laid out precisely this challenge:

> We must see increasing rents, bus fares and electricity charges as being only the smoke. Our work must be geared to extinguishing the fire which causes the smoke. Our goal must be to eliminate from this society all the causes of our hardship.

Rhodes also laid out a new, more political path:

> Most of our work to date has been in defence of the little we have. We have defended our right to continue living in District Six, in fact most of our work is in defence of

our living standards. The trade unions fight for improvements like higher wages, job security and improved working conditions. It would be pointless for unions to fight for higher wages if the increases will only go towards increased rents ... Our work in the community should ... go beyond defending our small bundles. Our demands like houses, security and comfort and rents we can afford, will only be attained if we in fact attack for these.

He also pinpointed the essential weakness of community organisations – their transitory nature. People tended to flock around the civics in times of crisis, like threatened rent hikes, but soon drifted away. So the organisations must move away from 'working around issues only ... Our organisations will be called on to play an increasingly important role in support of struggles on other fronts like workers on strike ... In short our organisations must strengthen themselves to ensure that we can meaningfully contribute to the advancement of the democratic struggle.'[18]

CAHAC was a complicated animal. Its leaders were political activists, albeit drawn from the communities they represented, but they were far ahead of most of their constituency. Many of its affiliates – the civics in various areas – were weak. It claimed to have up to 40 affiliates including, by early 1982, civics in some of the African areas, but according to the minutes of most meetings, only 17 affiliates were recorded.[19]

In a fairly candid secretarial report presented to the AGM, Manuel acknowledged these weaknesses:

CAHAC has ... become a household name ... people identify CAHAC with being at the forefront of taking up their struggles ... However this is not the occasion for patting ourselves on the back. We should ask ourselves how far we have actually grown where it counts, ie in the community ... Here the picture is not as rosy.[20]

Like Rhodes, Manuel warned against the organisation becoming purely 'issue driven':

Truly, people's organisations must provide a home for everybody in the community ... We should however be warned that our organisations have a common goal. This goal must not be lost sight of and our organisations must not become like problematic welfare organisations.

This was the challenge: the challenge of maintaining roots in often conservative communities, and of the need to strengthen the movement for the political struggle that still lay ahead. Leaders straddled two worlds, and often the more political one was invisible to the other.

This flourishing organisation in the coloured areas around the Cape was a major break with the past. Not only were there acts of resistance that were entirely new but it was the first time that, as Jonathan de Vries put it, a 'non-Non-European Unity Movement' political force emerged across the Cape Flats. This was real politics. It was tramping the streets and persuading people to come to meetings, rallying them to a cause both immediate and long term.

SIX MONTHS AFTER CAHAC was formed, Manuel gave up his job at Issel's urging. At first Lynne, his girlfriend, and his friend Goolam Aboobaker, both of whom worked in respectable jobs (Lynne was a teacher at Kensington High and Aboobaker was a medical physicist at Groote Schuur hospital earning 'serious' money) 'would stick their hands in their pockets and give me a bit of money to allow me to keep my mother going in the house, me going, get me some cigarettes and petrol ...'

For now, in the early 1980s, the seeds were being sown, foundations laid. The seeds did not always thrive, and the foundations often cracked. The civic organisations were still largely activist driven and controlled. But there was hardly a campaign run without an effort to bring ordinary people aboard. Street canvassing, door-to-door, house meetings, *Grassroots* stories, became the fabric of the civics. And with it came a particular brand of politics. The banners that went up around the Cape Flats proclaiming the demand for 'Houses, Security and Comfort' was strongly resonant with a community who either had none of these things or had lost them. That it came straight from a clause in the Freedom Charter was intentional on the part of the leaders, but not dwelt on by the community. It was as if by osmosis the political ideals of the African National Congress were absorbed into popular discourse.

Early in 1982 the local authorities that governed housing in the black areas of the Peninsula sent out about 14 000 rent notices notifying tenants of an increase. Some of the increases were astronomical – up to 150 per cent. In Bishop Lavis, one of the poorer areas, tenants got notice that their rents would increase by 65 per cent. Later the Divisional Council, which governed most of the outlying areas on the Cape Flats, admitted it had made 'an administrative error' in the notified increases. It had 'misinterpreted' the central government's rent formula which stipulated an increase of no more than R10 a month. What should have been a 25 per cent increase was mistakenly calculated as a 150 per cent increase.[21]

But the apology came too late. Tempers on the Flats frayed. In Elsies River tenants burnt rent notices; in Lavender Hill, a bleak flatland in the southern Peninsula, they held noisy placard demonstrations. Public meetings called by CAHAC were jam-packed with angry, worried tenants. At the largest, about 3 000 people urged the CAHAC leadership to press for a meeting with Pen Kotze, minister of Community Development (the apartheid government's euphemism for 'coloured affairs').

The way CAHAC responded to the rents crisis was perhaps its most impressive moment. Manuel was now its full-time secretary, eight months into his career as a professional activist. CAHAC circulated a petition objecting to the increases and demanding a meeting with Kotze. They collected some 40 000 signatures by walking door to door, calling mass meetings and organising in new areas.[22]

Kotze's response to the petition was at first dismissive: if the signatories had any grievances they should direct them to the Management Committees.[23]

The Management Committees were government-approved local authorities in Indian and coloured areas. There were parallels with the meat workers' demands for recognition of their own elected committees. Now the residents of the Cape Flats were effectively saying to the government, talk to *us* through the bodies *we* choose. CAHAC upped the ante, calling for a stay-at-home on 4 February, and flooding Kotze's office with telephone calls. There were marches too – not very well attended, only 600 people took part. But perhaps the embarrassment, perhaps the fact that the government was about to initiate a serious attempt to recapture the hearts and minds of the coloured people, and perhaps the fear of increasing protests swayed Kotze. At the end of that month he agreed to meet a delegation from CAHAC to discuss high rentals and the housing shortage.

On 1 March 1982, Kotze met a delegation from CAHAC in Cape Town. To its annoyance, CAHAC had been allowed to bring only six members after asking for a delegation of 43, which would include most of the areas affected by the increase. The leadership was also annoyed that the minister had brought with him not only representatives of the Divisional Council and City Council (fair enough as they managed housing in the city) but nine chairmen of the Management Committees. 'These "toothless dummy bodies", reported CAHAC to its affiliates, 'also presented individual memoranda. They pleaded with the minister to help them because if they were to leave empty handed (as happened so many times before) the people will further lose respect for them.'[24]

CAHAC's memorandum was a mature document for its time. Drawn up by Rhodes and Manuel, it explained that CAHAC cut across the lines of local authorities, representing, as it did, black tenants in all areas of the Peninsula and thus it wanted to negotiate with central government. 'Black communities have no say in the decisions made by the local authorities,' it said. 'The discriminatory and toothless bodies offered as representative, viz the Management Committee and Community Councils [their equivalent in African areas] have been completely rejected by the people. The people have therefore sought to build their own democratic organisations of which CAHAC is a natural outflow.'

It pointed out that tenants were never consulted about the rents formula and that the Divisional Council itself had revealed that some tenants were spending more than half their incomes on rent, despite the government recommendation that they should spend no more than 25 per cent of their incomes.

It detailed anomalies in the way the increases had been applied. For instance an income increase of R1 had resulted in some areas in a rent increase from R20,63 to R61,88 – an increase of more than R40! More than 100 000 tenants were given eviction notices that year. 'There is no clearer indication of the inability of tenants to afford the high rents,' CAHAC said. 'This powder-keg can only be defused by swift action on the part of the Minister to attend to the immediate problem.'[25]

Appendices detailed the housing shortage: more than 53 000 units in Coloured and Indian areas in greater Cape Town and an even worse backlog in the African areas, with allocation meeting not even normal population growth. The 'vicious' Group Areas Act had resulted in the removal of more than two million people, resulting in 'enormous social costs borne by the people', such as overcrowding, ill-health and crime.

Perhaps most notably, the memorandum distinguished between demands for short-term relief, medium-term demands and the eventual goal of ... well, democracy. The rent increases should be stopped, it told the minister. The central government should take responsibility for all housing and should provide bigger subsidies. And it called for 'the full participation of all people' in determining rentals.

The minister responded to some of these issues with an obtuseness that had come to characterise government. First, he asked whether by 'black', CAHAC meant coloured people as well as African. When the Council apologised in the meeting for sending out faulty accounts, he commented: 'People must not come to me about faulty accounts – it happens to my pay cheque every second month.' And on the worsening poverty of tenants: 'If you do not pay the rent (because of low wages), go speak to your boss. I cannot help.' On the Group Areas Act he said: *'Daar is nie meer verskuiwing van mense nie. Ons is klaar daarmee'* ('There are no more removals of people. We are finished with that'). And added for good measure: 'All people who have been removed are very happy ... Not one of them would want to go back to where they come from. My department has looked after them well.' When the petition was handed to him, he asked: *'Hoeveel van die goed het die skool kinders geteken?'* ('How many of the signatories were schoolchildren?'), and then warned Rhodes that he should not be led on a tow-rope (*sleeptou*).[26]

Perhaps he meant that Manuel was towing the rope, espousing the handy theory of agitators.

There was a half-hearted attempt to set up a joint committee to look at rent formulas but it never met and in any event the confidence of the CAHAC leadership in the whole process fizzled out. 'People in the leadership positions saw the exercise as futile,' wrote Manuel.[27]

At the end of that month a fake pamphlet was distributed in CAHAC's name. Purporting to be signed by Wilf Rhodes, it said that people 'can afford higher rents if we have smaller families, work harder for our bosses and spend our money wisely'.[28] It also called on people to support their local Management Committees.

Although the pamphlet was quickly disowned by CAHAC – and like many of the attempts at disinformation it was so crude as to give away its origins – CAHAC nonetheless called off the rents campaign. The struggle for affordable rents was not over, it said, but the community needed to be better organised to push for success.

Like the meat strike, the rents campaign looked like a failed battle. But it was another of those significant demonstrations of the decade, described by Lewis as protests against the illegitimacy of the apartheid government. The attempt to engage the government had been politically mature and in many ways a boost to the confidence of the organisers. It did not breach the huge gulf between the rulers and the governed. But it put indelibly on the agenda, both for government and for the Cape Flats community, the notion that people were no longer prepared to maintain the silence of the decade before.

MANUEL LED A LAYERED LIFE during this time. He was a leader of CAHAC, working around bread and butter issues, yet he was also at the forefront of political resistance that involved underground connections.

He had met Pravin Gordhan on a trip to Durban in early 1982, and drawn some lessons from him. Durban – at least the Indian and more middle-class African community – had more rooted connections to the ANC than there were in Cape Town. Several Robben Island prisoners, including people such as Mac Maharaj and Jacob Zuma, Ebrahim Ebrahim and Billy Nair, had been released there and had resuscitated organisation. 'It was a multiplicity of forces,' said Gordhan. The Congress movement, he said, was a little like 'these bulbous plants that stay underground when the weather is lousy and when the weather improves they start sprouting a bit'.

CAHAC was modelled on the Durban Housing Action Committee (DHAC), where Gordhan had found a political home. Goolam Aboobaker, Manuel's friend and sometime financial supporter, had been an activist in Durban before moving to Cape Town, so many of the ideas migrated with him. Through Gordhan, Manuel had seen how community organisation in the Indian community had worked. Like the coloured community it was both marginalised and oppressed (Indians too suffered great hardship under the Group Areas and other discriminatory legislation). It was also distanced from the majority African community, a distance that only deliberate political action could bridge.

One difference in Cape Town was that the coloured community was the majority of the oppressed in the area, and was generally more working class. So the stakes were higher. Manuel, like Gordhan, worked in small activist political groups that saw their links as being to the ANC, but also in larger community-based organisations.

'All of that helped us to mature,' said Gordhan later. '(It was) a process that actually generated a particular type of political culture, where you can fight, you can argue, you can rally people, you can contact the underground and keep your communications with the outside.' But at the same time, there was a realisation that the Indian and coloured communities wanted to take a stand against apartheid but were not, unlike the African community, prepared to take big risks at that stage. It was a culture that inspired both a revolutionary zeal and a patience born of trying to persuade the most timid that their future lay not in compliance but in resistance.

In that year too, Manuel made similar trips to Johannesburg and Port Elizabeth where he stayed with Qaqawuli Godolozi, one of the men from the group that became known as the PEBCO Three, abducted and killed in 1985 by the South African death squads which began operating in the mid-1980s (PEBCO was the Port Elizabeth Civic Organisation). 'We were organising separately but planning together,' he said. 'But that was the network that was being built, a solid ANC network.'

So in Cape Town in 1981 and 1982, there were the battles against rent, against increased bus fares, battles about issues as parochial as the due date of electricity bills and the location of washing lines in the flatlands of Lavender Hill. All these were central to the communities affected by them. But at the same time a much bolder political pattern was being stamped on the national canvas.

THE TURNING POINT CAME during Easter of 1981 when the ANC made its presence felt in a public way for the first time since it was banned in 1960. It was a strange and unexpected occasion.

In April that year Hennie Ferrus, then 40 years old, was killed in a car accident in the south-western Cape. He had lived in the Boland town of Worcester, about 100 kilometres from Cape Town over a jagged mountain pass known as Du Toitskloof. At first it seemed odd that Ferrus's life and death should have been the catalyst for a new era of defiance. He was a member of the Labour Party, which the bulk of the anti-apartheid movement rejected as collaborationist; he was even a member of the Worcester management committee, a structure explicitly rejected by the emerging civic movements on the Cape Flats.

Yet he had suffered years of imprisonment and restriction. His last banning order had been unexpectedly lifted a few months before his death. When he was 19, in 1959, he had joined the Coloured People's Congress. He stayed in the country after the ANC was banned but had been seriously harassed: a year's solitary detention in 1962, a charge of sabotage two years later (which was later dropped), and a house arrest order after his acquittal. He had even been on Robben Island. He was the prisoner who famously, one Sunday, asked a pastor if he could lead the prisoners in prayer, and urged everyone to close their eyes. While the pastor's eyes were closed, he nicked his Sunday papers, never breaking his full-throated prayer.

He was released in 1971, banned again, and then detained again twice under security legislation in 1976 and 1980.[29]

He was one of the few electricians in Worcester at the time. At Christmas his job was to put up all the holiday lights in the white town but because he was under house arrest he could never go to see them twinkle and shine.

It was in detention in Victor Verster prison in 1976 that Ferrus met his homeboy Johnny Issel. 'I really liked him, you know,' said Issel. 'He was really a charmer.' A poorly prepared cabbage bredie (a traditional Cape stew) in prison sealed a bond between the two men. Issel's mother had brought him the bredie, but there were no heating facilities in prison and a layer of crusty fat formed over the food. Issel put the food in a can and let hot water from the shower run around it till it was lukewarm. 'And then I offered Hennie this food and enjoyably he ate this food which made a huge impression on me because Hennie used to come from a very poor family and he shares this poor food with me,' said Issel years later. 'And he used to say to me, "Johnny! Our task as revolutionaries: we must harass them, we must embarrass them, and we must expose them." He always used those three words. Hennie!'

Ferrus was a bit of a mystery. He helped Lizzie Abrahams, legendary in the FCWU for her organisation of workers in the Boland during a major strike by workers in one of the battery chicken factories in Worcester. He had contact with the PAC, specifically through Barney Desai who had gone into exile months before Reg September when he (Desai) was still a member of the Coloured People's Congress (CPC). Ferrus joined the Labour Party in 1976, and in 1980, after his release from detention became a member of the management committee. But, above all, he supported the ANC. 'Ferrus … personified Charterist flexibility, energetically participating in the Labour Party and even segregated structures,' wrote Jeremy Seekings.[30]

The *Sunday Times*, one of South Africa's biggest circulating newspapers, was not so charitable: 'spy' they labelled him in a report on his funeral, a 'spy' for the ANC.[31]

The 'spy' appellation was a direct result of his funeral, which took almost everyone, including the police, by surprise.

Ferrus was buried by about 5000 people, most of them wearing khaki uniforms with black, green and gold epaulettes, under an ANC flag, his coffin draped in ANC colours. Manuel was there, wearing khaki. He had got word from Christmas Tinto and others of his comrades in the townships: 'This will be an ANC funeral.' 'I remember trying to work out this stuff in my head. There were clear instructions: *comrades will wear khaki.*'

It was astonishing, both at the time and in retrospect. No one had dared show the ANC flag for 20 years. Membership, or even 'promoting the aims' of the ANC, attracted a five-year jail sentence. It was an extraordinary show of courage and defiance.

Many years later, Issel said he was the main instigator. When Hennie died, he thought, 'I must give him a decent funeral.' He summoned two young activists, Cecil Esau (also originally from Worcester) and Zackie Achmat, to act on his behalf. Five years later Esau was sentenced to 12 years in jail for political offences, but released in 1991. Zackie Achmat would become one of the most vociferous activists and most trenchant critics of the government's Aids policy in post-apartheid South Africa and for his efforts was even nominated for a Nobel Peace Prize.

Then he was an angry young activist. He had shared a jail cell in detention with Issel and had impressed him with his 'violent temper' against the warders and his 'deep anger'. 'I had to subdue him sometimes because he'd be lying on the bed (in the cell) and decide that nobody the fuck is going to say to him what, what, what,' said Issel.

Issel feared the funeral might adopt a different political character, particularly because Ferrus had struck up a relationship with Neville Alexander while they were both prisoners on Robben Island. So he sprang into action. Banned and restricted, he could not travel, but roped in Achmat and Esau as well as Virginia Engel and Mildred Lesiea, an old ANC activist in the African township of Guguletu, and Lizzie Abrahams of the FCWU to go to speak to Ferrus's mother, Mrs Christina Ferrus (Auntie Stinnie). '*We* wanted to bury him. My resolve is that Hennie shall be buried with ANC colours, he deserves nothing less.'

Then Issel put his mind to making an ANC flag. Veronica Simmers, the wife of Willie Simmers, a CAHAC member, was an efficient and discreet seamstress. She was given that task. Next, there had to be a proper flagpole so that the green, black and gold banner could flutter in a fitting manner by the graveside. The flagpole was a wooden curtain rod from the Mitchell's Plain home where Issel lived with his then wife Shahieda and their three children.

When Veronica Simmers brought him the finished flag, he walked up and down his street with it, attached to his makeshift flagpole.

There were no instructions from outside, said Issel, no internal group, no discussion. 'I got the sense that people were prepared to go out and show their support for the ANC.' When nearly 5 000 people turned up at the funeral wearing khaki and ANC colours, it was like a Leninist epiphany to him. The time had been *right* to make the call. 'It worked! It just worked!'

Others are not so quick to apportion credit to one person. Yet even Virginia Engel, who spent the predawn hours of the days preceding the funeral in Worcester putting up posters with Zackie Achmat, cannot remember where the decision was taken to make the funeral an ANC one. She confirmed that there had been an attempt to hold a 'Unity Movement' funeral. She had spoken to Ferrus's wife Petronella, and to Auntie Stinnie. They were both in shock and mourning 'but accepted the fact that Hennie was an ANC person first and foremost'. In fact, even Nelson Mandela wrote a letter of condolence from his cell on Robben Island to the family. The letter was censored but nonetheless clear in its support for him: 'Hennie rests peacefully in the knowledge that he has done his duty to his beloved ones and ...' The rest of the sentence was blacked out by the prison authorities.[32]

Manuel also can't recall where the decision to hold an ANC funeral came from. But he wore khaki. 'Of *course* I wore khaki.'

As for the police, they were caught completely off guard. They certainly did not expect that the ANC's first show of force in the Western Cape would be in a country town on a Sunday in April at a funeral for a man who had been a member of the Labour Party. 'It was a big out-of-the-closet event for ANC people in the Western Cape,' said Manuel.

The *Sunday Times* excoriated both the deceased Ferrus as a 'spy' as well as the funeral organisers. He was an ANC agent who had 'infiltrated the Labour Party in 1977', it claimed. 'Let us admit it, Hennie has fooled us all,' the paper quoted a 'close relative' as saying. The Labour Party said the funeral had been 'hijacked'. But the following week Petronella Ferrus told the press that her husband's commitment 'was to nothing else but the total liberation of all the oppressed and exploited people in this country. I want to state emphatically that all arrangements for the funeral which took place on April 26, 1981 were made with my full consent and approval ...' Mrs Ferrus then affirmed her 'solidarity with Hennie's political life, his aspirations and everything he stood for. His struggle is my struggle.'[33]

THE FERRUS FUNERAL CATAPULTED activists such as Manuel into a more defiant phase. Later that month, the ANC colours were worn openly at meetings to protest the twentieth anniversary of the South African Republic. Later that year, the flag was to be flown again. It was not only a message to the government, at least not in the Cape. It was as much a message to the predominant political organisations in Cape Town who had long used political correctness as a cover for caution. But it also sparked a tussle *within* the broadly Congress-supporting bodies, including some of the trade unions, about the strategy of unfurling the flag in a way that could harm nascent organisation.

These conflicts came to a head in November, when the government announced that elections for the South African Indian Council (SAIC) would take place. The SAIC was, like the Coloured Representative Council (CRC), a discredited creation of the apartheid government. The anti-SAIC campaign took root in Johannesburg and Durban, both with sizeable Indian populations. In Cape Town, though, it was not as straightforward.

For a start, there were relatively few Indians in Cape Town and those that there were lived mainly in Rylands Estate, a middle-class Indian area just east of Athlone on the Cape Flats. The local civic there was run by Dullah Omar, the anti-apartheid lawyer who was to become a close friend of Manuel. Omar had represented a variety of anti-apartheid activists (including Taufie Bardien), but the Thornhill Residents' Association, which he chaired, was still closely aligned to the Unity Movement. In later years Omar was to become instrumental in moving less extreme members of the Unity Movement towards a Congress position, and eventually became one of the ANC's leading figures in the region.

The anti-SAIC campaign became a battleground between different factions in Cape Town's anti-apartheid movement almost as much as it was one between the apartheid government and its black opposition. Lynne Matthews (partly because of her Indian origins and looks) attended almost every meeting held in Rylands to plan for the campaign. She reported back faithfully to Manuel and her comrades, who advised on strategy. 'The first and biggest mistake they made,' said Manuel, 'was to give *Grassroots* control of the media committee.' *Grassroots* produced a campaign leaflet with a green and black masthead – colours of the ANC – and a huge picture of a chained Oscar Mpetha adorning the cover.

Mpetha, the veteran trade unionist and Robben Islander, had recently been arrested at Crossroads, the informal African settlement, and charged with terrorism. They were trumped-up charges, mainly based on his leading a crowd in a particular freedom song (*Nantsi 'bam bam e Angola* – 'There are guns in Angola') and seemed more of a vindictive campaign against the old man on the part of the security police than any careful political strategy aimed at weakening opposition.

The pain for the non-ANC aligned civics was that Mpetha was an unambiguously ANC man, yet they had provided the resources and money for much of the publicity material. Decades after, Manuel still laughs about it: 'Hey! You can't believe how livid these people were.' The planned rally for the first Sunday in November, a few days before the SAIC elections, was another point of conflict. Different groups took responsibility for organising parts of the rally. But the Congress-aligned people, such as Manuel, were more driven, better organised, and had more support from other parts of the country. As Lynne Matthews recalled, 'People were constantly flying up and down for meetings.' They included Valli Moosa and Zac Yacoob, both active in the Indian community in Johannesburg, and soon to become national leaders in the United Democratic Front. 'It was like a shadow group of the UDF.'

The Johannesburg group, which included Ismail Momoniat, at the time Moosa's best friend and later a senior official in the National Treasury, broke definitively with the Azanian People's Organisation (AZAPO) and the black consciousness groups around this time. 'We organised a massive stayaway (from the polls),' said Momoniat. 'We published the Freedom Charter, we really broke new ground in all the Indian areas in the Transvaal.' Fortuitously, Albertina Sisulu had just been unbanned. The anti-SAIC committee in Johannesburg arranged for her to speak at their rally, stamping it indelibly with an ANC identity.

So did Cape Town, much to the fury of the Unity Movement supporters. Before they knew it, posters were out advertising Sisulu and Paul David, a leader of the Natal Indian Congress, as the main speakers. 'Suddenly there were speakers and a programme and they were really seriously pissed off,' said Manuel. In a planning meeting they challenged the Congress supporters about who had contacted Paul David. Lynne raised her hand and said she had. 'What gave you the right?' they demanded. 'He's my uncle,' she replied, as though that would solve the conflict.

He wasn't and it didn't. The civic in Rylands had one card left up its sleeve. It had paid for the hall and had the receipt. Without the receipt the caretaker would not hand over the key. 'There was this big pow-wow, and they want to pull the plug on everything and disown the meeting. Huge debate!' said Manuel.

Omar trod a path between the two vociferously opposed factions, one of which included members of his own family. The Congress-ites had a plethora of affiliates supporting them – small organisations perhaps, but they added up. They were a product of the footwork of Manuel and his comrades. 'Of course we won,' said Manuel, 'because democracy had to rule.'

Yet it was only on the Saturday evening before the meeting that one of Omar's sisters handed over the receipt for the hall to Goolam Aboobaker, who rushed to collect the key. 'It was a great ANC occasion,' recalled Manuel. Albertina Sisulu spoke (she was banned again soon after that), the ANC flag was raised, and the Freedom Charter was everywhere on display.

It may have been a victory in the short term but it was a costly one, not only in terms of the relationships between the Congress-aligned and Unity Movement supporters, but between them and the trade unions too.

The trade unions, in terms of the constituency and economic muscle, were far more important to keep on side. They had put their names behind the anti-SAIC campaign in the belief that this was part of a non-aligned fight for democracy. When the ANC flag was raised they were profoundly displeased. 'Jan was livid,' recalled Aboobaker, speaking about Jan Theron, the general secretary of the FCWU. Others, such as David Lewis of the GWU, were also annoyed. Actually, Theron was not at that meeting. But he was, he recalled somewhat acerbically, in his office the next day when the security police raided it, looking for 'whatever they were looking for, but also conveying a message'.

It was an experience that was to colour the relationship between the unions, by far the biggest organised constituency, and the political activist organisations in the run-up to the United Democratic Front in the next few years. At the time, the unions were painstakingly setting up a national federation 'and we were gathering steam'. The 'fundamental tension', said Theron, 'was (over) the issue of some longer-term transitional agenda or short-term populist politics'.

This souring of relations was a setback because of the close relationships that been forged between the unions and the community organisations during both the Fatti's & Moni's and meat strikes. When Manuel and other political leaders began to talk to them the following year about one united movement against apartheid, they were deeply suspicious. '(They thought) we were reckless, that we brandished the flag.'

Theron's caution may well have been justified. Just two months later Neil Aggett, their Transvaal organiser, was killed in detention. There were fears that the relatively young independent union movement would be suppressed if it became too politically careless. The key for unionists at the time, said Lewis, was how to rebuild the union movement 'in such a way that it doesn't very quickly, if maybe gloriously and bloodily, get wiped out again'.

But there was another consideration, too, and that went to the heart of the manner in which the unions organised. Much effort went into ensuring that the rank and file membership was on board with every decision. Anything less would have exposed union leaders to being easily picked off by the security police, or their employers. The fact that many union leaders, including Theron who had joined the ANC on his post-university overseas trip, felt loyalty to Congress ideals, did not sway them from this position.

The leaders of the community organisations on the other hand had a different view: they felt that leaders needed to forge a path first and then take people with them. Johnny Issel, for instance, kept in the back of his mind something Oscar Mpetha had told him when they worked together in the FCWU in 1979. ' "We have to make a call on the people" ... he used to say that all the time.'

It was different styles of leadership, different styles of organisation. Even within the civic movement there were arguments about whether one should fly the flag – literally and figuratively – sooner to rally people, or later, once local organisations had been firmly established. On one side of this debate was Issel; on the other were activists such as Jonathan de Vries and Hedley King. Manuel fell somewhere in the middle. He believed in strong, rooted organisation and in taking people with him, but he believed that it was necessary to transcend the bread-and-butter issues of rent, electricity and bus fares, and quickly. Today a rents protest, tomorrow the demands of the Freedom Charter.

He debated these issues within the Congress-aligned group, sometimes with tolerance, sometimes not.

But when it came to the Unity Movement, Manuel had scant patience. So it was that the 1981 anti-SAIC meeting became a show of strength *within* the anti-apartheid movement. It was the point where the Congress-aligned organisations established their hegemony in anti-apartheid politics in Cape Town. Many of their leaders broke sharply with a past that had nurtured them. In retrospect, the anti-SAIC campaign was a strange place to win that battle in Cape Town, because of the small and largely conservative Indian population there. As Manuel ruminated, with some amusement: 'It was one of those great rip-roaring ANC occasions. We pissed off the opposition. We had everybody mobilised but we didn't have the Indians, you know ...'

It gave new meaning to the aphorism muttered by more sceptical leftists in those days that the community organisations had 'too many chiefs and not enough Indians'. They meant they were top heavy. In November 1981, it took on a more literal meaning.

By 1982, Manuel had a new job at an organisation that went by the acronym ERIC – the Educational Resource and Information Centre, one of those myriad organisations that sprang up in the apartheid era. ERIC, funded by a Scandinavian government agency, gave him a base, and a reason, to visit coloured and African areas and to distribute educational resources to community leaders. Some resources included practical advice – how to set up a civic and so on – others were more overtly political. In 1982, the tone was distinctly political. That was the year when Minister of Co-operation and Development (responsible for 'black (African) affairs') Piet Koornhof introduced a bill to deal with the escalating squatter crisis in the country that manifested principally in Cape Town.

THE ONGOING AND PAINFUL BATTLES between the large 'illegal' African communities in Cape Town were a world apart from the political activity in the rest of Cape Town. Crossroads, perhaps the most famous of the informal African settlements, took root in the mid-1970s. Many of the people who settled there had lived in Cape Town for longer than 10 years but had never acquired the precious Section 10 1(a) and (b) rights entitling them to permanent residence.[34] Many had been 'lodgers' in backyard shacks of the settled African townships. After a tussle with the City Council, which wanted to demolish Crossroads as a health hazard in 1976, it won the status of an 'emergency camp'. Church groups, such as the Quakers, and liberal civil rights groups, such as the Black Sash, rallied to the aid of Crossroads. Its high profile gave it a protection other 'illegal' Africans did not enjoy. In the late 1970s, after the destruction of Modderdam Road and Unibel, floods of refugees sought shelter in Crossroads. Official statistics – probably an underestimate – said that the population in Crossroads had grown from 16900 in June 1977 to 20000 by December that year.[35]

Bantu Affairs authorities tried to weed out the newcomers by increasingly harsh pass raids, and established the first divisions in the community by persuading the older residents to effectively police the community. Anyone who visited Crossroads in those days would understand the difficulty that the white authorities faced in policing Crossroads. It was a densely packed shack settlement situated on shifting sand dunes that were dotted with thick shrubs. Often the newcomers would erect shelters made of black plastic garbage bags in between the shacks, making the shackland even more impenetrable.

In effect, Crossroads and its satellite camps were a huge middle finger to the state's policy of influx control. The settlement became an international symbol of the suffering of Africans under the pass laws and the lack of humanity, especially towards women and children, of the apartheid government. But beneath this big picture lay a more complex one riddled with tensions and contradictions between rural tradition and urban organisation. There was a wedge between the Charterist organisations of the Cape Flats and African townships on the one hand, and their more oppressed brothers and sisters in the bush settlements on the other. This was exacerbated by the authorities who discovered that the area was impossible to police without making alliances – and giving concessions to – the most powerful faction. The Charterist organisations did not realise the depth of that alliance – or in fact that it existed at all. In later years, when UDF leaders, including Manuel, tried to bring Crossroads strongman Johnson Ngxobongwana into their fold, they made a fatal error of judgement, as we shall see.

But in 1982, the big picture obscured those details. When Koornhof introduced his Orderly Movement and Settlement of Black Person's Bill, it was primarily to try to deal with the growing squatter crisis – or failure of influx control – in the Western Cape. It allowed more rights to a permanent settled urban elite (those with 'Section 10' rights), at the same time cracking down harshly on 'illegals' by giving the government even more powers to lay waste the squatter camps and 'deport' people back to their putative homelands. For the Congress-aligned organisations the battle ahead seemed obvious.

AT THE SAME TIME, the first murmurings of a new constitution emanated from government corridors. It would allow coloureds and Indians limited voting rights and some form of representation in segregated parliaments, while at the same time cutting off the possibility of representation more completely for African people. It was a pathetic attempt at reform in hindsight, but Cape

Town's political leaders from the coloured community realised that unless they persuaded their constituency that this was a dead-end road, they could suffer significant political setbacks.

So Manuel, from his base in ERIC, began to distribute more directly political 'resource' material. A Disorderly Bills Committee, as it was called, was set up to oppose the Koornhof bills. It placed the focus once more on the national politics of interracial solidarity. Michell was among those who worked with Manuel at ERIC, producing posters and leaflets and booklets explaining why the new 'reforms' would bring more repression. As had happened in the rents campaign, the material was distributed community by community. Meetings were called to discuss the bills. The spidery network that had been set up grew longer arms as activists pushed into new areas.

'ERIC was not a place,' said Michell, 'but a mobile platform for training and politicisation.'

It was now overtly political work, but the community organisations still formed the basis for its propagation. '(ERIC) ... gave Trevor and me a platform to work legitimately at a mass level in civil society,' said Michell. 'It meant that we could operate in the underground quite easily, and didn't feel the pressure to separate these two structures. We just had to be careful we didn't get caught.'

The big gap, though, was that there was still no public, legal political organisation that could act as a leader in the showdown with the government that was surely coming.

AT THE END OF 1982 Manuel visited Durban, where he had forged close contacts with the Durban Housing Action Committee, and particularly with Pravin Gordhan. Around Christmas of that year he sat with Gordhan, who was now banned, on the little veranda of his flat in Durban's busy and historic Indian area in Prince Edward Street. 'We were talking about the civics and the question that arose was, what is the next step? PG said, why don't we go for a broad front, a kind of united front?'

Gordhan (still known as PG to his comrades from that era) had just come out of a particularly traumatic spell of detention but his interrogators had not managed to crack his ANC links. Now banned, he felt close to Manuel because they were in the 'same business' of tackling housing issues and building community organisations. But there was another level of that business too. 'The challenge was this,' he recalled. 'It's very easy to get socio-economic structures going, but how do you get overt political structures set up? And for many years the belief was always, if you try it, you'll die.'

The trick was to take the social capital built on the ground out of the 'reformist socio-economic organisations ... somehow extract political capital out of it ... and yet allow the ground to continue with its day-to-day work.' The other challenge was to establish African leadership at the forefront of such an organisation. So far, community-based organisation had flourished most prodigiously in the coloured areas of Cape Town and the Indian areas of Durban and Johannesburg.

To Manuel, it made perfect sense. He and Gordhan agreed that the relaunch of the Transvaal Indian Congress in Johannesburg in January would be a good place to make the call 'and we'd try to involve some of the ANC-aligned people around the country'. Gordhan also suggested that it would be a good move to involve 'this chap who'd just been elected President of the World Alliance of Reform Churches'. He was reputedly a powerful preacher creating a storm in his congregation in Bellville South and in rural areas around the Cape.

When Manuel returned to Cape Town after Christmas one of his first ports of call was to see 'this young priest'.

CHAPTER 12

All, here, now

T HE YOUNG CLERIC WAS nearly a decade older than Manuel. Then in his mid-30s, Allan Boesak ran a congregation in Bellville South, adjacent to the University of the Western Cape where he had been chaplain for nearly a decade.

Although he was an outspoken university chaplain, addressing students during times of unrest, he had astutely immersed himself in the politics of his church, the Nederduitse Gereformeerde Sendingkerk (Dutch Reformed Mission Church). And what politics they were.

His church, the Sendingkerk, was born directly out of racism. It had come into being in 1881, but as early as 1857 church members who were not white, many of them former slaves from the Cape, were asked to hold separate communion services. When the 'mother church', the Nederduitse Gereformeerde Kerk (NGK) first debated this, it had said: 'We know it's not scriptural, we know we don't have the Bible on our side, but for the weakness of some ...' Boesak told me this in 1989, more than a century later, still aghast at the language: 'That was the famous phrase – *"for the weakness of some"* – we will hold separate services for blacks.'[1]

The 'weakness of some' – white racism – became church doctrine in the mother church in 1947, a year before the apartheid government came to power. An NGK theologian, E P Groenewald, used Genesis 11 to argue that God had ordained apartheid:

> And the whole earth was of one language and of one speech ... and the Lord came down to see the city and tower, which the children of men builded/And the Lord said, Behold, the people *is* one, and they have all one language, and this they begin to do and now nothing will be restrained from them ... So the Lord scattered them abroad from thence upon the face of the all the earth.[2]

Boesak's God was different. Born in Kakamas, a remote rural village in the north-western Cape in 1945, Boesak saw his mother find comfort in a God that cared for the poor and powerless.

> *Die invloed van my moeder, met die gedagte dat die geloof onontbeerlik is in 'n mens se lewe. Mense soos ons wat arm was en geen mag gehad het ... ons inspirasie en troos moes put uit die Woord wat vir ons sê, dat God die Vader van die weduwee en wese is.*[3]

His family was too poor to provide their children with birthday presents: instead his mother read a Bible text to them on their birthdays: *'Ek het nie 'n present vir jou, my kind, maar die bybelwoord is groter as die grootste geskenk.'* ('I don't have a present for you, my child, but the word of the Bible is greater than the biggest present.')

So the church became a bulwark against a sense of deprivation and by the age of 16 Boesak had immersed himself in church duties as a sexton. By the time he was 23, he had graduated from the Bellville Theology Seminary and been ordained as a minister.

His influence grew precisely because he built his base in the church so effectively. He became a member of the *Broederkring* in the wake of the 1976 violence which had shaken him deeply, particularly when it exploded in the coloured suburbs of the Cape Flats. 'The government was willing to shoot at unarmed children with real, live ammunition,' he said. 'It showed how serious the situation was now.'[4]

The *Broederkring* was set up in 1974, some argue as a 'para-church' equivalent to black consciousness in the secular world.[5] Its aim was to allow clerics of the younger reformed churches, specifically the (African) NGK in Afrika and the coloured Sendingkerk to network. Its founders included Beyers Naudé, the white NGK cleric who had been one of the few to denounce apartheid and who was expelled from the NGK as a consequence, and the Reverend Sam Buti, the leader of the NGK in Afrika.

Boesak was elected chair of the *Broederkring* in 1977 and assumed responsibility for the publication *Dunamis*, significantly published in English rather than Afrikaans, the language of the church, as it was sent abroad. The aims of the *Broederkring* were also spelled out: to work for one united church and to oppose apartheid and racism as part of the church's 'prophetic task'. The *Broederkring,* with Boesak at the helm, began seriously to rock the white church, the spiritual bedrock of the Afrikaner community. In 1979 Boesak's church challenged members of the Broederbond, the secret Afrikaner society which was the driving political power behind the National Party, to choose between the church or the Broederbond. And then the *Broederkring* affiliated to the South African Council of Churches (SACC), an outspokenly anti-apartheid body (then led by Bishop Desmond Tutu), although the reformed churches themselves were not members.

Boesak's greatest coup in the church happened in 1982 just a few months before Manuel went to see him. At the Ottawa conference of the World Alliance of Reformed Churches (WARC), Boesak was not only elected the leader of the body; he also managed to drive a stake into the heart of the 'Moeder Kerk' at home.

'The struggle in South Africa is not merely against an evil ideology,' he told the conference.

> It is against a pseudo-religious ideology which is born in and is still being justified out of the bosom of the Reformed Churches. The importance of this for the future of the Christian church in South Africa is enormous, for ultimately, beyond denomination and tradition, the credibility of the gospel of Jesus Christ is at stake.[6]

Apartheid, he said, was not just political ideology. 'Its very existence as a political policy has depended and still depends on the theological justification of certain member churches of the WARC.' Apartheid should be declared a heresy 'contrary to the Gospel and inconsistent to the Reformed tradition'.

It was an extraordinary political and theological victory. It unravelled and undermined the entire moral base of white Afrikanerdom at the very time when black resistance at home was making life uncomfortable.

Boesak's 'heresy' call catapulted him from being a powerful local preacher in his Belhar congregation to an international figure. 'Articulate as he was – he was a great orator – he wasn't able to fill the Gaiety Bioscope before,' recalled Manuel. 'After he became President of the World Alliance, his crowd-pulling capacity changed. He became a big magnet.'

Boesak had another advantage, too. He had deep roots in the Cape rural areas, particularly among the poor and generally conservative coloured population. He had built his own, independent constituency. At the end of 1982, when the Charterist leadership offered him a national stage outside of the church, he was quick to accept. 'We built that stage for Boesak. It was there for the taking. He took it. He saw the moment, he saw the great opportunity and put every bit of himself into it,' said Manuel.

Manuel had taken Cheryl Carolus with him to speak to Boesak. A young, energetic activist, Carolus's political appetite had been whetted by black consciousness rather than by the Unity Movement. Through her uncle Steve Carolus, a prominent BC activist in the Cape in the 1970s, she had linked up with older activists such as Johnny Issel and Virginia Engel, and had even travelled to the Eastern Cape with Engel in 1977 to meet Steve Biko, not knowing then that Biko had been arrested at a roadblock coming out of Cape Town. She was detained for five months in 1976 when she was just 18, and by the end of the 1970s was a dedicated member of the ANC-aligned group that included Manuel.

When Biko was murdered in detention in 1977 in a most brutal way, it shook the country and the world. It also left young activists such as Virginia Engel downcast for months. 'I think a lot of us went lame for a while, like you had to work through a depression or a deep trauma before you could lift yourself again,' she said.

But the fact that there had been such close contact was a sign of the contiguity between black consciousness and the new Charterist activism that was emerging. Barney Pityana, one of Biko's closest friends and comrades, had a 'strong pedigree' with the ANC Youth League although he was also a 'loyal cadre' of the black consciousness philosophy that Biko espoused.[7] Black consciousness, said Pityana, never 'envisaged itself as an alternative liberation force ... because it was justly preoccupied with the middle passage'.[8]

It was this 'middle passage' crossed by black consciousness that provided many of Manuel's generation with the confidence to forge a new political organisation that involved their communities, rather than predominantly intellectual groupings. Where they broke with the BC groupings decisively was in the method of organisation.

The discussions about a united front consumed activists around the country for much of 1982. Manuel and Carolus travelled to Johannesburg that year where they met activists in the newly constituted Transvaal Indian Congress (TIC). Like their Durban counterparts, they had made increasing contact with mainly African activists who were in the wave of people being released from Robben Island at the end of their prison terms, among them Murphy Morobe, Eric Molobi and Amos Masondo.

Ismail Momoniat, then a young maths lecturer at the University of the Witwatersrand, had been among those who had pushed for the refounding of the TIC. His family had moved to Lenasia from Turffontein, a suburb in the south of Johannesburg, in the early 1960s, also victims of the Group Areas Act. He spent his school years, with his best friend Valli Moosa, later to become a cabinet colleague of Manuel's, immersed in black consciousness. Black consciousness was to the Johannesburg activists what the Unity Movement was to those in Cape Town. It provided their first political awakenings, but was not enough to sustain them in organised activism. From the late 1970s Momoniat formed part of a substantial group that committed to the ideals of the Freedom Charter. He was one of those arrested in the huge crackdown on ANC cells that ended with the conviction of Barbara Hogan and another white ANC member, Rob Adam, as well as the death of Neil Aggett, whom Momoniat had seen in his cell the day he died.

Momoniat and his Johannesburg comrades were a little suspicious of their Cape Town counterparts, such as Manuel and Carolus. 'You know, in Cape Town politics there were always so many divisions. So you talk to Johnny (Issel), you talk to Trevor, you talk to the others … we had all these secret links with people. Because of the police you didn't tell everyone who else you knew … unless you got involved in some activity together. It really wasn't possible … you didn't let people know you had a secret group … you just assumed everyone had their groupings.'

Yet he and his comrades in Johannesburg were clear that they wanted to work with people who had roots in the community. Manuel was one of these. 'We weren't interested in BC type activists and we had broken from them.'

So, in spite of political arguments – for instance, according to Momoniat, Manuel and Carolus challenged the TIC as an 'ethnic' organisation – they found common ground to lay the basis for a united front. The alliances made between Cape Town and Durban were paralleled in Johannesburg.

In this way the foundation was laid for Boesak's 1983 call. Newspaper articles, for more than a decade afterwards, would refer to the United Democratic Front as having been set up in response to Boesak's call. In fact networks around the country, those where Manuel now moved not only within but between, had laid that basis the year before.

And the government helped matters along with its constitutional proposals that galvanised, in particular, the Indian and coloured communities. Hand in hand with the Orderly Movement of Persons Bill, which clamped down on African movement, was a proposal for a new constitution aimed to co-opt the Indian and coloured communities. The attempts to ameliorate the effects of apartheid on these communities had been in the making since 1977 but were manifestly too little, too late. The refined proposals were driven by P W Botha, who became prime minister in 1980. He had been the minister responsible for coloured affairs in the 1960s, presiding over the destruction of District Six and hundreds of thousands of other Group Areas removals. The increased alienation of these communities, and the now militant opposition, posed a crisis of legitimacy for the government.

The separate organs government set up for coloured and Indian people had become unworkable, a point made clear with the abolition of the CRC in 1980. This collapse was partly spurred by the 'largely obstructionist role' played by the Labour Party.[9] Even those who were stern critics of the Labour Party conceded this: 'I have been a great critic of the Labour Party for its part in a separate institution like the CRC but in retrospect it has played a significant role in politicising the coloured people,' said Jakes Gerwel in 1978.[10] And indeed, at first, the Labour Party did not play ball with the government on the constitutional proposals. Allan Hendrickse, then leader of the Party, described the plans as indicative of 'decadence, immorality and a sick society, an attempt to entrench racism in the Constitution'.[11]

The proposals were to implement three separate chambers of legislators, one for whites, one for coloureds, one for Indians. The government did not forget its arithmetic. The numbers of representatives were in a ratio of four (whites) to two (coloured) to one (Indian). An electoral college comprising these representatives would elect a president who would have powers to override any legislation. It was a sop, at best, and at worst, a means of tightening control by the ruling party. When the Labour Party refused to participate in the commission investigating the proposals, P W Botha warned that if it didn't cooperate, he would find new coloured leaders who would. 'I want to give you a final warning. I say again: One man, one vote in this country is out. That is definite. And now I want to say something further: Don't try to do anything unconstitutional ... you will be sorry for yourself ... and any man who tries will be sorry for himself.'[12]

After its initial feistiness, the Labour Party succumbed to the pressure. At its meeting on 4 January 1983 in northern Natal, one of its leaders, David Curry, said: 'We in the Labour Party have decided we are going inside.'[13]

As much as government must have sighed in relief, it also left the field wide open for the anti-apartheid coalition that had been painstakingly built on the basis of rejection of the new constitution.

So three weeks later when Allan Boesak made the call for a united front at the Johannesburg rally to reject the SAIC and to reconstitute the Transvaal Indian Congress, it resonated around the country. 'He made a truly remarkable speech,' said Cas Salojee, one of the TIC's founders. 'He moved people in a deep way. He just created one helluva sensation.'[14]

Not even the anti-SAIC activists themselves envisaged the effect of the call. They decided to change the venue of the rally at the last moment to the Johannesburg City Hall. It was a significant move, escalating the cause from being local and ethnically based to a national one. 'Not in our wildest dreams did we think it was going to be so massive,' said Momoniat. 'We couldn't normally have a meeting at the City Hall but we had won that space, and we used it to launch the UDF.'

Boesak condemned the Labour Party for its collusion with government: 'From now on, they will share responsibility for apartheid, for the creation of yet more homelands, for the resettlement of black people, for the rape of our human dignity. From now on ... apartheid no longer has only a white face.'[15]

He introduced the theme that was to run through the UDF as a driving force, and to run through his speeches in the year to come: 'Three little words that express our seriousness in this struggle.' They were ALL, HERE, and NOW. 'We want ALL our rights ... we want our rights right HERE in ... a united South Africa ... We want our rights NOW. We have been waiting so long ... NOW is the time.'[16]

'This is the politics of refusal,' said Boesak, 'and it is the only dignified response black people can give in this situation.'[17]

Tucked in the middle of the speech was this invocation: 'We are all committed to the struggle for a non-racial, open, democratic South Africa, a unitary state in which all people will have the rights accorded to them by God. There is therefore no reason why churches, civic associations, trade unions, student organisations and sports bodies should not unite on this issue.'[18]

It was significant that O R Tambo, ANC leader in exile, made this same call about two weeks earlier in his 8 January statement on the seventy-first anniversary of the ANC. Tambo condemned the Labour Party for its intended collaboration and then made the following appeal:

We must organise the people into strong mass democratic organisation; we must organise all revolutionaries into underground units of the ANC; we must organise all combatants into units of Umkhonto we Sizwe; we must organise all democratic forces into one front for national liberation.[19]

For years afterwards, the police and government tried to smear the UDF by claiming it was a front for the ANC; liberal reporters, academics and civil rights activists 'defended' it: 'The UDF is a product of history, not of revolutionary conspiracy,' wrote Tom Lodge three years after its launch.[20]

The truth is it was both. The activists inside the country with links to the ANC, such as Manuel, had canvassed the idea thoroughly in the previous year. Some, such as Carolus, had even been out of the country to meet the ANC. 'At the end of the day,' recalled Manuel, 'how this thing worked ... all you need to know was that someone (not necessarily the person who'd had the contact in Lusaka) would say: "Comrades we've had contact with Lusaka. These are the views emerging from that." You couldn't do it formally in a meeting ... so we'd step outside, whisper to each other, this is the word from Lusaka, just take it forward.'

At the same time, there was a groundswell of dissatisfaction, borne of the years of deprivation and cyclical crises that had consumed the country since apartheid. Boesak's call fell on ground 'that was not just fertile, but already prepared'.[21]

The call also gave new meaning to the 'politics of refusal', as Boesak had tagged it, in the Western Cape. No more would it be translated into the traditional 'politics of withdrawal'. It heralded an entirely new era in offensive rather than defensive politics.

MANUEL PLUNGED INTO WORK when he returned to Cape Town. By this time he and Lynne Matthews had moved in together. They lived in Maitland, which adjoins Kensington, and was grimly holding on as a mixed residential area. They shared a house belonging to Philma Manuel's companion, Sylmore Poggenpoel, who spent several months each year at sea, and who by then was long separated from his wife.

The fight for hegemony within the anti-apartheid movement was not over. The Disorderly Bills Committee, formed to fight the Koornhof Bills, was still a site of intense political conflict. 'The Trotskyites were back again and there was a complete rift,' said Manuel.

There were arguments, too, in Manuel's base organisation. One of its affiliates, BBSK (which stood for Bokmakierie, Bridgetown, Silvertown and Kewtown), began to write fierce letters, detailed and bureaucratic, about the number of representatives they should be allowed in CAHAC. They argued that as BBSK represented four areas, not one, they should be allowed more votes. It was all part of a battle for a political voice, a clash between the old Cape left-wing traditions and the new. 'Some of these people were rolling along in their own little world,' said Manuel.

Much of the battle within CAHAC was whether it should affiliate to this new front. Some worried that their energies would be dissipated: instead of organising in communities they would be absorbed into a high-profile political organisation and their base would weaken, not strengthen. Many of these concerns were legitimate. Their most capable leaders, such as Manuel, Carolus, Issel, and De Vries, and the activists based in the African townships, such as Christmas Tinto and Mildred Lesiea, began working full time on forming the new front. Struggles over rising rents and electricity were put on the back burner. 'Those days I hardly saw Trevor, really,' recalled Matthews. Manuel effectively became a full-time organiser for the UDF under the convenient cover of ERIC, the organisation that employed him.

There was much to be done, not least persuading the different factions in Cape anti-apartheid politics of the benefits of a united front. The preparatory meetings began in May 1983: Dullah Omar, the lawyer who still straddled the Charterist group and the Unity Movement group, facilitated them. Manuel and his comrades met Kwedi Mkalipi, who had been a PAC member, they met APDUSA (African People's Democratic Union of Southern Africa) (a more radical breakaway from the Unity Movement which had given rise to Neville

184

Alexander's group), they met Mr Dudley from the Teachers' League, they met Neville Alexander himself, perhaps the most intellectually formidable of their critics who had the added cachet of having been a prisoner with Mandela on Robben Island. 'We had a myriad of these meetings,' said Manuel, 'trying to put to political factions in the Western Cape: let's build this broad united front. We've got a gap, we've got to allow political activity. And we were singularly unsuccessful.'

It was an exhausting period and Manuel teetered between enthusiasm and despondence. Alexander and his followers launched a rival front, first the Cape Youth League, then the Cape Action League. And when Manuel's comrades in Johannesburg approached the anti-apartheid icon Archbishop Desmond Tutu to back the UDF as a patron he, too, wavered, perhaps because he was close to AZAPO, the black consciousness grouping, thought Manuel. Many years later Tutu told me, 'I was chuffed that they should have invited me to be a patron.' He'd declined and had not even come to Cape Town for the launch because he was trying to maintain – and here he chuckled – a non-party political stance. 'I had a political stance but you tried to be as non-partisan as you could be. Because partisanship, as you know, was in fact a matter of life and death in so many situations.'

But more painful for Manuel, were the tortuous negotiations with the black trade unions. There were four major independent trade unions in the Western Cape: the General Workers' Union, which organised stevedores, steel workers and led the epic, but failed meat workers' strike; the Food and Canning (and African Food and Canning) Workers' Union, perhaps the most rooted union in the region and one with a history of ANC-alignment; the Cape Town Municipal Workers' Union, led by John Ernstzen, which represented mainly coloured workers in the municipality; and small branches of two FOSATU-affiliated unions that organised motor and components workers and textile workers. The civics believed they had painstakingly built relationships with those unions: they had campaigned for the Fatti's & Moni's boycott and the red meat boycott in support of strikes, they had even supported a strike at the Leyland motor plant in the north of Cape Town (hard to do when motor cars were not exactly a mass consumer item), and they had worked on a relationship with the municipal workers. There were two conferences with the unions in the months before the launch and endless talks. 'But we just couldn't make the breakthrough,' said Manuel.

The reasons for the impasse went to the heart of the different cultures of organisation. Perhaps the most important was that the trade unions themselves were involved in delicate talks to build a federation. It involved unions around the country, ranging from the politically cautious but well-organised FOSATU, the Cape unions, and a plethora of smaller, general unions in the then Transvaal and Eastern Cape. The Charterists thought of FOSATU as unashamedly 'workerist': it held political activists in no uncertain contempt. It was composed of strong industrial unions, with hundreds of thousands of members around the country. The Cape unions were more radical: they had spurned the idea of registration of unions, which the government had mooted in the Wiehahn Commission, unlike FOSATU, which saw Wiehahn as something of a victory. They were fiercely committed to worker control and to their own autonomy from any outsider, whether it be government or student activists. The up-country general unions were loud in support of the political struggle, but often disorganised on the factory floor. Outspoken and courageous, some had to deal with tyrannical 'Bantustan' authorities, who harassed their leaders relentlessly. So the project to build a federation involved robust meetings that often threatened to scuttle the dream.

Secondly, most of the unions were suspicious of the structure of the proposed front. If they affiliated to the UDF, they asked, would their organisations, with thousands of members, have the same weight as, say, an activist organisation with only a few hundred members? 'To take two concrete if extreme examples,' said David Lewis in an interview at the time, 'the ecumenical action group (TEAM) and the Detainees Parents' Support Group. The former is a grouping of progressive priests, and the latter is a group of individuals dedicated to opposing detention ... Let me be clear from the outset that both of these are laudable and necessary ventures, but neither bears any similarity whatsoever to the structure of a trade union.' Activist organisations, he said, were 'essentially groupings of like-minded individuals, who are brought together by a common political goal ... (and) ... have a great deal of freedom to manoeuvre in the extremely flexible parameters in which they operate. They don't represent members in the strong sense. Unions on the other hand are not organisations of activists, and union leaders are not activists in the same sense at all because they are representatives in the strongest sense. Union leaders don't claim to represent the views of the working class. They represent the views of their members.'[22]

Thirdly, there was a dissonance between the culture of the new workers' organisations that had emerged and the new activist organisations. Unions had, by their very nature, to be fairly open. There could be few hidden agendas or unspoken understandings. This was not necessarily so in the activist organisations, where various factors, not least a climate of repression, limited open discussion. Lewis hit on the Disorderly Bills Action Committee (DBAC) as a case in point: 'We found ourselves in the midst of extraordinary squabbles,' he reported. 'Sometimes they seemed to be squabbles based on straight power plays, straight questions of dominance between the two factions of the community organisations in Cape Town ... I recall a laughable situation where, in the same week that the Koornhof Bills were withdrawn, the DBAC met. They sat through an entire three or four-hour meeting without once mentioning the Koornhof Bills.'[23] (A function of the 'rift' with the 'Trotskyist' organisations Manuel had referred to.)

Years later, Jan Theron echoed this point: 'If you're trying to get people engaged in politics, then they don't need that kind of experience, where basically they're not respected and not part of the process and what they have to say isn't valued.'

Some of the general unions argued against this position. The general secretary of the South African Allied Workers' Union (SAAWU) Sisa Njikelana wrote, in response to Lewis, that it was vital that the working class not be isolated from the national democratic struggle at a time when the government was trying to co-opt 'sections of the oppressed majority and halt the advance being made in the struggle for a democratic South Africa'. (SAAWU was based in the repressive 'border' region of East London, and was one of the more militant of the general unions.) A front, he said, 'was an alliance of a broad spectrum of autonomous organisations of differing class origins who come together having identified a common political grievance. It is a forum, a rallying point, providing the structural form which guarantees the broadest possible unity in action of different social groups.'[24]

Alec Erwin, in years to come a cabinet colleague of Manuel's but then a national organiser for FOSATU, the most cautious of the African trade union groupings, reflected that there was no real 'hostility' on the part of the unions towards the UDF. 'It was a pragmatic position,' he told me. 'We felt there was a bit of adventurism, or a tendency towards adventurist positions in the UDF because they didn't have any actual organisations to lose. And you could just rotate and replace your activists all the time. But I think, rightly, we were protective of the organisational capacity of the unions, because you can't just replace and organise every five minutes.' (Erwin's position later, his centrality in the ANC and the government, is slightly ironic to some of his old and new comrades. 'If you wanted to earn the respect of "FOSATU types", like Erwin, said Lewis, 'you could not be seen as even close to "flag-waving types".')

What mattered to Manuel, were the unions in his own town. The irony was that both GWU and FCWU were close, in terms of their officials and their outlook, to an ANC position. The FCWU had even sprung from that tradition. He recalled Jan Theron saying to him in one of the planning meetings: 'The problem is that we're dealing with populists who are reckless. You people don't care about the lives of trade unionists. You'll raise the ANC flag, you'll bring everyone into the fold; then you'll bring attention to trade unionists who have the job of organising working people.'

In the end, there was a rather weak compromise position: the unions would endorse and publicly support the UDF but would not join. 'It was very sour,' recalled Lewis. 'There is no doubt about it that even if we went there (to the launch that was a few months off), it was not with a full heart. I sort of regret those things now.'

Theron has fewer regrets: If the mooted trade union federation had already been established and had joined the UDF it would have been different, he believed. But the quality of organisation 'on the ground' was distinctly different between the unions and community and activist groups. Manuel, he said, did not harangue the unions and was never abrupt: 'He was trying to be persuasive but wasn't being persuasive, I didn't feel he was listening to our concerns, or was prepared to.'

'Some of these things you can never unravel,' said Manuel later. But he was convinced then, as he remained, that an organisation that cut across class and race was essential to weaken the apartheid state. He was able to listen, willing to listen, and would try to engage. But in the end, then, as he does now, he would move ahead. 'It always characterised Trevor,' said Lewis later. 'He always wanted to be doing something and – bloody hell – things could happen *now* and here he was sitting and trying to persuade these people and listening to all these stories about whether we got consulted or didn't get consulted, and all he wanted to do was *do* things.'

THE SOURNESS IN THE RELATIONSHIP spread. A man who was to become central in the new democratic front – and in Manuel's life – experienced it first hand. He was Patrick Mosiuoa Lekota, then known universally as 'Terror', not for his political views or prison record but because of his legendary skills on the soccer field.

Released in 1982 after a seven-year jail stint, most of it spent on Robben Island, Lekota returned to Durban, the town where he had married. Born in 1948 into a poor family in the Free State town of Kroonstad, Lekota had matriculated at a Mariannhill school in Natal and then enrolled at the University of the North, one of the segregated apartheid universities. Bright and ebullient, he had soon become involved in the vocal black consciousness movement. By the time he was arrested at the end of 1974, he was the full-time secretary for the South African Students' Organisation (SASO). He was sentenced, along with seven other SASO activists in 1976, and went to Robben Island where he met the ANC Rivonia trialists, including Nelson Mandela and Walter Sisulu. Although the Rivonia trialists and the new SASO intake were not in the same section, they devised ways of talking to each other during exercise time, often clandestinely. Mandela would sometimes ask if Lekota could help in his section, and other prisoners had a packet of tricks to keep warders 'busy', so the new young prisoner could talk to the older men.

'First and foremost, when you arrive in prison you are a source of news,' said Lekota. 'So you narrate the things … : "Well, Steve Biko, by the way, what kind of person is he? What are his views on this? Where does he stand on unity? What's his attitude to the ANC?" Then those comrades make notes about this … so we make our own record.'

Lekota's 'conversion' from a black consciousness to ANC perspective is often assumed to have happened in jail through his conversations with ANC prisoners, particularly Mandela. In fact it began much earlier and was part of the contiguity between many elements of the BC groupings and the ANC. The high school group he had first joined, the African Students' Association (ASA), had roots in the ANC. When it was formed in 1971 SASO took in a mix of ASA members and PAC-oriented students from a school group called ASUSA (African Students' Union of South Africa).

An early discussion in SASO was about the attitude to whites. After huge arguments, the SASO Policy Manifesto, adopted in 1971, said that South Africa was a country in which both black and white live and will continue to live together, said Lekota. 'Like the Freedom Charter?' I asked. 'Yes, that's exactly what it was about. And the main architect of that document was Steve Biko.'

Thus, according to Lekota, there was no huge gulf between him and the ANC when he arrived on the Island five years later, and whatever gaps there were, were quickly bridged.

Shortly before his release, Lekota decided he wanted to go for military training when he got out. 'I was a very physically active person,' he said. But, exactly as had happened when Manuel wanted to become a soldier, the older ANC leaders dissuaded him. 'People like Comrade Walter Sisulu would talk to me. They wouldn't say, "Look, you mustn't go into exile in Zambia." They would say, "We've been thinking about things and we think you should stay." Then maybe Madiba would say, "Our comrades outside feel that we must strengthen the movement inside the country and they think that if you stay you will help …" And you'll find five or six comrades continuously repeating this. It was really an instruction but they would put it to you like a suggestion.'

On the eve of his release, the Robben Islanders put word out to ANC supporters inside the country that they must involve him in local organisations. One of those who rallied around him when he returned to Durban was Ismail Meer, the husband of Fatima Meer, an old friend of Mandela's. 'Before I knew it I got a job in the General Workers Union (GWU) in Durban.' The GWU by then had spread its reach from Cape Town to organise dockworkers around the country. It had a young, thriving branch in Durban led by an academic and unionist, Mike Morris, who had been detained during the meat strike. Lekota didn't realise then the extent of the antipathy between the independent unions and the emerging ANC-aligned organisations.

'I wasn't very tactful,' he admitted years later, 'because I didn't know the terrain very well. So I would talk to the workers about the ANC, tell them about the movement, link in the struggle of the shop floor to the general liberation struggle and so on. And this thing was spreading like wildfire.' Lekota, whose home language is Sotho but who is fluent in Zulu, the main language in Natal (as well as English and Afrikaans), soon attracted a steady flow of participants. His job was to collect subscriptions, not give political classes, and the steady and regular streams of workers to the office soon roused the suspicion of union officials. 'The class was growing in size, and they were coming every day. Then the officials began to ask, how come these guys are coming every day, they can't be paying subscriptions every day?'

Morris, who established a good personal relationship with Lekota, realised that while he was out organising factories, his administrative assistant was teaching workers about the Freedom Charter. 'So he decided I must travel around with him. That's how Mike Morris taught me how to drive. He gave me his car and said I must now drive. So I was benefiting but my classes were suffering!'

So Lekota hit on a new plan for political education. He began to use soccer, instead of subscriptions, as a cover. 'Well, I loved soccer of course, so it was good for me to be playing soccer, but I was anxious that as soon as we finished we must start class.'

But underground tactics did not work well in an above-ground union. Soon the national union leadership dispatched the union's president, Johnson Mpukumpa, a steel worker, to Durban to say 'I mustn't play soccer with these guys and I mustn't fraternise with them'.

That was the end of Lekota's enthusiastic but short-lived career as a trade unionist. Unlike his Cape Town counterpart, Virginia Engel, who moved quietly and carefully in her ANC group while working in the union, Lekota had plunged in a little too hastily. Many years later he was cheerfully rueful. His comrades had organised him the job 'because they thought Mike would fall in love with me' – and indeed the two had got on very well – 'but I wasn't tactful enough to play it steadily until we get the thing we wanted'.

Lekota then went to help Archie Gumede, an ANC veteran, do community work. The two men both lived in the vast Clermont township, west of Durban, which sprawls over the hills, and 'we were of the same school of thought'.

At first he didn't notice that many of the community organisers he met were actually part of the ANC's underground. Gumede was thrilled because he had a young man whom he could send into the communities to go and explain ANC policy (although they didn't identify it as such) which Lekota did in his fluent, if accented, Zulu. Like Manuel, he was supported by donations from friends and comrades and the church organisations.

Lekota was released at the end of 1982 when plans for the UDF were already well under way, particularly in the Cape, Natal and the Transvaal. He missed the Natal launch of the Front, which had happened soon after he came out of jail. But after his short stint in the union, the local Natal committee asked him to be publicity secretary, and he became part of the 'advance team' that travelled to Cape Town in July for the launch of the regional UDF in that divided region. 'I landed exactly in Trevor's hands,' he said.

LEKOTA WAS BOWLED OVER BY MANUEL, by his looks, his manner, even his car.

Manuel smoked prodigiously then – strong French cigarettes that added to an image he created for himself. He had a full head of dark brown hair, a generous beard and often perched a Che Guevara style beret on his crown.

But it was the intentness with which he devoted himself to organisation that was more memorable. Lekota was struck by the contrast then between Manuel's slightly wild outer appearance and his steely inner resolve.

The first shock for Lekota was Manuel's car. 'A certain reddish car,' said Lekota. 'I can't remember what it was. It was like these stock cars, you know, these cars they use for colliding with each other. I always thought he was a stock car driver of the Cape. That car! He was always starting that car and driving it like a mad thing. It didn't seem to me he cared whether he collided with one thing or the other. He just seemed to be going on and on.

'Now I always worried that it might stop at any time but he was absolutely full of confidence that this car could go anywhere. I don't know when he got rid of that car but, you know, he was always in it.'

The second thing that struck him was his appearance and an idiosyncratic habit he has retained of pausing mid-sentence and looking upward for minutes at a time. It is a habit that continues to disconcert journalists and officials, unless they know him well. Unnerved by the silence, they often interject. He always ignores the interjection and continues on the same thought track that began before he looked heavenward.

'He liked to hold his beard,' said Lekota. 'He had continuous plans. Always detailed planning. At this point we'll do *this*, then do *that*. Then he looks at the roof to get some ideas from there, and he'd say, "Comrades, you know what, comrades ..." And, you know, he left a bit of his moustache to look like ... Che Guevara.'

But despite the rackety car and the cigarettes and the beard, Lekota discovered that '... on the outside he didn't look as disciplined as what he was. With all that beard, with his car – I don't think that car ever got some water on it to clean it – (but) that this guy is *incredibly* disciplined. We must meet at *this* time, we must do *that* and so on. He WILL be there if the decision's been taken, make very quick notes, smoking a lot of Gauloises ... Something that brought me very close to him, were those two elements: the level of his personal discipline and his emphasis on organisational discipline. The meeting has got to be *there*, it's got to be *this*, it's got to be *that*.

'And, secondly, his firmness when it came to discipline was something I found extremely crucial. My father taught me that, years ago: that you can't have a team, a soccer team, and organisation if you don't have discipline. And I discovered that he had it. Hey, man, this guy! And I loved that.'

Lekota on the outside was the polar opposite: neat and conventional in appearance, but could never keep to a time or meeting schedule. Yet he was one of the most effective national organisers that the UDF could have hoped to have. He had been impressed with the 'discipline and coordination' of, of all things, the prison authorities when he arrived in his first jail cell in Pretoria Central in 1974. He told his comrades: 'You know, chaps, if we are going to beat this organisation, I can't see that we can beat it with this level of student discipline. This was tip-top. It was precision organisation.'

So Manuel was a breath of fresh air to him. 'He inspired me ... he was not afraid to take hard decisions, something that other comrades would dilly-dally about. He'd take a decision, and then this is the thing.'

It was this trait – this decisiveness that Lekota describes – that both his critics and supporters remembered. As much as it became a negative factor for the union leaders, for Lekota and other activist leaders in the emergent front, it propelled them forward. 'Sometimes it's just stubbornness,' Manuel himself reflected. 'Some of these tensions (in the Western Cape) were really, really, really tough.' Even with his mentor Johnny Issel, 'I had the most incredible stand-up fights, sometimes we threatened to physically beat each other. But you know we soldiered on through all that stuff.'

Manuel and Carolus were elected secretaries of the Western Cape UDF after the regional launch in July. Manuel himself successfully avoided (in public at any rate) any 'factional' tag. There was never a 'Manuel faction' in the Western Cape, despite his growing prominence. Oscar Mpetha, who was out on R1 bail after having been charged with terrorism, was elected UDF president in the Western Cape.

Then organisation started in earnest for the August 1983 national launch. The fact that it was in Cape Town, Manuel's home turf, raised his national profile considerably. Memories fray when it comes to the precise reason it was held in Cape Town. Johnny Issel, whose banning order had expired in mid-1983, evaded the police just long enough to go with Manuel to Johannesburg to discuss the launch. Ismail Momoniat said it was because there was more 'political space' in Cape Town: 'You could do things that we could never do in Johannesburg. I think it was a brilliant decision to have it in Cape Town because Trevor and company organised that launch. I don't think we would ever have been able to do such a big one because the cops would not have allowed it. But they also had a lot of style. They saw to everything.'

Moreover, the tricameral elections were on the horizon. Cape Town's demographics – coloured people were by far the largest population group

– made the constituency vital for the UDF. 'We needed a fillip for organising,' said Manuel. 'Everybody wanted the glory, and we said, "Well, you guys in the Transvaal have everything." '

Issel has a rather more romantic explanation. As he and Manuel checked in at the airport, Zubeida Jaffer, his then fiancée, and Leila Patel, then organiser of *Grassroots*, shouted at their departing backs to 'bring the launch to Cape Town'. And he felt compelled to, he said, because 'I'm in love with Zubeida and I really like Leila'. Moreover, he said, his heart was firmly in Cape Town. 'Whatever I do is here. I would get detained so many times but I would come back to this place … I would go into the rural areas and when I come down the N7, I see this mountain there when I hit Malmesbury. I mean, Cape Town! This is *Cape Town*!'

They argued the whole night, said Issel, the detractors saying, 'Cape Town is so divided, Cape Town has so many factions, and all that.'

He was 'really pissed off' by what they said about his beloved city but in the end, worn down by an all-night meeting, the up-country delegates accepted his proposal when he offered to work full time on the launch. His only problem was that the police were looking for him to renew his banning order. So as soon as he returned, to 'get the Boere off my back', he presented himself at Caledon Square police station with Percy Sonn, a clever and aggressive lawyer, in tow to personally collect his banning order.[25] This ruse worked, he said, and he was able to work without looking over his shoulder.

The Cape Town Charterists swung into action. Goolam Aboobaker hired more than a thousand mattresses from a wholesalers' store in Langa, he went to the mosques and churches to ask for sleeping space; Daphne King (whose partner Hedley King was then in jail) organised food for the thousand or so delegates expected. 'We got the youth, and they did all the peeling. And people went around and got vegetables and meat from the butchers. We got lots and lots of sponsorship. For example, in my area, the youth donated meat and veggies.'

Manuel called Lynne Matthews late one night from one of the preparatory meetings in the week's run-up to the launch, asking her to cook a rushed meal for the scores of delegates there. She drove across town without a licence to deliver a pot of curry made of tinned fish.

Ferdie Engel drove his little Beetle to Botswana (he worked for a rural NGO, which was a good cover for trips to Botswana) where his car was packed with banknotes hidden behind the radio panel. He drove back to

South Africa through the night and dropped R8 000 for the launch in the safe of Issel's sister-in-law.

Issel settled on a venue: the Rocklands Civic, a middling size hall in Mitchell's Plain where he lived. There was some symbolism to holding the launch in Mitchell's Plain too, as it had become effectively a vast resettlement township for many of those evicted from their homes under the Group Areas Act.

As the launch grew closer, he realised the hall was not going to be big enough. Because of the strict laws governing outdoor gatherings, he needed to erect a marquee, but in order to do this, the hire company had to drill a hole in the tar road outside the hall. Issel telephoned Eulalie Stott, one of the most liberal city councillors, who was among those who had met the CAHAC delegation the year before. He asked her to get urgent permission to drill into the tar. 'And she readily agreed.'

The logistics were awesome.

Hundreds of buses left Johannesburg, Durban, the Free State, the Northern Transvaal and the Eastern Cape on 19 August and trundled through the Karoo to Cape Town. The previous day the security police had distributed pamphlets in the Johannesburg townships saying the rally had been postponed until October. 'Don't go to Cape Town' said the pamphlet. But the injunction was roundly ignored.

Issel befriended local radio hams who provided walkie-talkies; off-duty security guards volunteered to stand on the freeway to direct the buses to the venue and watch out for the police. Strict instructions were issued to coordinators in each bus to phone a central monitoring number in Johannesburg from Bloemfontein and Beaufort West. Stops were to be limited to 15 minutes, people must remain on the same bus, and a list of lawyers' numbers was handed out. It was a feat of organisation, and remarkable that the only buses that didn't make it to Cape Town were some from the Free State that were stopped by the police. Eventually, hours late, tired and hungry, even some of those delegates straggled into the meeting.

The numbers were more than anyone expected: 1 500 delegates and about 500 observers came to the closed conference where the Working Principles were decided and the office-bearers elected. Manuel chaired a large part of the meeting, trying to hurry along the programme at the end to accommodate the throngs who arrived for the public rally.

Although the UDF was born out of opposition to the new constitution and the influx control bills, the meeting provided a unique opportunity to spell out both a litany of grievances about what was wrong with apartheid South Africa, as well as a vision of the new. Delegates spoke about inadequate housing, and poorly serviced sites; they spoke about the harshness of inflation and its effect on the paltry pensions of black people; they spoke about transport costs and the working class. Some demanded that workers should own the means of production; others asked that business organisations be specifically recognised as black business people were also among the oppressed. They spoke about migrant labour, the oppression of women, about Group Areas and the bitter taste it left, about their helplessness and rage.

'It would be better if apartheid was based on whether people were dirty or clean,' said a delegate from a youth group. 'Because by now we would all have gone to the shop to buy some soap.'

When Frank Chikane spoke, both in the closed meeting and at the rally later, he traced a line back to 1936, when the All Africa Convention was called to resist the removal of Africans from their land and from the vote. Chikane, a pastor from Soweto, had also begun his political career in the black consciousness movement and had been detained several times. In 1980, he was effectively 'defrocked' by his church, the Apostolic Faith Mission, because of his political activity. By the time of the UDF launch he was a prominent member of the Soweto Civic Association and had become committed to a Charterist vision for South Africa. In his speeches he located the UDF firmly within that tradition, tracking its roots to 1955, to the Congress of the People in Kliptown and to the Freedom Charter.

He spoke about apartheid's increasing repression, unable to contain resistance. In what seems to be a security police transcript of the meeting, it is clear that the transcribers struggled to understand some of his terms. The state, in his talk, is described as 'military sick'; the Bantustan policy as a Bantu Stand policy.[26] Manuel also referred to history. The common 'rock' in the names of Kliptown where the Freedom Charter was adopted, and Rocklands where, 28 years on, they were now launching the UDF, was no accident, he said: this was how firm the organisation was.

Pius Langa, then a prominent anti-apartheid lawyer in Durban, was the electoral officer. Born in the then Eastern Transvaal in 1939, Langa had started his working life in a factory, and then studied law and became an advocate. In Durban, he worked with Archie Gumede, who was to become one of the UDF presidents, and with Griffiths and Victoria Mxenge, the married couple who were human rights lawyers and supported the ANC. Both were assassinated by death squads – Griffiths in 1981 and Victoria in 1985.

'I know most of us are not voters,' Langa told the UDF's fist meeting. 'We have never voted in our lives. But I'll make a short explanation of how we are going to vote. This may sound like a complicated procedure but in fact it's very simple.'

It was simpler even than Langa realised. Almost every major position had been caucused beforehand. 'There was a big argument about who must be president of the UDF,' said Lekota. The Transvaal wanted Albertina Sisulu, legendary as one of the strongest, surviving ANC leaders in the country. With her husband Walter, Mandela's close friend and comrade, on Robben Island, and her own leadership well established, her position seemed unassailable. But Cape Town wanted its presence reflected, probably because the ANC tradition was weakest there. To build, they needed to have local leaders at national level. 'The Cape fellows felt we can't play second fiddle; then Durban said, you know, man, Natal is the home of the ANC and of Archie Gumede (a key activist in the formation of the UDF and also an old ANC member), then the Transvaal said, you know, Albertina … we said, *hey bani!* So we decided there would be three presidents.' They were Sisulu, Gumede and Oscar Mpetha, the old trade unionist from Cape Town, now seriously ill and facing terror charges. 'Actually the question of having three presidents saved us the question of who must be vice-president, deputy and so on. We just had all three,' said Lekota. 'Then there was a fight over who must be Treasurer. Transvaal wanted to be treasurer, Natal wanted to be treasurer. For Natal it was Mewa Ramgobin. For Transvaal it was Cassiem Salojee. Man! It was a toing and froing and toing and froing. Then we decided, no, we'll have two treasurers.

'Agreed, chaps, agreed! Two treasurers. Maybe we'll get more money, there's two of them.'

There was no battle about the general secretary. He was Popo Molefe, a Soweto activist baptised in the fires of the 1976 uprising when he was a matric student in Soweto; and the publicity secretary was the irrepressible Lekota himself.

So Langa's job was made somewhat easier. Whenever he called for nominations, Manuel informed him that the regions had met and chosen the presidents. Each region then elected two vice-presidents, two regional secretaries and two additional executive members. Manuel and Carolus were the Western Cape regional secretaries, both becoming members of the national executive.

'Discussing things through would have taken a hell of a long time,' reflected Langa later. 'And it was a process that was more inclusive than anything else. They concentrated on … two people, who, if they could do something together, then they put them together.'

By the end of the delegates' meeting, crowds were already swarming at the doors of the Rockland Civic Centre. There were more people than the organisers had ever envisaged: estimates ranged from 6 000 to 15 000. Realistically, there were about 12 000 people who crammed into every available space in the hall, spilling into the street and into the marquee.

Issel, who couldn't come to the rally because of his banning order, made his presence felt, driving around in his white Beetle Volkswagen with Bob Marley's 'Buffalo Soldier' blaring from speakers. The song refers to the black cavalrymen used in the wars against native Americans (*Buffalo Soldier,/in the heart of America./Stolen from Africa,/fighting for survival*), but Issel used it because it was major hit at the time rather than for any ideological reasons. He also set up his own 'narrowcast' radio station, fashioned on Radio Moscow, he told me, with two announcers, a man and a woman, who drove around Mitchell's Plain summoning people to the meeting. In his stead, he sent his nine-year-old daughter Leila who gave a brief but stirring message to the crowds on behalf of her father.

The atmosphere was festive despite the police attention and the extraordinary crowds.

Several times Manuel, who chaired the early part of the rally, had to appeal to the people crowding the streets to get into the marquee to avoid police action. Even more frequently he cajoled people to get off the beams of the roof of the hall. The caretaker had switched off the electricity supply as a precaution because people had scrambled up the rafters to get a better view. 'If you fall off you're going to kill people down below. So, please, everybody sitting on the beam up there, kindly move off.' As the thousands sang and chanted, he knew that the situation was potentially perilous. 'These people aren't even making an effort to get off. Please, people, you must get off! … Please don't rush … can the marshals form a chain across the door please … remember, we cannot fight with our own people, we cannot fight with our own comrades.'[27]

Reporters sat crammed on the stage, the only available space in the hall. 'The hall was packed,' recalled his mother Philma, who had taken Manuel a clean shirt that morning (he hadn't been home and hadn't slept). 'My godfathers, all those people! And people started going up on the beams and he said, "Come down from there, you're going to get hurt." And I was so amazed because people listened.'

It was the first time, said his mother, that she realised the extent to which Manuel had acquired both stature and authority, at least in his home town. It could have been a disaster. 'It was quite chaotic because there was no distinct stage and table where the speakers sat, and no rostrum that separated the masses. Everybody was just all over the place,' said Manuel years later. His concern about people perching on the beams came from his knowledge of construction: 'My fear was that you load a structure like that and it collapses and everybody's crushed. Or people fall off there into the crowd and kill themselves and other people.'

Remarkably, given the way the hall was packed, there was no disaster. Remarkably, although the police tried to stop a few buses coming into Cape Town and warned people not to stand in the street, they did not disrupt the meeting. The crowd, so used to speaking about the ANC in a whisper, heard Frank Chikane trace its history from 1936 to that day. It heard Archie Gumede, the only one of the three UDF presidents who was present (Mpetha was in hospital and Sisulu was in detention); it heard Francis Baard, a legendary figure who had spent years under a banning order hail them as 'a beautiful garden of flowers, the flowers in South Africa, the flowers in our motherland'; it heard Helen Joseph, an old white Charterist, still listed under the Suppression of Communism Act so the press could not quote her, say: 'We opened the doors but you must go forward'; it heard messages of support from around the country and around the world; it heard a young poet's voice reverberate as he recited:

Now is the time
Now is the time to review the burden of the soil of
Nature ringed by the winds of time ...
Now is the time to give me roses, keep them
Not for my grave ...
Give them to me whilst my heart yearns for jubilee
Now is the time.

Most of all, it heard Allan Boesak, the preacher and orator, sweep them away, bring them down, rouse them, and make them think, all in one speech, with oratory on a par with Martin Luther King. 'We shall never give up,' he said. 'Those in power in this country have made the fundamental mistake of all totalitarian regimes who do not depend on the loyalty of the people, but on the power of the gun. They have not reckoned on the determination of the people to be free because they depend on propaganda, on deceit and on coercion. They have forgotten that no lie can live for ever, and that the fear of the gun is always overcome by the longing for freedom.'

'*Dis die waarheid*' ('That's the truth'), responded the crowd.

The new constitutional proposals, he conceded, would 'modernise' apartheid. 'It will be streamlined and in its new multicoloured cloak it will be less conspicuous and less offensive to some', but it would be there, a thoroughly evil system that could not be modified. 'We shall not be satisfied as long as injustice reigns supreme ... We shall not be satisfied as long as those who rule us are not inspired by justice but dictated to by fear, greed and racialism ... we shall not be satisfied until justice rolls down ... like a mighty stream.'

He addressed the touchy question of white involvement in the UDF, the point that had driven the black consciousness groupings to set up a rival front: 'We have seen with our own eyes the brutalisation of our people at the hand of whites ... We have experienced the viciousness and violence of apartheid, we have been trampled on for so long, but we must also say that it is not true that apartheid has the support of *all* white people. There are those who have struggled with us, those who have gone to jail, who have been tortured and banned and there are those who have died in the struggle for justice, and we must not allow our anger, which is legitimate, for apartheid to become the basis for a blind hatred for all white people.'

'Yes!' responded the audience.

They'd been won. And then his 'three little words'.

ALL: 'We want all our rights; not just some rights ... we want all of South Africa's people to have their rights.'

HERE: 'We want (our rights) here in a united and undivided South Africa.'

And NOW: 'We want all of our rights and we want them here and we want them now ...'

'For too long,' he raised his voice above the murmuring, bewitched audience, 'we have been struggling ... we have petitioned for so long now, we have been jailed and exiled and killed for so long now, but we are saying today: "Now is the time!" '

It was a tour de force. As Manuel noted, he used the stage built for him by the activists to brilliant effect. 'He saw the moment, he saw the great opportunity, and he put every bit of himself into it.'

Now it was up to Manuel and the other drivers of the UDF, such as Lekota, not to let slip this new moment.

CHAPTER 13

'I beg you, please be ungovernable'

THE KEY TO THE UDF, reflected Manuel more than two decades after its launch, was 'the extent to which it captured the imagination'. It appropriated the space created by the new constitutional dispensation and filled a vacuum in extra-parliamentary opposition. The government had to be cautious. To clamp down too harshly on an opposition set up precisely in response to its reform proposals would have immediately undermined the legitimacy of the reform, not only with its opponents at home and internationally, but among those coloureds and Indians whom it still might win over.

But the UDF needed momentum. It was like riding a bicycle: only forward motion made it effective. But it was a somewhat awkward vehicle. It had been built specifically to oppose the 'Koornhof Bills' and the new constitutional proposals, yet it had to be bigger than that. The hundreds of delegates who had attended its inaugural meeting had spoken clearly: they wanted a coalition against apartheid. Their problems extended far beyond the new constitution. They were about rising food prices, inadequate housing, unequal wages and education, about the fact that they had no voice in government.

The first steps were to spread the UDF to where it was not. Remarkably, given its history of resistance, the UDF had not yet been launched in either the Port Elizabeth area or further north in what was then called the Border region around East London. The reasons were manifold. In the Border region, which included the Ciskei homeland, the UDF had to contend with a repressive Bantustan state, more naked in its violence than almost anywhere else in the country. The delegation of leaders from the East London unions, mainly SAAWU but also the GWU branch there, had been detained as they were about to come to Cape Town for the launch. In years to come they were handed between the Ciskei and South African security police like punching bags, tortured and harassed, and sometimes killed. Many of the ANC activists, who were to form the backbone of the UDF, had been restricted after being released from Robben Island. One was Steve Tshwete who had come off the Island five years before after a 15-year sentence. He had returned to his hometown of Peelton, near King William's Town, to which he had been restricted. His restriction order expired, allowing him to attend the UDF launch. But he was puzzled by this new phenomenon.

'Who are you people?' he asked a group of activists including Manuel and Lekota in his smoky voice. Lekota, who had known him in prison, replied, using his clan name: 'But you know us, Thangani.'

'Yes, but when I left the Island you were in SASO,' rasped Tshwete, smoking his Gold Dollar cigarette. 'I haven't been told about this thing.'

'Well,' replied Manuel, 'don't you want to talk to Lusaka? We are the ANC.'

Which Tshwete presumably did as after that he ploughed his not inconsiderable political weight into organising the UDF in the Border region.

Further west in the city of Port Elizabeth, the UDF was almost nonexistent. Lekota made it his first stop after the 20 August launch. 'He was a vanguard in the best sense of the word,' said Manuel. Whatever the job description of 'publicity secretary' was, Lekota was incapable of sitting in an office. He drove from town to town, met with people, organised them. 'It would be quite impossible to look at that period without understanding the profoundly important role Terror Lekota played in constructing a sense of national resistance.'

He was also unfazed by authority or scepticism. Many of the churches in the townships in Port Elizabeth (known to locals as PE), for instance, feared the UDF was a communist organisation. He told them he was a Christian too, and if the church and Christians were not prepared to stand up for the rights of those who were downtrodden and denied, then surely communists would take over the organisation.

'You have to be honey badger when you organise,' he told me later. 'You have to *believe* in what you're doing.' Walter Sisulu had told him on Robben Island that 'the masses of the people are never wrong'. If they don't support you, then the leadership is doing something wrong.

Certainly, he impressed the people in Port Elizabeth with his confidence. Once he had most of the community organisations, teachers' and church organisations on side, he set about trying to find a venue to launch the regional UDF there. There was no suitable hall in the African townships. So he decided to ask for the Feathermarket Hall 'in town', that is, the white part of town. 'The comrades looked at me, and thought, "This chap? Is his head right?" I could see that hardly anybody thought this was a sane idea.'

But the more he thought about it, the more sense it made. So, with one or two nervous activists in tow, he went to the white municipal offices and asked for the hall. When they refused to countenance it, as the PE activists knew they would, Lekota asked to speak to the 'person in charge'. He then confronted the senior official who came to see him with the following question: 'Are you saying you're defying the government?' Lekota asked him.

'I'm not defying the government,' said the official warily.

'Look the government has allowed the UDF to be formed. And it's not banned, it's operating. How can you refuse an organisation that the government has allowed to operate? Refuse that it must have a meeting? It means you are against government policy!'

He hadn't thought about that argument until the spur of the moment, he admitted later, but it worked. The council officials went into a huddle, asked him if they 'could make a few calls', and when Lekota said he wanted a decision at that moment, the official relented.

'So we launched this thing in the Feathermarket Hall. Not in the township hall. In the *town* of PE. Comrades were thrilled with this thing.'

Manuel joined Lekota for that rally in December 1983. The victory of the venue was, it turned out, the easiest part of the meeting. Manuel chaired it, and it was the first sign that the notion of non-racial unity might fracture. The government had mooted the idea of a referendum among the coloured and Indian population to test the new constitutional proposals. Many Indian and coloured community leaders were attracted by the idea that they would, at

204

last, get some sort of say in their future. The more strategic thinkers in the NIC and TIC thought it might be opportune to organise a 'no vote' to vanquish any legitimacy the new constitution might have. 'The key challenge,' recalled Manuel, was that many of them called for a 'flexibility of tactics' – in other words, no blanket boycott. We can be one united front, they argued, 'but be flexible about how we moved'.

The conference, said Manuel, 'was an unmitigated disaster ... This movement, this UDF, was so young, people didn't know each other, yet it was growing in leaps and bounds.' Several thousand people attended the meeting, they all 'slept rough' in church halls or schools, and 'because that was so unpleasant the meeting went on through the night, the singing went on through the night, everybody was tired, nerves were frazzled ... trying to keep a conference like that together was an impossible task that we'd set ourselves.'

'Africans,' recalled Lekota, 'were very, very bitter' at suggestions from their Indian and coloured comrades that there might be 'flexibility' when it came to participating in a vote that excluded them. Lekota had supported a 'no' vote in the whites-only referendum held the month before in November. 'We have to look at the strength of the whites with us and decide how best their vote can be used.'[1] But the white vote was not a major issue for the UDF as there were comparatively few members. The possibility that the coloured and Indian constituencies in the UDF might be split over whether to boycott a referendum was indeed an issue. And for Manuel and his Western Cape comrades it was even trickier, given the substantial tradition that the politics of boycott occupied in the tradition of the Western Cape.

But the Western Cape could no longer keep to its own pace. Nor could Manuel. Now a national player, there were different balances that had to be struck.

The tidal wave of mobilisation, the manic energy to keep the pace going after the August launch 'almost destroyed all of it' by the end of the year. 'The big spirit of non-racialism almost ground to a halt,' said Manuel.

The crisis drove the leadership back to organisational basics. In some senses, it vindicated a line driven by an important grouping within the UDF in the Western Cape, a group that had sometimes been at odds with Manuel. It was a view that echoed the caution and priorities of the trade unions. 'Trevor's approach to organisation was to convene mass meetings at which, basically, he and Boesak would speak,' said Jonathan de Vries, the student who had become regional publicity secretary of the Front in the Western Cape. He laughed when he recalled his then trenchant views: 'He had an appetite, he was in his element, he was on top form when he was standing in front of a crowd. And at the time I considered that an egotistical conceit.'

But De Vries's views moderated over the years: 'I think that is a sign of leadership. I have a broader view now ... We needed to do that (hold mass meetings) but we also (needed to) spend time developing leadership in every community, so apart from having mass meetings we should have small meetings, give people literature, discuss things at a deeper level, so that if we get detained, there is a stronger leadership based in communities. (You) don't just come and sing songs and then go home, you actually are potential cadres in the underground in the ANC itself.' That was the biggest bone of contention within the Charterist grouping in the Western Cape, he said. 'I think Trevor always thought that view was a bit of a distracting waste of time, like an intellectual point.'

Manuel absorbed at least part of this message. When he returned from the Eastern Cape that Christmas in 1983, he realised the fragility of a unity built only on mass meetings. He and the UDF executive immersed themselves in organising the small towns of the Western Cape, as well as in the urban areas. The rural areas most ripe for organisation were those where the Food and Canning Workers Union was strong, ironic perhaps when the union itself had refrained from jumping into the UDF tide. Unity between Africans and coloureds was strongest in the small fishing towns of the West Coast and in the places where there were major canning factories such as Paarl, Robertson and Ashton. On the West Coast, in particular, the coloured and African communities were far more closely united across language and cultural barriers than was the case in the city. Many African workers had changed their names to 'coloured' sounding surnames, such as De Bruin, to avoid the harshness of the laws that afflicted Africans on the West Coast.

One such activist, who was to become a comrade and jail mate of Manuel's, was Maxwell Moss. Born and raised in the fishing town of Saldanha, Moss's mother's surname was Nkosi. She was of Zulu origin, but to avoid an almost certain fate of 'deportation', she had quietly changed her name before 1960 when Moss was born. A fledgling news reporter for the local *Weskus Nuus* (West Coast News), Moss became a valuable organiser for the UDF partly because of his ability to speak both Afrikaans and Xhosa fluently and because of his roots in the two main oppressed racial communities there. Manuel had recruited him into *Grassroots*, urging him to write about the 'real problems' people faced rather than only report on the kind of social events he did for *Weskus Nuus*. By the time the UDF was formed, Moss understood that he was part of a growing spider's web of ANC activists who were part of what he called the 'Popular Mobilisation Pillar'.

Also critical was a network of graduates from the University of the Western Cape who returned to their small-town homes, some in the Northern Cape, and became teachers or priests and began to organise on their home turf. 'And we had orators like Allan Boesak, who didn't take day-to-day responsibility but, afforded a stage, would leave a community that same day entirely committed to a united, democratic South Africa. It was a truly, truly remarkable period.'

FURTHER NORTH, IN THE Free State and Transvaal, the UDF had a 'battering ram', as Manuel called him, in the form of Lekota. In the early stages of the organisation, Lekota and Popo Molefe, the general secretary, were the only full-time paid officials of the UDF. They were paid R600 a month each. When the UDF had raised a little more money, it bought two Toyota Corollas, one for Molefe, the other for Lekota. 'Believe you me, I was forever in that thing going at least 160 kilometres an hour,' said Lekota.

Lekota drove the countryside flat: he went to the Free State, to Kimberley, to the Northern Transvaal, to the Eastern Cape, delivering pamphlets, talking to people in the townships. He was not keen to go back to jail, and so he perfected the subterfuge and circumvention. He'd leave the UDF office in Johannesburg with a carload of UDF literature, drive as though he were going to Soweto, out-wait the police who had been tailing him and then, with the assistance of helpful young lookouts, leave when the coast was clear. 'BRRR!' he recalled. 'From Jo'burg to Kimberley, give some comrades the pamphlets there. Bloemfontein! Give some comrades a load of these things. By 6am, I'm crossing the Vaal again and by 8am I'm back in Jo'burg, and when the police are watching our offices I go in like anyone who's just come from home.'

In apartheid South Africa, it was the last days of legal space for the extra-parliamentary political opposition. The UDF used this space to its utmost, invoking the strange legal contradictions that existed whenever they needed to. One day, the security police stopped Lekota on the road as he was driving out of Bloemfontein. They wanted to arrest him, but it had to be for *something*. He had long since dropped off his load of UDF literature. The police were nonplussed for a while, and then glanced down at his tyres. 'Look, your tyres

207

are old,' they said. 'We're arresting you.'

'Tyres!' he laughed. 'No, man! Special branch turning into traffic cops all of a sudden!'

As it happens, he told the police, I was just on my way to the garage to get my tyres changed. 'You can't block me.' And Lekota did exactly that, stopping at a nearby garage, phoning his comrades in Bloemfontein from a payphone to bring him money to pay for the tyres, racing against time with the security police who busily phoned the traffic cops to get to him before the new tyres were on his car.

It was these mobilising efforts, around the country and in the Western Cape, that brought the UDF back on track. It had threatened to fall off the rails after the contentious meeting in the Feathermarket Hall at the end of 1983. 'It was incredibly difficult to rebuild the trust,' said Manuel. The first national executive meeting of that year held in Pretoria sat through the night in an effort to undo the damage. In a sense it was forced to: the impending elections in terms of the new constitution were now firmly on the horizon; the whites-only referendum after the UDF launch in 1983 had endorsed the new constitution. There was now a sense of urgency about keeping this sometimes fragile front together.

Manuel was a strong proponent of an active alternative campaign to the white referendum. It would help mobilise support and consolidate organisation, as well as providing an ideological alternative to apartheid's proposals. Fortunately for the UDF, the government had dropped the idea of a coloured and Indian referendum. It may well have torn the young organisation asunder had it happened, but the government was probably equally wary of risking more political turbulence to upset the 'carrot' proffered by then prime minister, P W Botha.

The Western Cape, driven in large part by Manuel, thought up the 'million signature campaign'. It was a simple declaration of support for unity and non-racialism, and against apartheid. 'I could never admit with hand on heart that we collected a million signatures but we put in a bloody good effort and part of that effort was to take a group of non-racial people into areas where they had never previously been, in a way that frequently shocked residents,' said Manuel. So whites and coloureds went to Crossroads, the vast informal settlement on the eastern edge of the formal African townships of the Cape Flats; Africans went to the working-class coloured areas of Bonteheuwel and Elsies River, even to white areas. People crossed the Group Areas borders in ways they hadn't done for the past 20 years.

In Crossroads they quailed a little before the demands of its putative 'mayor', Johnson Ngxobongwana, who wanted his photograph on the petition. The 'illegal' African residents in the various informal settlements relied almost completely on the protection and patronage of various 'mayors' for survival. These leaders collected taxes in the form of protection money and promised to get their names on 'lists' that were to be presented to the authorities as part of a deal to stay in the Cape. It was a system of local governance that combined rural and urban traditions, where the weakness of both was exacerbated by government repression and the insecurity of the squatters. Eventually Ngxobongwana would turn, violently, on not only the UDF but on thousands of African squatters under rival 'mayors', with the active collaboration of the security forces. But at the time the UDF leaders struggled simply to come to terms with local customs – the subterranean dynamics in the squatter camps evaded them. Manuel was intrigued by the formality of the meetings. On blisteringly hot Cape summer days, one had to wear a jacket if one wanted to speak. Those who didn't have jackets would borrow them from another in the meeting for the duration of their inputs. 'These were rural traditions that I didn't understand.'

Countrywide, the UDF collected not much more than 400 000 signatures, but the numbers didn't matter. The campaign burned the UDF into popular imagination; non-racialism became something that was seen in practice not simply espoused in principle; and it laid the basis for the opposition to the forthcoming coloured and Indian elections for the tricameral Parliament.

THE ELECTIONS AND THE RUN-UP to them were part theatre of the absurd, part dangerous circus. Mostly they were a diversion from a harder battle that was threatening.

There was a sudden burst of activity in the Labour Party's Athlone offices: generally stout men in unfashionable business suits shuffled in and out, in marked contrast to the singular lack of activity in the years before. Election meetings began to be held around the Peninsula. Many were broken up by the UDF.

In mid-1984, Manuel and several others went to an election meeting in Mitchell's Plain called by Peter Marais, a chubby, mustachioed politician, who later became a National Party MP in the Government of National Unity. He had formed a party that went by the hopeful if inaccurate appellation of the

People's Congress Party. Manuel and his UDF comrades arrived with a priest in tow, and as soon as the meeting had opened with a prayer, the UDF priest raised his hand: 'I want to ask a question,' he said.

'But there's nothing to ask. Nobody's spoken yet,' said the meeting's chair. The question the priest intended to ask was: Would they allow questions?

Theresa Solomon, by then an active resident in Mitchell's Plain, walked to the podium and said loudly: 'This man is a respected priest in Mitchell's Plain. You come from outside. You won't let the priest talk and he's a very important man in the area.'

'No,' insisted the chair. 'He said he wants to ask a question and all we've done is pray.'

It began a long, apparently illogical argument about when the priest should be allowed to ask questions. But there was stringent logic behind it. When Theresa Solomon tried to grab the microphone to hand it to the priest, the meeting organisers grabbed her, and then the rest of the UDF team grabbed them. Mayhem ensued and the meeting couldn't continue – which was the point. Manuel, Solomon and the rest were arrested and charged with public violence. One of those charged was Logan Wort, then a youth activist, later to work at the Treasury. Considerably shorter than Manuel, and eight years his junior, there is scant resemblance between them. In the trial, Peter Marais, who was the state's chief witness blamed everything on Wort, who was accused number two. He was the instigator, the troublemaker, the cause of the meeting's disruption.

Dullah Omar, who represented the six UDF members in court, asked him; 'Mr Marais, are you sure about this?'

'My Lord,' said Marais to the magistrate, 'I don't know what this lawyer wants. Of course I'm sure. It was accused number two.' Then Omar asked his clients to stand, and said again: 'Mr Marais, are you sure?'

Marais replied: 'My Lord, does he think that I don't know that number two there is Trevor Manuel, the secretary of the UDF?'

'Are you sure?' asked Omar.

'Yes, I saw him in Hanover Park, and someone told me, this is Trevor Manuel.'

Manuel looked back and smiled at the cops who knew their key witness had bumbled. 'You monkeys,' he mouthed.

'Will the real Trevor Manuel please step forward?' asked Omar, and when he did, he closed his case: 'I have no further questions.'

After the lunch adjournment, Marais returned and apologised. He had 'confused' Wort with Manuel, he said. It was quite some confusion, but the magistrate accepted it, convicted all of them and gave them suspended sentences.[2]

The elections themselves were similarly farcical. Reporters in Cape Town's newsrooms had fun writing stories about candidates running neck and neck 'with one vote each … voting is expected to pick up later in the day when the candidates' wives get off work.'

Statistics matched the anecdotes. On 22 August, almost a year to the day of the UDF launch, just over 11 per cent of registered coloured voters in the Cape Peninsula cast their votes. And just over half of all eligible voters had actually registered. In rural areas, the poll was slightly higher: one constituency in the Northern Transvaal, for instance, recorded a poll of 59 per cent. But that figure represented only 751 people.

The only battle that really counted was in the Peninsula, where the vast majority of coloured people lived. The leader of the Labour Party, Allan Hendrickse, whose constituency was in the small Eastern Cape town of Uitenhage, won his seat by a substantial majority of nearly 6 000 votes. But even then, less than half the eligible voters had registered to vote, so his actual mandate was less than 20 per cent, as the UDF pointed out.

Despite the massive dent to the legitimacy of the new dispensation, the government held fast. The low poll was because of intimidation or perhaps, as P W Botha charged, because 'coloured people showed no interest in exercising their political rights'. They are 'unaccustomed to democracy', said one cabinet minister.

The UDF was jubilant, proclaiming an 'overwhelming victory'.

The polls in the vote for the Indian chamber of Parliament, in elections held a week later, were as disappointing for government.

But as the UDF basked in its triumph, the government began to close in on the space that the new constitution had created. In August, the government detained several national UDF leaders, including Lekota. Popo Molefe went into hiding, but was caught by security police two months later outside the UDF offices in downtown Johannesburg. They were detained under Section 28 of the Internal Security Act which allowed for 'preventative' detention.

THE DETENTIONS CATAPULTED MANUEL into the national hot seat. He went to Johannesburg to become acting general secretary of the UDF. Without much

211

experience of working outside Cape Town, he was suddenly in a different environment at the centre of national attention. 'Those detentions are both in and of themselves significant but also in terms of my own development, being foisted with so much responsibility. I mean, hold on, I'm 28 years old. I don't have a fraction of the political experience that many others have. I don't know Jo'burg. My political development has been largely coloured but spills over into African areas in the Western Cape. But in political terms I'm incredibly green.'

Manuel had to deal with an entirely different dynamic of demography. In the Western Cape, the majority of people were coloured and many of those, particularly adults, had been cowed by the apartheid government. In the rest of the country, the majority was African. And much more militant. As Manuel made the move north, so huge and tumultuous demonstrations began in the townships of the Transvaal. It was the start of an entirely new period in South African history.

Sebokeng, Evaton, Sharpeville, Boipatong, Bophelong. Years later, Manuel could reel off the names of turbulent townships as if citing an epic poem. In many ways, it was an odyssey that gripped the country. On 3 September 1984, the day that the newly elected – if that is the word – Indian and coloured MPs were inaugurated, tens of thousands of Africans staged a stayaway in the Vaal Triangle, the dense, industrial area south of Johannesburg, to protest against rent increases. The rents in some of those areas were disproportionately high. For instance, the lowest rent in Sebokeng – R50 a month – was higher than the highest rent in Soweto, at R48 a month. On that day, 30 people in those townships died in clashes with the police.[3]

Local government in African areas was falling apart. The government sought to give greater autonomy to black local councils as part of its constitutional reform package, but the new legislation 'was more of a product of a constitutional conjuring act than of a real understanding of the material needs of the townships'. Firstly, the townships had no real fiscal base. The government had sharply reduced its contributions to town council budgets. But townships were really only 'dormitory towns' for white industry and households with no enterprises of their own. Thus rentals became the predominant financier. Many of the councils were in debt, with the Soweto Council by then budgeting for a R30 million deficit which it hoped to cover through increased rents and service charges.[4]

Secondly, the councils had no legitimacy. The elections, held the previous year, polled no more than 15 to 22 per cent of the vote. For such bodies to raise rentals during a time when the African working class was squeezed by inflation and recession simply exposed the bankruptcy of the scheme devised to contain black urban aspiration.

This was the climate that Manuel walked into when he took over the role of general secretary. He traversed the northern part of the country, following in Lekota's footsteps, organising and consolidating. He went to see Winnie Mandela, then banished to Brandfort in the Free State, he went to Kroonstad and Bloemfontein, to Vryburg in the northern Cape. He learned about a new country. When asked by a financial publication a month after the September uprising if the UDF was behind the unrest, he replied: '(It) is the harshness of the State and its complete lack of sensitivity in dealing with genuine grievances that are behind the violence. It is not the UDF that used the police against the people, nor does the UDF force people to carry passes or put up their rents.'[5]

His period in the national office coincided with the long sit-in in the offices of the British Consulate by six UDF leaders who were on the run from the police, including one of its presidents, Archie Gumede. It was excruciatingly embarrassing for the British government, then led by Margaret Thatcher, which the UDF saw as far too close to the Pretoria regime. But it drew daily attention to the question of detention without trial and the plight of detainees. The consulate officials made life as uncomfortable as possible for the refugees. There was no bathroom – the fugitives were escorted to the toilet for half an hour each morning; and consulate officials tried by persuasion, and irritation (one played scales on the piccolo all night) to get them out.[6] 'The UDF has made tremendous gains locally and abroad and has brought the question of detention without trial into sharp, effective focus,' said Manuel in an interview shortly after the men had taken refuge in the consulate. 'The consulate saga has at times taken on something of the character of a chess game: errors are being forced on the government.'[7]

Manuel used the opportunity to spell out the endgame scenario of the violence escalating around him. 'The government says the UDF is promoting a climate of revolution,' an interviewer put to him. 'Whether or not it is a fact, would the UDF like to see such a climate in SA?'

The UDF is committed to the achievement of a non-racial democracy by peaceful means. We believe that the strongest weapon in this is the organised voice of our people. The 'revolutionary' climate is in fact being generated by the heavy-handed manner in which the State at all times responds to reasonable demands … What is ignored is the fact that the situation in SA is unique and grossly unsatisfactory. It is unparalleled for a government to retain power for so long a period as the Nats have been in power without consent or legitimacy and buttressed by the gun. We must move away from the premise that white rule in SA is God-given or normal. The basic demand for all in SA to be included in the processes of decision-making in a unitary state is perfectly reasonable.[8]

This period saw the first wave of 'ungovernability' that swept swathes of the country, but not yet the Western Cape. The protests almost always started over local issues – rents, bus fares, removals of shacks, or grievances of schoolchildren. Manuel told the press that it was the heavy-handed manner in which the police dealt with the protests that led to the violence. Black schools were in disarray. It was the beginning of the people's insurrection which Issel had dreamed of.

But the UDF was unable to give it cohesive national leadership. Many of its leaders were in detention, it was involved in a high-profile and stressful campaign in Durban with the holing up of the 'Consulate Six', and it didn't have the necessary roots to control or give leadership to the masses of increasingly angry people. And while the ANC in Lusaka called for its supporters to 'intensify the struggle' and for 'the sharp conflicts now raging in Sharpeville, Evaton, Sebokeng, Lenasia … (to be) widened and extended to other areas',[9] the ANC operatives inside the country struggled with a more brutal reality on the ground. 'There was always a tension,' said Murray Michell. 'Always, always, always a tension. We didn't control everything … you knew you had to encourage it, knew you had to spawn it. And it was fine in the build-up … because you knew you were talking about rendering the apartheid regime inoperable, ungovernable. And it didn't matter how you achieved that. But how do you exercise your discipline through that and emerge at the other side, providing leadership?'

This was the major contradiction for the UDF leaders. The insurrection that many of them had pushed for threatened to gallop ahead without them. Even the ANC, which had pushed for ungovernability, seemed shocked by the extent of the internal violence, in addition to the police violence, visited on communities. When Manuel was in Johannesburg, the first 'necklacing' – the brutal method of burning to death suspected informers or collaborators

214

– was still a year away. When it happened, it shook the nation, including those in exile. In 1987, when Pius Langa went to the Harare conference on children in detention, the ANC leader Oliver Tambo called the South African delegation aside and said: 'Wherever I go, people confront me about this. I don't want to dictate to you, but don't you think it's time to stop?'

'That made an impact on people,' said Langa.

The problem in this period was that instructions from the ANC might get to the first, even second or third level of leadership, but in the townships in the grip of battle, actions, and reactions, were largely spontaneous.

There was a major exception to this, though, in the Vaal Triangle and East Rand because, at last, local UDF affiliates had found common cause with the large black industrial trade unions. Most were affiliates of the Federation of South African Trade Unions, which had been wary of throwing in their lot with the 'populist' UDF a year before. But now the gravity of material hardships, plus some focused political work, especially by Lekota and Molefe, had changed the climate. The two UDF leaders had, after much lobbying, been allowed to address a regional FOSATU meeting earlier in 1984. They arrived before the appointed time, to find some of the union officials explaining to their members why it would be a mistake to align with the UDF. Lekota asked politely whether he could just clarify 'a few things'. 'It was a real *tsotsi* move and effectively he just took over the meeting there and then,' said Cheryl Carolus, Manuel's co-secretary in the Western Cape UDF. It helped that Chris Dlamini, the president of FOSATU, had two children who were members of the Congress of South African Students (COSAS) and who had recently been detained by security police in an ongoing clampdown. Dlamini was sympathetic. A few months before he'd told a union congress: 'We must unite to fight the bosses in the factories and we must unite in the communities. We are facing increases in rents every day and our children are facing terrible conditions and bad education in the schools.'[10]

On 5 and 6 November hundreds of thousands of workers stayed away from work across the Transvaal. Estimates ranged from a conservative 300 000 to about 800 000 who stayed away.[11] In addition, about 400 000 students boycotted schools. It was a significantly different show of strength than any previous demonstration, and prompted big business for the first time to consider a political way forward. 'It is difficult to establish just how great the support for the ANC is among blacks,' Tony Bloom, the chief executive of the Premier Milling Group, told the Wits Business School later that month. 'But I venture to suggest it is very substantial. There is an inherent inevitability of talking to the ANC. It is not a question of if, but rather when.'[12]

For the government, though, it was still a question of 'if'. In December of that year, the Consulate Six came out from their retreat in Durban. Five were arrested and charged with treason.

That month, too, Manuel came back to Cape Town and his co-secretary Cheryl Carolus went up to Johannesburg to take over the reins of the national UDF. Carolus and Manuel were close, politically and emotionally. When they were elected joint regional secretaries of the UDF in 1983, they decided that they would either both do the job, or neither of them would. There were similar sharing arrangements in the Transvaal, 'but ours was a *pact*', Manuel said.

Manuel returned to the start of what would become a violent war in Crossroads. It began with a threat from government that all the African squatters in Cape Town would be moved to Khayelitsha, a new township in the Cape about 30 kilometres from the city, set on windswept dunes even more barren than where the established townships had been built.

With the tumultuous uprisings in the townships of the East Rand in 1984 fresh in his mind, Manuel addressed a meeting at St George's Cathedral early in 1985 in a decidedly more militant tone than he had adopted before. If the government tries to touch the people of Crossroads, he said, 'we will make Sebokeng look like a Sunday school picnic'. Manuel by then had become vaguely aware of the power struggles and protectionism that ruled in Crossroads: the township's activists in the UDF were even more wary of Ngxobongwana. But what mattered to him then was whipping up mass resistance to the proposed removals to Khayelitsha.

There was not much space then in Manuel's reality for a nuance that would develop in later years. The aim was to use almost every threat by the government to try to mobilise opposition. Yet it came in a context where divisions within the anti-apartheid movement in the Western Cape were still deep. One sign of these was the visit of Senator Edward Kennedy to South Africa in early 1985. Archbishop Desmond Tutu had invited him and Allan Boesak had joined the invitation. But it sparked a noisy backlash from black consciousness groups in Johannesburg and Unity Movement groups in the Cape.

In retrospect, it was a brilliant move on the part of Tutu, building as it did the international movement towards sanctions against South Africa. In less than two years, the US Congress was to pass the Comprehensive Anti-Apartheid Act, which hurt South African business and the government more deeply than any demonstration at the airport against Kennedy possibly could have.

But in South Africa it sparked a major debate on 'imperialism', and even the UDF, which in the end backed the invitation, reported ambivalently on the event. 'Only 26% of the American voters actually supported (then President Ronald) Reagan,' reported *Grassroots*, in a story that barely quoted Kennedy.[13] It was a reminder of the traditions that shaped political struggle in the Western Cape. 'The politics of Cape Town were so unique,' recalled Lynne Matthews. 'What we marvelled at … there just weren't the kind of *issues* you had to deal with in other communities (in other parts of the country). Here there were always added issues around political lines and affiliations. It was so much easier to work in those communities where everyone was just ANC.'

The luxury of divisions was becoming harder to sustain in the face of an entirely new era of repression launched by the government. Although it released most of the UDF and union detainees on 10 December 1984, the authorities also charged the most prominent UDF leaders with treason, including two of its presidents, Albertina Sisulu and Archie Gumede. Several leaders were still in hiding, and soon a more sinister type of containment would emerge in the form of the apartheid death squads.

In April, the UDF General Council met at Azaadville, an Indian township outside Krugersdorp. The theme of the meeting was 'From Protest to Challenge, from Mobilisation to Organisation'. The intent of the UDF was to somehow govern ungovernability. It also broadened the Front's working principles to include clauses that articulated opposition to any legislative programme that clashed with democratic principles.

In other words, it shifted from being a Front set up specifically to oppose the new constitutional proposals to one that opposed the system of apartheid in its entirety. It was now effectively the main internal opposition to the apartheid government. It did not see itself as an alternative to the ANC. Rather, it was 'another link in the process of liberation'.[14] Molefe and Lekota were re-elected but the jailed treason trialists were replaced.[15]

The UDF also appointed full-time organisers in some areas. In the Transvaal, it appointed Murphy Morobe, who had been a student and organiser of the 1976 Soweto uprising. Another was a young schoolteacher in Cradock, a small farming town in the Eastern Cape hinterland. His name was Matthew Goniwe. He was a maths and science teacher, one of the best qualified in the inferior system of Bantu Education. He had been a political prisoner for four years in the Transkei and was married with two young children. He was dedicated to his teaching, but also found time to organise the youth and a civic group to counter rising rents in the township of Lingelihle where he lived. The year before he had been transferred to a school in Graaff-Reinet. He refused to go and was dismissed. After that he was appointed a full-time organiser for the UDF, a task to which he proved himself equally dedicated. In Cradock he established a model of community organisation, setting up street committees and organising house meetings. Cradock became one of the best organised communities in the country despite the heavy hand of the Eastern Cape security police, which monitored him continuously and detained him frequently.

In the Western Cape there was a strong move to consolidate the affiliated organisations, the backbone of the UDF, which had become weaker as their best leaders were absorbed into the Front's leadership. At its March conference, just before the Azaadville meeting, there was considerable shake-up in leadership. Carolus and De Vries were among four executive members who declined nomination, saying they had decided to focus on building up the UDF affiliates. Oscar Mpetha was not re-elected as president. He was replaced by Zoli Malindi, an ANC veteran and member of the Western Cape Civic Organisation based in the African townships. Mpetha's ousting, said the press at the time, 'was partly as a result of political conflict in Cape Town's townships over recent months'.[16]

Manuel retained his position as regional secretary but was joined by a young township activist from the United Women's Organisation, Miranda Qwanashe, and Ebrahim Rasool, who had come to prominence through the Muslim Students' Association.

In the following months, Manuel moved between Johannesburg and Cape Town, filling in for Lekota and Molefe who had gone back into hiding after their UDF comrades had been charged with treason. Lekota had grown close to Manuel. He'd stayed with him in Cape Town, taken meals at his mother's house, even run with him between meetings. He often outran Manuel, said Lekota, although he could see that Manuel thought of him as 'this dumpy so-and-so'. Indeed Lekota was solidly built, and short, but extremely fit in those days. He was struck by the contrast between Philma Manuel and her son. 'It's difficult to see how such a gentle soul, such a gentle person, can have almost a ruffian for a son like Trevor,' he told me. 'The guy is well cultured but very *hard*.'

He was to experience Manuel's hardness during this period when he desperately wanted to leave the country. 'Because, really, man, I don't want to go back to jail and I can see these guys are going to lock me up again.' But, *'Hey*, Trevor put his foot down. We had a hell of an argument, but we failed to persuade him. That's when I decided I must go to Natal.' It was too dangerous to leave the country without the consent of his comrades, said Lekota, because 'that would raise the question of whether you may not have been sent on a mission of the old order, the regime. That of course is something I was not prepared to risk.'

So Lekota stayed and hid out on his home turf in Natal until he made a cardinal error. On 21 March 1985, the anniversary of the Sharpeville massacre in 1960, the police gunned down more than 30 protesters in the Eastern Cape township of Langa outside Uitenhage. Many of them had been shot in the back. In April, Lekota was asked to go to the area to speak to 'the structures' together with Curnick Ndlovu, the new UDF national chair, and Molefe. Molefe telephoned him to tell him where to collect his plane ticket. He was arrested as he landed at Port Elizabeth airport – proof that the phone was never safe as a means of communication.

As for Molefe, he didn't even make it to PE. He sat in the airport lounge in Johannesburg, heavily disguised, reading the *Citizen*, a pro-government newspaper. When the security police found him they said exultantly, 'Hey, Popo!' Molefe stuck his head further into the paper, and they said: 'Hey, Mr Molefe.' Molefe raised his head to enquire who they might be looking for and they replied: 'Please man, Popo, the game is up.'

It was. Both men were arrested and charged with treason. The subsequent trial, long and drawn-out, became known as the Delmas Treason Trial after the small Eastern Transvaal town where it was held.

CAPE TOWN, THOUGH, WAS still relatively untouched. Manuel and the UDF busied themselves with preparations for the rally to commemorate the thirtieth anniversary of the Freedom Charter. The rally was set down for 30 June, a Sunday, four days after the anniversary of the adoption of the Freedom Charter on 26 June 1955.

On the Friday, a UDF activist from the Eastern Cape phoned Manuel to tell him that Matthew Goniwe, his fellow organiser, Fort Calata, and two others, Sparrow Mkhonto and Sicelo Mhlauli, had disappeared on their way back to Cradock from a UDF meeting in Port Elizabeth. Manuel, and most of the nation, held their breath. Manuel had met Goniwe and Calata before the UDF launch in Port Elizabeth, and again in Grahamstown, a little university town about 100 kilometres from Port Elizabeth. They were 'a very impressive twosome', thought Manuel. There had been a few mysterious disappearances in the Eastern Cape before, notably the three men of the local civic organisation, known as the 'PEBCO Three', including Qaqawuli Godolozi, with whom Manuel had worked and stayed. They had disappeared without trace the month before.[17] But there was always doubt. Perhaps they had skipped the country, gone to join MK? The doubt showed just how new this era of repression was.

On the Friday, two days after their disappearance, Fort Calata's wife Nomonde got copies of the local *Herald* newspaper which she distributed in the township. On the front page was a picture of Goniwe's car which the men had been travelling in; it was a charred shell. On the Saturday the bodies of two of the men were found, Mkhonto and Mhlauli. Everyone feared the worst for Goniwe and Calata. Their bodies, burnt, stabbed, mutilated, were found on the outskirts of Port Elizabeth two days later. 'That Sunday,' said Manuel, 'I was quite beside myself. The rally was in Athlone and I had to tell people what I'd heard. I went to that rally completely distraught.'

The guest speaker at the rally was also an Eastern Cape activist, Mkhuseli (Kusta) Jack, a militant and articulate member of the student group COSAS, who would also be frequently detained and badly tortured by the police. Perhaps the full import of what had happened to the Cradock Four hadn't sunk in then; perhaps the new turn the government had taken hadn't been grasped.

Jack had come from the tumultuous townships of the Eastern Cape, where community councillors had been chased out (one had been brutally murdered by the 'necklace' method), where a consumer boycott of white shops was in full force, where almost nothing was functional in the townships.

On the heels of the awful news, Jack calculated the odds. This is what he said: 'Comrades of the Western Cape, please, I beg you, please be ungovernable. If the Boers open the door, you close it; if they close the door, you open it; but please, please, please, comrades, be ungovernable. You are the last part of the country that is not ungovernable. Now we've lost our comrades from

Cradock and I beg you, please be ungovernable.'

That night Jack slept at the Maitland house where Manuel and Matthews lived. All night Manuel heard noises at the window. He was convinced there were police outside the house. He had not feared detention before, or arrest. But that night he was full of fear. He, Jack and Matthews slept on mattresses in the passage, away from all windows. 'We thought, this is death now, you know.'

The atmosphere in the country changed sharply from that day. It was not only a new horror that was induced – as Manuel said, the four men had died 'a *terrible* death' – there was also a newfound sense of defiance. The legal niceties were gone.

By the time of the funeral of the four men on 20 July 1985, it was clear that the resistance movement felt the same. Almost 70 000 people attended – remarkable, given the repressive atmosphere and the fact that in some regions, the Western Cape for instance, the UDF leaders asked people to pay for their own transport. Beyers Naudé, the Afrikaans cleric who had been excommunicated from the NGK for condemning apartheid, was there. So was Allan Boesak. So was Archbishop Tutu. So was almost every anti-apartheid activist in the country. 'We are facing in this government the spiritual children of Adolf Hitler. The four leaders did not die by accident or mysteriously. Our people know who did it. Our people believe it is the police who did it and this government must stop protecting those who did it,' said Boesak. But he called for restraint and discipline as did the other church leaders.

'We are dying left, right and centre under apartheid,' said Victoria Mxenge, a lawyer and UDF executive member from Natal. Her husband Griffiths had been murdered only four years previously. Before a month had passed, she would be the next victim of hit squads.

That day, in that small township tucked between the khaki-coloured koppies of the eastern Karoo, two enormous flags were unfurled: the green, gold and black of the ANC, and more defiant still, the red flag of the Communist Party. It was a moment when everyone caught their breath, not least the churchmen who stood under the hammer and sickle as they spoke, a fact that state television made much of afterwards.

The UDF executive got word at the funeral that a State of Emergency was going to be declared that night. Most of them decided not to go back on the buses to their respective towns. Manuel, Carolus, Valli Moosa and Murphy Morobe crammed into a large hired Audi driven by Derek Swartz, then secretary of the Eastern Cape UDF. He had been one of the last people to see Goniwe alive at the meeting he attended in Port Elizabeth. As they drove down through the mountain passes to the coastal city of East London, they saw police erecting roadblock after roadblock. When they arrived in East London, Swartz said to their horror: 'Comrades, I'm so relieved because I've been driving with this ANC and SACP flag from the funeral.'

'Madness, complete madness,' said Manuel, to do that in a climate that now spelled death.

They made their way up to Peelton, a village not far from East London on the edge of what was then the Ciskei 'homeland' where they held a frantic executive meeting in Steve Tshwete's village. The Ciskei, as nasty as its authorities were, was still not under a State of Emergency so technically they could meet legally. As far as Tshwete was concerned it was a declaration of war. Three weeks later, he spoke at Victoria Mxenge's funeral in Peelton. She had been brutally stabbed to death outside her home in Durban.[18] He broke with all calls for restraint. 'If we have to liberate ourselves through the barrel of a gun then this is the moment.'[19] A Ciskei soldier was killed at the same funeral. It was Tshwete's last speech in South Africa for several years. Shortly after that he fled over the Lesotho border, heavily disguised.

There was still one small legal space: the Western Cape. No State of Emergency had been declared there. Manuel and his comrades grabbed the gap. Within a month, the Cape Town activists decided to organise a march to Pollsmoor on Wednesday, 28 August, 'to fetch Nelson Mandela'. It was both extraordinary and cheeky but it 'actually gripped the imagination'. It also marked the moment when Dullah Omar, the thoughtful advocate, threw in his lot squarely behind the Charterists, leaving his old Unity Movement connections behind. He attended the press conference on the Friday, five days before the planned march, where Manuel told the gathered journalists that 'on Wednesday we will march to Pollsmoor from everywhere, we will go fetch Nelson Mandela'.

The group who drove the plan was the core ANC/UDF group that included Manuel, Issel and Carolus. It fired up a city outraged by what had happened in other parts of the country. Scores of groups pledged to march: students from the townships, civic groups, workers, academics and students from the mainly white University of Cape Town. 'The Boere got a fucking big skrik (fright),' Issel recalled, when they saw the widespread support for the march.

After the press conference, Manuel drove Zo Kota and Miranda Qwanashe, both UDF executive members back to Guguletu, where they lived. There was a police roadblock at the entrance to the township. He dropped them just outside to avoid the roadblock, and watched as they walked towards the police. That was the last time he saw them for several years. They were both detained and afterwards went into exile.

Manuel then went to Athlone to the office of Essa Moosa, an activist lawyer who worked closely with Omar. When he arrived there, one of Moosa's colleagues, Ebi Mohamed, gripped his arm, hauled him inside and said: 'You might be the last one out.' He then heard that almost all of his comrades had been detained under security laws that now allowed for 'preventative' detention. Even Allan Boesak, whose clerical and international role had always been a protection, was detained in Malmesbury and later charged.

Issel discovered the news the same way when he had bumped into a fraught-looking Cheryl Carolus 'with a big parcel of fish and chips' at Moosa's office. He phoned his home and was told that 'there are a lot of cops in the house. With big guns. They're waiting for you.' Manuel had a similar message from Lynne. 'I had one instruction and that was that I couldn't go home,' recalled Manuel.

So he moved silently from house to house for the rest of the weekend and into the next week.

On the Wednesday people from all over the Peninsula tried to march. Police set up roadblocks to stop them from going to Athlone Stadium where the march was to begin, so they just marched from wherever they were. The police deployed themselves around the Peninsula and beat and arrested would-be marchers wherever they found them. 'Riot police and SADF (the army) waded into ordinary people – mostly non-violent demonstrators, including middle-aged nuns – with sjamboks, tear gas and plastic bullets, as well as those responsible for the stoning and petrol bombs. Casualties – dead, wounded, missing, detained, arrested – run into countless hundreds,' wrote Margaret Nash a few months later in the journal of the Black Sash, a civil rights lobby group.[20]

A setback or a victory? Issel, who had a slightly apocalyptic view of escalating conflict, was excited: 'The police did it for us. The police smashed the march ... So that became the event!'

But Manuel, who hid out in a house in Hanover Park, was frustrated. He knew it spelled the end of the political space they had tried to occupy.

For the next two months he disappeared into the shadows.

CHAPTER 14

'Say not the struggle naught availeth'

I N MANUEL'S LIFE, LYNNE MATTHEWS was like an anchor at the end of a very
long chain that bobbed through some turbulent surf. This intense round
of political activity kept them apart. His travels had intensified the absence.
Moreover, orthodox fidelity was not something predominant in the cultural
milieu of the interlocked Cape Town activist circle at the time.

Manuel was attractive in many ways. He was powerful in the alternative
world that the resistance movement created for itself; he was lean and tall
with a thick crop of dark hair. His slightly affected dress sense – the beret, the
revolutionary T-shirts – made him look a little like an exotic Cuban soldier
who had wandered south from his comradely duties in Angola.

He also liked women, not in the sense of pretty young things whom he
could have wooed. He enjoyed the company of intelligent, independent
– and powerful – women. Perhaps it was because he had grown up in a
household with six women when he was a child, four after his father and
two grandmothers died. He had seen the women in his life hold difficult
emotional and financial situations together. His mother had worked hard to

get him into one of the best available schools, and his two older sisters, Beryl and Pam, had gone out to work at a young age to help keep the finances flowing at a crucial stage in his life.

His relationships were fluid: he maintained his attachments even as he began others. But during this period his seven-year relationship with Lynne began to falter. Partly it may have been the intense way in which he sank himself into political activities. Partly, too, it was because of the similar intensity with which he engaged others, including women. He and Cheryl Carolus were close during this time, politically, intellectually, emotionally. They both had the same ability to network with small groups, to persuade large ones, and to charm and rouse crowds. They both respected each other's space. They both put their political lives before almost anything else.

But the combination of all this put a strain on his relationship with Lynne and by the time he went into hiding, he and Lynne had broken up. 'She wanted kind of nothing to do with me,' he said. In fact, so disordered was his life at the time that he wasn't even quite sure whether she'd moved out of their shared house in Maitland.

But then this Friday 23 August, 'happened'. He went from the street into hiding. Circumstance, and perhaps Lynne's emotional solidity in this turmoil, brought them back together.

For the two months he spent on the run, he was reliant on Lynne as his base as he moved from house to house, keeping one step ahead of the security police. 'At the end of the line would be Lynne who would get my clothes, take them to school (where she taught), leave a key, and someone would pick them up.' Whatever her feelings of disaffection at the time, she rallied, stayed in their Maitland house, and made sure he got what he needed. Some of the time Manuel donned Muslim garb, sometimes a workman's overalls. He cut his hair short, wore a fez, and drove an old bakkie – a pick-up – so he looked like one of Cape Town's many Muslim artisans.

Sometimes he miscalculated, unable to quite get into the spirit of his disguise. Wearing the flowing robes of a devout Muslim one Friday noon in Grassy Park, he strolled down the street to a corner café to buy cigarettes. It was a moment when every other Muslim man in the neighbourhood was in Mosque. The café, owned by a sympathiser with the resistance movement, was often monitored by the security police. This was one such day. When Manuel saw their car, he realised his theological oversight and hoped the police didn't. He quickly turned a corner and then 'lifted my dress and ran like hell'.

It was in these months that 'ungovernability' descended on Cape Town and other small towns in the Western Cape. Mitchell's Plain was ablaze. Night after night, blazing barricades blocked the enormous arterial roads that carved through the vast township. Local reporters learned how to make their staid company cars mount the high pavements to escape the fires or the police, whichever was more immediately threatening. The townships in the outlying areas were rocked by protests and dissent, and then invaded and occupied. In Zwelethemba, the depressed little African township outside Worcester, school students boycotted the only high school and stoned and petrol-bombed the house and car of a councillor for the local black authority. 'Many areas in the Cape Flats, Paarl (Mbekweni) and Worcester (Zwelethemba) are in an intermittent or semi-permanent "state of war"', wrote Margaret Nash.[1]

One of the reasons for the relative quiet in Cape Town in the first half of that year was precisely the new constitutional dispensation that the UDF so bitterly opposed. 'The New Deal meant handouts to the coloured community and major construction projects. Both stimulated the Western Cape economy and protected it from the worst effects of the countrywide recession.'[2] In addition, the government had eased tensions in the African squatter communities by announcing a moratorium on influx control. More significantly, State President P W Botha had announced that the coloured labour preference policy was to be scrapped.

It should have been a monumental announcement, but for Africans in small townships in the outlying areas, little changed.

Africans in Worcester, for instance, could still not get jobs as bus drivers – so they boycotted the buses. The tiny four-roomed houses were crammed with an average number of 11 to a house, and, to become self-financing, the local black authority had raised service charges by 25 per cent in an area where more than half the community was without jobs.

Police reacted with vengeance to the subsequent protests, sealing off Zwelethemba twice in 10 days in September, patrolling the streets with quirts and guns and arresting nearly 150 people. In Ashton and Robertson, small towns in the Boland where canning factories had been organised by the FCWU, protests were met with similar harshness. At times, youths were picked up by the police and made to stand in the hot midday sun in a police yard, their heads covered with black garbage bags.

By mid-1985 the atmosphere changed sharply in the Peninsula itself. The sweeteners in the form of construction contracts to small companies had petered out, and African people still suffered marked economic deprivation and political frustration.

This time, too, the police were more systematically brutal, particularly in coloured areas. In just one month after the disrupted Pollsmoor march, at least 33 people were killed in political violence, most of them by the police.[3] And there were tales of a gratuitous show of force on the Cape Flats.

In Bishop Lavis, a poor coloured working-class area, a 15-year-old was shot on his way back from the shops while walking past a burning barricade. His name was Ivor Constable. As he crawled to his gate, bleeding heavily from stomach wounds, his 17-year-old sister tried to help him. She was warded off by policemen who brandished rifles at her. Then they pulled Ivor by his feet and threw him roughly into the back of a police van. He survived the shooting but his digestive tract was severely damaged. In Elsies River, another vast working-class area on the Cape Flats, people sitting in their tiny front gardens were set upon by patrolling police and whipped.[4]

The government dispatched a battalion of Zulu-speaking policemen from the eastern seaboard province of Natal to help quell the protests. This battalion knew no local people, did not speak the local languages well, and were particularly alienated and brutal.

Meanwhile the students around the Peninsula had taken to heart Kusta Jack's words: it had stung them when another student leader from the Eastern Cape had accused them of 'living in a holiday resort while the rest of the country is fighting for liberation'. First, they boycotted schools and universities. When Carter Ebrahim, the new coloured minister of education in the tricameral parliament ordered the closure of schools in early September, they tried forcibly to reopen them. 'If the Boers open the door, then close it; if they close it, then open it,' Jack had said.

Teenagers, 15, 16, 17 years old, were arrested on the streets on their way to school, taken into police stations and beaten up: 'I was slapped through the face and told to shut up. I was so exhausted I collapsed to the ground. I was pulled by my hair by the black policemen and continuously slapped through the face. My breast was punched several times and I was ordered to stop crying which I found it impossible to do. The same policeman hit my knee with a quirt with tremendous force.' This was the experience of 18-year-old Colleen Fick of Athlone, related by her 19-year-old sister to a press conference because Colleen was too distraught to speak.[5]

Hardly a day went by in those months without tear gas, protests, beatings, sometimes death.

But on 15 October, amidst all the daily brutality, there was an incident that fissured the routine unrest by its premeditation and callousness. On that day, an orange freight truck belonging to South African Railways cruised slowly down Thornton Road, one of the main north-south roads of the middle-class suburb of Athlone. Thornton Road was fronted by neat, modest houses with patches of front gardens. It was – is – a street punctuated by small trading stores where neighbours meet and chat. Midway is Alexander Sinton, the local high school. It represented the quintessence of an established, modest, lower middle-class coloured neighbourhood, unlike some of the newer more desolate areas further east on the Cape Flats.

But the conflict in Cape Town had grown to such a pitch that even this quiet area became a battleground. Alexander Sinton students were at the forefront of vociferous protests and boycotts, which sometimes erupted into sporadic stone-throwing. On this occasion, a small group of students had gathered on the corner of Thornton and St Simons Roads, near Alexander Sinton, which had already been raided and tear-gassed by the police when the schoolchildren and parents tried to reopen it in defiance of the government order.

There was a tension in the air that day. Amina Abrahams, a young mother, sensed it and went to fetch her children early from the nearby Muslim school. On her way home, she had even thought it prudent to take shelter in her friend Zainab Ryklief's house, on that very corner. There were other children in the Ryklief home that day, friends and cousins of theirs. But one was nervous of the protest outside and wanted to go home. Sixteen-year-old Shaun Magmoed, who lived further down in Thornton Road, said he would accompany him.

At that moment, the railways truck which had cruised once down the street and turned, was on its way back. As it passed the corner of St Simons Road, a stone hit it. The crates on the back of the flatbed opened and several policemen jumped out and opened fire. Shaun had turned back to the house as the shooting started. He had pushed the children with him inside and run to the bedroom.

It was only later when Amina Abrahams ran to the bedroom that she discovered that both of her children, aged seven and ten, had been shot and wounded, her friend Ryklief, who had given her shelter, had been shot in the shoulder, and Shaun lay dying on the bed.

Two others were shot dead in the street – 11-year-old Michael Miranda and 21-year-old Jonathan Claasen.[6]

Zainab Ryklief's home was marked by gunfire, its windows shattered and its walls pock-marked. The police had stormed into the house and levelled guns at them as the children lay gravely wounded, with Shaun already dead. Three local reporters and photographers and an American CBS crew had followed their instincts when they saw the railways truck cruising slowly down the street and stayed put rather than rush after the rest of the press corps covering unrest in Wynberg. The television pictures of armed policemen leaping out of crates and shooting children were beamed around the world. 'The fact is that they were committing a crime,' said a police spokesman the next day. 'We will use any method to combat them.'

Notwithstanding the disproportionate punishment – death and maiming – for the crime of stone-throwing, the fact remained that most of those dead and injured were children, and some had even been indoors at the time.

The next day everything in Cape Town changed. What had been a series of demonstrations turned into low-level warfare. Members of the white parliamentary opposition, the Progressive Federal Party, visited the Magmoed family. While they were in the house, a police van drove down the street and was immediately surrounded and shaken by an angry crowd. The police shot their way out of trouble and soon the neighbourhood was surrounded by Casspirs (armoured police vehicles), which shot canister after canister of tear gas into the street. Even the parliamentarians had to dive for cover behind the low walls of the Thornton Road front yards. 'If this continues the Western Cape will enter a period of civil war in the very near future,' warned Jan van Eck, a PFP member.[7] That night, as police patrolled the streets of Athlone outside a local mosque, they were shot at from the mosque. At least one policeman was seriously wounded, and Abdul Fridie, who was 29 years old and lived in Athlone, was shot dead in the mosque.

On that day, too, Manuel, still on the run, came to the Magmoed house in his Muslim disguise to pay his respects, under the nose of the police who surrounded the house. And the day after that he appeared at a press conference in Hanover Park to say that the UDF wanted 'the entire civilised world to be made aware of what was happening in South Africa'.[8]

Four days later, the three youngsters and Fridie were buried in a funeral attended by about 12 000 enraged mourners. Manuel was there again.

Thousands of people marched down Voortrekker Road to the cemetery, three blocks from his childhood home. 'Death to Apartheid' read some of their banners. And when a military helicopter hovered over the procession, reported a local newspaper, it 'provoked a forest of clenched fists and a torrent of abuse as it buzzed above the crowd'.[9]

The Trojan Horse incident, particularly because it was broadcast around the world, made an immediate impact on world opinion. Like its predecessor in classical history, this Trojan Horse was, above all, a consummate act of treachery even given the stark battle lines that apartheid had drawn. The fact that children were the main victims made it more outrageous.

But it was a time when no trend seemed to be absolute. Days after the funeral the government released most of the Western Cape detainees. 'Fine,' thought Manuel. 'They've found nothing on these guys; it's safe for me to surface.'

MANUEL RETURNED TO WORK at the UDF office in Longmarket Street in the city centre on 23 October. The police found him there almost as soon as he'd walked in. Four burly policemen took him down to street level in the cramped old elevator, while Veronica Simmers, his colleague who had sewn the ANC flag for the Ferrus funeral, ran down the stairs, pushing the elevator button so it stopped at every floor. As it stopped, little groups huddled at the elevator doors, bearing witness to his detention. Manuel and the four policemen crammed into a Daihatsu Charade, a small economy car new on the market. There was an advertising jingle for the Charade at the time that went: 'Some call it impossible, we call it the Charade.'

As the packed little car drove through the gates of the Caledon Square police station a few blocks away, a police officer at the gate gasped at the squeeze: *'Som noem dit ontmoontlik maar ons noem dit die Charade,'* he said, repeating the tagline in Afrikaans and breaking some of the tension inside the car.

Manuel was taken to Pollsmoor where he was subjected to long hours of interrogation. 'It was clear they wanted to link me with the Boesak sedition trial,' he recalled (in the end the charges against Boesak were withdrawn). Manuel was already well known; both the warders and security police were careful not to allow 'something to happen' to him, as it had with others. 'But it was clear that these guys had done their homework,' he recalled. 'They knew when I'd crossed the border (to Botswana in 1979), they assumed I'd made contact, they knew I'd been there again in 1980, they knew that I'd applied for a passport after it had expired and that it had been turned down.'

But it was all circumstantial. The police could not make a case that he had joined the ANC, and they had no definitive proof to link the UDF to the ANC. Manuel was somewhat protected by his public profile, now not only in the Cape but nationally, and also by the fact that he was in a prison rather than the more isolated and lawless police cells. He developed an instinct for what to admit, and how to mask his real activities.

So, yes, he'd been to Botswana, he told them. The first time he'd hitch-hiked there and met this woman – God, such a beautiful woman, he fell completely in love. Completely. Her name? Edith Modisane. This was going to change his life. *She* would change his life. He would go back to Botswana and marry her, and, oh, by the way, he was a civil engineering technician, he could build roads and bridges and dams, and Botswana needed young people with skills, and this way he could contribute to the development of Africa and spend his life with the woman he loved.

And so he went back, four months later to marry her. But his dream crumbled. Edith wasn't what he'd thought her to be. He discovered, to his sadness, that he was just one of many men in her life.

Maar jy lieg vir ons. Wat van die ANC? (You are lying to us. What about the ANC?)

The ANC? There was no ANC there. Guys! Guys, you were 24 once, didn't you ever fall madly in love?

And he would answer them in Afrikaans, Afrikaans speakers who bristled with insecurity about their status and their language, and then suddenly switch to English. 'It's a big mind game, but normally it's their mind game, but I think I was reasonably mature enough to be able to manage them. I wasn't afraid of them.'

He had been really afraid when he had spent the night on the floor of his passage with Lynne and Kusta Jack, soon after the murders of the Cradock Four, but now he wasn't afraid.

It was a calculated boldness – his critics may say recklessness – that was to carry Manuel through every decision he made in his political life: through the years of the Emergency and prison, through arguing with a bruised and suspicious constituency that negotiations were the only way forward to, later, introducing an economic policy that had many of his old comrades singing derogatory songs about him at mass meetings.

While he was in Pollsmoor the State of Emergency was extended to the

Western Cape on 26 October. He didn't know at the time. He was in solitary confinement, with no visits from family or lawyers, and no newspapers. But he did have one visit that moved him profoundly. One day there was a rustle at the grille of his cell. He looked up and there was an older man he didn't recognise. 'Psst! Comrade Trevor,' said the visitor. 'I'm Comrade Kathrada. Trevor, you're doing well. All the comrades upstairs, Comrades Sisulu, Mbeki, Mhlaba, and Mlangeni all send their best. Be strong!' And then he was gone. 'Long, long after he walked away I stood in a state of total shock,' said Manuel more than two decades later.[10] Kathrada understood the trauma of isolation and had come to give him succour.

Ahmed Kathrada, Nelson Mandela's jail mate, had by then been moved from Robben Island with the other Rivonia trialists to Pollsmoor Prison. Christo Brand, a warder who, in Kathrada's words, was simply 'a wonderful human being', had brought him to see Manuel on his way to the doctor.[11]

In November, just before Manuel was released, Kathrada sent him a Christmas card and a poem, copied in his 'amazingly neat, fine hand'. By Arthur Hugh Clough, it read:

> Say not the struggle naught availeth,
> The labour and the wounds in vain,
> The enemy faints not, nor faileth,
> And as things have been they remain.
>
> If hopes were dupes, fears may be liars;
> It may be, in yon smoke conceal'd,
> Your comrades chase e'en now the fliers,
> And, but for you, possess the field.
>
> For while the tired waves, vainly breaking,
> Seem here no painful inch to gain,
> Far back, through creeks and inlets making,
> Comes silent, flooding in, the main.
>
> And not by eastern windows only,
> When daylight comes, comes in the light;
> In front the sun climbs slow, how slowly!
> But westward, look, the land is bright![12]

Manuel was released three weeks before Christmas. The police could find nothing to charge him with. Instead, they restricted him under a strict banning and house arrest order – 'six-six, report to the police station', like the one imposed on his childhood mentor Taufie Bardien for so many years.

He also discovered that many of his comrades were still in jail. But there were still pockets of 'ungovernability' despite the Emergency. In Athlone there would be small weekly protests, and by the middle of December the remaining detainees went on a hunger strike. Manuel fasted in solidarity. He would go daily to the Buitenkant Street Church, opposite Caledon Square. His aunt Hester, now a widow, had moved into a flat above the church after being evicted from District Six. 'I'd talk to her for hours, sitting there on the steps, fasting, sunrise to sunset.' And every Sunday evening he would break his banning order and go to a service in the church, which was becoming known for its outspoken opposition to apartheid. 'I wanted them to arrest me for coming to church.'

When he came out of jail, he also discovered that Lynne was pregnant. The baby – their eldest son, Govan – must have been conceived in the period when he was on the run.

It was a circumstance that changed both of their lives. Lynne was teaching and in the days of apartheid – as hard on women as it was on people of colour – single, pregnant teachers were dismissed. She had been through six weeks of agony, not being able to communicate with him about the enormity of what lay ahead, nor knowing whether he was safe. 'It was really, really awful,' she recalled.

Manuel threw himself into the relationship with renewed commitment and the two decided to marry. Lynne, a feminist and agnostic, was at first dubious. She had decided that it was better to live together 'for a few more years'. But she relented when he said to her mother: 'Mrs Christian, I'd love to marry Lynette.' And of course there was the issue of her job security.

And so they were married in a small ceremony at the Kensington home of Manuel's sister Pam. No party, no big do, because so many of their friends were still in detention. They found a priest sympathetic to Lynne's alternative views on religion and tradition to conduct the ceremony. Lynne wore a 'cottage dress' and sandals, no stockings, much to both their mothers' disapproval. There was no ring, and she didn't change her surname, which upset them even more. 'I was always independent and it was my way of preserving my independence,' she said.

'It was very low key,' said Manuel. Only their immediate family were there, as well as the Von Söhnen sisters from Stellenbosch. Later he said: 'We didn't want to attach too much importance to it. We were actually quite hard. Hard on ourselves. Hard on our view of life.'

≡ PART FOUR: Emergency ≡

1986-1989

CHAPTER 15

'The enemy faints not nor faileth'

IN 1986, MANUEL WAS ABOUT to enter a period that would challenge him to go beyond being a militant political leader with a sharp tongue. It was a period that was to hone his temper and emotions. His bravado was supplanted by a more strategic courage. The years of the Emergency, when he was forcibly taken out of circulation, forced him to focus on what leadership meant in a situation where the more vulnerable shared living quarters with him on a daily basis.

But at the start of that year, Manuel was beset by boredom. Now under a banning order, he was forbidden from going to the UDF offices or to any public gathering. Partly to irk the security police, partly out of enervation, Manuel would stand on the corner of Corporation and Longmarket Streets in the city, outside the building that housed the UDF offices. 'The security police watched me doing this and I'd wait for comrades, and walk with two comrades around the block.' He wasn't breaking his banning order: he stayed out of the office, he remained in the Cape Town magisterial district, and he was in the company of no more than two people at a time. 'They'd get really pissed off. A lot of it was show.'

The State of Emergency persisted in most areas. By the end of 1985 more than 10 000 people had been detained and more than 1 000 were still being held.[1]

Manuel's ennui was soon shaken. Now there were signs that the murder of the Cradock Four was not an anomaly but heralded a new era of extra-judicial and internecine violence, stoked by the police.

In 1986, four union shop stewards in Mpophomeni, a little township near Howick, north of Pietermaritzburg, were murdered. They had been workers at the British Tyre and Rubber subsidiary Sarmcol, part of a group fired en masse after a legal strike. The workers, staring starvation in the face as Sarmcol was the only factory in the area, set up small-scale manufacturing co-operatives in a way that was so creative it galvanised the whole community. 'If the government does not build factories here, then we must make our own,' said Phineas Sibiya, shortly before he was murdered.[2]

Alec Erwin, then a senior official in the union to which the Sarmcol workers belonged, recalled countless attempts at peace talks with an increasingly hostile Inkatha, led by KwaZulu homeland leader Mangosuthu Buthelezi. 'The violence started (in Pietermaritzburg) just after Mpophomeni. So we had to do two things: we had to begin trying to defend our shop stewards, but we also felt it was important that we begin talking.' Partly this was to stem a rising tide of violence from young UDF comrades, who began launching ferocious attacks on areas they perceived to be Inkatha strongholds. Several meetings between unionists and senior Inkatha officials resulted, all of them secret. Eventually, they got to a point in about 1987 when Erwin and Jay Naidoo, the general secretary of the Food and Allied Workers' Union in what was then the province of Natal, began to work in earnest on a meeting between Thabo Mbeki, then head of international affairs in the ANC, and Buthelezi. 'It was going to be in London, and we'd set it all up,' said Erwin. But then a pamphlet, claiming to quote Mbeki but which probably emanated from the security police, was circulated in the Natal townships. It excoriated Inkatha and Buthelezi, and the latter just used that as a pretext to say 'no, he's not coming'.

By then the Congress of South African Trade Unions (COSATU) had just come into being – the united federation that unionists had worked so hard to create during the previous four years. At its inaugural conference in Durban in December 1985, its new president Elijah Barayi had made the cardinal mistake of calling Buthelezi a 'dog', a huge insult in Zulu culture. Notwithstanding the careless speech of Barayi, local union leaders such as Erwin and Naidoo worked hard with more moderate Inkatha leaders to create a climate of peace. The security police worked equally hard to undo their efforts. A senior union leader, Maxwell Xulu, was discovered in 1991 to have been working for the security police. He used his position in the union, under the guise of radicalism, to discourage peace talks and to fuel hatred between Inkatha on the one hand, and the UDF and COSATU on the other.[3]

In Manuel's home town, there were also signs of more sinister containment of opposition. In March 1986, seven suspected guerrillas were shot dead at a crossroads in Guguletu. Police told the media that the men were 'terrorists' who were planning an ambush on a police bus and they were killed in the shoot-out that ensued. But it was clear even on that day that this was not true. Reporters interviewed residents of the Dairy Belle hostel, positioned directly opposite from where the killings had taken place. Some had seen the entire incident. They said the police shot some of the men at point blank range as they lay wounded on the ground.

Chris Bateman, a *Cape Times* reporter, interviewed several people. One, Mr General Sibaca, told him a policeman had 'kicked' one of the wounded men on the ground, and then 'sort of turned around and looked for some kind of confirmation which he got from a – I imagine – a senior officer. This is General's relation of events to me, and he turned back around and then shot this guy at virtual point blank range'[4].

In the post-apartheid era, there was evidence that not only had the police shot them in cold blood, but the police's own agents may have been responsible for supplying them with weapons in an agent provocateur operation. The same thing had happened in Duduza on the East Rand the year before when angry and untrained youths were given faulty hand grenades which blew up in their hands. Their supplier was Joe Mamasela, who worked for the security police.

On the night of the shooting of the seven young Guguletu men, state television showed grisly footage of the aftermath, including a scene where a man named Christopher Piet had a rope tied around his waist and was dragged to a police van 'like a dog'. Years later his mother told the Truth and Reconciliation Commission that she had quickly switched off the TV. For days afterwards, police invaded her small house in Guguletu, ostensibly searching for weapons. On one occasion an officer asked why she always had a candle burning in her house: 'I cannot live without switching on my candle because I am always in prayer,' she told them.[5]

Violence, and defiance, swept Cape Town in waves that year. As cold-blooded as the killing of the Guguletu Seven had been, there was little to compare with the chilly collusion between the security forces and leaders from the Crossroads squatter camps that turned Cape Town's vast informal settlements into a war zone for more than half of that year. Ironically, the main collaborator in the subsequent destruction of all the satellite camps that surrounded Crossroads was none other than the leader the UDF had adopted as its own – Johnson Ngxobongwana.

Since the end of 1985 there had been sporadic conflicts between members of Ngxobongwana's committee and 'comrades' who were loyal to the UDF. The death of a community councillor in the adjacent formal township of New Crossroads on Christmas Eve in 1985 – he had been hacked to death then set alight in his car – had provoked calls for revenge from some of Ngxobongwana's supporters.

For years, Ngxobongwana and his committee had set themselves up as an informal – if powerful – local authority in Crossroads. They collected tithes from residents in exchange for protection from the white authorities, but also for protection from themselves. The previous year, Ngxobongwana and 169 women had been arrested in New Crossroads, a new township built to resettle some of the older Crossroads residents. They had been arrested after protests against rent increases. Ngxobongwana and his committee raised money from both Old and New Crossroads to pay the bail. When they were acquitted, not all of it was returned to residents. This sparked a violent series of clashes: one of Ngxobongwana's lieutenants who lived in New Crossroads, was wounded in a hand grenade attack. In response, Ngxobongwana's supporters burnt down a crèche in one of the satellite camps that was used as a meeting place for 'comrades', and 'arrested' three members of the United Women's Organisation, holding them captive for several days in a container shed. 'The children are being very disrespectful to the fathers ... If the government (or) police say they have any help for us, they can come and help us. We want to find the guys who have the hand grenades,' said one of Ngxobongwana's supporters.[6]

Sam Ndima, a committee member loyal to Ngxobongwana, echoed these sentiments. 'The maqabane (comrades) have to stop making petrol bombs and holding "kangaroo courts". We will not allow them to beat and punish their own people.'[7]

In fact there were real grievances among many of the older residents. Many had been the victims of rough justice dispensed by the youth in the townships. Consumer boycotts were mercilessly enforced during the 'Black Christmas' period when white shops were boycotted, and older people were assaulted and humiliated by the youth, sometimes being forced to drink vegetable oil or eat soap powder.

The conflict coincided with a promise by the government to 'upgrade' Crossroads, but only on condition that the satellite camps were cleared and their residents relocated to Khayelitsha. In February, Ngxobongwana's committee set up and policed their own 'local authority' elections for a new committee, in which Nxgobongwana claimed 3629 votes (a Mr Langa who came second in the poll, won only 522 votes). But less than 10 per cent of the area's 80000 residents actually voted at all.[8] Ngxobongwana used his new authority to push the government to upgrade Crossroads and clear the surrounding areas (which housed his enemies).

The year before Ngxobongwana had told me that all the people from the surrounding squatter camps should be moved to Khayelitsha. When I asked the UDF spokesman whether this was not against policy, Ngxobongwana's comment was denied. It was not UDF policy, but clearly it was Ngxobongwana's policy and he happened to find a perfect coincidence of interests with both the security forces and the government authorities responsible for black affairs.

In late March 1986, shortly after the massive ANC funeral for the Guguletu Seven, a war began in the informal settlements. One Thursday Crossroads men were hailed by Sam Ndima, told to bring whatever weapons they had and go to Ngxobongwana's office. They were to wear white cloths on their heads and legs so they would be recognisable to one another. From then on they became known as *witdoeke*. That night about 300 *witdoeke* invaded New Crossroads and seven of them were killed in the ensuing battle. Police vans accompanied the *witdoeke* on their mission but did not intervene. UDF affiliates, including the Western Cape Civic Association (WCCA) said after the attack that Ngxobongwana 'through his actions, has brought grief to the families of these seven men who died away from their homes ... Our people must resist being made cannon fodder by people like Mr Ngxobongwana.'[9] The hard irony was that Ngxobongwana was in fact the chair of the UDF affiliate, the Western Cape Civic Association, at the time.

By mid-May, the conflict had turned into a war. Hundreds of *witdoeke* invaded the neighbouring satellite camps, burning shacks and attacking those who resisted. Again, they were accompanied on their mission by police in armoured cars, and sometimes soldiers. 'The police at no stage attempted to stop the vigilantes from burning our houses,' said one Nyanga Bush resident in an affidavit. After they had burned about 200 houses, some of the residents returned to try to put out some of the fires. 'The police had not left and when we attempted to get back to our houses, they fired on us.'[10]

By the second week of June, despite a court interdict restraining the vigilantes and police from attacking squatter camps, every satellite camp had been destroyed. About 70 000 people were left homeless and about 100 were dead. In the end, many of the refugees were forced to move to Site C, an informal settlement near the hated new township of Khayelitsha.

The Crossroads war significantly shifted the terrain of political battle in Cape Town. The UDF in the townships suffered a major defeat, and there was little their beleaguered comrades in the coloured areas could do to help them. And although the State of Emergency was lifted on 7 March, the legal space to organise, not only in Cape Town but around the country, was now massively constrained by a new, deadly level of violence and internecine conflict stoked by the police.

In the midst of this gloom, there was a sliver of hope when the Eminent Persons Group (EPG) visited South Africa. Co-chaired by Olusegun Obasanjo, the past military ruler of Nigeria (who'd handed over power to an elected government) and Malcolm Fraser, a former prime minister of Australia, the EPG was conceived as 'a united Commonwealth response to the challenge of apartheid'. Effectively, it was a compromise as British Prime Minister Margaret Thatcher was vociferously opposed to sanctions.

'None of us was prepared for the full reality of apartheid,' began the Eminent Persons Group's report on its mission. 'As a contrivance of social engineering, it is awesome in its cruelty. It is achieved and sustained only through force, creating human misery and deprivation and blighting the lives of millions.

'The degree to which apartheid has divided and compartmentalized South African society is nothing short of astounding.'[11]

On the day the Guguletu Seven were shot dead, the EPG began a series of meetings, first with several cabinet ministers, then with Allan Boesak.

On Sunday, 9 March 1986 they met members of the UDF's National Executive in Johannesburg. Manuel, in defiance of his banning order and taking advantage of this newly created space, flew to Johannesburg for the meeting.

The following Thursday, 9 March, back in Cape Town, the UDF executive in the Western Cape met the EPG delegation at a Newlands hotel. The Commonwealth Group had seen Nelson Mandela in Pollsmoor Prison the day before. 'He impressed us as an outstandingly able and sincere person whose qualities of leadership were self-evident. We found him unmarked by any trace of bitterness despite his long imprisonment. His overriding concern was for the welfare of all races in South Africa in a just society; he longed to be allowed to contribute to the process of reconciliation. We all agreed that it was tragic that a man of his outstanding capabilities should continue to be denied the opportunity to help shape his country's future, especially as that is so clearly his own profound wish.'[12] After meeting the EPG, the UDF delegates reported back to the General Council of the organisation at the Lutheran Youth Centre in Athlone. In the middle of the meeting, Noel Williams, Maxwell Moss's fellow activist from the West Coast, burst in, called Manuel aside and said: 'There's shit. I've just been to your house. The cops have your house covered front and back. I don't know what you're going to do.'

Manuel and Lynne Matthews, who was then nearly six months pregnant, were still living in Sylmore Poggenpoel's house in Janssens Road, Maitland. The house was a semi-detached cottage – similar to his mother's house in nearby Kensington. There were two things he could have done, Manuel reflected later. He could have stayed out and gone on the run again. But Lynne was pregnant and there was no telling for how long he'd have to stay underground. Or he could go home and make his undoubted arrest politically costly for the government.

While he considered the options, he went with Williams to his sister Pam's house. She also lived in Kensington, near their mother, with her husband Calvin Barron and her first-born child, Dylan. He drank a cup of coffee, then made his decision. First he asked Williams to go to the Cape Sun hotel in the city where the EPG was staying. Williams was to ask for its secretary, Mary Mackie, and tell her that he had been arrested for reporting back to the UDF General Council on the meeting with the Commonwealth Group. Then he asked his brother-in-law to drive him home. They circled the block, Manuel crouching low in the seat, as Barron described the cars he saw parked around the house.

One block to the north of Janssens Road is Royal Crescent. First Avenue cuts across both streets, and on the corner of First Avenue and Royal Road was a field that stretched to the back of Manuel's house. Two coloured police officers in an unmarked car were keeping watch in Royal Crescent near the field. Manuel crept up on them from behind, rapped sharply at the window and spoke to them in Afrikaans.

'Hey, man! Wat soek julle ouens hier? Vir wie hou julle dop? Wat gaan aan? Ek stap hier verby en ek sien julle hier sit. Wat maak jy?' (What are you looking for here? Who are you keeping watch for? What's going on? I'm walking past and I see you sitting here. What are you doing?')

After they'd recovered from the start he had given them, the two struggled to hide their embarrassment. Here was the fugitive, the wanted man, chatting to them, not running from them. He knew that the more senior security police were stationed right outside his front door. One was a large officer called Jan Louw, whom Manuel had got to know well over the years and would get to know even better.

Manuel continued addressing the two sheepish coloured officers: 'Look, you see that fence over there,' he said, pointing to the back of his house. 'I'm going to walk across that field and then I'm going to jump over the fence and then I'm in my house. OK? You didn't see anything. Voetsak!'

'You can't do that!' shouted one of the cops in alarm. 'Jan's there in front … Hy's daar voor. Moenie kak maak nie, asseblief. Anders moet ons jou skiet!' ('Please don't make trouble, otherwise we'll have to shoot you!')

Manuel ignored them and began running across the field. Instead of going over the fence the back way, he ran around to the front. His house was one away from the corner. To pass it, he had to run across his neighbour's driveway. Two cars were in front of his house; the third, with the two coloured policemen, had driven around to the front. 'Now I'm running: I know I'm running home.' One of the cars tried to block him as he tore across the neighbouring driveway but he leapt over it. Then Jan Louw – pronounced by the Cape Town activists always with a soft 'coloured' 'J', as opposed to the white Afrikaans 'Y', to Louw's apparent annoyance – began running after him. He grabbed Manuel from behind, one arm around his neck, a shotgun in the other hand. As much as he yelled at Manuel to stop, Manuel kept moving – walking now, not running, dragging Louw behind him. Then he shouted, calling the neighbours to come out. 'Look, they're going to shoot me in the street!' Manuel carried on, dragging Louw to his front gate. By this time, two other officers had come to his assistance. 'I can't let you get in,' said Louw.

'I need a jersey, that's what I need. That's why I want to go home!' yelled Manuel. He called for Lynne at the gate: 'Hey! I need a jersey.' Lynne, alarmed by the fracas outside her gate, came out with a jersey. Later she admonished him: 'Are you mad? How can you misbehave like that?'

Manuel knew why. As he was pulled to a police car, he called again to the neighbours: 'Come see! I want you to see that I'm healthy and strong. If I don't come back, look at their faces!'

The police took him to Maitland police station, the same cells where Imam Haroun had died in custody 15 years earlier. Manuel was beside himself with anger. He turned on the police and told them: 'This police station has a history. This is where Imam Haroun was murdered by your predecessors.'

Louw promised him that he would be there only a few days and would appear in court the following Monday on a charge of breaking his banning order. 'Not on your life,' replied Manuel. 'I will not stay here even for one night.'

'When you appear in court on Monday,' replied an equally irritated Louw, 'we'll see who has won this round.'

'We will see,' said Manuel.

Meanwhile Lynne had called the lawyer Essa Moosa's office. An attorney rushed to the police station. And Williams had undertaken his mission to find the EPG secretary. Manuel, in the back of the station, knew that he had set himself a major challenge. He could not stay in the police station without losing face. He continued 'stirring' with the police. Eventually they put him in back office, not even a cell, with one cop to guard him. At about 1.30am the following morning, the policeman in the front office came to call him. His lawyer stood in the charge office beaming. He'd come to bail him out. He was to appear in court the following day. Louw, red with anger, was also there. He said: *'Jy dink jy's te groot en belangrik maar ek sal jou nog kry.'*

When Manuel appeared in court the next day, it was packed with supporters and journalists – and almost the whole of the EPG secretariat.

The case was postponed. Later that month, in a completely unrelated but fortuitous event, Winnie Mandela and Henry Fazzie, also restricted under similar Emergency banning orders, went to court in the then Transvaal and had them overturned. So Manuel, from then on, assumed he was no longer

245

banned either and resumed his daily political work. His court case was struck off the roll.

By now he had developed a reputation for taking the security police head on. At a public meeting in Johannesburg shortly after this incident, he was 'deployed' by his comrades to tell a suspected security policeman to '*fokof*'. 'But it's a public meeting,' objected the policeman. 'I said: *fokof,*' said Manuel. The policeman turned around and went out.

Manuel may have acted out of instinct to some degree – he was known then, and later, for a quick temper. But it was also, crucially, a lesson in calculated risk-taking. He knew that if he had gone on the run, he would have been incapacitated perhaps for months. His wife was pregnant and that was also a major consideration. His best chance was to be arrested precisely when the EPG was in town. He also knew that his defiance and subsequent temper tantrum was about establishing the limits of power when he had the chance. 'I grew up in an area with gangsters. All you needed to do with a gangster was to look him in the eye and say, fucking take me on. Call it street wisdom, call it whatever, but relative to cops, the whole issue of power is very important.'

It recalled the time he and his friends had taken on the armed gang in the train a decade before. 'Same stuff,' he reflected. 'It's that stuff that lives with you.'

For one small moment, at the onset of the most repressive era in South Africa's apartheid history, the enemy had, in fact, failed.

CHAPTER 16

'Unnecessary noise'

THE EMINENT PERSONS GROUP LEFT THE COUNTRY in May 1986, a pall of smoke from the shanties around Crossroads embedded in their memories. The group had been struck by the apparently random violence of the police. 'While we were in South Africa, we encountered or heard of violence and its manifestations nearly everywhere we went. We did not have to seek it out: it was a daily phenomenon.'[1] The Group recounted an incident where it accompanied a white lawyer and distraught black mother looking for her child in the Northern Transvaal.

> He had reportedly disappeared after a bus in which he had been travelling to a funeral with a youth group had been stopped and its occupants fired on by police. After encountering denials at one police station, we tracked the boy, of about 14 years, to the Groblersdal police station. Although the duty officer was helpful initially, it took the lawyer over two hours of persistent effort to overcome the reluctance of successive police and security men to produce him. Threatened with a complaint to his Minister, the senior officer finally produced the boy. He

was limping; his face was bruised; and his shirt was splattered in blood. He said he had not been fed or given medical attention: his injuries had been received while he was being arrested, but he had also been slapped at the police station. He was denied bail on a charge of 'trespass' (he had been found taking refuge on a white-owned farm). We could not imagine that the boy's mother would have had any chance of overcoming the police's obduracy when it took an experienced and skilful white lawyer so long to do so.[2]

In Cape Town, police invaded Arcadia High School in Bonteheuwel after pupils demonstrated. They beat the children with the heavy rubber whips known as sjamboks. 'The School Committee reported that the police seemed to take "particular pleasure to damage the faces of the pupils" and that "children had to drag themselves between two rows of policemen as the sjambok blows rained down on them." Five were hospitalised; a number were scarred for life; and one reportedly faced the likelihood of losing an eye. Two pupils were charged with "public violence" but released two days later without any allegations against them.'[3]

On 19 May 1986, just before the Commonwealth Group left the country, South Africa launched military raids against the capitals of three neighbouring countries – Zambia, Botswana and Zimbabwe. All three were Commonwealth countries. The raids were ostensibly aimed at ANC bases but several civilians, and citizens of those countries, were killed. It may have been part of a war of attrition against the ANC, but mainly it was the manner that the reactionary forces within the South African government had chosen to show their contempt for the Eminent Persons Group.

South Africa sank under a welter of violence. The UDF tried valiantly to continue its work, but it was severely weakened by repression and – certainly in Cape Town – by its own internal differences. The national leadership had been knocked by the detentions and by the two treason trials going on. In addition to the Pietermaritzburg trial, Lekota, Molefe, and several others were now standing trial for treason in Delmas, a small town in what was then the Eastern Transvaal.[4]

In Cape Town, the ANC underground, acting in the name of SACTU, the ANC-aligned trade union, set up the Clothing Workers Union (CLOWU), mainly run by Johnny Issel and his then wife Zubeida Jaffer. It spelled hope, initially – an attempt to stamp a presence among the majority of the working class in Cape Town, the garment workers. But it soon caused friction, particularly between Manuel and his old friend Murray Michell, and between Issel and several other UDF and ANC leaders, including Michell. Michell had been drawn into CLOWU through the underground structures but soon realised it was being used as a 'recruitment centre' for armed activists outside the discipline of existing underground structures in the country.

It was 'a kind of an erratic, rabble-rousing attitude towards politics. There was no sober appraisal of organisational tasks and no kind of systematic plan,' said Jonathan de Vries, who also clashed with Issel at the time about whether COSAS, the national school students' group, should organise in Cape Town. (De Vries, who thought COSAS was basically a 'recruitment ground' for the ANC's military wing, Umkhonto we Sizwe, was in favour of more locally based organisation with deeper roots in the community.)

UDF leaders, for their part, worried that the Front, as the central political resistance body, was being denuded of strategic support. Underground ANC activists, who had worked closely with the UDF from its formation, were also concerned about a proliferation of underground structures, often with no accountability. Michell was even called out of the country at one point when the ANC leadership realised the dangers of 'small structures' like the new union being used to spawn military recruits.

Certainly, within the next three years, there would be several young Cape Town activists, notably from the coloured areas, who would die violent and untimely deaths either in armed operations, or at the hands of the police who intercepted them. Some were recruited through these networks, hastily set up and without proper support. The victims, brave beyond their years, were fresh out of childhood. Some complained that they came back from military training and had hidden out for months without being given basic tasks.[5] At least two, Robbie Waterwitch and Coline Williams, were blown up by faulty explosives. But as porous as the networks may have been, the main blame undoubtedly had to be laid at the door of the police who had turned so many black schools into places of terror rather than places of learning. The angriest and the bravest were easy targets for recruitment from networks that were not necessarily secure.

One victim of a police execution was Ashley Kriel. Only 20, he had grown up in a poor home in the working class area of Bonteheuwel. He had boarded with Issel and Jaffer for a while before going for military training. When he returned, he lived under a pseudonym in Hazendal, an area in Athlone. 'A curly haired, lean, intense, beautiful and fun-loving youth whose life and laughter was cut short by a bullet in the back at point-blank range,' as his friend and fellow activist Zackie Achmat described him.[6] 'He was loved not only by his family but by many of us who saw in him the embodiment of our hopes,' writes Zubeida Jaffer in her memoir.[7]

More than 10 years later, during the hearings of the Truth and Reconciliation Commission, Jeffrey Benzien, an officer with the police anti-terrorist unit, applied for, and got, amnesty for the murder of Ashley Kriel. A well-known torturer in the Cape Town police, many aspects of Benzien's story raised more questions than answers. Kriel's housemate, who returned home from an errand minutes after the young activist was shot dead, said he had seen handcuffs on Kriel as he lay with a bullet wound in his head.[8]

Kriel's funeral was made more traumatic for his family and friends as the police tried to pull the ANC flag off his coffin and then shot rounds of tear gas into a church hall where the wake was being held. His mother sat in a car for most of the service, unable to deal with this unseemly tussle over her dead son's coffin. 'I walked away from the funeral because they didn't include the family,' said Jonathan de Vries. 'The comrades hijacked the funeral. I just thought it was in bad taste ... I was very big on this highfalutin idea that one must never allow the struggle and the *boere* to narrow our humanity ... [Here] there was a lack of respect for the dead.'

The lack of more mature leadership was never more evident in Cape Town. Manuel may have been able to intervene in ways that would produce less cruel outcomes for the teenage recruits. But that is all in the realm of hypothesis because, for almost the entire period of the extreme violence of the late-1980s, he was isolated from the daily events unfolding in the Cape.

BETWEEN THE END OF MARCH 1986, when he became effectively 'unbanned', and early June, Manuel worked full-tilt with other UDF leaders to plan a commemoration for the tenth anniversary of the Soweto uprisings. He was hardly at home during that period, lying low and working. In the month before the June 16 memorial 'the security police were literally camping outside our place', said Lynne. June also heralded a personal milestone. Manuel's first child was due then. The impending birth was the main reason he had acquired a pager – a technology widely used by journalists and doctors in the pre-cellphone age. Messages could be relayed to a pager by phoning a central number. In those days, they were not even text messages: they were relayed via an operator.

He adopted a bogus name for the pager – Arthur – because of the volatile political climate. On 12 June, it sounded as he sat in one of the final planning meetings for the June 16 rally. *Beep, beep, beep.* He pressed the button and a voice said: 'Arthur, don't go home. Your place is surrounded. Repeat: don't go home, your place is surrounded.'

The operator who had taken the message had been perplexed when Lynne had phoned to convey it. 'What are you saying?' he asked. 'Just send it,' she said.

Fortuitously, the message came through to Manuel while he was in a meeting with most of the UDF leadership. So they, too, knew something was amiss. Afterwards, it emerged that most of the activists who had not been in that particular meeting were detained. Those in the meeting with Manuel escaped into hiding. Some, such as Cheryl Carolus, escaped the police for the entire Emergency. By the next day, 13 June, at least 1200 people had been detained across the country.[9] Louis le Grange, the minister of law and order, described the detentions as 'normal operations' but later that afternoon President P W Botha declared a nationwide State of Emergency. The previous one, which affected only certain areas of the country, had been lifted on 7 March, just before the visit of the Eminent Persons Group.

This Emergency was not only more widespread than the previous one, its terms were more severe. Any member of the security forces – army, police or railways police – could arrest anyone on a suspicion that they may be involved in 'unrest'. The security forces were immune from prosecution or civil claims. Public rallies of most of the opposition organisations were banned. By 1988, most, including the UDF, were declared 'affected' organisations, meaning they could not operate. Schools were subject to strict regulations, both to stem the boycotts and also to prohibit alternative education programmes which the National Education Crisis Committee, a UDF affiliate, had arranged. The media were severely restricted: no detentions could be reported without confirmation from the police, and reporters were forbidden from even being present at any incident the police defined as 'unrest'. There were reams of regulations about detainees, among them prohibitions on being 'disrespectful' towards officials, being 'idle' or refusing to clean his place of detention, or 'singing, whistling or making unnecessary noise'.[10] (Zackie Achmat, who was to become a vociferous Aids activist in the post-apartheid era, was once charged under the latter provision during a spell in detention. It prompted Ebrahim Patel, a fellow detainee at the time, to reflect later that the minister of health in the post-apartheid government, whom Achmat had bitterly clashed with over the provision of antiretroviral medicines, might wish for a similar prohibition on 'unnecessary noise'![11])

By the end of August, the Detainees Parents' Support Committee estimated that about 13 000 people had been detained under the Emergency and a further 2 000 under 'normal' security laws, more than half of them under the age of 18. (Government released a list at around the same time, saying that 8 551 people had been detained under the Emergency.)[12]

'It's clear that our country needs political solutions during this period (*tydstip*),' wrote Manuel in an article in the Afrikaans newspaper *Rapport* five days before the Emergency was declared. 'And it's clear that the government is not in a state to find those solutions because the initiative is not in its hands. Thus the State makes draconian laws *om hul magsposisie te handhaaf en te behou*' (to reinforce and maintain their power.[13]

His comment was prescient, both in terms of the forthcoming State of Emergency and the subsequent clampdown that was to last more than three years, and also with respect to one of the most significant reform measures the government had yet made. The fact that it went unacclaimed, if not unnoticed, proved the point. In May the government announced it would abolish influx control – for so long the most hated and oppressive law affecting Africans. But the announcement came in the context of the warlike destruction of squatter communities around Cape Town, and the severe restrictions on movement on a much wider swathe of the population. What should have been seen as a major concession left the government no better placed to win the hearts and minds they needed in order to govern. The tricameral parliament had proved its toothlessness when the Emergency was declared in June. The Coloured and Indian chambers of Parliament opposed the measures and they were quickly overruled by the white chamber, as indeed the UDF had predicted they would be three years earlier.

'As someone who has been locked up myself,' wrote Manuel in *Rapport*, 'I feel that detention without trial is criminal.'

AFTER 12 JUNE 1986 MANUEL was forced to go deeper underground. Political activity ground almost to a halt. The mainstay of political resistance was now the more strongly organised trade unions, which pulled off two massive stayaways – on 1 May and then again on 16 June, involving at least 1,5 million workers on each occasion. But even the unions were not unscathed and by the end of the year at least 2 500 union officials and workers had also been detained under the Emergency.[14]

'What a year that was,' recalled Lynne. 'The police coming around quite regularly and pushing me around there in Maitland. And I was really highly pregnant at that stage.' She eventually abandoned Sylmore Poggenpoel's house when her family said she should not be living alone, and went to stay with her sister in Kensington. Manuel had meanwhile gone to a friend in Athlone, Huxley Joshua, where he lay low. But he was aware that nets were closing in, and both he and Lynne were anxious that he would miss the birth of his firstborn. The couple set up a code to be used on the pager when Lynne's labour started, using her mother's name, Myrtle. Their doctor was sympathetic both to their political principles and their plight and promised that if labour had not started by the following Sunday, 22 June, he would induce it. Lynne asked her friends not to use the phone to discuss her condition as she feared it would tip off the security police to intercept Manuel at the hospital.

Lynne's labour began in the early hours of Friday, 20 June. 'Myrtle has arrived,' came the message on Manuel's pager. He went straight to City Park hospital, a private hospital in the city centre just below Bo-Kaap and, ironically, directly opposite the security police headquarters in Loop Street. Manuel arrived at the hospital dressed in a Muslim robe and fez. He had cased the hospital beforehand, so he knew exactly where to park and how to get to the ward in the quickest, least conspicuous way. When he arrived, Lynne was already there, in heavy labour.

Their baby, a healthy boy, was born just before the sun rose. They named him Govan, after Govan Mbeki, Mandela's fellow Rivonia trialist sentenced to life imprisonment in 1964. Manuel was there for the whole birth and for about three hours afterwards, and then he left still wearing his disguise.

How did he feel not being able to spend more time with his newborn? 'There was nothing you didn't expect,' he said. 'These things were always going to be hard. The small mercy for me was that I could be *there*. Because many other people couldn't.'

Manuel walked out of the hospital into the hidden corners of Cape Town. For a time he hid in the house of his older sister Beryl, a risky choice as she lived opposite his mother's house in Kensington. Fortunately the house had an enclosed garage, and at night Beryl and her husband Roy would leave the boot of their car open so if the need arose he could hide there and perhaps be driven out. 'He used to go out disguised as an imam ... he wore a long outfit,' recalled Beryl. 'And once in the house, he didn't move around or go over to Mommy.' It was nerve-racking, she said, but even the children became used to stringent security measures. Manuel's small nieces and nephews knew never to use his name either in the street or in the house.

Lynne stayed another ten days in hospital, mainly because she could not cope with a new baby by herself when she was being hounded by the security police. When she was discharged, a colleague of Manuel's sister Pam took them in to their home in Heathfield. 'They didn't know me at all,' said Lynne. 'But they put their lives and their family at risk by letting us live with them for a few weeks. They insisted we take over the bedroom and gave us all the support and comfort we needed.' Manuel sneaked in to stay with his wife and child during that period. It was good, he recalled. He learned how to take care of his newborn, did the major chores like nappy-changing – at one stage he admonished Lynne that she'd have to learn to deal with 'poo nappies' because he could not stay for long – and took this precious gap to bond with his son. After about four weeks he moved out and on. For his part, he was afraid to expose Lynne and Govan to the security police although Lynne 'begged him to stay longer'.

'He felt he had so much to do,' she said. 'There was so much activity and he just had to go do it. And Trevor really is a political animal.'

MANUEL MOVED INTO A HOUSE in Grassy Park in the southern Peninsula. But most of his political work was in Mitchell's Plain, and the long trip across the Peninsula from the southern suburbs to the eastern Cape Flats was risky. So he moved to Mitchell's Plain, where he stayed with a sympathetic, but low-profile activist, Donny Jurgens, and his wife Eunice.

A few weeks previously, Manuel's UDF colleague Logan Wort had stayed with the Jurgenses. The house had been raided and Wort detained. Going by the rather uncertain principle that lightning doesn't strike twice, Manuel thought Jurgens's house would be a safe bet. He was wrong.

After a meeting with students one afternoon in August, he returned to the house, he thought, undetected. That night he heard his hosts' dogs barking persistently. It must be the cops, he thought. He went to his hosts' bedroom to ask them to help him hide in the ceiling. But they, as he diplomatically put it years later, were 'busy with marital affairs'. So he returned to his room and thought: 'OK, I need to be very alert.' He sat on the bed, his back against the wall, his legs stretched in front of him. He would ask for help when the moment was more opportune. And he promptly fell fast asleep.

When he awoke he saw four pistols pointed at his head. A distressed Eunice wept loudly. 'It wasn't very smart of me, I suppose, to stay there,' said Manuel. 'But be that as it may. The only thing I know is that from a very high mental alert, I went like *that*' – and he snapped his fingers to illustrate the sudden transition from vigilance to narcosis.

His bête noire, Jan Louw, led the band of four or five officers to arrest him. Manuel quickly regained his senses and his familiar anger with the police. He discovered they'd been to the Maitland house, intimidated the hapless Uncle Sylmore and during their search had unpacked his wife's underwear drawer. 'I was fucking angry with him,' he said.

It was 15 August. The following day, some newspapers ran a story headlined 'Trevor Manuel goes missing'. 'Monitoring organisations yesterday added the name of Mr Trevor Manuel … to their lists of people missing during the State of Emergency.'[15] The report epitomised the cryptic way newspapers learned to deal with the restrictions on reporting detentions.

He was taken to Loop Street police headquarters, opposite the hospital where he had witnessed his son's birth two months earlier. Then to Sea Point police station, where he was kept for about a month in solitary confinement. 'It was pretty tough. A Bible, soap, bread. Occasionally Lynne would bring me food and when she brought it she'd wrap it in the previous day's newspaper and say, please try take him his food while it's warm.'

The police didn't interrogate Manuel at all that month. They just left him – alone – which was his main source of anxiety. He saw Lynne once and his lawyer Ebrahim (Ebi) Mohamed twice. 'You must get me out of solitary,' he pleaded with Mohamed.

After about a month, a security police officer came to fetch him, cuffed him, put him in the back of a car and told him: '*Hou jou bek; sit net stil.*' ('Shut up and just sit still.')

As soon as the car hit the N1, the main northerly road out of Cape Town, he knew where he was going and was delighted. He was on his way to Victor Verster in Paarl, a prison where the authorities had detained many of the black men held under Emergency regulations in the Western Cape. There he found Wilfred Rhodes, his CAHAC colleague; Leslie Maasdorp, president of the SRC at the University of the Western Cape; Logan Wort, with whom Peter Marais had confused him in their trial for disrupting an election meeting two years earlier; Christmas Tinto, the old Robben Islander and UDF leader from

Guguletu; and several young African activists from the Boland townships of Paarl, Worcester, Ashton and Montagu.

Manuel arrived at Victor Verster at the tail-end of one of the first in a series of hunger strikes held by the detainees to demand their release from indefinite detention. There was an 'inquiry' among them because a *frikkadel* (a meat ball) was missing from two of the plates. Who ate on the hunger strike? It was a constant ploy of the prison authorities. Whenever there was a hunger strike they would make an effort to produce extra nice food, weakening the resolve of a hungry detainee.

That strike was called off after a couple of days, and Manuel began to adjust to the routine of prison life. At least he had companionship. One was Maasdorp, about ten years his junior, arrested at the UWC hostels on the eve of the Emergency. 'We had no chance,' he said. 'We had these manuals about what to do if you get detained, what your rights are, etc. You can pack a bag and so on. But they just took us. They were quite harsh.' He spent his first night in the Bellville Police Station, the lights burning all night and 'people just coming in all the time'.

After the initial fear faded, prison became a 'collective experience, a shared deprivation'.

About the time Manuel arrived, the more 'senior' detainees were moved from communal into single cells. The atmosphere was spirited. The detainees spoke about 'our struggle, the national democratic revolution, what we were really fighting about', said Maasdorp. There were many young militants in jail – people picked up from townships, and from the satellite camps around Crossroads that had been targeted in the *witdoek* attacks. 'At that stage, within the ANC, while non-racialism was a very strong principle the approach to class content ... the national democratic revolution, was the hub of the debate. Those senior guys like Trevor were very active and led those discussions.' They were 'hardcore' debates, recalled Maasdorp, 'about whether you were a communist, if you want to put it crudely'. They spoke about racial capitalism, about colonialism of a special type: 'I don't think we fully understood what it meant but if you think about it, it went to the heart of the nature of change we were fighting for.'

It may have been Manuel's leading role in these debates, or it may have been that Jan Louw, officially his 'investigating officer' simply became bloody-minded. But one month after his arrival at the prison he was taken by Louw to an office in the prison building. Louw reached into a packet, and took out a brand new dictaphone. It was still in its box, wrapped in plastic. He put in the batteries and said: 'Now I'm going to interrogate you.'

Manuel's response: 'Fuck off, man.'

Louw was flummoxed.

'I said, fuck off. You want to interrogate me? You don't know the first thing about interrogation.'

'No,' replied Louw. 'I'm just going to ask you questions' – as though the word 'interrogation' itself was the stumbling block.

'I'm not interested,' replied Manuel. 'I'm not going to answer any questions. Take your machine, put it back in its box, and piss off.'

Louw was taken aback. 'But this is very unfair,' he said. 'If you must be looked after during the night, if your place must be watched, or you must be arrested at 4am, then I'm good enough. But I'm not good enough to interrogate you?'

'That's your problem, not mine,' retorted Manuel, and it was the end of the session.

In later years, Manuel reflected, with amusement rather than sympathy, that Louw was indeed 'deeply hurt by this thing'.

But the police officer was to exact revenge. Two days later, he appeared in Manuel's cell and said, *'Pak jou goed!'* During those long days of indefinite detention *'pak jou goed'* could mean anything. It could mean you're going home, it could mean a transfer to another prison, it could mean interrogation by a more efficient interrogator.

In this case it meant a trip to a grim single cell in a police station in Kraaifontein, one of Cape Town's northern suburbs. The Kraaifontein police station was old and dilapidated with a makeshift holding cell for suspects picked up from the street. It had no natural light, a peephole at the door, and was filthy. There were no showers and no exercise yard. Where will I shower? Manuel asked the station commander. *'Ons sal vir jou van tyd tot tyd 'n kom warm water bring om te was.'* ('From time to time we'll bring you a bucket of hot water so that you can wash.')

Manuel asked for a Government Gazette that listed the plethora of rules about the holding of Emergency detainees. 'It says I must shower. It gives me the right to shower and the right to exercise. I'm not staying in this place.'

The three men – Manuel, Louw and the station commander – stood in the filthy, barely lit cell. The toilet overflowed – 'there was shit all over the place' – and the one blanket they gave him stank. He grabbed the blanket, dragged it over to Louw, took him by the shirt and said: '*Sou jy onder die kak slaap?*' ('Would you sleep under this shit?') The two policemen were distinctly nervous now. They were not part of the more lawless death squads roaming the land. Their role was to obey rules. They stood silent for a while until Manuel said in Afrikaans: '*Een ding. As Oliver Tambo kom, gaan jy kak!*' ('One thing. When Oliver Tambo comes you will shit!')

Without a word, the policemen left him there but came the next morning to fetch him. This time they took him to Brackenfell police station, in a nearby suburb. The cell was better-sized. There was a courtyard and a shower. There he stayed in solitary confinement for 64 days. Day and night, the overhead bulb burned. Manuel began to get severe headaches, and the police took him to the district surgeon in Kuilsriver. The prison was cold. It was the end of a Cape winter, which drags itself out stubbornly when spring is already flourishing in the rest of the country.

'What's wrong?' asked the doctor.

'I've got the flu,' Manuel replied.

'Uh-uh. It's my job to diagnose. Tell me what is wrong.'

'Well, doctor, I've got headaches, my throat is sore, my nose is blocked ...'

'UH-UH!' The doctor shook his head. '*Net twee kwale in een week.*' ('Only two complaints a week.')

'*Net twee kwale in een week!*' Manuel was amused by it years later, this odd medical orthodoxy in the prison service.

It soon became clear to Manuel that he was there because of the political education classes he'd run in Victor Verster. 'I wrote papers about the Freedom Charter, about the ANC, about the Kabwe Conference. They knew all the topics I'd covered. We used to deal with the four pillars of the national democratic revolution – the mass struggle, the underground, international support, the military (the fifth, which was still to come, was negotiations). They knew about those things which we ensured people understood.'

So somebody in Victor Verster must have been an informer. There was no respite from them even in jail.

Apart from brief enquiries about the 'political education' classes, there was no interrogation at Brackenfell. Occasionally Louw would come to see him. More frequently there would be an English-speaking security policeman who was a university graduate, Lieutenant Godfrey Tom, a tall, 'smooth' man, who had also visited Manuel's mother when her son was in hiding. She had sent him packing with a brief biblical lecture: 'If God is for you, who can be against you?'

He had few visitors. His mother came once, Lynne twice, and Ebi Mohamed, his lawyer, more regularly. It was Mohamed who persuaded a local magistrate that Manuel, whose headaches were getting worse, needed to see a private doctor. So one blue and breezy early summer's day the security police came to fetch him and drove him slowly along the Sea Point beachfront all the way to Camps Bay, along the rocky, blue Atlantic coast, a trip reminiscent of the one Nelson Mandela's jailers took him on at around the same time. Then they drove him back to City Park hospital. There he saw a physician, who was to become his regular doctor even after he left jail. He checked his blood pressure and found it to be a little high but not dangerously so.

On Christmas Eve, Tom came to see Manuel with a box of dried fruit and told him how bad he felt that he was in jail, but that this decision was not in his hands.

Manuel stayed in Brackenfell through Christmas, through New Year. One afternoon, early in February, Manuel's evening meal did not arrive. They had to bring it from a nearby hotel as there were no kitchen facilities in the prison 'and you must have the same food as a police constable has – that's what the Gazette says'. The next day, again, his food didn't arrive. When he asked the station commander what the problem was, he replied that there was a shortage of vans because certain police officers had to go to rugby practice in Pinelands. 'When they go with the vans we don't have any way of getting the food.'

'That's your problem,' replied Manuel. 'I'm now on hunger strike.'

Strangely, this reverence for rugby among the prison warders and police had also resulted in an early release from prison for Manuel's UDF colleague Jonathan de Vries. He had been detained in Pollsmoor, in the southern Peninsula, the year before under 'normal' security legislation which allowed for two weeks' detention unless the order was extended by the minister. His two-week period ended one Saturday afternoon, and there was no sign of the security police with another order. They were all at the Currie Cup, a major provincial rugby match. So were many of the warders. De Vries pressed the emergency buzzer in his cell continually and told the few remaining warders on duty that unless he was officially re-detained, he was now being held illegally and he could sue for kidnap. Worn down by threats, the junior warders on duty released him. He phoned his mother from a public phone booth outside the prison, and then sprinted through the leafy neighbouring suburb of Tokai to the highway where he met his parents. That night the infuriated security police began looking for him again but by then he'd moved to a safe house.

Now it was rugby that scuttled the police's plans to keep Manuel in solitary away from his comrades. On the third day of his hunger strike – in protest at no food delivery – Tom came to see him to remonstrate with him. 'Be reasonable,' he pleaded. 'It's give and take.'

'Then give me my freedom and take me home,' said Manuel. When he saw that was not going to happen he pressed Tom. Either release him right then, or take him back to Victor Verster. There were rules. The Government Gazette said detainees had to be fed at certain times. He understood that policemen had to get on with their rugby practice, but they could not expect him to adjust his diet around the rugby.

That afternoon, Jan Louw came to fetch Manuel and drove him back along the N1 towards the mountains of Paarl and Victor Verster prison.

CHAPTER 17

'You're supposed to be smiling'

IT CANNOT BE OFTEN that returning to prison comes as a relief. 1987 was one such time for Trevor Manuel. He arrived back at Victor Verster from 64 days in isolation in the late afternoon, after lock-up.

'Hey, I'm back!' he called cheerfully through the cells to his jail mates.

Most of the detainees he'd left behind were still there. Many of those the police considered leaders were in single cells, but they saw each other during the day.

'By that stage we'd developed a rhythm,' said Leslie Maasdorp. 'After about four months you begin to get a rhythm of prison life.'

The older detainees, such as Christmas Tinto, who had experience as sentenced prisoners on Robben Island, began to set a pace for their younger, more impatient comrades. 'When you wake up in the morning, you think this could be your day,' recalled Maasdorp. 'I woke up every day thinking this could be my day, and then you get so *gatvol*. And when you see these (older) guys starting their walk in the courtyard, walking, reflecting, there's a mellowness about all those older comrades that on one level was quite inspiring, but on another level – you didn't want to become too comfortable in this bloody place!'

Veterans such as Tinto persuaded the detainees to demand better conditions: milk with the morning porridge, for example, proper toilet paper. The younger, more radical detainees, including Maasdorp, railed against it. To argue for better conditions in prison was to accept the right of the authorities to lock them up in the first place. 'We don't want to reconstruct prison life to make it more comfortable,' they said. But the older leaders persisted, saying there was no basis for not wanting better food or conditions.

It is hard to understand now exactly how debilitating emergency detention was, not only for the thousands of individuals who were detained, but for the entire opposition movement. But its psychological effects on hundreds of individuals – some mere children – were as detrimental to the movement as any of the harsher bans on meetings or organisations.

'This long-term detention without trial was probably the single most effective thing the old government did. It was much more damaging to people than going to Robben Island for five years or ten years,' said Willie Hofmeyr, a radical student leader who was banned in 1976 for five years and then became a UDF executive member in 1987. He was detained for long periods in 1988 and 1989, and came close to the point of death at least twice through a sustained hunger strike that saw his weight drop as low as 30 kilograms.

Uncertainty was the weapon the government wielded during the Emergency. Previously, when people had been detained there were always certain landmark dates: two weeks, 90 days, 180 days. Easter. Maybe Christmas. But now days in prison stretched ahead with no horizon. Young, inexperienced activists were arrested simply for handing out political pamphlets – pamphlets that were not even banned. 'They'd get zapped and stay in detention for two weeks or four weeks or four months ... nobody knew quite how long it would be,' said Hofmeyr.

Even for the more senior leaders, who had steeled themselves for worse, it was a debilitating period. As a sentenced prisoner, one could make adjustments, register to study, arrange support for one's family. The uncertainty around detention without trial meant that, at least in the first year of the Emergency, few people made any long-term arrangements. Many simply floated between hope and despair, day by day.

'It had a devastating personal cost for people at an individual and psychological level until they got to grips with the sense ... that they must just accept now that they are in here for a long time,' said Hofmeyr.

For Manuel, it was a period that forced him into rapid maturity. He had inspired and protected younger detainees by being fearless in front of the security police and prison officials.

'Trevor just made life unbearable for these guys,' recalled Maasdorp. Out of jail, if he was arrested on marches, 'they would need five cops to hold him because he would literally *bliksem* them … he was like a madman when they tried to arrest him.'

In jail, too, he stood up to the prison warders. One senior warder had the nickname of 'Sametime' because he punished supposed transgressions immediately without any process. Spare diet, solitary, whatever – he would make the decree then and there. But Manuel could stand his ground. One time, for a reason Maasdorp can't recall, the prisoners refused to go back to their cells from the yard when it came to lock-up time. They linked arms and the warders approached them with dogs. Manuel stood firm and kept the other terrified detainees with him. Eventually, when the dogs were called off, they agreed to go inside.

THE PERIOD IN JAIL TEMPERED MANUEL. 'He went in fighting and kicking, but he learned how to be a leader in there,' said Logan Wort, who spent many of the long months with him. If they were in for the long haul, with so many more vulnerable younger activists, it was crucial that he find a way that they could all manage the jail time. There were problems, too, for the older detainees. Wilf Rhodes's wife was diagnosed with cancer while he was in jail. Zoli Malindi, also elderly, suffered from diabetes. In both cases, and in countless others, there was intensely personal pain that had to be dealt with under hostile conditions.

Those who were registered students, such as Maasdorp, eventually got permission to continue their studies. Jakes Gerwel, who had recently become rector of the University of the Western Cape, fought in court for the right of the students to continue their studies. Suddenly the students could get books in jail – other than the Mills & Boon romances and westerns that populated the small prison library – and even taped lectures. Maasdorp wrote his final exams in a little courtroom inside the prison under the South African flag which symbolised all that he opposed. The lecture tapes had to go to the security police who checked there was nothing 'subversive' on them. Who knows what they may have learned? Despite the difficulties, he passed with distinction even though he had attended hardly any lectures that year.

Manuel himself got permission to register through Unisa, South Africa's correspondence university, for certain courses, mainly in law and public administration.

'I think that provided me with a measure of sanity,' he said.

It was ironic that he chose law. Years before his mother had discouraged him from studying law because she feared he 'would end up on Robben Island'. But in life the sequence occurred quite differently. Prison led him to law, rather than the other way round.

He also encouraged other detainees to study.

The detainees began to play regular games – mainly sport, but also chess. Manuel had a reputation for being aggressively competitive. He did not like losing. The detainees made themselves a makeshift tennis court of unrolled grass. The prison authorities provided a net.

'Now Trevor,' recalled Maxwell Moss, his comrade from Saldanha Bay who was a keen sportsman then, 'he was a bastard. He wouldn't want to lose. He does *not* want to lose. He was almost like John McEnroe. If an umpire calls wrong, according to him, he would shout. Trevor almost fought with comrade Lizo Kapa (a fellow detainee from Worcester) when they were playing tennis.'

He would play with his shorts on, nothing on top, recalled Moss, an intent figure darting around the court, battling for every point, disputing those he thought were unjustly awarded to his opponent. 'He wants to win because he believes he's right!'

It was a mark always of Manuel, and even if he had moments of self-doubt in his political career, he seemed to have none in his short-lived tennis career.

The conditions were hard – so many men locked up together for who knew how long. They sometimes got on each other's nerves, especially when one intruded on the private inner space of another. Moss, for instance, used to pray before he ate – even though the meals were uninspiring at best, often 'pap' and soya beans. He would pray quietly to himself and one evening Manuel, who was sitting with him, asked him what he was doing.

'I'm praying,' Moss replied.

'Why are you praying?' asked Manuel.

'I'm saying thanks to God for the food.'

'No, man,' said Manuel, 'it is Vlok (Adriaan Vlok, then minister of law and order) who gives you food. It is Vlok who holds the key. He can decide whether to release you or not, to charge you or not.'

'*Yinne*, I was so cross,' said Moss. 'You know the frustration building in me! Here was this man saying to me ... I was so cross!' Moss opted not to engage but rather to bottle his anger.

Manuel was hard, then, in his beliefs. The detainees set up a committee – partly to discuss conditions among themselves, but also partly as a disciplinary committee, 'although Trevor was more often a defendant' than an adjudicator, said one fellow detainee. Sometimes his temper got the better of him. The detainees' committee agreed that Muslim prayers would be Wednesdays and Fridays, and Christian prayers the rest of the time. Manuel objected that there should be a time, too, for agnostics and atheists where they could read a tract of philosophy. Agreed: Thursdays were set aside for this. On one Thursday Manuel read an extract from Bertrand Russell. When he was done, just before lock-up, Wilf Rhodes began to pray. Manuel objected, saying this was not a 'Christian' day, but Rhodes persisted and the two came close to a physical fight.

When quarrels like this threatened to brew too strongly, one of the older men, often Christmas Tinto (known as Com T), would call them together and say: 'You know, comrades, prison is one of those things. You might feel like this now, and I understand why you sometimes feel like this, but you must remember that we are all comrades, and at times prison eats you! You just get frustrated. But you must not take out your frustration on your fellow comrades.'

But parallel to the bristles of personality that prison conditions evoked in Manuel, there was also a maturity that was developing that allowed him to see himself – and others – through this period.

'His period of national leadership in the UDF ... experience in national leadership beyond the borders of the province ... helped him in prison. It said a lot about the insular nature of politics in the Western Cape then and today,' said Logan Wort who spent more than a year in jail with Manuel. 'He could relate to senior ANC stalwarts ... in a quiet and deep way, because he had the time. The experience *did* mature him but he didn't become less radical; all the revolts we had, he was in the forefront. But he started to learn to use it more tactically and appropriately.'

The older activists realised their responsibilities when they learned that in the larger, communal cells some of the younger detainees – many were just children – spent the nights crying for their parents. 'We had to negotiate with the same cops that we were fighting to allow us in with the youngsters after lock-up time, in their interests, so we could sort out their problems; and we had to do that in a non-antagonistic way,' said Wort. 'Part of surviving this period is you've got to work with them in a way that benefits us (the detainees), and that kind of leadership was aptly displayed by him.'

Manuel taught himself calligraphy in jail. This, after a handwriting that his comrades described as, 'Oh, worse than a doctor!' (In an age before, his boss at Murray & Stewart had also chastised him for his bad handwriting.) His mother brought him calligraphy pens and by the Christmas of 1987, he was sending carefully crafted handmade cards from the prison to his family.

More than that, though, he took responsibility for the poorer detainees who had little in the way of resources. 'It was in Victor Verster,' said Moss, 'where Trevor started to become the minister of finance.'

Church groups, support groups, family, would deposit small amounts of money in detainees' accounts every month. They were allowed to draw money once a week to buy small luxuries at the prison shop – chocolate, cigarettes, soap and toothpaste (the prison-issue soap was a hard laundry soap and the small tube of toothpaste did not last long). The flood of new young detainees who had been picked up from the townships often came from families without the resources to deposit money, and anyway most didn't have bank accounts. Manuel would calculate every week how many detainees there were, and how much those with money should draw to allow every detainee to have something in their pockets.

'Everybody would get the same amount of money,' said Moss. 'It was amazing. But it was also like socialism; everything must be shared equally no matter who you are, as long as you're there.'

In the second week of June in 1987, a small group of the detainees, including Manuel, Tinto, Malindi and Maasdorp, were called aside and told: '*Pak jou goed.*'

Maxwell Moss had been released a few months earlier with heavy restrictions. They were taken to Ravensmead police station in one of Cape Town's peripheral northern suburbs. For a night they slept 'sardine style' in one cell. The next morning, a police major came into the cell and said: 'I know your life has been hard this past year. Well, I have good news and bad news for some of you. The good news is that the State of Emergency is ending today, and so I have the privilege of releasing all six of you.' He then named

266

them, one by one, telling them they were free. 'However,' he continued, 'a new State of Emergency has been declared and so I have the responsibility to detain the following people.'

He then named all of them except Maasdorp, who had just turned 21 after a year in prison.

Maasdorp's head was in a spin. A month before he'd been separated from the group for interrogation. *'Pak jou goed,'* they'd said, and he'd thought he was going home. Instead he was taken to Brackenfell police station for a week. This time he was told he was free, as were the others. There were two tables in the police station. At one they released the detainees. At the next they re-detained them. In between the tables, they were free for a few minutes. He was the last one to be processed. He saw what had happened to the others. As he arrived, gloomily, at the second table, the police didn't look up from their papers.

'They were just sitting there doing their stuff, and I'm getting irritated,' he said, 'because I knew the vans were waiting outside to take people back to prison.' One policeman looked up and said: *'Jy moet gaan.'* ('You must go.')

He felt lost. Far from home (his parents lived in the Eastern Cape), he didn't know where to go or what to do. He had R20 in his pocket. He went outside, found a public phone, and called a friend at the university to come and pick him up. 'But I can't tell you how terrible I felt. Because Zoli Malindi was really sick – he had diabetes. And I was a youngster. I thought if there's someone who deserves to be out, it's these guys, even if you want to be free yourself.'

Some Emergency detainees were brought from Pollsmoor or other prisons and they went through the same process. Noel Williams, the UDF organiser from the West Coast was among them, as was Roseberry Sonto, a youth leader from Guguletu, and Mountain Qumbela, a former Robben Islander.

All of them were taken to Victor Verster. They found the prison practically empty when they returned. The authorities had moved most of the other prisoners out except those who worked as cooks and cleaners. The Emergency detainees were the only people there.

'We realised then,' said Manuel, 'that this was a different ball game now.'

THE DIFFERENCE WAS THAT their lives had to move out of a holding pattern. They had to deal with the possibility that prison was at least their medium-term future.

'Guys,' said Noel Williams, after they had been back in jail for about a week, 'prison is getting the better of us now. Sure, we all wanted to go home, but we haven't gone home. We're here … The best thing we can do now is to take hold of our lives again (because) pity's not going to work here.'

So that's what they did. Manuel became serious about his studies. He would try to sleep for a few hours in the afternoon, save one or two pieces of bread from supper for later in the night, and then study until the early hours. In any event, sleep was always erratic in jail. The lights burned 24/7 and distracting noise was a constant feature.

At the same time, the detainees fought for better conditions and for medical and dental care. Manuel had been both amused and amazed by the district surgeon who had allowed prisoners only 'twee kwale per week'. Now he needed a dentist and the practices in prison seemed just as archaic. When the prison authorities finally brought in a dentist, all he wanted to do was to extract their teeth.

'No!' said Manuel. 'You're out of your mind. I want proper dental care. I want fillings.'

'I come to prison and I extract teeth,' replied the dentist obtusely.

Manuel refused the treatment. He and a number of his fellow detainees wrote to the head of prisons and their lawyers demanding proper dental care. A few months into their second year of detention, they won this small but basic demand. For a few weeks he and Noel Williams would be taken to Tygerberg Hospital on Tuesday mornings, sometimes in a car, sometimes in the back of a van. Stellenbosch University had a dental faculty at Tygerberg run by final year students. The woman who attended to Manuel and Williams was young, Afrikaans, and not unsympathetic to their plight. Her father happened to be the doctor who treated Nelson Mandela for tuberculosis when he was in a private clinic in Cape Town undergoing treatment in 1988. (Manuel continued seeing the dentist for a while after his release, and it was through her that he found out that Mandela had been admitted to hospital in August 1988.)

As hard as it is to talk to dentists, Manuel managed conversations with her. For her part, she drew out the appointments: clean the teeth one week, the next week do one filling, the week after another filling. So Tuesday trips to the dentist became something of a ritual, and certainly something that made prison life more bearable.

In August Williams was released. (He was replaced almost immediately by his neighbourhood comrade Maxwell Moss who was re-detained in

September 1987 after being involved in toyi-toyi after a rugby match in Saldanha Bay that had spontaneously erupted into stones being thrown at policemen's houses.)

Manuel meanwhile continued with the Tuesday trips to the dentist. One day he sent a message to Lynne: Tuesdays at Tygerberg. The police officer who transported him to Tygerberg, 'Essie' Esterhuyse, the same man who had first driven him from Sea Point police station to Victor Verster more than a year before, would usually handcuff him. This time, for some reason, he didn't.

And on this day Lynne arrived outside Tygerberg with Govan, then about 14 months old. When Manuel saw Govan, he scooped him up and held him. 'Los daai kind' ('Leave that child'), snapped Esterhuyse. Lynne turned on him, asking: 'Are you a father? Do you touch your children?'

Manuel had not touched any member of his family for more than a year. He had not held his son since he was an infant. Eventually, under Lynne's barrage, Esterhuyse relented and allowed Manuel to hold Govan until a crowd gathered around them. 'We must go,' he said tersely. But he did not handcuff Manuel in front of his wife and child.

Lynne Matthews had spent a hard year with a baby and without her husband. Manuel was allowed one visit every second month, initially – later, one visit a month. She and his mother took it in turns visit. She had decided to further her studies in education and to scale down her political activities to avoid being detained as well.

'There was no way that I'm leaving a young child that *we* brought into the world to be left without both parents. There was no way I was going to do that,' she said, despite the fact that some Cape Town activists criticised her decision.

She tried to make things more bearable for Manuel in jail. She brought him news – real news – writing down the major political news in point form on her hand and holding it up to the window between them when the guard wasn't watching. She would take Govan on every visit. 'He would put his hand on the glass panel separating us from Trevor. When he could speak, he would say, "Daddy kiss my hand", and I could see Trevor breaking.'[1] She had pinned a picture of Manuel above Govan's cot. 'Whatever we did, we included Trevor in the arrangement. So that Govan would say goodnight to me, and then kiss his daddy goodnight. Kiss the picture goodnight.'

Philma Manuel took her son's detention badly. 'Trevor is the apple of her eye. He's someone she is very devoted to and proud of,' said Lynne. Mrs Manuel credits Lynne with giving her sufficient strength to pull through those long and anxious months. But Lynne, like Manuel, was manifestly realistic about their situation. 'There was no point looking for sympathy,' she said, 'because this was a lifestyle we *chose*. We chose to get involved politically.' If she wept at the loss of 'camaraderie, support and friendship and love', she did so privately.

So when Esterhuyse tried to stop Manuel from holding his son on that Tuesday in the spring of 1987, he'd hit a particularly raw nerve with both of them. The next week when he came to pick up Manuel for his weekly dental appointment, he said: 'I hope we're not going to have the same problems as last week.'

Manuel replied, 'I don't know what you call problems. I'm sorry, you know, but you guys are there (with me), I listen to you talk every week. It's clear to me you are a Christian. You go to church every week. You play a role in the church. And you say to me that as a Christian, as a father, you detain me. You take away my rights, you deny me access to my family, and you say that is your Christian duty.'

Esterhuyse was silent. He did not cuff Manuel when they got out of the car. He did not cuff him on the way back from the dentist. As he drove back to Paarl, just before he got to the prison, he stopped the car outside a little shop. He and the other policeman went in, leaving Manuel alone. It was reminiscent of Mandela's trip through the brighter side of Cape Town, when his warders left him alone in the car while they went to buy him a Coke. Manuel did not know that yet, of course, but exactly the same wild thoughts that Mandela had played through his mind. 'He (Esterhuyse) was breaking the law, and I'm thinking, "Do I run? Where do I run to? Is this his ploy? Does he want to put a bullet in my back?"'

It took him only minutes to make the call: 'No, no, I must not run, this is not the moment to run.'

When Esterhuyse got back in the car, he handed him a can of Coke and a little sweet – friendship sweets, children used to call them, with 'corny messages' on them. This one said: *'Maak vriende'* ('Make friends'). He said to Manuel: *'Ek hoop dit sal so wees.'* ('I hope it will be so.')

After that, when they went on the dental trips, Esterhuyse would stop outside the CNA, a news agency, at Manuel's request so that he could 'buy a writing pad'. Manuel would buy the newspapers too, stuffing them in his pants. 'He (Esterhuyse) knew what was going on, but something had broken in him. Something had turned him like that.'

It was a small moment, but of huge import: both men, from different sides of the political divide, had found the humanity and decency in each other in one simple gesture.

Esterhuyse left the police force in 2000. I tracked him down to Springbok in the Namaqualand area of the Northern Cape where he worked for an agribusiness. He was taken aback by my call, but managed to say that the years of the Emergency were not pleasant, and that he still struggled to come to terms with those memories.

Less than two years after Manuel's spell in Victor Verster prison, in 1990, in a country that was palpably different, Manuel led a march to promote the newly unbanned African National Congress in the little Northern Cape town of Calvinia. As the march passed the police station an officer strolled out and walked next to him. It was the same man, Esterhuyse, now a station commander in Calvinia.

'I was never a security policeman,' he said to Manuel. 'I hope you have a good day in Calvinia, Trevor.'

To survive indefinite detention, the detainees had to start reasserting control over their own lives. One way of doing this was to study. Manuel had passed his first lot of Unisa courses 'quite well' and now decided he wanted to study constitutional law 'because I know some time we're going to have to write a constitution'.

Who said so? No one could say, but it was this relentless optimism that kept him focused. Many detainees fell apart under the conditions. Many went to psychiatrists hoping they would be able to get out of jail that way. Even Manuel went to a psychiatrist at Tygerberg but 'by then I knew I was in full control ... I wasn't even seriously depressed.' He understood by then that 'this was a battle that was going to be won in your own head'.

By early 1988, some 25 000 people in total had been detained in terms of the Emergency. About 400 of those had been in jail since the first national Emergency was declared in June 1986. Others came and went, such as Wilfred Rhodes and Maxwell Moss.

Hunger strikes were also ways to reassert control but they would not be used to their full dramatic (and dangerous) limits until the following year. More useful for Manuel was a court application he and several other

271

detainees launched soon after he was re-detained in June 1987. Although it was marked as an urgent application, it was not heard by a full bench of the Cape Supreme Court until the end of that year. To this day there has been no judgment on the application.

Manuel had secured several court judgments in prison on the grounds that he was studying law through Unisa. He pored over Government Gazettes, Acts, other precedents set by the courts. 'Part of my sanity came from this pretence that I knew the law.'

By June 1988, when the second national Emergency was coming to an end, and the third about to be declared, the security police called him into the prison office. 'Well, Trevor,' said a major, 'we get to that point again. The State of Emergency has been lifted so I can release you. But a new State of Emergency has been declared.'

'You mean you're not even going to give me the joyride out this time?' asked Manuel. 'In that case,' he said, 'I'm going to have to ask you some questions.' From his readings of court judgments he knew that somebody in authority had to 'form an opinion' that he was a danger to law and order. The police were surprised. 'We don't have to answer questions,' they said. 'You see, you're a detainee and we're not.'

'The law requires you to answer questions,' said Manuel. 'I didn't bring a pen and I don't have paper so would you be kind enough to give me a pen and paper because I'd like to write this down.'

Then proceeded an inverse interrogation – the prisoner questioning his captors. What informed your decision to re-detain me? he asked. Who formed the opinion? Have you considered the following? He wrote it all down and asked each of the security policemen to sign his account of the questioning. Each refused.

As he went out, two of his fellow detainees were waiting to see whether they would be released or re-detained: Whitey (Mzonke) Jacobs and Maxwell Moss. These are the questions you need to ask, Manuel told them. Jacobs successfully posed all the questions and wrote the answers down at length.

However, when Moss's turn came he did not even get a chance to ask anything. 'His' security police from the West Coast were somewhat less sophisticated. *'Fokof, jy's in die tronk'* ('Fuck off, you're in jail'), they retorted when he asked the first question.

So Manuel launched another application for his release on the basis that the police couldn't form a fresh opinion. His lawyers were doubtful. After all, the Emergency allowed the police almost unfettered powers. But Manuel was stubborn. The police could not have formed an opinion, he said, because the original matter – his first application – was still before the court. 'How can this guy (the security police major) form a fresh opinion when the judges are still sitting on this thing and I've not been engaged in any political activity?'

His lawyer, Ebi Mohamed, said he would try his best. Part of the problem was finding an advocate prepared to take the case because they didn't like taking on sure losers. But he'd found one, appropriately named Pat Gamble, who thought Manuel had done a 'bloody good job' of drafting the papers. Jacobs joined the application but Moss, because the police refused to entertain his questions, had nothing concrete to go on.

A few days later, an amazed Mohamed appeared in his cell. 'You're not going to believe this but you're going home,' he said. The minister of law and order had said he was not going to contest the application – it did not even go to court.

On 7 July 1988 Manuel was released, after 695 days in detention. Whitey Jacobs was released after nearly 18 months in detention. He, too, had a small child – a 14-month-old daughter – whom he held in his arms for the first time that day. It was only the third time Manuel had held Govan since he had been detained. Mountain Qumbela was also released after 188 days in detention. Maxwell Moss was to stay another two months before being charged with three charges relating to public violence, and released. All the former detainees were served with heavy restriction orders.

After he was freed, Manuel went straight to his childhood home in Kensington where a banner saying 'Viva Trevor, Welcome Home' was hung across the front door. His mother and sisters were waiting for him outside. 'When his mother Philma saw her son unfold his long frame from the car which brought him from Paarl, she started weeping,' reported a weekly newspaper. 'Don't cry,' he told her. 'You're supposed to be smiling.'[2]

Manuel himself smiled. 'I secured my own release,' he told me. 'For me, that was such a big victory.'

CHAPTER 18

'Forcing the sun to rise ...'

B Y THE TIME MANUEL came out of jail, Lynne had moved with Govan to a converted garage, one large room, attached to a Kensington house.

She had not told him while he was in prison because she had not wanted to upset him 'but the environment was totally *deurmekaar'* (in disorder). She was living out of boxes, so when streams of activists came to greet Manuel, she had no glasses or plates or cups or anything to entertain them.

Among their visitors were Huxley Joshua and his family, who brought a large chocolate cake. They had sheltered Manuel just before Govan's birth. Apart from the unprepossessing and cramped environment in which Manuel now had to live, he was also unhappy because his banning order restricted him to the Cape Town magisterial district, in which Kensington and Maitland fell. It provided narrow options as far his social and political contacts went. The Wynberg magisterial district was much broader, including many of the southern suburbs and most of the Cape Flats where the coloured and African townships were located. It thus became imperative for him to move.

As it happened, there was a three-bedroomed vacant house next door to the Huxleys in Albemarle Street, in a good part of Athlone, just below the railway line. Huxley spoke to the owner who agreed to rent it to Manuel and his family, and the police allowed Manuel to change his magisterial district.

From a personal point of view life looked a little better, but Manuel was still subject to heavy restrictions. He had to be indoors at night. He had to report to the local police station twice a day. He was not allowed to be quoted, to attend any meeting, or be in the company of more than two people at a time. The police frequently checked up on him at odd times: during supper, at bedtime, or sometimes at 4am.

Govan turned two that June. He was an angry little boy, said both his parents, partly because he had first been deprived of a father, then because he had to share a relative stranger with his mother. He got angrier when the police did their random checks. 'He was very aggressive against the police,' recalled Lynne. 'He'd call them pigs!'

In August, about six weeks after his release, some of Manuel's comrades came to visit him. They needed to plan how 'to take the struggle forward because our people have been battered now'.

So they set about organising a wide-ranging anti-apartheid conference, mustering up support from the left to the centre, this time even more significantly across race and class lines. Manuel became a low-level organiser, sending emissaries such as Goolam Aboobaker to speak to Jakes Gerwel about using the UWC hostels, speaking to Franklin Sonn, then rector of his alma mater Pentech about similar logistical support. Although the conference itself had been reported in the press, Manuel's role was quiet and careful.

But not quiet or careful enough. Before dawn on 21 September there was a sharp knock at his door. It was a contingent of three security policemen; one was Warrant Officer Janse van Rensburg, known as 'Rooies' because of his crop of red hair. Manuel was nervous because he had, only the day before, secreted some banned publications – *Sechaba*, the ANC magazine, and the *African Communist* – under his mattress. He knew it was a foolish thing to do as the police were looking for any excuse to charge him, but it was too late now to do anything. So he played for time. 'I'm sleeping now,' he complained.

No, insisted Rooies, I must see you.

Calling him by his nickname, Manuel replied: *'As ek jou naam ken, as ek jou bynaam ken, wie anders kan dit wees?'* ('If I know your name, and I know your nickname, who else can it be?') 'I must see you,' insisted the policeman, and as Manuel opened the door, he put his foot inside and came into the living room. Manuel asked Lynne to go next door to fetch Joshua, his neighbour, who was a lawyer. 'Huxley!' laughed the police. *'Hy's lankal weg!'* ('He's been gone a long time!') And indeed when Lynne got to his house she found his wife and daughter in tears because he had been detained.

Govan was doubly angry. Although he was only two years old, he'd absorbed his father's diction in the 10 short weeks he'd been at home. The police were 'pigs' he said, who should 'fuck off'. But they didn't. The three told Manuel they were detaining him again under the Emergency regulations. Manuel asked one, a Captain du Plessis, who had 'formed the opinion' that he should be detained; he was told that it came from 'higher up'. When he asked who 'higher up', he was told that it was irrelevant.[1]

Manuel was taken to Loop Street police headquarters, processed, and then taken to Sea Point police station. He dreaded the prospect of another spell of solitary confinement.

In the 10 weeks he was out of jail, his friend Cheryl Carolus, who was then working for a group that provided medical support for ex-detainees, had urged him to get a proper medical and psychological check-up. As much as he had insisted that he was all right, she had insisted that he do this. 'We have to demonstrate to the younger comrades who may be emotionally scarred that there's nothing wrong with it,' she'd said. So Manuel saw Professor Frances Ames, professor of neurology at the University of Cape Town, who was well known by then for challenging and exposing the two district surgeons who had allowed black consciousness leader Steve Biko to be transported naked in the back of a van a thousand kilometres to Pretoria when he was suffering from brain damage as a result of torture.

Ames was a strong proponent of human rights: she and Manuel got on well from the start. As soon as Manuel was detained she spoke to the state psychiatrist Dr T Zabow and pressed him to prevail on the police to take Manuel out of solitary. It worked. Less than 36 hours later, Manuel was taken from the single Sea Point cell to Pollsmoor Prison.

At first Manuel thought that this was a holding operation on the part of the police – they would wait until the dates for the Anti-Apartheid Conference, scheduled for 24 and 25 September, had passed. Most of his fellow detainees – including Mountain Qumbela and Zoli Malindi – had been involved in its planning. But the dates came and went and they were still inside. Then his neighbour Huxley Joshua, who was also his neighbour in jail, was released on 4 October. Joshua had recently had a heart bypass operation and was still

ill. Then other organisers were released – Amy Thornton, a prominent white activist and Harald Harvey, a unionist. But still Manuel sat in prison.

Pollsmoor, a huge prison that stamps a punctuation mark at the foot of the mountains that begin a spinal journey down the southern False Bay shoreline, was different from Victor Verster. Where at Victor Verster the detainees had fought for and got various rights – milk and beds being two – here they had to start from scratch. Manuel soon realised that the prison worked on an elaborate system of corruption and patronage.

When the detainees insisted on a cup of milk a day – here, it's in the Government Gazette, they told the warders – their guards relented but pleaded with them not to tell the other prisoners. All the milk was being stolen and sold off. Even those warders who tried to play it straight soon crumbled in the face of systemic corruption. A new head of prison had been brought down from the Transvaal to try to clean up the corruption. He had a grey poodle, recalled Manuel, and would walk around the prison while his subordinates held their guard dogs fast. He was determined not to bend. But his subordinates knew better.

'Let me tell you how this works,' one told Manuel. 'One of these days somebody will bring him a box of bananas. And he's not going to touch it. The bananas will go off. Then a man will bring a second box and say, *"My baas. My seun is hier. Jy moet net vir hom mooi kyk."* ('My boss. My son is here. You must just look after him nicely.') Eventually the smell will get to this chap, and the day he touches the first fruit, just one, everybody in this prison will know ... That's how it works ... Soon someone will come to him and say: *"My oubaas, ek sien jy ry daai mooi Skyline. Maar ek sien jou tyres is glad. Nou dit is nie so in die Transvaal nie maar hier in die Kaap is dit nat in die winter en Oubaas moet nuwe tyres laat soek. One wil hê dat niks moet gebeur met Oubaas nie."* (The speech is a Cape patois. Translated loosely: 'I see the old boss drives that nice Skyline. But I see your tyres are smooth. Now it's not like this in the Transvaal, but in the Cape it's wet in winter. You must get new tyres. We don't want anything to happen to you.') A bribe or a threat? Who would know? But one day "Oubaas" would go to the retread shop in Retreat where he was promised a "good price", and that price would be nothing.'

Manuel and his comrades used the system to good effect. Ebrahim Rasool (who was later to become premier of the Western Cape) brought in a hot-plate. They had a TV and a video machine – they even watched the con-cert celebrating Nelson Mandela's seventieth birthday live from Wembley

Stadium. They had a radio.

In October, Manuel and six others, including Malindi, Qumbela and Theresa Solomon launched a court application for their release. In his affidavit, Manuel argued that he had nothing to do with the Anti-Apartheid Conference, nor had he any thoughts on the forthcoming October municipal elections, the first all-race (but still segregated) municipal elections, which the UDF had decided to boycott. 'Captain du Plessis asked me if I had spoken to people about the conference,' said Manuel in his affidavit. 'I informed him that socially I had because it was in the newspapers and was topical. Captain du Plessis then asked me about my views on the conference to which I responded that I was ambivalent. Captain du Plessis asked me what effect the conference would have on the October municipal elections. I told him from what I had read in the newspaper, the conference had nothing to do with the elections.' He used Zabow's name to plead that his continued detention 'will further affect my mental well-being'.

In any event, the Conference itself was banned by the government and therefore the reasons for his detention ceased to exist.

In a replying affidavit, Minister of Law and Order Adriaan Vlok said Manuel had been involved in 'so-called "people's education" which was an important form of the ANC's strategy of "people's war" and "people's power".' The purpose, he said 'is to dismantle the existing education system and to replace it with an alternative one' (*'onderwysstelsel af te takel en 'n alternatiewe stelsel in plaas daarvan, daar te stel'*). It was directly related to involving the youth in the revolution. He had also propagated a 'full-scale and open revolution' in South Africa 'modelled (*geskoei*) on the revolution in Nicaragua about which he had made a profound study'. Vlok's opinion was that despite his previous lengthy detention and despite the restrictions imposed on him, Manuel was 'so ideologically *'oortuig'* (convinced) that a revolution should take place in South Africa that he was not diverted from his ideals while he was in detention (*dat ek nie glo dat hy van sy ideale afgesien het terwyl hy in aanhouding verkeer het nie*). It was his opinion that Manuel should spend the rest of the Emergency in detention.[2]

Fortunately for Vlok he didn't have to prove his suspicions in any court, leaving aside the injustice of the laws in the first place. The detainees lost their application with costs.

Early in 1989 some 300 detainees held in indefinite detention began a hunger strike. It was a planned but desperate act. On 16 February Archbishop

278

Desmond Tutu, then Archbishop of Cape Town, the highest rank in the Anglican Church in southern Africa, went to see Vlok with a large church delegation that included Frank Chikane and Allan Boesak. They likened the situation of the hunger strikers to the plight of the Irish prisoner Bobby Sands, who had starved himself to death in jail. Vlok disagreed. To the amazement of the church leaders, he said the South African detainees' plight was worse: 'Sands had been convicted in court, whereas the South African detainees had never been charged.' He told the church leaders he would review the detentions and begin to release detainees.[3] The next morning, Manuel and the other detainees heard on their little radio about the church leaders' interventions. That afternoon Ebi Mohamed came to fetch him. 'I'm taking you home,' he said. Manuel was aghast. 'But you can't leave these old men here,' he said, referring to Malindi and Qumbela. 'They're going home soon,' said Mohamed. 'I didn't know how to deal with that,' said Manuel later.

Manuel 'packed slowly and made sad goodbyes to his cellmates'.[4] He was again released with heavy restrictions, including one that forbade the press from quoting him. 'I'm happy that he is home,' Lynne Matthews told a local reporter. 'But it is very sad that detainees had to take such drastic steps before they were released. I salute all who went on hunger strike in demand of their freedom.'[5]

LYNNE WAS PREGNANT AGAIN. Their second son, Pallo, was born two months after Manuel came out of Pollsmoor on 7 April 1989, nine months after he was released from Victor Verster. But there was to be little respite. Less than three months after Pallo's birth, the UDF executive decided that they should defy their banning orders.

'It was really to enable us to win back space,' said Willie Hofmeyr, who had also been held for nine months in detention at Pollsmoor. Because he was white, he was almost alone, except for seeing Ivan Toms occasionally. Toms was a doctor who worked in the Crossroads clinic. He had been sentenced for refusing to do military service, mandatory then for all young white men.[6] Hofmeyr had also been on a hunger strike. Thin already, his weight plummeted. The young Afrikaner, determined and stubborn, had refused to give up his fast until he was released. 'It was really important to get the leadership out of jail from a strategic perspective,' he said. 'When they came out they were quite scared of going back in, so even though we got about 200 to 300 leaders released during this process, there was little revival in internal political activities.' The UDF in the Western Cape had operated for some time after it been effectively shut down in the Transvaal, but by February 1988 heavy restrictions forced its work to a halt.

The quest to win back space put the UDF activists on a new collision course with the government. They planned to break their restriction orders and, if rearrested, would start a hunger strike straight away. 'So the weapon of detention couldn't be gained back,' explained Hofmeyr.

Lynne, not surprisingly, was less than enthusiastic about the plan. She had spent the past two years bringing up a small child alone, and now had another infant. But Manuel 'talked her through (the fact) that it was a collective decision'. There had already been a sharp spotlight on detention without trial in Johannesburg as three UDF leaders there – Murphy Morobe, Valli Moosa, and Vusi Khanyile, chair of the National Education Crisis Committee, had made a dramatic escape from prison in September 1988 and taken refuge in the US Consulate. They had feigned illness and escaped from hospital. Morobe later described the escape as 'one of the highest moments of my life'.[7] When they left the Consulate six weeks later, the government kept its word not to re-detain them.

In Cape Town it looked as though the battle for political space was going to be more tumultuous. Yet, strangely, there was no better time to wage it. The government was dancing to a score of discordant counterpoint. Unknown to the UDF leaders then, Nelson Mandela had been having secret talks with the government, including even the hard-line P W Botha, for the past four years. They did know, though, of the delegations of white businessmen, journalists and academics, particularly Afrikaans academics, who had trekked northwards to meet the ANC, and the political dent this made on the ruling party.[8]

It was an economic crisis that had forced white business to consider their options. In 1985, shortly before P W Botha's hard-line 'Rubicon' speech which, against all hope, promised only a harder fist, Chase Manhattan 'had prompted an international crisis of confidence in South Africa's finances when it stopped rolling over the loans to South Africa's borrowers'.[9] A year later, thanks to the focused and connected anti-apartheid movement in the United States, the US Congress imposed comprehensive sanctions against South Africa, and even overrode the veto of President Ronald Reagan. There was a total ban on new US investments in South Africa as well as new loans, a ban on landing rights and on imports of strategic minerals essential for South Africa's balance of

Manuel on his release from Victor Verster prison, 7 July 1988

(Photographs courtesy Benny Gool/Oryx Archive)

Above: With Govan, his first-born son, his mother and Whitey Jacobs

Left: With Govan and Lynne Matthews, Whitey Jacobs in the background

Below: With his lawyer, Ebi Mohamed

Top: Manuel at Cape Town airport after his release from Grootvlei prison in Bloemfontein in September 1989. He is holding his second son, Pallo, and Reggie Oliphant is on his left

Middle: Protest demonstration against violence in Natal, 1990

(Photographs courtesy Benny Gool/Oryx Archive)

Bottom: Manuel being warned by a policeman for participating in the demonstration

Top: Manuel with Nelson Mandela and Reg September at Cape Town airport, 1990 (courtesy Benny Gool/Oryx Archive)

Middle: With Allan Boesak and Nelson Mandela, Langa, 1993. Nosiviwe Mapisa-Nqakula is on the far right

Bottom left: With Dullah Omar, 1990 (courtesy Benny Gool/Oryx Archive)

Bottom right: With Walter Sisulu, 1990 (courtesy Benny Gool/Oryx Archive)

Above: With Govan, about 1990

Left: With Pallo and Jaimé, 1991 (courtesy Trevor Manuel)

Below: Christmas 1994, with Pallo and Jaimé (courtesy Trevor Manuel)

*Above: With
Pallo Jordan and
Fidel Castro at
Nelson Mandela's
inauguration as
president, May 1994*

*Left: Swearing in,
Parliament, 1994.
From left: Winnie
Madikizela-Mandela,
Mosiuoa 'Terror'
Lekota, Pallo Jordan,
Geraldine Fraser-
Moleketi, Trevor
Manuel (courtesy
Benny Gool/Oryx
Archive)*

*Bottom: Manuel
with his mother
and Steve Tshwete
at the opening of
Parliament, 1994
(courtesy Benny
Gool/Oryx Archive)*

Above and left: Kensington 'homecoming' meeting with 'Titie' (Auntie) Patel, the chair of the Kensington civic, soon after Manuel was appointed Minister of Trade and Industry in 1994. Wilf Rhodes is seated next to him

Below: With schoolchildren in Parliament, 1996

(Photographs courtesy Benny Gool/Oryx Archive)

Top: First Budget speech, 12 March 1997

Above: Mosiuoa 'Terror' Lekota congratulating
Manuel on his Budget speech

Left: Manuel and his family - his mother Philma,
Lynne, and his sons Pallo, Jaimé and Govan
- with President Nelson Mandela after Manuel's
first Budget speech

(Photographs courtesy Benny Gool/Oryx
Archive)

Top: Tiananmen Square,
Beijing, while attending the G20
meeting, 2005. From left: Lesetja
Kganyago, Trevor Manuel,
and Tito Mboweni and Monde
Mnyande of the Reserve Bank

Left: Personal Finance
cartoon by Colin Daniel, 2004
(Copyright Personal Finance and
Independent Newspapers)

payments. Sports sanctions were almost comprehensive and the few rebel teams that came to South Africa were subject to moral opprobrium at home and in South Africa.

Capital fled – much of it illegally – to the extent that some analysts estimate that South Africa lost more than R50 billion in the period 1985-1992.[10] Manufacturing, which had grown impressively during the 1960s behind a barrier of protective tariffs and was boosted by the reservoir of cheap labour created by apartheid, had been in decline since the 1970s. From the 1980s it rapidly shed jobs and little new investment was forthcoming.[11]

The country teetered in every respect. The government itself was deeply divided. On the one hand, certain senior officials gave the nod to talks with the ANC; on the other, its security forces, which under P W Botha had become the most powerful branch of the state, unleashed the most brutal campaign ever against the legal anti-apartheid opposition. Indefinite detention was one weapon in the arsenal of the state. But there were also judicial executions (from 1985 to 1987, 101 people were sentenced to death for politically related offences), and disappearances and assassinations, many of which would only be revealed years later in testimony before the Truth and Reconciliation Commission.

It is likely the reformists in government had a plan: they thought that if their counterparts in the police and army contained the internal opposition, they would be able to control the pace of negotiations and the political reforms they had come to believe were necessary for survival. It is just as likely, though, that the plan went awry, not only because they did not succeed in quelling the internal opposition but also because of the deep divisions in its own ranks. If the rulers were struggling to tread water, then so was the internal opposition, although it had more confidence that history was on its side. It was an interaction, as Manuel later described, it 'with a maelstrom moment of history. You can't write script for that stuff.'

In fact, the script, such as it was, seemed to have gone askew in 1985 already. Then, significant parts of the traditionally anti-government English press had cautiously supported the State of Emergency as a necessary prelude to reform. 'Organised commerce and industry (and ordinary black urbanites) have accepted the need for drastic short term action to break the cycle of violence and to restore law and order,' said the business publication, the *Financial Mail*, in an editorial. '(But) reform remains essential as a long-term solution to our woes. Reform however needs a return to something approaching normality in the townships – quickly.'[12]

Four years later, most of the English newspapers despaired of the repressive plan coming together: 'The re-imposition of the state of emergency is an admission of failure,' wrote the *Argus* in an editorial in June 1989 when the Emergency entered its fourth successive year. 'It shows the government is unable to run the country without suspending fundamental human rights and that it is unable to win over the general support of the populace to govern by normal means. The securocrats have again won the day.'[13]

But they hadn't quite, because the reform impetus in government was getting stronger. As early as 1981, enlightened Afrikaners such as Ton Vosloo, then editor of *Beeld*, had written that the ANC was the 'mother body of organised black politics ... The day will yet arrive when the South African government will sit down at the negotiating table with the ANC.'[14] He had argued that this was contingent on the ANC accepting a 'federal structure', yet the point about negotiation with the prohibited body was so overwhelming coming from an establishment figure, albeit a courageous one, that the details did not matter.

He was prescient. In 1985 a group of whites – including Afrikaans editor Harold Pakendorf, publisher Hugh Murray, and businessmen Gavin Relly, Tony Bloom, and Zac de Beer of the powerful Anglo American Corporation – met Oliver Tambo and his colleagues in Zambia. In 1987, Frederik Van Zyl Slabbert, the leader of the parliamentary opposition who had resigned from Parliament in despair and disgust, led a delegation of 50 Afrikaner intellectuals and journalists to meet the ANC in Dakar. Granted, most of them already opposed apartheid – they were not the establishment – but it significantly dented the perceived armour of Afrikaner unity. And around the same time, Professor Willie Esterhuyse, a political philosopher at Stellenbosch University, took Afrikaner colleagues and business leaders from Consolidated Gold to meet ANC leaders, including Tambo and Thabo Mbeki.[15] Esterhuyse then began a complex reporting relationship to the National Intelligence Service which was, internally, opening lines of communication to Nelson Mandela who was by then in Pollsmoor Prison.

By 1989, Mandela was already deep into talks with the regime. In early July of that year, he even saw President P W Botha, who amazed the jailed leader by pouring the tea himself. 'They talked relaxedly for half an hour about South African history and culture ... At the end, Mandela, more tensely, asked for the release of all political prisoners, which Botha politely refused.

But they agreed about the need for peace, prepared a minimal statement, and parted genially.'[16]

Mac Maharaj, then on the ANC's weighty Politico-Military Council, was a key operative in Vulindlela ('open the road'), an underground ANC operation inside the country launched in the mid-1980s. He was instrumental in helping Mandela get messages about his talks with government to Oliver Tambo in Lusaka. Maharaj met with some of the key UDF leaders to persuade them that Mandela was not 'selling out'. The clandestine meetings were dangerous. Most of the UDF leaders who were not in jail were either in hiding or restricted. And Maharaj himself, a wanted man if there ever was one, was in the country illegally and under cover. 'In South Africa today it is not possible to find former struggle activists who are prepared to admit that at one time they believed Nelson Mandela was selling out,' writes Maharaj's biographer, Padraig O'Malley.[17]

'Selling out,' explained Maharaj, 'meant that he would settle, and hence so would the black masses, for something less than majority rule.' Maharaj himself describes how a document from Mandela, meant for Tambo, had mistakenly landed in the hands of Jay Naidoo, then COSATU general secretary. Maharaj tracked down Ismail Momoniat in hiding and told him to bring Valli Moosa and Sydney Mufamadi, also a COSATU unionist who was then a member of the ANC underground in the Transvaal, to a meeting with him. Moosa met Maharaj at a coffee shop in Rosebank, Johannesburg. Line by line, Maharaj went through Mandela's letter: 'There is no sell-out here,' he told Moosa. 'He is urging PW to have talks with the ANC in order to resolve the conflict in South Africa. He is not negotiating for himself.'[18]

THE WORD 'NEGOTIATIONS' began to ripple through the Mass Democratic Movement (MDM) in 1989. The MDM was a loose alliance between the UDF and its affiliates and COSATU. Partly, it was a term coined in 1988 that reflected a new and important relationship between the political movement and the unions; partly it was a way to get around the heavy prohibitions the government had placed on the UDF.

For Manuel, in the middle of this 'maelstrom moment', he and his comrades battered by jail and by restrictions, it was an intellectually perplexing time. 'Liberation? I could never conceive of it.' The moment was about mobilisation, about keeping up the pressure. 'When the message came in about the Harare Declaration (you think) this is a sell-out. You had no conception. This was completely unprecedented.'

The Harare Declaration, adopted by the Organisation of African Unity (OAU) in August 1989, was driven largely by the ANC in exile, and particularly by its leader, Oliver Tambo. It grew out of a network of talks – between white business and the ANC, between the internal resistance movement and the ANC, between Tambo and African leaders such as Kenneth Kaunda and Julius Nyerere, and between Nelson Mandela and the government:

> We believe that a conjuncture of circumstances exists which, if there is a demon-strable readiness on the part of the Pretoria regime to engage in negotiations genuinely and seriously, could create the possibility to end apartheid through negotiations. Such an eventuality would be an expression of the long-standing preference of the people of South Africa to arrive at a political settlement.
>
> We would therefore encourage the people of South Africa, as part of their over-all struggle, to get together to negotiate an end to the apartheid system and agree on all the measures that are necessary to transform their country into a non-racial democracy. We support the position held by the majority of the people of South Africa that these objectives and not the amendment or reform of the apartheid system, should be the aims of the negotiations.[19]

Despite their surprise at the Harare Declaration, UDF leaders sensed that 'the armed struggle wasn't very successful' and that 'people were becoming tired'.[20] They had seen terrible violence in the townships, many had been locked up or restricted for years with no light on the horizon. The late 1980s were palpably different from the early part of the decade when the struggle was a compelling, life-forming adventure. In Cape Town, as in other towns, there was no life outside of it. *Grassroots*, the newspaper, held regular 'gumbas'.* These social events cemented the bonds between activists. They worked together, attended meetings together, shared houses and socialised with one another. 'We had no life outside of each other,' recalled Manuel. 'We had no material possessions to distract us.'

But by the late 1980s the harsh repression had forcibly severed many of those bonds. Some 30 000 people in total had been detained since the 1985 Emergency, many of the leaders, like Manuel, for three years or more. There was not much fun any more, just a focused earnestness to survive. 'There was

---

* Parties, usually held for fund-raising purposes.

a lot of despondency about the state of our struggle,' a Cape Town student activist, Febe Potgieter, told me at the time.[21]

What they needed, she said, was an 'inspiration'. They found it in the most basic and simple contradictions of an apartheid state that claimed to be reforming. Yet it took enormous reserves of energy to mobilise for what would be the last push against repression.

HOSPITALS, BEACHES, ARBITRARY LAWS: these were the key targets of what became known, after the ANC's 1952 campaign against racial laws, as the Defiance Campaign. On 2 August, hundreds of black patients 'successfully presented themselves for treatment at hospitals reserved for white people'.[22] In Durban, about 2000 people gathered at Addington Hospital, a large state hospital on the beachfront, in support of the 200 patients who demanded treatment.[23] There were smaller protests in other parts of the country – notably, Pretoria, Johannesburg, and even Welkom in the Free State.

In Cape Town, the campaign was preceded by the searing funeral of two young Athlone activists, Robbie Waterwitch and Coline Williams, 20 and 22 years old respectively, who had been blown up, apparently while trying to attach limpet mines to government buildings. The police put severe restrictions on the funeral, including the condition that only ordained ministers could speak.

The restriction was ignored. 'The time comes in the life of any nation where there remain only two choices: submit or fight. That time has come to South Africa.' Peter Mokaba, the voluble leader of the South African Youth Congress echoed the words of Mandela defending the establishment of the armed wing of the ANC 28 years before. Even the presiding priest repeated the phrase. ANC flags covered the coffins and when a handful of police armed with shotguns strode into the churchyard making straight for the ANC flag draped over the waiting hearse, youths formed a wall between it and the intruders and pushed them back into the street.

Archbishop Desmond Tutu was at the funeral. He put himself then, and later at the cemetery, between the police and the youth. When the police tore off the flags at the graveside, new flags emerged and the coffins were covered once more. As the police and the youth rushed at each other again, Tutu urged the 'comrades' back, telling them in his inimitable style that they were not 'running away' but 'marching to freedom'.

Something happened to the police that day, though: suddenly, at the cemetery, they dropped back, apparently on orders. The two young people were buried draped in the colours of green, black and gold. It was partly Tutu's intervention, but also would become a harbinger of police behaviour in the next six weeks. They would attack with ferocity on some occasions, but then just as surprisingly retreat. It was also a sign of the central role that the church, and particularly leaders such as Tutu and Boesak, was to play in this campaign that was eventually to politically weaken the government to the extent that it ran out of options.

The Defiance Campaign was essentially a moral one. This was not simply a Christian aversion to violence, despite the central role of the Church, but a strategic decision. 'The regime is always pushing us to the terrain of violence, where it is strongest,' a restricted (and hence unnamed) black leader told *New Yorker* writer Ray Bonner. 'We thought there was a dire need of new, creative ways of confronting the regime – not on the basis of violence but on the basis of morality.'[24]

And indeed the brazen defiance that was to take place in Cape Town was always centred around the most simple, most moral demands, and often in the sanctuary of the churches. On 6 August 1989, Cape Town activists embarked on their first brazen act of defiance. Former detainees – all of whom were heavily restricted – decided to defy their house arrest orders by going to a church service one Sunday and praying and singing well into the evening. The church was in Athlone, within walking distance of Manuel's house in Albemarle Road. All the former detainees had to be in their houses from 6pm to 6am, but some, such as Manuel, had weekend restrictions too. 'If one of my children gets sick at night,' complained Hilda Ndude, a UDF leader who lived in Guguletu, 'I can't even take them to hospital.'[25] Ndude, who had also spent several months in jail, lived alone with her five children.

The church service, which started at about 4pm, was packed with activists who had come to support their restricted comrades. Yet despite the bravery, there was a hint of anxiety in the air. For the first time in several months, those who had been in hiding, such as Cheryl Carolus, surfaced and were on the platform. One by one the former detainees declared their intention to defy their bans: 'This restriction order is the fourth I've had since I tried to put myself in the sun in this country,' said Christmas Tinto, one of Manuel's former jail mates. 'But today I've given myself freedom.'[26]

Tutu told the crowd about his negotiations with Vlok in February when he had persuaded the police minister to release Manuel and the others:

I told Mr Vlok: 'You know you have lost.' I said it nice and quietly, I didn't shout like now. I said 'You know you have lost, you know it from your own history. You believed you were being oppressed by the British and in the end you became free. The lesson you must learn from your own history is that when people decide to be free, nothing, just nothing, absolutely nothing can stop them.'[27]

Well after sunset the congregation, many embracing such religious fervour for the first time, continued to pray and sing until one of Manuel's neighbours walked on to the podium and whispered to him. A buzz went up on the platform where the banned leaders were sitting. Manuel whispered to Carolus and Tinto, held Carolus's hand briefly, and then turned back to the congregation. Uniformed police were strangely absent during the service when the 3 500 congregants sang praises to God and to the resistance. Foreign networks and local journalists crammed into every spare nook in the church. By then all the former detainees knew that police were outside Manuel's house in Athlone, and also at others' houses. When this was announced, the congregation broke off their service and accompanied Manuel home with the other detainees. Most of them had warning statements read to them but no one was arrested that night. 'It's very hard to arrest someone for being in church,' said Manuel later. 'You've got to understand the psychology of it. They've got to hold their own people. There's a TV camera right there ... and they're going to arrest me for having gone to church? And this thing is going to be played to Christians and Muslims all over the world and they're going to say, what bastards!'

After that most of the detainees ignored their restriction orders. Hofmeyr got arrested twice, charged, and released on bail. On the third occasion, he was refused bail because he had 'a history of disobeying his bail conditions'.

'I had stood up in public and said I'm going to continue doing this. It shows how weak the criminal justice system was that I actually got bail at all!' said Hofmeyr who became a fervent law enforcement official himself in the post-apartheid era. But the failure to lock him up initially was more a reflection of the ambivalence of the government in this interregnum.

Manuel also experienced this ambivalence. He had managed, through Franklin Sonn, then the rector of the Peninsula Technikon to get a job at the Mobil Foundation of which Sonn was chair. Sonn actually created the job for him as a 'policy coordinator', which gave him a pretty free hand to think about a future. It was here that he began to think more seriously about an economic future for the first time. He organised seminars on co-operatives, on black business ventures – a forerunner to Black Economic Empowerment (BEE) – and on education. Still under restrictions, he had to get permission to work, even to travel to work. But it was relatively easy. The police were not keen to put him back in jail, as they had shown with Hofmeyr. They were afraid that a renewed hunger strike might lead to a death in jail and they could ill afford this possibility.

So they tried everything to get Manuel to abide by his restrictions without actually arresting him. One afternoon, a few days after the defiant church service, Manuel loaded his two little boys in the car to drive to Buitenkant Street to attend a party for his Aunt Hester's eightieth birthday. Buitenkant Street was out of his magisterial district. Instead of arresting him when he had already broken the law, the police decided to prevent Manuel breaking it in the first place. They simply stood in his driveway and blocked his exit.

This apparent eagerness to maintain control while avoiding open confrontation spoke of a government in profound crisis. It was caught in the contradiction of trying to clean up its international image on the one hand, while placating its own conservative constituency on the other.

White establishment politics unravelled. This became apparent in the week following the Athlone church service, where former detainees unbanned themselves. The anti-apartheid newspaper, the *Weekly Mail*, revealed in August that Nelson Mandela had held secret meetings with senior government officials for the past three years.[28] Mandela's famous 'tea' meeting with P W Botha a month before was public knowledge. 'South Africans, black and white, were stunned.'[29]

Four months earlier the government had announced that there would be an election on 6 September, mainly to try to consolidate its support in an attempt to re-establish control and then institute reform. The Emergency had cost it support among whites to both the right and the left and now it hung dangerously on a precipice without a stay.

Botha, the grizzled old leader known as the 'Groot Krokodil' by friend and foe alike, had hung on to the presidency through his declining health, even though F W de Klerk had been elected party leader in February of that year. But in August De Klerk precipitated a showdown, announcing that he planned to visit Kenneth Kaunda, the president of Zambia, who had openly and solicitously sheltered the ANC in exile for the past 35 years. 'It was a meeting that De Klerk wanted as part of a long-range strategy to improve

South Africa's international standing. The next day, President Botha issued a terse statement saying he was 'not aware in terms of the rules governing overseas journeys by ministers of the proposed meeting. With this bizarre public rebuke to the Party leader ... the cantankerous Botha created a crisis that accelerated rapidly.'[30]

The showdown that De Klerk needed happened over the next two days and on the following Monday, 14 August, P W Botha resigned with a petulant speech broadcast live on state television. 'Zambia is the centre where the ANC plans and coordinates its military and political activities against the Republic of South Africa,' said Botha. 'In view of the general election of September 6, 1989 and the general attempts at disruption, I am of the opinion that it is inopportune to meet with President Kaunda at this stage.' He went on to reveal with unparalleled candour that his cabinet had asked him that very morning to step down. 'I asked them what reason I could offer for such a step ... They replied that I could use my health as an excuse. I replied that I am not prepared to leave on a lie.'[31] He would leave office the very next day, he said.

And he did. F W de Klerk took over as acting president. The National Party's right wing may have been a constraint on him, but the immensity of the effect of sanctions on the economy was more compelling. Just the year before there had been an outflow of R6,7 billion in capital (about $2,5 billion then) and the ANC, with huge international support, was pressuring foreign banks not to extend short-term loans due to be renegotiated the following year. 'It's getting through to the government that sanctions are working,' said Mike Daly at the time. 'The pressure is working.' Daly was the chief economist for Southern Life, then one of the country's largest financial houses.[32]

Strangely, at a time when conservative whites stood to lose everything, they had become more, not less intransigent. Boksburg, a small mining town about 20 kilometres east of Johannesburg, had become a minor battleground between the National Party government and its right-wing opposition, the Conservative Party. The Conservative Party municipality began to enforce the Separate Amenities Act fiercely, barring blacks from public parks and swimming pools. Black people in the nearby township responded with a crippling boycott of white business. The National Party used the conflict to paint a gloomy scenario to its voters about what would happen if the CP ran the country. In Zeerust, a farming town near the Botswana border, the local council did not bother to put up 'whites only' signs at the public park. They simply fenced it off. 'If you want to feel proud of your park, you must close it,' explained one white resident to a bewildered foreign correspondent. 'Then nobody can use it.'[33]

What better, then, than for the MDM to test the limits of reform on one of the most basic – and easily eradicable – apartheid laws: separate amenities. The hospital protests, particularly in Durban, had been a notable (and peaceful) success, as had protests against beach apartheid there. In Cape Town, beaches had already been largely desegregated. But at least two fell outside the municipal boundaries. They were situated in predominantly Afrikaans-speaking areas, and were still restricted to whites.

On Saturday, 19 August, MDM activists in Cape Town heeded a widely publicised call to 'desegregate' a long, sandy stretch of beach at the eastern end of False Bay, known as the Strand. Signs still proclaimed: 'BEACH AND SEA; WHITES ONLY.' The 'black' beach around the mountain range was a small stretch of pebbly sand on a rocky, precipitous stretch of coast with dangerous currents.

The police also heeded the call, and when the MDM activists arrived at the Strand in their hundreds, they found a new sign on the beach, right next to one that said 'DOGS NOT ALLOWED'. It said: 'DANGER, NO ENTRY, SAP DOG TRAINING' (SAP stood for South African Police). And, indeed, on the other side of coils of barbed wire, scores of armed riot police walked their guard dogs along the pleasant stretch of sand. Many local whites were shocked by the display of force. 'This is a sad day for South Africa,' said one young white father.[34] Desmond Tutu arrived, walked on the beach, and then led a small demonstration of the people who had gathered there, many with picnic baskets, expecting, perhaps, a rather more pleasant demonstration than what was to be. As soon as the Archbishop left, the police laid into the crowds, beating many and arresting cameramen and journalists. It was an extraordinary display of brutality, witnessed by local white people and later the world who saw the footage that foreign networks managed to secrete from the police.

But the leadership was not there. Manuel and the more prominent leaders of the MDM had decided 'we need a Plan B'. Plan B was to gather at Blaauwberg Strand, across the Peninsula on the Atlantic coast. The ocean temperatures are much cooler than on the False Bay coast but it is a beautiful beach with a classic postcard view of Table Mountain and Robben Island. And it was still proclaimed for whites only. As soon as Manuel and his comrades heard about the barbed wire and the police dogs, they put Plan B into action and buses ferried hundreds of activists there. Tutu got a message to go there directly from the Strand. When Tutu arrived, there was already mayhem. 'They really beat people up,' recalled Manuel.

An Anglican priest was severely injured. 'They climbed into him,' Tutu told me. 'Daggers were drawn. When I got there I said to the people, look you have made your point, now you've got to demonstrate to these people that you are disciplined. In fact, I asked the police if I could use their loudhailer.' He laughed at this recollection. 'I don't think they were overkeen but they realised that the situation was very tense. And I got the people to sing *Nkosi Sikelele* [the African hymn that was the anthem of the liberation movement], and then I said, let's just show them how disciplined we are, get back on the buses. Which they did!'

At a church service the next day Tutu summed up the excruciating quandary the government found itself in: 'They say that apartheid is dead but really it's one of the most extraordinary corpses I've ever seen … They had dogs, they had tear gas, they had quirts. To do what? To stop black people walking on God's beaches.'[35] And then he hailed the MDM's victory: 'If we got to the beaches we won; if we didn't get to the beaches we won, because you are saying to the world, 'If we do not get to the beaches, we have been stopped by apartheid, we have been stopped by dogs. Dogs can walk on God's beaches. Black people cannot walk on God's beaches."'[36]

Manuel and his fellow strategists were keenly attuned to the government's dilemma. A few months before, UDF leaders had been invited to visit US President George Bush and British Prime Minister Margaret Thatcher. (Manuel did not go as he had not been granted a passport.) Albertina Sisulu led the delegation. The test of reform, they had told two of the South African government's most tolerant international supporters until then, would be whether there was a climate for free political activity.[37] That Saturday on the beaches, the government dismally failed that test.

The MDM did not let up the pressure. At a service in the Cathedral after the beach incident, which was attended by about 4 000 activists, Manuel took over the pulpit as soon as Tutu had finished his sermon. 'AMANDLA,' he shouted, his right arm in the air, his fist clenched. The Cathedral reverberated as the crowd responded: 'AWETHU.'

'Comrades,' he said, 'there's an old Kikuyu proverb. No matter how long the night, the day is sure to come. We are gathered here today to unban our organisations. We have been through three years of a very dark night ... but the actions of our people around this time and more especially yesterday show us that we are forcing the sun to rise in our country.'

It was a speech that was on the face of it militant and defiant. But it was also a more measured call on activists to reorganise and even to begin to rebuild the country. 'The challenge to us today, comrades, is to move from the joys of the toyi-toyi to the hard work of rebuilding our street committees. The challenge to us today, comrades, is to move away from the mere flashes of excitement and enthusiasm to the long, hard slog that will bring light to our country. That light, that bulwark against state attack, is our community-based organisations, which, with our allies COSATU, will effectively improve the quality of life. Because we must always remember that the masses of our country are not engaged in struggle because of any ideas in our heads. They are engaged in struggle to improve on the quality of their lives ... We want to unban our organisations not as a publicity stunt, but as a solemn commitment to our intention to build democracy in this country from the bottom up.'[38]

One by one, those organisations that had been banned during the Emergency, came to the altar and unfurled their colours, the last being the UDF which unrolled a gigantic yellow, red and black banner.

The next Sunday Manuel and his fellow banned leaders went around the Peninsula, from church to church, through Athlone, through Silvertown, urging ready congregations to march with them. The police, as befitted their schizophrenic behaviour of the past several weeks, held off. The country was now on a cusp of change as it had never been before. 'There's a state of high alert. We've got this sense now,' said Manuel.

The next morning, there was a hiatus in that high alert because at 4am the security police came to his house and detained Manuel for the fourth time in as many years. Many of his fellow MDM leaders were detained at the same time. Hofmeyr was arrested the same day for breaking his restriction order by picketing outside a major bank that was sponsoring a rebel rugby tour. So was a UDF leader and lawyer in the African township of Guguletu who had recently returned from a three-year semi-exile stint in Geneva. His name was Bulelani Ngcuka, and he was later to become Hofmeyr's boss in the post-apartheid National Prosecuting Authority.

The agreement between activists was that they would go on hunger strike the moment they were re-detained. Manuel said he wasn't properly consulted – a statement had been made to the press before everyone had agreed.

Nonetheless, he could not break ranks, so when he saw the district surgeon (now routine after being detained) and the doctor asked if he was going on hunger strike, he said yes. He was kept for the first few days alone in Manenberg police station. 'Very bad,' he said. The cells were inside the building so no natural light came in and the corridors echoed eerily. Every time a policeman picked up the keys, he could hear. Three nights into his detention, he heard the yard door unlock, and then his cell door. He sat up and saw two white men at the door 'pissed out of their skulls'. One said to him: *'Jou vark, jy's wakker.'* Then they locked the door and left. It was the first time, through all of his detentions, that he had thought that the police were going to 'take me out'. It was part of the sinister ambivalence of the time that resonated around the country.

Two days later, he was woken before dawn by security policemen he knew. They told him, *'Pak jou goed'.* They bundled Manuel, handcuffed, his hands behind his back, into a car and made for the N1, driving north. No Victor Verster this time. They drove past Paarl, over the imposing Du Toitskloof Pass that forms a natural barrier around the Boland, past Worcester and on through the arid Karoo. On the way the policemen ate *'padkos'* packed by their wives – the previous night's braaivleis (barbecue), sausages and chops and rolls. They offered their prisoner food but he would not eat. By the time they reached the central Karoo town of Beaufort West, about 400 kilometres from Cape Town, Manuel's wrists were bleeding from the tight cuffs and his hands were swollen. They uncuffed him to allow him to use the bathroom and then put them on again, but this time more loosely and in front, and drove to Bloemfontein, some 1000 kilometres from his hometown. 'We're just doing our job,' they told him as they drove. 'Please don't hold it against us.'

In Bloemfontein he was put into Grootvlei Prison, a 'godforsaken place'. One of the warders who spoke good English tried to befriend him, confiding that he wanted to get into Intelligence and that he didn't believe in God. Manuel resolved not to talk to him about religion, at least not with the same candour as he had discussed the subject with his fellow detainees at Victor Verster. He did not trust the man or the circumstances at all.

One by one other detainees, all of them on hunger strike, joined him: a teacher from Grahamstown, who arrived shaken after the police car he was driven in had skidded across a road into a dam, with him in handcuffs. The police couldn't find the key as the car slowly submerged so they'd had to drag him out of the water. Then came a man from Duncan Village, the old township near East London. Then his fellow Cape Town activists, Bulelani Ngcuka and Tsili Mososoli who had been in detention with him before.

None of them ate.

Back in Cape Town, Manuel's fellow executive member Willie Hofmeyr gave his captors headaches. He, too, stopped eating; his weight plunged. The security police tried to transport him to Kroonstad, a small town in the northern Free State, even further from Cape Town than Bloemfontein. But his lawyers fought for him to be admitted to hospital instead as he began suffering painful stomach cramps. The second day into his hunger strike he had begun drinking juice, more because of a cool-headed calculation about the political situation outside than because of weakness. By then, there were massive demonstrations every day, and he realised that publicity was a major weapon on the side of the hunger strikers. If anything distracted press attention from them, the point of their suffering would be blunted.

He drank juice for five days and then switched to water only. He had read about the effects of a hunger strike – in fact, many of those who risked detention knew the Bobby Sands story well. Sands, the young Irish Republican prisoner, had died after 66 days on a hunger strike. Minister Vlok had been correct when he told Desmond Tutu that at least Sands had been tried and sentenced, unlike the South African detainees. But Sands had fasted to get political status for Republican prisoners who were treated as criminals by the British authorities.

'You feel terrible for the first few days,' said Hofmeyr. 'You feel really hungry, but by about day five your stomach collapses, which is what happened to me.'

If one gets through the first few days, a hunger strike becomes easier in many respects, although more dangerous. After a few days on a water fast, the liver starts to convert fatty acids into fuel, producing ketones in the blood. 'This stage is called ketosis and among its many by-products is a build-up of acetoacetate, which is believed to produce mild intoxication, and a release of beta endorphins, which are linked to satiety. Ketosis may explain an experience common to fasters and anorexics: the disappearance of hunger, accompanied by rushes of elation.'[39]

Certainly, in the case of the South African detainees, the hunger strike provided focus. 'It's much more empowering than sitting in detention on your own for six months,' said Hofmeyr. 'One of the really debilitating things about detention is your incredible dependence on people outside. If you need a pen, you must remember to tell people when they visit, that the next week, when they come, among all the other hundred things they are doing, they must remember to bring you a pen. If they don't you can't write for a week! So the nice thing about a hunger strike is that you have a sense of taking your destiny in your own hands and being in control.'

While he was starving, Hofmeyr launched several court applications: one to stop him being chained to his hospital bed, and when the prison authorities responded that he was being treated just as other prisoners were, his lawyer, 'Lang Dawid' (D P) de Villiers, replied that the authorities were not 'applying their minds' to his situation: after 18 days on a hunger strike he was hardly a flight risk. Doctors at Groote Schuur hospital contrived to drag out tests so that the police could not move him to Kroonstad.

Hofmeyr's father Arend, himself from an old Afrikaner family in the Cape, eventually managed to see Minister Vlok, Basie Smit, senior commander of the security police, and General Johan van der Merwe, then the commissioner of police, to plead for his release. Twenty-one days into his hunger strike, the police said they would release him if he agreed to abide by his restrictions. Hofmeyr said no. His father was devastated, 'but I was very stubborn in those days'. After 28 days, weighing just 30 kilograms (66 pounds), he was released unconditionally. 'Essentially,' he said, 'we achieved our objectives because after that the UDF, and then the ANC, was unbanned.'

While Manuel, Ngcuka and their cell mates were starving themselves in Bloemfontein, the MDM leaders intervened to stop their health deteriorating. Phumzile Mlambo-Ngcuka, Bulelani's wife, who would become a cabinet minister and deputy president in post-apartheid South Africa, visited Ngcuka in Grootvlei. She had a strong message for the detainees. The comrades had met, she told them, the Detainees Parents' Support Committee had met. They were angry with them because of the hunger strike. Why were they imposing this hardship on themselves? What did they want to achieve? They must stop it now. This was not a request; this was an instruction.

Slowly the prisoners began eating again: drinking juice, then a nutritional supplement, then a thin 'pap' (porridge). Two days later Ngcuka and Mososoli were released. Two weeks later, on 27 September, Manuel was released. Lynne and his lawyer, Ebi Mohamed, came to Grootvlei to take him home. That night he flew back to Cape Town to a tumultuous welcome. 'Hundreds of jubilant supporters packed the arrivals section of D F Malan airport last night to welcome Western Cape UDF member Mr Trevor Manuel who had been released from Grootvlei Prison in Bloemfontein,' reported *The Argus*.[40] 'The huge toyi-toyiing crowd, which held banners proclaiming "Viva Trevor" and "Welcome Home", sang as Mr Manuel, who appeared cheerful, entered the airport building.'

'Clearly,' recalled Tutu, 'what that was saying was that this was significant young man.' Tutu himself was not there but his wife Leah was. 'It was pandemonium at the airport.'

MANUEL RETURNED TO A changed country. Reform ebbed and flowed like an undercurrent beneath repression, but in the month he'd been in jail, that current had strengthened.

Cape Town itself had suffered and triumphed alternately. In Mitchell's Plain, schoolchildren emerged from their corners to defy the Emergency laws. They rallied and marched, but the police resorted to the tactics of terrorising a whole neighbourhood. One victim was Ricardo Adonis, then just 14, who came out of a shop to find himself in a crush of schoolchildren fleeing from the police. 'They said we must all run from the Boers, so I ran and jumped over a wall. Two (police officers) caught me. One fisted me. Then they threw me back over the wall on to the cement and then into the van on my head. When I told them I didn't riot, they said "Don't talk shit." '[41]

On 2 September, a few days after Manuel and the other UDF leaders had been arrested, a march in town was brutally broken up the police, who whipped and beat bystanders, including a group of foreign tourists. Near St George's Cathedral, the centre of the Anglican congregation in the country and also an important centre of resistance, the police mounted a water cannon and sprayed the protesters with purple dye. The idea was that those stained with purple would be easy targets for arrest later. In a scene that echoed one at Tiananmen Square in Beijing earlier that year, when a lone protester scrambled on to a military tank advancing on protesters, in Cape Town a protester climbed on to the water cannon and turned its nozzle away from the people towards buildings, which were drenched in purple dye. Furious, the police then resorted to their more traditional weapons of batons and tear gas, injuring scores of people. Medics who tried to attend to them were arrested. Many of the victims took refuge in the Cathedral and Tutu was summoned to protect them from further assault. He negotiated with the police to allow them safe passage, and gave the shocked and battered protesters some hope with a simple message about their humanity:

'Say to yourselves, in your heart, God loves me. In your heart: God loves me, God loves me, God loves me … I am of infinite value to God. God created me for freedom … My freedom is inalienable.' Straighten up your shoulders, he urged them, 'like people who are born for freedom'.[42]

(A graffiti artist displayed a keen sense of humour after the event, scrawling on a city wall: 'The purple shall govern.')

Two days later it would have appeared to any outsider that the country was on the edge of complete dictatorship. A meeting called under the banner of 'Free and Fair Elections' was banned. Then the organisers arranged a church service at the Buitenkant Street Methodist Church on Monday, 4 September, two days before the elections. The Methodist Church brought an urgent interdict against the police that very night as security forces whipped would-be churchgoers and passers-by alike as they walked down Buitenkant Street. The church service was declared legal at 11pm that night but not before scores of people had been injured, and clerics, including Boesak and Tutu, arrested. The Reverend Jackie Jooste, the presiding minister of the Methodist Church, was denied entry into his own church. That early spring evening in Cape Town was heavy with terror. I recall walking down Buitenkant Street towards the church when a car full of strangers stopped beside me and urged me to get in. 'They'll beat you if they find you on the street,' said my rescuers. And, indeed, even the 13-year-old daughter of Charles Villa-Vicencio, a religious studies academic, later a senior official at the Truth and Reconciliation Commission, was badly injured by police with sjamboks as she made for her mother's car outside the church. The streets emptied. The spirit of defiance, it seemed, had been extinguished.

Two days later, the segregated elections were held. They were sheathed in a dark violence that gripped Cape Town's townships throughout the day and into the night. Roads in Mitchell's Plain and other townships were almost impassable because of burning barricades. By the next morning, at least 20 people had been reported killed by the police.

When Tutu received this news, he wept and spent much of the remaining day in his chapel at Bishopscourt. The next day he was to make a decision that changed the atmosphere in Cape Town so profoundly that it turned the whole country inside out. At the memorial service for the dead, on Friday, 6 September, he told his personal assistant Matt Essau that he had decided to call for another protest march, right through the centre of the city of Cape Town. 'He blanched a bit,' recalled Tutu, and said couldn't it be a little later to 'give us more time'. The idea for the march, Tutu told me, had 'just happened, almost *goops*, like that'. After he had come out of his chapel prayers 'the idea of marching just sort of hit me'. The UDF leaders still out of jail, such as Cheryl Carolus, were doubtful. 'I think they were a little upset that I'd gone ahead and called it (without consulting them). It was at the time of "Well, do you have a mandate",' he reflected years later, with a throaty chuckle. He told his biographer John Allen that he had told Carolus: ' "God told me and I'm afraid we can't argue with God." ... It looks as though you are arrogant and presumptuous, yes, but the trouble is that I knew I was not my own master. At least *I* believed that.'[43]

Whatever the role of a higher being, Tutu judged the political climate more accurately than most of the activists embroiled in day-to-day battles with the police. De Klerk's first act as de facto head of the country (he was installed as president on 20 September) was to send in the troops to keep blacks off the Cape beaches. It cost him dearly at a time when South Africa badly needed international economic and political support to break the long impasse. Moreover, senior figures in the white establishment now, more than at any time before, expressed their revulsion and despair at the security forces. The newly installed mayor of Cape Town, Gordon Oliver, who had attended the Friday memorial service, told reporters he would join the march. White opposition members of parliament also expressed support for it. Both Margaret Thatcher and George Bush told Tutu they were pressing the government to negotiate. Tutu and Boesak briefed ambassadors and asked them to monitor the behaviour of the police.[44]

The government itself was split: the police tried to persuade the political leaders to interdict the march organisers; some cabinet members, such as Pik Botha, argued that the march should be allowed. Then followed a flurry of negotiations between Tutu and Boesak on the one hand, and emissaries sent by De Klerk, such as Johan Heyns the moderator of the (white) Dutch Reformed Church. Heyns suggested that the church leaders go with him to De Klerk to ask for permission to hold the march, but was politely rebuffed. The police minister, Adriaan Vlok, phoned Tutu to ask him to cap the number of marchers and to apply for magisterial permission to hold the march. Tutu was in his offices at Bishopscourt at the time, as John Allen writes, in a meeting with leaders of the MDM. He put Vlok on speaker phone. 'He refused both requests and, to the amusement of the gathering, told Vlok that he didn't mind if policemen lined the march route, as long as they kept their hands in their pockets.'[45] Two days before the planned march, De Klerk said the government would allow it: 'The door to a new South Africa is open. It is not necessary to batter it down,' he said. It was, writes Patti Waldmeir, then the *Financial Times* correspondent in South Africa, 'the first irreversible step to a new South Africa'. De Klerk's fellow cabinet member Gerrit Viljoen told Waldmeir later that it was a 'more fearful leap into the dark than any the president had made later – including the release of Nelson Mandela'.[46]

For their part, the leaders of the march and MDM marshals entreated their supporters not to provoke police action. In a brief service at the Cathedral before the march, a cleric warned them that they would be considered 'agents of the system' and removed should they 'resort to violence' or do anything to disrupt what was intended to be a 'disciplined, peaceful march'.[47]

Nobody knew how many people would turn out. By 11am on 13 September, two hours before the advertised time of the march, the Cathedral, which was the rallying point, overflowed. Press reports estimated that that a further 8000 people jammed the streets outside. By the time the march began, more than 30000 people followed its leaders, who included Tutu, Boesak and Gordon Oliver; Jakes Gerwel, the rector of UWC; Sheik Nazeem Mohammed, president of the Muslim Judicial Council; the Reverend Colin Jones, Dean of the Cathedral; and Jay Naidoo, the general secretary of COSATU. Office workers hung out of windows and over balconies. White businessmen such as John Drake and Ian Sims, managing director of Shell and chairman of BP Southern Africa respectively, marched, as did white members of the parliamentary opposition.[48]

'The MDM leaders disperse the police,' read one headline, and although a few uniformed police officers took up positions near Parliament, they left the marchers alone as they thronged their way to the City Hall, about one and a half kilometres away. As they started out, the Reverend Lionel Louw of the Western Province Council of Churches addressed them: 'We are assembled here today as a city to express our outrage at what we've seen the past two weeks … We shall march towards our freedom in this city and all other cities. This is our day today.'[49]

And it was. Posters ranged from the poignant to the humorous: 'Stop Killing Our People', read several; 'Stop Vlokking Us About', another.

UDF banners were festooned, as were the colours of the ANC, the same colours that less than a month before the police ferociously ripped off the coffins of the two young cadres buried in Athlone.

The crowd snaked and swarmed its way through the streets of Cape Town. By the time the end of the line reached the destination, two and a half hours had passed since they left the Cathedral. Boesak and Tutu addressed the crowd. Tutu, with his unique way of maintaining both discipline and enthusiasm in a crowd, invoked everyone to hold hands and then said: 'Mr de Klerk, please come here. We are inviting you, Mr de Klerk, we invite you, Mr Vlok, we invite all the cabinet. We say, come, come here, can you see the people of this country? Come and see what this country is going to become. This country is a rainbow country.'[50]

A rainbow country. It was the first time Tutu had used the expression that was to become a visionary driver throughout the often painful transition to come. 'Our freedom will be beautiful when it comes,' said a woman from the Cape Flats who was standing next to me in the crowd, her voice choked with tears.

THE MARCH SPARKED SIMILAR MARCHES across the country, most of them led by the clergy. It was into this new narrative of impending freedom that Manuel landed when he stepped on to the tarmac from the plane that had brought him from his prison in Bloemfontein. 'The country was a different place,' he recalled. 'The banning order was kept but it was mere form then.'

In October 1989, De Klerk released all the Rivonia trialists, except Mandela. Govan Mbeki, the oldest of the group of men who had been sentenced to life imprisonment with Mandela in 1964, had been released in 1987 as his health deteriorated. In spite of pleas by the government not to stir up crowds, the Rivonia men were welcomed by thousands of people at a rally in Soweto, and not long afterwards they were granted passports to consult with the ANC leadership in Lusaka. Change now developed a momentum of its own.

In November, Manuel was granted a temporary passport to go to a conference in Paris organised by the Danielle Mitterrand Foundation. It was an entirely new experience for him. It was the first time he'd been out of the country except for his two exploratory trips to Botswana a decade earlier. He didn't even have a proper coat to protect him against the European winter. 'I've never been so cold in my whole life.'

'It was bloody cold,' recalled Alec Erwin, who was also there. He had unsettled some of the South African delegates, according to the former opposition leader Van Zyl Slabbert by 'thundering': 'You fat cats have had your chance. When we take over, there will be no private property, industry will be fully nationalised, and the state will be the only real instrument for economic development.'[51] Erwin told me there was 'a large dose of poetic licence' in this account. He presented a paper that drew heavily on the two groups of economic researchers loosely convened by the union movement. 'Since neither of these adopted such a position it is unlikely that I said this … frankly, I don't recall any such thing, particularly since such a caricature has never been my position.'[52]

Nonetheless, the perception of the clash over economic policy was a forerunner to some of the conflicts in which Manuel would be embroiled in the years of the transition. But then, he was only pleased to be out, outside of jail, outside of Cape Town, outside the country, meeting ANC leaders such as Thabo Mbeki, Barbara Masekela and Brigitte Mabandla who formed part of the ANC delegation, and disappearing into bars with some of the harder-drinking South African journalists who were also there. The way the South Africans took advantage of their newfound freedom on the streets of Paris rattled the Parisian police assigned to protect them. It was only a few months before that Dulcie September, the ANC representative in Paris, had been assassinated.

But it was a heady time, as Manuel described it. 'Heady. Heady. Because then you knew this was over. But you didn't know what quite next.'

CHAPTER 19

The narrative of freedom

O N THE MORNING OF 2 FEBRUARY 1990, Trevor Manuel stood on a makeshift podium in Greenmarket Square, the cobbled plaza that is one of the oldest parts of Cape Town. He was badgering a young reporter from the *Cape Times* to get an advance copy of the speech President F W de Klerk was to deliver to mark the opening of Parliament. The reporter demurred, saying it was embargoed. In fact, only accredited reporters in a 'lock-up' in Parliament had access to the speech, so close were its contents kept. Manuel believed the day would not disappoint him. But he wanted to make sure. 'We didn't have the exact detail, which is why we wanted the speech.'

It was important because in the past four months – since coming out of jail at the end of September – his political activity centred round persuading MDM supporters that the time for negotiations had come. 'By the time 2 February came this was our line, this was our mandate.'

The alacrity with which the idea of negotiations was embraced was remarkable. It showed the extent to which communication lines between the exiled ANC leadership and the internal leadership were maintained, even during the harsh crackdown during the last days of apartheid. 'Amazingly brave things were done by people just to pass a message,' Murray Michell told me. 'A lot of it was then left to autonomous, independent decision makers of the sub-structures because of the difficulties of coordination and communication. It was rough, it was very rough.' By 1990, Michell was in a 'coordinating' position in Vula in the Western Cape.

Manuel was aware of the Vula activity in Cape Town, but it appeared as a flurry in his peripheral vision. Both he and Michell knew it would be too dangerous for him to be 'in the loop', although he did meet Mac Maharaj, who was operating underground, at least once when he was in Cape Town. The underground structures were vertically defined where one would operate on a strictly 'need to know basis'. Then there was the broader political space 'and Trevor was one of the people who was there, in the limelight, making decisions'. If there was tension between the decisions taken by the legal, if restricted, resistance organisations and the underground, Michell would be one of the people who would engage Manuel. 'There was always a tension. From time to time there'd be a one-on-one engagement – "Trevor, just explain this, how the hell have you arrived at this decision" … (But) for me it was a test of that loyalty. You've got to hold the line. You've got to trust a person's integrity.'

Michell, together with two other ANC activists in the underground, prepared a booklet at around this time called *The Weapon of Negotiations*. But they also continued to prepare back-up plans for armed insurrection. It was not that the two policies were in contradiction of each other; rather, they ran on parallel paths.

Michell's contact with Manuel became more circumscribed in 1989 partly because, while Manuel was restricted, Michell himself was suddenly the target of a major police surveillance operation. 'I had squads of 24 cars monitoring me all the time. I couldn't *move* without this huge contingent. I'd get on the plane and there'd be six people on the plane with me.' Vula's strength was that it had focused on using technology that could match, if not outmatch, the police.[1] Michell and his comrades managed to penetrate the police radio signals, and when he realised that they were close on his trail, Michell went to ground for a few crucial weeks and stopped seeing Manuel.

The government played much the same game as the ANC: it moved towards talks and a steady liberalisation after September 1989 on the one hand, and shored up violent counter-resistance on the other, increasingly through the medium of disaffected non-ANC supporting black people. The *witdoek* war in Crossroads in 1986 was an early indication of this strategy.

Far more serious and sustained was the conflict in KwaZulu-Natal which, although it had a basis in real differences between the supporters of the MDM and Inkatha (mainly, but not exclusively, based on divisions between urban and rural people), was mercilessly stoked by the security forces.

By mid-1989, KwaZulu-Natal (it was then the black 'homeland' of KwaZulu and the province of Natal) was by far the hardest hit in terms of Emergency detentions. A total of 828 people were being held under the Emergency there, out of a national total of 2 386 detainees. The urban areas around Johannesburg and the Vaal, by far the most politicised region, had slightly fewer at 820, and the Western Cape had only 84 people in Emergency detention at that time.[2]

COSATU was instrumental in trying to broker talks between the increasingly hostile camps of the UDF and Inkatha, partly because many workers were, at least at one stage, sympathetic to the more traditional values of Inkatha. But as much as they tried to get peace talks off the ground, the security police seemed to scupper them. Alec Erwin, a senior COSATU official, was one of the peace brokers. Erwin and Diliza Mji, an important UDF leader in Durban, worked hard to organise a meeting between Chief Mangosuthu Buthelezi and the ANC's Thabo Mbeki, but it was derailed by the false pamphlet purporting to come from the UDF which flayed Buthelezi.

Later that year, South Africa's small but feisty alternative press produced evidence that Inkatha warlords, who had created havoc in several townships around Durban and Pietermaritzburg, were being funded and armed by the government. This was later confirmed by the Goldstone Commission which found that a 'third force' in various townships, including those in KwaZulu-Natal, had been supported by the security forces. But by the late 1980s, the collusion of the police with Inkatha was clear to their opponents in the UDF and COSATU. As the peace talks floundered, the MDM opted to set up 'self-defence units'. In mid-1989 Erwin and Murphy Morobe, from the Transvaal UDF, travelled to Lusaka to collect R50 000 to fund these units. They brought the cash back to South Africa in a suitcase.

By some fortuity, they received a message en route that instead of alighting in Johannesburg, their original plan, they should continue to Cape Town. Mbeki wanted them to pass a message to Manuel and his UDF comrades that Maggie Thatcher might visit South Africa for talks with P W Botha, and that if she did they should hold off on demonstrations in the hope that she may persuade Botha to start negotiations. So with the money still in their travel bags, Erwin and Morobe hopped on another flight to Cape Town as soon as they landed from Lusaka, evading the security police waiting for them at Johannesburg airport. It was there Erwin met Manuel for the first time, in a brief window period in 1989 when he wasn't in jail. The atmosphere in Cape Town was 'pretty rough' then, recalled Erwin, and it was difficult to discuss any sort of message of conciliation.

But the incident summed up the necessary ambiguities of the time. A mission completed to get cash to set up 'self-defence units' on the one hand, and one to transmit a message of tolerance on the other, towards one of apartheid's most fervent international apologists.

These were the two strands that continued well into the 1990s on both sides. But by the end of 1989 the ANC decided, irrevocably, on talks as the first line of struggle. All the rest was back-up.

When the released Rivonia trialists visited Lusaka towards the end of 1989, Alfred Nzo, the ANC's secretary-general, was acting for ANC leader Oliver Tambo who was recovering from a stroke. He famously mixed up two key speeches written to mark the occasion. One was meant for the ANC's NEC, and was an internal acknowledgement that the armed struggle had merely been armed propaganda and that negotiations were the only path to political power. The other was an exuberant exhortation to strengthen the ANC, intended to be delivered at a public rally to welcome the Rivonia men and at which the Zambian President, Kenneth Kaunda, was due to speak. Nzo mixed up the speeches. He gave the one meant for the NEC at the public rally. Old activists, including those who had travelled from South Africa, and the press, were astonished by his apparent candour. The press corps rushed off to file their stories without waiting for Kaunda's speech.[3] The struggle stalwarts, accustomed to canvassing these issues behind closed doors, scratched their heads. But while it may have been a gaffe, the message about the ANC's willingness to negotiate filtered through to every level both inside and outside the country.

IN DECEMBER 1989 THE ANTI-APARTHEID conference that Manuel was arrested for the previous year took place. This time it was called the 'Conference for A Democratic Future'. It was held at the University of the Witwatersrand in Johannesburg. There was a second conference in January, hosted by the Kagiso Trust, called 'From Opposing to Governing: How Ready is the

Opposition?' 'Just 18 months before,' writes Jeremy Seekings, 'it had been almost inconceivable that either conference could have been held: the state would not have allowed them and the UDF-MDM would not have imagined the themes worthwhile.'[4]

It was more broad-ranging than any such conference had been for several years. It included the unions, the UDF, and the black consciousness groupings, such as AZAPO. Liberal business organisations, such as the Consultative Business Movement, opposition parliamentarians, and even Bantu Holomisa, the progressive military ruler of the Transkei – oxymoronic as that may sound – attended as observers. More than 4 000 people from about 2 000 organisations attended and its key purpose was to examine the role of negotiations in the quest to end apartheid.[5] Using the language of the revolution, as the ANC continued to do, the aim was to persuade its constituency to change tack. Negotiations were now 'a terrain and method of struggle'. Walter Sisulu, released after 26 years in jail and an ANC leader with impeccable credentials and acute political insight, gave the keynote address, endorsing negotiations as a way forward. Itumeleng Mosala of AZAPO was more wary, and it was clear by the end of the conference that the black consciousness groupings were deeply suspicious of the Harare Declaration.

The UDF/MDM expected such opposition. In a pre-conference caucus, Manuel offered to play the role of 'bad cop' to get a crucial resolution on negotiations through. When AZAPO refused even to entertain discussion of a negotiated settlement, Manuel intervened: 'We cannot be held back by people who were not in the trenches with us.'

'The house came down,' he recalled. The AZAPO delegation walked out in anger and the resolution on negotiations was passed. 'Our mandate was the Harare Declaration,' said Manuel. This included the unbanning of organisations, the release of political prisoners and the cessation of hostilities. 'So this conference at Wits had to capture that and raise the profile of the entire exercise.'

At the Kagiso conference the following month, a lower profile but more strategy-driven meeting, Manuel gave the opening speech. He spoke an entirely different language from the old discourse of opposition and defiance. Once power had been 'secured', he said, the movement had to discuss 'retaining power'. He warned against 'all the glib talk about our strength' (much like Nzo had done, inadvertently, in the full glare of the public spotlight a few months earlier). 'We lack the boldness to differ with our constituency, to challenge and debate key issues. We lack the boldness to move our constituency in the direction that secures the future. We lack the boldness required for transformation.'[6]

He re-echoed a theme that had grown stronger in his discourse since 1986. But now it was more pertinent. The most important requirement for a 'smooth transition' was 'organisation: organisation that is solid, impervious to state strategy, organisation which is rooted and accountable, organisation which is capable of regenerating leadership at all levels'. He cautioned about the 'balancing act' required 'between destroying and … beginning some sort of process of reconstruction'.[7]

This was not an easy view to articulate to a battered following. Just as Mandela had risked his credibility and constituency in starting talks with what was then a brutal regime, the MDM leaders had to break from their constituency to take it forward. In some ways, they were fortunate that until the Emergency, and often during it, there had always been a tradition of negotiation in South Africa. The trade union movement, for instance, put considerable muscle behind the right to negotiate: such as the cases of the Fatti's & Moni's workers or the meat workers in Cape Town, or tens of thousands of others around the country. Their militancy, at least in the medium term, was aimed at securing a structured, respectful relationship between them and their bosses. In the community organisations, as far back as the early 1980s, the aim had been to get local authorities to recognise and talk with civic organisations. The 'ungovernability' and 'defiance' period had been deep in impact but short in duration. So there was a basis in history and practice for the calls the leadership was now making to embrace this ultimate negotiation – for political democracy.

Yet in the political climate of the day it took considerable courage to risk breaking with a people who could easily have been swayed by the more militant arguments of the black consciousness groupings. The unity that prevailed was a tribute to the roots the UDF and the trade union movement put down in the early 1980s. It was also a tribute to the rude courage many of the leaders, such as Manuel, had displayed when confronted with a government that exercised, for a period, extraordinary power.

F W DE KLERK, the new president of the country, faced the same challenge with his constituency. At the time the Conference for a Democratic Future took place in December, he was meeting with his cabinet in a *bosberaad* in a remote private game reserve near Ellisras (later renamed Lephalale), in the northwest of the country. But he spent most of the South African summer holidays alone, contemplating his speech, and had ended up drafting the final part at midnight on 1 February.[8] He told only his few closest advisers the main points. 'I didn't even tell my wife what I was going to announce,' he said.[9] (Probably wisely: Marike de Klerk, his first wife, was renowned for her conservative views and unreconstructed racial prejudices.)

Although no one was quite sure what he would say, expectations had never been higher than they were on 2 February. Foreign correspondents from around the world descended on South Africa. Western TV networks brought out their expensive news anchors. Newspapers, small and large, sent reporters. And the ANC waited outside on tenterhooks.

As De Klerk began speaking, it was clear that the tone was different from any previous government speech. In the second line, he mentioned a 'negotiated understanding' among 'representative leaders of the entire population ... The alternative is growing violence, tension and conflict. That is unacceptable and in nobody's interest. The well-being of all in this country is linked inextricably to the ability of the leaders to come to terms with one another on a new dispensation. No one can escape this simple truth.'

He spoke of 1989 as a year of 'change' and 'major upheaval' for South Africa and the whole world; about the collapse of the Soviet Union, the clampdown at Tiananmen Square, about the new relations in southern Africa that the demise of the Soviet Union would bring.

'The season for violence is over. The time for reconstruction and reconciliation has arrived.'

And then he did what the world had waited for: he lifted the ban on the ANC, the South African Communist Party, and the Pan Africanist Congress; he rescinded the Emergency restrictions against 33 organisations including the UDF; he said that political prisoners serving sentences only because they were members of banned political parties would be released; and he lifted the restrictions on all 374 of the former detainees, including Manuel. He announced that the government had taken a 'firm decision to release Nelson Mandela unconditionally'.

He concluded by calling on the international community to 're-evaluate its position and to adopt a positive attitude towards the dynamic evolution which is taking place in South Africa' and on the 'Almighty Lord to guide and sustain us on our course through uncharted waters'.

It was a moment when emotions of relief overwhelmed educated expectation. Everyone expected it, yet everyone was surprised. The dream so distant just a few months ago was today, here, now. The narrative of freedom that echoed around the world began in Cape Town.

Manuel, then working for the Mobil Foundation, was so convinced that this day would change everything that he'd asked his boss Franklin Sonn if he could cram a planning meeting he was responsible for into one day instead of two, on 1 February. The meeting ran into the early hours of the morning, and he'd hardly slept when 2 February dawned.

Eight days after De Klerk's path-making speech, Manuel got a phone call from the office of General Johan Willemse, the commissioner of prisons. Could he be at the H F Verwoerd building in the parliamentary complex (the Cape Town offices of cabinet ministers) at 2.30pm? Bulelani Ngcuka got a similar message; so did Dullah Omar. Saki Macozoma, then a young activist with the South African Council of Churches, was in town. The three Western Cape leaders took him along.

'General Willemse told us that the president was making the announcement now. Nelson Mandela was going to be released tomorrow, here in Cape Town. We must prepare to receive him.'

That afternoon, Manuel and other UDF leaders drove to Victor Verster and met with Mandela to discuss his release. They asked Willie Hofmeyr and others to convene a meeting at the University of the Western Cape to brief activists on the release. It was a meeting that alternated between wild excitement and frustration because, while there was so much to do, there was so little that could be done in the short time available – a mere 24 hours' notice for an event that the country had been waiting for for years.

'By that time,' recalled Hofmeyr, 'we were fairly experienced rally-putters-together because we'd been doing it through most of the Emergency, but this was a real last-minute thing.' They had to organise posters, pamphlets, buses, sound systems, and all on a Saturday afternoon. At 3am on the Sunday morning, Hofmeyr was on the phone to cardboard manufacturers to persuade them to open because Allies, the movement's printers in Athlone, had run out.

They could not rely on the SABC, the state broadcaster, for publicity, and the announcement came too late to make some of the Sunday newspapers, so a lot of effort went into publicising the rally which, as Hofmeyr admitted, 'in the end turned out to be unnecessary'.

Mandela wanted to be released in Cape Town, his home for the past 27 years. The Cape Town leadership decided the homecoming rally would be on the Grand Parade, the large public space in front of the City Hall in downtown Cape Town, where Tutu and his fellow clerics had led the 'rainbow nation' in the mass march just four months before.

The rally was advertised for 3pm, the time Mandela was due to walk out of jail – he'd opted to walk rather than be driven out. The roads to the city centre were already thick with traffic by 11am. 'That's the first time I realised we may be in trouble,' said Hofmeyr.

To make matters worse, the Johannesburg contingent assigned to fetch Mandela from jail was late. Manuel had spent the whole night trying to organise the reception from the Cape Town end. Cyril Ramaphosa, the leader of the National Union of Mineworkers and a key figure in the MDM, was in hospital with pneumonia at the time. He pulled the drips out of his arm and walked out of the hospital. 'I was not discharged by a doctor,' he told me. 'I just pulled out the drips and told them that I'm out of here! And off I went.' Desmond Tutu was in Soweto baptising his first-born grandson. He missed a seat on a chartered flight and cadged a lift with a BBC crew instead.

Mandela's wife Winnie, who had rocked the MDM after she was implicated in a sordid case involving the kidnapping and assault of children supposedly under her 'protection', refused to get on the same plane as Murphy Morobe. Morobe, publicity secretary of the MDM since Lekota's imprisonment, had the unenviable task of publicly distancing the MDM from her actions about a year before.

So they chartered two planes instead of one. But they were propeller planes, not jets. 'What did we know about planes?' said Ramaphosa, who years later became one of the wealthiest black businessmen in the country. 'What we knew about planes was as dangerous as what we knew about RPG launchers! What did we know?' So the Johannesburg contingent boarded the 'slowest planes in the world' that took four hours, not two, to reach Cape Town. 'One would have thought that when one was going to receive Mandela one would have gone in a Concorde!' said Ramaphosa.

Meanwhile a crowd of at least 50 000 gathered on the Parade soon after midday. It was a sweltering day. People wilted, tempers frayed. Some collapsed in the heat. And soon a group known in the townships as 'com-tsotsis' – gangsters who used political protest as a cover for thuggery – took over. They looted a liquor store and several shops in a nearby shopping mall.

Riot police on the edges of the crowd opened fire. Standing in the centre of the crowd one could hear the shots: Crack! Crack! Nobody knew whether it was ammunition, rubber bullets or tear gas. Later, reports said four people had died that day. The reek of tear gas drifted in from the edges of the Parade. UDF marshals battled valiantly to maintain order.

One of the problems, Hofmeyr said afterwards, was that they had not managed to get walkie-talkies – the technology they had used so successfully during the UDF launch seven years before. And this time the crowd was at least five times bigger. 'Our marshals were just overcome, and we were not used to having to deal with people who would come in with knives and fists to get to the front of the crowd.'

A platform erected for photographers and TV crews was overrun by impatient youngsters hoping to get a glimpse of Mandela. Cameramen are known to be a brave breed. When the last of them jumped off, so did the marshals. Even more people scrambled up the structure which withstood their weight for another 10 minutes or so before bending and buckling and spilling its usurpers into the dense crowds below.

It was now well past 3pm. Still Mandela didn't arrive. An angry murmur went through the crowd that this was all a trick by De Klerk to confuse the oppressed masses.

All the time the crowd swelled in size. At one stage, Tutu and Boesak offered to lead a march of people away from the City Hall in an attempt to disperse the now dangerous build-up. The clerics led them to St Mark's Church, situated in the middle of the rubble that was once District Six. But they were not fooled for long, and when they began to get volubly angry, Tutu and Boesak led them back to town.

Then the sound system broke down. The crowd now numbered well over 60 000, and the 'most aggressive were right in front', recalled Hofmeyr. 'We were seriously contemplating using fire hoses just to spray them down. People were fainting in the masses, in the crush and the heat, which just dragged on and on.'

At 4.15pm, Nelson Mandela finally walked out of Victor Verster prison, an hour and a quarter behind schedule, 27 years after he was first arrested at a roadblock outside Pietermaritzburg. He was both triumphant and dazzled by the attention, especially by the aptly named rifle-mikes that camera crews pushed towards him. 'Every time I moved away, they would come closer,' he told me shortly before his eightieth birthday.

Manuel helped him pack his belongings into one of the waiting vehicles and got into a car behind his. Then they drove the back roads to Cape Town. Hofmeyr had heard over the traffic cops' radios that Mandela's convoy was on its way, but now there was mayhem outside the City Hall. He rushed to the freeway turn-off to warn them not to come into the city centre. His T-shirt was ripped to shreds and hung in strips around his emaciated figure. 'We'd all been involved in physical combat for hours!'

Manuel spotted him at the turn-off. 'He still hadn't recovered from his hunger strike, and he said, "Comrades stop! They're killing people in the city."' So Manuel drove ahead to the Civic Centre, which is on the other side of the freeway from the City Hall and Grand Parade. He spoke to the security guards there and told them that in a few minutes the convoy would arrive and they should let them in. Then he, Cyril Ramaphosa, Valli Moosa and Jay Naidoo went to the City Hall to scout for a safe route to take Mandela there. They found a way in, but when they got back to the Civic Centre, they discovered to their horror that the car carrying Mandela had disappeared. 'They didn't come in here,' said the security man at the gate. A traffic cop stopped them at the gate, told them they were at the wrong venue and redirected them to the City Hall by a route that took them to the edge of the impatient crowd.

A newspaper reported afterwards that Mandela's cavalcade had 'roared' into the city just after 5.20pm. 'A huge crowd ran wildly alongside his car as it wound through the city, beating on the windows and chanting. A group of women jostled and pushed, desperate to see their leader. They wept and laughed simultaneously. The press of the crowd slowed the motorcade to jogging pace and Mandela, in the back seat with his wife Winnie, looked out at the mad crush of faces. He was impassive, with his fist raised stiffly in salute.'[10]

Mandela may have looked impassive but his driver panicked, edged out of the crowd, and took the first turn out of town. He sped along the freeway to the southern suburbs not knowing where he was going, and landed up in Rosebank, a suburb near the University of Cape Town. There they pulled up outside a house and knocked on the door. A woman who had been watching the release on TV looked out in astonishment. The man she had just seen walking out of jail was now here outside her house. Her name was Vanessa Watson. Coincidentally, she happened to be an urban planning researcher who had written extensively on the parlous state of black housing in the Cape, information that had been used by Manuel's organisation, CAHAC, in the early 1980s. Instead of watching the rest of the chaos on the Grand Parade on TV, she chatted to the freed leader while he played with her newborn twins.

The diversion may have given Mandela's minders breathing space, but it didn't help the organisers. The sun faded and still there was no sign of their leader. They were terrified about what might happen. A few hours earlier, US Senator Jesse Jackson had come to the City Hall 'through the people', although the organisers tried to persuade him to go in the back way. 'He thought everyone would just say, "Hello Jesse!"' Manuel told a class of Princeton students years later. 'Except his car was mobbed, and by the time we got there later that day, the trunk and the roof and doors of the car were just one level. There was none of the car left! Jesse and his wife were gone. And into that crowd they took Madiba!'

Jackson managed to make his way to the front wall of the City Hall but couldn't make it through the crowds to the steps. The wall from the balcony of the Hall is about three metres high. In the end, he clambered up, being pushed from the bottom and hauled from the top. 'And then his poor wife couldn't go through the crowd so she had to go over hands,' recalled Hofmeyr. 'Now you must appreciate that the most aggressive, violent young men had managed to get right to the front, so she was going over their hands, and also had to be dragged up the wall. So she was pretty traumatised.'

When Mandela disappeared, Manuel was 'beside himself'. 'How could we lose Madiba on the day of his release? How would you write that thing in history?'[11]

At around 6pm, a traffic cop near the City Hall beckoned Manuel and said there was 'someone who wanted to talk to him' on his two-way radio. It was a colonel in the security police whom Manuel knew from his frequent detentions. He said: 'Trevor, you must go fetch Mandela. If you don't bring him here the city will burn down and hundreds of people are going to be killed. Go fetch him!'

By this time Mandela was having tea in Rondebosch East with the family of a local Cape Town activist whom his driver knew. The colonel directed Manuel, who raced to fetch him and brought him back to the city along the less congested De Waal Drive which winds along the mountainside, and through the back streets of the city. This time they got him into the City Hall through its back entrance. With the late summer evening fading to darkness, Mandela addressed the crowd on the Parade and millions more around the

313

world who had been waiting for years for this moment.

'I stand here before you today not as a prophet but as a humble servant of the people. Your tireless and heroic sacrifices have made it possible for me to be here today. I therefore place the remaining years of my life in your hands.'

Many criticised the speech afterwards as having been written by a committee – cobbled together by the leadership of the MDM and reflecting a myriad different interests. The press complained that he had promised to 'intensify' the armed struggle and had called for continued sanctions.

De Klerk had told the world that he (Mandela) was committed to peace. At the following day's press conference held in the well-tended gardens of Tutu's official residence, Bishopscourt, a journalist asked him: 'Last night you committed yourself to the intensification of the armed struggle. Would you care to comment?'

'There is no conflict between those two statements,' said Mandela. 'I have committed myself to the promotion of peace in the country but I've done so as part and parcel of the decisions and campaigns which have been taken and launched by the ANC. There is no conflict whatsoever. There is not a single political organisation in this country inside and outside parliament which can ever compare with the ANC in its total commitment to peace. If the government gives us the opportunity, if they normalise the situation, we are ready to make a positive contribution towards the peaceful settlement of the problems of this country.'[12] In fact, Mandela had called on his supporters to 'intensify the *struggle* on all fronts'. On the armed struggle, he said: 'The factors which necessitated the armed struggle still exist today. We have no option but to continue.'

For the most part, he spoke about the need for negotiations: 'I myself have at no time entered into negotiations about the future of our country except to insist on a meeting between the ANC and government. Mr de Klerk has gone further than any other Nationalist president in taking real steps to normalise the situation. However there are further steps as outlined in the Harare Declaration that have to be met before negotiations on the basic demands of our people can be met,' he said on the Grand Parade.

There were no policy statements in the speech other than to pay tribute to a host of resistance organisations, including the trade unions and white anti-apartheid groupings, and to emphasise that 'the march to freedom is irreversible'.

At the press conference, he was more specific. The 200 or so journalists who clambered over the flower beds at Bishopscourt ranged from representatives of the world's most important and powerful newspapers and TV networks to those from local 'struggle' publications, eager to impress him with left-wing questions. He was asked about his views on redistribution of wealth.

'The question of the nationalisation of the mines and similar sectors of the community is a fundamental policy of the ANC,' he replied. He elaborated on a remark in his speech that the economy of the country lay in 'ruins': 'There are three important aspects we must consider when we are discussing the economy of a country. The question of full employment, the question of productivity, and the question of social responsibility. Once we can guarantee that there is progress in these three aspects, then the economy of the country is performing very well. But it is my impression that it is not performing well.'

Manuel was at the press conference. He didn't know then how heavily Mandela's words on the economy would weigh on him.

At the time he had more literal weights on his mind. After nearly 48 hours without sleep, he collapsed into bed at around midnight after the rally only to be awoken at 4am by a phone call from Mandela. 'Trevor, where are my weights?' asked the old man.

They had been packed into one of the vehicles that had left Victor Verster prison the day before. Manuel tracked them down before driving Mandela to the airport that afternoon to see him off on his homeward journey to Johannesburg.

'Goodbye, Comrade Chief,' he said. He hugged him and handed over his weights.

≡ PART FIVE: Transition ≡

1990-1995

CHAPTER 20

'Corner boy'

I F THERE WAS A HEADINESS in the weeks preceding Nelson Mandela's release, the sense of exhilaration consumed Manuel even more in the weeks after.

To his delight, Cyril Ramaphosa, secretary general of the National Union of Mineworkers and an increasingly important figure in a reviving internal ANC, asked him to be on Mandela's team as he travelled around Africa and Europe greeting old comrades and touching bases in the exiled organisation.

Kenneth Kaunda provided a plane for the delegation: they flew to Lusaka, the Zambian capital, and met leaders more iconic than real in South Africa due to the three-decade exile of the ANC: Chris Hani, Joe Modise, Joe Slovo. Mandela stayed in State House, a guest of the Zambian president; the others stayed in a nearby government guest house. Most of the African heads of state came to pay homage to Mandela, now quickly finding his way in a new world. 'Quite, quite, *quite* incredible,' recalled Manuel.

Then to Harare, where Mandela was given the freedom of the city by a mayor who wore a red velvet cloak and a horsehair wig in 35-degree heat, the sweat pouring off his brow. Zimbabwean President Robert Mugabe, who had been in power for the past decade, was in election mode – the first Zimbabwean elections accused of being 'rigged' were held later that year and Mugabe garnered 80 per cent of the vote. Mugabe may have thought that Madiba's appearance beside him boosted his campaign, but more astute observers noted the occasion more for the contrast between the two leaders. 'Mugabe introduced Mandela with a self-serving hectoring speech denouncing his rivals,' wrote Anthony Sampson, while Mandela, as one reporter wrote, 'spoke with the quiet, dignified assurance of a great leader and appeared decidedly calm beside the sweating, twitching Mugabe.'[1]

In many ways the post-prison trip paralleled Mandela's clandestine sweep through Africa in 1962, but now colonial rule had gone, and African leaders could publicly fête him. Some of his travelling companions – for example, Ramaphosa, Manuel, and Jay Naidoo and John Gomomo of the trade union federation COSATU, would just have started primary school when he made his first trip.

They flew from Harare to Tanzania, then to Zanzibar. At a camp in Iringa, Tanzania, they were photographed taking the salute in military uniforms. In Lusaka, Manuel attended a formal meeting of the National Executive Committee of the ANC for the first time. It was also the first time that the three strands of the ANC were brought together – the exiles, those who had been imprisoned and those, like Manuel, from the internal resistance wing. It was at this meeting that Mandela was officially elected deputy president of the organisation. They went to Somafco, the ANC school in Tanzania, to Morogoro, and to Mazimbi. Manuel's head spun. Occasionally he was called on to baby Mandela's wife Winnie out of a tempestuous mood, but largely that was left to Chris Hani.[2]

But the highlight of the trip was out of Africa, to freezing Stockholm, where Manuel witnessed the reunion between Mandela and the ailing Oliver Tambo, then recuperating from a stroke in a Swedish clinic. Trevor Huddleston, the priest who had played a crucial role in Tambo's youth before he was deported by the apartheid authorities, was also there. Mandela and Tambo had last seen each other nearly three decades before. 'That must have been one of the most special moments of my life,' said Manuel. His meeting with the gentle, erudite leader invoked a different image from the one he had used in another age, albeit just two years earlier, when he he'd threatened his recalcitrant prison warder with Tambo's name: 'As Tambo kom, dan sal julle kak.'*

---

* 'When Tambo comes you will shit (yourself)'.

'Oliver was not well,' wrote Mandela in his autobiography, 'but when we met we were like two young boys in the veld who took strength from our love for each other.'[3]

Manuel returned to South Africa three weeks later. He had won a special place in Madiba's heart by then, one that was to steer him through his early years in government. 'Madiba is the type of person who recognised, almost instantaneously, good talent, and in Trevor he picked it up immediately,' recalled Cyril Ramaphosa. 'I wouldn't be able to recall the key moment, but what I do know is that just in terms of coming on that trip (it meant that) Trevor's stature was on the rise, and hence we had this feeling that he needed to come, not only to ... represent the Western Cape but in his own name and right. He was beginning to emerge as a leader in our eyes.'

But the euphoria in the wake of Mandela's release quickly dissipated in the roughness of Western Cape, and transitional, politics after Manuel returned home.

BACK IN THE CAPE, the ANC grappled with its new role as a legal organisation. Manuel formed part of what was called an interim leadership core. Reg September, not yet back from exile, had been tasked with organising the region. But until he was home, Manuel had to 'hold the fort'.

Ties of solidarity are often stronger in times of adversity than when the scent of power is in the nostrils, as Manuel discovered. He knew he had to start somewhere building a branch structure for the ANC, so he began with a list of about 300 activists whom he invited to a meeting at the Peninsula Technikon one Saturday evening in April. They signed the 'oath of allegiance' to the ANC and promised to recruit additional members. But those who had been left out of the initial meeting, more by accident than design, were furious at their exclusion. The sour epithet attached to Manuel's 'core group' of the 1980s – the 'High Command' – bit him again. 'Jesus, was I unpopular!' He paid a price. He made it on to the regional executive of the ANC which was elected later that year, but not in a senior leadership position.

Fred Robertson, who had become much closer to Manuel since his release from jail the year before, and who by then was running a small insurance business, was at that meeting. 'He was sidelined almost,' he said. 'Considering the work he'd done ... I could just see the disappointment in his face. Our eyes caught one another's ... It was a *huge* disappointment for him.'

It was not altogether a personal rejection. Willie Hofmeyr, who had fought on the frontlines for much of the Emergency, was not elected on to the regional executive at all and recalls how he, too, was 'a bit hurt'. The Khayelitsha branch had wanted to nominate him but the Guguletu branch moved to close nominations at that point. Guguletu prevailed. The tensions over these elections reflected a division in the Western Cape ANC that was to deepen, sometimes to crisis point, in coming years. The branches from the established, 'old' African townships (unlike Khayelitsha which housed many of the relative newcomers to the Cape who had been driven out of the Crossroads area four years earlier) had long murmured that the UDF was 'too dominated by coloured (and white) leadership'. Now the new space allowed for what was an essentially Africanist backlash, especially from old ANC activists in the established townships who laid special claim to the ANC.

But the contradiction in the Western Cape was this: most ANC members in the Cape were indeed African, and it was logical that they should wish to see those demographics reflected in the leadership. Yet the majority of people in the Western Cape, the majority of the working class, was coloured. This contradiction, and the ANC's inability to manage it, played out in the first democratic election in 1994 in a way that shocked ANC leaders.

THERE WERE STILL COMPLEX organisational overlays within the ANC itself. For one thing, Operation Vula had rooted itself in various areas around the country, principally Durban, Johannesburg and Cape Town, in the previous few years. The sensitivity of the operation lasted way into the interregnum. The reporting line, at least for those in Cape Town, was to Joe Slovo. It is mistakenly thought that Vula was conceived of as an alternative to negotiations, as a plan for an armed insurrection around the country. This is partly true but fails to capture its complexity. It began as a way to establish ANC leadership inside the country in the midst of the popular uprisings of the 1980s. Until then, ANC 'core groups' had liaised with the different leaders in Lusaka or Botswana and Swaziland, but there were no ANC leaders inside the country. 'The key was to bring and prepare an internal leadership of capability. You can't run an insurrection or anything like that from kilometres away. So we had to build reception capability and survival capability in the country,' said Pravin Gordhan, Manuel's UDF comrade and fellow housing activist, who had become part of Vula in Durban in 1988.

There are other misconceptions about Vula: one is that it was a relatively late intervention in the ANC's battle against apartheid. But according to Ivan

Pillay (who in the post-apartheid era worked for the South African Revenue Service where he successfully took on major tax offenders), the genesis of Vula went back to 1981 when Area Political Committees (APCs) were established in the wake of the Anti-Republic Day protests. 'There was a continuous battle to locate senior leadership inside the country,' he told me. 'The happenings of the mid-80s drove home the point that it was not possible to run things by remote control from Lusaka.'

The other misconception was that it was a project undertaken outside of the formal structures of the ANC. But Pillay said the decision to locate senior leaders inside the country was taken in about 1985 by an NEC meeting. Oliver Tambo and Joe Slovo were tasked with responsibility for the plan. In 1986, after Pillay had been clandestinely in South Africa for a few months, he was summoned to Lusaka and asked to coordinate the project. In 1988 a number of leaders came into South Africa – Janet Love to Johannesburg, Mac Maharaj and Siphiwe Nyanda ('Gebuza') to Durban, and Charles Nqakula and an operative still identified only as 'Little John' to Cape Town. After a while this leadership connected to 'separately run units' and so began, said Pillay, to 'shape national leadership inside the country'. Pillay said he regularly reported back on these projects to the NEC in Lusaka although he was, of necessity, hazy about details and locations.

It is also a myth that Vula was against negotiations. It may have been a rather ambitious 'back-up' plan, but the ANC leadership, including that in Vula, was at one on the necessity for negotiations. The booklet titled *The Weapon of Negotiations*, which Murray Michell's Vula cell produced, came out in early 1989, for instance. It was discussed throughout the underground structures. 'There was a strong sense that, hey, things are happening fast, and we've got to be abreast of it and understand it and deal with it appropriately,' said Michell.

The Cape Town Vula operation continued throughout 1990. Ironically, after Mandela's release, the surveillance of Michell increased considerably, so his contact with Manuel was both intermittent and cautious. (Later that year, Mandela asked De Klerk to instruct the security police to stop their harassment of Michell.)

'I tried to make it my business to ensure that Trevor was kept in the know and in the loop of those underground developments without giving him the details,' said Michell. 'So you'd have these convoluted discussions explaining what was going on without revealing names, and where and how, and he

323

would respond in an equally convoluted way and you'd have to suss out what he's trying to say. The two of us – talking without talking. It was just bizarre, bizarre!'

Manuel's 10 years in a related but separate underground structure, combined with his work in the above-ground legal structures had taught him, if nothing else, when to be cautious and when to take risks. It was one thing to be truculent as hell with the security police, but with Vula, 'he would make damn sure he wasn't going to get into a corner over it', said Michell.

But when the Durban, and then some of the Johannesburg, nodal points of Vula were uncovered by the security police, the ANC leadership involved in the negotiations were embarrassed and distanced themselves from the operation. This was to become a major source of tension within the movement.

Whether the Vula arrests were due to sleuth police work or simply bad luck for the operatives is still a matter of conjecture, but it appeared that misfortune was the main mover. According to Maharaj, a Durban operative, Charles Ndaba, was recognised at a Durban taxi rank by an *askari* (a 'turned' operative working for the police) who happened to be driving past with the security police. Ndaba was arrested, as was his comrade Mbuso Shabalala. The only thing their Vula comrades knew at that point was that they had disappeared. Ndaba was supposed to be at a meeting on Saturday, 7 July in the Durban township of Inanda. He didn't arrive. Gordhan had planned a meeting with the two on Monday, 9 July. Neither turned up. Gordhan, who had survived the entire State of Emergency underground without being caught (and had even secretly married his second wife, Vani) was arrested at a flat in the Indian area of Brickfield Road on Thursday, 12 July. Only Ndaba and he had known about the flat. Nyanda, a senior commander in Umkhonto we Sizwe, who had come into the country with Maharaj, was arrested on his way to another hideout, a flat owned by Shabir Shaik, the brother of Mo Shaik, one of the ANC's top counter-intelligence officers.[4]

Maharaj supposes the police must by then have known the car Nyanda was driving.[5]

Gordhan was taken first to the local security police headquarters and later to a prison cell in Bethlehem, a small town in the eastern Free State. A fellow operative, Rajin Pillay, a doctor, who had run a printing press for Vula, had also been detained there. By the time Gordhan arrived, Pillay had 'created a communication line' – in plain language, he had bribed a cop to carry out messages. Gordhan wrote a note to a now deeply worried Maharaj telling him what his 'cover story' was so that the others could corroborate it. 'This is my story, this is what I'm saying,' wrote Gordhan: he had been recruited by George Naicker, who had by then died, and he was meeting 'two mysterious characters, I didn't know who ... I spun it in a way that no one could get stung by it.' He laughed ruefully when he told me this because when Maharaj was detained two weeks later, the police found the note in his shirt pocket.

After that, mainly as revenge, Gordhan's torture began, the worst of all his frequent detentions: beatings and suffocation. His torturer was a Durban security police officer, H J P (Hentjie) Botha. Botha was one of the policemen who were later to apply for amnesty for the murder of Charles Ndaba and Mbuso Shabalala, the two Vula operatives they had arrested initially.[6]

Gordhan knew the police were simply trying to break his spirit in revenge for smuggling out the note. Most of his questioning was about the first SACP meeting in the country in May on the south coast of Natal. One of the more sympathetic warders had shown him a newspaper article about the meeting, before he was interrogated. So he knew the police knew about it. Still they tortured him to tell them about it. And even though he knew they knew, he refused to budge.

Gordhan, Maharaj, Nyanda and five others were charged and released on bail in October of that year. It was an awkward time for the ANC; there was ambivalence in the movement about the fact that while it was trying to negotiate an effective ceasefire so that talks could start, the government had scored an embarrassing PR coup by hitting a Vula nerve. But there were many Vula operatives who were not hit, despite a perception that by July 1990 'Vula existed far more powerfully in the mind of Maharaj than in fact'.[7] The Cape Town operation was one example: it survived the crackdown. But the arrests *did* lead to countrywide confusion among the operatives, who went even further to ground. Many of the Vula structures were kept intact, at least until the elections in 1994, according to Michell, but there was a 'lot of confusion between the lines of command and the lines of communication between the different respective structures'.

For the government it made sense to clear the decks of any underground operatives, be they Vula or MK (they were effectively separate structures in operation at the same time), 'both to weaken the ANC but also that in the event that the negotiations collapsed they wouldn't face an assault from a source they hadn't predicted or understood'.

THERE WERE OTHER AMBIVALENCES TOO. Barbara Hogan, sentenced to 10 years in 1982 for clandestinely reporting to the ANC, much as Manuel had done, was 'catapulted' out of prison in late 1989, at Mandela's insistence after the other Rivonia trialists were released. She had immersed herself in economic studies in her last years in jail and was about to start a master's degree through Unisa with a young economics lecturer called Maria Ramos as her supervisor. But her 'love affair' with economics was put on hold. To her dismay, she was not deployed to any of the new policy-making commissions of the ANC in 1990 but to the interim leadership core of the Transvaal, where she dealt with escalating and distressing violence. 'I was dealing with blood on my hands every day ... Taxi violence, train violence; they were trying to kill us.'

And many other prisoners were still in jail. Some political activists even *started* jail sentences in this period. Maxwell Moss, Manuel's old jail mate and comrade from the West Coast, was one of them. He was sentenced to three years for public violence, charges that had arisen out of incidents in the late 1980s. When his appeal failed, he went into hiding. Manuel advised him not to leave the country as 'everyone' was coming back. When the police finally caught up with him, just before the end of 1990, he was taken to Pollsmoor in chains, 'like a criminal'. He was released after four months when the ANC negotiated a general amnesty for him and scores of other political prisoners still in jail.

Manuel himself was arrested – again – for 'illegally' demonstrating against the Vula arrests. There'd been a fracas during the arrest, and one of his charges was of resisting arrest. His lawyer Ebi Mohamed told the court that the police 'had severely manhandled' his client, tearing his clothes, bruising his left leg, injuring his thumb and scratching his body.[8] But, years later, Manuel told a slightly different tale to some of his staffers as he rehearsed a Budget speech. He recounted how proud his then four-year-old son Govan had been because 'my daddy had kicked a policeman in his penis'. A headline in *Vrye Weekblad*, a left-wing Afrikaans weekly, summed up the police's dilemma neatly: '*As jy Trevor will stil hê, sluit hom op.*' ('If you want to keep Trevor quiet, lock him up.')[9] Manuel was released on warning – and the charges were eventually dropped in 1991.

PERHAPS IT WAS THIS BRAND of street-smart wisdom that landed Manuel a crucial backroom role in the meetings that culminated in the Groote Schuur

Minute, signed in May 1990, four months before his fracas with the police. It was negotiated against a backdrop of ambivalence, suspicion, and violence, particularly in the Transvaal and Natal. Groote Schuur was the stately Cape Dutch mansion in the leafy upper reaches of Rondebosch which had been the official residence of South African prime ministers since Cecil John Rhodes bequeathed it to the government in 1902.[10] It is now a museum.

Three senior ANC members were effectively smuggled into South Africa at least two months before the talks, according to Manuel. They were Jacob Zuma, the ANC's intelligence chief; Penuell Maduna of the ANC's legal department, and Gibson Mkanda.[11] Manuel's job was to chaperone them, in particular Jacob Zuma. It was a risky mission as none of them had indemnity from arrest or prosecution.

On Friday, 28 April 1990, an official ANC delegation, including Thabo Mbeki and Joe Slovo, arrived from Lusaka. Manuel was one of the hundreds of people who went to Cape Town airport to meet them, but the new arrivals were hastily dispatched on to a bus by the police and driven away. They were closeted in a luxury hotel, the Lord Charles Somerset, at the foot of the Hottentots Holland mountains in Somerset West. Journalist accounts at the time chronicle how the delegates' behaviour made logistics a nightmare for the security officials tasked to protect them. 'Motorcades would zoom in and out of the Lord Charles Hotel in Somerset West while frantic security men tried to find out where they were headed.'[12]

The man who gave the security men such headaches was Manuel. His main job during the early negotiations was as fixer – and stirrer – of trouble. Kader Asmal, the constitutional lawyer who returned from exile in Ireland a few months after this, met him for the first time in 1991: 'He looked like a corner boy,' he said. 'An Irish corner boy! A small-time thug!'

Soon after the return of the official ANC delegation, Manuel arrived at the hotel to take care of them. It was a dangerous time and deep distrust still lingered on both sides of the apartheid divide. On that day in late April, when the newly arrived exiles had settled into the hotel, Manuel asked the colonel in charge of security where the ANC could caucus. 'Come, I'll show you the room,' said the colonel. 'We've given you a very nice room.'

The somewhat bewildered and overwhelmed exiles had come almost directly from Lusaka to the Lord Charles. There was a 'disastrous' homecoming ANC rally in Mitchell's Plain on Sunday, 29 April, where Manuel had introduced the returned leaders, including Thabo Mbeki and Joe Slovo. 'It was a large rally,' Manuel recalled, 'but we'd hoped that the crowd would have been of the order of magnitude that received Mandela.' It wasn't. And then back at the Lord Charles Manuel advised them not to use the room the security chiefs had earmarked for their caucus meetings.

Anglo American, who owned the nearby wine estate Vergelegen, offered it to the ANC for its first legal meeting on South African soil. Manuel did not tell the police. He put everyone in cars, Mandela last, and when he saw that they were ready, he passed word down the convoy: 'Vergelegen. Let's go!'

When they returned to the hotel, the police complained bitterly: 'Ah, but I can't do this to them. They've got responsibility for our safety and I must give 24 hours' notice.'

Where are you going tomorrow? they asked. 'I said, look I'm still waiting for another call.'

The police chief then let slip precisely what made the ANC delegates so suspicious. 'But we're *listening* to your phones,' they told Manuel. 'And there've been no calls.' (There were no cellphones then and listening to hotel phones provided almost no challenge to security police skilled in these techniques.)

The following day, Manuel took the ANC delegation to the house of a well-to-do businessman in Athlone. He had a squash court in his house and he'd agreed that the ANC could use it to caucus. Manuel led the delegation to the house, but on the way one driver went to the wrong house. In a fine display of cheek, Manuel phoned the flying squad helicopter station in the nearby suburb of Pinelands and told them where he was. 'Just get a chopper to fly overhead and I'll wave at them. Then you can lead the delegation here. Which the police helicopter pilots obligingly did, to the irritation of their colleagues in Somerset West. 'Were they angry again!'

The third day, 1 May, Manuel took the delegation to an Anglican bishop's house in Kenilworth, a white suburb, again two steps ahead of the security contingent assigned to guard them. He caused more havoc on that day, because he'd asked the Western Cape Traders' Association to sponsor the suits that the men in the ANC delegation were to wear to the talks the next day. He led them to Queenspark, a retailer attached to Rex Trueform, using a zig-zag route to avoid the police. 'Look, these people have just come from the bush,' he told the Traders' Association. 'They don't have nice suits.' The retailer was a middle-market chain and Thabo Mbeki, a fastidious dresser, joked with Manuel years later about 'that shit suit I bought him'.

Throughout the preparations for the Groote Schuur meeting, Manuel parried with the police. He had grown up on the streets of the Western Cape, and for the most part could outsmart and outrun the police, and knew exactly how to talk to them, an art that many of the exiles had lost after spending years out of the country. He was also assigned to look after some of the most powerful ANC figures: Mandela, Zuma, Mbeki among them. It allowed him the space to build relationships with them that were to become critical later when he had to take on many of his own constituency in implementing an economic survival and growth policy for the country.

He was not involved in the substance of the negotiations. Not the Groote Schuur Minute, which laid the basis for the release of political prisoners and the return of exiles, in return for the ANC's 'considering' the suspension of the armed struggle. Nor in the Pretoria Minute three months later, where the ANC agreed to suspend the armed struggle.

Did it worry him?

'No. I was quite OK with it. I was where the adrenalin was. The other process was a political process, preparing for the Pretoria Minute about the cessation of hostilities. That was a very big decision from the ANC ... That took a lot of persuasion.'

But he was crucially involved in clearing space for the ANC leaders in the Western Cape, sometimes even physically. In 1991, when Mandela visited Stellenbosch University, a group of right-wing students protested vociferously and threatened to break up the meeting. Before Mandela arrived at the venue Manuel and a few of his comrades waded into the hall, identified the potential disrupters and bodily threw them out. They challenged the other students to declare whether they were with them. Nobody did. Mandela summoned Manuel and the rest just before the meeting to ask what they had done. They were nervous, thinking they had gone against Mandela's quest for reconciliation. But to their relief and surprise, he said: 'Boys, you did the right thing.' There had to be some sort of historic equivalence for Manuel in his rough-arming the white supremacists: 50 years earlier his great-grandfather, Maximillian von Söhnen and his son Leonard had sat on their veranda and watched as the ideological ancestors of these students laid waste to coloured people's homes in protest against South Africa's siding with the Allied forces in the Second World War.

By then, Manuel was established in the leadership of the Western Cape ANC: later in 1991 he was elected publicity secretary, a more senior position than he held before. But before then, by the time the ANC held its national consultative conference at the end of 1990, at Nasrec outside Soweto, he had established relationships with the national leadership that in important ways insulated him from the volatile and vituperative politics of the Western Cape.

'A moment of hope', is how the ANC described that conference on South African soil for the first time in more than 30 years. The ailing ANC president Oliver Tambo had arrived in the country the previous evening. The sight of him and Mandela together at home underpinned that hope, even though the formal documents prickled with suspicion and distrust. Sanctions must stay; the violence in the country was a counter-revolutionary plot to derail negotiations; the four pillars of struggle was still the ANC's creed. But its main political task – amid the fighting discourse – was to formalise the ANC's commitment to negotiations and to bring its supporters, from exile and from home, into a fold that allowed this to happen. The ANC leadership had already made the commitment to talks a few months earlier, when it signed the Pretoria Minute and, crucially, agreed to suspend the armed struggle.

Six months later the ANC held its first national conference in the country since 1959. Its main task was to elect a 60-member National Executive Committee (NEC), the governing body of the party, which would steer it through the unknown terrain of the transition. Manuel went up as a delegate from the Western Cape and shared a shabby hotel room with unlikely bedmates – Johnny Issel, who had been both his mentor and nemesis in the 1980s; Ebrahim Rasool, who came from the anti-apartheid Muslim youth movement; and Johnny de Lange, a truculent young Afrikaans lawyer who had fought several political trials.

Nominations for the NEC can be made before the conference, by branches, or from the floor if 25 per cent of the voting delegates indicate support. Manuel's name had 'already gone forward' (he didn't know who nominated him). He himself, sensitive to the criticisms of insufficient African leadership in the Western Cape, nominated Tony Yengeni from the floor. Yengeni was a young MK militant, who came from the African township of Guguletu, and had spent four years in prison facing trial – and terrible torture – for his underground military work. Yengeni didn't make it.[13]

But Manuel came nineteenth in the poll of 50 directly elected members. (Chris Hani, the popular MK commander, topped the poll.) His fellow Western Cape comrades, Cheryl Carolus and Dullah Omar, were also elected on to the executive whose members were equally distributed between returning exiles, on the one hand, and former political prisoners and internal leaders from the 1980s generation on the other. For Manuel, it was a 'joy' to be on this national body.

The first NEC meeting took place in Soweto a month later. Its task was to elect the 15-member National Working Committee (NWC), which makes the day-to-day decisions about the organisation. Manuel's name was put forward, as was Carolus's. As they had in the days of the UDF, the two friends decided that only one of them would take up a position on the NWC if both were elected. Anyway, Manuel, in deference to his long-suffering wife, had promised that he would spend more time at home. But both Carolus and Manuel were elected on to the governing body. They caucused with the Cape Town ANC leadership. By then several exiles had joined that core, including Kader Asmal, the eloquent law professor, Reg September, and Pallo Jordan, one of the ANC's most expansive intellectuals. 'And they were saying, no, no this is a big honour, you must go – and in the end we were elected on to this NWC, both of us.'

Nominally still at his job at the Mobil Foundation, Manuel spent much of his time in Cape Town lobbying for and organising the logistics around the release of political prisoners. Several hundred had been released in April 1991, but there were still some remaining on Robben Island until well into that year.

The Mobil Foundation's offices were in a tall building at the harbour end of Long Street, walking distance from the quay where the ferries to and from Robben Island docked. This helped. It also helped that Willie Hofmeyr, by now an articled clerk in a firm of attorneys, worked in the same building. He, too, was campaigning for the release of the rest of the prisoners, seeing out the cause that he had nearly starved himself to death for two years earlier. As Hofmeyr had done, those who lingered in jail embarked on a sustained hunger strike to focus the minds of the authorities. They were all released a few months later.

Because of this campaign, Manuel was unable to go to an NWC meeting held in Johannesburg at the end of July 1991. That night his phone rang. It was Cyril Ramaphosa, who'd been elected the ANC's general secretary at the June conference in Durban in a move that was seen as a victory for the internal leadership.

'Bru, we've got a job for you,' said Ramaphosa.

'Yeah?' asked Manuel.

'The DEP. You can head it.'

'What?' asked Manuel. 'What's the DEP?'

'The Department of Economic Planning.'

'But Cyril, you can't expect me to head that! I know nothing about it.'

'No, this is the decision of the NWC,' replied Ramaphosa.

'I wet myself,' said Manuel later.

Ramaphosa had proposed Manuel for the position. There was no opposition. When I asked Ramaphosa why the NWC had chosen Manuel to head the economics department, he laughed. 'Don't even ask me why. Why? *Why?* Why did we choose Trevor? I've been thinking about that since I saw your letter. [I'd written to him before I spoke with him.] Was it because he represented to us, somehow, a guy who had worked in industry? Is that what we were looking for?'

Ramaphosa echoed the fascination expressed by David Lewis, the student-cum-trade unionist who had met Manuel more than a decade earlier. ('I didn't know anyone who even had a *job*!') 'I mean I'd never worked, most of us had never worked.' Ramaphosa chortled as he told me this. 'I'd come out of university, was a little bit into law, and then into the union movement. He ... represented somebody who had *worked* in the belly of the beast.'

Moeletsi Mbeki, who had returned from exile, mentioned the same qualities to explain why Manuel was appointed minister of Trade and Industry less than three years later. He had a technical background, he explained, which few ANC people had. 'It had all the sociologists and historians, blah blah, so they needed someone who knew *something* about SA industry ... all those PhDs in history and sociology, but they've never seen the inside of a factory!'

There was another reason too, perhaps one that only became apparent later. It was his ability to provide political leadership at a time when the ANC's economic policies were under intensive construction and an ability, mentioned by several friends and colleagues, old and new, to *listen* to new ideas, and to the concerns of people in the differentiated communities that made up the country.

But some of his friends were as anxious as he was about the new assignment. Fred Robertson, who'd nursed him through the disappointment of missing a senior leadership position at the first regional ANC executive meeting and seen him 'bounce back like a rubber ball' when he was elected on to the NEC, feared this was going to be another bruising for his friend. 'They'd given him a poisoned chalice,' said Robertson. 'It *was* a poisoned chalice.'

CHAPTER 21

The 'guru with matric'

THERE MAY NOT HAVE BEEN poison in the chalice but certainly the contents were not sweet.

Some writers have argued that the appointment was part of a 'coup' by the internal wing of the ANC, which gave key positions on the executive to the internal people such as Manuel and Carolus.[1] But Cyril Ramaphosa dismisses this. 'The issues of the economy were not yet so prominent at the time. What was more prominent was intelligence, foreign affairs and so on.' The exiles – people like Joe Nhlanhla, Joe Modise and Thabo Mbeki – were given those positions. Social welfare, which went to Cheryl Carolus, and economics which went to Manuel, were seen as 'soft positions' then.

But Manuel was determined not to play it soft. In early September 1991, he walked into the office of the Department of Economic Planning on the twenty-first floor of the ANC's hectic downtown Johannesburg building, located near a train station and a taxi rank. The building, purchased from Shell for R25 million, was known then as Shell House. More frequent visitors began to drop the first letter of its name to give it, some thought, a more apt appellation. When Manuel arrived he discovered a team of people who had been busily planning new aspects of the ANC's economic policy. He was not, at first, enthusiastically received. He did not have an office. He sat at a desk in the corridor for a while until two of the researchers, Khetso Gordhan, the nephew of Pravin, and Viv McMenamin, invited him to share their office.

Also there was Tito Mboweni, one of the ANC's bright young economic stars, who had recently returned from exile. Born in 1959 and raised in the then Northern Transvaal in a working-class family, he'd attended a poorly equipped 'Bantu education' school in Tzaneen, across a river from his village. Most days the children waded across, but when the summer rains came, 'if the river was full you couldn't go to school'. On matriculating, he'd enrolled at the black University of the North, or Turfloop, in 1979, but he left the following year 'because it was a war zone there ... there was a lot of academic terrorism'. He'd applied to study at the designated 'white' University of Natal but permission was refused. Soon after that he went into exile. Genial, outspoken, a man possessed of a razor-sharp intellect, he still resents the way that apartheid stymied his education. 'I wasted a lot of time. If I'd started properly in 1979 and completed in 1982 I would have finished my first degree and been able to do a PhD before I got too old. So it was always a grudge for me,' he told me.

But he had an intellect that was not to be outdone and soon after going into exile, he graduated with a degree in Economics from Lesotho University and then won a scholarship to the University of East Anglia in the United Kingdom where he did his master's degree in development economics. He had been one of the ANC members whose interest in economic policy was sparked in the late 1980s when '(we thought) the *possibility* of a post-apartheid situation might arise'. So he had gone back to Africa, stationing himself at the ANC's Lusaka headquarters, where he began researching policy for the ANC's Constitutional Guidelines, published in 1988.

He worked with a group of left-wing economists in London, both South African and British, on this ongoing project. Among them were the exiled South African banker, Vella Pillay, and the British economists, Ben Fine and Lawrence Harris 'who had been researching and writing papers on the South African economy, structural issues, the debt standstill issues, the lack of access to international capital and so on and I thought they were a very important group because they also introduced quite a number of the younger people, including myself, to the rigours of empirical economic research and analysis.'

He was not initially enthusiastic about Manuel's appointment. 'In the beginning it was not well received. There was a feeling that it was a political imposition.'

Another who was lukewarm about Manuel was Ismail Momoniat, who'd been a central contact figure for Mac Maharaj during the underground Vula days in the late 1980s. Momoniat, a mathematician by training and profession (he lectured at the University of the Witwatersrand), had drifted into economics while in hiding from the police. 'When you worked in the underground we all operated from our cars and you would wait for *ever*, for hours on end. And I decided that although I was always trying to do a master's in maths, it's really difficult to read maths (in a car) and I had quite liked economics. So for fun I just registered with Unisa to do Economics 1, 2, and 3 and I did it just while waiting around.' The only trick was to avoid the police at examination halls, which he did by registering at multiple addresses. When 1990 came, he was tired and burnt out from politics – he'd tried to run the UDF office in Johannesburg when it was restricted – so enrolled at the London School of Economics to do a master's in economics. He was about to leave for England when Manuel was appointed. When he heard the news, he wasn't sorry he was going. 'I thought what a joke. To head Economics? Trevor! What the hell does this man know about economics?'

Some of the media concurred: *'How a guru with matric plans to fix the economy,'* read one headline.[2] You don't need a PhD in economics, Manuel retorted, to realise that the government had made a mess of the South African economy.

The 'guru' took over the DEP, which now included agricultural and land policy as well, from its incumbent head – and trained economist – Max Sisulu. Sisulu is the eldest son of Walter and Albertina Sisulu. He had run the DEP for the past two years, beginning when the movement was still in exile. An 'intelligent, quietly confident man (he) managed to win the confidence of a range of mostly younger economists who looked to him for leadership and direction'.[3] Sisulu had spent 26 years in exile – he left the country after being detained when his father was on trial with Mandela. He narrowly missed being killed in 1974 by the parcel bomb which killed his comrade John Dube. He'd studied in the Soviet Union, in Amsterdam and at Sussex University, the same university where Thabo Mbeki had studied. He had been away from his family so long that when his mother Albertina stopped over in Lusaka in 1989 on her way to see US President George Bush as head of the UDF delegation, she started when she saw him. 'I was surprised. Why is Zwelakhe (her youngest son) here? He didn't tell me he was going to follow me. Only when I came near, I noticed it was Max.'[4]

Nobody had told Sisulu that Manuel was coming to take over his job. As it happened, he was on his way to Harvard University, but the moment was awkward and although he welcomed Manuel to the office, there was certainly, as Manuel put it, 'some measure of disaffection'.

Another economist whom Manuel encountered in the DEP was a bantam-sized woman with dark copper hair. She was a close friend of Tito Mboweni, who, since his return from exile, had been sharing a house with her and her then fiancé. Mboweni had returned from exile 'back to reality', as he put it – the reality of racism that made it almost impossible for him to find his own apartment in the Johannesburg suburbs. Maria Ramos offered to accommodate him.

Ramos was born in Portugal in 1959, and moved to South Africa with her family when she was five years old. She learned to fight her battles early in life. The oldest of four daughters, her father was a bricklayer and her mother brought them up at their home in Vereeniging in the southern Transvaal. 'Like all immigrant families it's a struggle to make ends meet, it's a struggle against discrimination and exclusion, sometimes it's a struggle against the people that come from the same country ... they tend to be pretty conservative. Certainly the Portuguese community was pretty conservative so we didn't really fit in there either.'

In 1978, after she'd finished school, she went to work as a clerk at what was then Barclays Bank (it later became First National) because 'there was no money to go to university'. She hadn't been there long when she realised that 'there was this fantastic scholarship' the bank offered: it sent you to university, paid your fees and kept a job open. So she applied, to be told that it was open only to men. 'They tried to explain that it was because women go to university and come out and have babies ... you know the kind of stuff that was impossible to understand ... So I thought this was complete and utter discrimination and I just took them on,' Ramos told me.

As Manuel had done 15 years before with his supervisor at Murray & Stewart, she badgered the bank. 'Eventually I made such a nuisance of myself that they agreed to see me.' The managers at the bank's head office in Johannesburg said that if she passed all her bankers exams, they would consider her for the scholarship scheme. In record time, she passed them all, and returned to the head office.

'I've kept my side of the bargain, where's yours?'

Yes, well, said the managers, we've just started this new scholarship scheme at Unisa, where you can study part-time ... Ramos demurred. 'That's not what you committed to. I want a fair shot at the ordinary scholarship scheme.'

And so in 1984, seven years after matriculating, she found herself at the University of the Witwatersrand doing a Bachelor of Commerce degree. She was the first woman the bank had sent to university.

But she realised that accounting was not her passion. Economics was. She asked if she could do Economics Honours, and now, with a more progressive CEO at the bank (Chris Ball, known for his anti-apartheid views, became head of Barclays Bank in 1984), the bank agreed. She returned to the bank for a while, and then left in 1987 to teach economics, first at Unisa (where she almost supervised Barbara Hogan's thesis), and then at Wits.

Ramos's academic career galloped ahead. She won the economics prize for her honours thesis – 'something quite obscure' – on Clower's dual decision hypothesis and Keynes's general theory. She won scholarships to do her master's and was appointed a visiting fellow at the London School of Economics. She found a political home at Wits and began writing papers for the Centre for Development Studies, a policy think tank, on the economy. 'But there wasn't that much ANC stuff on the economy to read at the time,' she said. She'd read the Freedom Charter, the 'political stuff', but there were few pointers to economic policy. Like several other young economists in the country who were sympathetic to the ANC, she began intensive research on what an economic future might look like, which was how she found herself at the Harare conference of the ANC in 1988, which drew up the Constitutional Guidelines. There was little about the economy but what there was referred to a 'mixed economy, with a public sector, a private sector, a co-operative sector and a small-scale family sector'.

In 1989, when change looked real, she went to a conference held in Montreux in Switzerland, where ANC-aligned economists met business people and even some South African government officials. It was there she met Mboweni. With him and others, including Khetso Gordhan, she helped establish the DEP in the ANC offices even before Max Sisulu returned.

She had not known 'this Trevor Manuel fellow', except by reputation, when his appointment to head the DEP was announced. But the day he walked into the DEP offices on the twenty-first floor of Shell House, she did not think he was either a joke or an imposition. 'I thought to myself: anybody who thinks this man is only here occasionally and we were just going to be able to do whatever it is we were doing without much reference to him, I think we've underestimated the situation here quite grossly!' The fact that he didn't have an office might have sent a subliminal message to Manuel that the experts didn't think he would be around much, but Manuel had other ideas. Something in his body language, said Ramos, his confidence, told her that was not to be the case. 'I can still see him walking in there,' said Ramos, 'and I thought, oh shit, here we are.'

THERE THEY WERE: a clutch of talented, but inexperienced, young economists from inside the country and those who had returned from exile, led by a street-fighting politician who, by his own admission, knew hardly anything about the economy. The policy experience Manuel had gleaned from his stint on the Western Cape regional executive was scant, and it was in health issues – 'very nice doctors and nurses and stuff like that ... people who came along and wanted to share in ANC policy'. It hardly prepared him for what he was about to undertake.

Ramos for her part says she was not fazed by his appointment. On the contrary. 'The great thing was that it was going to be somebody who was going to champion these issues at the NEC. And at the time that's exactly what we needed,' she told me.

In fact, the ANC had been working quite intensively on economic policy issues since the late 1980s. There were no fewer than seven major international conferences between 1988 and 1993 that involved ANC-aligned economists and policy makers to sketch out a new economic vision for a post-apartheid South Africa. To a significant extent – at least in the 1980s – this process was driven by the exiled ANC. In fact, a key policy maker who returned from exile told me, somewhat disparagingly, that Nelson Mandela's Grand Parade speech on the day he was released from jail had taken such an uncompromising line on nationalisation because 'it was written by the Cyrils and the like' – (a reference to Ramaphosa and the MDM leadership), who were out of synch with the policy debates in the ANC in exile.

Ramaphosa bristled slightly at this charge, telling me that, indeed, he had been a co-drafter of Mandela's speech (with Valli Moosa and Murphy

Morobe), but that it was a reiteration of ANC policy at the time. 'In our view the policy of the ANC was encapsulated in the Freedom Charter. But we also tested it, by the way. What Madiba said that day was not a thumbsuck. It was tested ... with him (and) also with comrades in the ANC outside the country ... We were not just flying by the seat of our pants.'

But he acknowledges the fluidity in thinking of economic policy that came in the next few years, spurred by a sea change in the world. 'It was less to do with our own understanding of economic policy at the time, but more in line with the broad thinking internationally (about) whether one could still pursue those naked socialist-type solutions of blanket nationalisation. Many people were beginning to feel more and more comfortable with a mixed type of economy.'

Certainly, for those in exile, the real jolt came when the Soviet Union began unravelling. The USSR, unlike the West, had invested considerable resources into supporting the liberation movements in Africa, including the ANC. The South African Communist Party (SACP), an ally of the ANC, so close that its leadership overlapped in the most important respects, had since its inception been allied with the Soviet Union. But the fraying economy and polity there had given many of the brighter ANC leaders pause. When I asked one, Moeletsi Mbeki, the brother of former President Thabo Mbeki, when he first realised that the Soviet system was unsustainable, he laughed and replied that it was when he had flown Aeroflot, the Soviet airline, for the first time.

But a more permanent fissure was established in 1990 when Joe Slovo, the general secretary of the SACP, esteemed in liberation songs at home, wrote a seminal article, 'Has Socialism failed?' Slovo, 'a pillar of the armed struggle', confronted head-on the uncomfortable legacy of Stalinism, not only in the Soviet Union but in most of Eastern Europe as well as some of the cruder 'socialist' dictatorships, such as Cambodia. 'Socialism is undoubtedly in the throes of a crisis greater than at any other time since 1917,' he wrote.

> It is not enough merely to engage in the self-pitying cry: 'we were misled'; we should rather ask why so many communists allowed themselves to become so blinded for so long. And, more importantly, why they behaved like Stalinists towards those of their comrades who raised even the slightest doubt about the 'purity' of Stalin's brand of socialism.[5]

He still managed to find faith in a Marxist vision of a classless society free of exploitation, but was trenchant about the way the 'dictatorship of the proletariat' had translated into authoritarianism at best, and real dictatorship at worst. He quoted Rosa Luxembourg, approvingly, who said: 'Freedom is always and exclusively for the one who thinks differently', thus placing real value on the notion of individual human rights.

The paper did not dwell on economic policy but rather it was 'the intellectual equivalent of a sudden supply of pure oxygen to a person who had been slowly asphyxiating'.[6]

It also gave impetus to a more nuanced economic vision that had begun to be expressed in the ANC in the mid to late 1980s. Both the ANC's Constitutional Guidelines of 1988 and the Harare Declaration of 1989 expressed support for a mixed economy.

But the roots of a more flexible economic policy in the ANC go back further. Joel Netshitenzhe, who left the country in 1976, recalls ANC study groups in exile that discussed the Freedom Charter. Principally a humanist and nationalist document that did not delve deeply into economic questions, it talks, on the one hand, of 'the mineral wealth ... the Banks and monopoly industry' being transferred to 'the ownership of the people as a whole'; on the other hand it proposes that people have 'equal rights to trade where they choose, to manufacture and enter all trades, crafts and professions'.[7]

Jack Simons and his wife Ray Alexander (a founder of the Food and Canning Workers' Union), both committed communists, gave Netshitenzhe and his comrades in the ANC camps lessons on the economic meaning of the Freedom Charter. Here is Netshitenzhe's recollection of the study groups: 'Jack would explain, how does capitalism evolve? And he would say, if you were to ... do the things that the Freedom Charter says: the land shall be distributed amongst those who work it, for instance – such is the evolution of capitalism that some among those (to whom) you have redistributed the land will succeed, and others will fail. Those who fail will get swallowed, so big capitalist owners will emerge from that. Yes, you talk about monopoly industry but the Freedom Charter also says one will have the right to trade where they want and so on, and the small capitalist will develop, even black (small capitalists), into big capitalists. So he was arguing, don't ever think the Freedom Charter is about socialism. This is Jack Simons teaching us that!'

The fluidity of ANC economic policy in the late 1980s and early 90s was precisely a reflection of its vagueness during the organisation's exile years. Shortly after Mandela had endorsed nationalisation on the day of his release,

Thabo Mbeki, then the ANC's chief of international affairs, and still in exile, gave an interview to the South African state broadcaster. Clearly not wanting to seem at odds with Mandela, he chose his words carefully: 'The economy would need restructuring and I'm saying it would be wrong, from the beginning, to exclude consideration of the element of nationalisation or the element of public property.' Misleadingly, this statement was translated into a newspaper headline that read: 'Mbeki argues for nationalisation.'[8] A few days later, in another interview with a South African newspaper, Mbeki was clearer: the truth, he said, was that those clauses in the Freedom Charter that suggest nationalisation are only 'guidelines'. There was no hard policy. But the economic system in South Africa had created gross inequalities and imbalances and 'any democratic government will have to alter the structures inside the economy to create a system that can redress these imbalances'. The newspaper reporter wrote a breezy introduction to this story, which may have laid some fears of business to rest but again did not reflect the nuances of Mbeki's words: 'Those who have not understood the African National Congress policy on nationalisation can cheer up – the truth is the ANC does NOT have a nationalisation policy.'[9]

The truth, in fact, was that economic policy for the ANC was a work in progress. It had only been in the past five years that ANC intellectuals such as Mboweni began seriously to tackle such questions. Mboweni became involved in a study group known as EROSA (Economic Research on South Africa), first in England, with the British economists Fine and Harris and the exiled South African Vella Pillay, later in Lusaka. Much of the work was based on 'hard studies' – empirical research into the structure of the South African economy, the effects of the debt standstill and so on – rather than just wish lists for a new economic order.

'In the middle of all that, we then had to begin to make sense of what is meant by this mixed economy. And the thinking, more and more, was directing us to these models in Scandinavia, to Scandinavian social democratic thinking,' Mboweni told me. 'You must recall, as well, the difficulties of the East European model by 1985. By 1988 (when Mboweni relocated to Lusaka) it had all but collapsed. So the need to examine this social democratic model became very important. And within that philosophic context of a mixed economy (we were) to develop the basis for most of the economic policies that were to be debated later.'

At home, similar policy groups emerged from the late 1980s, when liberation could be spotted on the horizon. The trade union federation COSATU had gathered around it a group of sympathetic academics and economists in 1986 and set up the Economic Trends Group. Alec Erwin, then education secretary in COSATU, was a key driver of this group.

The Economic Trends Group was coordinated first by David Lewis, later by Stephen Gelb, a young Canadian-trained economist. Initially its brief was to assess the effects of sanctions, but this quickly expanded to a study of the whole economy. In 1990, the group made contact with Max Sisulu, then head of the ANC's Economic Planning Department who was studying in Britain.

The union movement had developed an approach to economic policy by then that was born of its three-decade battle for its members. Not surprisingly, most unionists and workers linked their political oppression to an economic system that allowed them no mobility and little freedom. Slabbert's memoirs that had Alec Erwin 'thundering' about nationalisation at the Marly le Roi conference in 1989 may have relied on 'a large dose of poetic licence', as Erwin said, but nonetheless the fact that Slabbert recalled such a robust encounter showed just how fractured the country was over the question of economic policy.

THE FISSURE WAS HARDLY SURPRISING. This new debate took place against the backdrop of the implosion of the centrally planned economies of Eastern Europe on the one hand, and the complete economic stagnation of South Africa on the other. If communism had failed in Eastern Europe, then capitalism, at least as far as most blacks in South Africa were concerned, had failed too.

When Mandela affirmed that the ANC's economic policy included nationalisation just hours out of prison, he was reflecting not only the disillusion of many black people with the capitalist system, but also the ascendant voice of the trade unions within the Mass Democratic Movement. He was also reflecting, albeit unwittingly, the gap between the internal resistance movement and the ANC in exile which had moved ahead in terms of nuanced economic debates. As early as 1988, when the Constitutional Guidelines were drawn up, the ANC expressed itself in favour of a mixed economy.

'At a very empirical level,' said Netshitenzhe, '(you have) a Mandela who was not in touch with those debates and who is assisted in drafting his release speech by people who were not aware of those debates and not fully informed about ANC policy positions, so he talks about nationalisation as a fundamental policy of the ANC.'

Ramaphosa's point – that he and his colleagues consulted ANC members in exile before the speech – actually highlights differences within the ANC itself rather than only between the internal resistance and its exiled comrades. But the debate that Mandela's remark sparked was in fact useful fuel for the energetic policy making in the years that followed.

Initially, though, it 'started badly', as Gelb wrote in a newspaper two weeks after Mandela was released from jail. 'There has been widespread panic and hysteria in the financial media and more ominously in the financial markets following Nelson Mandela's unsurprising support for nationalisation.'[10] Gelb warned that it would be disastrous if the debate continued along what he called 'Simplistic Ideology' lines.

And a nervous National Party government, on the verge of losing power, threw further toxins into the mix by gearing itself to sell off key public assets in the early 1990s. Partly, it argued, this was to help pay off some of its mounting debt. The suspicion this aroused was exacerbated by provocative comments by, among others, the former police spy (by this time a major in the security police) Craig Williamson who said: 'What we are trying to do is make sure that no future government has the power we did.'[11]

The prospects of power spurred a new thoughtfulness in ANC-aligned economists. 'It was quite an intense time,' recalled Ramos. 'Because we knew at some point that we were going to have to go into government and there were all of these big issues that we were going to have to confront and it was really quite a battle between, on the one hand, the ideology that we all felt and the things we all felt very close to, and (on the other) the reality of having to deal with a range of very tough economic choices.'

Those choices turned out to be tougher than even the harshest critics of the apartheid-run economy had imagined. But even then it was clear that 'horse trading' alone, as one commentator put it, was simply not going to cut it when it came to solving the severe crisis that awaited the new rulers.[12]

The COSATU economists met their ANC counterparts for the first time in Harare in May 1990. Some of the EROSA researchers, based in London, also attended and, despite the many divergent viewpoints, the paper that was produced out of that – *ANC and COSATU Recommendations on Post-Apartheid Economic Policy* – was a sign of the seriousness with which both groups struggled to transcend easy ideological positions. The document defined the role of the state in a post-apartheid economy broadly but, importantly, stated that a 'future non-racial democratic government would not replicate the recent practice of using borrowings to finance current state expenditure'. It expressed itself on macroeconomic planning (a yes) and on inflation (a no) and on the regulation of capital markets to 'encourage appropriate investments' (a strong yes).[13] Nationalisation was mentioned as a possibility, but flexibility on this point was contingent on the NP government not proceeding with its own privatisation programme (by then it had already sold off most of Iscor, the state steel company and Sasol, its oil company). 'The threats worked,' writes Hirsch in his book that explores the development of ANC economic policy. 'Privatisation ceased between 1990 and1994.'[14]

Five months later the ANC economists met again in Harare. This time there was no official COSATU representation, and no economists from outside. That meeting produced a document called *Forward to a Democratic Economy*. It dealt with logistical issues – such as proposing that the DEP be relocated to Johannesburg. It examined the daunting challenges the ANC was about to inherit: South Africa's extremes of poverty and wealth (at that time some 5 per cent of the population owned 88 per cent of the wealth); the 30 per cent unemployment rate and the fact that over half the population lived below the minimum subsistence level.[15] It also noted the steady stagnation of the South African economy: between 1983 and 1989 the economy had grown by an average of only 1,4 per cent a year while the population had grown by about 2,5 per cent, which meant that, on average, every South African had grown poorer. To create jobs, to haul people out of poverty, the new economy had to grow. And the engine of growth? Not 'a rising demand for luxury goods by a minority of wealthy consumers', said the document, but 'the growing satisfaction of the basic needs of the impoverished and deprived majority of our people ... we thus call for a programme of growth through redistribution, in which redistribution acts as spur to growth and in which the fruits of growth are redistributed to satisfy basic needs'. And then, towards the end, the ANC acknowledges that 'private business has a major role to play in the economy of a democratic, non-racial South Africa and that a new government 'should actively strive to build confidence with the private sector'.

It also called for 'high standards of financial management and discipline', noting that a large budget deficit, high inflation and deficits on the balance of payments can have a detrimental impact on people's living standards. And on nationalisation? 'A future democratic government will need to act to transform the public sector into a vehicle for development. But this does not mean creating large, profligate public corporations and parastatals.'[16]

And so by the end of 1990, the ANC had adopted an altogether more considered approach to an economic future. There were still to be plenty of battles, but a new narrative had been constructed.

This was almost upset just over a year later when Nelson Mandela, urged by Mboweni, attended the World Economic Forum (WEF) in Davos for the first time. He had been suspicious of the Forum because Klaus Schwab, its executive chair, was seen by the ANC as close to its political rivals, F W de Klerk and Mangosuthu Buthelezi, both of whom were attending. But Mboweni persuaded Mandela that he could have his 'own programme' and that it was critical for him to meet with some of the one thousand executives there, as well as other political leaders 'invited like zoo animals to be scrutinised', as one diplomat put it, in 'this exclusive club of capitalism'.[17]

When Mandela and Mboweni arrived in Davos, the chintzy ski resort that hosts the annual WEF meeting, Mboweni discovered to his annoyance that the economic section of the speech – for which space was left in the draft – had been penned by one of the left-wing ANC-aligned economists based in London. Worse, it had already been distributed to the media.

Some journalists were careful. Quoting the 'prepared text', they reported that Mandela said: 'Nationalisation in our view does not mean a universal blanket policy or sticking rigidly to an old dogma. It means examining selected major enterprises on a case-by-case basis. Our starting point would be those bodies and corporations already in state hands.'[18]

It may have been a compromise for the London-based economists, but it did not sit comfortably with Mboweni, wise to the possibilities and pitfalls of international political sympathies at this crucial early stage of South Africa's transition. Then only 31 years old, he showed the maturity of an elder in wresting control of the speech. 'It's the wrong platform,' he told Mandela. 'You can't deliver this speech here … You can't go in front of a thousand business executives and talk about nationalisation … We've moved on. We now talk about a mixed economy.'[19]

He and Saki Macozoma, an Eastern Cape-born former Robben Islander, sat through the night and rewrote Mandela's speech. 'These people (at Davos) consider you a hero,' Mboweni told him. 'Don't disappoint them.'

When the day came, Mandela gave a 'conciliatory and moderate' speech, pledging to work together with his fellow South Africans. De Klerk and Buthelezi echoed the message. 'Mr Mandela took his softest approach to nationalisation so far, assuring the industrialists that their investments would not be endangered by nationalisation', wrote one reporter. The most controversial aspect of his visit to Davos was the fact that he complained that he was not given equal speaking time with De Klerk .[20]

What sticks in Mboweni's mind is this: during the Davos forum, Mandela met Li Peng, who had been installed as Premier of China a few years earlier. That country then was on the verge of an economic renaissance.[21] The conversation came around to nationalisation. Li Peng, according to Mboweni, was puzzled. 'Madiba,' he said, 'I don't understand why you're talking about nationalisation. You're not even a communist party. I am the leader of the communist party in China, and I'm talking privatisation.'

'So, yes, really!' Mboweni exclaimed when he recounted this to me.

The conversation stayed with Mandela a long time. At every ANC discussion on the economy, he would remark on it. 'This thing was stuck in his head, you know. He kept on saying: "Even *Li Peng*, general secretary of the Communist Party doesn't believe in nationalisation. Who are we? We are not a communist party." '

THE FACT THAT SOUTH AFRICANS were suddenly players in the world burst a bubble of self-absorption. Partly because the struggle against apartheid was so intense, partly because the transition was tortuous and miraculous, South Africans frequently saw themselves as unique, as though there had been no history before them or without them. But the problems that confronted the country on the eve of its reconstruction echoed those in other societies that had remade themselves. It is dangerous to generalise about recipes for economic success, but one common thread seems to be an eschewing of ideological solutions.

In the twentieth century the ideology of the free market was a fashionable explanation for the economic success of England and America, two and three centuries before. History is often seen through the prism of the present, and at the height of the Reagan and Thatcher eras in the late 1980s, the market was lauded as the panacea for economic problems. But in fact the free market was last on a list of solutions for these countries at the time. Had England, for instance, followed the dictum of nineteenth-century economist David Ricardo, who argued for a free market and free trade based on 'comparative advantage', the Industrial Revolution may well not have happened. With England's edge in wool production, would it, asked one Harvard professor,

346

have 'perhaps been better off … setting up academies to train shepherds', instead of what it did – which was to import technologies, protect them, enhance its linen production and throw up a naval wall of steel to keep cheaper imports from India out.[22]

When Alexander Hamilton became the first Secretary of the Treasury in post-revolutionary America in 1789, he agreed, within days of his appointment, to pay back the debt accrued by the colonial government – a highly unpopular decision. He also established a national bank to promote a common currency and to manage new debt. In the short term, this seemed lunacy. Why pay debts incurred by the colonial government that the revolutionaries had gone to war against? Why a national bank when the revolutionary values were of freedom and independence for all the 13 separate states? Hamilton pushed the point. Through repaying the debt, he managed to raise more money from places such as Amsterdam. With the new capital, the federal government built infrastructure to link the hitherto disparate 13 states of the federation. Hamilton mobilised further financial resources through taxation, and threw up a wall of tariffs around the domestic market while promoting free trade between the states.

Some of his fellow revolutionaries were bitterly opposed to many of these moves. Thomas Jefferson and James Madison, both co-authors of the Constitution with Hamilton, opposed the repaying of debt; they opposed the establishment of a central bank and one currency, and they opposed tax on farmers. They were the era's populists, ardent campaigners for individual liberties and economic equality, particularly for small farmers who had been the backbone of the revolution. In fact, the tax burden on the farmers – then the majority of the population – probably was unduly heavy. And Hamilton's plan to refinance the state using federal bonds may have raised the total cost three to four times.[23]

It caused huge political ructions (the revolutionary party split into two, ultimately the Republicans and the Democrats), but by 1900 the United States market was the largest in the world and the richest in terms of per capita income.[24]

Two centuries later, Japan would emerge from bitter defeat in World War Two, many of its factories and cities damaged or destroyed and its merchant marine wiped out. Its GDP was less than half that of the UK's; its savings were moderate; its exports weak. American experts at the time predicted that the country would need long-term foreign assistance. 'Regardless of the political and economic system she eventually chooses (it is doubtful) whether (Japan) can maintain any satisfactory standard of living in the future,' said one.[25] Thirty years after this prognosis, Japan became a founder member of the G7, a group of the most highly industrialised and economically powerful countries in the world.

How did it happen? How did Japan pull itself out of penury and defeat to become a global economic power?

For one thing, its planners looked at tomorrow's opportunities, not only the day's exigencies. The country mobilised its own economic resources, instituted a policy of forced savings in the 1950s, kept its currency undervalued, rebuilt its basic industries and developed its own manufacturing industries until they were internationally competitive.

In Brazil, nearly five decades after that war, the former academic – a sociology professor at that – Fernando Henrique Cardoso, was given the unenviable cabinet position of finance minister. Unenviable because inflation was running at about 2 500 per cent a year and government consistently spent much more than it earned in revenues: in 1994, the deficit was $20 billion out of a budget of about $90 billion. It also simply printed money when it needed it. The problem, as Cardoso records in his memoirs, *The Accidental President of Brazil*, was this: powerful people benefited from inflation. One group was politicians ('as long as there was inflation they never had to say no to anybody. No spending request was too large: just print more money'); the other was the banks who made a substantial profit from a process they called 'floating': holding back on transferring people's payments for just three days could result in as much as 8 per cent profit because of the rapid devaluation of the currency.

The real victims of inflation, writes Cardoso, were the poor and the powerless. Despite populist arguments, including those of the unions, that inflation spurred economic growth and was good for workers' wages, the real truth was that 'inflation acted like a regressive tax that made poor people poorer'.[26] And investment shrank, particularly foreign investment, because 'how could anyone make a deal when they didn't know the value of something as basic as money'. Cardoso engineered an economic recovery plan called the *Real* Plan, after the new currency, the *real*. The central bank's task was to steady it by buying and selling foreign reserves when appropriate. Cardoso introduced severe budget cuts. He presented his ideas to the country's legislators. 'Naturally everyone hated it,' Cardoso records. 'From the left and the right, from inside and outside Brazil, there was a hailstorm of criticism and mockery.'[27]

When the *real* was introduced, fortuitously at the same time as Brazil won the 1994 Soccer World Cup, Cardoso had left the finance ministry and was campaigning for president. His principal opponent was the charismatic trade union leader Luis Inácio Lula da Silva, more popularly known as Lula. The two men had been allies during the struggle, in an earlier era of Brazil's history, against the military dictatorship, but now they were bitter opponents. And economic policy was the great divider. When Lula lost the election to Cardoso in 1994, he fumed that the victor was 'the executioner of the Brazilian economy, responsible for one of the greatest economic disasters in the history of Brazil'.[28]

But Lula was wrong. Perhaps it was the soccer that distracted people from their current economic woes and thus protests. At any rate, the euphoria, and the public forbearance that came with it, gave the government the space it needed to implement the plan. Inflation plummeted and then dropped steadily to only two per cent by July 1994. And for workers, who were Lula's principal constituency, the value of the average wage in Brazil increased by 30 per cent.[29]

And then there was South East Asia, whose rocketing economies in the three decades after 1960 made the rest of the world draw breath. The eight aptly but dully named HPAE (High Performing Asian Economies) grew, from 1960 to 1990, twice as fast as the rest of East Asia, three times as fast as Latin America and sub-Saharan Africa, and outperformed the major industrial economies and the oil-rich countries of the Middle East and North Africa. Amazingly, they increased their income equality at the same time. As a result of the combined effects of growth and income redistribution, poverty took a severe knock in all the previously poor South East Asian countries. For instance, the proportion of people living without the basic necessities of clean water, food and shelter dropped from 58 per cent in 1960 to 17 per cent in 1990 in Indonesia, and from 37 per cent to less than 5 per cent in Malaysia.[30]

In most of the South East Asian 'miracle' countries, the banking services improved, private investment increased and expenditure on primary and secondary education rose considerably.

The rest of the world was both enthralled and puzzled by this phenomenon. A World Bank analysis concluded that the 'miracle' was due to two main factors: one was getting the fundamentals right in terms of macroeconomic policy (low inflation, positive but low and stable interest rates, property rights and predictability); the other was by selective government interventions to support particular industries that could compete in the world market.

Savings were harnessed – it was hard to buy on credit in many of those countries – human capital was trained and enhanced, and investments were made in better and more modern technology.

When the miracle became clear for the world to see in 1990, many of the more intellectually progressive ANC economists such as Mboweni began to look with keener interest at what exactly these countries – many of them former colonies – had done to improve their lot. The planned economy experiment of the Soviet Union and Eastern Europe had ended in tears – it was clear that, apart from the political and cultural repression that accompanied those regimes, most could not meet the consumer demands of their citizens and certainly could not compete in a changing world, as Moeletsi Mbeki's negative experiences with Aeroflot testified.

The sustainable economic successes, in different times and places, depended not on the ideology of either the free market or socialism but on a combination of both, a worldly knowledge, and particular government interventions. The interventions were determined by history, place, culture, and the balance of political power. There was, is, no easy one-stop solution to economic reconstruction. Often, the remedies are deeply unpopular, as Cardoso discovered in Brazil and as Hamilton found two centuries before him in the continent to the north. But none of them were 'ideological' solutions in that they were tailored to meet the popular demands or ideas of the time.

On that September morning in 1991, when Trevor Manuel walked into the ANC's Department of Economic Planning offices, he had not considered any of this. He had had no need to. Jail had matured him; his role in the early talks about talks had sparked new views about a solution to the South African crisis. But his heart was still on the streets in combat mode. Then, he was probably more a Jefferson than a Hamilton, more a Lula than a Cardoso. For him, the challenge was to acquire a little of the 'other' while remembering the streets that he came from.

'I'M NOT A TRAINED ECONOMIST,' Manuel told a newspaper reporter days before taking up his new ANC position in August 1991.[31]

But he went on to talk about sanctions – they should stay until political change was irreversible – and that job creation and service delivery would be the two biggest challenges facing a new government. It was not sanctions that were responsible for the frighteningly high unemployment, he said. 'I think our economic problems emanate from economic mismanagement particularly during our boom years … Unless we are going to provide the goods and services that will improve the quality of life for our people, the notion of liberation will not be worth the paper it is written on.'

He was cautious about nationalisation, too – even though this was a few months shy of Mandela's watershed appearance at the World Economic Forum. 'Nationalisation has always been one of our options. It is now less prominent in our economic documents.'

But nothing was certain. Manuel walked into not only a new world on the twenty-first floor of Shell House, but a highly contested one.

In the wake of the two Harare economic conferences of the year before, a plethora of small economic study groups had clustered around the ANC and COSATU. One was the Industrial Strategy Project, linked to COSATU, which developed a vision for development that was 'less Keynesian and more Asian in its approach', meaning it outlined a policy of growth that involved increasing productivity to compete in the export markets.[32] The more 'Keynesian' alternative – following the ideas of the British economist John Maynard Keynes – was of 'growth through redistribution', which the earlier ANC policy documents had endorsed. In fact the ANC slogan 'growth through redistribution' could have accommodated both paths and it was convenient, perhaps inevitable, at that early stage of policy formulation that the ANC would have fudged any finer distinction between the two.

More contentious was the Macro Economic Research Group (MERG), set up by the ANC. Nelson Mandela had asked Canadian prime minister Brian Mulroney 'to help us strengthen our capacity for economic research and policy formulation' and the Canadians' response was to get its International Development Research Centre* to fund MERG. Until then expertise and research within the ANC on fiscal and monetary policy had been lacking. The critical question was how to fund the dire social needs apartheid had left in its wake, how to correct decades of structural inequality, discrimination and enforced poverty, and at the same time to drive economic growth.

MERG fell squarely into the ANC's policy-making project. Manuel chaired it, and Pillay managed it. Manuel described it later as a 'fascinating experience

---

* An independent government-funded body.

because you had these teams at different universities trying to collaborate on new policy'.

It was a serious attempt to get to grips with the challenges that faced a new government and to move away from the rhetoric that dominated, as Mandela put it, the 'vigorous, if not rigorous' debate about the economic future.[33] By then the ANC had settled on the idea of a 'mixed economy ... that includes both the role of the state and the market in directing redistribution of wealth and promoting growth of the economy.'[34]

But MERG was deeply divided on the economic way forward, and the project ended in a bitterness that lingers to this day. Gelb, initially a part of MERG, characterises the split in the group as being between 'people, on the one side, who accepted that we lived in a globalising and globalised economy and we needed some kind of openness to that economy in order to grow,' and those on the other who 'took a closed economy, Keynesian position. In other words,' he told me, 'they assumed the economy would remain cut off from the rest of the world and you could have a growth strategy based on government spending and government intervention.'

To be fair, it was a complex process and Pillay's task was to converge various analytical strands into a single macroeconomic policy. The divergence, not only in views, but also in the analyses done, made this a near impossible task at the time.

MERG was to present its final report amid fall-outs and acrimony some two years later. It drew in some of the best economic brains inside and outside the country, all of whom were sympathetic to the massive project of democratic reconstruction that confronted the ANC. But the editing of the final report involved only one South African-based economist – the rest had withdrawn – and, in the end, neither Manuel nor Mandela gave it any official endorsement. In fact, at the last moment Mandela pulled out of the planned function to launch the report. Manuel did speak at the launch, but said later that the problem with official endorsement was that it was hard for the ANC at that stage to take detailed analytical work on board as formal policy.

Manuel may not then have understood the precise economic formulations and arguments that came from different quarters. But he certainly understood the political trust that had been placed in him. 'I have to ensure that our policy is not formulated by technocrats,' he told City Press a month after he assumed his new post. 'That contributions by ordinary members are also acknowledged, with the mysticism of the economy removed for them.'[35]

And what did he mean by 'mysticism'? It was about the economy's centre. '(Some) say it is about value, money flow, the gold price, foreign exchange. But it is wrong. It centres fundamentally around people.' Showing a sense of what was to come, he added: '(People) say they want more houses, they want pensions to be equalised [across race groups], and they want to create more jobs. Then they see they have to tax people more to do it, but they also don't want to do that. Expectations are very high and we have to teach them to wrestle with these problems so that expectations can be tempered.'

Does one have a capital gains tax, he mused to the reporter. Heavier corporate taxes and less burden on individuals? What policies would lead to a capital outflow, and what would keep business on board? How does a country move from exporting raw materials to manufactured goods?

The social needs at the time were as daunting. How does a society move from one that grinds hope by absorbing only 10 per cent of school-leavers a year into the market to one that nourishes it? How do you defuse the anger in a country where the richest 10 per cent received nearly half the country's income, and the poorest 10 per cent just over one per cent?[36]

What Manuel brought to the DEP in 1991 was the ability to harness political capital. Some of the economic experts may have had their noses out of joint when 'the guru with matric' walked in to take charge, but not many took this view for long.

Mboweni's 'niggling feeling' that this was an imposition faded. Manuel's appointment was 'a blessing in disguise', he told me. 'To try work through the issues ... and he's very bright, got a very good brain, so he's able to pick up issues very fast.'

Ismail Momoniat, who was among a large handful who thought Manuel's appointment a 'joke', is sheepish a decade and half on. 'I would eat my words now,' he said.

The ANC office, somewhat hastily re-established in Johannesburg in 1990, was 'a mess' at that stage. 'Such a shambles,' recalled Momoniat. 'People didn't know how to handle answering phones, and you know all these old *toppies* (fellows) came and they were nice old *toppies* but they just didn't understand ... And there was no prospect of the ANC delivering, and we just felt we really needed someone smart.'

The first someone was Cyril Ramaphosa, whom the internal liberation movement backed strongly for the position of general secretary; the second was Manuel, elected to head the DEP a few weeks later at the NWC meeting.

'A surprise,' said Momoniat, 'but we never realised these appointments were so powerful.'

MANUEL IMMERSED HIMSELF in the rapidly changing world of international finance. At Mboweni's urging, he went to a southern African meeting of the World Economic Forum in Geneva. And then, again at Mboweni's behest, to Bangkok which was hosting the annual meetings of the International Monetary Fund (IMF) and the World Bank.

South Africa had been a member of the Bretton-Woods institutions since their inception in 1945. But in this interregnum between apartheid and democracy, neither Manuel nor Mboweni had any official standing at the IMF meeting and no protection against mishap. 'I had the idea that we needed to expose as many of our people as possible to different local and international organisations such as the IMF and the World Bank, as well as the markets,' said Mboweni. 'So that when we develop policies, we must take account of all the views that are out there, but still be governed by our basic philosophical approach to a mixed economy.'

The two arrived in Bangkok with hardly any money in their pockets. In those days, explained Mboweni, when you travelled for the ANC you got a flat rate of $40. '*Qhwe!*' he exclaimed using the explosive Nguni palatal click to emphasise the point. Whether you were going to Benoni on the East Rand or Bangkok in South East Asia, it was the same amount.

Then there was the question of getting into Thailand. Mboweni was traveling on a UN passport which the Thai immigration officials regarded with deep suspicion. 'They kind of took him away, as if they were going to arrest him,' said Manuel. 'I really had to argue and … these people couldn't understand anything – so I kept on saying *"Mandela"* and *"South Africa".'*

A lot of rubbish, recalled Mboweni. 'Trevor started talking a lot of rubbish, a lot of rubbish I'd ever heard, about do they know Nelson Mandela, we were sent here by Nelson Mandela, he's going to be upset if they don't allow us in. A lot of rubbish! But that helped a lot because they eventually gave me an entry visa.'

The immigration officials who finally let them in introduced them to a taxi driver and asked him to 'Drop us at a reasonable hotel, not a rich place because we didn't have a lot of money,' said Mboweni.

The taxi driver took them straight to a brothel. As soon as they realised where they were, they rushed outside, found another taxi and said: 'IMF!

World Bank!' in much the same way that Manuel had mouthed the 'Mandela' mantra to the immigration officials at the airport. Somewhere near the meeting venue, they found a 'marginally' better hotel, called Comfort Inn. It was cheap, but tried to live up to its name.

Then to the meeting, where there was more awkwardness. They had no accreditation and weren't part of a country delegation. South Africa was represented by the then finance minister Barend du Plessis and Reserve Bank Governor Chris Stals. Tim Tahane, an old university colleague of Mboweni's from Lesotho, was a vice president of the World Bank at the time (he was later to become a deputy governor of the South African Reserve Bank and then finance minister of Lesotho), helped the two get into the meeting. South Africa's director-general of finance, Gerhard Croeser, was friendly enough and offered to register them as part of the South African delegation but, as Manuel said, 'that would have been the end for us'.

So the two walked around alone, 'quite wide-eyed. Nobody knew us ... we were very much on our own trying to take stock of this big world that we didn't understand.'

THIS BIG, NEW WORLD had confronted Manuel even more uncomfortably just weeks earlier when he attended an investment conference at the Notre Dame University in Indiana, in the United States.

The conference was jointly announced by the ANC and by the University of Notre Dame in October 1991 as a 'landmark' one: 'Officials of the ANC will meet with US government representatives and executives of more than 40 major US corporations, and a small group of academic scholars who are actively involved in the South African issue, to discuss for the first time a policy for investment in post-apartheid South Africa.'[37]

It came at a critical time for both the US and South Africa. The US anti-apartheid movement had won a resounding political victory in the mid-1980s by enforcing sanctions against South Africa at congressional, not just state, level. The Comprehensive Anti-Apartheid Act (the CAAA) had passed through Congress not once, but twice, the second time by a two thirds majority after being vetoed by President Ronald Reagan. It was an extraordinary victory for the anti-apartheid cause in the United States, particularly because the movement there was not a cohesive national body: rather, it comprised a myriad local church, trade union, political and, later, celebrity groups. Its success turned to a large extent on the pivot of domestic politics, particularly the strong African-American lobby that had been forged in that country's own racist past and present. As writer and anti-apartheid activist Bill Minter put it: 'The debate on sanctions became in effect a referendum on racism.'[38]

After Mandela's release there was a body of opinion that called for the lifting of sanctions. But most of the anti-apartheid groups insisted they stay until democracy was irrevocable.

By 1987, more than 200 US companies had withdrawn from South Africa.[39] In defiance of the call for comprehensive sanctions, some US companies remained under an uneasy compromise known as the Sullivan Principles. Leon Sullivan was a Baptist minister who proposed a set of ethical business principles in 1977 as an alternative to disinvestment and divestment which he feared would harm black workers in South Africa. The principles, he believed, 'would offer corporate interests an opportunity to reject the mandate of apartheid in the operation of their business interests in South Africa'.

But the compromise became increasingly unpopular as the liberation struggle dragged on, both in South Africa and in the United States. The push towards majority rule became the bottom line and nothing short of harsh economic punishment for the South African government seemed capable of bringing that about.

Manuel inherited this view, along with a deep suspicion about the motives of big business. US President George Bush lifted US sanctions in mid-1991, although local anti-apartheid groups kept the 'pressure on', as the slogan went, until Mandela gave the nod for the lifting of sanctions two years later. But what many of the anti-apartheid activists did not appreciate sufficiently was that the challenge would be not so much how to maintain sanctions but how to attract investment. And the smell of victory that came with the release of Mandela distorted the ANC's sense of its own power internationally.

Perhaps it was this sense of inflated power, or perhaps it was just Manuel's street-fighting instincts that led to what he himself would call 'complete disaster' at the Notre Dame conference.

The conference organisers, Father Oliver Williams, the provost of Notre Dame (a Catholic institution), and George Schroll, a consultant on South Africa to Colgate-Palmolive, one of the Sullivan companies, had met the ANC leaders, including Thabo Mbeki, Walter Sisulu and Manuel, earlier that year in Johannesburg. 'They (the ANC) said ... we would like you to help us to generate interest for new investment in South Africa after the first election ... our big worry ... is running a government and not having sufficient investment to create the jobs to keep the forward morale going here,' Williams told me.

'And they said we understand investment decisions are made a year or two in advance so we want to give it enough lead time, and to let people know that we *do* want investment. We're not interested in a command economy or socialist or Marxist ideals.' Mandela, who at the time was distracted by his then wife Winnie Mandela's court case that concerned the abduction and murder of the 14-year-old activist Stompie Seipei, had popped in to the meeting to assure them on this point.

The planning for the conference raised hackles on both sides. Notre Dame, sponsored by its business allies in the venture, offered to pay for 10 members of the ANC to attend. But the ANC, according to Williams, also asked whether the PAC and AZAPO could send representatives as they were at the time part of the short-lived 'Patriotic Front' with the ANC. However, it objected to Chief Mangosuthu Buthelezi's Inkatha attending on the basis that it was not part of this Front.

There were other reasons too: Buthelezi had long opposed sanctions and had been an active supporter of the Sullivan Principles. Buthelezi, who knew both Schroll and Williams well, was 'incensed' that he was not invited and made such robust objections that the entire conference seemed to be in jeopardy.[40]

Ten days before the start of the conference, the ANC reluctantly agreed that Inkatha could be present. The Inkatha representative was Sipho Mzimela, a prickly man who was later to be the minister of correctional services in Mandela's first Government of National Unity cabinet.

Manuel, along with Thabo Mbeki and Penuell Maduna, a lawyer who had spent several years in exile, were among the ANC delegation. The tone of the meeting, writes Williams, was 'best captured by headlines in the *Washington Post* – "An uncertain re-entry into South Africa: US companies fear sanctions, possibility of nationalisation", and *Business Week*: "The ANC to US Investors: On Your Mark, Get Set … Not Just Yet".'[41]

The conference began on 6 October with an address by the US State Department's Herman Cohen, as well as Thabo Mbeki. Cohen warned those about to assume the mantle of power to be 'realistic … This is a competitive world. It will not be enough for a post-apartheid government to say 'here we are', and then wait for the flood of investment capital. The international economic climate into which South Africa is emerging is different from the

357

one from which South Africa was excluded.'

Mbeki gave an address described by one participant as 'eloquent and conciliatory'.[42] Mbeki said the ANC had not 'to the best of my recollection ever condemned capitalism'. But he spoke about the need to create a more equitable economy. One way to do this was to ensure rapid economic growth, more equal distribution of wealth, and 'some sort' of affirmative action programme. 'Now is the time to begin making preparations for entry or re-entry into South Africa. It is important to us that South Africa is on the agenda of the US corporate world. We are looking for new investment.'[43]

He did not give the nod to the lifting of sanctions – there were still 142 state and local government authorities in the US that had restrictions on doing business with South Africa and the ANC considered this to be critical leverage in its negotiations with the white minority government.

But generally the US executives there seemed pleased by what they heard.

That was Day One.

'Had Mbeki's presentation on new investment been the final word on the matter, the Notre Dame meeting would have ended on a high note.'[44]

But it wasn't. There was still Day Two. That was when Manuel spoke. His intervention nearly unravelled the conference.

Manuel's temper was already frayed by Sipho Mzimela. Inkatha was resentful at being invited as an afterthought, so Mzimela attacked Mbeki for being a 'communist': 'Sipho was, I thought, very inflexible in his thinking,' said Williams. 'A very bright ideologue, who was really difficult to get along with.' He 'continually intervened', recalled Williams, even while Mbeki was talking.

'The meeting got very difficult,' said Manuel. The next day he took his brooding mood out on the would-be and actual US investors.

'He suggested that the ANC might reward those firms that had left South Africa (in response to the disinvestment call) and penalise those firms that had remained there in opposition to the ANC's call to disinvest. His remarks seemed to resonate with those of the other seven members of the ANC delegation and left a decided chill on the discussion of new investment. Moreover, the ANC delegates at this session had such a poor understanding of international finance that many business leaders in attendance were wondering why they had bothered to come to Notre Dame.' The ANC seemed to believe that investment could be turned 'on and off like a faucet (a tap)', and that once it was in power, new investment would 'flow like a river after a spring thaw'.[45]

Manuel remembers his intervention being even blunter. 'I said, "You don't want to listen to us? You know what's going to happen? We're going to take over the country and we are going to kick you guys out." '

Stephen Gelb, who also attended the conference, recalled such an uproar after Manuel had threatened to 'punish' those firms that had broken sanctions that the organisers called a tea break. Far from his remarks resonating with other members of the ANC delegation, as Williams thought, Gelb said that most other ANC members tried to put a polite distance between themselves and Manuel's remarks. 'My view was that first of all it's not that easy *to punish* firms … but even if you *are* going to do that, the last thing you do is tell them ahead of time … It was a major PR disaster. The rest of the meeting was spent trying to get back to square one.'

Mbeki was not there during Manuel's outburst. He was packing to go to Germany for another visit to potential investors. Williams told him at lunch that the meeting had 'basically fallen apart … you obviously haven't briefed Trevor Manuel because he wasn't talking the same language you were talking'.

Mbeki, according to Williams, sighed, and asked what he'd said. Then he spoke to Manuel. His words had some effect because after lunch Manuel, if not exactly apologising, told the executives he had been 'misunderstood' and denied there was 'any threat on our part'.[46]

'That's how polished we were!' said Manuel 15 years later, well into his third term as finance minister. He had told me the story initially. Gelb, who confirmed it, was amazed at his candour. When I told Manuel a few months later that I had spoken to Williams about the incident, he smiled and said, 'Did he tell you what an arsehole I was?'

Williams had. But he had also said that he had posed a few questions to him at lunch the day before his outburst. 'As a long-time teacher I'm very good at assessing intelligence … and I thought this guy's extremely bright.'

Leaving aside the notion that it is the prerogative of citizens of the richer countries to 'assess the intelligence' of those of the less powerful, Williams nonetheless pinpointed those characteristics of Manuel's that were to carry him from being a radical civic leader from the Cape Flats to a politician who could grasp the possibilities, and boundaries, of power in the unforgiving world of global finance. 'He's a quick study – he learns on the job, and (learns) by surrounding himself with very bright people,' said Williams. 'One of the marks of a good leader is that you can surround yourself with people smarter than you are. In other words you're not threatened … If you criticise him, he *thinks* about it and maybe he changes his mind.' Not everyone can do that, said Williams. Manuel could and can 'because basically he's a pretty secure person'.

ACTUALLY, MANUEL TOLD ME IN 2004, he was 'uncomfortable' then. 'I was scared … I was young and insecure.' Although he admitted it to few at the time, he rose at 4am most days to read through economic policy papers and the theories of economic development that the DEP 'technocrats' were themselves grappling with. In 1992 came a whirl of workshops, conferences, trips, speaking engagements with business and with the unions.

In the midst of this, in January 1992, his third son Jaimé was born. He was at a World Bank workshop on fiscal management in Berlin with Mboweni at the time. It was the first baby born in his household where Manuel was not on either side of a stint in prison. Yet he was absent as ever during Jaimé's early months, travelling the world, or working in Johannesburg where he rented a little flat in Berea, an inner-city suburb that borders Hillbrow. He worked from dawn to well after dark, and used the predawn hours to read.

Among his copious reading was an article on Zimbabwe, then 10 years into independence, but now beginning to come under the whip of the IMF in a structural adjustment programme. In its first decade of independence, Zimbabwe had spent money on a lot of 'very good things', such as education. It ran a considerable deficit on the budget. In 1991, Zimbabwe had to borrow from the World Bank and the IMF, and the latter imposed a tight structural adjustment programme on the country, curtailing its land reform programme and other social priorities it had identified. By 2006, Zimbabwe was in arrears to the tune of several hundred million US dollars to the IMF, the World Bank and the African Development Bank. If there were, and are, lessons to be drawn for South Africa from the economic and political disaster in Zimbabwe, it is not so much in the increasingly authoritarian politics practised by the ruling party but in imprudent and enthusiastic spending early on to the extent that it had its political autonomy undermined by its creditors in the form of the IMF.

In May 1992, Manuel and the ANC galloped into the *Ready to Govern* conference, perhaps the most critical ANC policy conference in the transition period. Mboweni and Ramos had begun intensive research on macroeconomic and Central Bank policy. It was in this period that some of the more critical differences between various ANC economists were crystallised.

Vella Pillay, for instance, who coordinated MERG, argued forcefully that the Central Bank in a new government be subjected to political control by the ruling party. Both Ramos and Mboweni opposed this position. Both were to argue at Codesa,* the multiparty negotiations that paved the way for democracy, that an independent Central Bank was essential to maintain price stability and to contain inflation. Ramos distinguishes between 'goal' independence and 'instrument' independence: it was the latter position they backed. A Central Bank would implement a democratic government's goals, but with instruments of its timing and choosing.

It was not a popular view in ANC circles. Apart from the MERG report, which recommended the opposite, even the ANC's leading negotiators were iffy about the idea. Ramos recalled how at one meeting, prominent ANC leaders, including the articulate and persuasive constitutional lawyer Kader Asmal, opposed Central Bank independence. 'As only Kader can do, he made an impassioned plea about why we shouldn't allow this to happen. I stood up and said that I knew that Comrade Kader was a brilliant constitutional lawyer, but when did he have time to learn anything about Central Banking and Central Bank independence?'

Asmal, who became a firm supporter of the economic policies adopted by the ANC, and a close friend of both Ramos and Manuel, was suitably chastened.

By the time of the *Ready to Govern* conference in mid-1992, Manuel was in a position to steer the DEP's economic policy through the organisation. It committed the ANC to an effective social-democratic policy: equalising social welfare, education and health across racial groups, eliminating poverty, boosting job creation projects. It proposed a two-pronged strategy to achieve this: redistribution, and restructuring of the economy to enable it to reach sustainable growth.

There was nothing in the *Ready to Govern* document about the independence of the Central Bank – that would come later when the interim constitution was finalised in 1993. But there were two crucial aspects of policy that were enunciated. One was to change somewhat once the ANC was in

---

* Convention for a Democratic South Africa.

power; the other was, and would remain, a matter close to Manuel's heart for the next decade and a half.

The first was about who precisely would determine macroeconomic policy. 'The democratic state,' said the document, 'will have ultimate responsibility – in cooperation with the trade union movement, business and other organs of civil society – for coordinating, planning and guiding the development of the economy towards a sustainable economic growth pattern. Emphasis will be placed on macroeconomic balance, including price stability and balance of payments equilibrium. The policy surroundings will be characterised by the principles of transparency, consistency, predictability and accountability.'[47]

The basic elements of that policy would remain throughout the constitutional negotiations and the first decade of democratic government. But both the unions and business were somewhat neutered as lobby groups in the post-1996 period when the government effectively took control over macroeconomic policy.

It was a position that Manuel was to articulate just over a year later, in July 1993, at the first meeting of the National Economic Forum (NEF) a tripartite forum between labour, business and government. It was later to become the National Economic Development and Labour Council (NEDLAC). Ebrahim Patel, by now a leader of the SA Clothing and Textile Workers' Union, which had emerged from the debris of the left-wing Clothing Workers' Union of the 1980s and the conservative Garment Workers' Union, was one of its conveners, as was Derek Keys, the newly appointed minister of trade and industry and economic co-operation. Keys was a blunt and realistic businessman who had been brought into government by De Klerk.

By the end of the apartheid era, the unions exercised an influence in the political milieu which far outweighed their strength on the shop floor (particularly given South Africa's high levels of unemployment). As Patel wrote at the time: 'Organised labour has been able to exercise power through effective shop floor organisation, a strong and militant membership, a talented leadership and strong links with community groups. It has been able to change wage standards ... affect government policy in the labour market through general strike action and alter consumer behaviour through a series of consumer boycotts ... The movement was compelled to develop this capacity for it had no institutional arrangement through which to affect policy.'[48]

Now the NEF provided precisely the potential for this kind of 'institutional arrangement'. It was a first in the fractious industrial relations that had predominated in South Africa, even though its work was stalled for several months following the breakdown in political negotiations as a result of escalating violence in the country, much of it stoked by a security force-backed 'third force'.

By 1993, the NEF was back on track with membership comprising 17 business organisations, 55 trade unions with two million members, the government, as well as representatives of the transitional authority which by then had been established at the Codesa talks.

There were high expectations then that the union movement would become a major player in the making of economic policy. Moeletsi Mbeki, who had come back from exile into a communications job with COSATU, told me, 'What COSATU wanted in reality was two parliaments: they wanted an economic parliament, which ended up being called NEDLAC, which had pretty much the same sovereignty as the political parliament. But the sovereignty of NEDLAC would be over economic matters and the national parliament would have sovereignty over political matters. That's actually what they wanted, however they articulated it.'

But it was always unreasonable, he said, to tie a future ANC government to policies that the unions had agreed with 'the Nats and big business ... At the end of the day a ruling party is elected on it own manifesto. It has to draw up its own manifesto according to what it believes in.'

And South Africa, like other developing countries, had a far wider constituency to serve than simply the most vocal and well-organised lobby groups in the formal economic sector. There was a vast underclass that had largely been confined to rural areas as a result of apartheid laws, there was an informal sector to which few rules applied, and a rapidly growing urban underclass, all of whom hoped to secure a better life under an ANC government.

Manuel understood this by then. When he addressed the NEF conference that year, he dampened any expectation that such a forum would have a major hand in determining macroeconomic policy. 'There are vested interests in the Forum,' he told the conference. 'In some sectors, business and labour may be united in an attempt to retain the present inefficiencies in order to guarantee profitability and save jobs as a trade-off in marginal industries. Such decisions may not be in the national interest.'[49]

Who in the Forum, he asked, represented the interests of the unemployed? Who in the NEF gives consideration to price, as opposed to wage, issues? Yes, there must be consultation with unions and business as 'governments do not possess a monopoly on wisdom'. The NEF had a crucial role to play, but its existence could not be 'entrenched' in the constitution, 'because we may have to make concessions which are in conflict with the overall democratisation of the economy'.[50]

Many years later, in 2004, Manuel told me that his insistence that the creation of macroeconomic policy must be the preserve of the democratic government was made without 'any pretension' that he might one day be minister of finance – 'I had nothing going for me'. But he could not imagine, even then, interest groups such as the unions, or business, sitting and 'negotiating endlessly with government about what the deficit should be'.

His stance did not warm his relationship with the trade union movement.

It is a constant contradiction and irony in Manuel's political life that his relationship with the trade unions has often been awkward. It began in the 1970s with the rejection of his offer of help by the General Workers' Union, on the mistaken assumption that he was a Unity Movement supporter. It grew in the 1980s with his failure to persuade the most powerful black unions to join the UDF. It was cemented in the 1990s with his stance, first as head of the DEP, later as trade and industry and finance minister that democratic governments have a brief wider than that of organised labour, even if the labour movement is an ally. It was an observation that Tito Mboweni made soon after he returned from exile. Manuel, he said, played a critical role in being able to argue complex economic policy issues in the leadership of the ANC. And despite a crusty relationship with business, he could help the DEP interact with it. 'But he wasn't particularly good at interacting with the trade union movement and that still is the case today.'

Actually, by Mboweni's own admission, he too got impatient with the trade unionists in those early years of policy debate in the DEP. 'There was a huge concern particularly from COSATU that we had to work on the *process*. We were the "process people". What process? ... I can understand process but we must produce a policy document ... the process (becomes) more important than the outcome! These people are going to drive you mad you know,' he said, recounting his exasperation at the time.

But in Manuel's case, there was a painful irony in this difficult relationship. He was one of the UDF leaders who came from a deeply rooted working-class background. His mother, a garment worker all her life, lives in the same modest house today that Manuel was born in. Her pension, after working in the clothing sector for 36 years was negligible and each year since 1997, she, like other pensioners, waits expectantly on Budget Day to see what increase her son will announce for state pensioners.

When, in the early years of his trade and industry ministry, Manuel lowered tariffs on clothing and textile imports, he was particularly riled at a union demonstration outside Parliament that mentioned his mother on a placard. According to a colleague, he demanded that the COSATU parliamentarians who were present at an ANC caucus meeting apologise for what he considered an insulting invasion of his family. They did.

IF THE FIRST CRITICAL POINT in the *Ready to Govern* document was about who determines macroeconomic policy, the second became a lodestar for Manuel. It said: 'Relationships with international finance institutions such as the World Bank and the International Monetary Fund will be conducted in such a way as to protect the integrity of domestic policy formulation and promote the interests of the South African population and the economy. Above all, we must pursue policies that enhance national self-sufficiency and enable us to reduce dependence on international financial institutions.'[51]

He piloted its inclusion into the manifesto. It reflected, in two sentences, his concern about the effects of unmanageable debt. His readings about Zimbabwe had prompted a fear in him that soon after South Africa won its hard-fought-for political independence, profligate spending would send it into a downward debt spiral that would undermine the new government's sovereignty.

A few months after *Ready to Govern*, in August 1992, Manuel participated in the Mont Fleur Scenarios organised by Pieter le Roux and Vincent Maphai, both academics from the University of the Western Cape. They were directed by Adam Kahane, a Canadian (who later married Allan Boesak's ex-wife Dorothy) who had done scenario planning for Shell in Canada. A local economist with Shell, Khoosum Kalyan, an ANC supporter, brought him to South Africa to discuss scenarios of change with a group of politicians and academics. Among those who took part were Rob Davies, an ANC economist recently returned from exile; Saki Macozoma, then a spokesman for the ANC (later to become a parliamentarian and then a businessman); Gugile Nkwinti, an Eastern Cape community and UDF activist; Sue van der Merwe, then of the Back Sash, later an ANC deputy minister; and Tito Mboweni. 'Scenarios describe alternative pathways into the future,' explained Kalyan at the time. 'They project a range of possible outcomes and enable people to think about the future in different ways. They do not predict what will happen but identify what *may* happen.'[52]

Initially, the atmosphere was not easy. Manuel introduced Kahane as a 'representative of international capital', Kahane recalls. 'I could see this scenario meeting was not going to be like the Shell ones I was used to. We were not working on an ordinary problem of organisational strategy but on an extraordinary national transformation.[53]

The team first thrashed out a definition of the problem. Politically, the answer was fairly obvious: a government with no legitimacy, mistrust of the security forces, repression, collapse of black local government, and no faith in the judicial system.

Economically the problems were also simple to spot: high unemployment, inability to deliver health and education to most communities, rapid urbanisation and alienation of the youth.

It took longer to agree on the answers.

Four scenarios were presented by various participants. All had avian characteristics. Two were no-hope scenarios: the ostrich and the lame duck. In the ostrich scenario, the minority government dug in its heels, prolonged the transition, and tried to form a 'moderate' alliance with non-ANC black groupings. This was unacceptable to the liberation movements. As a result, sanctions continued, resistance increased, the government failed to deliver to the people, violence escalated, and even a 'Lebanonisation' of South Africa resulted. The 'lame duck' scenario painted a picture of an overly long transition. Uncertainty ruled, investors held back, and the majority of the people remained dissatisfied.

But both these scenarios seemed unlikely at this stage. A referendum among whites, called by De Klerk, had overwhelmingly endorsed negotiations. A transitional government was within sight.

More likely was the third scenario, named for the Greek mythical figure Icarus. Although he was not a bird, Icarus flew – briefly. According to the myth, he had been imprisoned in a labyrinth with his father Daedalus, a brilliant craftsman, by the resentful King Minos. Daedalus crafted two pairs of wings and attached them to their shoulders with wax. He warned his exuberant son not to fly too close to the sun or the wax would melt. But an excited Icarus, scenting freedom, flew closer and closer to the sun until the wax melted and he plummeted to his death.

The fourth scenario was the Flight of the Flamingos. It was premised on a political settlement and subsequent good governance. This created the conditions for a slow, but sustainable, economic recovery and take-off. Confidence in the economy would boost investment and allow the government to deliver social services to the most deprived under apartheid. 'The government adopts sound social and economic policies and observes macroeconomic constraints. It succeeds in curbing corruption in government and raising efficiency levels.' Flamingos, it was explained, 'characteristically take off slowly, fly high and fly together'. Initially, the growth rates are much slower than in the Icarus scenario. There, the government embarks on a 'massive spending spree' to meet all the backlogs created by apartheid. 'It implements food subsidies, price and exchange controls and institutes other "quick fix" policies. The initial results are spectacular growth, increased living standards, improved social conditions, little or no increase in inflation, and increased political support. But after a year or two the programme runs into budgetary, monetary and balance of payments constraints. The budget deficit exceeds 10 per cent. Depreciation, inflation, economic uncertainty and collapse follow.'

Economic crisis spurs political chaos. The government then has to cut back on its social spending and turn to the IMF and World Bank for assistance. If it is threatened politically, it may turn authoritarian. 'The most sobering aspect' is that the 'intended beneficiaries of the spending end up worse off than before'.[54]

Manuel presented the Flight of the Flamingos scenario. If he was sceptical of the exercise before, he now feared the very real possibilities of an Icarus scenario. It had already happened in parts of the developing world, particularly in Latin American countries. Argentina grew spectacularly for a few years after the Second World War, and then collapsed economically, ushering in a military government. Peru did likewise. Most tragic, perhaps, was the case of Chile, where Salvadore Allende's government made sweeping reforms that included nationalisation of all the major mining and industrial companies, import substitution, wage increases and price freezes. In the first year GDP grew, employment grew, and inflation came down. But before long basic commodities disappeared from the shelves, GDP plummeted to a negative growth rate and, unable to repay its debts, the country defaulted.

There is no doubt that the heavy hand of the United States played a central role in the tragedy that followed, as did the falling price of copper – Chile's main export – on the world markets. But it would be naive to argue that the economic collapse that came as a result of Santa Claus-type economic policies did not spur internal dissatisfaction, even among some workers' groups, students and small businesses. The internal political upheaval opened the way for the US-backed coup by the military dictator Augusto Pinochet in 1973 and 17 years of his rule of terror.

Chile was perhaps a worst-case scenario and its fate was governed to a large extent by its proximity to the United States. But there were examples closer to home of government getting into economic hock, losing effective sovereignty over spending decisions, and then resorting to authoritarianism to maintain order. Zimbabwe was on that path.

Some years later, after Manuel had introduced the first macro-stabilisation plan of the ANC government, he said: 'It's not a straight line [from Mont Fleur to GEAR]. It meanders through, but there's a fair amount in all of that going back to Mont Fleur ... I could close my eyes now and give you those scenarios; then you probably carry it for life.'[55]

COSATU's economic policy thinkers – principally Alec Erwin and Jay Naidoo, then general secretary of the federation – had not gone to the Mont Fleur sessions 'because they thought it was a waste of time', said Manuel. It was a pity in many ways because the learning experiences that were formative in Manuel's thinking were not shared by his union allies. One of the biggest differences that would emerge later between the liberation government and the unions was whether, and how, the new rulers should restrain spending in the short term to protect sovereignty in the long term.

A VISIT TO THE WORLD BANK in the northern hemisphere spring of 1992 rubbed in the dangers of an exuberant spending spree which landed a developing country 'in the pouches of these people', as Manuel put it.

Many in the ANC were suspicious of the IMF and World Bank and thought the ANC should have nothing to do with them. But Manuel argued that 'we'd better try to understand these animals otherwise we're going to make big mistakes'. Mandela concurred and he asked Lewis Preston, then President of the World Bank, to take a group of ANC policy makers to Washington so they could get some experience of the Bretton-Woods institutions. Among the large ANC delegation that went with Manuel were Mboweni, Cheryl Carolus and COSATU trade unionist Jayendra Naidoo (not to be confused with Jay

Naidoo, although the two were union comrades and later business partners). The course was two weeks long. Thabo Mbeki joined them for the last few days of the trip.

Their host at the World Bank was the Bank's vice-president for Africa, Edward 'Kim' Jaycox. Jaycox had studied African development at Columbia University in New York in the early 1960s, and had then hitch-hiked around newly independent Africa, giving apartheid South Africa a miss in his peregrinations. He joined the Bank in 1964, rising to vice-president for Africa by the time Manuel and his comrades visited. One of his first decisions as vice-president in the late 1980s was to fund the Lesotho Highlands Water Project, which provided water to the heartland of industrial South Africa in what was then the Transvaal. It prompted criticism from anti-apartheid activists on the grounds that it kept the economy of apartheid oiled.[56] But Jaycox defended the decision when I met him in Washington in 2006, pointing out that water was a 'tremendous export' for Lesotho 'and there was no reason in the world why we shouldn't have supported Lesotho. The idea was that $120 million a year in revenue was going to come in to Lesotho and what were they going to do with it? They only had a million people. It could double per capita income in Lesotho. The real worry was that this would end up in people's pockets rather than for the benefit of the people. So we escrowed a certain proportion of it and used (that) as a development fund for education, health and the like.'

When Manuel first told me about this trip to the World Bank – in 2004 – he recalled Jaycox as being a 'large Texan', bearded and wearing suspenders. It was not only his appearance that made an impression. When the ANC team asked how and why the Bank and the IMF imposed structural adjustment programmes on poor countries, Jaycox replied: 'When you go to a bank to borrow money to buy a house, the first thing they'll do is to check that you are capable of repaying the loan and if, in its estimate, you can't, it'll charge you more interest. And if you don't repay at all, it will repossess your house …

'Now when the World Bank lends money to a country to, say, build infrastructure, and that country cannot repay us, we know we can't repossess a dam or a country, but by God, we'll teach you how to budget.'

When I met Jaycox in 2006, I was struck, first, by the fact that he was not large – he was quite a trim man – and, second, that he was not from Texas. He was born and bred in Ohio and had gone to Columbia University in

New York: a middle-class, decidedly unbrash man reared in the Mid-West and educated on the north-east coast of the United States. I was puzzled by Manuel's memory as he, as his friends and colleagues will attest, has a razor-sharp recollection for dates, people, places and events.

Manuel attributes the dissonance between his memory and reality partially to a successful diet Jaycox undertook. But more importantly, it was the largeness of what Jaycox said that stuck in his mind rather than his physical stature – the extraordinary implications of winning freedom for your country and then surrendering it to international financial institutions who 'teach you how to budget' if your country's purse strings are too loose too early.

'The things that fell into my head then were all related to the Zim experience,' Manuel said nearly two years after our first conversation about his visit to the World Bank. 'Part of what I needed to understand is what happens if you end up in the pouches of these people.'

It is ironic, perhaps, that some of the fiercest critics of the Growth, Employment and Redistribution (GEAR) economic policy that Manuel was to pilot through government just three years after this encounter, damned it for being subordinate to the exigencies of the IMF and the World Bank. For instance, Patrick Bond, a Canadian academic based in South Africa, wrote that the 'Bretton-Woods institutions were extremely influential in determining South Africa's economic and social policies'.[57]

Jaycox scoffed at this notion, as might be expected. 'God, we are *really* powerful ... incredibly powerful,' he said sarcastically. 'I wish it had worked in Zaire (which abandoned an imposed structural adjustment programme in 1990). I guess SA is just weaker intellectually than Zaire. That's ridiculous. Come on!'

In fact, Jaycox told me, many senior officials in the Bank advised the new South African government to spend more, faster. 'The political window is limited,' he told me in 2006. 'There've been two presidents and how much has been done in terms of curing these problems of discrepancy? I mean how much will the people put up with? When are they going to turn? They can say, hey, it's been 15 years what have you guys done?'

In fact the Mandela government, of which Manuel became part, spent time in the early years explaining to the IMF and World Bank that it did not want their money, no thank you, and that it would rather determine its spending priorities itself.

On the other hand, Jaycox was acutely aware of the fact that extravagant spending in much of Africa had resulted in the hardships – and unpopularity – of structural adjustment programmes. The phrase was a 'dirty word' by the late 1980s, he conceded. 'We were forcing through conditionalities, forcing governments to cut back on expenditures in general, without reducing the budgets for education, road maintenance and a few vital areas, and it was causing tremendous political problems. Many countries just couldn't stand it. I mean we didn't have coups d'etat or anything like that, but many of the governments just couldn't do it. So there was just a general feeling of crisis, it was unrelieved and people, of course, pointed to the suffering of the people. They were suffering even worse as a result of lack of adjustment but that didn't make a difference. And a lot of this was believed as gospel by the ANC.'

There was also the example of African countries that had gone into substantial deficits without being able to finance them. Many countries that took World Bank loans – Zaire (now the DRC), Uganda, Tanzania, Ghana, to name a handful that Jaycox dealt with – had fallen into the 'vicious little cycle' of allowing their Central Banks to print money to finance the public sector and parastatals which 'covered up all types of inefficiencies ... These economies were in free fall and they were going to hit the pavement.'

Local currency became worthless in some countries. Jaycox recalls being at a meeting in Mozambique with the Central Bank after the civil war, which had been fuelled by apartheid South Africa, when he asked the Governor and his top brass whether he could look at their currency. 'Nobody in the room had any of the national currency in their pockets. They had rands, they had dollars, but no metacais.'

This was the Central Bank! Little wonder that if you wanted to flag down a taxi cab in Maputo at the time, 'you'd have to get to the side of the road and pull out a packet of cigarettes ... (and hold up) two, three depending on how far you wanted to go. People would almost crash getting to the side of the road to pick you up.'

Jaycox still keeps a Zairean note, worth five million zaires, to remind him of the essential uselessness of printing currency to resolve economic crises. 'It couldn't buy anything. People just laughed when you took it out of your pocket.'

So, coincidentally, does Manuel. He was given three of the notes, all emblazoned with the face of Zairean dictator Mobutu Sese Seko at a conference he attended in Nairobi in 1992. The note was actually worse than useless: it sparked the beginning of Mobutu's downfall. Issued in 1992, ostensibly to solve a liquidity crisis, it was refused as tender by many of Mobutu's political opponents in the north-eastern part of the country. Some cited a (French) grammatical error on the note: it stipulated it was worth *'cinq millions zaires'* instead of *'cinq millions de zaires'*. But the opposition to it was more fundamental than pedantry. In less than a year, reported *The New York Times*, it was worth about two US dollars at the official exchange rate. The Zaire government used it to pay the already hard done by military and when soldiers discovered that the notes could not buy anything, they rioted in the capital causing hundreds of deaths.[58] Ironically, the note is worth more today on E-Bay, where it retails for just over four US dollars, than it was in Zaire in the early 1990s when it was currency.

Manuel gave one of his three Zairean notes to Tito Mboweni, the other to Thabo Mbeki; the third he kept for himself. He didn't know then that the notes would be in the hands of the future president, the future governor of the Reserve Bank, and the future finance minister. They were all ANC 'function-aries', as he describes them, at the time. But the notes served, and continue to serve, as a salutary reminder of what can happen when an accelerating deficit, coupled with a lack of accountability, takes hold of a country.

South Africa, on the cusp of transition, looked very different from the outside. There seemed to be a certain 'probity', as Jaycox put it, a financial infrastructure, a conservatism in the financial sector that several of the ANC economists were beginning to appreciate. It was going to be tough reconstructing the economy after more than four decades of apartheid and its attendant inequalities, but it was not about to sink into an abyss. The parameters of a new economic policy would be wider and more flexible than many other developing countries in Africa.

But were they? And how far off, in 1993, was the brink?

CHAPTER 22

What is G?

A CTUALLY, THE ECONOMY was in much worse shape than even the harshest critics of apartheid had imagined in the 1980s. South Africa's economy was founded largely on massive gold reserves extracted by politically oppressed cheap labour. But in 1971 the world abandoned the gold standard and the price began to fluctuate. Add to that a steady decline in gold production, and gold, instead of being a 'foundation (became) a wild card'.[1]

Manufacturing had grown rapidly under an import-substitution regime, again oiled by ready supplies of cheap labour, but began to decline steadily from the early 1980s. Whereas initially consumer industries thrived under protective barriers and 'booming white incomes', in the end, when gold exports could no longer be used to pay for imported capital equipment and fuel the consumer boom, manufacturing industry became inward-looking, unable to compete in a new globalised environment where the successful developing economies, such as the South East Asian Tigers, grew on exports.

The costs of maintaining apartheid also got more burdensome. Sanctions and disinvestment meant that the government spent increasing amounts on parastatals in an attempt to be self-sufficient in food production, energy, weapons and telecommunications, not to mention the increases in defence and police spending.[2]

Moreover the economy, even internally, grew increasingly uncompetitive. In the climate of disinvestment by foreign firms, 'a small number of South African conglomerates seized almost total control of the economy'. By the end of the 1980s, five groups controlled companies worth nearly 90 per cent of all stock market value.[3]

'The impression that sticks in my mind was that South Africa was a fascist economy,' one international financier told me. 'Almost 50 per cent was owned by the government, and the rest was owned by five companies – big mining companies and their trusts – owning things down to dry-cleaning level. It was not an economy that had growth or distribution as its objectives. It was clearly a fascist economy.'[4]

As the internal war against apartheid intensified, capital took flight, the tax base grew weaker, and increasing amounts of government money went to maintaining the repressive structures necessary to protect the white minority government from the general uprising spilling out all over the country.

Capital fled and new capital cowered. Government's consumption spending grew from 15 per cent of GDP in 1983 to 21 percent a decade later.[5] In the first five years of the 1980s, foreign debt rose from 20 per cent to 50 per cent of GDP.

After P W Botha's ill-received 'Rubicon' speech in 1985, international banks refused to roll over South Africa's loans and as a result the flight of capital intensified with some R50 billion estimated to have left the country between 1985 and 1992.[6] Government reneged on its foreign debt and interest rates rose to 25 per cent soon after that.[7]

Even when the numbers were written boldly on the wall, even when apartheid government ministers tried to do the right thing, they were stymied by their own politics. In 1986 the finance minister, Barend du Plessis, invited Rudolf Gouws, an articulate and personable banking economist, to give a slide presentation to cabinet that showed some frightening facts about what would happen to the country if the deficit kept on rising. Du Plessis told Gouws later that P W Botha had telephoned him afterwards and berated him: *'Jy sal nie sulke mannetjie nooi vir ons te kom sê wat te doen nie.'* ('You must not ask such a little man to come and tell us what to do.')

Worse, in 1988, when Du Plessis was in Berlin for an IMF meeting, Botha announced a 15 per cent pay rise for civil servants, without consulting him beforehand. This was despite earnest promises by Botha at the beginning of that year that government would freeze the wages of civil servants. Gouws, who has been analysing South African budgets since 1971, was with Du Plessis in Berlin. 'Barend understood the stuff far better than people thought and he went ashen … He just had to find the money. So that laid the foundation for the disaster that followed in the years after that.' Botha had announced the handout a month before the municipal elections, and left the hapless Du Plessis to find the R4 billion required. This was against a backdrop of escalating government expenditure that threatened to come in 22 per cent above the projected level for the fiscal year, and an 'unprecedented' deficit of R17,4 billion or 7,5 per cent of GDP.[8]

The panicked reaction by government in response to the deep structural crisis caused by apartheid hastened the piling up of a national debt that the old – let alone a new – government could ill afford.

To make matters worse, the black 'homelands', satellites of repression and patronage, sucked up money. In the 1993/94 budget nearly R17 billion was allocated to the homelands, an increase over the previous year of more than 20 per cent.[9] 'It is not just the rate at which these allocations to the TBVC* countries and the non-independent homelands are rising that is cause for concern,' commented a major financial weekly. 'More serious is that the SA government, and therefore the taxpayer, has no control over how these transfer payments are used.'[10] By then, the deficit was heading higher than 8 per cent, or about R30 billion, in a shrinking economy. By 1994 – when the democratic government was slated to take over – the interest charge alone would be R20,7 billion (or more than 18 per cent of expenditure), and the interest-bearing debt R186 billion (or an astonishing 42 per cent of GDP), estimated one private sector economist.[11]

In 1993, the ANC's team of economics negotiators had to grapple with three fundamental issues around the debt. One was who 'owned' it – in other words, who were the main creditors? The second was whether a new government could or should accept the liabilities of the old government. The third – and most alarming – question was: how much was it?

In the main, according to Maria Ramos who worked extensively on the

---

* TBVC countries: The so-called independent 'homelands' of Transkei, Bophuthatswana, Venda and Ciskei.

debt question in the transitional period, the government had borrowed most heavily from the state employees' pension fund. So it was domestic debt that, had it not been honoured, would have resulted in a political and economic crisis for a new government. That fact alone provided most of the answer to the second question: would the ANC government accept it? 'It was clear that we were basically going to have to accept the assets and liabilities of the previous government. We couldn't walk away from it without plunging this country into a complete crisis. And if you did that and you wiped out the assets of a pension fund, can you imagine the welfare problem that would have been just compounded. And who was going to lend us money then and how were we going to finance the deficit?'

The ANC's talk was bolder in the early 1990s before it knew the extent of its problems, but also more confused. In the same week that Mandela told the gathering at Davos in early 1992 that an ANC government would repay the debt, the ANC's Department of Information and Publicity (the DIP) issued a 'hard-hitting' statement saying that a new government would be 'compelled to weigh with great care' its obligations to service debts contracted by the 'illegitimate' apartheid government. Mandela then told the gathering at Davos that those were the 'opinions of individuals'.[12]

At the end of the day, the Hamilton line prevailed: debts would be honoured, not only because most of the debt was domestic, but because reneging on it would have blackened its book in the international markets at the precise time when a new government needed to finance a costly reconstruction programme.

What focused the minds of the ANC economics negotiators more acutely was the extent of the debt. 'What was quite interesting, and I suppose quite shocking, at the time was that there were no proper records as such. No one could tell us for certain what the extent of the liabilities of the TBVC states was. There was no sense. I kept saying to these guys on the other side, is it R5 billion, is it R10 billion, and they didn't know. They had no memory of it,' recalled Ramos.

Then there was the problem of the forward book: contracts had been issued to the giant electricity utility parastatal Eskom, which could, unlike the South African government, borrow on the international markets in the fading years of apartheid. These contracts guaranteed Eskom a particular rate of exchange at a time when the South African currency was plummeting. The difference between the guaranteed and the actual rate was for the account of the government. What was the extent of this forward exposure? What were the contracts behind it? Ramos asked these questions repeatedly at meetings with government representatives. 'And there were no answers.'

What is G? This was a question asked repeatedly by a young economist who had joined the Unit of Fiscal Analysis set up in the Department of Finance in 1993. Andrew Donaldson had grown up in the Eastern Cape 'border' town of Grahamstown, gone to university there, and lectured for a while at the University of the Transkei. He was one of the first of those economists described as 'progressive' to join the Finance Department, even before the new government had taken over the reins. The job of his unit, set up by the then director-general (the most senior civil servant) of the Department, Estiaan Calitz, and run by Frederick Fourie (an academic who went on to run Free State University) was effectively to cost the transition, including the equalisation of racially discriminatory budget items which included just about everything from health to education to pensions. Donaldson, who became a senior Treasury official under Manuel, was an infusion of new blood into a basically demoralised Finance Department, many of whose officials were looking for early retirement.

But before Donaldson and his team could do any costing on the programme for reconstruction and development adopted by the ANC at its policy conference of 1993, they needed to know the liabilities of the outgoing government.

What is G? they asked. G is the symbol for government expenditure in the standard Keynesian model taught to public policy economics students the world over. 'And we said, well, do we add up the homelands, do we add up extra budget expenses? These are things that had not ever been done before because the budget had been such a fragmented exercise,' recalled Donaldson.

Alec Erwin recalls a meeting that included Manuel and Mboweni, among others, with then Finance Minister Derek Keys and Calitz. They asked the same question. Keys had been candid about the financial crisis and said they needed to manage it into the transition 'very, very tightly'.

'We agreed with him,' said Erwin, 'and asked, what is our debt? And Calitz and he looked at each other and said, 'We don't know, we just don't know.' We walked out of there thinking, 'Fuck! Have we got problems now!'

Mostly the problem was in the amount of money that had been pumped into the wasteful and corrupt administrations of the black homelands scattered around the country. The debt itself was scattered, and it would take at least 18 months into the new government to consolidate it into one national account. Before then, no one knew quite what 'G' was.

In early 1992, an exhausted Barend du Plessis announced his retirement. A few months earlier, F W de Klerk, who had come to appreciate the thin blades on which the economy now slid, had appointed mining businessman Derek Keys as the minister of trade and industry and economic co-ordination. De Klerk had asked Anton Rupert, one of the more far-sighted of Afrikaner businessmen, for advice. Rupert was a member of the Gencor board, which Keys chaired, and recommended the latter to De Klerk as a person who would have the confidence of business through the transition. In the northern hemisphere spring of 1992, Keys was in Beijing when De Klerk called him (at 3am Beijing time) to ask if it would make his job easier if he were also minister of finance. 'I said, yes, it would, it would, yes!'

Keys was born in Johannesburg in 1931 but spent most of his early childhood in what was then the Eastern Transvaal where his father was a country branch bank manager. His father died when he was seven years old; his mother returned to Johannesburg with her children 'where by some miracle on a bank manager's pension she managed to bring us up'.

Trained as a chartered accountant, Keys worked first for the Industrial Development Corporation (IDC), then as a consultant where he handled major company mergers with enough panache to be noticed by the business community. In 1986, Marinus Dalling asked whether he would like to become chair of Gencor, the mining conglomerate. 'And I was sure I wouldn't but it was such a nice potential offer that I decided to keep it to myself for a week before I tell them no.' By then, though, his arm was sufficiently twisted into accepting.

When De Klerk 'scooped me out of there' in 1992, he said, 'the economic problems were so big you couldn't help seeing them'.

'I'm the minister of the bloody obvious,' he told reporters 11 months into his appointment. 'I see myself as somebody who jollies people along to do what common sense dictates they ought to do.' Now that De Klerk was in charge, Keys felt that he was able to deliver the necessary message to government: the economy must be radically restructured; government consumption spending must fall, civil service costs must be cut, unions need to agree to a virtual wage freeze, and interest rates must remain high to counter inflation. When asked what his recipe for health was in such a stressful job, Keys replied: 'It's my daily exercise ... on my knees twice a day.'[13]

Keys made a significant breakthrough in the fraught years leading to the transition. He managed to win the confidence not only of business (which he already had), but of the ANC and COSATU too. 'He's very bright,' said Manuel. 'I actually became quite close to him.'

Keys had an instinct and sensitivity for the culture of the South African left that few other businessmen displayed. Alec Erwin recalls how Keys once arranged a meeting with him and his COSATU colleague Jay Naidoo at the Rand Club. When the two unionists arrived at the Club, the epitome of the Johannesburg business establishment which maintained a strict dress code, they were stopped by the doorman. 'You must be Mr Keys's guests,' he said. He handed them each a tie which Keys had left for them. 'I knew you bloody fools would come with no ties,' Keys said when they met him inside.

Neither Manuel nor Erwin is alone in saying that Keys's critical role in the transition has not been properly credited. Gill Marcus, who came from the tough world of the exiled ANC, who chaired the finance committee in the first democratic Parliament and was to become Manuel's deputy, said: 'I think that Keys was very, very good, I must tell you. He's probably underestimated in the role he played.'

Keys, according to Erwin, made some critical interventions, among them starting the ETC, and being a main driver (with Ebrahim Patel) of the National Economic Forum. What did ETC stand for in the alphabet soup of acronyms that dotted the growing industry of economic policy making? 'Look, I don't care what it stands for,' he told Manuel. 'Maybe Economic Transformation, maybe Economic Trust, but let's just call it Et Cetera.' Whatever it stood for, it was the first genuine multiparty chamber that discussed economic policies at a government level.

More than a decade after leaving government, Keys still had the same laconic manner and wry humour that those who worked with him remember. A creature of habit – like his twice daily prayers – he stops whatever he's doing at precisely noon to drink a glass of champagne. When I went to see him in his bright Johannesburg apartment with views north and south, he told me that when he accepted the job as finance minister, he had promised himself that he would not try to reform the system, 'for which obviously I did not have the time or mandate. I really just used my intuition, if you like, to paddle my way through the deficiencies.'

In mid-1992, when the delicate multiparty Codesa negotiations about the transition threatened to wobble off their narrow track, the economic talks between the ANC, government and COSATU chugged on. In the midst of extreme violence around the country – and well-founded suspicions that elements in the government were backing an effective third force – Keys consulted COSATU and the ANC on negotiations with the American banks who had withdrawn their lines of credit from South Africa a few years earlier as part of the sanctions campaign. The talks between the banks and the Reserve Bank was about the terms of repayment and involved a committee representing the 140-odd banks, on the one hand, and a Reserve Bank team briefed by a South African delegation on the other.

'Whereas in the past, banks had insisted that there be no political involvement, this time they insisted there *must* be political involvement,' Keys recalled. 'So that created my first opportunity to have an all-party meeting as to whether the final agreement was in order ... and that brought Trevor in.'

Manuel had already impressed Keys: 'Trevor was appearing marvellously and really building my confidence in him, which he's never disappointed, I'm happy to say.'

POSSIBLY THE MOST DECISIVE MOMENT, not only in the relationship between Manuel and Keys, but in the transition, came that winter weekend in 1992 when Manuel participated in the Mont Fleur scenarios. It was a moment that nudged the faltering political negotiations from the rocks on which they had jammed. Keys had gone to Mont Fleur, with representatives from other political parties, to observe the 'scenario' talks.

He went equipped with an update of Rudolf Gouws's slides which showed the dangerous debt trap into which South Africa was sliding, and its weakening economy. Gouws had sat next to Keys on a plane trip earlier in the year and showed him the slides. The finance minister had then taken them to a cabinet *bosberaad* in July, 'in which I had to present my view of what was wrong'.

There was no scheduled slot for Keys to present his slides. But he found space on a Saturday afternoon, when many of the participants went off to watch a Currie Cup rugby match between the Western Cape and Natal. In later life, Manuel was to become a rugby enthusiast (his three sons excel at the sport) but at that time his politics held sway. In the old South African resistance tradition, he still boycotted South African sports teams and, at any rate, the international sports boycott had not yet been called off. Rugby, in particular, bore the mark of an obstreperous apartheid culture, so much so that Manuel volubly and controversially declared his support for the New Zealand All Blacks against the South African Springboks in 1996, more than two years into democracy.

In 1996 he attracted opprobrium: even a left-of-centre newspaper exhorted him to follow Mandela's example and 'play the game' in the interests of nation-building. Then, more sourly, it commented: 'If he will do so, we will continue to play our part ... by pretending to believe our minister of finance has the faintest clue about economics.'[14]

Ironically, in 1992, it was his disdain for South African rugby that opened his eyes to certain economic realities. He was around on that Saturday afternoon for Keys to show him how close to the brink South Africa actually was.

'Filthy pictures,' Keys called them at the time. They showed that the deficit could top R30 billion for the year – more than 8 per cent of GDP – the largest in South Africa's history. And that the economy had shrunk by 5 per cent during the second half of 1992.[15] Barely a month after this report, the influential *Economist* magazine reported gloomily on the legacy waiting to be inherited by a new government: 'There is much talk of babies and bathwater, and geese and golden eggs,' commented the *Economist*. But it was not a case of Africa's only dynamic economy in danger of being destroyed 'in a fit of retributive vengeance (by) a government of wild-eyed socialists ...

'A more apt description of the country's predicament is that a post-apartheid administration will inherit an economy prostrated after decades of incompetent management, over-government and subordination of economic goals to political ones.'

The misery is breathtaking, said the magazine: 40 per cent of the labour force could not find work in the formal sector, gross fixed investment was down to a 'feeble' 16 per cent of GDP, just enough to replace worn-out machinery, and although inflation was down, it was only, as Keys explained in his cheerful and disarming way, because the economy was 'buggered'.[16]

Manuel, reported the *Economist*, was no 'firebreather. Right now he talks more about busting cartels and unbundling industrial giants than taking them into public ownership – some revolutionary.'[17]

By then, undoubtedly, it was a different and more sober Manuel who spoke to business than the angry contrarian who had berated potential international investors at Notre Dame just 18 months before. At a business forum in Durban in April 1993, he spelt out a nine-point plan on economic policy that had been approved by the ANC. It included building up the manufacturing sector, rather than relying on exports of raw materials; 'demonopolising' the private sector (he pointed out that 85 per cent of shares on the Johannesburg Stock Exchange (JSE) were owned by just six conglomerates'), enshrining 'free and fair competition' that would include lowering tariff barriers, broadening ownership, and reviewing budgeting and monetary policy. When he was asked whether this meant that the ANC had 'softened its line' on the redistribution of wealth, he replied that its budgetary and anti-monopolistic policies were 'unashamedly redistributive'.[18]

In September of that year, Manuel, along with some of the COSATU team, made his first real governance decision, even though the ANC was not yet in power. It was thanks to Keys. A severe drought gripped the country for most of the year. With the other fiscal crises, it was clear that the government could not, on its own, provide the necessary relief. Manuel accompanied Keys to the annual meetings of the Bretton-Woods institutions that year. Keys had told Manuel earlier that year that the government wanted to get an IMF loan. Manuel argued the case to the ANC which supported him.

Unlike most IMF loans, this was a 'contingency' loan – designed to get a country through a bad patch – without conditionalities attached. It was a concrete sign that the different parties could work together in a time of crisis.

By then, the economic crisis in the country had focused Manuel's mind. Political power was just a first step. The country was on the verge of a debt trap: having to borrow money just to pay its extant interest by the time political power changed hands.

Manuel's colleagues in the DEP became increasingly alarmed as they grappled with the figures that were now coming to light. It was the numbers – not only the debt but the 'multiple billions of dollars' that the Reserve Bank owed on its net open forward book – that spurred Maria Ramos to argue so forcefully at Codesa for an independent Central Bank, at least as far as monetary instruments were concerned. 'It's easy to forget now, she said, 'but at the time one of the things we were facing as a (future) ANC government was a credibility gap, especially around economic policy. And we really felt that if we had a sound and rational and appropriate set of institutional arrangements around fiscal policy, and fiscal policy management and Central Banking ... that in itself would give us a lot of credibility.'

And South Africa needed that credibility because there was no doubt that the country would continue to run 'big deficits' at least for the first few years, to address the immediate racial inequities and hardships of the majority of people. It needed to be able to borrow either on the domestic or global markets.

All of these were hard-fought, contested issues, Ramos told me. 'There's this complete myth that somehow a bunch of people sat … in a quiet room somewhere and spoke to a bunch of economists in Washington and formulated economic policy in that way. Nothing can be further from the truth. These were contested, *intensely* contested, debates and issues and ideas.'

And Manuel, the 'guru with the matric', encouraged them, as long as the end goal was kept in mind. 'The one thing that is consistent about Trevor, and has been in all the years I've known him, is how were the choices we were making going to make this a strong economy, because you had to deliver to the poor, you had to create jobs, you had to deal with the unemployment problem,' Ramos told me. 'Remember at that time we didn't even have equal pensions for black and white people in South Africa. How were we going to do that? Where were we going to get the funds to do that? Were the choices we were making going to inhibit that in any way?'

The fact that Manuel wasn't an economist 'didn't mean anything', she said. He'd be more prepared on an issue than most of the professionals, and never be afraid to debate them. 'But that's Trevor's hallmark. If you want to stand your ground, you'd better have done your homework, because you can bet that he's done his.'

In the course of his 'vertical learning curve', Manuel read John Maynard Keynes, the left-wing, though not Marxist, British economist whose writings influenced a generation of policy makers since the 1930s. From Keynes he learned a dictum that he was to quote frequently throughout the next decade and half. Keynes had been asked why he had changed his opinion on monetary policy after the Great Depression of the early 1930s. 'When the facts change, I change my mind. What do you do, sir?' Keynes had replied.

And it was this attitude perhaps, which gave the 'guru with matric' the confidence to start fixing a shattered economy. The interregnum had been, for Manuel, a period of rapid intellectual and political consolidation. 'I don't know if you could ever subject people to such a steep learning curve like that ever again. It was a truly phenomenal experience.'

CHAPTER 23

Losing home

O N AN EARLY APRIL DAY IN 1994, Nelson Mandela addressed a rowdy election rally in the coloured township of Kleinvlei in the northern suburbs of Cape Town. Trevor Manuel was with him.

'I was born far from here,' Mandela said. 'Where no one spoke Afrikaans and where no one learned it and where there was no Afrikaans literature. But you,' he told the wary crowd, 'are my own flesh and blood.'

With that he turned to Manuel, sitting behind him on the stage. Proudly, he called him to the podium. 'Just come here and let them see you,' he said. Manuel stood beside him awkwardly. Again Mandela addressed the crowd: 'I send him all around the world to America, to discuss with the World Bank and the IMF. Do you think that a man like this should agree that Africans should take the homes of coloured people in this country? Do you think he should agree?'[1]

Notwithstanding Mandela's frank charm, it must have been a moment of dissonance for Manuel. Here he was, a man who had spent more than a decade fighting on the streets of the Cape Flats for better living conditions for the poor, but more importantly for a democracy that rose above race. In the discourse of the UDF, the word 'coloured' may have been implied but it was seldom heard. In fact, amongst many activists of the UDF, particularly those whose early political education had been in the Unity Movement, even the word 'coloured' was anathema. And now here was Manuel's race, his 'colouredness', being used as an election tool; worse, as a pacifier to those who feared African majority rule.

If the UDF had closed its eyes to this phenomenon, Mandela was acutely aware of it. Back in 1991, when he addressed the students' meeting at Stellenbosch and the right wing had taken him on (and been successfully countered by Manuel and his comrades), Mandela had shown the same sensibility to race. 'Having regard for our background,' he told the mainly white students, 'it may not be enough to work purely on one-person-one-vote, because every national group would like to see that the people of their flesh and blood are in government ...

'I am sure you would like to see a Terreblanche in government,' he told the students (referring to Sampie, the Stellenbosch professor of economics, not the deranged right-winger, Eugene). 'And Trevor Manuel, however democratic he is, would like to see his flesh and blood in government, and so would Thabo (Mbeki) and Ahmed (Kathrada).'[2]

Now three years later, Mandela again invoked this idea of 'flesh and blood' in the Western Cape: people there must see their own 'flesh and blood' in government. The ANC, he assured them, *was* their 'flesh and blood'. They were *his* 'flesh and blood'.

For Manuel, who has eschewed race in the past and who was to rise above it in the future, who was so *South African* rather than ethnic, it must have been a peculiar if not painful moment. Mandela was doing what was necessary: he was building one country in an environment torn apart by racial fear and hatred. It was to become one of his abiding legacies. But for Manuel, and his other UDF comrades, it signified a failure, at the end of this era, to truly unite people across racial lines in the Western Cape.

This was not the fault of the UDF, or at least not its fault in a principal sense. But the reality was that when the ANC took over from the UDF in 1991, it could not fill the lacuna in the Western Cape left by the dissolution of the lively resistance movement that had its roots in the day-to-day struggles of people on the Cape Flats.

'I think the UDF had a pretty sophisticated strategy with regard to the coloured population,' said Willie Hofmeyr who worked fervently for both the UDF and later for the ANC in the Western Cape. 'There was very good appreciation that it was, socially, a quite conservative part of the population. Things like the church play a really important role in the community. The UDF had a strategy of essentially organising people and politicising (them) around grassroots issues not by feeding them a political ideology and saying "Believe!" '

It was precisely the same point that Manuel had realised years earlier, when he had launched his civic organisation: 'You can't just go in there,' he had said of the middle-aged tenants in Factreton, 'and say "*Now*, comrades"!'

There had been a fierce argument among ANC leaders before the UDF's official dissolution in 1991 about whether the UDF, particularly in the Western Cape, should remain part of some sort of federal structure in alliance with the ANC. Western Cape activists – even some prominent ANC members – were cautiously in favour of this approach. But it was rejected out of hand, principally by Steve Tshwete, then also newly returned from exile. Although he had been part of the UDF leadership in the Eastern Cape before going into exile, he had always seen the UDF as a front for the real organisation of liberation which was the ANC. Many UDF leaders, including those in the Western Cape, would have conceded this point during the 1980s. Yet the UDF had an identity and life of its own and from 1991 onwards, many coloured people in the Western Cape did not identify with the ANC in the same way as they had with the UDF.

Partly, this was because there was a schism in the political culture between the two parties. Mandela had instinctively picked it up when he called Manuel before the gathering at Kleinvlei and explained why, being born 'far away', he had not grown up speaking Afrikaans. Even by 1996, according to the census, by which time many more African people had moved to the Western Cape, Afrikaans was still the first language of nearly two thirds of the population; English of only 20 per cent and isiXhosa (Mandela's mother tongue) of 15 per cent.[3]

Yet in the post-1990 ANC in the Western Cape, little Afrikaans was spoken. There were few songs, or pamphlets, or posters in Afrikaans. Moreover the UDF's birth, in the eyes of many Western Cape people, had been midwifed by men of the cloth. Allan Boesak was then a deeply respected and charismatic cleric who could appeal to the strong religious element in the Western Cape. 'Coloured people,' said Hofmeyr, 'could see it (the UDF) coming out of their struggles, their issues. It was *their* organisation in a way that the ANC could never ever be, however sophisticatedly the ANC positioned itself.'

And the ANC was not very sophisticated in the early 1990s. 'Everything became English – all the speeches, all the talking; all the songs were in Xhosa, it lost all connection with coloured culture, not only with the organisational background but in the way it conducted itself,' said Hofmeyr. It was no surprise that the UDF activists and leadership, people such as Hofmeyr, Manuel, and Cheryl Carolus, threw their weight behind the ANC. But the people who had been part of the street committees, or the enthusiastic participants at civic protests did not automatically follow them there.

'Is this an organisation for people like us?' This was one of the questions posed to focus groups around the country by Stan Greenberg, a Harvard-educated political scientist then based at Yale University who had been an adviser and pollster for Bill Clinton in his successful presidential campaign of 1992. Greenberg was contracted to help the ANC in its election campaign. It was he who helped the erstwhile underground liberation organisation transform itself into a political party with a forward-looking vision; it was he who helped the party frame the aspirational campaign slogan: 'A better life for all.'[4]

However, in the first election in the Western Cape, a 'better life for all' would not have, in itself, sold the party to the electorate. More fundamental was the simple question of identity and cultural affiliation. Hence the question: 'Is this an organisation for people like us?'

The hard answer – hard at least for the ANC activists to hear – was no. The idea of focus groups to complement polls was Greenberg's. He knew that polls could often be misleading. And in the Western Cape they were. The early polls showed that 70 per cent of the coloured population were 'undecided' about who to vote for; 25 per cent supported F W de Klerk's National Party, and between 5 and 15 per cent supported the ANC. But the ANC were not despondent. Indeed, it thought: we can still win.[5]

Until, that is, Greenberg persuaded some of them to sit in on the focus groups.

Hofmeyr was one. Without fail, he recalled, one of these 'undecided' voters in the focus groups, would 'pipe up and say, if only they had not released Mandela from jail, we would not have all this trouble. And everybody would agree that the solution would be to put Mandela back in jail!'

More telling was the question: who do you trust? Or mistrust, because the one is not necessarily the opposite of the other. Greenberg believed this was the best predictor of voting behaviour.[6] 'And De Klerk came out with about 90 per cent support – that is, the people who said they trusted him; Mandela only had about 20 per cent, but he didn't have such a heavy "against".'

Of the ANC-aligned leaders, the cleric Allan Boesak scored the highest number of 'trust' votes – about 30 per cent, but also scored a high 'against' (or mistrust) proportion of over 50 per cent. And the UDF leaders, such as Manuel or Carolus? They hardly blipped on the radar screens of the voters who took part in the focus groups.

One person who scored highly in the 'trust' question was Franklin Sonn, the newly appointed rector of the Peninsula Technikon, where Manuel had studied. He was later to become Nelson Mandela's ambassador to Washington. A high proportion of people said they trusted him – about 60 per cent – and a few mistrusted him (about 5 per cent). 'Sonn personified the values (of the coloured community) in a very deep degree,' said Hofmeyr. 'He was a good, upstanding, religious citizen.'

When the ANC campaigners discovered the degree to which he commanded respect they got his permission to put his face and name on their election posters. When the next focus group survey came around, a few weeks later, the number of people who said they 'trusted' him had gone down to 30 per cent and those who 'mistrusted' him had soared to about 40 per cent. 'Just because he was now supporting the ANC. There was no other reason,' said Hofmeyr.

Yet, the ANC activists who took part in the *huisebesoek*, the time-honoured tradition on the Cape Flats perfected by Manuel's civic organisation, would report back to the ANC's Western Cape headquarters that the party was going to win. 'We were delusional,' said Hofmeyr.

It was not that the ANC nationally did not put a lot of effort into the Western Cape, and into reassuring coloured voters. Apart from Mandela's efforts, bolstered by Manuel at his side at most of the final campaign meetings, Terror Lekota had campaigned intensively in the Western Cape the year before. Lekota had been appointed head of the ANC's election campaign, an inspired move, given his excellent organisational capacities, and certainly wiser than his first 'deployment' into ANC intelligence. Lekota is fluent in many of South Africa's languages, including Afrikaans. He campaigned early and vigorously, for example, in Hanover Park, a working-class coloured township. There, he spoke only Afrikaans: 'Now it's our task to walk the last mile,' he told an elderly woman, whose arthritis had made almost any walking difficult. Yet he struck a chord with a tone familiar yet respectful, as though he'd grown up next door.[7]

Mandela, in those last frantic days before the election, tried valiantly to address bread-and-butter issues – or more specifically domestic issues. At one meeting in Grassy Park, in the southern Peninsula, he delighted the women but horrified the men by stressing that household chores should be shared. In the new South Africa, he assured them, you'll earn enough to buy washing machines and then the laundry tasks can be equally divided.

He tried to get the same message across at a meeting later the same day in Manenberg, a rougher area where gang rule was almost unassailable. But most people there hardly heard the message because they focused instead on bricks flying over the closed gates of the sports field where the meeting was being held. The gangs had taken sides in the election campaign, and several in Manenberg had decided to take on the ANC physically. The press, in particular, was distracted, not listening to Mandela's message. 'What did he say?' asked one reporter, who'd been counting the flying bricks. 'The same, exactly the same,' replied another. 'But now it's tumble driers too.'[8]

In fact, just as gangs had posed a danger for the civics in the early 1980s as they tried to organise streets committees, so they now queered the pitch for the ANC campaigners. Two gangs in Manenberg, the Dixie Boys and the Schoolboys, opposed the ANC. Another, the Hard Livings, supported the ANC, to the party's evident embarrassment in an area where almost every resident put gang violence at the top of their problem list.[9]

Then there was the fear among many of the poorer elements of the coloured community of a new influx of Africans. They feared that houses they had been waiting for, and jobs they needed, would be taken by Africans.[10]

The National Party (and later the Democratic Alliance who absorbed a significant element of the National Party) openly played on these fears, as well as fears of the 'godlessness' of the ANC. Shortly before the election, the National Party distributed a comic book on the Cape Flats that depicted a respectable coloured woman on her way to church in a hypothetical 'ANC' future, being waylaid by thuggish African youths who tell her: '*Jy sal nie meer kerk toe gaan nie. Daar is geen God nie. Die regering is jou god.*' ('You won't go to church any more. There is no God. The government is your God.')[11]

Crude as it was in its propaganda, the National Party – the party which had removed tens of thousands of coloured people from their homes, which had denied coloured people any job mobility, which had split families through the Prohibition of Mixed Marriages Act and other racist legislation, won the election in the Western Cape. It was a 'great political paradox', wrote American journalist William Finnegan at the time. 'In the Western Cape, at least among the coloured majority, the ANC, the historic movement of the poor and oppressed, could apparently only count on support from the small educated elite, while the National Party, the infamous citadel of white-minority rule, had captured the illiterate masses.'[12]

Perhaps, at heart, it was just too difficult to bridge the cultural dissonance that existed between the old UDF and the newly arrived ANC. Even though Allan Boesak was chair of the party at the time, it was an insufficient condition to convince most Cape Flats residents that this was an organisation for 'people like us'.

One of the people who could have bridged the racial and cultural divide, at least on the West Coast where he lived, was Manuel's old jail comrade Maxwell Moss. He was one of the few campaigners who spoke isiXhosa, Afrikaans and English with equal ease. He had a network of sports and teaching and political contacts, and it was no surprise that the ANC asked him to work as an organiser in 1993. He drove from small town to small town, enlivening the ANC campaign. On 11 November, he took a back road between Lamberts Bay, a fishing village, and Doringsbaai further up the coast. On the way, his car overturned. He went through the windshield and landed on his neck. His injuries were so serious that a helicopter had to transport him to hospital, where he spent the next eight months getting used to the idea that he was now a quadriplegic. (Moss has since recovered much of the strength in his arms; in 1996 he was elected an ANC ward councillor for his area on the West Coast, and in 1999 became a Member of Parliament.)

Another was Manuel, who had worked intensively in poorer communities for the better part of a decade and half, had credibility in the African townships, and had national stature too. But he was brought into the campaign from his Johannesburg offices at a relatively late stage, just three weeks before the election. 'In typical fashion, he walked in and said, what's going on here. This is a mess! You need this, you need that. (He) laid down the line and created a lot of animosity,' said one comrade. But Manuel was right, he added: 'These people had been working in the most wishy-washy way imaginable.'

In a sense, it was the absence of the kind of leadership that people like Manuel and Carolus had provided that made mobilising the coloured community so difficult. Both had been swept up into the national leadership level of the ANC and left the streets of the Cape Flats.

When the votes were counted, the ANC garnered one third in the Western Cape – better than the pollsters had originally predicted. De Klerk's National Party got over half. Nationally, the ratios were more than reversed, with the ANC receiving 62 per cent of the votes and the National Party just over 20 per cent. It showed how different the political rhythms were in the Western Cape. Interestingly, though, the ANC won in Mitchell's Plain, the birthplace of the UDF, with 68 per cent of the vote, and did significantly better in those small towns where the Food and Canning Workers' Union had actively organised across the racial divide than in other Cape towns.

If the ANC activists had been 'delusional' before the election, they were 'shell-shocked' afterwards, as ANC treasurer Ebrahim Rasool put it. 'We somehow didn't believe that the (coloured) community of the Western Cape would, in the worst days, be able to vote for the National Party.'[13]

Manuel had little time to reflect on what had happened in the Cape, though. Shortly after the results were announced, he was back in Johannesburg, listening as Nelson Mandela announced his first cabinet.

CHAPTER 24

New world

Four days before Nelson Mandela was inaugurated as South Africa's first democratically elected president, he called a meeting of the National Working Committee (NWC) of the ANC. 'I want to advise on my choices for cabinet,' Mandela told them.

He said he still had to talk to the National Party about positions – it was to be a Government of National Unity for five years – and to the Inkatha Freedom Party which had been promised a place in government. 'I've thought long and hard,' Manuel remembers Mandela saying, 'and Thabo (Mbeki) will become deputy president with De Klerk. Some of the people I'd like to go in with me are Zola (Skweyiya) for public service, Dullah (Omar) in justice. Mac (Maharaj) in transport, Derek Hanekom, land affairs, Tito, labour, Trevor, trade and industry, and Kathy (Ahmed Kathrada), prisons.

There was some jubilation, some shock. Cyril Ramaphosa, who had steered the constitutional negotiations steadily and cannily for the past three years, had hoped he would be deputy president,[1] but he had been outmanoeuvred while he was focusing on getting the interim constitution approved.

There was some discussion at the NWC about whether the choices could be improved on, but Mandela appealed to them not to negotiate 'this matter'.

Manuel went back to the DEP office and found his colleagues Mboweni and Hanekom there (neither of them were members of the NWC) and told them the news. 'They were completely over the moon,' he recalled, 'although I didn't quite know if Tito would appreciate what the labour thing would entail.'

As Mboweni remembers it, he was absorbed in documentation, 'trying to tie together a bit of a programme of action around trade and industry issues', when Manuel walked back into the office. Manuel walked over to Mboweni's desk and said: 'Congratulations to the minister of labour.'

'Oh, congratulations,' replied Mboweni, thinking that Manuel had been appointed to that portfolio.

When other colleagues began to congratulate him on his appointment, he said: 'No, no, you've made a mistake. Trevor is the minister of labour, he's just told me.' No, they pointed out; Manuel was the minister of trade and industry – ironic news for Mboweni who had been working out the details of a programme in that field.

Because Manuel had worked hard on macroeconomic issues in the past years, he had thought he might make deputy minister of finance. As it happened, Mandela dispatched Alec Erwin to be deputy minister to Derek Keys, who he kept on as minister of finance in a move to settle markets which, while enthusiastic about political change, were somewhat jittery about a predominantly black government.

Actually Keys thought there was a higher hand in Erwin's appointment. His twice daily prayers had not been in vain and, as the first rough months of the new government kicked in, he said he believed that 'God sent me Alec Erwin as a deputy'.

Certainly there was another hand in Manuel's appointment, and that was Thabo Mbeki's. Jakes Gerwel, then rector of the University of the Western Cape, who was to become the first cabinet secretary and the head of Mandela's office in the new government, said Mbeki played an important role in helping Mandela identify new cabinet ministers. 'He would have had a lot to do with Trevor being in that first cabinet, and I know he had a lot to do with the identification of Trevor as a future finance minister.' In fact, said Gerwel, contrary to Mbeki's reputation, 'he's more inclusive than people understand in terms of keeping constituencies together'.

Manuel represented more than just an 'internal resistance' constituency. Importantly, he came from the Western Cape, where the ANC had a fragile foothold among the coloured majority. His mother bore first-hand witness to just how fragile that foothold was. At first, when she was told the news of Manuel's appointment to cabinet by her daughter-in-law Lynne, she tried to suppress her desire to shout the news on the streets. Two days later, when the announcement was official, she recalled that 'the phone didn't stop ringing!' But some of the callers were relatives who had been silent and absent in the long months when her son was in jail or restricted. 'After I got my breath back, I said, ooh, we've got lots of family now. But where were you, when we needed you?'

In spite of Mandela's injunction 'not to negotiate this thing', there was still horse-trading going on until the last moment. The day after the inauguration, there were new faces in the circle of would-be cabinet ministers. One was Kader Asmal, the erudite constitutional lawyer who'd unwisely tangled with Maria Ramos on the question of Central Bank independence. He was hoping for the justice portfolio, had been promised constitutional affairs, and in the end was given water affairs. Constitutional affairs went to Roelf Meyer, the National Party's chief negotiator at Codesa, after De Klerk asked Mandela to include him in the Government of National Unity. As it happened, Asmal took the apparently pedestrian portfolio of Water Affairs and turned it into the 'sexiest portfolio' in government, as Manuel remarked in a farewell speech for him when he left Parliament in 2008. He drove a programme that saw nearly four million new households provided with clean, piped water during his tenure, and earned an accolade from the United Nations Development Programme that remarked in 2006 that South Africa was one of the few countries that spent more on water and sanitation than it did on defence.[2]

The other was Jay Naidoo, Erwin's union comrade. He took up a post that was not initially envisaged in the original planning for the new government: minister without portfolio in charge of the Reconstruction and Development Programme (RDP).

The RDP was originally conceived as a policy rather than an office. But COSATU, nervous that its priorities may be overlooked, insisted that a portfolio be created and that one of its own be appointed. And Ahmed Kathrada, one of Mandela's oldest friends and old jail comrades, gracefully bowed out of the prisons portfolio to accommodate the Inkatha Freedom Party (IFP). The IFP, which put up a monumental fuss before the elections and came in at the last moment, agreed to become part of the Government of National Unity. The Prisons portfolio went, now, not to Kathrada (who had had 26 years' first-hand experience of South African jails), but to Manuel's old antagonist who had piqued him so bitterly at Notre Dame University, Sipho Mzimela from the IFP.

IN THE TWO DAYS between Mandela telling him that he was to be the new minister of trade and industry, and being sworn in, Manuel flew halfway across the world to Warsaw. Directly after Mandela's announcement, Mbeki asked him to go to a meeting between the G7 trade and commerce ministers and their Eastern European counterparts. He told him that he would 'give him a young man' to accompany him, who would ensure that he got back in time for Mandela's inauguration.

The young man was Peter Matlare, a British-educated black South African who was a rising star in a local business world that was still dominated by white men. At the time he was a young executive at Anglo American. He had met Manuel briefly when he had been part of a mining industry delegation – along with his boss, Bobby Godsell, who was later appointed CEO of Anglo-Gold – to confer with the ANC about its mineral policy.

The trip to Warsaw had been conceived at the ANC's post-election victory party held at the house of Douw Steyn, the insurance tycoon who had doled out hefty chunks of generosity to Mandela and the ANC in the pre-1994 period. At the party was an aide to Ron Brown, Bill Clinton's Secretary of Commerce, who urged Thabo Mbeki to send a delegation of the yet-to-be installed new government to Warsaw for the G7 meeting of trade and industry ministers. Matlare, who was part of the conversation, told Mbeki the proposal made 'humungous sense' because many South Africans, as he put it later, were 'uninitiated … we didn't understand the complexities of the world'.

Mbeki agreed, and invited Matlare to accompany him. The initial plan was that he (Mbeki), Matlare and Mboweni would travel to Warsaw. Matlare pushed the envelope by asking Godsell whether Anglo would fund 'three first-class tickets'. (Godsell demurred on funding all three tickets, but approved Matlare's trip.) Shortly before they were due to leave, Mbeki told Matlare that Manuel, not he, would be going on the trip and thus Manuel found himself on a plane to Warsaw (first class) with Matlare, just hours after his appointment as minister of trade and industry had been announced.

When Matlare first encountered Manuel the year before, at the meeting between the ANC and the mining industry, he was struck by his grasp of detail on the one hand, and his emotional distance on the other. 'When Trevor doesn't know you, he's not the warmest character in the world.' It's a view echoed by Kader Asmal, who shared a Pretoria government house with him for 10 years: 'He's not someone who sets up friendships very quickly.'

So it was with some wariness that Matlare set out on the whistle-stop trip to Poland with Manuel next to him. But he was impressed by the gracious way in which Manuel accepted congratulations from a range of people, including the head steward on the South African Airways flight, and white South African businessmen. He was also struck by the fact that when they arrived in Warsaw and Manuel discovered a button missing on the shirt he intended to wear to the meeting, he whipped out needle and thread in the car ('I don't know where he got it from') and fixed it himself. Most of all, Matlare was struck by Manuel's 'propensity to *listen*'.

'Remember, he hardly knew me. He didn't know me from a bar of soap. He could easily have said, look I'm busy, I need to prepare,' recalled Matlare.

A few years later, when he was finance minister, Manuel instituted 'Tips for Trevor', suggested at first by a current affairs programme on a national radio station, as a forum for the public to give input on the annual Budget. He reads them all. 'They may give him 50 lousy ideas, or one great idea, but here is someone with the facility to listen,' said Matlare.

The meeting was both exhilarating and sobering for Manuel. Here was South Africa, flavour of the month, the first black president about to be inaugurated, yet the principal focus of the most powerful countries in the world was on the Eastern European countries, such as Poland, the host of the meeting. Now set adrift from the Soviet bloc, they were considering integration into the European Union. 'For South Africa to put its case in the face of the former Eastern bloc countries, you'd have to make a very compelling case,' said Matlare.

But the prize for Manuel at that meeting was not to get undying commitments to South Africa from the industrialised rich: he had not expected that. His prize was more unexpected: it was the bond he established with Ron Brown, the key figure at the meeting, who introduced him to everyone and then invited him to fly back to South Africa on his plane as he would be attending the inauguration. It was a small plane: they had to stop twice on the way home. Manuel cemented a relationship with Brown, described by Matlare as 'a most remarkable man', that lasted until the latter died two years later in a plane crash over Croatia. But it was a crucial relationship in the early years of the new government. A week after the Warsaw visit, said Matlare, 'Trevor would be sitting in a new office somewhere in Pretoria, Ron Brown would be back in Washington and I would be back in my rabbit warren', but somehow the world they had encountered had changed and everything in front of them was new.

IF WARSAW REPRESENTED THE CUSP of a new world, downtown Pretoria still lurked in the old. The Department of Trade and Industry was housed in a featureless building opposite the State Theatre – two rectangular blocks linked by an air bridge, painted a shabby blue. Manuel found his office bare – not a single photograph or picture on the wall, as though the old officials had wanted to strip the walls of any clue of their past.

Manuel had phoned Gerrie Breyl, the acting director-general of the department, just hours before he was sworn in as a cabinet minister – the DG, Stef Naudé, had resigned shortly before the elections – and asked him to convene a management meeting on the Monday morning. 'I'm going to need to bring some people in,' he told the department's senior managers. 'You can't do that,' said one. 'Oh yes, I can,' replied the new minister.

It may appear now as a simple assertion of authority of the new over the old, but in fact many new ministers were cowed by the fuddle of bureaucratic rules that kept the old machinery ticking over. Political power may have been in the hands of the ANC, but actual control was not.

Manuel would not settle for this. He set about establishing a team of people who had the insight and skills to shake up the moribund South African economy. He also needed like-minded political souls around him. It began with the bodyguard assigned to him by the VIP protection unit, a police officer who had worked in the old regime.

'I have just two questions for you,' said Manuel. 'One is, what is your name? The other is, who is the president of South Africa?'

'My name is Sergeant Ashford Smith,' replied the bodyguard. 'And the president of South Africa is Nelson Mandela.'

'All right,' said Manuel. 'We're going to be OK.'

'One slip and he would have been gone,' said Manuel later. Mandela had only been president for three days at that point, but for Manuel the question was a test of Smith's acceptance of the new. He passed, and a decade and half later, Ashford Smith was still firmly and (mostly) enthusiastically with

Manuel.

Then Manuel began to harness the skills he'd left in the ANC's DEP. Before he'd gone to Warsaw, Zavareh Rustomjee had given him a series of documents detailing policy proposals for industry, for trade, and for the encouragement of small and medium enterprises. These were distilled from policy work that had been developed since the late 1980s by academics, trade unions and anti-apartheid activists within and outside of South Africa. 'This is the first one hundred days,' Rustomjee told him.

Rustomjee is a chemical and industrial engineer with a PhD in economics from the University of London. He worked as an engineer in South African industry from 1980 to 1988, taking a sabbatical to study industrial development and economics in the UK. He returned to South Africa to work in the DEP, coordinating the trade and industry desk. He hails from a family with strong ties to the ANC. Frene Ginwala, who was a close aide to Oliver Tambo and the first Speaker of the democratic parliament, is his aunt; his mother Khorshed, a medical doctor who spent many years involved in community health struggles in KwaZulu-Natal, was one of the first crop of ambassadors in the new dispensation.

'I remember him saying they were useful,' said Rustomjee of his policy proposals, 'because until then he'd focused more on finance issues than trade and industry issues.'

A few months later, Manuel phoned Rustomjee, who was still faithfully going to the DEP office in Shell House most days. 'I need you here,' he said.

'OK,' replied Rustomjee, calculating it would take about an hour for him to make the trip from downtown Johannesburg to Pretoria.

'No, I need you here in the department,' replied Manuel. And so Rustomjee moved over as an adviser, becoming director-general when the post was advertised a few months later.

He recruited his private secretary in a similar manner. Patti Smith had grown up in Athlone, and had known Manuel through his community activism. She had, for a time, shared a house with his ex-girlfriend Daphne Williams. They were not close friends, nor even close fellow activists, but Manuel had an instinct that she would make a good secretary. At the time of the elections, she was working for Pius Langa, later the President of the Constitutional Court, but then the president of the anti-apartheid National Association of Democratic Lawyers (Nadel). A colleague at Nadel had given her tickets to the opening of the first democratic Parliament and in the swirl of excitement that day, she bumped into Manuel. A few days later he phoned her and asked her to come and work for him. Before she knew it, he'd asked Langa to release her before the month was out. She started working for him on 16 June 1994 and has been with him since.

Then he recruited several others who had worked with him at the DEP: Alistair Ruiters, an activist and economist to work on small business development; Faizel Ismail, Mfundo Nkhuhlo and Alan Hirsch, local economists who'd worked in the DEP, to work on trade policy, and later Paul Jourdan, a geologist who had worked on the mining sector in the DEP. Jourdan came in as Manuel's adviser as soon as Rustomjee moved up to become director-general. Their task was to transform a department that had been a refuge for bureaucrats who protected almost any sector that requested it, into an engine to overhaul the economy. Most of the new officials were in their thirties and brand new to government.

The way Manuel assembled this team has been a mark of his leadership in government ever since. Oliver Williams, the American business academic whom he had so alarmed with his outspokenness two years before, saw this in him even then. 'One of the marks of a good leader is that you can surround yourself with people smarter than you are,' he said. 'You're not threatened. If you look at the great leaders that's one of the skills they almost all have, they're not threatened by very bright people, and he isn't. He finds the brightest people he can get. And if you criticise him, he *thinks* about it and maybe he changes his mind.'

Several of the civil servants from the previous government stayed on. Some were 'openly hostile', recalled Rustomjee; others, including Gerrie Breyl, who had been acting director-general, were 'more supportive'. Some had a 'very racist attitude' at first, but 'I think it changed over time because we *did* know more than they expected'. Under Manuel, the new and old guard found something in common: many of the old civil servants had an ethos about serving the public. The shortcoming – the great and reprehensible shortcoming – was that the public they envisaged was largely white. Now suddenly they had to serve the whole country. But the principle of public service, which inspired many of the first generation recruits to the new democratic government, was not alien to some of those who already occupied the positions.

But there was something else Manuel brought which was quite new to them: his resistance to lobbying. In the past the Trade and Industry Department had been a watering hole for special interest groups: it was 'protection on demand', said Rustomjee. 'Some of them (the civil servants) ... were quite outraged by the way in which the integrity of the policies they were custodians of were just violated by their previous political heads. And when they started to see us operate consistently where we take a policy position and it's endorsed politically ... and when we start confronting some of the powerful vested interests that we don't back down ... some of them found a new lease of life and they were able to start enjoying what they were doing.'

Early on in Manuel's term, the department made some changes to the regulations that (inadvertently) affected the scrap metal industry. Clearly used to getting their way in the past, the industry badgered officials, phoning and writing daily. Manuel, one Friday afternoon, instructed his officials to 'batten down the hatches' – an instruction that, according to Rustomjee, impressed particularly the old guard, who had become used to being leapfrogged by businessmen with direct access to politicians.

And then there was Manuel's personality, the way he interacted, which was entirely new to them. 'Trevor used to *engage*; we'd have these workshops and he'd come in and talk quite openly. He was relatively casual; he wasn't stuffy like the ministers tended to be in the past. He would also rave a little bit so there was probably a mixed response ['rave' is 'leftspeak' for 'expound at some length']. Some of them didn't understand what he was talking about, but others found it quite stimulating. And (they liked) his approachability. He's a very personable kind of guy and they liked that.'

But while Manuel may have won over some of the older civil servants, and surrounded himself with bright, new ones, his task was daunting. For years, Trade and Industry had been a department whose main task was to protect uncompetitive industries. Now he had to take that same department and turn it into an engine to fundamentally restructure a moribund economy and propel it into the modern world. As Mark Gevisser put it, writing as Manuel's term there ended: 'His victory was to take a department whose sole raison d'être was to stifle competition and to make it the vanguard of the 'liberalised' market economy.'[3]

Rustomjee thinks this is too 'simplistic' a characterisation. 'At the time I remember us grappling with steering a path that was appropriate for the mixed economy that we inherited – there was a place for liberalisation, but it was only one instrument among many.'

Whatever the case, Manuel's task was peppered with fights.

The first was with business. In early 1995, he spoke 'off the cuff' at a business breakfast in Cape Town about his plan to introduce tough new anti-monopoly legislation to distil the high concentration of ownership in South Africa. 'Some of the people who call themselves capitalists in South Africa would function best in the planned economy of the Soviet Union after 1917 … We have capitalists who don't like markets, capitalists who don't want to compete, capitalists who don't take time out to look at what world markets have to offer.'[4]

It was a delicious 'reversal of ideological roles'.[5] Manuel, the activist who had once styled himself on the revolutionary Che Guevara, attacking the suits for betraying the essence of capitalism.

He clashed frequently with big business in this period. At one meeting, after similarly sharp words about monopolies, Michael Spicer, then an executive director of one of the country's largest firms, Anglo American (later he became CEO of Business Leadership SA), snapped: 'Fortunately, ministers have a short shelf life.'

Manuel gritted his teeth and replied: 'We'll see.'

More than a decade later, Spicer thought that Manuel used language that was inappropriately 'violent'. He once said that conglomerates 'should be dismembered, torn limb from limb', recalled Spicer. 'And I said that kind of violent language is not going to get us anywhere.'

At first, business feared that Manuel and his department were 'mooting wholesale implementation of anti-trust policy', Spicer told me. 'And we were saying that's great, but the United States has a market of 250 million and here we have a very small market. Can you have 26 banks here? It's just not going to happen.'

Spicer told me that his relationship with Manuel had improved considerably over the years, but he still thinks that he – and the government – did not do enough to open up the state-run sector of the economy. Some of the large state-run enterprises have taken anti-competitiveness to a 'stellar level', he said.

As it happened, Manuel could not after all introduce his proposed competitions law that year and it fell to his successor, Alec Erwin, to pilot it through parliament in 1998. Manuel had too many other issues to deal with, too many other vested interests to butt heads with.

Central to increasing competitiveness in Manuel's view was boosting small business. This would serve both to create more jobs and to promote black businesses in particular. Among apartheid's many litanies of wrongs was the way it suppressed black business people. Even before the National Party took power in 1948, there had been restrictions on black business, but after 1948 almost every path for independent African business was blocked. In 1955, Africans were allowed to trade only in areas designated as black townships. Soon after that, the Afrikaanse Sakekamer complained even about this, and in 1963 a government edict to local authorities decreed that Africans could assume no right at all to trade in any urban area, nor could they own commercial property, nor run more than one business. 'So, for Africans, the capitalist path to progress through accumulation as an entrepreneur was erased by the apartheid regime.'[6] In addition, the job colour bar and deliberately inferior education blocked most paths of economic betterment for Africans in particular. Indians and coloureds had their business opportunities stymied by the Group Areas Act which severely restricted their trading rights.

By the end of the 1980s the government either backtracked or turned a blind eye to small African traders. By the end of that decade there were at least half a million African-owned businesses in the country, comprising informal taxis, hawkers, vendors, backyard manufacturers and owners of taverns (known as 'shebeens') in South Africa.[7]

In 1981 the government, together with a number of private corporations, had set up the Small Business Development Corporation (SBDC) to provide loans for small business people, including a few black businesses. But too few in the eyes of the new government. In his bid to shake up the stranglehold of the conglomerates on the economy and to stimulate small businesses, the SBDC fell into Manuel's line of fire in the first few months of his appointment.

There were two major issues for him: one was racial. In 1994, the bulk of loans went to whites rather than to black businesses. The other was accountability: in spite of putting up about half of the SBDC's budget, the government only had a 25 per cent vote on its board. Alistair Ruiters, then Manuel's chief director for small business development, accused the SBDC of being 'racist'. The SBDC, for its part, protested that it needed to be independent from government to be effective.

Before the end of 1994, Manuel and his officials had produced a White Paper* on small business development that promised a R1 billion injection into its development and proposed to curtail the SBDC's powers by creating new

---

* A government policy document that precedes legislation.

institutions that could better respond to the needs of small black businesses.

History goes round. The SBDC was chaired by Johann Rupert, the Afrikaans entrepreneur whose father Anton had made a fortune initially from his tobacco business. Manuel's great-grandfather, Maximillian von Söhnen, had once been the Rupert family's plumber. The Ruperts had increased their fortune; the Von Söhnens, in contrast, had lost their most valuable asset, a sprawling property and business in the middle of Stellenbosch, under the racially discriminatory laws of the country.

But when the two met in early 1995, neither mentioned the inter-generational journey that had brought them to opposite sides of a table where, now, Manuel held the upper hand. But Rupert, in contrast to some of the SBDC's executives, saw the need for change and agreed to substantially restructure the SBDC. The government, for its part, withdrew nearly R700 million of its assets leaving it with an asset base of about R500 million. The funds were transferred to a Small Business Development Agency located in the Department of Trade and Industry.[8]

FAR TOUGHER WAS THE BATTLE to cut through the Byzantine system of tariffs that had protected the largely uncompetitive manufacturing industry in South Africa. The tariff structure was 'both complex and opaque'.[9] It reflected the obsessively protective import-substitution policies of the apartheid government and had the effect of 'not only discouraging imports but also of taxing exports by raising production costs'.[10] There were more than 200 different rates and they took a number of different forms. It was 'really a dog's breakfast', Rustomjee told me. 'It was high, but there was no logic to it. In some cases you found you had higher protection on inputs than on the outputs in value chains. Because that was the way it worked: people just came and it was protection on demand.'

There were also, supposedly, subsidies to encourage exports, but they too had little logic. The biggest and most expensive was GEIS (which stood for the Generalised Export Incentive Scheme). Launched in 1990 'amidst deep economic panic', it was effectively a government subsidy to encourage exports to shore up the sinking economy. It was 'fraught with fraud and backlogs', and very difficult to budget for because the department never knew quite who would claim on it.[11] The strangest enterprises used it. I once worked for small but prestigious magazine with perennial cash flow problems: the GEIS subsidy was often the business plan for getting through the month. But the main beneficiaries were manufacturers of intermediate products such as paper and steel, which now got huge tax-free bonuses on goods they would have exported anyway.

Derek Keys, Manuel's immediate predecessor, had removed the tax-free exemption from the GEIS handout and realised at the time that it was 'completely unsustainable'. But when Manuel became political head of Trade and Industry it still consumed two thirds of that department's budget of about R3,5 billion. It was one of the first things that the new guard decided to scrap. But nothing was easy. When Manuel and his officials tried to get rid of this 'wasteful' (as Rustomjee described it) subsidy, the most affected firms lobbied hard – but not initially with government. Instead they went to the unions, and threatened that if GEIS was scrapped, they might have to retrench workers.

The DTI lobbied the trade unions as assiduously. Rustomjee recalls that at Manuel's urging he met with the COSATU leadership, including Mbhazima Shilowa, then general secretary, and Enoch Godongwana. They agreed to support the termination of GEIS if the DTI in turn supported other supply side programmes.

Still the battle was harder than anticipated and in the end it took three more years to terminate; even then the government had to rely on a provision of the General Agreement on Tariffs and Trade (GATT) that restricted export subsidies.

That exports were essential for growth was not an issue. But GEIS did not efficiently encourage exports, nor did it force South African companies to do what Manuel urged: to overcome the 'almost seismic fault ... in the inability of local firms to produce high volumes or to seek, establish and exploit niche markets'.[12] And, more importantly, there was a principled issue for Manuel of 'taking taxpayers' money' to try to solve the export problem.[13]

Frustratingly for Manuel – and his ANC colleagues – in terms of GATT South Africa had been defined as a 'developed country'. The average income – which took into account the relatively high white income – put it in that category although, as he put it then, 'the statistics for black South Africans mirror those of the developing countries'.[14] Concretely, it meant that South Africa was excluded from the special tariffs and dispensations enjoyed by those countries defined as 'developing'.

'We're arguing about the relative poverty of South Africa,' he said at the time. 'But it's a hard battle. People come here, stay in top hotels, have lunches

404

with business people in good restaurants.' But the proof to him that South Africa was essentially a developing – if not backward country – was found in its basket of exports. Two thirds of them were 'primary commodities – that which we dig from the earth, shake from the trees, put in boxes and send overseas.'[15]

A few days before the first democratic election, South Africa had re-entered the fold of international trade. It signed the Marrakech Agreement on 24 April 1994. Kader Asmal went to Morocco with Derek Keys to sign the agreement which concluded the Uruguay Round of GATT. To send Asmal – not then a representative of government – with Keys was a sign of the maturity of ANC economic policy at the time. It was a signal to the world that the ANC was committed to reshaping the economy as a competitive and fair one.

World trade negotiations were – and are – notoriously complicated: the spirit of free trade is often clouded by convoluted measures to protect politically powerful lobby groups in countries with the most clout. And when import duties are relaxed, there is no guarantee that the rich countries won't give their own constituencies (especially farmers) relief in the form of generous subsidies to protect them from cheaper imports from poorer agricultural countries.

The Marrakech Agreement established the World Trade Organisation in place of GATT. For South Africa its significance was that it was back in the international trade fold after the long chill of isolation in the sanctions era. It also led to a major reduction of tariffs around the world and allowed better access for textiles and clothing from developing countries into the richer markets.

But it was not altogether gratefully received in South Africa. There were powerful local industries which employed several thousand people in a society where unemployment was already high, which would have suffered tremendously had they been subject overnight to rigorous international competition.

One was the motor industry.

The components and auto industry had established itself in South Africa in 1924 when Ford first invested in Port Elizabeth. It expanded until the mid-1980s on the basis of a bet that didn't pay off. The bet was that the market for cars would grow steadily with the growth of a middle class. By the early 1980s, there were at least 11 motor car manufacturers in South Africa – more than in the whole of Europe – producing 250 versions of passenger cars and

120 versions of light commercial vehicles for a shrinking market. Whereas in Australia, a country with a comparably sized market to South Africa, motor vehicle sales had increased in the first half of the 1980s from 358 000 to 402 000 a year, in South Africa the trend was the opposite. Sales shrank by 33 per cent in that period from 301 000 in 1981 to 200 000 by the end of 1985.[16]

The problem, to put it simply, was that apartheid had simply made most South Africans too poor to provide a market for the car manufacturers. Car ownership by the mid-1980s was about 450 per 1 000 among whites and less than one tenth that – 40 per 1 000 – amongst blacks.[17] Combined with increasing pressures for disinvestment and the subsequent withdrawal of foreign companies, this had put thousands of motor workers on the streets, particularly in the Eastern Cape, one of the most economically depressed areas.

In a desperate attempt to protect the declining industry, the old regime had placed tariffs on imported motor cars, some of them as high as 125 per cent.[18] And still prices were not competitive. Excluding the tariffs, locally assembled motor vehicles still cost 65 per cent more than their imported counterparts. There had to be something wrong, Manuel told a South African Chamber of Business convention in Port Elizabeth in 1995.[19]

Business may have been peeved – they were already irritated that he'd dropped tariff levels in some instances to below those agreed to at Marrakech – but if Manuel was right about one thing it was that South African industry was alarmingly lacklustre.

So what to do about the motor industry? Despite huge lay-offs, it still provided several thousand of the better paying jobs in impoverished areas such as the Eastern Cape. One option was to close it down. This is exactly what the pre-1994 industrial strategists clustered around Alec Erwin had thought likely.

But research (conducted by the DTI with University of Cape Town economics professor Anthony Black) suggested a third way: tariffs were cut, but steadily and slowly; auto manufacturers were encouraged to streamline their production, so as to produce higher volumes of fewer models. For instance, Samcor (which bought the Ford plant in Port Elizabeth) made 92 variations of a light pick-up truck (known in South Africa as a *bakkie*) at the time, as Manuel told a reporter.[20] In return for chipping away at the tariff wall, motor manufacturers who exported their goods, would be able to import other models duty free. 'The rationale was to make the industry more competitive,

406

lower car prices and give consumers more choice,' said Black who wrote his PhD thesis on the transformation of the industry.[21] The plan was known as the MIDP – the Motor Industries Development Programme.

BMW became a shining example: it used to make the 3, 5 and 7 series in its South African factory. But small volumes and a limited domestic market made it uncompetitive. Under the MIDP, it expanded production of the 3 series, while being able to import the 5 and 7 series with minimal duties. BMW South Africa is now one of the largest exporters of right-hand-drive BMWs in the world.[22]

Another danger with a complex system of tariffs, as Manuel found out, was how easy it is to defraud the system. So at the very moment he introduced the MIDP, just 18 months after he had become minister, he found himself doing battle with his counterparts in the Southern African Customs Union (SACU) member country of Botswana over a fantastical scheme that 'Billy' Rautenbach, a man still wanted in South Africa on various charges of tax avoidance and fraud, had cooked up.[23]

Rautenbach and a business partner took full advantage of the complex tariff differentials. In the industry parlance, the CBUs (Completely Built-Up Units) attract the highest tariffs; tariffs are lower on the SKUs (Semi-Knocked Down Units) and CKUs (Completely Knocked Down Units). Rautenbach bought fully assembled Hyundais from Korea, imported them into Mozambique (which was not part of the Customs Union), took out the air-conditioning units, used his own trucking company, Wheels of Africa, to transport them to Botswana, where he reassembled them and sold them, duty free, on the South African market. He employed Mozambicans to take out the aircon units (so the authorities there were not keen to upset the scam), and employed Botswana citizens to reassemble them. And he paid low duties, as though they were SKUs or CKUs. When the South African authorities cottoned on to this, Manuel and his officials had to persuade a doubting Botswana government that they were not simply fronting for South African manufacturers.

By 1997, Rautenbach had declared insolvency. This after the Botswana Development Corporation had invested heavily in a paint and assembly plant at Rautenbach's urging to assemble his imported Hyundais. He also had the Asset Forfeiture Unit pursuing him, trying, with varying degrees of success, to confiscate his assets.[24]

FOR MANUEL, A BATTLE FAR CLOSER TO HIS HEART and to his home was in the clothing and textile sector. Initially the plan was to try a similar carrot-and-stick method that had worked with the motor industry.

But it was far harder to reduce tariffs at the rate that the Uruguay Round of GATT required. Before he was even president, Nelson Mandela telephoned Bill Clinton, at the behest of the South African Clothing and Textile Workers' Union (SACTWU), an important election ally for the ANC in the Western Cape, to ask him to support a more gradual phasing down of tariffs for clothing and textiles than stipulated in GATT. The United States had argued against South Africa being given 'developing country' status which would have meant a more gentle reduction of protective tariffs. Mandela asked Clinton to agree to extend the down-phasing of tariffs to a 12-year, rather than five-year period.

In 1994, the clothing and textile industries employed about 200 000 workers. In the Western Cape, many of them were women, like Manuel's own mother who spent 36 years working in the industry. The industries had grown out of step with the low-cost, mass-producing industries in Asia.

Tariffs on imported clothing and textiles were mostly in the region of 100 per cent but in some cases were as high as 400 per cent.[25] In addition to GEIS, there was also a rule in the tax schedule called the 470-03, which allowed enterprises to claim a rebate on imports in return for goods they exported. Then there were the Duty Credit Certificates (DCCs) which, unlike the 470-03s, were actually tradable. In other words, if a clothing manufacturer had a DCC worth R1 million, but could use only R500 000 of the rebate for imports, he could sell the value of the remainder to another business, not necessarily even another manufacturer. In fact, many DCCs were sold to retailers, who could then import clothing at cheaper rates – undermining the entire reason for the existence of this complex protection in the first place.

Manuel's instinct was to abolish both rebates, along with GEIS.

In practice, this was not so easy. It took the new government another two and half years to phase out GEIS. Then it tried to do the same thing in clothing and textiles as it had done in the motor industry. The 470-03s and the DCCs became part of a package of incentives that gave local manufacturers some protection for a limited period, allowing them, theoretically, enough time to restructure and compete in the global markets. But the DCCs are still vital in keeping alive some factories and tens of thousands of jobs among South Africa's poorer neighbours – Lesotho, for instance, which qualifies under the AGOA (African Growth and Opportunity Act) for access to the United States market.

Manuel relied on his own history to persuade clothing and textile workers that if the industry didn't make the necessary changes then it might well be extinguished by the global markets. 'Partly because of my interpersonal relationships (in the industry), partly because I could persuade people that we needed trust in this environment, I've never been afraid to stand up and face clothing and textile workers. And I've faced hostile meetings!'

The DCCs lingered on long after Manuel would have liked to see them go. Even though many rebate certificates ended up in the hands of retailers, directly threatening jobs in the ailing industry, the union seemed afraid to relinquish them. Why? Because, said Rustomjee, they gave the union important leverage in wage negotiations and allowed them to set off the textile manufacturers against their downstream industries, clothing manufacturing and retailing.

Ten years into democracy, eight years after he'd moved on from Trade and Industry, Manuel addressed the Fashion Imbizo in Cape Town, an event hosted by the union run by his old UDF comrade Ebrahim Patel. The Fashion Imbizo is an attempt to highlight successful niches which the South African industry may occupy: innovative design, short runs, and understanding, as Manuel told me, 'that the market in clothing is … segmented; that those parts of the industry that either China or the export processing zones in Eastern Europe would take was low-end, and it was never going to be where we were playing. On the other hand, there was Savile Row which was highly exclusive and where we were never going to play. But between these polar extremes there (are) a series of niches that we can claim successfully, but firms need to be supported in order to do that. And that comes with training and worker organisation and competitiveness rather than narrow subsidies.'

At the Fashion Imbizo he spoke in a manner that he himself described as 'tough love'. 'Take nothing for granted,' he said. A decade ago, governments around the world told the new South African leaders how they were rooting for the country's success. 'Ten years on … we can rightly ask what happened to those promises. The harsh reality is that the emotional appeal of post-apartheid South Africa struck no chord in the cabinet rooms and boardrooms where decisions … are taken. The same message, perhaps amplified many times, is evident in the clothing and textile sector. So, we can wring our hands and weep. We are free, and capable of name-calling. We can try and shame our competitors. Regrettably, none of those actions will guarantee the fashion industry in South Africa a future. We will have to rely on the hard road of striving for competitiveness by understanding both threat and opportunity.'[26]

He spoke to the audience – many of them leaders in the union – about China as one of the 'tough realities' the industry had to deal with. At the time, the industry was deeply worried about the amount of cheap Chinese clothing imports coming into the country.

'China's custom is never to blame others for our own problem.' Manuel was quoting Li Ruogo, the deputy governor of the People's Bank of China. 'For the past 26 years we never put pressure or problems on to the world. The US has the reverse attitude: whenever they have problems, they blame others.'

He may well have said South Africa, and this was the point Manuel wanted to make. 'Chinese manufacturing expansion in an environment of low wages is a major irritant to the clothing and textile industry of South Africa. But we should not become irritated. Rather we should ask how to engage with that reality.'

At question time a worker stood up and said to him: '*Ja*, Comrade Trevor. Let's not panic about China. It's going to be there. It's not going to go away.'

'I had a sense,' he told me, 'that there was more uphill from the bosses than from the workers.'

Despite a strong union, there are some things over which workers exercise no choice: 'They don't select the kinds of machines they use, they don't plan work organisation (in the factory), and the failures (manifesting in lack of competitiveness) are largely management failures.'

For whatever reason, the pockets of success in the car industry have not been emulated in the garment or textile industries to the same extent. The sense of anxiety and loss in those sectors, particularly in the Western Cape, cuts deep.

In 2005, Rex Trueform, where Manuel's mother had begun her lifelong career as a garment worker, announced that it would close down. For generations it was the landmark factory in Cape Town, its building like an enormous ship on the main road of Salt River, Cape Town's industrial heartland, in an earlier age. In the same year, the women's clothing factory in Maitland where Philma Manuel had spent the last 18 years of her working life went on 'short time' for three months. Then it, too, announced it was closing down. Maitland adjoins Kensington, where Mrs Manuel lives. She encountered the local manager in the street one day shortly after the announcement was made. She asked him why the factory was closing. 'You know, Mrs Manuel,' he said to her, 'we just had to close.'

'He always used to call me on my (first) name,' she told me a few weeks after this encounter. 'But since Trevor, he calls me Mrs Manuel.' She didn't complete the phrase about her son, but the message, and its ironies, lay heavily on her few words. Here was a woman who gave her life to the industry, and who had to wait more than 36 years to get the respect of being addressed by an honorific. And then it was in circumstances that summed up the limitations of power that her now ostensibly powerful son faced. 'You're OK, but these girls,' she told the manager, 'they've got bonds to pay. And children!'

When Rex announced that it would close, it led to an emotional outpouring from a coalition that included SACTWU, its parent body COSATU, the churches and other civic bodies which denounced 'unfair international trade rules which put profits before people'.[27] The clothing market had been flooded with 'inexpensive goods' made under sweatshop conditions, they said. Workers in China earned less than R200 a month, for 15-hour days with one day's leave a month. 'No person who supports dignity, equality and fairness should buy products made by labour under these conditions, especially when they destroy jobs in poor communities in South Africa and elsewhere.'

How do you bar the goods of the world's fastest growing – and one of its most innovative – economies, and hope that it will provide a solution to the huge challenges facing the clothing sector in Cape Town?

Well, the industry tried. In 2006, the clothing industry (against the strong wishes of the retailers) managed to legally limit Chinese clothing imports. In dollar terms, Chinese imports dropped by about 40 per cent that year.[28]

But that was a short-term measure. Far more difficult to track, but more fundamental in its effects, is the plethora of 'backyard' shops that have emerged, not only on the Cape Flats and around the country, but in South Africa's neighbouring states: CMT shops – cut, make and trim – that supply some of the biggest retailers. So when the union estimated that 17 000 jobs had been lost in the industry since 2003, they described them as 'formal' jobs. Rustomjee estimates that the number of jobs in the sector has stayed constant, even increased, but those that have been created are in the 'backyard' operations.

'Backyard' is a misnomer. Some operate out of the city centre of Durban, others in small towns in KwaZulu-Natal, still others out of smaller premises in the Cape. I spoke to a clothing manufacturer who had closed down two of his South African plants, eliminating 1700 'unionised' jobs, and moved to a neighbouring country. He was nervous about speaking to me at all, enquiring several times whether I was 'from the union' and ending each statement with the phrase, 'Are you with me?'

'The jobs are lost for one reason alone: the cost of labour is too high. Are you with me?' Not a single factory established in the past eight years has been 'compliant' in terms of the industrial relations bargaining council that SACTWU belongs to, and which determines wages and working conditions. He told me the retailers – the bigger chains – were 'very supportive' of the smaller industries in the region because they could get quality clothes at economical prices.

This manufacturer has a 'state of the art' factory, he told me, that pays 'China rates' and he still has people queuing up for work. Was I with him?

Yet there is something intangible, more than just economic opportunity, that has been lost in the Cape with the closure of so many factories, especially Rex Trueform. It was 'like family', Philma Manuel told me more than once. It seemed an indelible part of Cape Town. 'Every family on the Cape Flats has a member who at one time or another has worked for Rex Trueform. Every family in South Africa who has bought formal wear for their fathers and sons has proudly worn the products made by the workers of Rex Trueform.'[29]

This is probably true. Trevor Manuel's mother worked for Rex. So did Ebrahim Patel's mother. So, too, did the mother of Fred Robertson, one of Manuel's closest friends and today a successful entrepreneur, head of the empowerment company Brimstone.

So it may have been good business sense, but it was probably tempered with history and sentiment when Robertson's company signed a lease agreement with Rex, as it was closing, whereby they could continue to produce a limited range of clothing, so saving about 250 jobs of the thousand. It also helped that his holding company owned House of Monatic, an upmarket men's clothing factory, just down the road from the Rex factory.

At the end of 2006, a few months after the agreement was concluded, I went with Mrs Manuel to visit the plant. It is not the flagship building where she had worked all those years, but one across the road. The factory no longer produces its own range of clothes, but does short runs to particular orders from retailers. The day I visited, they were manufacturing snatched-in-the-waist short grey jackets and matching pants for Truworths, one of the largest South African clothing retailers. 'The customer gives us the material, patterns, they supply the buttons – everything,' said Wendy Nathan, the director of Human Resources at House of Monatic, who showed Mrs Manuel around the new plant.

Almost everybody – the 'girls', as the women call themselves – know who Mrs Manuel is. Her claim to fame is only partly through her son; it is equally that she worked at Rex for nearly two decades.

Leonard Messenheimer comes to greet her. He is the floor manager of the factory and has worked there 35 years, although he is a few months shy of his fiftieth birthday. Like Mrs Manuel, he started at Rex when he was 14 years old. Although she is a generation older than him, and left Rex before he even started, they talk about the people they both knew. 'Mrs Manuel, do you remember Jack Whittaker?' he asks. 'Yes? He still pops in here, refuses to walk on his cane. He's very old but very gay also (he means cheerful), and doesn't want to walk on his cane yet: he's that fit!'

The 'girls' flock around her: she was one of the first generation to work at Rex; they get her to sit at a pedal sewing machine – 'It still feels the same,' she says – and jostle to get their photograph taken with her.

There is indeed a feel of family about the whole encounter. When Manuel is introduced as a 'son of the industry' at union meetings, there is no rhetoric in the statement. His first job was in the garment industry; his mother and sisters worked there.

This makes the reality much tougher for him. He has faced angry workers. He agreed to go to a COSATU conference at Vista University in 1995 shortly after the tariff reductions were announced. 'I thought, you know, they're going to have my balls for dinner. It was a very scary moment. (But) I went, and it wasn't so bad.'

And afterwards he took the SACTWU leadership out to dinner at a fish restaurant in Melville in Johannesburg, where the discourse went to a level beyond the polemic of union meetings. 'There was outward posturing, but inside we could still talk about the issues. That has never broken down.'

In fact Ebrahim Patel does not opt any more for the simple route of protection when it comes to plans to save the industry. Trade liberalisation, he acknowledges, has created more growth and more jobs in most parts of Asia. But not in all regions. In Latin America, for instance, exports have grown but employment hasn't. Secondly, there has been a dramatic increase in foreign investment into some developing countries in the era of trade liberalisation, but not all.[30]

'There is sometimes a false choice that is posed to us. The choice is not between two kinds of fatalism. The first kind of fatalism among those who are opposed to globalisation has a view that virtually says stop the world – I want to get off. And a fatalism among those who support globalisation – who say, we can't change the world and we must fit in. What the lessons have shown is that there is some policy space. There is policy space available to utilise and we have not always, as South Africa, pushed the policy envelope.[31]

It is almost, but not quite, the same language Manuel spoke the year before when he told the union members at the Fashion Imbizo that he was 'painfully aware' of just how tough life in the industry is. 'We can and must pull out all the stops to transform the fashion industry … But the changes will have to be informed by realism, not pity, not an appeal to justice, not complaining over Chinese wage rates. The realism has to include an acceptance of what we can do better, and do it well … Government will back you but you must demonstrate the vision and leadership.'[32]

Occasionally when he has been faced with tough decisions in governance, Manuel has gone back to his early days of reading groups when he and his young comrades absorbed the teachings of Marxist philosophers into the early hours. In this case, his lodestar is Antonio Gramsci, the Italian Marxist philosopher who wrote about building hegemony. 'It has always meant for me a fairly soft, persuasive hand which results in approaches where I try not to use the power of the state to force people to do certain things,' he told me.

'How much baggage you shed as you go through life, I don't know, but what I am very consciously aware of is that you need to be able to take decisions; some of them will be unpopular, and you need a frame of reference you can go back to.'

The frame of reference for Manuel was based in what Kader Asmal has called his 'rootedness' – his history in the Western Cape, his 'son-of-the-industry' status. He has urged the industry to find a path for growth, not mere survival. He has listened to the fears of workers who stand to lose their jobs, but he has also told them of the realities of a new twenty-first century world against which neither he, nor anyone, can protect them for long.

It was this mixture of empathy and toughness, 'hegemony-building', and an ability to take unpopular decisions, that would drive him through the turbulent first few years as finance minister. In the ensuing years he would have to shake up, not just a few industries, but an entire economy that still wavered on an edge.

≡ PART SIX: Power ≡

1995-2007

CHAPTER 25

Amorphous markets

ONE SATURDAY MORNING IN JUNE OF 1994, there came what Manuel called a 'transition point' in his career. Nelson Mandela telephoned and asked to meet him. When Manuel arrived at the president's house in Pretoria later that day he found the deputy president Thabo Mbeki and his fellow cabinet minister Tito Mboweni also there.

Mandela told them: Derek Keys has said he wants to resign. He needed a replacement, and 'I don't think we're ready yet for an ANC appointment.'

He'd applied his mind, and thought Chris Liebenberg should be the new minister of finance.

Two days later, the French president Francois Mitterrand made his first state visit to South Africa. At the state banquet in Cape Town, Mandela sat at the main table with Mitterrand until halfway through the evening, when he beckoned Manuel. 'Trevor, sit here and act as head of state,' he said. 'I'm going to see Chris Liebenberg now. He's come to Cape Town to see me.'

The next day he told Manuel: 'Chris said he must talk to his wife Elly, but I think he's going to be OK.'

Derek Keys had prepared the 1994/95 Budget just before the election and was working on the next. He had also produced a financing scheme for the ANC's election manifesto, the Reconstruction and Development Programme (RDP), costing it at about R2,5 billion for the first year with R2,5 billion added to that for the following five years. 'Which I knew would have to be abandoned after a couple of years,' he told me. 'But at the time nobody knew that.' Why? Because the money could only come from other government departments. 'And once the ministers had turned into the champions of their departments, they sure weren't going to provide money for the Reconstruction and Development Programme.'

Keys indicated when he first took the finance ministry post that he wanted to stay only one year to help through the transition. De Klerk had asked him to stay two years. In the end he stayed nearly three. He had never seen his appointment as a long-term commitment. 'I always knew it was going to be cataclysmic.'

Mandela tried to manage the transition between finance ministers as tightly as he could. He would not announce Keys's departure before he could announce a successor. And word was already leaking out to jittery markets. So speed was of the essence in persuading Liebenberg to take the post.

Chris Liebenberg comes from a humble background. He is a smart but unpretentious man whose modest lifestyle belies his status at the helm of one of South Africa's major banks for nearly two decades.

He was born in 1934 in Touws River, a little town near Worcester in the Western Cape 'which immediately tells you what my father did'. Touws River was one of the country's biggest railway junctions at the time. This was where his father worked.

Liebenberg started at Nedcor Bank – in those days it was called Nederlandse Bank – as a messenger in 1952. Like Manuel, he had no university degree but a natural intelligence and an empathy for others. He came from a 'strict Afrikaans background' but his conscience was troubled when he saw how District Six was razed by the relentless enforcement of the Group Areas Act. By then, in the 1960s, he was working in Cape Town, and he knew the District well because he delivered letters to the bank's clients there. It was, he told me, 'a watershed realisation' for him.

In the next 30 years he worked his way up through the ranks of the bank first to managing director, then to CEO. He had just retired from that position in 1994 when he received 'that fateful phone call from Madiba' at four in the afternoon. He was chairing a Credit Guarantee board meeting at the time. Mandela said he'd like to have a word with him. Fine, he said, where shall I meet you? 'At Westbrook,' said Mandela (the president's Cape Town residence which was later renamed Genadendal). So Liebenberg took the next flight to Cape Town.

'Did you tell him it was going to be OK?' I asked him.

He laughed. 'You can't say no to Madiba. He gave me 24 hours (to decide). I said to him, look, I've never belonged to a political party and I had given my wife an undertaking I'd never go into politics. So I said I had to speak to my wife. And he said, no, he'd speak to her. And I said, no, you leave that to me. I'll speak to her.'

Which he did, and 24 hours later he accepted the post with certain conditions attached.

Among those were that there be a 'market-related' economy with strict fiscal and monetary discipline, that he would not join a political party, and 'that we put all our efforts into redistribution through the RDP'.

Mandela agreed and because of Liebenberg's refusal to join a political party, he was compelled to change the Constitution to accommodate him in cabinet. (Keys had, somewhat reluctantly, joined the National Party.)

The meeting between Mandela and Liebenberg late on the night of the Mitterrand banquet was one of only a few times the two had met. Liebenberg had first met Mandela soon after he came out of jail and 'started making noises about the nationalisation of banks. And I, as a banker, didn't think that was a very clever idea so I asked to see him.'

He had met Manuel on more occasions, mostly when he was still head of the Department of Economic Planning (DEP) in the ANC. Manuel had addressed the executives of Nedcor one evening so persuasively, according to Liebenberg, they thought he was 'from the PR unit', not the economics unit.

Like Keys, Liebenberg praises the way that Mbeki and Mandela supported him. He was not a member of any caucus: he was in a political wilderness yet a key member of the new government. 'I saw myself as the financial director of an organisation.'

But what an organisation! The Budget deficit hovered near six per cent of GDP. Net government debt in 1995 was just over R244 billion. It had climbed since 1993 and now reached nearly half of GDP. This situation was aggravated by having to absorb the liabilities of the old Bantustan states and to cover losses on the Reserve Bank's forward book.[1] In addition to this burden, the new government had to pay nearly R15 billion in 'extraordinary transfers' to government pension funds to cover early retirements.

It would have been a nightmare for any finance minister. For a new government concerned to bridge racial inequalities and to spend money on education and welfare, it was even more daunting. The difference between expenditure on debt interest and education in the 1995/96 budget was a mere R4 billion. Manuel, then and in later years, would often remark how wrong it was to spend on 'yesterday and not tomorrow'.

Liebenberg began to 'talk that we must get the deficit down to three per cent'. He had no political clout, and did not attend caucus meetings, 'but Mbeki and Mandela really held their hand over me'. He got similar support from the three ANC ministers who dealt with economics: Manuel, Erwin, still deputy minister of finance, and Mboweni. 'The biggest pleasant surprise that I had was to walk into the cabinet room and see the determination of people to do the right thing.' He told his wife one night that although he had never known 'this Erwin fellow before, if I listen to what he says and he listens to what I say, and we're so close to one another, then I too must be a communist!'

In Liebenberg's first Budget, he had to equalise the tax system – married women were taxed more heavily than men. In doing so, 'we were short of something like R3 billion in our Budget that we had to make up,' said Liebenberg. It was the 'toughest' Budget. The government had to raise taxes. It could have repeated the 'one off' five per cent levy that Keys had used to kick-start the RDP but Liebenberg felt – and the ANC agreed – that to repeat a 'one off' would seriously dent its credibility.

And then there was the inherited profligacy of the old Bantustans. All of them were incorporated into the new provinces. Liebenberg and Erwin flew to Bisho one day to speak to provincial staff in the Eastern Cape about the overspend there. 'It was just too horrific.' They landed at the pompously named Bisho International Airport, the only airport in southern Africa with a snow plough because a European company had built it for the old Ciskei government to European standards. The provincial and local governments in the Eastern Cape had just voted themselves increases, which they were not authorised to do. Erwin spoke to them about the importance of containing expenditure, the start of a long engagement with the provinces that the Finance Ministry under Manuel would continue. Erwin, said Liebenberg, played a key role in getting all the provincial ministers for finance to 'toe the line'.

The state of the country's finances at the time left Liebenberg horrified.

'I was shocked,' he told me. 'Absolutely shocked. I came home one night and said to my wife, I don't know what I let my head into but this country is bankrupt.'

'Yes, it was,' agreed Gill Marcus, who was the first chair of the portfolio committee on finance in the post-apartheid Parliament. 'We were virtually in a debt trap ... we were virtually having to borrow to pay interest.'

Once the deficit was at the level it was, she told me, 'the argument that you grow the deficit doesn't hold, because if you grow the deficit you're borrowing more, if you borrow more you can't even meet your interest repayments'.

Like Manuel she was not an economist. But she also has a keen intelligence and a workhorse ethic. Her lack of formal training advantaged her, she believed. 'I could look at the numbers and say, guys, it's simply not doable. We're borrowing more, we're going to have to borrow to pay interest and you're not going to be able to deliver a single thing that we need to deliver.'

Marcus was born in Johannesburg in 1949, the second of four children. Her parents Nathan and Molly were both ANC activists and her father was restricted in terms of the Suppression of Communism Act in the 1960s. In 1970, while she was studying at Witwatersrand University, her family decided to leave the country. Her parents were granted passports to visit Germany and England on business. 'Why don't we all go?' they suggested. So they did. And because their entry into Britain was contingent on them being self-employed, they set up a little sandwich bar in Knightsbridge.

In 1970, Marcus began to do volunteer work for the ANC's London office and a few years later was appointed full time. She produced a weekly news briefing on behalf of the ANC, which was distributed at the United Nations and to parliamentarians in Britain and Europe.

Marcus became a significant voice of the ANC in London, so much so that in 1982 the undercover police agent Craig Williamson planted a bomb in her office. It was only by sheer chance that she was not there that day. The bomb went off at 9am on a Sunday, usually a time when she would have been working. It was placed next to her office wall. But there was an anti-apartheid march in London planned for that Sunday and her mother suggested that she work late on the Saturday night, instead of going in to the office as she usually did on Sunday mornings. After the blast, Williamson sent her a postcard that said: 'Oh, you're still around?'[2]

Marcus returned to South Africa in May 1990, after being summoned from London to Lusaka with two days' notice in February. She was due to come back a week later with Joel Netshitenzhe and Jeremy Cronin, a leading member of the South African Communist Party, but the authorities declined to let her in. The trio returned three months later and found themselves lost in Johannesburg, now a new city to them. They slept on people's floors and had hardly any money, and were so busy 'we didn't come out of the office for months'. She set about re-establishing the ANC's communications office in South Africa. She had not thought about economics and had little to do with economic policy in the interregnum when Manuel was appointed head of the DEP.

She was elected to Parliament in 1994 and opted to join the finance committee. 'I thought about it and said, you know I've done communications all my life but that's not the challenges going forward … If I want to under-stand the challenges it's actually going to be about the economy.' She also joined the audit committee that scrutinised government finance.* Probably because of her legendary diligence, she was elected chairperson of the finance committee.

There was no Budget then – Derek Keys presented the first Budget of the new government later that year – but as the new MPs 'knew nothing about it', she decided that every government department needed to appear before them to explain what they did and how much it cost. This would establish the authority of Parliament. Some were refractory, especially those departments long used to secrecy, such as the police and the defence force.

But their recalcitrance did not faze Marcus. 'I discovered the committee had in its original powers, powers of subpoena and I simply said to people: Fine, you *will* come and we *will* ask you, and therefore we could create that climate of accountability from the outset.'

The finance committee also began to look at tax issues. Derek Keys had appointed the lawyer Michael Katz to investigate South Africa's tax system and Katz told the committee there was a gap of some R19 billion in revenue that could be collected if systems were better. It was clear, said Marcus, that the issue was not about raising taxes but about better administration.

It was also clear to her then that the government had 'very narrow room

---

* This became the Standing Committee on Public Accounts or SCOPA.

to move'. There was no blank slate on which to write the future.

LESS THAN A YEAR after Liebenberg was appointed, in the winter of 1995, Manuel had another call from Mandela, asking him to come to his office. Thabo Mbeki was there when he arrived. As Manuel recalls it, Mandela said: 'Chaps, look, Chris has come to me and says he needs to leave.' He had agreed to do the job for a year and the year was up, but Mandela had asked him to table the next Budget in March 1996. Liebenberg had agreed 'that that was fair to him and fair to the country'. But when that's done, said Mandela, 'I think I must appoint Trevor. I think the world is ripe for an ANC appointee.'

He asked Mbeki if he agreed. He replied, 'Yes, Mr President.' He asked Manuel whether he would take the job. Manuel said, 'Yes, Mr President.'

Mandela said he would tell Liebenberg but that it was critical to 'keep this thing under wraps'. And, 'Trevor,' he advised, 'you must use this time wisely to learn about what happens in the Finance Ministry.'

It did not come as any surprise to Mbeki. He had earmarked Manuel as an economics minister before the 1994 elections and had suggested his initial appointment to Trade and Industry.[3] And there was an urgency now to have a politician at the helm of the Finance Ministry, one with political capital to wield, if the government was to make the necessary reforms. Liebenberg said he had recommended the appointments precisely: Manuel as minister, Marcus as deputy minister and Erwin to Trade and Industry. 'I feel quite proud that the recommendations that I made were followed. Because Madiba said to me, if you go, who should take over from you ... and the recommendations that I made to him were what he followed in the end ... So I felt quite chuffed. But I'm not that naive. It's not because I suggested it. But my analysis of the situation was in line with the party's analysis.'

Mandela told Liebenberg he would appoint Manuel, but no one else knew. They kept the secret for nearly seven months. 'Which was absolutely amazing,' said Liebenberg. 'That cabinet was porous as a sieve with news ... You had a cabinet meeting on Wednesday and on Thursday you read the press ... in inverted commas are things that people said. I was absolutely shocked that this could happen.'

One reason was that the cabinet of the Government of National Unity comprised ministers of three parties – the ANC, the IFP and the National Party. Frequently the media was used as a weapon to advance party interests in cabinet. But this secret stayed secret.

Manuel took Mandela's advice and spent hours during the ensuing months with Liebenberg. 'Chris and I would meet privately, at his house, we'd go out for tea, go out for lunch ... For the Budget that was tabled in 1996, I knew all the details, but not the speech, because that would have put me in touch.' (Liebenberg's officials, who crafted the speech, would have known who was reading it.) He didn't go the IMF annual meeting in 1995, in case questions were asked about his presence. It was the first meeting he'd missed since 1991.

In the 1996/97 Budget debate, Liebenberg told Parliament that he'd dented the debt, to the extent, as he put it, that the deficit fell from 91 per cent of the amount allocated to the RDP to 68 per cent in two years. 'We cannot at this stage spend ourselves to prosperity,' he warned. 'We are not heading for a debt trap but the margin of error is very small. We only have to miss some of our milestones and we will be in a so-called debt trap.' Government spending had dropped from 33 per cent to 31 per cent of the GDP in the past three years, and the deficit had almost halved. 'So I think the government has done the right things.'[4]

Importantly, Liebenberg had scrapped the financial rand – a parallel exchange rate designed to lure investors in the time of sanctions. 'I was a little nervous for a while because we expected the currency to take a significant drop, but it was not nearly as bad as we thought it could be,' he told me.

Many parliamentarians were not happy at the cut in expenditure, or the reduced deficit, and some complained to him during his term. But, oddly, the same critics had then asked him for personal financial advice. One even asked him to be his financial adviser. 'With their own money they trusted me, but not with the country's!'

There was no question that the path Liebenberg took was firmly backed by the new government, not least Mandela and Mbeki. When Mandela rose to speak at the end of the debate, he commented that the government 'has demonstrated its commitment to the pursuit of goals which the country has set in order to ensure that we handle the public finances in a manner that is consistent with the objectives spelled out in the RDP'.

He showered praise on Liebenberg, to the extent that when Liebenberg replied, he said: 'I wish my mother were here.'

'I had tears in my eyes when I walked back to my seat,' he told me.

But Mandela had something else to say, and he did it with his customary languid humour. He thanked Liebenberg and wished 'my dear colleague and friend, good health, happiness and success in all your future endeavours.[5] To replace the Honourable Chris Liebenberg as minister of finance of the democratic republic, I have chosen – allow me to pause for a sip of water – I have chosen the Honourable Trevor Manuel who is presently serving as minister of Trade and Industry.'

Erwin would take Manuel's place at the helm of Trade and Industry and Marcus would be Manuel's deputy. And because the ANC now had one too many ministers in the Government of National Unity, 'I have decided to assign the Honourable Pallo Jordan other tasks outside the cabinet.' Jordan, one of the most outspoken of the ANC intellectuals and leaders, was clearly taken aback. He had been minister of Posts, Telecommunications and Broadcasting. It was the only blight on Manuel's big day. After all, he remarked to me later that day, he had even named his second son after Jordan.

'His place ... will be taken by – I am no longer thirsty – the Honourable Jay Naidoo.' Naidoo, the former COSATU leader, had been 'minister without portfolio' running the RDP office. That office would be closed, said Mandela, and its funds relocated to the Ministry of Finance. 'I have taken this decision because of the evolution in Government ... as a result of which the various departments of State are better placed to focus their activities on the realisation of objectives spelled out in the Reconstruction and Development Programme. I trust that this change will help to concentrate our attention on the fact that the RDP is not the responsibility of some specialised department but the compass, the lodestar, which guides all Government activities.'[6]

In later years, the closure of the RDP office was often conflated with the introduction of the macroeconomic stabilisation policy known as GEAR. In fact that policy was only introduced three months later but the two events were woven together in a narrative that was to put Manuel (and Mbeki) squarely in the centre as villains of the tale.

IN THE WEEKS THAT followed Mandela's announcement there were different reactions. Mostly, his ANC colleagues were enthusiastic. 'I thought it was brilliant,' said Barbara Hogan who served on the parliamentary finance committee. 'Because of all the ministers around the economy, he had been the most focused in Trade and Industry.'

Not everyone shared this view. The rand began to tumble. 'Do you know where your office is?' Mbeki asked Marcus after she and Manuel were sworn in. 'Yes? Well, you better get there because the rand is falling.'

'And we didn't come out for six weeks,' she said.

The rand lost more than 2 per cent of its value soon after Manuel was appointed and then kept going south, losing 9,4 per cent in the next month.[7]

Manuel took office on 4 April. Shortly after that, he held a press conference, partly to reassure the financial press, some of whom doubted his ability to manage the economy. The sharp fall in the currency after his appointment reflected that doubt.

Manuel has rarely played a race card, nor tried to elicit sympathy on the basis of his background. Throughout his days in the UDF, later in the ANC and government, he always behaved with an expectation that he would be afforded the respect of an equal, no matter whether he dealt with the police, with fractious comrades, business leaders or international financiers. But the refrain in the discourse that he 'was not a trained economist' rankled and at his first press conference as finance minister, the attitude of several of the journalists, as he parodied it, was: 'Who the hell is this coming to look after our money?'

'It was one of those terrible press conferences – and you know the questions! Financial journalists can be very cocky, (they) like to show off.' But he, too, was 'cocky', he conceded later and what could have been a gentle spark became abrasive.

At the time, the rand was falling steadily, confirming a narrative of failure before the job had even begun. When he was asked a question about the rand, Manuel responded with an answer about Purchasing Power Parity. He used the acronym: PPP. 'So what's PPP?' a journalist asked. 'Define it.'

'Now, you know, it starts like that and it keeps going, keeps going and they say, you're the finance minister, are you going to lift exchange controls?'

'Who's asking this?' he asked.

'The markets,' replied one.

'And I say *what* is this market, you know. And they say, the *market*! And I say what is this *market*? What is this amorphous entity that sent you here, huh! *Who* sent you here? On whose behalf do you speak about these issues?'

Recounting this years later, he still thought it was 'exceedingly glib and arrogant for journalists to purport to be this market'. But then 'things spun, and it was very tough'.

The phrase 'amorphous markets' was thrown back at Manuel for years, sometimes seriously, often in affectionate but patronising jest. 'Look how much he's learned,' was the subtext.

426

Ramos, who in later years often had a steadying influence on Manuel's volatile temper, was sympathetic to his predicament at the time. As soon as she heard the reporter asking him to define purchasing power parity, she thought: 'What a stupid question, actually.'

And the minute Manuel had finished his sentence about the amorphous markets, 'I could see from people's faces that they hadn't got the point and that this was going to be an issue. You can see … you've been around financial journalists for long enough to know exactly what angle they're going to take. They were looking for something. They needed to say that this person who's just been appointed minister of finance knows nothing.'

Oddly, the then deputy president, Thabo Mbeki, with a master's degree in economics from Sussex University, had said much the same thing about the markets just two days earlier. He was speaking at the 120th birthday celebrations of the *Cape Times*, a gathering that included a number of journalists. 'Over the recent past, including this very day, we have watched as the rand has done somewhat of a mad dance, gyrating to the music of a band of faceless, odourless and non-corporeal musicians who are described as the market.'

The market? Faceless, odourless, and non-corporeal? Sounded suspiciously like 'amorphous'. But no one paid any attention.

The reason is contained in Mbeki's next sentence: 'As I tried to listen to the music this band has been playing, I thought I heard lyrics which contained the refrain – this, after all, is just another African country! … All this happens because there seems to be an accusation … that it cannot be that a majority black government can properly manage an economy as sophisticated as ours is. After all, look at the rest of Africa!'[8]

But he was 'only' the deputy president then and he could say it. Manuel was the new minister of finance and he, in the atmosphere that Mbeki so aptly described at the time, could not.

SOME SENIOR OFFICIALS in the Department of Finance were also less than enthusiastic about Manuel's appointment. One was the director-general, Estiaan Calitz. On the day Mandela was to make the announcement about Manuel's appointment, Manuel and Liebenberg were the first two people to arrive in the National Assembly. Liebenberg whispered to him: '*Boetie*, you owe me one.'

'Why?' asked Manuel.

Liebenberg replied that he had told Calitz he was leaving, and Calitz had asked who his replacement would be. On discovering it was Manuel, he asked for his contract to be renegotiated so that he could leave his post earlier. 'I'm sure that's what Minster Manuel would want as well,' replied Liebenberg.

When Manuel moved to the Department of Finance offices in Vermeulen Street in the centre of Pretoria, he found the same tattiness of the Trade and Industry offices, with one difference. Whereas at the DTI there had been no pictures on the walls, here there was a gallery of pictures of every finance minister from Jan Hofmeyr, who had served under Jan Smuts during the Second World War, to Barend du Plessis, the last finance minister in the apartheid era.*

But no picture of Derek Keys, and none of Liebenberg. 'Those pictures must come down,' Manuel told his senior officials. Calitz replied that the pictures were 'part of our history'.

'They may be part of your history, Estiaan,' said Manuel, 'but they're not part of mine.'

When Calitz objected that he could not 'destroy state property', Manuel retorted that if he was so attached to the pictures he could take them home. 'You pack them along with your other things. You can put them up in your study at home. I will sign them out to you and explain to the auditor general.'

It was soon clear that the relationship between Manuel and his most senior official was not going to work, not even until August which was when Calitz intended to leave. 'I don't want to split the loyalties of the staff,' he told Calitz. 'And I'd rather have a clean plate.'

There was a handful of new people in the department already, but they were dispersed and not very powerful. Andrew Donaldson had been there three years and had begun the first serious work on financing the reconstruction programme. Ismail Momoniat had joined in 1995, and was 'miserable ... I was given nothing to do', and not even a parking place, he complained.

Maria Ramos was recruited in mid-1995 to become deputy director-general (DDG) to an apparently reluctant Calitz. She had gone back to LSE in the South African summer of 1994/95 to teach and to start work on a doctorate. Erwin and Manuel urged her to apply for the position of DDG, but instead

---

* Technically, Derek Keys was the last finance minister under the old government, but he was appointed in 1992, in the interregnum stage when negotiations towards democracy had already begun.

428

Calitz had offered her a post as a deputy director, about five rungs from the top in the bureaucratic hierarchy. 'I said thanks, but no thanks,' and she went back to London.

But Erwin, at Manuel's urging, raised the question of her appointment again with Calitz.

'This is time to put your foot down,' Manuel told Erwin. Manuel knew then that he was to take over the ministry, and he wanted to establish his own team. Erwin's insistence worked. Calitz agreed that Ramos should apply for the DDG post. Cabinet approved her appointment and within a few months she manoeuvred herself out of her teaching contract with the London School of Economics and returned to South Africa. It helped, too, that Liebenberg was fond of her and admired her. 'My little daughter,' he still calls her.

But nothing was easy. Ramos arrived at the Finance Department to find she had no office. So she sat in Calitz's because he was in Cape Town. 'I asked for the organogram. There was no one there to tell me what my job was going to be – nothing.' She called in various people whose names appeared on the organogram. One of them was a man from human resources. He walked into the office where she was sitting, and remarked: 'What a big office for such a little girl.'

Ramos is renowned for her charm towards journalists but is brutal if she thinks the situation requires it. The HR chap went on stress leave soon after that, as she puts it, and did not last much longer in the department.

But recalcitrant personalities were just the tip of the iceberg. There were much bigger problems. One was that government expenditure fell within the purview of the Department of State Expenditure, not the Department of Finance. Information flows were slow, so the department that drew up the Budget for the following year had little idea what expenditure was for the preceding one. Another was cash and debt management. Partly because the apartheid government had been under siege, it borrowed as much money as it thought it needed at the start of the financial year, most of it from the government pension fund. Andre Roux, who joined later in 1996, and became head of the Budget Office, explained that government would borrow for all its cash needs at about an 18 per cent interest rate, then put it in the bank at 12 or 13 per cent. Like borrowing money for a car or a house before you actually buy them and paying the interest. 'It was just a crazy system, but nobody said "this is madness".'

The first person to do so was Derek Keys, who stopped it, and then

Liebenberg, who made further reforms. But the lack of information between expenditure and budgeting was still apparent.

Calitz, Manuel's reluctant director-general, also introduced important reforms. It was he who equalised social grants in 1993. A socially, if not politically conservative man, 'he had the courage to try to engage in the challenges of transition ... There's a fair amount of criticism of Calitz that he wasn't accommodating, but I think in his own way, given who he was, he was forward-looking,' said Donaldson.

But it was not enough for Manuel. He needed, as he said, a 'clean plate'.

Before he began an overhaul of the department, Manuel and Ramos went on a short trip to Europe and the United States with Liebenberg. Liebenberg had offered to introduce Manuel to central bankers, investors, ministers and financiers in London, Zurich and Frankfurt, and New York and Washington.

Would-be investors were both charmed, and puzzled. Some wanted more certainty on economic policy. 'Everyone has a pretty good idea of what the problems are and it does not take a genius to foresee the dangers of continuing to lollygag around key decisions concerning the growth and competitiveness of the economy when nearly half the black working-age population under 30 is chronically unemployed,' wrote Simon Barber, the acerbic but perceptive *Business Day* columnist from Washington.[9]

Barber was also unamused by Ambassador Franklin Sonn's joke that Liebenberg had come to hold the new minister's hand. 'It was not very funny. The last thing South Africa needed last week was a finance minister perceived as needing to have his hand held.'[10]

Liebenberg, though, believed that many investors and bankers were suspicious of politicians and 'suspicious of what might happen once politicians start getting hold of the budget. So I wouldn't say there was a fear, but there was a doubt. But I had no doubt that Trevor would handle it and handle it well.'

But mostly investors and bankers were intrigued by this somewhat odd trio. In New York, Liebenberg told me, the billionaire investor, currency speculator and philanthropist George Soros had insisted on meeting them. At first Liebenberg was not keen. Eventually he relented, and the three of them had dinner with Soros in his Fifth Avenue apartment. A few weeks later, a banking colleague of Liebenberg's said he had met someone who worked for Soros. '(Soros's employee) said he had met these three South Africans. A funny lot. There was this Portuguese fellow, Manuel (pronounced the

Portuguese way, ManWELL), a Brazilian girl, Ramos, and this little Jewish guy, Liebenstein.'

It may have been an inadvertent reference to the 'rainbowness' of the new South Africa, but it also showed South Africans exactly how little was known about their country in the tough world of the international markets. They may have been amorphous, but they were quick to form an impression, even if it was the wrong one.

The impression Manuel left on Liebenberg was this: that he was a man who combined an enduring kindness with an impenetrable toughness. 'He's one of the toughest politicians I know,' said Liebenberg. At times he was embarrassed by the ferocity with which Manuel attacked political opponents in Parliament. 'But as a man, as an individual, he can be ... sensitive and tender.' Liebenberg's observations arose out of a letter that Manuel wrote to him as the trip came to an end. 'These past 8 days have been a period of intense and accelerated learning for me,' Manuel wrote on the notepaper of the Watergate Hotel in Washington. 'In a sense, your "contacts" were by the way. What was far, far more impressive was learning the real Chris Liebenberg – the quiet, unassuming, humble, gifted individual ... South Africa is a special place and South Africans a great nation. Having Madiba helps. I am sure though that it is people like you and Elly that inspire our greatness.'[11]

Manuel's note echoed what Mandela had said in Parliament on Liebenberg's retirement. But it was a letter that showed something more: Manuel's awareness of the need to build a new country out of the fractious strands of the past. The 'Portuguese fellow', the 'Brazilian girl', and the 'little Jewish guy' were an indelible part of this new world on the southern tip of Africa.

CHAPTER 26

The outsider

FOR MANY MONTHS AFTER his appointment as finance minister, a sense of 'oneness' escaped Manuel. On the contrary, he confessed, 'I was the outsider. It was a kind of existential problem. I was the Camus outsider, really the outsider.' First, there was the alienation from the financial press.

He was the outsider internationally, too. His trip to the Western capitals with Liebenberg had been partly successful, but many investors had responded warily to the new South African finance minister, and the currency continued to roll downhill. 'Nobody is asking for a perfect solution,' wrote *Business Day*'s Barber. 'All that is needed is commitment to a credible programme, including a schedule for the elimination of exchange controls, which shows government is intent on setting up an environment where investors, foreign and resident, will feel happy holding rands … The fact that Manuel was unable to offer anything approaching such a statement in his meeting with bankers and investors here last week undoubtedly took a toll.'[1]

But an even bigger sense of alienation came, not from local business, not from the financial press, nor from Washington bankers. It came from inside his own constituency and was to start as a murmur and grow into a crescendo in the following two years. It was sparked, ironically, by doing the very thing that Barber had slated him for not doing: putting a stabilisation plan on the table that would help steady an economy ailing under the burdens of debt, lack of competitiveness, and unemployment.

Actually, the debate that raged between the government – in the incarnation of Manuel – and the union movement and the ANC's left-wing often hinged around just one aspect in the plan that was tabled, albeit a key aspect: the reduction of the deficit. But in coming years the bitter tone in the arguments around economic policy were more over the fact that the unions felt slighted by what they thought was a lack of consultation. This became a lingering resentment.

For the first 18 months after the introduction of the economic plan, Manuel felt that 'I was not even the ham in the sandwich. I (was) just dragged out of the sandwich, abandoned by left and right.'

'It's interesting,' he told me, 'because these are not factors that you have control over. (My) activism was born of circumstances. I approached things in a particular way. I was harder than the rest. If my route into activism had been through universities, it may have been different. If I'd opted to go into exile when I wanted to be nothing but a soldier, I may have come back as a functionary or as a bodyguard. An intelligence operative! In many respects that period of the 80s was the furnace.'

Was he telling me that his emotions and his political sense had been soldered by this period, that he'd grown a sufficiently thick political skin to ride out a wave of unpopularity? Or that the intensive community organisation he'd undertaken in the hostile environment of the 1980s had made it easier for him to empathise with recalcitrant constituencies than it was for many of the better qualified ANC leaders who had returned from exile? Perhaps the latter. He may have had a tough hide, but in the end the rousing union songs, reworded to decry the new economic policy and him in particular, the personal attacks, particularly the label 'neo-liberal', one of the worst pejoratives in the lexicon of the left, needled through that skin. 'Things had really become very, very ugly.'

Unlike Camus's hapless anti-hero Mersault, a man outside *himself*, who faced down the world, and even his own impending death with a stubborn emotional indifference, Manuel was hurt by the jibes in the long battle of nerves that followed.

At one stage he did something quite of character. He went to Thabo Mbeki, then deputy president, and offered to resign. In writing. He said he 'was happy to go because the ANC and the Alliance (with COSATU and the Communist Party) was bigger than Trevor Manuel'.

Mbeki told him not even to think about it. 'This is fundamental.'

So he bore the political weight of the government's new economic policy. Manuel was not part of the policy's conception. But less than three months after his appointment, it became his task to deliver it.

A FEW MONTHS BEFORE Manuel walked into the Finance Department as minister, a team of economists had begun working on a macroeconomic stabilisation plan. They had been pulled together by Alec Erwin, then deputy minister. The project was coordinated by Andre Roux, who was still at the Development Bank, and Iraj Abedian, then an economist at the University of Cape Town. Ramos, the newly appointed deputy director-general, drove it.

It began in late 1995 and came amid two other policy documents, one produced by COSATU (*Social Equity and Job Creation*) and another by the business sector in the form of the South Africa Foundation (*Growth for All*). Thabo Mbeki, whose office had taken over much of the economic policy work, seemed irritated by both. Jeremy Cronin, who was appointed deputy general secretary of the Communist Party in 1995, summed up his attitude thus: 'Who are *they* to tell *us*?'

At the time, Cronin himself lambasted business's plan for suggesting less government involvement in the economy, a reduction of government spending, deregulation and privatisation. 'These measures will strip government of any effective strategic role in the economy,' he wrote. 'We have just installed the beginnings of democracy and already we are being asked to replace elected government by an unelected market.'[2]

The proposals were heartless in the face of the damage that apartheid had caused. The *Growth for All* authors, wrote Cronin, were 'horrified' that among the recipients of state old age pensions were those who live in households with per capita income close to or above the minimum living level. Actually, these were very poor households indeed: to qualify for the 'minimum living level' in 1996, per capita income in a household had to be just R168 a month, a notion Cronin described as 'barbaric'.[3]

Labour, in the form of three major trade union federations, the largest being COSATU, responded with its own plan two months later. It was poles apart from the business document. It proposed more government involvement – not less – in, for instance, job creation through huge public works programmes. It wanted an end to job cuts in the public sector. It wanted to boost demand in the domestic market by increasing wages in return for increased productivity. It vehemently opposed the *Growth for All* proposal of a low-wage sector to create more jobs. The unions, not surprisingly, wanted more labour market regulation, not less, a higher deficit and taxes at 55 per cent for those earning more than R200 000 a year.[4]

The government itself produced an economic plan known as the 'Six Pack', introduced by Chris Liebenberg in October 1994 shortly after he was appointed. It was a simple plan, designed to save 'tens of billions of rands to help the RDP and reduce the government debt mountain'.[5] Its key proposals involved 'belt-tightening' by cutting and reprioritising state expenditure, examining privatisation options that would release money for the RDP, and trimming down the public service.

But it was not sufficient to calm international investors as Alec Erwin discovered when he and Liebenberg went to Europe to raise the first global dollar issue for the new government. No amount of good sentiment towards South Africa would persuade investors to part with their money if they were not sure it would be safe.

'We spoke and we spoke,' recalled Erwin about their meeting with a major Italian pension fund. And then (he imitates the Italian accent) one of the fund managers, responded thus: 'Of course we *love-a* South Africa. Everybody *love-a* South Africa. Not to *love-a* South Africa is like shooting the Red Cross.' Then the sentiment vanished. 'I deal with money,' she told them. And what made them think that within a few weeks or months, all the prime lenders would not want to sell their South African treasury bonds because nobody knew quite what the country's policies were. 'And then I'm sitting with a bond worth nothing.'

Likewise, in early 1995, this time in Scotland, where he and Manuel (who was still Trade and Industry Minister) tried to sell a 10-year Treasury bond to the Scottish Widows' Pension Fund. The Scottish Widows' Pension Fund, despite its quaint name, is huge. In 2007 it had an investment portfolio of nearly £98 billion.

'We got *hammered*!' recalled Erwin. 'We just got criticised by everybody, because they said, what is this macro balance you're talking about? What do you mean? What's your policy on the exchange rate? What's your policy on the interest rate? What's your inflation policy? And we just realised that we couldn't answer that successfully. So our credibility in the capital markets was low.'

For a country faced with a massive task of reconstruction and instituting racial parity it was critical to be able to borrow money on the most favourable terms. As Manuel had discovered in his brief two weeks at the World Bank in 1992, the more risk associated with a country, the higher the interest that country will pay. With debt service costs – that's just the interest – at R28,6 billion, or 18,6 per cent of the 95/96 budget, it was a cost the new government could ill afford.[6]

It was not surprising, then, that both the government and the ANC decided to put their minds to a coherent macroeconomic stabilisation policy. In late 1995 the ANC called for the formation of a 'single, central, macroeconomic authority'.

'The need for macroeconomic authority at a central level cannot be over-emphasised,' it said in a document entitled: *One Year of Government of National Unity.*[7] A year before, government had appointed a four-man committee to draft economic policy guidelines.[8] Manuel was on that committee, as were Liebenberg, Mboweni and RDP Minister Jay Naidoo. Mbeki's office was tasked with coordinating economic policy.[9]

There was an attempt at formulating an economic policy in early 1996, called *The national growth and development strategy.* It was initiated by the RDP office. Andre Roux, then at the Development Bank of Southern Africa, worked on it. Roux, who earned postgraduate degrees in maths and economics from both Oxford and Cambridge, went on to become one of the most effective managers in the Department of Finance. His work, his intellect and his ideas merged closely with Ramos's, and the two worked energetically to overhaul the budget and drive the new economic policy. Mbeki sank the first economic policy that came out in February 1996, Roux told me, 'and quite rightly so because it was a completely incoherent document'.

It was effectively a 'wish list' cobbled together from various departmental inputs with little emphasis on either growth or development. Ramos had also voiced her objections to it.[10]

In late 1995 a team began working on the policy that later became known as the *Growth, Employment and Redistribution* policy (GEAR). It was pushed, largely by Mbeki, with Erwin taking political responsibility for it in the early stages. Driven by Ramos, Roux and Abedian, it also drew in officials from the

Department of Trade and Industry (there is a lengthy section on tax holidays and incentives in the document), from the Reserve Bank, 'a few funnies from the Labour Department', and academics.[11]

The team worked quickly. By early 1996, the policy began to take shape. Later, as the fall-out with the unions grew bitter, there were accusations that the policy was engineered by the World Bank and the IMF and informed by the 'Washington Consensus'. There were, in fact, two World Bank economists involved. One was Richard Ketley, who went on to work at the Treasury. The other was Luiz Pereira da Silva. According to Roux, he was one of the most left-wing thinkers in the group. 'There was nothing World Bankish about Luiz,' said Roux. Later, he joined the Finance Ministry in Brazil in the government of Lula, the ardent trade unionist who became president after Cardoso.

The document that eventually emerged is both forthright and complex. It spells out a vision of job creation, service provision, redistribution in favour of the poor, and a fast-growing economy. The 'core elements' of the strategy were outlined as budget reform to 'strengthen the redistributive thrust of expenditure', a faster reduction in the fiscal deficit to contain South Africa's burdensome debt obligations, an exchange rate policy 'to keep the real effective rate stable at a competitive level', and a relaxation of exchange controls. It also recommended reductions in tariffs, tax incentives to 'stimulate new investment in competitive and labour-absorbing projects', a restructuring of state assets, an expanded infrastructure programme, and 'structured flexibility' within a collective bargaining system.[12]

Several of the economists who worked on the policy were skilled technicians who could model scenarios based on a variety of possible numbers. So they modelled a vision of what South Africa might look like if the government were to increase the deficit by boosting expenditure. A higher fiscal deficit would boost growth in the short term but would also 'reproduce the historical pattern of cyclical growth and decline'. Employment would rise in the short term, mainly because the public sector would expand, but real wages would be eroded by higher inflation. Interest rates would also rise because of the extent of government borrowing and 'in the present climate of instability ... would precipitate a balance of payments crisis ... Without attention to more deep-rooted reforms, there is no possibility of sustainable accelerated growth.'[13]

Although the strategy called for a 'competitive' exchange rate – to boost non-mineral exports which it saw as the driver of growth and employment in the economy – it was trumped by the markets, amorphous as they were, which sent the volatile rand on a continuous downward slide.

The rand first lost value early in 1996 when an ambulance was seen outside Tuynhuis, the president's Cape Town office, and wild rumours ran through the currency markets about Mandela's health. Then De Klerk's National Party announced in March that it would leave the Government of National Unity. That sent another jitter through the markets. And Manuel's appointment and his remarks about the 'amorphous markets' accelerated the slide.

Much of the discourse that followed GEAR, even years later, was that this was a classic 'free-market' or 'neo-liberal' policy that had 'replaced' the RDP and effectively sold out the ANC's left-wing allies. But the policy incorporated strong elements of state intervention to boost job creation: 'supply-side industrial measures' to contribute to investment; public investment to upgrade municipal infrastructure, and hefty redistribution through state expenditure and training policies.

The substance of the policy – apart from the issue of the deficit – was rarely the subject of rigorous debate. But it was the 'process' – that word that had irritated Mboweni so much during the transition period when he dealt with the unionists – that alienated many key constituencies within the ANC.

When I repeated Alec Erwin's story to Cronin about the hammering he had faced at the hands of the expressive Italian fund manager and by the more dour managers of the Scottish Widows' Pension Fund, Cronin said he understood the international pressures the economics ministers in the ANC were facing. But, he asked: 'Why couldn't Alec have come and said to the NEC, this is what investors are saying? And why couldn't we have had a debate about that?'

Manuel's political skill would be tested to its limits in trying both to contain the fall-out and 'stay the course'. He was not altogether successful. But his critics in the Communist Party and the union movement acknowledge the attempts. While Mbeki, said Cronin, was trying to use the debates around GEAR to 'sharpen the conflict ... Trevor was trying to win us over'. More than a decade after GEAR was introduced, after the Polokwane conference when Mbeki was defeated in the leadership race, Manuel was still engaging, still debating, still arguing. Many of those who criticised GEAR were acutely aware of the need, as Cronin put it, 'to disentangle Trevor, and Trevor's role in macroeconomic strategy from a broader strategy that was the Mbeki strategy'.

But few doubt the immense courage it took to drive an economic policy of fiscal austerity at a time when most South Africans had emerged from a deep and long period of deprivation. Manuel himself had to be persuaded that it was the correct route to take at a time when the debt burden was so severe it threatened to overwhelm political independence. 'I think initially he was a bit lukewarm,' Roux said of Manuel. 'But maybe he just didn't want to give us an easy ride.'

'I needed to ask questions because I needed to understand what the hell this thing was about,' Manuel told me. He first met the team at the Development Bank, where Roux was based. Erwin and Mboweni were also there. 'They walked us through this issue called the balance of payments constraint. And it was quite a scary story but one that I don't want to pretend now that I understood in the detail.' This was within days of his appointment. The numbers convinced him: South Africa's economic growth would remain on the boom-and-bust cycle of the past so long as growth depended on imports. But more than that, he had come into the debate with 'my own issues about not wanting to get the country into hock with the Bank or the Fund. I come with my own issues about the Washington Consensus, all of those things I bring with me, so there's a kind of abstracted policy discourse, something that sits in my head that is hard to articulate: I know what we *don't* want; it's harder to see what we do.'

The road ahead was also muddied by a rand that was 'tanking', to use Roux's expression. Manuel, anxious about the currency, asked for a meeting with Mbeki. He, Ramos and Gill Marcus went to his house in Pretoria one evening, as the rand threatened to break R4 to the dollar. Mbeki's response was: 'So?[14]

'One of us, probably Maria, tried to explain that this was a psychological barrier, because once it passed four, five was in reach and then six, and then …'

Mbeki interrupted: 'Whose psychology is that?' He calmed them sufficiently to dissuade them from reacting precipitously. Manuel said he began to understand then 'just how fallible those kind of indicators are and how they can mess you up'.

More importantly, he realised that the ANC government needed a 'policy response' to a crisis that went much deeper than the rand's roller coaster ride.

For Marcus it was also manifestly clear. The debt crisis had become real to her when she chaired the portfolio committee on finance in Parliament. Debt service costs were swallowing large amounts of money that should have been put to better use to clear the backlog of inequality. It would take time, of course, she said, 'but if we didn't do that we were likely to land up in the hands of the IMF because we would not have the resources. And then you are punished. And we certainly had not worked this hard for our liberation to hand it over to the IMF.'

The financial crisis focused their senses. Had the currency continued to decline, said Marcus, the country may not have been able to pay its debts. 'We were getting to that point ... So we had to put something on the table and we had to do it very quickly. And it was not complete in the sense of doing all the research that you needed but it was at a sufficient point to give a stabilising effect and that's why it was handled the way it was. Everyone forgets the context in which that was. Was it perfect? By no means. But it gave you a framework to operate in; and it stabilised; it gave us goals.'

The awkward meeting with the Scottish Widows' Pension Fund had been a 'big education' for Manuel. He had gone with Erwin and Chris Stals, then Governor of the Reserve Bank. The two newcomers to the world of international finance had looked to Stals as the more experienced. But when the fund managers had asked them what the new government's inflation policy was, Stals replied, in Manuel's recollection: 'I'm a central banker; I only rest when inflation is zero.'

Bullshit, said the managers, or words to that effect.

'So it was clear,' said Manuel, 'that trying to be more Catholic than the Pope didn't work either. You needed more rational responses.'

THE POLICY TEAM WORKED hard through May, often late into the night. They thought then, as Roux put it, 'this thing was real'. The pressure to produce a coherent policy was now unrelenting. In mid-May they gathered at the Presidential Guest House in Pretoria, a stately old building that borders on a golf course on the estate where most of the cabinet live. Mbeki was there, as were Erwin and Mboweni. Manuel presented the details. It still did not have a name, and he himself seemed a little unsure of parts of it. 'I didn't feel that Trevor owned it,' said an official who was present. 'There wasn't a great deal of conviction in his presentation but he'd obviously cleared it beforehand, the details, with Mbeki. Mbeki's body language made it very clear that this thing was going to go. He made it very clear.'

440

Election campaigning on the West Coast, 1999. Maxwell Moss, Manuel's jailmate in Victor Verster prison, is seated in a wheelchair behind Manuel in the middle picture (Photographs courtesy Benny Gool/Oryx Archive)

Above: With Mandisi Mpahlwa, his deputy minister of finance, 1999-2004

Below: In a pensive mood

Above: With Cheryl Carolus at a party in her honour, 1995

Right: With Thabo Mbeki's mother, Epainette. The occasion was a visit by Mbeki to Ngcingwana, after being elected president of the ANC in December 1997

Bottom: Celebrating Archbishop Desmond Tutu's 70th birthday, 7 October 2001

(Photographs courtesy Benny Gool/Oryx Archive)

Left: With Jim Wolfensohn, former president of the World Bank, 2004

Below: With Thabo Mbeki

Bottom: With Nelson Mandela at the launch of the Homecoming of the Elders campaign in Distict Six. The then mayor of Cape Town, Nomaindia Mfeketo, is on the left, Ebrahim Rasool is standing behnd Mandela and Anwar Nagia is to Manuel's left (courtesy Benny Gool/Oryx Archive)

Top: Trevor Manuel in Camps Bay, 2006
(courtesy Trevor Manuel)

Above: Conducting the orchestra at the
International Investment Council meeting,
Cradle of Humankind

Left: Manuel became a keen golf enthusiast; this
photograph was taken in 2003 (courtesy Benny
Gool/Oryx Archive)

Above: Manuel gave the inaugural Global Economic Governance lecture at University College, Oxford, in March 2004. With him is Professor Ngaire Woods

Below: Receiving his first honorary doctorate at the University of Stellenbosch, 2001, with previous ministers of finance Derek Keys (back left) and Chris Liebenberg (centre). With them are Silma Keys, Elly Liebenberg and Philma Manuel (courtesy Anton Jordaan, SSFD)

Above: Trevor Manuel with his sons Govan, Pallo and Jaimé, 2004 (courtesy Trevor Manuel)

Below: Trevor Manuel and Maria Ramos at the presidential inauguration, 2004

Above: Janet Love, a former Vula operative who was among those arrested in 1990, with her baby and Trevor Manuel at Parliament

Right: Trevor Manuel with a visiting schoolboy outside Parliament, 1996

(Photographs courtesy Benny Gool/Oryx Archive)

Mboweni on the other hand looked uncomfortable with parts of the policy that proposed a 'regulated flexibility' in the labour markets. This was in a context of an official unemployment rate of 33 per cent, a productivity level that made the country far less competitive than its emerging counterparts in Asia, a lack of skills and training, and a situation where about one third of new jobs were being created in the 'unregulated low wage sector'.

Mboweni was then minister of labour. If he was discomfited (he himself did not put it that way when I spoke to him), it was because much of the labour market policy relied on a social compact with South Africa's powerful trade union movement, an important component of the ruling party alliance. He did concede to me that the 'GEAR process was difficult' and he thought that NEDLAC, the tripartite bargaining chamber, was not taken sufficiently seriously by the Finance Department, or by Manuel. The contradiction stemmed from what Moeletsi Mbeki had noted when he worked for COSATU before the 1994 elections: the unions believed that there would be an 'economic parliament' where their voice would be, at least equal with those of government and business. 'When one reflects what the difficulties were,' Mboweni told me, 'it (becomes) clear that expectations on both sides were not correct.'

There was no political discussion at that May meeting about whether the unions would like the new policy or not. The talk was purely about the economics of the plan and whether the econometric modelling stood up to scrutiny.

From the government's point of view, endless negotiation about what the deficit should be, or what the inflation policy should be, was not only not practical but not desirable. As Manuel had said six years previously, before he even entertained the notion of being finance minister, the ANC government had responsibilities broader than only the unions, or business, or those in the formal sector. It was government's job to govern, to take the decisions that were necessary to put the country on a path to growth. 'We needed, as a country, to take control of the situation,' said Ramos, 'and that's what we did.'

For Gill Marcus, the rookie deputy minister, there were few alternatives. Fortunately, the ANC had won the 1994 election with a huge majority. There was no threat of being unseated in a coming election. 'We had the leeway to take the harder decisions for the longer term.'

For Manuel, the political leader responsible for driving the new economic

441

policy, the next five years would be a relentless balance between trying to bring a myriad constituencies on board, while 'staying the course', even when he himself had moments of doubt.

JUST DAYS BEFORE MANUEL launched the new economic policy, it was still without a name. It had been decided to launch it during his departmental budget vote (not to be confused with the National Budget vote that happens in February). The departmental budget is the occasion when ministers report to parliament on their progress during the year and their plans for the next.

That winter, the days in the office got longer; the nights down to the minimum needed to nap briefly, shower and eat. Manuel's budget vote was on Friday, 14 June. By Wednesday, the team still didn't have a name for the policy. It was Marcus who eventually suggested they call it the Growth, Employment and Redistribution policy. It gave it an acronym too – GEAR. And then there was the speech that just didn't come right. No one slept the night before it was presented. The officials wrote and rewrote the speech, 'a hundred times', incorporating Manuel's comments. 'It just didn't flow,' said Roux. 'It was a horrible speech. It had nothing of the confidence of the subsequent budget speeches.'

The only cheer they had was the reaction from Mandela. Ramos had taken him the final document a few days before and he had sent it back with comprehensive notes in the margin – a clear sign that he'd read it all – and with a positive endorsement.

At the last moment, Manuel decided to change the word 'privatisation' (referring to state assets) in the speech to 'alienation'. He did so in the early hours of the Friday morning – around 5am – just before he gone home after another all-night session in the office. It was a small point, but it was a word he felt comfortable with, a word familiar in leftist discourse. He did not tell his officials, who saw it only in the final version of the speech as they sat on their benches in Parliament. As Manuel waited for his turn to speak, perched on a waiting bench between the president's bench and the officials' parliamentary box, they began to mouth and gesticulate to him. 'Who put that word in?' one of them asked. 'I did,' he mouthed back. Roux and Ramos were nervous. 'The markets aren't going to like it,' they whispered. 'Take it out.'

'There was a hiss and banter from their bench,' recalled Manuel. 'And I'm bloody nervous about this thing! They're saying "take it out, take it out". And the last thing I did before I stepped up to speak was to say no, no! It's a legal term for sale. Ask Johnny de Lange.' (De Lange, an ANC member and advocate, chaired the parliamentary justice committee.)

Mbeki was at the podium introducing the policy while the hissing exchange happened between Manuel and his officials. He began by talking about the RDP: 'It is about the fundamental transformation of society in all its aspects. It has to do with the construction of a truly democratic, non-racial, non-sexist, prosperous and stable South Africa, positioned within the rest of the world community, not as a pariah of the past, but as a responsible international citizen and an example of what a people-centred society should be.'

The RDP, then, was not a 'conglomeration of particular projects' but 'an integrated and sustainable vision for the creation of the post-apartheid society … Its abiding feature is revolutionary change. Its ethos is an all-pervasive optimism for a better life for all our people.'[15]

Mbeki had long argued to his cabinet colleagues that the RDP, as it was first formulated, was more of a wish list than a policy with defined, deliverable goals. It was easy to promise two million houses. But if you didn't figure out where the money would come from, where the bricks and mortar would come from, if you didn't 'run the numbers', to use one of Manuel's expressions, the promise was empty.

Now in parliament he said that the government had a macroeconomic policy that was 'based on concrete reality and therefore sustainable'. It was, he said, 'the central compass which will guide all other sectoral growth and development programmes of government aimed at achieving the objectives of the RDP'.

When Manuel rose to speak, the speech turned from what Roux had feared would be 'catastrophic' to a message he was able to deliver with 'real aplomb'. It was 'Trevor, the politician,' he said, 'who can actually communicate with people around him, and he did it fantastically well'.

Manuel focused first on the unemployment crisis: 'We want employment and a decent life for all – from Mamelodi to Manenberg, from Malabar to Matjiesfontein. This can only be achieved through the sustained higher growth of our economy.' By early in the new century, the hope was that there would be a 6 per cent growth rate and 400 000 additional new jobs a year.

He held his audience. If the country continued down the same road, employment creation would be limited, and scope for public spending curtailed. He explained why the balance of payments was a 'structural barrier to accelerated growth', the concept he himself had battled to come to terms with.

He held them through exchange control relaxation, through the expansion of a public infrastructure-investment programme, through, remarkably 'structured flexibility in the collective bargaining system'.

And then through the deficit reduction – the plan to take the deficit down to 4 per cent of GDP in 1997/98 – a 'great stride', and control of inflation. 'Without fiscal prudence and in the absence of declining inflation, higher real interest rates will remain. They have undesirable consequences. For me, they are detrimental to economic growth and to job creation ... (H)igher real interest rates also affect the Government's ability to deliver social services. Debt servicing will constitute the highest proportion of the Budget in the following year.'[16] He mentioned 'alienation' only once and that was in the reply to the debate.

The ANC whips had mustered the heavy-weight of the left to speak in the debate: Jay Naidoo, the former unionist, now minister of posts and telecommunications, and Phillip Dexter, then a provincial leader of the Communist Party.

'The key positive aspect' of the new macroeconomic policy framework, said Dexter, 'is that it builds on the RDP ... It is about unlocking resources for investment, i.e. creating jobs. The other very important aspect is that there is now a strong commitment to the Government intervening in the economy, and leading the process of reconstruction and development.'

He addressed himself to the 'left', his own comrades. '(They) will probably read a different message into the document, thinking that what we are in fact going to have is deregulation, but I think that it is very clear that the Government has made a firm commitment to creating jobs that people are going to benefit from.'

He did say, though, that he was unhappy with the deficit reduction 'if this is to be done at the cost of delivery of basic services ... To make sure that this does not happen, we are going to have to ensure that the required economic growth does take place'.[17]

In the narrative that followed the introduction of the new policy, two aspects became central. One was that the new policy eclipsed the RDP; the other was that a low deficit was a betrayal of the people's needs. The fact that not only Manuel, but Mbeki and Dexter had said, from their respective corners, that the new policy was to enable the RDP to work, was not addressed by the critics. As for the deficit, the arguments would continue to rage for the next 12 years, even after spending on social services increased substantially. As we shall see, to Manuel's continual frustration, several government departments were unable to use the extra money effectively.

A higher deficit is often held up as an article of left-wing faith, yet it was not only the left who encouraged government to borrow more. Tony O'Reilly, the Irish billionaire who bought the largest English-language group of South African newspapers in 1994, urged the government to borrow heavily to 'jump-start' the economy.[18] So did conservative economist, Brian Kantor.[19] So had several officials in the World Bank.[20]

A major reason for the disjuncture between the left in the ANC and the government – the disjuncture that rendered Manuel an 'outsider' – was actually more a case of hurt feelings than any article of faith. And the word that caused the pain was 'non-negotiable'.

'CALL ME A THATCHERITE.' Thabo Mbeki rapped the table sharply at Tuynhuis before he and Manuel briefed the press on GEAR after the parliamentary debate. The remark was meant – mainly – as a joke. But it was also designed to protect Manuel from some of the political fall-out that would follow.

The day before the policy reached Parliament, at a background briefing for the media, Ramos said the policy was 'non-negotiable'. She had direct support for this position from Mbeki.

Interestingly, Manuel never put it this way. He knew that the meticulous modelling within the framework may well fall apart if 'the numbers' were separately negotiated. But he told Parliament that although the 'framework was integrated … it sets the parameters for change (and) the parameters are not up for negotiation at this stage', he hoped the ANC's social partners would work through the details with government. It was a slightly different way of putting it. 'You can't actually negotiate those numbers,' Manuel told me later, 'because if you move one, the others fall flat. It wasn't actually my call. It was Maria's call, but in retrospect it was the correct call. She'd raised the matter with me, but also with the then deputy president (Mbeki), who said that's a call you've got to make … And clearly it was a shock to the system.'

Some of Manuel's aides believe there was tension between Manuel on the one hand, and Ramos and Mbeki on the other, over the extent of consultation. But perhaps it was more to do with Manuel's style of politics, which reached back to the days when he tried to persuade a recalcitrant and cautious union movement to join the UDF. First prize was to have them on board. But in their absence, he nonetheless went ahead with a decision he felt was both correct and timely.

Five days before GEAR was presented in Parliament, a number of unionists and Communist Party members gathered at Nelson Mandela's Johannesburg house where they were briefed on GEAR (it didn't yet have its name). Zwelinzima Vavi, then assistant general secretary of COSATU (he became general secretary after Mbhazima Shilowa was appointed premier of Gauteng province in 1999) was there. A number of SACP officials were there too.[21] 'We discussed it,' said Manuel, 'and I'll be pretty frank and say that none of us in that room had the economics to go through this thing. There was a measure of suspicion partly because of the closure of the RDP office. There was a concern that we were selling out to Washington.' There was a lot of concern about cutting the deficit because bigger deficits 'appeared to be a left-wing thing to do'.

Zwelinzima Vavi remembers it thus: 'They told us they had been working on a document which in their view required closing of the ranks by the Alliance, and the document was such a radical document it was going to cause an uproar, business was going to be up in arms. And so we said no, no, no, you can't just ask us to endorse a document we have not seen, give us more details. Obviously, they said, we can't give it to you, it's a sensitive document, if it is leaked it will cause such a row in the markets and so forth. Well, we insisted and Mandela agreed that we must be given more details. But there was no time for that.'

A few days later, there was a similar meeting at Shell House, the ANC headquarters in downtown Johannesburg. Cronin, who attended, is still annoyed that the NEC of the ANC was not formally briefed. 'I've been an NEC member since the Durban conference in 1991, when Trevor would have become a member. And I received a briefing as an SACP official a week or so before the public announcement, but I never received a briefing as an NEC member. So there were problems with the process.'

Some of the drafters of GEAR agree. Stephen Gelb, then an economist at the University of Natal who had come into the process belatedly, was worried about the possible fall-out. He was invited to an ANC Economic Transformation Committee meeting in Cape Town – a flurried, last-minute invitation – about a month before GEAR's completion. There, he found himself in an invidious position: Mboweni was chairing the meeting and asked him to brief them 'on the new economic policy'. Unsurprisingly, none of the key drafters of the policy were there, certainly not Manuel or Erwin.

'So I'm sitting there knowing we've all been sworn to secrecy, and there was a fear of the rand disappearing to the South Pole, and here I'm sitting with the minister of labour and the leaders of the organisation. So what do I do?

'So I just decided that actually these people have a right to know, they're political leaders, so I gave a kind of summary of the whole policy as it was then … and it just led to total pandemonium.'

Gelb wrote to Roux after that to suggest that Mandela introduce the policy with Mbhazima Shilowa of COSATU on one side and Gavin Relly of Anglo American on the other, 'just to have the signal go out that business and labour were on board with government. I thought it was absolutely crucial.' But it was too late for such an intervention then, and anyway may well not have worked.

If the lack of sufficient consultation united leaders such as Vavi and Cronin, they differed on the details of the policy. Cronin told me: 'Something was needed – a macro-stabilisation intervention was needed, and signals to markets. Even as an "ultra-leftist", I must concede that was necessary.' And an emergency plan to devalue and stabilise the rand, he said, could not, should not, have been the subject of 'democratic debate'.

But 'when it came to a complex document with a whole set of assumptions about job creation and growth as a result of a particular stabilisation intervention' – that needed to be debated.

Mbeki's remark about being a Thatcherite aside, Cronin said: 'What we have seen is not a Thatcherite government but a government that's delivered two million low-cost houses, electricity connections, water connections, social grants now at 12 million (in 2008). Tax policy had been used as an instrument to redistribute wealth, and economic growth had returned. Although Cronin criticises it for being a 'rather top-down kind', he admits that 'it's not this nasty Reaganomics of "the market will do everything" '.

Vavi did not laugh at Mbeki's 'Thatcherite' joke. 'We were devastated,' he told me. He was not only irked by the lack of consultation but would have had different policy proposals had he had a say. An engaging man, Vavi occasionally has two different personas. One is reserved for when he is on a stage or behind a microphone. Then he has frequently taken extreme positions that accentuate any gulf there may be. But there is another persona: when he is grappling with issues in a one-on-one engagement he is far more thoughtful and conciliatory. He told me that despite NEDLAC not being 'the economic parliament' the unions hoped it would be, workers have nonetheless

447

attained hitherto undreamt of rights under the ANC government. 'The rights of workers in the constitution are enshrined, the right to strike, the right to form unions, the right to collective bargaining, even the right to union security arrangements ... No constitution in the world contains such rights for workers.'

Moreover, the ANC government passed laws that 'tilted the balance in favour of workers', such as employment equity, occupational and health and safety laws, 'too many things ... very good interventions'. Beyond that, the poor have benefited from government's social delivery programme: 'water for millions, electricity for millions, and access to health care ... We are free as a nation.'

Yet Vavi does not buy the argument that the debt crisis was so severe in the 1990s that one needed a fiscally prudent policy. In his view the austerity programme designed to escape the clutches of the IMF was like, as he used to say as a child, 'pinching yourself before the bully boy pinches you'. Also, in his view, if the government had run up a higher deficit, 'economic growth would have been above 8 per cent by now'. (It was the end of 2006 when I spoke to him, and growth had reached 5,4 per cent, its highest level in two decades.) Vavi's number may be pulled from somewhere but certainly GEAR's careful econometric modelling exercises showed that a 10 per cent increase per annum in real government expenditure would have boosted growth in the short term but it would have fallen by the year 2000; inflation in the same year would hit nearly 15 per cent, and the Budget deficit would reach 16 per cent of GDP. Employment would grow because of an increase in government employment, but real wages would be eroded by inflation. And growth? Far from hitting 8 per cent, it would have been 2,9 per cent in 2000 instead of the (then) projected 3,3 per cent.[22]

While Cronin and Vavi may have differed on the exact economic policies to follow, they were equally irked by the lack of consultation. In the short term, they took out this irritation on Manuel, but in the longer term, they turned it on to Thabo Mbeki who became the country's president after the 1999 elections. What differentiated Manuel for them was that his roots in internal activism, and their own, were similar. Each of them understood what had shaped the other.

ZWELINZIMA VAVI COMES FROM the poorest of poor families. The tenth of 12 children, he was born on a farm in the Northern Cape, where his parents were both labourers. As a small boy, he worked: he dipped cattle, clipped sheep, picked fruit – stole fruit, too, he told me, and still has the scar on his back from the barbed wire fence he had to wriggle under to escape the farmer.

He attended primary school erratically. In 1971, his family was removed from the farm to a grim resettlement camp called Sada in the north-east of the Ciskei homeland. Bitterly cold in winter, searingly hot in summer, Sada housed thousands of former farm workers who had been expelled from white farms. There was hardly any work there, no running water; people lived cheek by jowl in zinc shacks in a rural slum. When I visited there in 1981, I was struck by the listless depression that hung like a fog over those who were trapped there.

For Vavi, though, the grimness brought a ray of light. He managed to complete high school, the first in his family to do so. In 1984 he got a job as a clerk on a mine in Klerksdorp, about 160 kilometres west of Johannesburg. There he discovered the National Union of Mineworkers, started by Cyril Ramaphosa two years before. It had grown exponentially from 14000 at its inception to 120000 workers on 85 mines by 1985.[23] The union had natural gravitational pull for Vavi, who carried, and still carries, a sense of outrage at the deprivation of his childhood, and at his parents' powerlessness in the face of humiliation. In 1987, when more than 300000 workers came out on a lengthy strike, marked by violence, arrests and mass dismissals, Vavi was one of them. Three weeks later, more than 50000 workers were dismissed. Vavi was one. 'The devastation, the demoralisation, and the loss of hope to the union, and management's success in fully intimidating members,' he said trying to recapture the mood. But he did not give up. He stayed on the mine, working as an unpaid union organiser under a pseudonym to evade management. 'We have to start a-scratch. To get a shop steward elected took three meetings and nobody wanted to (stand). When it comes to the point where you must elect shop stewards, the hall just becomes empty and you have to go to the rooms and beg with people to stand for elections.'

After a few months, he got his first monthly paycheck as a union organiser: R350, signed by Ramaphosa. But it was not the end of his personal suffering that emanated from the strike. His mother had a stroke soon after he was dismissed. He had supported her, as his older brothers were by then married with families of their own. 'It was quite a devastation for her.' She died a year later.

JEREMY CRONIN COMES FROM a quite different background: white, English,

449

middle-class (by his own description). Like Manuel, he also lost his father – a naval officer – at a young age and his mother raised him and his brother on a pension. Cronin has the kind of mind that seldom stops working, exploring, questioning, so it was perhaps not surprising that he began to dip into revolutionary philosophy at a relatively young age. In the early 1970s he studied in Paris and was strongly influenced by the structuralist movement in Marxism. And he was inspired, as were many of his generation, by Rick Turner, the visionary intellectual and activist who was assassinated at his home in Durban in 1978. By the late 1960s, Cronin was actively involved in one of the few remaining underground communist party cells in South Africa, producing propaganda and educational material.

He continued his underground work while lecturing in politics at the University of Cape Town until he was arrested in 1976 with two other members of his 'cell', David and Sue Rabkin. Their arrest came after a series of 'pamphlet bombs' in Cape Town, which proclaimed the continued existence and fighting spirit of the ANC and the SACP. He was jailed for seven years.[24] In jail, Cronin continued his studies and philosophical readings to the extent that he was able to, and wrote poetry, much of which was published when he was released.

Strangely, Cronin had never been an activist in the sense that either Vavi or Manuel was before he went to jail. He was imprisoned for being a member of the ANC and SACP, but he had never been to an ANC meeting, nor sung an ANC song. In fact, his handlers warned him to stay away from such meetings, and to eschew interracial friendships for fear of attracting unwarranted attention from the security police.

When he was released from jail in 1983 he emerged into an entirely new world. Now mass struggle was firmly on the agenda, and a militant non-racialism was being forged. He walked out of Pretoria Central Prison a few months before the UDF was launched, and immediately became involved. 'My impressions were that it was quite a factionalised Western Cape and it was hard for someone like myself, coming out of prison, to read it all. I was a rank amateur,' he told me. 'But I was treated like I was a veteran of the struggle because I'd been in prison!' Although he'd been in the underground since the late 1960s, 'in practice I'd had zero experience of popular organisation, going into townships, women's organisations and so on. So I had lot of grand theory and very little practical political experience and found it quite a bewildering reality, actually.'

But in this bewildering reality, and in the factionalised Western Cape, he recalls Manuel as being 'absolutely central in getting the structures and the organisation moving'.

Cronin rejoined an underground cell – one that included Tony Yengeni – and when several of its members were arrested in 1987, he left the country on a borrowed passport. It was also the middle of the Emergency so he was actively being sought as a UDF leader. He oscillated between London and Lusaka for the next three years, growing close to several exiled ANC leaders, in particular Joe Slovo, and he returned to the country in 1990.

In spite of this period in exile, Cronin's experience in politics was shaped 'on the ground', much like Manuel's.

This common experience of activism in communities, or among workers, forged different lessons from those learned in exile where the constituency was mainly political activists under discipline. It was an experience that formed an umbrella large enough to contain a Manuel, a Vavi, and a Cronin.

Vavi regrets some of the language that was used against Manuel in the union movement's critique of GEAR. In about 2000, he had called him 'the blue-eyed boy of capital'. 'Which was mistake,' he told me, 'because he's a very likeable fellow. He has a passion.' It was a mistake to question 'the bona fides of each other'.

And Cronin, although he is harshly critical of the 'state technocrats' whom he thinks have driven policy, isolates Manuel from his critique. 'Trevor's got an activist's heart and experience,' he told me. Although there was chill around the time that GEAR was introduced, after a few years the two resumed 'an affable, homeboy' kind of relationship that allowed for engagement about policy issues.

Manuel may have felt an outsider in the early period of the new economic policy. But in fact he had a store of political capital that he had not quite realised.

Ten years after Gear was introduced, I asked Manuel if he'd ever had a moment of doubt either about the policy or about his ability to survive the political fall-out.

He sighed and said: 'You know at one level, the strength for me came not from sitting in government but from being more directly involved in ANC policy work. When you have to deal with this matter in order to debate the issue in ANC circles with comrades who were sometimes hostile ... you needed to dig pretty deep and read as widely as you could and shore up every bit of argument you had. It was necessary to win the argument and to hold the faith, but the problem is it *becomes* a bit of faith. And the risk of that is that the persona of the individual and the issues become too intertwined. And it was that that affected me.'

A year after GEAR was introduced, it hadn't delivered. 'We're in the middle of an Asian crisis, we're quite panicked, the currency begins to fall out of bed – it's a very difficult period,' recalled Manuel. 'Because now we're trying to maintain a strength of discipline. The biggest sell-out in the minds of some was that we decided to cut the deficit. So we cut the deficit, we're not seeing the foreign flows; we're seeing the currency heading south ... it's a very, very difficult period.'

To see through the policy in the face of criticism, muted in 1996, but more strident in 1997, *did* become a measure of faith. The targets were not being met. The deficit in the 1997 budget remained at 5,1 per cent instead of the 4,5 per cent projected in GEAR, the currency continued to fall throughout 1996, the rate of real gross investment dipped from 10 per cent in 1995 to 7 per cent, and interest rates increased to 17 per cent. Capital inflows slowed down, mainly due to the volatility in the foreign exchange markets, from R19,2 billion in 1995 to R3,9 billion in 1996.[25]

Much of what had happened in the months since GEAR was introduced was due to factors beyond government's control. There was a global crisis that preceded the Asian crisis that had resulted in money flowing out of emerging markets the world over.[26] The currency was being driven 'by something else', as Andre Roux put it, and the spending cut – and reprioritisation – was hobbled by a massive wage equity deal that Alec Erwin had concluded just before he left office.

'It was a historic agreement,' said Kuben Naidoo who joined the Treasury in 1998, 'because it equalised pay across racial categories.' It was inevitable that any new government would have to do this. In education, for instance, there were 16 education departments under apartheid and almost as many categories of teachers. Each province had an education department, each of the 'homelands', and each racial group in the cities. The lowest paid teacher then was an African female in the Transkei, the highest paid a white male in the old Transvaal Education Department (the TED). 'And so everybody was bottomed up to a TED teacher. The person in the Transkei got a 56 per cent salary increase. In addition everybody got a 7,5 per cent increase so the whole band went up. It was hugely costly. It pushed up labour costs in education and health by 15-20 per cent.'

Naidoo comes from a family with a long political pedigree: his uncle, Indres Naidoo, was jailed on Robben Island for several years, and his father Prema was a key underground ANC activist who was detained several times, including during the anti-ANC swoop that netted Barbara Hogan.[27] Born in 1971, Naidoo spent his childhood and youth on picket lines and at mass meetings. He believed that South Africa required radical transformation. Yet even he was aghast at the effects that an overnight equalisation would have on the fiscus at a time when it most needed to cut its debt. 'I think it would have been better to say, look guys, this is the budget constraint, let's take five years to equalise salaries and it would have been far easier to absorb the costs.'

At the same time, the government's personnel salary administration system (known as Persal) began to discover enigmas on the payroll, particularly in the provinces that encompassed the old homelands such as the Eastern Cape and KwaZulu-Natal. There were people in positions that no longer existed and vice versa, literally dead or absent people still on the payroll.

The controls over spending were, at best, lax.

In the face of these obstacles, Manuel still managed to produce a Budget in 1997 – and in particular to deliver a Budget Speech – that, in Roux's words 'won Mandela's heart. I think that was the moment when people said, 'he is our man, we are going to back him'.

Manuel began his Budget Speech by talking about a 'people-centred society'. Government needed to 'feed the hungry, clothe the naked, shelter the homeless, secure our streets and homes, shield the weak and vulnerable from violence, give impetus to the producers of wealth, and encourage all citizens to meet their social obligations.'[28]

He used a teleprompter for the first time, enabling him to make eye contact with parliamentarians and with those in the public gallery and, through the television screen, with a much wider audience. He introduced indigenous languages into his speech, speaking about poverty alleviation in Zulu and SeTswana. Most of all, he spelled out the vision of economic reform. 'This Budget tells the story of a government determined to effect deep transformation and to live within its means ... It demonstrates unequivocally that the success of the RDP is dependent on the successful implementation of GEAR.'

The expenditure figures gave some credence to the argument. Defence was cut back significantly to allow for a massive boost in education expenditure to more than 21 per cent of the total budget. Health harnessed nearly 11 per cent of the budget.

In spite of this boost in education spending, there was, in 1997, an even smaller gap between education and the spending on debt interest than there had been in the years before – just R1 billion. Debt interest cost the country R39 billion that year and the education spend was R40 billion. It was a 'big turning point', he said later, for the ANC. 'Without an intervention, we would have been spending more on yesterday than today.' It was this that 'jogged the collective mind of the NEC'.

Still the deficit became an ideological bone of contention, and by the end of 1997, the debate had sharpened into the shrillness of union songs and protests. That, and privatisation (even though the RDP document, too, supported it in certain circumstances) became lodestars of the left.

The problem was a political one. After the first vocal objections in 1996, Thabo Mbeki had said to Manuel that they needed to get a group who would sit 'under a tree' to talk. It was a reference to the age-old African tradition of meeting in the open to discuss disagreements, but also a more modern reference to the ample shade provided in the garden of the deputy president's official residence in Pretoria.[29] The meetings involved, principally, Mbhazima Shilowa, the general secretary of COSATU, Enoch Godongwana, the general secretary of one of the largest trade unions, the National Union of Metal Workers (NUMSA), and Vusi Nhlapo from the public service union. Mbeki convinced them of the perils of debt. But the mistake he made, according to his biographer Mark Gevisser, was to exclude the more radical critics of GEAR from those meetings.[30]

So while Shilowa may have been convinced of the argument, and received recognition for this in the form of his appointment as premier of Gauteng, South Africa's most powerful and wealthiest province, there were others, such as Vavi, who were left outside.

Manuel was aware of this. He mentioned it to me in 2006, describing it as 'a major error'. But the divisions were only sharpened by Mbeki. They already existed within COSATU itself.

So the first tier of union and party leadership was brought on board in the early meetings about GEAR but that tier would soon go into government. The more radical critics were excluded from Mbeki's 'inner sanctum'.[31]

Manuel was affected both by this division in COSATU, and by the cooling of relations between Mbeki and the left within the ANC in a peculiar way. At first, Vavi told me, 'he sort of withdrew' in the face of attack. 'I know he took it very, very painfully to be attacked by own allies. It was a pain.' There are arguments Vavi has had with Manuel, such as over the deficit, that the unionist says will 'never be resolved ... They think they were right until today, we think they were wrong till today.' Those arguments 'we will take to the grave, me and Trevor'. But on the other hand, there is still that 'soft spot', as Vavi describes it, which distinguishes Manuel from others in government who took a hard line about GEAR. There is a soft spot and there is, extraordinarily, pride.

'As a black person he had made all of us very proud. He was the first black minister to be given the most important portfolio and he has run it very, very efficiently, and he has grown tremendously as a person ... Trevor had no official training as an economist. He has learned everything walking, and he has done wonderful self-training and self-empowerment, and he is now one of the best economists in the world. He would not be found wanting. He's regarded as one of the most efficient ministers in the world.'

Vavi told me this in 2006 after Manuel had become one of the longest-serving finance ministers in the world. It was a notable tribute from one who is cast in the popular discourse as Manuel's main antagonist.

Manuel appeared, then, to have escaped the opprobrium reserved for Mbeki that became apparent in the latter's second term as president.

But in 1997, when he was still under fire for a risky, untested and unpopular new policy, Manuel relied heavily on the support of both Mandela and Mbeki. 'You never had a query in cabinet or otherwise that would not be dealt with by (Mandela or Mbeki) to say, that's our policy. So you had clarity of purpose and thinking from the top that allowed us the room,' Gill Marcus told me.

That 'clarity of purpose' expressed itself in 1997, between the ANC's policy conference at Gallagher Estate in Midrand and its 50th National Conference in December held in the North-West town of Mafikeng. It was the first 'hard' conference of the ANC in government – 1994 was still a 'honeymoon period', according to Manuel. Certainly it was one of the biggest tests of policy that the ANC government faced in its own constituency.

After the policy conference, the ANC leadership produced a document called *The State and Social Transformation*, authored principally by Mbeki. Critics of his government commented wryly that it skilfully used the language of

Marxism to defend a 'capitalist road'.[32]

Perhaps more importantly, it argued against the notion of 'voluntarism' – or, to use Gill Marcus's term, a 'blank slate' on which the ANC could now write its own history. It pointed out that what was already written on that slate was a rising public debt that then stood at 65 per cent of GDP, a massive drop in capital expenditure during the last years of apartheid, and escalating debt service costs that would continue to rise unless the deficit was brought down. In the language of Lenin, the document affirmed that 'the democratic movement and state must never entertain the notion of voluntarism with regard to economic questions, according to which the concept takes hold that the subjective can assume ascendancy and preponderance over the objective, in violation of the laws of motion governing the objective sphere ... It is this lurch into subjectivism which, in the history of human development, led to such experiments as "The Great Leap Forward", which was, in reality, its own opposite.'[33]

Equally, it eschewed the 'right-wing' philosophy of 'economic determinism'. This was defined as a view that the creation of wealth is governed by a 'mystical' market, 'which is amorphous, disembodied, colourless, odourless and ethereal'. The relationship between the subjective wish to transform society, and the 'objective conditions' – the most central being that capital is still largely in private hands – made social transformers 'neither prisoners of ineluctable forces of "free market" capitalist development, nor free agents of popular empowerment who can write any letter of the alphabet as they wish, because what they have in front of them is a *tabula rasa.*'

No blank slate, in other words. Social transformers had to understand the objective world in which they worked in order to change it. 'The enemy of dogmatic certainty is that social transformers are neither slaves nor free agents: they are both slaves and free agents!'

That is the essence of the document. It also encapsulated Manuel's struggle, since his early days of anti-apartheid activism, to come to grips with a world that he had not made but that he wished to change. How does a human being, trapped in the circumstances of history, act to change it?

Mafikeng acquired added significance for Manuel. The Economics Commission convened there was, according to Alec Erwin, 'massive', one of the biggest the ANC had ever had, so large it split into three groups. 'And contrary to the expectation that there would be a war over GEAR, there wasn't,' he said. In fact there was more discussion on rural development which took a fair amount of space in the resolution on economic policy that was eventually accepted.

Shortly before the Mafikeng conference, a group including Erwin, Manuel and at least two SACP leaders, Enoch Godongwana and Jabu Moleketi, met at Erwin's Johannesburg house to 'hammer out the bare bones of the resolutions'.[34] At the conference, Mboweni and Erwin wrote a first draft. Shilowa, then still COSATU general secretary, wasn't happy and amended it. The wording was nudged along by Moloketi, Godongwana and Erwin, with input from Shilowa. The final draft was written by Mboweni and Shilowa. They tested it with the commission 'late, late at night' and then with Mbeki. Manuel deliberately stayed out of the drafting and the presentation 'because then the heavies would try to take me and not deal with the arguments'.

Yet the resolution on Economic Transformation adopted at Mafikeng starts with the words Manuel had first used in an interview six years earlier when he was appointed to head the economics desk of the ANC: *Economics is about people.*

'Economics is about people; their work, their ownership of productive assets or lack of it, their share of what they produce, what they buy and sell, their accommodation, their recreation, in fact every element which we describe as quality of life, flows from the structure and management of the economy.'[35]

More critically, the central tenet of the resolution brought RDP and GEAR together, as Mbeki had tried to do in June 1996 when he introduced GEAR, and as Manuel had tried to do in 1997 when he presented his first Budget. 'The emphasis in the RDP on macroeconomic balance has been a consistent part of ANC policy and has been mentioned in every policy document since 1990. The strategy for Growth, Employment and Redistribution (GEAR) aims at creating the environment of macroeconomic balances required for the realisation of the RDP. In this, therefore, the GEAR does not seek to displace the RDP.'

The idea that reconstruction and development – RDP – was the vision and that GEAR was the instrument to effect it was 'always there', said Manuel. 'It was always there. In my mind it was never an issue, there was never a question about it.'

It may have begun with Nelson Mandela's first State of the Nation address to Parliament in May 1994, when he spelled out the new government's commitment to creating 'a better life for all'.

Precisely because we are committed to ensuring sustainable growth and development leading to a better life for all, we will continue existing programmes of fiscal rehabilitation. We are therefore determined to make every effort to contain real general government consumption at present levels and to manage the budget deficit with a view to its continuous reduction.

Similarly, we are agreed that a permanently higher general level of taxation is to be avoided. To achieve these important objectives will require consistent discipline on the part of both the central and the provincial governments.

Furthermore, this disciplined approach will ensure that we integrate the objectives of our Reconstruction and Development Plan within government expenditure and not treat them as incidental to the tasks of government, marginalised to the status of mere additions to the level of expenditure.[36]

The big difference this time was that this policy went to the conference floor and became ANC policy. 'It was a reconfirmation of the rationality of the ANC.' Given that the organisation had agreed to suspend the armed struggle at a time when their members were still in jail or in exile – a much harder ask – it seemed as though that sense of vision and rationality had stamped itself again on the organisation. The scant difference – of R1 billion – in expenditure between education and debt interest focused the conference into the realisation that 'we would spend more on yesterday than tomorrow' if debt were not curtailed.

In his 'more narcissist moments', Manuel regarded the economic policy debate in Mafikeng as 'a kind of referendum. It was incredibly hard. How do you deal with this thing? Because for 18 months, you've immersed all of what you are into this thing, you've taken the flak. What's the ANC going to do?'

If the ANC had 'booted this out', he would have had to resign.

As it happened, the resolution was accepted. As it happened, Manuel was elected again on to the National Executive Committee coming seventh in the list of 60 NEC members. (Mboweni came in just above him at sixth place and Ramaphosa, who had by then left the public service, topped the list.) It was the moment when he came in from the outside.

'ONE OF THE THINGS we haven't talked about sufficiently in our country,' said Maria Ramos, reflecting on that period, 'is the quality of our leadership. Because you had the quality of leadership in that cabinet all the way down from the president at the time to the deputy president to people like Trevor as the minister of finance – just the courage to make decisions under very difficult circumstances and to stick to those decisions, to see them through.'

Ramos had sat through a conference of international bankers in New York in the late 1990s, where the Argentinian minister of finance had to explain why his country was defaulting on its loans. Argentina's politicians had been very popular for a while: valuing the peso at an equal rate to the dollar which made imports cheap, borrowing heavily to spend, and giving huge subsidies to particular industries. Popularity was one consequence. After a few years there were others, too: the overvalued currency killed exports, the heavy borrowing drove up inflation, and the hefty subsidies, when they became unsustainable, drove up unemployment. Interest rates were sky-high and poverty increased in the early years of the twenty-first century. It was clear, said Ramos, two years before that crisis, that the Argentinian minister of finance could not do 'what needed to be done' because his eye was on the next election.

In South Africa, while there were 'intense, intense debates, they were always about the issues. I can't think of a single occasion where Trevor, or the deputy president (Mbeki) or Madiba sat in those meetings and said, what is this going to do for our popularity? It was always, what is in the best interests of our country? How we going to fix this situation? As South Africans, we are incredibly lucky.'

CHAPTER 27

'Good luck being in charge'

IN APRIL 2006, MANUEL CAME TO PRINCETON UNIVERSITY, where I was teaching at the time, to address students, and to give a public lecture. He had come straight from the spring meetings of the IMF and World Bank in Washington DC. The students were bright and engaged and wanted to know everything from the effects of the oil price to how many people actually voted in South Africa's last elections.

One asked him what it was like having Zimbabwe as a neighbour 'whose economy was in such dire straits'.

Inflation in Zimbabwe was then about 700 per cent. Its economy was imploding, and unemployment was close to 80 per cent. In the following two years things got steadily worse. The group of 20-somethings, including one young Zimbabwean student, fixed on him as he spoke.

'Zimbabwe,' he began, 'is one of the big tragedies of our time … The achievements in the years 1980-1990 were actually quite remarkable, their investment in people quite incredible. A lot of it was done with money borrowed from the World Bank and IMF and in 1991 the IMF started calling in loans.'

The country faltered on meeting its loans. Then it faltered meeting the conditionalities set out for it by the IMF. 'So you've got to try to understand this thing. Understanding economics is a bit of a longitudinal rather than a snapshot view ... What you're seeing now is the culmination (of the past 15 years) ... They are going through a tremendously difficult period because if your inflation is running over 700 per cent, your interest rates are probably 800 per cent. You can't do anything with figures like that.'

He spoke about the long, steady flight of skilled people as the country deteriorated. Then about the way Zimbabwe 'went about the land redistribution issue ... They've destroyed the agricultural potential of a country that actually has the most amazing climate and soil conditions for agriculture. Tobacco's a big export crop, floriculture, but also, certainly, a variety of grains.

'So there's no money. People may have land but there's no training about what to do with the land, no money for input costs, no diesel to drive tractors, there's no seed to plant, there's no money to repair irrigation systems that may have disappeared or just fallen into disrepair. And many of its people, skilled and unskilled, have fled to South Africa. (There's a part of Johannesburg called Hillbrow, and they say you couldn't throw a stone down a street there without hitting a Zimbabwean.)

'My position on Zimbabwe is quite a sober one,' he went on. 'We must help people but we can't just put money down the chute. It's not *my* money. It's not my inheritance.'

If there was an inkling of change in Zimbabwe, then perhaps it was worth taking the risk. 'Without wanting to preach, the bottom line is self-belief. It's the ability to understand that unless you take decisions – and you know the problem with politics is that if it were only popular decisions I wouldn't have a job like this – you've got to take some exceedingly unpopular decisions. If you don't the impact is doom.'

The Zimbabwean minister of finance, he told the Ivy League students, had a doctorate from Harvard University. 'My brother (the then minister Herbert Murerwa) has a doctorate from *Harvard*! I mean, hold on! There's a hell of a lot *he* can teach *me*. But knowing it and taking decisions is not the same thing.'

The students were struck by his frankness on Zimbabwe, but there were several subtexts to what Manuel said. His constant worry about what excessive debt does to a country is measured by the economic fate of Zimbabwe.

461

South Africa's stabilisation programme was, for him, vindicated by the civil and economic collapse of its neighbour. There was another subtext that he continued to raise back home, especially when politicians and civil servants were in the audience: 'It's not my money.'

At the cocktail party after the 2008 Budget where luminaries and potentates gather, he reiterated this theme: Parliament must be responsible for ensuring that government departments are 'accountable for the taxpayers' money which is not *our* money'.

And, lastly, this subtext: that tertiary education, even from Ivy League institutions such as Harvard, does not mean that a minister of finance will take the right decisions.

Manuel spoke at Princeton as he marked his tenth year as minister of finance. He was an altogether more confident, less frantic man than when he'd first walked into the Vermeulen Street building in Pretoria. Vavi said, 'He learned by walking.'

In the first few years, he learned more by running.

THE FIRST PROBLEM THAT had to be solved was the massive debt. It was not so easy to simply cut the deficit – although it was indeed cut – in a country whose new democracy demanded reconstruction. It was also a matter of pricing the debt differently, and of finding the spending cuts that could be made.

Debt was hopelessly overpriced under apartheid. Because it was not easy for the apartheid government to borrow, bonds came at a price. It also borrowed erratically.

Phakamani Hadebe, who joined the Treasury in 1996, and the debt management division in 1998, explained: 'Government will wake up today and realise that they need R550 million. So immediately they will (issue) a new bond, something totalling R550 million, then they get the cash, then they sit, use the money, continue with the day-to-day operations. The week after, they realise that we need another billion. Then they announce again, we have this new bond, one billion and the guys will give them a billion.'

Or they borrowed a load of cash at the start of the financial year, and sat on it, paying more interest than they earned on it.

In addition, there were the enormous negative reserves the Reserve Bank had built up, often in its futile defence of the currency. These had accumulated as a result of 'huge unfunded forward cover' – in other words selling dollars it didn't have – said Andrew Donaldson. 'Monumental numbers that had just

462

not been disclosed ... it was a great black hole.' By the time Tito Mboweni was appointed as governor of the Reserve Bank in 1999 (after a year spent as adviser to the governor, Chris Stals), the negative reserves – in other words what the bank owed and what was added to the country's debt – was $25 billion.

The black hole had been there for a while, but got worse in 1998 during the currency crisis sparked by the collapse of the emerging Asian markets. The Reserve Bank, unwisely many thought at the time, tried to shore up the currency by selling the dollar short. The gamble didn't pay off: it didn't help the currency and the overall debt mounted.

In the last years of apartheid, Treasury bonds had also been issued at huge discounts. This means that in addition to paying high interest on the loan, the country doesn't even get the amount of money that the bond is worth. So if a $1 billion bond is issued at a five per cent discount, the country gets only $950 million but has to repay it as if it had borrowed $1 billion. Some of the bonds issued by the apartheid Bantustans had discounts as high as 18 per cent, so desperate were they. Many of the bonds were also illiquid, meaning they could not be easily traded in a secondary market. If bonds trade, the discount often comes down.

Keys and Liebenberg made some dents on the capricious borrowing habits of government, trying to borrow in a more careful way rather than, as Liebenberg put it, simply to 'issue more paper to the (government) pension fund ... (which) held the bulk of government debt, and had not another investment to speak of'.

So the key to cutting debt costs was not only to borrow less, but to borrow smarter. Maria Ramos was skilled in debt and risk management and she set about building a formidable department to manage this. She kept the best of the old Treasury officials and attracted sharp new talent. Skilled young black economists and bond traders joined the department. Hadebe, who is from the Natal Midlands, had the good fortune of having visionary parents who sent him to Adams College in Durban, one of the best schools available for Africans. He was an economics lecturer at the University of Durban-Westville for a while, where he did his master's degree; he got another master's at Sussex University, and returned in 1996 when he joined the Department of Finance, just as Manuel was appointed. A decade later he was managing billions of dollars of debt and has helped bring the country's debt service costs down from 5,6 per cent of GDP in 1998 to 3,2 per cent in 2008.[1]

Lesetja Kganyago was another young recruit in the department. He arrived in August 1996. Born in Alexandra township near Johannesburg in 1965, he grew up with his paternal grandmother in the then Northern Transvaal, escaping some of the serious political disruptions that affected scholars of his generation by attending a Catholic boarding school. 'Eventually', he said, he 'got to Wits' (Witwatersrand University) where he studied for a Bachelor of Commerce. He completed an economics degree only in the late 1980s through the University of South Africa, the correspondence college, because of the continuous political rumbles that disrupted the education of black students.

Kganyago worked for First National Bank, overlapping with Ramos (although he didn't meet her then), and then went to work for the union federation COSATU as an accountant. When the ANC was unbanned, he found himself in the peculiar position of being one of the few 'numbers' experts in the movement and quickly got involved in ANC economic policy making, where he first worked with Manuel. He went to London in 1993 to do a master's in economics at London University, specialising in South African debt, and returned to a job in the Reserve Bank where he developed his skill as a bond trader. But he found the bank still mired in the culture of the old, and an unfriendly place to work, so he was delighted when Ramos hired him in 1996.

Intense, but possessed of a sharp humour, Kganyago is a man who gives short shrift to ideological holy cows. When told once that the churches had issued a call to renege on the 'apartheid debt', he retorted to a fellow official that they should rather concentrate on the Bible and leave debt to the people who know about it.

Kganyago knows about debt. Under Ramos, he and a team that included Hadebe, Coen Kruger, who had been in the department previously, and Brian Molefe, who went on to become the chief executive of the Public Investment Corporation (it manages the massive portfolio of the now fully paid-up government pension fund), waded into the international capital markets. Their task was to fundamentally alter the structure of South Africa's debt. They began by restructuring the department, which ran out of the 'ill-lit' nineteenth floor of the Vermeulen Street building and was divided into three branches: those responsible for raising international bonds, those responsible for paying it back, and a domestic debt branch.

'These chaps,' said Kganyago, 'I called them sanctions busters because the way in which they approached foreign debt was in a very secretive way. They

464

used to go to all of these dodgy foreign places like Luxembourg because they were scrambling to just grab whatever money they could lay their hands on during the sanctions era.'

Once the department had consolidated these branches, they began to consolidate the debt. The team switched nearly R44 billion worth of illiquid bonds into benchmark bonds, trading liquidity for a lower interest rate. So the investors could more easily trade their bonds and government paid less interest on the debt. Then they repurchased another R4,6 billion of illiquid bonds. Initially investors didn't bite. 'They were just looking at the coupon,' explained Hadebe. The coupon is the guaranteed interest paid on the bond. At that time it was 12 per cent. 'They were saying, you guys are now issuing 8 or 9 per cent coupons, we are not interested. But ... we just announced that we were never going to issue these bonds (again). You keep them for life. Now there's nothing that scares an investor more than holding something he can't get out of. '

By the early 2000s, there were no illiquid bonds left in the market. Then the department began diversifying its funding instruments, introducing inflation-linked bonds, retail bonds and variable rate bonds – an array of new instruments that served to both reduce the debt costs substantially over the next five years, and to build a domestic capital market. The total South African bond market turnover increased from about R5 trillion in 1997 to R11 trillion in 2000, with the government bond proportion increasing from 55 per cent to 91 per cent of the market in the same period.[2]

It is hard for mortals outside of the esoteric group of bond-market traders and Treasury specialists to understand the details of switching, buy-backs, coupons, discounts and yield curves. Manuel, a politician, was not in that group either when he became minister of finance. But he pored over the documents and listened to advice from his officials. 'You see,' Hadebe told me, 'it's not just the technical stuff. For the minister to have agreed ... to sit and listen to me saying I would like to switch R60 billion, and these are the cost implications. You know the guys (bond traders) trade on a day-to-day basis, they will try to play. But the minister was so confident that he agreed to do this.' Initially, the objective was simply to build a capital market. South Africa was a 'price-taker'.

But once the Treasury officials were 'comfortable' in the market, 'we said, now the objective is reducing debt subject to acceptable risk levels. Then we take a position,' Hadebe explained. 'We announce the auction and they give us a crazy price, we don't take it. Whereas earlier we used to take whatever price they were giving us. But over time, over time, you start playing the game they're playing.'

By the mid 2000s, South Africa was considered one of the most successful countries in consolidating debt, so much so that some 30 countries, mainly African but also India, Israel and Brazil, have visited the South African Treasury for advice.

A country's ability to borrow, without discounts, and at a reasonable interest rate, depends in large part on the investment ratings it gets from the four main international rating agencies.* By the mid-2000s, South Africa had won a favourable investment rating from all four, and this brought down the cost of borrowing.

But it was not easy in Manuel's early days, and it took time for that trust in his officials to grow. He would get upset and irritated about having to go and put on a show for, as Kganyago put it, '25-year-olds controlling billions of dollars who would ask all these silly, crazy questions'. In 1996, Manuel went on one of his first roadshows as finance minister, to Hartford, Connecticut. It was the first time South Africa was raising a Yankee bond (sold to US domestic investors). The roadshow nearly came off the tracks because of Manuel's irritation.

He and his team, including Ramos and Kganyago, planned to talk to investors who controlled, between them, upwards of $500 billion. Manuel was already angry because news had just come through that Standard and Poor's had refused to upgrade South Africa's investment rating. In those days, the governor of the Reserve Bank, Chris Stals, usually accompanied the department on its roadshows. At Hartford, Manuel listened as official experts, including Stals, tried to persuade investors that South Africa was a good investment. But 'everything went wrong', said Kganyago. 'We were doing a multimedia presentation using laptops and one back-up laptop. And we were running them at the same time, and the laptops bombed one after the other. And we then switched to a carousel, and it ran for about two or three slides, then it jammed.' As Kganyago told me this, he made an explosive, grinding noise to illustrate the enormity of the embarrassment. Eight investors, $500 billion at stake, a rattled and irritable minister, and three broken machines. Not a good start. 'Trevor was upset! He was upset!'

---

* Moodys, Standard and Poor's, Fitch and R&I.

Then they flew to Boston for another pitch. This time, Manuel, even though he had flu, decided not to rely on the officials with their broken laptops and economic niceties but took over the presentation himself. 'He went through the whole presentation on his own and he finished the presentation with "Buy South Africa. Buy!" Like in a rally type of thing. And the investors actually applauded.' At question time, he took charge, not referring questions to anybody else. 'Because these investors,' said Kganyago, 'keep on asking the same questions; they want to see if you are consistent.'

They managed to raise the money they were looking for in New York, but it was a close call.

By the following year, Manuel's irritation at the roadshows had not waned but his confidence in his officials had increased. Even so, he still found it hard to accept the attitudes of the 'amorphous markets' to South Africa. In June 1997 he and his officials went to New York to launch a Yankee bond. On the mornings on which deals were to be launched there was always palpable tension in the finance team, but this day was particularly bad. At first, Manuel said he was not going to do the 'one-on-one' meetings with investors. Ramos headed off on her own to meet an investor who was abrupt with her because she was not the minister. It was as though, Kganyago said later, Manuel had a sixth sense. A rude investor would have rattled him more.

Worse news was still to come. Just before Ramos left for her meeting, she had a phone call telling her that the Philippines was launching a 30-year bond priced at a spread of 175 basis points. 'A *very* good price,' said Kganyago, and below what the South Africans were planning to price their bond at: between 180 and 185 basis points (that's 1,8 to 1,85 per cent above the benchmark US Treasury rate).

The investment rating of the Philippines was below South Africa's but the Philippines had priced their bond to pay substantially less interest than South Africa would. Ramos left Kganyago and his colleagues to try to soothe Manuel by 'doing the numbers'. They tried to explain to him that, in fact, the Philippines bond was unrealistically priced and that it would bomb. 'Put away those numbers,' Manuel replied.

'He was upset!' recalled Kganyago. 'You see GEAR was taking a hammering back home, people were criticising it and COSATU was singing about it. He said, 'How do I go back to South Africa and tell them that Philippines borrowed money at 175 and I borrow money at 185? What is the use? I have put GEAR on the table and I'm still borrowing money more expensively.'

Usually, Treasury officials have to sell a story to investors and convince them that the price of a bond is right. This time, it took all their effort to sell the story to their minister. 'The Philippines will regret their behaviour,' Coen Kruger told Manuel, 'and the markets will punish them. We can't go home without a deal.'[3]

In an office at Merrill Lynch, the bank that was managing the deal, Ramos presented the case 'in a calm voice' to Manuel, while Kganyago 'chewed his fingers'. Manuel's mood was unrelenting. But not his recalcitrance. 'You can do the deal,' he said to her, and walked over to the fridge and took out a Pepsi. 'But this is not a champagne deal. It's a Pepsi Cola deal.'

Before he could change his mind, his officials bolted to the trading floor one level below, shouting 'press the buttons, press the buttons!'

'Bang! We had a deal at 183 bp for an amount of $500 million,' recalled Kganyago.

That afternoon, Manuel met with Jerry Corrigan, former president of the New York Fed, who congratulated him warmly on the deal, but Manuel had still not chilled. And as they were leaving for the airport, the banker who facilitated the deal, and who had witnessed Manuel's bitter 'Pepsi' comments, walked to their car with a bottle of champagne. 'We want to tell you this is a champagne deal. You must be very proud of your team.'

On the way to the airport, the South Africans learned that their bond was doing so well, it was now trading at 180 basis points. On the plane back to South Africa, Manuel walked from his first-class seat to business class where his officials were sitting and said: 'Well done, I'm very proud of you. I'm not sure this thing is a champagne deal, the jury is still out, but well done.'

'The deal was a blow-out', wrote Kganyago later and subsequently became the Yankee deal of the year. And the Philippines deal? It became the 'dog deal' of the year, he told me with no uncertain satisfaction.

Nine years later in Princeton, where Manuel spoke to the students about making the right decisions, he had lunch with a number of local luminaries, including the banker who had facilitated the deal, Chris Shade. 'What was the name of the banker who did the Pepsi Cola deal?' Manuel's assistant, Dumisa Jele, asked in a text message to Kganyago shortly before the lunch. 'His name is Chris Shade, and it wasn't a Pepsi Cola deal. It was a champagne deal,' replied Kganyago.

IF THE PEPSI COLA/CHAMPAGNE DEAL dichotomy shows one thing about Manuel it is that he takes the advice of the experts he trusts, even sometimes when his mood leans in another direction. A senior civil servant in the South African government told me that this was not common among politicians, 'who think they know everything', and it was why they make so many mistakes.

Building this body of expertise was largely Ramos's task as she painstakingly brought into the department some of the most skilled economists in the country. It was Manuel's task to cement those relationships between himself and his team of officials. He also had to cultivate relationships of trust with political leaders in the provinces, with other cabinet members, and with the two other arms of his operation: revenue collection and the statistical service. That would come. But in the late 1990s, when he was fiercely trying to reduce the debt, debt management and investment upgradings went only so far. In the provinces, in particular, spending was often both merry and uncontrolled in an environment where government had embarked on a programme of fiscal austerity and reprioritisation.

In the first two years of Manuel's term, expenditure was hard to cut because of the 1995/6 wage agreement. Personnel expenditure still totalled 51 per cent of non-interest expenditure at the time of the 1998 budget.

The provinces in particular were out of control. Provinces, as the first sites of delivery, get well over half the national allocation of money from national government. In terms of the constitution, they are obliged to spend it on education, health and welfare services. Provinces have little revenue of their own. They are almost entirely dependent on the national Budget, and when spending goes awry, as it did in the mid to late 1990s, it dents the national coffers.

Five of the nine new provinces incorporated large tracts of what were once the old Bantustans, inheriting with them lacklustre and often corrupt administrations, and a marked lack of governance ability.

There were scant controls over the personnel administration system, and in some provinces, such as the Eastern Cape, almost anyone could be hired without regard to budget. So loose were the controls that even after people left the civil service or died they often weren't removed from the payroll, resulting in hundreds of 'ghost workers' in some provinces. By 1997, it looked as though spending was going to be way above budget. 'Our back of the envelope calculations,' said Kuben Naidoo, who had come into the Treasury as a director of education finance, 'was that you were going to have to close down one in six schools and one in six hospitals.'

It didn't quite come to that but he and others still spent days in the provinces, particularly the Eastern Cape, going through their accounts, 'looking how to balance the books, looking where we could cut'.

'We were ruthless,' he told me, 'absolutely brutal.'

By the end of 1998, provincial overspending had reached between R6 and R7 billion, a large amount then, totalling some one per cent of GDP. 'There were thousands of cheque books floating about,' he said. 'Just no financial controls.'

That year, both the Eastern Cape and KwaZulu-Natal were placed under the Department of Finance's control in terms of Section 100 of the Constitution which allows national government to intervene in a province when it cannot 'fulfil its executive obligation'.[4] Those were the two worst cases, but there were other provinces that made naive errors. Limpopo (the Northern Transvaal), for instance, had a teacher shortage of about 20000. It also had a classroom shortage. Instead of building classrooms, and then hiring teachers, it simply hired 20000 teachers only to find there were no classrooms for them. Then they hurriedly built about 3000 classrooms, overspending in the process, but still it was not enough. So they had to retrench many of the new teachers. Likewise, the Western Cape had to retrench a proportion of its teachers. It made no sense in a country that had prioritised education, but likewise it made no sense to spend in a profligate fashion in a country that had decided to dramatically reduce its debt. Partly, the generous but precipitous wage increase settlement made in 1995/96 was to blame for the rapid increase in personnel spending.

If it had continued, the government would have overshot its deficit target, and GEAR would have lost its credibility. 'We closed the tap,' said Naidoo. 'And there were unintended consequences of the way we cut spending – losing teachers, losing health workers. The voluntary severance packages got rid of the most experienced and best teachers. There's no doubt there were costs involved. But I think if it wasn't for the Treasury (it would have been worse) ... In public finances, if you increase spending and there's no capacity, the money just gets wasted. And that was part of the problem. Any cuts in spending have a negative effect, but I think had we increased spending at the time it would have had no positive effect.'

And indeed, even in this time of austerity, there were rollovers of unspent money from the provinces – as much as R6,1 billion in the 1998/99 budget.[5]

The fallout from the Asian economic crisis in 1998 did not help matters.

470

Capital continued to leak from emerging markets, including South Africa. As a result growth was lower than GEAR had predicted. In 1998 it was just 0,1 per cent.[6] And as the currency lost value, interest rates rose steeply in an attempt – many said short-sighted – to defend it.

But by 1999 there were some successes in tackling the enduring legacy of apartheid. In the 1998 budget, expenditure rose by 6,4 per cent – way above the level of economic growth. Of this, 60 per cent went to social services, including education, health and welfare grants. In 1999, despite another year of paltry GDP growth, expenditure increased by 7,2 per cent. At the same time, Manuel's department cut tax rates and reduced the deficit, showing that even in an age of austerity and economic stagnation, there was so much room to reprioritise that spending on social services could increase significantly.

'The Budget is about people not numbers,' said Manuel in his 1998 Budget speech, repeating a refrain. 'It is an opportunity for us to reflect on the goals and aspirations of our people; to reflect on the South Africa that now exists; the South Africa from which we have come; and the South Africa which we are building for our children.'[7]

'The Budget that we table in this Parliament today bears testimony to the fact that as a nation we dared to dream,' he said in 1999. 'That through our tormented past we kept the dream alive. We understood then as we do now that the fruits of progress come slowly, one harvest a little richer than the last.'[8] It was an audacious dream in the circumstances. It bore fruit in the vigorous new spending plan and in the tax cuts. But the dream was somewhat stymied by a new and hefty expenditure entirely unforeseen by Manuel's department when it had drafted the economic stabilisation plan.

JUST AS MANUEL'S OFFICIALS were pencilling out line items on some of the overblown provincial budgets, cabinet began a discussion on the procurement of new arms to re-equip the Defence Force at a cost of some R30 to R40 billion. It evoked disquiet from the start, not least within the Department of Finance.

There was also substantial fall-out both in the ANC and in the country in the decade that followed, with allegations and counter-allegations of corruption and wrongdoing among senior government officials and politicians. It was the long slow fuse that resulted in Mbeki dismissing his deputy president Jacob Zuma in 2005, thus putting the latter in a pivotal position to harness growing anti-Mbeki sentiment in the ANC and defeat him at the ANC national conference in Polokwane in 2007. Eventually it was to be a substantial factor in the unseating of Mbeki from the presidency.[9]

The arms deal also exposed the frailty and venality of some struggle heroes who fell prey to petty but ostentatious greed, such as accepting discounts on luxury cars from arms bidders. It broke faith with some ANC members and ended their political careers. It sparked years of investigation by the law enforcement authorities that, by 2008, have resulted in two convictions (including Tony Yengeni, Western Cape ANC leader) and a set of charges against Jacob Zuma, the man who would become president of the ANC.[10]

Throughout it all, Manuel, the minister charged with financing the deal, walked a tightrope between his own sentiments and his cabinet obligations.

Two issues are often conflated in the ongoing debate about the defence procurement of the late 1990s. One is whether the spending on military equipment was justified at all in a country where unemployment and poverty were still substantial; the other is on whether the deal was 'clean' – in that the best decisions were made in the interests of the country.

Since becoming finance minister in 1996, Manuel assiduously cut the defence budget by almost R1 billion a year for three consecutive years. 'It was the right thing to do at the time because we were cutting everyone and it made sense to cut defence rather than education and health but the negative consequence of that is you strip defence of their capability … so when they came to reassess (that), there was a big price tag attached,' said Naidoo.

The decision to spend so heavily on arms at a time when the finance officials were 'just beginning to see the light' in terms of getting spending under control, was 'demoralising'.

The pressure for the re-equipment of the defence force began in 1994 when the navy asked government to supply it with four Bazan Spanish corvettes at a cost of R1,7 billion each. A rear admiral had made the presentation to cabinet and Manuel asked 'some very tough questions'. It intensified in Parliament in 1996 with a process that ended in a Defence Review and White Paper on Defence – a formal policy document that recommended re-equipment of the defence force.

The first minister of defence in the new democratic government was the late Joe Modise, who had been the commander of the ANC's military wing, Umkhonto we Sizwe, for nearly 30 years. Even in exile, he stirred controversy. The TRC heard evidence of how he had fiercely suppressed a mutiny in the ranks; an ANC internal inquiry cited him as being responsible for human rights abuses that had occurred in the military camps.[11] Yet he was also, according to Mbeki's biographer Gevisser, an 'early believer in a negotiated settlement' and 'an ardent defender of Mbeki both in exile and in the turbulent first years back home'.[12]

So when, as South Africa's first black minister of defence, he campaigned for the upgrading of a defence force that now incorporated former enemies in arms, his word held strong sway. When Mandela and his cabinet nixed the purchase of the Spanish corvettes in 1995, he was devastated. It was 23 May, his birthday, and he was disconsolate as he told Manuel that the president had said government couldn't go ahead with the arms deal. 'I don't know what it's going to do to the defence force,' Manuel recalls him saying. 'To the morale of the defence force. We're building a unified defence force, but the president has said we can't do it.'

In fact the defence force was one of the toughest state institutions to rebuild in the post-apartheid era. Modise had the unenviable task of trying to integrate some 27000 mainly black guerrilla fighters into the existing force – to make up a military force of about 65000 'in which the enlisted men were mainly black volunteers and the officers overwhelmingly white'.[13] And during the apartheid days, the army, as opposed to the navy or air force, got the bulk of defence spending, reflecting the political bias and affiliations of the apartheid defence minister Magnus Malan and President P W Botha. There was reason for the navy and air force to feel deprived.

By early 1998, when Parliament completed the Defence Review and endorsed a strategic arms acquisition, in Manuel's view cabinet was bound to consider the matter. 'Once you had that, the acquisition wasn't really optional. You could debate when you could take delivery, you could debate the financial terms, you could debate all manner of issues, (but) once there was a subcommittee that was convened to deal with the implementation of the process, a democrat is *bound*. And part of our responsibility as a Treasury is not ever to assume we were the Defence Ministry. Our job was to look at the financial modelling, and part of the modelling exercise was to look at the downside risk.'

The downside risk was substantial: at the time 'the rand was a one-way bet', and as the purchases were all imported, there threatened to be a huge impact on the balance of payments.

I asked Kader Asmal if it were true that he and Manuel, in particular among cabinet ministers, were 'less than keen' on the arms procurement package. 'More than less than keen,' was his reply. 'My view is that we never had a proper discussion on the arms deal.'

'You know, I wasn't at the front of the queue, the happy bunny about this,' Manuel told me, 'but I understood the Constitution bound us to have a defence force, and if you want a defence force and it needs a certain capability, once you had the Defence Review process, once all those things were in place, you needed to (equip it).'

Other Treasury officials are more outspoken. 'I don't think Trevor was willing to fight it all the way. He gave up, essentially. It was a big defeat for Treasury and I personally was very sad the way we got beaten there,' a former senior official told me. Manuel backed off, perhaps, because it was clear that Mbeki wanted to go through with it.

The procurement also went to the heart of an ongoing economic policy debate that continued for more than a decade between Alec Erwin, minister of Trade and Industry at the time of the arms deal, and Manuel. Broadly, this is the debate about precisely how the state leverages itself into the economy in a way to promote economic growth. Erwin saw the arms deal as an opportunity to extract promises of industrial offsets out of the successful bidders.

To this end, Erwin sent Paul Jourdan, who had been Manuel's adviser in the Department of Trade and Industry, and still worked for the department, in to bat for the best offset deal. Jourdan is a well-trained, knowledgeable intellectual who joined the ANC in exile, fleeing security police attention after a stint in student politics at UCT. A geologist and oceanographer by training, he spent most of his exile years in Mozambique and Zimbabwe, where he was involved in local economic development projects.

Jourdan decided to 'hit British Areospace the hardest' as they were the sellers of the most expensive items in the arms package – the Hawk and Gripen planes (the contract was a combined one with BAE Systems and the Swedish company SAAB, which makes the Gripen). He was specific about which industries it should invest in – not ferrochrome, for instance, which the company initially wanted, because South Africa was already one of the world leaders in ferrochrome production. He went to Finland, which had negotiated a similar offset deal, to see how it worked. Finland, it turned out, was one of the few countries where an offset deal had actually been successful. Why? he asked. Because, his Finnish hosts told him, the Finns are a homogeneous people and a cohesive society. More importantly, they also passed a law saying that if there was any reneging on the offset deals, the Finnish government would never do business with those firms again. And, thirdly, Finland joined the European Union at around that time, which gave it added clout to enforce the offset deals.

South Africa had none of these advantages. Even when Jourdan urged politicians to draft legislation prohibiting further business with arms companies that reneged on the offset deal, he was unsuccessful.

Then, when it became clear the offsets were not flooding in, the government stretched the conditions. Ferrochrome valorisation – in a huge new stainless steel plant that was supposed to be established in the industrial development zone of Coega – became a carrot that the South Africans tried to tempt BAE into. 'But they chickened out,' recalled Jourdan.

By 2006, out of the 64 000 high-end jobs promised in terms of the offsets, no more than 13 000 had materialised.[14]

'I remain as sceptical of (offsets) now as I was then,' Manuel told me in 2007. And for years after the deal, each Budget Day when he had to face the press, he would often snap at his officials who asked him what he was going to say about offsets, that 'Trade and Industry' could answer that question.

'Alec wanted it, he's the guy who sank us,' said a former Treasury official who had helped with the costing.

And indeed Erwin confirmed it was one of the major disagreements between him and Manuel. 'It was basically three of us who argued we must proceed on this matter,' said Erwin (Mbeki, himself and Modise). 'We must go ahead. And the Treasury was arguing it was not affordable. It turns out that they were wrong. And we kept saying to them, you're wrong! You're being too cautious.'

As it turned out, the arms deal first soared in cost because the rand declined in value but by the mid-2000s the repayment portion of the package was a relatively small item on the Budget (by 2005 it was about one per cent of the total Budget) – 'We're spending that much on the rail commuter corporation,' said Naidoo, himself an arms-deal sceptic.

Yet Treasury officials are still irked by the timing of the arms deal: 'We had been through three years of very, very tough Budgets,' said Naidoo. 'We were just beginning to see the light at the end of the tunnel. The fiscal space that was starting to open up should have been spent on education or housing. Instead, it was another two to three years before we had the space to spend on the things we wanted to spend on.'[15]

The issue of cost was contentious, mainly because of the subsequent allegations of corruption that emerged in the wake of the deal. South Africa bought the Gripen and Hawk aircraft from British Aerospace/SAAB, four corvettes from the German Frigate Consortium (GFC), 30 helicopters from the Italian manufacturer Augusta and three submarines from the German Submarine consortium. One question that won't go away is why the Hawk aircraft, which was nearly double the price of the Italian Aeromachi aircraft, also then in the hat, was chosen, particularly as the air force said it preferred the Aeromachi.[16] But the subcommittee of cabinet that dealt with the procurement excluded cost as a criterion apparently at the insistence of Modise. 'The odour of impropriety,' writes Gevisser, 'emanated directly from Modise.'[17] The other question is why the cabinet committee rejected the Bazan bid on the corvettes, first mooted in 1994, in favour of the more expensive GFC corvettes.*

The chief procurement officer of the defence force at the time was Chippy Shaik, who came from an illustrious 'struggle' family: his brother Mo had been an operative in Operation Vula effectively ferreting valuable information from a double agent in the security police during the 1980s; another brother Shabir was Jacob Zuma's financial adviser and a director of African Defence Systems (ADS), half of which was owned by Thompson, a French company subcontracted by the GFC to provide the combat suites for the ships.[18]

Shabir Shaik was convicted of fraud in June 2005 – for paying Zuma irregularly to try to influence him to protect the Thompson's part of the deal. Mbeki dismissed Zuma in the same week. The government maintained steadfastly that while there may have been irregularities in the secondary contracts, there were none in the main contracts.

But the Treasury officials who were involved in working out the financing of the deal felt a sense of discomfort throughout. One of them told me that when they talked about, for instance, cutting the number of Gripens, 'Chippy goes berserk, he absolutely goes apoplectic.' They were even more discomfited by the news that Mo Shaik had been sent to Germany as consul-general in Hamburg at the precise time that the deal was being negotiated. But suspicion is not the same as proof, and in the end the Treasury officials, and Manuel, had to accept that it was Mbeki's prerogative to push the deal through. His arguments about South Africa's role in the rest of Africa – as a peacekeeping force – were compelling. All the Treasury officials could do was to remain resolutely above board. When they went to London to sign off the

---

* Although some government officials involved in negotiating the deal argued that the GFC corvettes were better suited to the navy's needs.

final package with BAE, 'we acted with absolute integrity, we never took any entertainment, our guy didn't even go to watch rugby matches in London, he sat in the hotel. We made absolutely sure that we were squeaky clean, and so was Trevor.'

The irony, though, was that Manuel, one of the great sceptics about the arms deal, was hounded with particular assiduousness by a banker turned Christian anti-apartheid, then anti-arms, activist. Terry Crawford-Browne had worked for the international banking sanctions against apartheid with the blessing of Archbishop Tutu and Allan Boesak.

In the post-apartheid era, he took Manuel to court at least three times between the arms deal being signed off and 2008, sparking retaliatory litigation from Manuel to recover costs and, eventually, in 2008, to interdict him from continuing to accuse him of corruption and fraud. It was an expensive, and mostly wasteful, battle. Crawford-Browne argued that because Manuel signed the loan agreements, he not only condoned any corruption in the arms deal, but also 'sold' the country to international banks and the IMF, leading it into classic 'third world debt entrapment'. It is a particularly ironic charge against Manuel who has spent a lot of his career in government putting the case to his left-wing constituency against debt entrapment. It also took on an intensely personal tone, with Manuel accusing him of being a 'gorilla on my back' and Crawford-Browne stating that Manuel should be charged with corruption. The minister of finance, he wrote in an affidavit, 'is directly accountable for the arms deal scandal because he failed to meet his obligations of public office', through, among other things, signing the loan agreements 'despite numerous warnings that finalisation of these agreements would be fraudulent'.[19]

Crawford-Browne won a minor court battle – the copies of some of the loan agreements turned over to him – but lost his major one, which was to overturn the deal on the grounds that the loan agreements were fraudulently signed. Manuel tried to recover costs against him. They amounted to almost a million rand, and Manuel thought it wrong that the taxpayer should pay for what he saw as unnecessary litigation. When Manuel tried to sequestrate him, Crawford-Browne said his only asset was a 'rusted' 1993 Fiat Uno.[20]

Crawford-Browne may have a case that the arms deal was wrong for South Africa and that the offsets were a misleading trap. But his argument is often undermined by his own conspiratorial hyperbole. He peddled extraordinary allegations in his court documents. One, added in handwriting to his 2005 affidavit, was that Modise, who had been on medication for cancer before his death, had been poisoned 'to speed up his demise against the premise that "dead men don't tell tales"'; the other was to question the 'curious death' of one of Jacob Zuma's wives, Kate, presumed to have committed suicide in 2000 from an overdose of anti-malaria pills and antidepressants. Coinciding with this, he said, 'Jacob Zuma's stance on the arms deal investigation veered by 180 degrees. Previously he was in favour of an open investigation.' But then, in January 2001, he signed a 'blistering' letter to Dr Gavin Woods, chair of Parliament's standing committee on public accounts, warning him off further investigation of the arms deal.[21] But there is no obvious connection between Zuma's wife's death and his subsequent letter to Woods; and there is no evidence proffered to show that Modise was 'poisoned'.

After seven years of litigation, Manuel applied to have Crawford-Browne declared a 'vexatious litigant'. The former banker accused him several times of fraud and corruption and Manuel argued that, without proof, to accuse a finance minister of fraud not only undermined his name but the standing of the country internationally.

There was a personal twist to the vitriol, too. The two men were not strangers to each other. Crawford-Browne's wife Lavinia has worked for more than two decades as a personal assistant to Archbishop Desmond Tutu. Manuel was a frequent visitor to Bishopscourt in the late 1980s. Tutu himself has never joined any of Crawford-Browne's applications or publicly supported him, although he, too, has criticised the arms deal. 'I think that is something that we should not have done and ought to try get out of it as soon as possible. It's totally contrary to the things for which we all were striving and for the things which they say they stand for. I mean our greatest enemy is not external to us. Our greatest enemy is this poverty. And I do not myself think at the present time we are tackling it in a way that gives you hope that we are going to resolve it,' he told me in late 2006. But at the same time he is enormously fond of Manuel and thinks he 'has been quite amazing in his giftedness'.

Manuel, for his part, is quite firm that once cabinet had made a decision, his job was to implement it. 'Once we were satisfied that we understood what the downside risks were, and we understood what the financing arrangements were, signing the contracts was not an option,' Manuel told me. 'I couldn't refuse. I'm bound by collective (cabinet) decision. And you know it's as basic as that: if you don't like that collective, you step aside. This is not a prison sentence: you leave if you want to leave.'

The Defence Department made the final decision about what aircraft, or corvettes, or submarines to purchase and Manuel was, reluctantly, persuaded that even at a greater price tag, having made the decision to re-equip the defence force 'there was no point in spending all of that money on yesterday's technology'.

There was also the question about the extent to which the criticism has been generated by losing bidders.[22] 'I had people knocking on my door from Brittany in France who told us they could build these corvettes, from Bazan in Spain because they were the (initial) favoured contracts. But the one thing that was very clear to me was that these losers would continue to generate bad blood.'

The bitterness still lingers, not only in the unanswered questions about Chippy Shaik's role and Modise's interests, but also in a battle over similar large-scale economic interventions by government to leverage high-tech investment in the economy. But that Manuel himself could be accused of impropriety is hardly credible on the evidence.

'Incorruptible,' replied Kader Asmal, himself a critic of the arms deal, when I asked him for the most appropriate word to describe Manuel. 'Total, absolute incorruptibility.'

THE PROBLEM WITH SPENDING – whether it be on welfare, or education, or even on arms – and cutting the deficit at the same time is that another source of revenue had to be found. It was clear to Gill Marcus soon after she was made chair of the finance portfolio committee in 1994 that more revenue had to be raised internally. And even clearer, in the light of the Katz Commission report into taxation, that it was neither necessary nor desirable for the new government to raise taxes.[23] There had already been the once-off RDP levy, and Liebenberg, when he took over from Keys, was reluctant to reimpose it because it would break faith with the taxpayers even though the government was running a deficit that bordered on dangerous. The Katz Commission reported that there was gap of between R15 billion and R21 billion between actual and potential revenue. The revenue service was simply not tapping into the tax potential.

When she was appointed Manuel's deputy, Marcus took responsibility for the revenue services, which Liebenberg had begun to reform. Just before he had left office, he appointed Trevor van Heerden as the Commissioner of the Revenue Services, a man whom Marcus described as 'technically very competent' in tax affairs but who 'was unable to see strategically where we wanted to go'. In late 1997, Marcus suggested to Manuel that they approach Pravin Gordhan to fill the spot of deputy commissioner. 'It was quite counter-intuitive,' said Manuel.

So counter-intuitive that Gordhan was puzzled. A pharmacist by training, a long-time underground and community activist, he had since 1994 chaired Parliament's constitutional affairs committee. Before that, he had chaired the negotiations – Codesa – that navigated the transition to democracy. Marcus had seen him at work during the Codesa negotiations, 'a strategically complex and organisationally complex' task. She had been deeply impressed with his skill. 'And therefore when I looked at the Revenue Service and saw what was required, I said we need someone who has the strength of character and that strength of purpose … (and) the ability to organise people. The only person who could make it happen was Pravin, and Pravin was very reluctant. It took a lot of persuasion. It took months!'

'It seemed like such an obvious choice,' Manuel reflected after Marcus had canvassed him on the possibility. 'But when we approached him he said, Oh my God, you're trying to take me out of politics. Is there an agenda here?'

'Yes,' confirmed Marcus. 'He couldn't believe I was saying to him this is the most important job in the country.'

'It was out of the blue,' Gordhan told me. 'I didn't know what SARS (the South African Revenue Service) was, I didn't know what SARS did, I didn't realise the impact that SARS could have.'

A somewhat bemused Gordhan was appointed deputy commissioner in March 1998. In November that year, after Trevor van Heerden resigned, he became commissioner. (It's a sign of the confidence that Gordhan developed that when Van Heerden, after a few unhappy years in the private sector, asked to return to SARS, he took him back as a consultant.)

In 1998, Gordhan walked into the Revenue Service, where he found his office on the twenty-first floor of the Department of Finance in Vermeulen Street in downtown Pretoria, five floors below the minister, three floors above the commissioner. 'It was fascinating, but I was sidelined immediately.' One man in charge of Special Investigations – investigating tax fraud – told him he did not have to report to him. Others were, at best, dubious about his abilities. A considerable number of the older generation of civil servants tried to help him understand the business, but several others told him nothing at all. 'But I wasn't the type who would just sit and wait for something. I would go out and look for stuff ... it didn't faze me. As far as I was concerned it was another terrain of struggle. And I must just get on with what I have to get on with.'

There was a lot to get on with. For a start, there was scant tax morality in the country. Many small black businesses had effectively boycotted the tax system – not unreasonably when they were not part of the political system, but the culture of non-compliance persisted. In 1995, Nelson Mandela addressed a meeting of quarrelling bosses from the black taxi associations in Pretoria, and urged them to regulate their chaotic and violent industry by registering as businesses. The taxi owners were aghast. 'But aren't you leading us to the taxman?' one asked. 'We don't want to be taxed for what we don't know what for.' Whereupon the even more aghast Mandela gave them a short lecture on good citizenship and tax compliance.[24]

Some of the owners of bigger businesses displayed the same contempt for the tax laws without even the political excuse to do so. The arcane system of taxes – where internal retailers paid value-added tax (VAT), but exporters could claim it back – led to some odd export practices. Trucks would arrive at the border post with a consignment, get 'stamped through', turn around, then claim back the VAT. The two systems – one that processed VAT claims, the other that charged it – didn't 'talk' to each other, so there was no monitoring system. The department that administered income tax was separate from customs, which charged import duties and VAT. Add to that, corruption among customs officials widespread enough to make a significant dent in potential revenue, coupled with a lack of skill and empowerment in regional offices (a manager in East London, for instance, could not make a simple decision without approval from Pretoria), and it amounted to a tax net in shreds.

Marcus and Gordhan drove the reform, enthusiastically backed by Manuel. There were three priorities Gordhan identified: making the Revenue Service more 'client-friendly' – a challenge to any taxman; rooting out corruption especially around VAT, and enforcing the law against the big offenders; and thirdly to prosecute recalcitrant 'clients' who did not file tax returns. Marcus and Gordhan decided to learn from 'the best': they went to Sweden, where income tax compliance is estimated at 98 per cent, to Britain, which Marcus described as world leader in customs compliance. Gordhan learned from the Swedes the art of changing 'the *attitude* of the public'. The other side of the smile, though, is the stick. He and Marcus visited every key border post where there was a customs office, from Beit Bridge on the Zimbabwean border to

Punta D'Oura on the Mozambican border. 'When we saw corruption, we pursued it,' said Marcus. 'And the guys went to jail.' They went around regional offices in small towns to see where the holes were.

Importantly, they made SARS a sexier place to work. Shortly before Gordhan arrived it was split off from the public service and began paying market-related rates to big-hitting accountants, who could ferret out tax fraud. Shortly after his arrival, SARS moved out of the soulless Vermeulen Street building into airy new offices in the upmarket Pretoria suburb of Brooklyn. And where they saw rot, they went for the jugular in a spectacularly public way.

Gordhan managed to retain the best of the old, while hiring sharp new sleuths. First he brought in Judy Parfitt from the Eastern Cape, whom he described as an excellent human resources person who sought out the best talent. For a while, said Gordhan, she was his only 'soulmate'. It was Parfitt who suggested Gordhan hire Ivan Pillay, his old struggle comrade and one of the leaders of Operation Vula. Pillay was appointed the head of enforcement. In his first two years, he and his team recovered nearly R300 million for the fiscus from two firms alone. One was Metro Cash and Carry, which had claimed refunds in VAT on goods supposedly exported. These included 107 000 bullet-proof vests supposedly exported to Mozambique, as well as 48 000 army tents. Most improbably, though, the company claimed to have exported 76 million bras to Lesotho, a country with a population then of two million people, not all of whom, it is safe to assume, wear bras. 'The great Basutho lift,' Manuel called it later.

'The bra, it seems,' said Gordhan at the time, 'has replaced the blanket as Lesotho's national dress.'

After months of litigation and appeals, Manuel and Gordhan finally won the day when the Constitutional Court, in 2000, overturned an Appeal Court ruling in favour of the company, vindicating Gordhan's view that firms must 'pay now, argue later'. The company paid up: R267 million in back taxes and penalties.

Gordhan and Pillay also spearheaded an investigation into the electronics industry, where some companies were notorious for under-invoicing their exports. Several customs officials were found to have been involved in the scam, apparently having received 'televisions, cellphones, furniture, airline tickets, holidays, cash and, in one instance, a rifle'.[25] That operation netted R26 million for the fiscus.

A year after his appointment, Gordhan was able to report a 10 per cent increase in revenue, exceeding the budget target by more than R2 billion.[26]

Tax forms were simplified – by 2007 they were just two pages long, and one million taxpayers submitted their returns online. A decade after he joined SARS, revenue had grown from R184 billion to R558 billion.[27] Corporate tax rates fell from 35 per cent to 28 per cent, and personal income tax went steadily down in all six income tax brackets. The threshold below which no tax is payable went up from R18 500 in 1998/99 to R46 000 in 2008/09. It was an indication of a much wider net.[28]

Gordhan told me that part of his success – and of Manuel's – in exceeding even the ambitious targets set, for revenue collection is embedded in both of their 'activist' pasts. Like Manuel, he trod the streets and knocked on doors to organise communities, taking little for granted about people's political sentiments. Like Manuel, he became used to thinking strategically. 'I suppose there's an intellectual and personal chemistry that allows for both a difference of views, on the one hand, but synergies among our views as well. That enables us to work in a fair amount of harmony.'

If there are differences – and there have been, for instance, over the revenue targets set or over the budget allocated to SARS to pull in the cash required – neither man will speak publicly of them. In that way, Gordhan said, the two are moulded from the same ANC clay that took them through the apartheid years. 'If you want to describe me crudely, I will not break ranks publicly. I'm a very disciplined individual. And so watch me. I will never say anything … That's how we grew up.'

He was describing Manuel as well as himself. The finance minister can do bloody battle in his own ranks, but when it comes to facing the world, he can be inscrutable.

AMONG THE BLOODIEST INTERNAL battles Manuel had were those with the statistical services agency that was added to his growing finance empire in late 1996. Initially, the then Central Statistics Service (CSS) reported to Jay Naidoo when he was the minister responsible for the RDP. After that office closed, Manuel inherited it and with it the first post-apartheid census, known as Census 96.

Mark Orkin, an Oxford and Sussex-educated economist and sociologist, with a doctorate from the University of the Witwatersrand, was appointed statistician general in 1995. Previously he had run a small, but dynamic, statistical research agency called the Community Agency for Social Research (CASE), that produced 'high quality social research for the resistance movement', especially numerical social research. He started CASE in the mid-1980s, at a time when the traditionally Marxist left were suspicious of anything to do with numbers. Jürgen Habermas, the European Marxist theorist, had written that 'big science', including statistical surveys, was mainly undertaken by the 'economic, industrial military elite who can afford it, and they use it to manipulate the citizenry in terms of dominant ideology'.[29]

This was 'seven-tenths' true, Orkin told me. 'But it doesn't necessarily follow from that, that numerically informed social science is reactionary (just because) ... fiendish guys are misusing it.'

So in the face of initial scepticism from his peers, Orkin set up CASE and went on to produce some path-breaking knowledge on education, on health and even religion. One survey in the early 1990s examined whether the youth that had come of age during the worst excesses of apartheid really were a 'lost generation', as they were dubbed by the media. And CASE found that only a small percentage was badly marginalised, really 'lost'; the rest, even those severely disadvantaged, were aspiring and hopeful. Nine years later, Manuel bore this research in mind when he hit two mutual insurance funds for a hefty one-off tax when they demutualised. He used these funds to set up Umsombomvu, a foundation for young, disadvantaged entrepreneurs. 'And I thought, isn't policy research fantastic, because ... it has consequences in unintended arenas years (after) it was written,' said Orkin.

Orkin loves numbers: 'If you've got big enough data, it speaks to you. You aren't doing it any more. The world is talking through those numbers and your techniques, and you *know* when that's happening. It's bigger than you and it comes through, and out.'

So he was well suited for the job as the first post-apartheid statistician general. But little could prepare him for the huge challenges ahead. For a start, he was catapulted out of his cosy office in Braamfontein, where he ran an NGO of 25 like-minded people, to the dour surroundings of the Central Statistical Services in downtown Pretoria. At the time the staff numbered some 800. Most of them had never been involved in a real census, in the sense of counting every single person. The numbers of black people were mainly estimated by aerial surveys, or by employment figures, both unreliable measures. Measurements of economic activity were largely confined to the white population, as most black businesses ran on the margins of the formal sector – posing the problems Gordhan described of creating a single tax morality and tax base. 'We haven't yet understood what it means to govern a country of 47 million by just four million,' Pali Lehola told me. Lehola was Orkin's deputy until 2000, and took over the post of statistician general after Orkin left.

Lehola, born and raised in Lesotho, studied demographics in Ghana, and quite by accident, en route from Lesotho to Botswana whither he was fleeing political violence in his homeland, landed a job in the statistics office in Bophuthatswana, one of the nominally independent black homelands. That was in 1982.

In 1995 Orkin and Lehola took charge of the first all-inclusive census in South Africa. At the same time, Orkin had to 'transform' the service – a South African euphemism for getting a more representative racial mix in management – which meant negotiating retrenchment packages for some of the older, white managers and recruiting new black talent. And they had one year to prepare for the first major census. Most developed countries, even middle-income countries such as Australia and Canada, have a lead time to plan a census of between two and five years. 'In any country it would have been an insanely short time,' said Orkin, 'but in our country in a state of transition with a fundamentally different approach from the past, it was even more insanely short.'

But the new government was intent on getting the numbers right so that it could plan a future. 'If you can't measure it, you can't manage it,' Manuel would say to his officials. And because the statistics service was also responsible for producing economics statistics, such as inflation and unemployment figures, it seemed logical that it move, in 1997, into the domain of what Lehola called 'the most difficult minister, because he's a perfectionist'.

Everything that could go awry with Census 96 did. The demographers were confronted with a complete unknown. Not only had most people never been enumerated, many had no addresses. So the statisticians hired pilots to fly over informal settlements and rural areas on the same day to map areas through aerial photography. But when the day came to fly, it rained. It rained throughout that summer of 1995/96 so the mapping was delayed. When detailed mapping finally began, Statistics SA (as it had been renamed) provided nails to its field workers to affix numbers to rural huts and semi-urban shacks. But the nails were too short to go through the walls of mud huts. The field workers tried to spraypaint numbers on huts, using

485

a different colour for each Enumeration Area (EA) so census counters could more easily demarcate areas. And one colour of paint would run out, so they would continue spraying huts with the same colour paint, seven million all told. When census day came it was hard to distinguish one EA from another. 'This is where the calamity is on addresses,' Lehola recalled. 'We can't go on like this. For heaven's sake, we need addresses!' In fact, most people were happy that at last they had numbers on their houses. It was a sign that the government recognised their existence.

On the urging of government, the statistical services hired unemployed matriculants as census takers. Lehola would have preferred to have hired teachers, but government felt it would do more social good to give the matriculants a chance. They asked 'university people' to train the enumerators, said Lehola, which may have been a mistake because the academics would get lost in such theoretical debates as 'what is night?' (The census counts how many people are in each household on one particular night, in this case the night of 10 October, 1996.) As in the case of SARS, there were consultants, in this case the Swedes and the Australians. The Swedes had advised the statistical service to have nine provincial centres to collate the figures instead of one national centre. In this way, the local people would 'own' the results. Which was all very well, said Orkin, 'but it meant that we had nine problem areas instead of one, nine strikes instead of one'.

There were indeed strikes and disruptions; there was even a hostage-taking incident. One night, shortly before Christmas, enumerators held their supervisors hostage in Limpopo because their cheques were late. They threatened to drive to Pretoria that night to get their money. Lehola promised to 'fax' them the money. And he did: a cheque for R2 million to the local bank. They were mollified and agreed to wait until the bank opened the next morning, by which time real money had been deposited in the account.

By the time Manuel inherited the Statistics Office, the count was done. The statisticians were doing a Post Enumeration Survey (PES), a sophisticated check on the actual numbers. It is beyond the capacity of many developing countries to do this: in fact South Africa was the first African country to do so. It is a detailed check of a one per cent sub-sample to make sure that the numbers calibrate. In South Africa, however, unlike developed countries, the PES had to consider such questions as: is this hut, with this colour spray paint, and 13 people in it, the one that was enumerated, or is it the one 15 metres down the dust road with 17 people in it?

Orkin, Lehola and their international advisers assumed that there might be an undercount. Whites in suburbs with high walls had been difficult to access (a leading financial weekly at the time actually urged whites to boycott the census); white farmers refused to cooperate; black youth in informal sectors had been suspicious and were thus undercounted. Then there were whites who had left the country but no one could be sure whether they had actually emigrated (most did not say so).

When the PES turned up a 2,7 million undercount, about half of which was in the Western Cape, the experts were not surprised. But before the statisticians could recalculate the count, the government pushed them to release the preliminary census numbers. Which they did, against the advice of their international consultants.

That September morning in 1998, when Orkin, Lehola and one of the Australian consultants met Manuel to brief him on the results, they were quite pleased with themselves for the methodological rigour with which they'd worked. 'We'd found the 2,7 million and we were really rather proud of that,' said Orkin.

They were blown to pieces by Manuel's reaction. As Lehola tells it, interspersed with robust guffaws: 'He goes . . .' And with his hand he simulates an upward spinning motion. 'Julia (Evans, the Australian consultant) was sitting behind me and Mark when he rose. She just disappeared into the wall . . . I couldn't see her. She just *disappeared*!'

'He was *absolutely incandescent*,' recalled Orkin. 'It was more startling because we knew we hadn't made a mistake. We'd done our best in terms of the preliminary statistics but against all advice we'd delivered them.'

On reflection, Orkin said 'incandescent' was not the word: *ballistic* was a more accurate description. 'He literally just blew up. He went through at full volume.'

'How do I face the president and this nation and tell them this?' yelled Manuel. 'I'll have to resign.'

'Mr Minister, I'll have to resign before you do,' replied Orkin.

'Going through my mind,' reflected Orkin, 'was the thought that we were just going to have to stay put and talk this through.'

Which they did. Manuel calmed down. He started talking about what to do about it. 'And then he blew up for a second time!'

For Orkin, it was a rough baptism into the world of *realpolitik*. 'I was an experienced public sector social statistician, but was not experienced around the political process,' he said. 'I did not understand the excitement the opposition would have in attacking a black majority government for any instance of incompetence … about the legitimacy of the public statistics, for instance.'

'So what has to be done?' Manuel asked them when he'd cooled down the second time. The government communication services and a PR company released a statement explaining the discrepancy in the statistics. Manuel asked Orkin to explain the correction to the provincial premiers (who have a great interest in population numbers in their provinces as it determines their slice of the national budget). 'I was hugely impressed by how professional he was,' said Orkin. 'This was the first diagnosing of results … and then he mobilised resources that we needed. He was with us all the way.'

Statistics SA was always a potentially explosive point for Manuel. When it produced numbers that reflected the economy in a less than flattering light, he had to sit on his hands not to interfere. At the same time, he wanted an agency whose accuracy was unassailable. Take unemployment figures: the bane of the macroeconomic stabilisation plan in its first five years. Some time in the late 1990s, Manuel told Orkin that if their instruments were better, they would pick up more employment. There was some truth to this. Roz Hirshowitz, a survey designer who ran the October Household Survey, which measured employment, realised that the questionnaire did not cater for employees of small businesses in the informal sector, such as house painters or construction workers. Once she included that question, the statisticians picked up half a million more employed people.

Manuel even sent the questionnaires to the International Labour Organisation at one stage to check on how they compared internationally. 'Well, we were delighted, and he wasn't, because they sent it back and said, this is extremely good; it is much more thorough than most of those we encounter, especially in a developing country,' said Orkin.

At the same time, Manuel was a stickler for accuracy. When Orkin decided, independently, to change the definition of unemployment to the 'narrow' definition – which excludes people who are not actively looking for work – in line with more than three quarters of other countries in the world, Manuel was horrified. But Orkin held his ground, pointing out that South Africa would be disadvantaged compared with other countries when it came to investment ratings if it didn't measure unemployment in a comparable manner. In the end, the statistical service produced two figures: the classic definition of unemployment as well as the broader one.

It was only after Orkin left Statistics SA in 2000 that the employment figures began to show genuine improvement. As the bearer of sometimes unwelcome news before that, Orkin had been subjected to several ear-bashings by Manuel in his years as statistician general. 'But although he felt quite free to talk in my ear at 6.30am about a result that he thought was wrong, he would never pressure us into changing anything,' said Orkin. 'Ever.'

WHILE MANUEL HAD TO build the components of a team that worked – in finance, in the revenue and statistical services – the real challenge was to get political buy-in from the provinces and from other cabinet members for budget decisions. Team Finance, as he called it, was, crucially, the provincial legislators in charge of finance, and his cabinet peers.

This was not always easy. Cabinet ministers, but particularly provincial ministers of finance, had to be recruited to this cause in the wake of the sometimes brutal interference in their expenditure in 1997/98. Three were effectively managed by the Treasury between 1997 and 2000 (Eastern Cape, KwaZulu-Natal and Mpumalanga).

There were times when Manuel was upbraided in cabinet meetings by ministers unhappy with their budgets. Sometimes – unlike the implementation of GEAR – Manuel did not get support from Mbeki, then deputy president, if the complainant was politically close to him. There were other instances, too, when he felt uneasy, such as the time when cabinet, at the urging of then health minister Nkosazana Dlamini-Zuma and Mbeki, agreed to give R5 million to Zigi and Olga Visser, the Pretoria doctors who were pioneering Virodene as a cure for Aids. It was later found to contain a toxic industrial solvent. One insider described the decision to disburse the money as 'totally irregular'.

His solution to disaffection among politicians was an old activist one: to bring them on board so the Budget became not 'his', but 'ours'. Kuben Naidoo, who spent two years working in the United Kingdom Treasury, says the South African budget stands out as an example of a 'collective, collegial one'. Gordon Brown, who was then the Chancellor of the Exchequer, 'certainly didn't have that view', said Naidoo. 'His (was), "This is my budget. I'll tell you what you're going to do".'

It helped that Manuel read every single cabinet memorandum before meetings. Few cabinet ministers did – in fact after F W de Klerk left government in 1996, Kader Asmal said only he (Asmal) and Manuel read every cab memo, as they are known in the parlance of government. But Manuel had to, as did his officials. It is the fiduciary duty of the Treasury to know the financial implications of any government proposal. When Manuel walked into cabinet meetings on Wednesdays he was one of a handful who knew 'everything in cabinet', according to Andre Roux who headed the Budget Office until 2000.

'So in the contest around money, he was always at an advantage, given his own knowledge, his memory and the capacity under him that he could actually mobilise,' said Roux. Manuel's memory is legendary among his colleagues. 'It's so powerful as an official to work into. You can't always make sure that (information you give him) lands with him at the right moment. In politics, it kneads around, in cabinet it pulls backwards and forwards. Ministers come to him when there's a social occasion and ... say, I need more money for this and so on. How do you react? Trevor would have in his memory, this is the story ... and he would be able to say, "Well, we can talk about it, but how about this thing, it's something I wanted to raise with you ..."

'And immediately the conversation puts them on the back foot.'

His great strength, Andrew Donaldson told me, is a 'ruthless' resistance to 'special pleading' whether it be from business interests or from cabinet colleagues. Donaldson, who had been in the department since Keys was there, said this resistance was also characteristic of Keys and Liebenberg, Manuel's predecessors. 'The queues of people who used to line up outside Trade and Industry, or Finance, with special interests have disappeared.'

In 1998, Manuel introduced the Medium Term Expenditure Framework (MTEF) – three-year rolling budgeting plans that allowed Parliament and cabinet to make an early input. Manuel resisted the demands of some parliamentarians and COSATU that they be allowed to change the Budget in its current year. In law, it can only be accepted or rejected, to avoid a stalemate that could hold up government programmes. 'The MTEF will enable Cabinet to make decisions based on ... policy ... rather than expenditure,' Ramos told the parliamentary committee on finance in late 1997.[30]

It was part of a massive overhaul of public finances. In 1999, the Public Finance Management Act[31] was passed. It was driven largely by Ismail Momoniat and held heads of government departments and public enterprises accountable not only for over-expenditure, but for 'wasteful and fruitless' expenditure.

And in 2001, the Department of Finance formally merged with the Department of State Expenditure (although they had been effectively working together for some time) to become the National Treasury, with Maria Ramos at its head. At last there was a formal system to match expenditure with budget policy and to monitor expenditure throughout the year.

The quest for transparency was aimed at mustering domestic political support when some tough budget decisions had to be made. But it had international payback. In 2006, the Open Budget Index, a non-profit organisation in Washington that monitors public finance systems around the world, named South Africa the fourth most transparent country in terms of Budget information, scoring 85 out of a possible 100 points. (The top three are France, the United Kingdom and New Zealand.)[32]

'Trevor's skill,' Gill Marcus said, 'was that inclusiveness. You create the cabinet cluster of ministers, you create your Minmecs (committees comprising national and provincial ministers), you create the question of getting people involved in the decision. But it is something that you could not have done if your clarity of thinking and purpose was not there from the president or deputy president.' Nobody, she said, could go to Manuel 'on the side', and say 'I need this or that'; nobody could go to the president or deputy president and complain that 'these people are too harsh ... That was crucial to the success. In most countries you find that the minister of finance who needs to make reforms is held out on a limb.'

Those who have worked at the Treasury since Manuel's appointment, describe it as a place where intellectual argument is as valued as diligence. 'If you provide a well structured, well thought-out argument you'll be listened to. Similarly if you talk bullshit you'll be told so,' said Kuben Naidoo, who rose steadily in the ranks at the Treasury to become head of the Budget Office. Preparing for the 2005 Budget, for example, he had an ongoing argument with Manuel about whether to cut the corporate tax rate. Naidoo proposed cutting it by 2 per cent from 30 per cent to 28 per cent; Manuel was opposed to any cut. 'But he didn't say, look, I'm the minister of finance, and I've told you 10 times, will you shut your mouth and get on with the job. Trevor didn't say that. So I went and found data on cash reserves of the corporates. And I said: here, they're holding cash reserves.' Naidoo told Manuel that mining companies were not investing for political reasons, and other companies were not for financial reasons. At the next Budget meeting, he pushed his point. Manuel did his own research. 'So it was a discussion, but it was a discussion

491

based on evidence, on research.' At one point, said Naidoo, Manuel 'got very irritated'.

'You're swimming with crocodiles,' he told Naidoo.

'So in my next memo (about the issue) I entitled it "swimming with crocodiles".'

In the end, Manuel cut the corporate tax rate – not by two per cent but by one per cent. But for Naidoo it was a salutary lesson in how to have an argument: 'Nobody putting their egos on the table' – but with research and facts and evidence.

Several officials in the Treasury will tell stories about politicians who treat officials like skivvies – one even asked Naidoo to fetch her ice cream during a workshop to discuss the Budget. 'Trevor would never do that, never ever. He values intellectual input.' Civil servants talk to each other, and know those politicians who behave as if they've been enthroned rather than elected. One calls her bodyguards at all hours of the day or night for no apparent reason, and makes her officials stand when she enters or leaves a room.

'Within government,' Donaldson told me, 'the Treasury is an unusually creative place to work. There's a lot of room for ideas and for engagement with ideas and that's one of Trevor's great strengths. He welcomes debate, he's willing to engage with people, he takes advice, he's actually very cautious about taking decisions without advice, and that's healthy … (it) creates an atmosphere where people feel there's space to raise issues and he will take it seriously.'

Not all relationships in the Treasury have worked so well. Deep rifts developed in the relationship between Manuel and his first deputy, Gill Marcus. Neither will talk about it. A former colleague of Marcus's told me that she (Marcus) felt 'abused' by both Manuel and Ramos – partly perhaps because she considered herself senior to Ramos in the ANC and felt the latter didn't respect her. 'I just think there was no chemistry between them at all,' said her colleague.

Yet, neither Marcus nor Manuel will mention this. In fact, Marcus herself remarked soberly: 'What we had (then) was a single-mindedness of purpose because we were building a country. None of us were thinking, am I a glory boy or not? That was not in the equation.' Tensions are inevitable when you put four 'incredibly strong and driven people together'. (She was referring to Manuel, Ramos, herself and Gordhan.) 'But we are all able to see the big picture, we all (had) a very strong political sense of what was doable and how

492

we needed to get it done.'

Manuel said, yes, there had been 'stand-up rows' in the Treasury, including one between him and Ramos, on one occasion, over tax policy. His concern then, as now, is 'the risk that inequality will widen'.

But, then as now, his attitude was: 'You debate the issues, you listen to the arguments, you look at the numbers, you test and test and test. And part of what we need to do is to test (policy) against our vision of society.'

Perhaps a university degree, even a doctorate from Harvard, such as his Zimbabwean counterpart had, would have been a waste of time. Manuel, more than any other South African cabinet minister, has shown an unusual openness in drawing on local and international academic and policy experts. It was he who invited Sir Nicholas Stern to present a report on the effects of climate change on the international economy to cabinet in 2007; it was he who assembled and commissioned the 'Harvard Panel' – led by Harvard economists Ricardo Hausmann and Dani Rodrik – to investigate new growth paths for the South African economy; and it was he who launched the World Bank Growth Report in South Africa led by Nobel-prize winning economist Michael Spence (on whose commission he sat).

He told the Princeton students in 2006 that 'knowing it' and 'taking decisions' is not the same thing. The question is, how do you do both?

In 2004, Manuel got a letter from Ashlin Anderson, a child at Tafelberg School in Cape Town, who comes from Heideveld, a poor township on the Cape Flats. 'I would like to be the Minister of Finance,' she wrote, 'but I would like to know how to become the Minister of Finance.' And then, some advice for Manuel: 'You know when the rand goes down everybody should get more money, and when the rand goes up, the people must get less money ...'

'Good luck being in charge,' she ended cheerfully.

'You ask me how you become the Minister,' Manuel wrote back to her. 'Well, there is no special school for Ministers. You are appointed by the President of the republic and once you are appointed there is lots more hard work.' He encouraged her to continue studying EMS (Economic and Management Studies) at school, and, if she could, economics at university. 'But to get into university, you will need good results at school. Good results can only be attained through hard work. I know all this talk of hard work is very boring. It does not have to be – it is possible to work hard *and* play hard.'[33]

CHAPTER 28

Choice, not fate

As the century turned so did Manuel's personal life. On a Friday afternoon in April 2001, after the markets had closed, he and Lynne Matthews announced in a press statement that they had separated and were to begin divorce proceedings. They asked for privacy to protect their three young sons who were then 14, 12 and 9. President Thabo Mbeki issued a statement saying the matter had no bearing on Manuel's role as finance minister.

For more than a year before there had been a ripple of rumours, among politicians, journalists and even in the amorphous markets, that Manuel and Maria Ramos were involved in a relationship. Shortly before the announcement of the divorce, an intrepid reporter called Manuel on his cellphone while he was on the golf course to ask whether it was true that (a) he was getting divorced and (b) he was about to marry Ramos. The reporter felt the full brunt of Manuel's legendary temper, as much because she'd dared to interrupt his golf game as for the question.

The suggestions and innuendoes intensified after the divorce announcement. Notably, there was a cartoon on the cover of *Noseweek*, an irreverent, investigative magazine – that had them sitting in a swimming pool together, their faces grafted on to swim-suit clad bodies, Ramos in a bikini and Manuel in swimming trunks. 'If they knew anything about the two of us,' Ramos told me drily, 'they would know that neither of us can swim.' Sitting around a swimming pool was not exactly something they did 'on a daily basis'.

The magazine came out shortly before Ramos won the award for the Businesswoman of the Year. She had not seen the magazine when she was interviewed, ostensibly about the award, on a radio talk show, and was clearly taken aback when the presenter asked her whether she and Manuel were 'an item'. 'I kept saying this is about the work I have done. And, no, I'm not going to discuss my relationship with you, my private life, I already have so little privacy.'

Manuel was enraged and phoned the presenter and blasted him. 'None of your bloody business,' he said.

In fact, it was remarkable that the couple managed to keep their relationship under wraps for so long. It had started early on in their time in the Treasury, soon after Manuel was appointed minister. At first, the press didn't pick it up and, later, those who did, with the exception of *Noseweek*, kept quiet about it. It is a point that Ramos acknowledges. '(The media) were incredibly respectful of our privacy – and I'll always be grateful to them for it – I really felt they treated us with dignity.'

It was an on-off affair for some years, partly because of Manuel's family, but also partly because of the fact that they worked together in two of the most critical positions in the country. So discreet were they that few of their colleagues in the Treasury knew about it. Even Kader Asmal, who shared his Pretoria house with Manuel for 10 years when they were in cabinet together, claimed not to know.

When there were odd speculative stories in the media, Kuben Naidoo told me, 'I'd say to myself, no man, I don't believe this. They managed it in an incredibly professional manner. Maria is a workaholic and she set a culture in the Treasury that I enjoyed.' Only occasionally did he feel the need for a personal life of his own, such as the time he was on a first date with a girlfriend, eating ice cream on the steps of the Union Buildings, when Ramos called to tell him there was one word wrong in a cabinet memo. He went back to the office, changed the document, reprinted it, and left at about 2am. (His relationship survived.)

Andre Roux echoed this. 'They were quite discreet. I didn't know whether they had become partners or not. (But) there was no question that Maria could influence Trevor, we were all completely aware of it.'

Manuel, he said, is 'without a doubt the most impressive person I've ever worked with. But he's difficult. He can at times be quite moody and unsettle people around him, and there were some meetings … where, quite honestly, in my view, Trevor would try put you on your place. Unnecessarily. Sometimes I felt very irritated.'

But often when the officials lost a battle or had been put 'on their place', 'Maria would go to work on him and sometimes he would change his mind.'

For Ramos's part, she said she made a decision early on to keep the relationship and her work 'quite separate'.

'I can't remember a single instance when I went into a meeting with Trevor, even after he and I were more openly in a relationship, when I did not go in with the team to bat for the team. So I never actually felt professionally compromised. I never took a decision or any position in any discussion or debate with Trevor that I felt I was taking because we were now in a relationship. It was never about that. Even when we were in a relationship, and people knew we were in a relationship, we had some very intense disagreements and arguments – about issues, about work.'

During the heated argument about tax policy that Manuel recalled, they were 'virtually screaming at each other and everybody else stood in awe, too petrified to intervene. And my difficulty was that their loyalty to her was stronger than their individual loyalty to me.'

In other circumstances, if the two had perhaps not been dedicated to their work, or if they had palpably failed, or been arrogant and dismissive of the media as some South African politicians have been, their private lives may not have escaped critical public glare. But both worked abnormally long hours, both recruited and maintained some of the most talented officials in government, and both kept their staff aware of their obligations to the public. As a result, barely a whisper of suspicion came out of the Treasury itself. Manuel's sharp tongue may have dissuaded all but the most persistent outside enquirers from pursuing the matter.

But then there was the more serious matter of how they felt about each other. For Ramos, by the end of 2001, it was no contest. She had considered 'walking away' from the relationship, but then thought that 'it's not about that … It's not so easy in life to find someone you can connect with at so many levels. So it wasn't going to be case of simply stepping down ... and walking away from it. I kept thinking well, I'd rather leave the job and walk away from *it*, if it ever came to that.'

But it didn't. In 2003, Ramos resigned from the Treasury and went to head Transnet, the vast transport public enterprise, which she soon began to overhaul. She also told me that it was the 'first time she had felt happy at a personal level', once the commitment between them was clear and the relationship on solid ground.

Manuel, for his part, is more taciturn: 'All these things are organic, people grow together,' he said.

And yet, in the months when I interviewed one of them, usually at their comfortable kitchen tables in either their Pretoria or Cape Town government homes, when the other walked into the room both visibly brightened.

It was not an easy time, least of all for Lynne Matthews, who had stuck with Manuel through the travails of the struggle and jail time for more than two decades, nor for his immediate family, who valued her as a pillar during a time when they anguished about his safety. Matthews is still special to Manuel's family. She still occupies an important place in his mother's heart and mind. Yet there is a depth of reflection in their acceptance of his new situation. 'They (he and Ramos) are very happy together,' his mother has told me. And although she and his sister Pam felt deep empathy for Matthews, they eventually accepted Manuel's new relationship with reluctant grace.

When Ramos left the Treasury after seven years, her colleagues produced a glossy tribute to her in the form of a magazine, entitled simply 'Maria'. Kganyago recounted the Pepsi Cola/champagne deal story; Phakamani Hadebe recalled her irritation at how, in 2003, he managed to get her lost in London trying to find the Standard & Poor's office (which was about to upgrade South Africa): 'If you can't find the physical address how are we going to put people on the moon?' she'd asked him. Manuel wrote a piece titled simply with her full name: *Maria de Conçeição das Neves Calha Ramos*. It gave a glimpse of how central she was to him in the early days of building a new Treasury. He recounted how many memos, with grammatical or spelling mistakes, she red-penned with the words: 'DON'T GIVE ME THIS RUBBISH!' and how the 'new diktat' in the Treasury corridors became 'Don't write rubbish and don't miss deadlines'.

'Could the environment be any tougher? Of course not. Could it be a more pleasurable environment for economists committed to transformation? Of course not. Will her legacy live on? Unless the vandals arrive to destroy it, the cultural change that has bombarded the Treasury has been internalised and will be permanent. Will we miss her?'[1]

THE NEW CENTURY ALSO brought a change in Manuel's political stature. It rose on the changed fortunes of a country that after five years of austerity began a more robust spending programme.

Manuel began his Budget Speech in 2001 with an extract from the poem 'Afrique' by David Diop, the French-born West African poet.

> That tree there
> In splendid loneliness amidst white and faded flowers
> That is Africa your Africa
> That grows again patiently and obstinately
> And its fruits gradually acquire
> The bitter taste of liberty.[2]

'The *bitter* taste of liberty?' Manuel asked. 'Does the lemon always ripen before the sweet plum? Or do we have it in our power to determine for ourselves the quality of liberty we earn from struggle?'

Diop was writing at the brink of decolonialisation of his ancestral home. Manuel was speaking more than 40 years later, halfway into the first decade of his country's independence. Post-colonial Africa was already, in parts, a legacy of broken dreams. The indebtedness of many countries had trapped them in new relations of subordination. Diop's words were strangely prophetic because he was killed in 1960, in a plane crash off Dakar, aged just 32, at the first light of African independence.

'The Budget we table before the House today,' said Manuel, 'is the story of an irrevocable and powerful transformation. It is the story of a nation which has worked without rest to build a new history for its children. Like Diop's young tree at the edge of the ancestral savannah at the dawn of our continent's independence, ours is a story of patience and obstinacy. Of determination and hope. Of activism, not atavistic tolerance. Of choice, not fate.'[3]

'When will our suffering bear fruit?' he had asked in his Budget Speech in 2000, quoting Nigerian poet and novelist, Ben Okri. The answer was to be found in 2001, in a Budget which Manuel described as the 'fruit of the macroeconomic transition'. He handed out apples to legislators that year.

It was the first fruit of the new economic policy. Real non-interest spending increased by 4 per cent, taxes dropped by a total of R8,3 billion, and the economy grew by 3 per cent, the fastest rate of growth recorded since 1996.[4] The deficit had come down to just over 2 per cent of GDP. 'It is instructive to reflect on how different things might have been,' Manuel told Parliament. 'Debt service costs rose during the 1990s from 15 per cent to over 20 per cent of the Budget in 1998/99, steadily eroding the resources available for the delivery of services. If that trend had continued, the headlines for today's Budget would have been "Interest on debt now R10-billion more than spending on education and rising." But we reversed that trend. Next year we will spend R10 billion more on education than on debt and, by 2003/2004, R15 billion more. Interest on debt will have retreated in three years' time to 16,4 per cent of consolidated spending.'[5]

Infrastructure spending increased substantially too for the first time since 1994, by a total of more than R6 billion. Social grants increased, both in size and in terms of the number of people eligible for them. By 2006 there were about 12 million people receiving social grants. South Africa must be the only country in the world where there are more social welfare recipients than taxpayers. Twenty-five per cent of the population receive social grants – the highest proportion in the world – not, Manuel told me, something of which the country should necessarily be proud.

By 2001, GEAR had shown some significant successes: the deficit was down, and with it the horrendous debt-service costs; as a result interest rates had fallen to 7,5 per cent from nearly 15 per cent just two years earlier; inflation had fallen to about 7,8 per cent, despite a rise in oil prices; and an increase in state expenditure – particularly on the poor – had increased significantly in real terms.[6]

The reduction of debt accelerated after Tito Mboweni was appointed Reserve Bank governor in 1999, with Gill Marcus, who had been Manuel's deputy, as deputy governor. During the 1998 Asian crisis which had rocked the South African markets, and had sent the currency on a downward spiral, the previous governor, Chris Stals, put substantial resources into stabilising the rand. This meant not only raising interest rates, but also effectively betting the rand against the dollar. The Net Open Forward Position (NOFP) – the country's uncovered foreign exchange liabilities – had reached a monumental negative of $25 billion by 1999.

Although there has long been a personal rivalry and sometimes friction between Mboweni and Manuel, and although Mboweni has jealously guarded the independence of the Reserve Bank, the two worked tightly together to coordinate monetary and fiscal policy. Thus by 2001, the NOFP had been reduced from minus $25 billion to minus $10 billion, and by 2004 it had been eliminated altogether. 'It's an extraordinary story,' said Marcus. 'This was a cooperation between Treasury and ourselves, ja? So you had an alignment of policy between Treasury and Central Bank. Not an influence, but a question of saying how do we complement each other?'

'All that forward book nonsense is all gone, finished,' Mboweni told me in late 2006. 'It's all paid back. The strategic issue was to get rid of the thing because the structural overhang had caused a lot of unnecessary volatility in the market. It was piling up and we had to get rid of that.'

Instead of selling dollars it didn't have, the Reserve Bank embarked on a different strategy: buying excess dollars whenever they were available. But it did not chase them. So, for instance, when Anglo-De Beers restructured in 2001, the Reserve Bank creamed off a substantial portion of the excess dollars that flooded into the market as a result of that transaction.[7]

'All the dealers in the market know that when the Forex market has excess dollars in the market, those dealers come to offer us those dollars. When there's no excess in the market we don't buy,' Mboweni told me. It's not a currency intervention, such as the Reserve Bank of old did. 'We just want to buy when there are excess dollars. Some call it creaming off. Creaming off dollars, the excess. If there's no cream, we don't drink!'

By 2006, South Africa had foreign exchange reserves of $25 billion: that represents a turnaround from the mid-1990s of $50 billion. Manuel and Mboweni may sometimes prickle each other's egos, but when Mboweni reported this quite remarkable achievement to the parliamentary finance committee that year, both men shared a common irritation. One of the few questions from a politically correct but otherwise less than clued-up committee member was: 'Is there a woman involved in managing the reserves?'

'Bloody hell,' said Mboweni. 'I was really irritated that day.'

It was the combination of closing the forward book, the careful restructuring of debt by Ramos and her team, and of course the huge boost in tax collections that allowed the first fruit of 2001 to be harvested. 'This is the basic story,' Michael Katz, who chaired the tax commission, told Manuel in 1997. 'You take away all of the lobbying through a myriad incentives, you lower the tax rate and you get bang for the buck.' That was what happened in 2001, and although sufficient growth was not yet there to solve South Africa's huge unemployment problem 'it felt like we were on safer ground and therefore we could spend', Manuel told me.

'What 1996 was all about,' said Andrew Donaldson, 'was taking the long term view … and although (it) was tough it was undoubtedly the right thing to do. This was an economy that had forgotten how to grow, an economy that no longer knew how to invest, an economy that for 10 years had not maintained its roads and not replaced its locomotives and allowed industry gradually to stagnate.' There had been a slow decline in living standards, a dwindling of investment to 'almost nothing'.

'Reform brings pain,' said Rudolf Gouws. 'The tribute to Trevor is that, first as minister of Trade and Industry, and then as minister of Finance he was willing to inflict the pain because he knew that in the end the pain would yield gain.' Gouws, who has monitored every Budget as a banking economist for the past 35 years spoke to me in 2006. At that point, for the first time in his career, growth exceeded inflation and the South African economy had grown consistently for the past 84 months 'the longest recorded phase of economic growth'.

By 2001, GEAR had done its job, albeit imperfectly, and new economic strategies could be implemented. 'Right at the heart of GEAR,' said Manuel 'was (that) the minute growth reached 3 per cent, a balance of payments constraint kicked in. That was the epicentre of this thing. And you needed to deal with the balance of payments constraint so you could lift growth levels in order to create the employment.'

GEAR made the mistake of assuming it had control over more instruments than it actually did, as Manuel later acknowledged. It assumed lower (but positive) interest rates that would stimulate growth. This did not *begin* to happen until 1999. In fact, in the wake of the turbulence caused by the Asian market crisis in 1998, the Reserve Bank put up interest rates no fewer than eight times.

That inhibited investment and with it employment. It was only in 2001 that employment figures began to show a steady growth from 11,2 million in 2001 to 12,8 million in 2006. But, perversely, unemployment rose too, reaching a high of 31 per cent in 2003.[8] More and more people, mainly African women, now free to move to cities, were actively looking for work. Unemployment declined to 25,5 per cent in 2006 and 23 per cent in 2008 (by the narrow definition), but nonetheless its climb during the first few years of GEAR gave ammunition to Manuel's critics.

Part of the problem is that South Africa's education system does not produce people with sufficient skills to enter growing industries. In 2006, the Institute of Justice and Reconciliation (a Cape Town based NGO) assessed education thus: 'By 2008/9 South Africa will be spending R112 billion per year on public provision of education. This amounts to nearly 20 per cent of non-interest expenditure, the largest spending on a single sector, and is over R26 billion more than the current fiscal year's allocation. (Yet) nearly 80 per cent of schools provide education of such poor quality that they constitute a very significant obstacle to social and economic development.'[9]

Manuel quoted this report at the annual lecture[10] to commemorate his fellow activist Ashley Kriel's death, 20 years after the young Bonteheuwel man had been gunned down by police in Hazendal, where Manuel lived out the last months of his heavy restrictions after being released from jail.

He recalled the revolutions that had so inspired Kriel and his generation: Cuba, Nicaragua, and those of the former Portuguese colonies, Angola, Guinea-Bissau and Mozambique. He quoted Jorge Rebelo, the Mozambican poet of the revolution. It begins thus:

Come, brother, and tell me your life
come, show me the marks of revolt
which the enemy left on your body ...

And ends so:

... later I will forge simple words
which even the children can understand
words which will enter every house
like the wind
and fall like red hot embers
on our people's souls.

In our land
Bullets are beginning to flower.

Then, in front of the generation that had been the most ardent defenders of revolutions, he deromanticised them: Nicaragua had been 'overrun' by

502

United States-backed Contras; even though Daniel Ortega, the Sandanista leader, was latterly elected into power he had now even fewer resources to satisfy his citizens; Angola's new leader, Jose Eduardo dos Santos, had been described as among the 'world's most crooked and predatory presidents'; Guinea-Bissau was barely functioning with civil servants receiving only three months' pay in the past year; only Mozambique was making steady progress from an albeit dismally low base.

And here in South Africa? Did 'bullets begin to flower?' Well, not exactly, and part of the reason was the low matric pass rate, particularly in maths, which condemned young people to a life without tertiary education and skilled employment. 'Should we not pause to ask what these abysmal outcomes are about?' asked Manuel. 'I have used the example of education, but I could as easily have referred to the provision of health care or policing or the construction of communities where once townships existed. But I have used education consciously because it provides such a tangible link between our collective past and future, where our present actions will determine the outcomes. I have used education deliberately, too, because it was so important a site of struggle for the youth in places like Bonteheuwel where the leadership was provided by the young like Ashley Kriel. But I have also used the example of education because we should all understand that if we fail in this area, we will fail this generation of young people, who will be unable to find employment.'

Manuel did not absolve the government from responsibility, but asked where the partnership was between strong communities, committed public servants and a 'developmental state'. Somehow, there is a hiatus between government putting money in the right places, and the delivery of those services. It amounts to a breach of contract with a new generation of citizens.

If there is a single factor that exacerbates unemployment it is that South Africa, more than a decade into its democracy, still lacks sufficiently skilled people. It is a matter of considerable frustration to Manuel and his officials that as much as they could allocate money to key social services such as education and health after 2001, money in itself is no magic wand. Six years later, the disjuncture between expenditure and delivery was still pronounced enough for Manuel to ask whether the bullets of the past had indeed begun to flower.

Some of the drafters of GEAR, such as Donaldson, believe government missed an opportunity to provide jobs for low-skilled workers in broad-based public employment programmes in much the same way F D Roosevelt's government had done during the depression years in the 1930s in the United States. 'Partly there was an argument (in government) that broad-based employment programmes are just temporary and we have a structural problem.' But it was a mistaken view, he told me. Partly it came out of a position in cabinet that South Africa could not afford to go the way of the soaring South East Asian economies 'which pay slave wages, and compete successfully internationally on the strength of that' so it would rather put all its eggs in the basket of a 'high-skilled growth strategy', in the 'mega-projects' that Manuel was sceptical of even in his days as Trade and Industry minister. But the reality, said Donaldson was 'that we had an education system that was highly deficient, (and) we had a highly unequal society with a large number of comparatively unskilled people needing work'.

Manuel found it hard to hide his frustration with the fact that in spite of pouring money into education, in the hope that it would begin to dent unemployment, the system was not delivering results.

After the 2008 Budget, he made this point again. At the bustling annual cocktail party held across the cobbled street from the National Assembly where he delivers his speech, he told the parliamentarians, cabinet ministers, union leaders, and business people gathered there: 'Once the money is allocated it is only the beginning. We make the repeated plea today that the money gets to where it needs to get to. If the money is committed to education infrastructure, that is classrooms and schools and libraries and ablution facilities, then all of us ... must ensure that the money actually buys what it's meant to buy. It's a task in the first instance of parliamentarians, but it's a task of all South Africans because we believe that, fundamentally, education is our future.'

It's not our money, he reminded them.

FINANCE MINISTERS ARE GUARDIANS of other people's money – mostly taxpayers' – but sometimes they are charged with looking after the money of shareholders or bank depositors. In the early 2000s, Manuel was faced with the country's first serious banking crisis in post-apartheid South Africa. The wrong decisions can cost billions, but dithering can destroy investments and trust in the country's financial system.

The banking regulation system in South Africa is complex, and involves the registrar of banks, who reports to the Reserve Bank, the Treasury and, on occasion, the toughened-up Competition Commission.

In 2000, Nedcor, the country's fourth largest bank in terms of banking assets, made a hostile bid to take over Stanbic, the country's second largest financial group. Nedcor already owned just over a quarter of Stanbic stock. Such a merger would have led to the new merged entity controlling more than one third of deposits, mortgages and credit cards in the South African market, and the 'big three banks' (the merged entity in addition to First National Bank and Absa) would have controlled three quarters of these key markets. By any international standards – particularly of like middle-income countries such as Canada and Australia – the concentration would have exceeded the boundaries. Such a merger would also have meant that South Africa had a 'three-pillar' banking system – in other words three major banks of note rather than the 'four-pillar' system favoured by such countries as Australia and Canada. 'The fewer banks you have the more exposed you are because those big banks, if they fail, then you are obliged to bail them out. But if you had four big banks, if one goes belly up, you still have three that could sustain the thing,' explained Lesetja Kganyago, who succeeded Ramos as Treasury director-general in 2004.

The merger also may have led to a loss of jobs – between 10 000 and 15 000 according to Stanbic, which rejected the hostile bid.[11] But there was persistent lobbying by some of the banking interests in the country arguing that government should not interfere with shareholders' wishes and, moreover, the merger would catapult the new bank into the international market as a significant player. They also argued that the high costs of technology in banking would have been cut because a merger would create an economy of scale.

In June 2000, when Manuel decided to block the merger, he found himself on the opposite side of the table from his erstwhile mentor and immediate predecessor Chris Liebenberg, who became chair of the Nedcor board after leaving government four years earlier. If South Africa's big banks could not rationalise, a newspaper quoted him saying at the time, 'they may bleed to death'.[12]

So Manuel's decision to block the merger was deeply unpopular in certain quarters. Two years later, he had to make an even tougher call when he put Saambou, South Africa's seventh largest bank, under curatorship after a run on deposits had depleted it of R1 billion in one day. In a relatively small country such as South Africa, the risks of contagion were great.

Kganyago worked closely throughout the period with both Gill Marcus, who was responsible for banking supervision at the Reserve Bank, and the Registrar of Banks, Christo Wiese. There was fierce disagreement between the Treasury, the Registrar and the Reserve Bank about whether Saambou's problem was one of liquidity, or of solvency. If it was a liquidity problem, the Treasury, on the recommendation of the Reserve Bank as the lender of last resort, could have injected funds to stabilise it. But a solvency problem meant something different: a decision to stabilise such a bank with taxpayers' money would not have been justifiable.

But the Reserve Bank feared that if Saambou were put under curatorship it would have a systemic effect – in other words undermine confidence in other banks in South Africa. There were about 500 000 depositors in Saambou – 'ordinary working-class South Africans ... good, sound depositors', as one official close to the process described them. Curatorship could create a crisis of confidence in the banking system among ordinary South Africans.

There is a duality of authority in bank supervision in South Africa. The Registrar of Banks is housed in the Reserve Bank and supervises banks under the eye of the governor and deputy governor. But he also has a reporting line to the minister of finance, and a range of day-to-day issues, such as bank licensing, need ministerial approval. So when anything is amiss with a bank, the Registrar and Reserve Bank are likely to pick it up first, and recommend to the minister what action to take. Gill Marcus won't discuss specifics of the case, but she did tell me that in times of crisis, such as the run on Saambou and the fall-out that followed in other banks, the relationship between the Bank and the Treasury is of critical importance. It did not matter so much to her that she, Mboweni and Manuel (as well as Kganyago) had all been comrades in the ANC and thus had a political relationship. 'The material question is that you can work together. That you trust each other enough, you trust (each other's) judgement ... you may well have different views about what you need to do, but once you've taken the decision you've got to ... make it work. But I think the heart of it is building relationships because it's not just between Treasury and the Bank, it's with the banks themselves.'

In the Saambou case, this relationship became crucially tested. Because, when it came to the final decision, Manuel had to take it, and he took it against the advice of Reserve Bank officials.

The turning point for Treasury officials was a letter they found in the fat files of documentation on Saambou. It was from the financial director of the bank addressed to both the bank's auditors and the Registrar of Banks saying that the returns Saambou had been filing had been falsified and that he could no longer live with such an unethical practice. That letter, at least for the Treasury officials, gave new insight into whether the problem at Saambou was simply one of liquidity, or a deeper solvency crisis. The letter itself never emerged in the prolific press coverage at the time, although after the bank was put into curatorship, there were reports that Saambou's directors had sold some of their shares a few months before the fatal run on deposits.[13] More than a year later reports emerged that gave an inkling of the deep disagreements between the Treasury, on the one hand, and the Registrar of Banks and the Reserve Bank on the other, over whether, and how, to rescue Saambou. 'At the time,' reported a financial journalist in 2003, 'the Treasury vetoed a plan – put together by Investec and supported by the Reserve Bank – to bale out Saambou, opting instead to put the ailing bank under curatorship.'[14] Wiese, the registrar, went further. On the eve of his retirement, he blamed the Treasury for sparking the crisis and 'set(ing) back the banking sector in SA by 20 years.'[15] There was also an implication that Manuel and the Treasury had decided to cut Saambou loose, because it was an 'Afrikaner' bank. 'All sorts of crazy things,' Kganyago reflected six years later.

Manuel and Mboweni put Wiese out to graze within days of his making this statement, three months before his official retirement date, a sign perhaps of the dictum that Marcus spelled out: 'Once you've taken the decision, you've got to make it work.'

In some ways the Reserve Bank fears of Saambou going into curatorship were vindicated. There was a particularly fearsome run on some of the A2 banks, and then more ominously on BoE, an A1 bank with deposits worth some R46 billion, about double those at Saambou. Some R14 billion worth of deposits 'flew out in just a few days'.[16]

Marcus phoned Kganyago on a Friday evening, asking him to an urgent meeting at the Reserve Bank. But this time there was not any dispute about whether to rescue it. 'BoE was a solid bank,' said Kganyago. 'It was solvent, we were not going to put it into curatorship.' Government guaranteed its deposits, and soon after that, Nedcor bought it 'lock, stock and barrel'. In the end Saambou depositors were also saved when First National Bank bought its home loan book and its retail depositors' book (valued at a total of about R18 billion) for just R1. No depositors lost their money.

The Reserve Bank may have been right about the systemic crisis that followed Saambou's collapse, with the run on small banks. But Treasury's decision to rescue BoE stemmed that run. The aftermath of that crisis was pronounced friction between Treasury and the Reserve Bank, personified by the institution's leaders, Manuel and Mboweni. At one point, shortly after the crisis, Manuel began to float the idea of a 'super-regulator' for banks that would fall under the Treasury, but the Reserve Bank was, unusually publicly, antagonistic to the idea. Manuel quietly shelved it.

For Kganyago, though, the point is this: a finance minister always needs to take decisions, often quickly, and often on the basis of incomplete information. It was good, he comments somewhat wryly, that Manuel was known to be a bold decision maker in his days in the UDF. 'But here he doesn't have an *option*. You don't have an option! You must take a decision; this bank is here, it is solvent, it is not solvent. There is an analysis that is done for you that tells you it is not solvent, here is the advice. If you do not take a decision one way or another, the run continues on the bank … so it was a big benefit that he's a man who can take decisions, who is bold and, more importantly, will live with the consequences of his decisions.'

And then, more trenchantly, Kganyago compares that mandatory decisiveness with other cabinet ministers who have dithered about key decisions. What should have been a fairly simple matter about which company should get the licence to run the national lotto, for instance, was not made in time, resulting in the lotto being temporarily shelved and its beneficiaries suffering. And the minister responsible for communications sat on a crucial decision about who should get the licence to run a second national telephone network. That hesitation is reflected in South Africa's pricey and inefficient telecommunications infrastructure. 'The worst position for a minister of finance would be indecision,' said Kganyago. 'If you decide that you not going to make a decision on the lotto, you can go on … or on some licensing thing for a cellphone operator or a second national operator. In finance, you get to make the decisions and you've got to make them quick and most of the time on the basis of incomplete information. What's important is that you've got to show that you used all the information at your disposal.'

Five years after Manuel put Saambou into curatorship, one of South Africa's most insightful economic columnists, Hilary Joffe, compared the way South Africa's banking authorities, including Manuel, had handled its domestic banking crisis with the way Northern Rock, a regional bank in the United Kingdom, had gone down in the midst of the subprime mortgage loan crisis. 'The banking crisis that hit SA in early 2002 was probably more serious than anyone realised. Yet it was resolved with less noise and certainly less controversy than has been the case in the UK,' she wrote. 'SA didn't do too badly in 2002. Depositors didn't lose their savings and the crisis was averted. Ironically, perhaps, the mess was sorted out because so much of it was behind closed doors.'[17]

On a Sunday evening in February, before the 2008 South African Budget, the government of the United Kingdom announced that it would nationalise the ailing Northern Rock to protect its depositors. Manuel had not had to do that, so it must have been with some satisfaction that he and Pravin Gordhan watched the announcement live on Sky News from his Cape Town home. His senior officials had gathered around his large dining room table to fine-tune the Budget Speech he was to give in Parliament three days later. It was in the middle of these discussions that Gordhan and Manuel disappeared into the living room to watch TV, leaving an impatient Kganyago complaining that 'unconstitutional UK mortgage holders are now holding up the South African budget'.

When Manuel returned to his meeting he grinned and confirmed that indeed the nationalisation of the bank had happened but the British were calling it, rather, 'temporary public ownership'.

CHOICE, NOT FATE. Six months before Manuel used the phrase in his 2001 Budget Speech, it assumed added significance when he became the first South African to chair the Board of Governors of the International Monetary Fund. It catapulted him into the international spotlight at a time when the multilateral financial bodies set up by the Bretton-Woods agreement in 1945 were under attack as never before.

In 1944, at the establishment of the Bretton-Woods institutions, US Treasury Secretary Henry Morgenthau had postulated that 'prosperity, like peace, is indivisible ... poverty where it exists is menacing to all and undermines the well-being of each of us'. Then, Morgenthau was referring to the 'great economic tragedy of our time' – the pre-war depression. Now, more than five decades later, the economic tragedy was poverty, said Manuel.[18] Much of Africa was in worse shape economically now than it had been at independence, he said. Manuel was addressing the 2000 annual meetings of the IMF and World Bank in Prague.

Five years later, the Africa Commission Report also wrote of Africa's declining fortunes. 'When the sun began to set on Europe's foreign empires, and former colonies across the globe began in the 1960s to prepare themselves for independence, nobody was that worried about Africa. The anxiety was all for Asia. After all, Africa was a place of great mineral resources and vast agricultural fecundity. Asia, by contrast, seemed to have only problems and population.'[19]

Today, 'Africa is the poorest region in the world. Half the population lives on less than a dollar a day. Life expectancy is actually falling.'[20]

'All of us today face the urgent task of making sure that the benefits of globalisation are equally spread,' Manuel told the meeting at Prague. 'Growing inequality poses the greatest risk to the future of the global economy.'

Sir Nicholas Stern, who was then the chief economist and vice-president of the World Bank, had attended several such meetings of the IMF and World Bank. Normally, he told me, 'there is always a hubbub of private conversations. There must have been a thousand people in the room, it was teeming. And he said "Ladies and Gentlemen", and there was just silence.'

It may have been the seriousness of the topic he addressed. Partly, too, said Stern, it was Manuel's 'talent at seeing the big problem', and 'his enormous faculties and powers of speech'.

There may have been silence inside the hilltop Congress Centre where the annual meetings of the IMF and World Bank were taking place, but it was pretty rumbustious outside. Thousands of protesters gathered on a knoll opposite the Centre. Czech police blocked off the bridge and the only road leading to it, but despite being out in force (there were 11 000 officers around the city, according to newspaper reports), they did not see the steady trickle of demonstrators who made their way down the steep, grassy hill on the opposite side of the Congress Centre, up the other side. To the surprise of police officers relaxing on the lawn below the walls of the Centre, demonstrators were suddenly at its walls.

They were a disparate bunch. There were members of Jubilee 2000 and pro-African aid organisations who were outraged by the deep debt into which many African countries had sunk; there were 'anarchists from the Czech Republic, Italian communists, British schoolteachers and German truck-drivers'.[21]

Like the protesters in Seattle at the World Trade Organisation six months before, they represented a range of interests: from egalitarian left-wingers who wanted debt cancelled, to conservative protectionists who (in the case of the WTO protests) wanted more, not less, protection for first-world farmers, to disaffected anarchists. 'I hate the police and they hate me,' one 19-year old Czech anarchist told a reporter. 'I would like some real fighting to happen.'[22]

It did. That day protesters trashed a McDonald's in Prague's famous Wenceslas Square, and then tore up the cobblestones, several centuries old, that had survived the Nazis, decades of Communist rule and then the 'Velvet Revolution' of 1989. That night the thousands of delegates, officials and staff at the annual meeting were escorted out of the Centre by police on a dedicated subway line to the other side of the city.

Before he left for Prague, Manuel had been somewhat dismissive of the demonstrators. Perhaps the memory of the more farcical aspects of the Seattle protests were in his mind when he answered a question from Ben Turok, the left-wing ANC MP in a parliamentary committee meeting. Turok asked what South Africa's attitude to the protesters would be and what he thought their point was. 'Well, you know, if you ask one of them why he's wearing a bunny suit today and not a turtle suit, he may tell you that his turtle suit is in the wash,' said Manuel, implying that not even the protesters knew what 'anti-globalisation' meant.

But Prague was different from Seattle. At Seattle, many of the African trade ministers who were keen to drive home new deals to dismantle what the Africa Commission would call the 'disgraceful barriers in the markets' erected by developed countries, were effectively derailed by the protesters, some of whom had scant sympathy for African farmers. At Prague there was a significant group of NGOs both from the industrial countries and Africa, deeply concerned by African poverty. They honed in on the issue of debt.

In his opening address, Manuel said debt 'remains one of the major obstacles to sustainable growth and development'. Debt, as the Africa Commission was to report five years later 'casts a long shadow over the continent's development prospects'. It caused political resentment because much of it had been incurred by dictators (such as Zaire's Mobutu Sese Seko) who had plundered their countries' natural resources and public funds. In the first years of the new millennium, for every dollar of aid that went to Africa, at least 50 (US) cents were returned to the developed countries in the form of debt repayment.

Manuel was sympathetic to many of the NGOs and met with a large group of them, including Jubilee 2000, on two occasions in Prague. The first time, the day before the formal opening, he was with his South African officials. These

511

included Cyrus Rustomjee, who was about to become the Executive Director for the 'Africa One' group at the IMF.

To understand the voting rules of the IMF you need to wrap your mind around an arcane set of rules and, if you are African, suppress a sense of outrage. At Manuel's urging, Rustomjee, who had been the deputy director for 'Africa One' for the previous two years, explained the position that African countries found themselves in at the IMF and World Bank.

There are 24 executive directors on the IMF's Board of Governors, he told the NGOs. Some represent one country; others represent a group of countries. The 'Africa One' director represents 21 countries in Anglophone Africa. The Africa Two group comprises 24 countries in Francophone Africa and also has one executive director. Between them, they constitute 27 per cent of the membership of the IMF, but have less than 5 per cent of the vote. The chairmanship rotates between six regions: Africa One – that is the entire 21 countries as a group – gets a turn once every 10 years. Africa's voice in the IMF is, at best, muted.

So when the issue of debt, and debt relief, comes on to the table of the IMF Board of Governors, African countries have little sway in the formal meetings. The 12 or so NGO representatives at the meeting with Manuel listened intently. The organisations ranged from the European Network on Debt and Development, to the Catholic Relief Services, to the Zambian branch of Jubilee 2000, to World Vision in Uganda. They were Africans, Europeans, and British people who were angry about debt entrapment and poverty. But as the listened to Manuel and Rustomjee, it was clear they had not grasped quite how unequal the world actually was.

The Highly Indebted Poor Countries Initiative – HIPC – was agreed to by the Bretton-Woods institutions in 1996. There were 10 countries that qualified for debt relief, including Mozambique, Uganda and Tanzania. But by the time of the Prague meeting in 2000, not a single country had been accorded the promised relief. This was because once the 'decision point' (in IMF parlance) that a country is eligible is reached, there is another three years before the 'completion point' comes. To get to the 'completion point', Rustomjee told me, 'they have to do a zillion things'.

Some of these conditions seem noble. Manuel opposed most of them. He told the NGOs in Prague that to impose them on poor countries actually undermined governance and accountability. So, for instance, one of the conditions imposed on Mozambique was that it build a certain number of clinics. But many were damaged or destroyed in the devastating floods that hit the region in 2000. The bureaucrats of the IMF, ticking off their checklist, almost ruled Mozambique out of the running for debt relief on the grounds that it did not have sufficient clinics. They may have been successful had it not been for the intervention of the then new managing director Horst Köhler, who reportedly said: 'This is crap. You can't tell a country that it's not complying with the conditions when it's God who brought the floods.'[23]

'When we got to Prague, debt was on everyone's minds,' Rustomjee recalled. 'There was a framework but no actual relief.' Manuel's instinct may have been to simply endorse the protests. 'But it was a good example of Trevor and the way his mind worked, because he could have been drawn into the street activist type role but he looked far beyond the immediacy of that. He could also just have said, "down with this institution", but there was another immediacy too and that was debt relief.'

The debt issue was 'a nice thing for him (Manuel) to latch on to', but the main battle in the global economy 'is about structural issues that lead to debt'. For Manuel, the key structural issue was the massive disequilibrium in the IMF between Africa and the developed world in terms of voting rights.

Many of the NGOs were not aware of this. Nor did they realise the size of the huge barriers that block African trade. At the first meeting with the NGOs, Manuel and Rustomjee told them that the tariff barriers in the developed world blocked trade worth $350 billion a year. 'That's the equivalent of the whole GDP of sub-Saharan Africa,' Rustomjee told them, and raised his arm high in the air. 'It's a wall, so high that you can't even see the top of it.'

Rustomjee is a mild-mannered, soft-spoken man with an extraordinary grasp of detail. The brother of Zav Rustomjee, Manuel's first director-general in Trade and Industry, he was an adviser to Alec Erwin when the latter was deputy minister of finance, and then worked for the World Bank before becoming the Africa One executive director on the IMF. His challenge to the NGO representatives from the developed countries was not explicit but it was there: dismantle the enormous protection in your own countries so that Africans get a fairer shot in the world markets.

After the formal opening of the IMF meeting, Manuel met again with NGOs and protesters, this time with Czech President Václav Havel, a writer and playwright and an architect of the Czech 'Velvet Revolution'. Manuel and Havel, two revolutionaries, now world leaders, disarmed many of the more vociferous protesters by expressing sympathy with their cause. Some protesters were upset that their message had been drowned by the violent protests of the anarchists who had set about wrecking the old city. Manuel hammered home the point about the hypocrisy of rich nations whose barriers cripple participation of poor countries in the world agricultural market. Wealthy countries pressed poor nations to embrace free markets, he said, 'while often protecting their own markets from the goods that developing countries produce'.[24]

'Trevor really hit the sweet spot with his interventions. With words such as, everyone is entitled to demonstrate and part of his struggle he fought was to have the right to do so,' Rustomjee said. 'But you have to have some kind of strategy because if you don't, you lose the opportunity, lose the moment.'

Manuel took the moment to the Africa Commission. The Commission was chaired by former UK Prime Minister Tony Blair. Half of its members were African, including three ministers of state. Nick Stern, who led the team of writers who wrote the Commission's Report, said all three, including Manuel, were 'very experienced, highly intelligent and thoughtful'. All had gone through difficult times on the path to power. (The other two were Benjamin Mkapa, former president of Tanzania, and Meles Zenawi, former prime minister of Ethiopia.)

The Report contains some far-reaching economic and social research about the continent. It slams the wealthy countries for not doing enough to relieve debt or to open up trade, but equally, it emphasises that good governance in Africa, including the building of strong, independent institutions such as the media and the judiciary, is crucial to development. Lack of transparency and accountability has led to gross corruption in some states where political leaders of resource-rich countries have stripped their states of wealth. 'Trevor always had the broad strategic understanding of what mattered and what made a difference, beyond merely narrowing it down to (specific) economic projects,' Stern told me. 'But fundamentally, it's about building the economy, improving accountability and changing economic policies; about transparency and openness ... He emphasised seeing the big problem ... This was his great talent.'

The Africa Commission supports a change in the voting quota in the Bretton-Woods institutions; it also recommends that the top jobs of both the World Bank and the IMF should be open to foreign talent. Since their inception, the IMF Managing Director role is open only to Europeans, and the World Bank presidency to Americans. Stern, who worked as second permanent secretary for the UK Treasury before taking up the World Bank vice-presidency, had just taken up a new chair at the London School of Economics when I spoke to him. After writing the Report for the Africa Commission, he wrote a report on the economic effects of climate change which quickly impressed itself into international consciousness.

Manuel, he said, had taken the lessons from Prague into the IMF Development Committee (he was elected chair in 2001 for a four-year period) and into the G8 meeting in Gleneagles in 2005, when the richest nations promised to back the Millennium Development Goals for Africa – a doubling of aid to Africa, ending export subsidies, and writing off the debt of the 18 poorest countries.

Then he took the quest for a bigger African voice in the international financial institutions into the G20 which he chaired, jointly with Tito Mboweni, in 2007. The G20 was established in 1999, an initiative of the Clinton administration in the US, and includes the G8 countries plus those considered 'systemically important'. Apart from South Africa, they include Australia, Brazil, India, China, and Turkey. So the battle was taken out of the tortured bureaucratic structures of the IMF and World Bank, and into the G20, where the new economic powers such as Brazil, China and India could flex more political muscle.

One does not need a doctorate in mathematics to understand the voting ratios in the IMF, but it would help. There are 'basic votes' – 250 each – which were allocated at the inception of the institutions. 'So whether you're Vanuatu or the United States you get the same number of basic votes.' Then additional votes are allocated according to economic size of the country. But economic size has until recently been measured purely in terms of an economy's market exchange rate, not in terms of its purchasing power parity. There are also political factors that determine a country's voting power although they are not visible to the naked eye. In all, there were five overlapping formulas to commute voting power. 'It was a garbled mess,' said Rustomjee, who was a consultant to the Treasury in the G20 meetings.

Manuel and the South African team used the G20 – which comprises 70 per cent of the IMF's voting power – to make critical alliances with the emerging economic powers such as China, India and Turkey, to lobby to get a new measure of the size of economies. 'We got together with other emerging markets and said we're going to give it a hell of an impetus and work like mad.' Manuel was advantaged, being the longest serving finance minister in the G20, and his stature was 'immeasurably higher than if he had just come in'.

When the G20 summit took place in Kleinmond, a seaside village in the southern Cape in November 2007, 'we had all the elements on the table'. In 2006, the annual meeting of the IMF in Singapore agreed to examine the 'out-of-lineness' (that is a real IMF term, incidentally) of certain countries, so 'the button was pushed there'. In Kleinmond in 2007, the G20 adopted a unified stance on the matter. And by the spring meetings of the IMF and World Bank in 2008, 'the deal was done', said Rustomjee. The 'basic votes' were trebled from 250 to 750 and economic size was redefined to include purchasing power parity (ironically, the same term Manuel had been asked to define when he became minister of finance). For the first time, there was a real shift in voting power in the IMF and World Bank. About 135 countries, most of them in the developing world, gained, and although in real terms it was far from earth-shattering, about three per cent, 'bloody hell ... there was enormous pride that we did it'.

Manuel had taken the popular outrage expressed over the debt issue in Prague, seen a strategic advantage in focusing on Africa's voice, or the lack of it, in the Bretton-Woods institutions, and pressed the issue, 'as part of a careful, well-planned, multi-year strategy', said Rustomjee. 'You can shout at the top of your voice, but that alone is not going to get you anywhere.'

In fact, Africa gained relatively little from the change in voting quotas: most of the countries that benefited were the rising economic powers such as Turkey, Korea, Mexico and India. But the change in the formula was a rupture in a set of rules that, for five decades, had been determined by a handful of rich countries.

Manuel has been pivotal in pushing for greater debt relief and aid for Africa. This is partly because South Africa is one of the few African countries that requires neither, so it is not beholden to the richer nations. Yet, whenever there appear to be breakthroughs, disappointments follow. He was appointed the United Nations secretary general's special envoy for development financing at the Monterrey Conference in 2002, a year after being elected to chair the IMF's Development Committee on Financing. In Monterrey, the richer nations made a commitment to double aid and halve the debt burden of Africa. The Monterrey Consensus was a pact: on the one hand developed nations would help with aid and debt relief and reduce their own trade barriers; on the other, African countries would introduce reforms that included institution building, macroeconomic stability and better governance. It was a commitment echoed at the Gleneagles G8 meeting in 2005. But 'tragically', as Manuel reported in 2006, 'we have made little progress on much of the Consensus. Far too many of the policies and practices of developed countries weigh against it – cultural exclusion, economic protection, political manipulation and favouritism have not disappeared with the dismantling of the Berlin Wall.'[25] And the details of aid can be diabolical. In the year following the Gleneagles agreement, the G8 countries increased their aid to developing countries by $21 billion. 'However $17 billion of this went into writing off debts in Nigeria and Iraq.'[26]

In 2008, Manuel was appointed the UN general secretary's special envoy on development financing where he found, in the face of gloomy economic outlooks in the developed world, even less enthusiasm to implement the Monterrey or Gleneagles agreements.

Yet, unusually for an African finance minister, Manuel has been able to get development issues firmly on to the international agenda. When he was appointed to chair the IMF's Development Committee in 2001, he elevated the role of the committee, according to Kganyago, to a position of influence within the IMF. And when he left the position in 2006, Gordon Brown, then still the UK Chancellor, praised his 'rare ability to manage the detail as well as focus on strategic issues'.[27] Manuel, with Brown, initiated an international finance facility for vaccines against debilitating, communicable diseases in children. 'Through working together we have started to see progress; the international finance facility for immunisation has raised funds to immunise more than 500 million children and save 10 million lives by 2015.'[28]

Ian Goldin, whom Manuel recruited to head the Development Bank of Southern Africa in 1996 and who later became a senior official at the World Bank, saw Manuel's role in the Development Committee through the prism of the bank's head office in Washington. South Africa had been isolated from the world financial institutions during apartheid, and the ANC had not grasped the extent of their power. 'So I think it's all the more impressive. A comparable example is China that also came through a very rapid transformation; or Russia,' said Goldin. 'But South Africa is *way* ahead of Russia in its leadership role in the world on economic policy. It's *way* ahead. It's in the league of the G8 countries and I think that makes it all the more remarkable.'

Rustomjee believes Manuel could have done 'better for himself' in pushing harder on the tariff issue, even though 'it is a trade and industry matter'. It is of limited use for poor countries to get debt relief if they cannot export their goods to earn foreign exchange. Stern said that the constant pushing on trade barriers, both by Manuel and by his successor in the Trade and Industry ministry, Alec Erwin, had seen them lowered since the mid-90s and the protectionist lobby were 'now on the back foot'. But when Rustomjee spoke to me, midway through 2008, he predicted the tariff barriers of the developed world would get worse, not better, because of a looming recession in the developed countries. 'The tariffs will go up, and the last thing they will be concerned about is the poor farmers in Mali.'

Then there is the African side of the development equation: good governance. It is an essential part of the Gleneagles pact that Manuel helped to broker. The rapid deterioration of Zimbabwe due to profligate and unaccountable leadership will not help the subcontinent's quest for a better deal for its people.

Manuel has carved a strong profile in the international finance community. After Paul Wolfowitz, the president of the World Bank from 2005 to 2007, a man better known for his commitment to US President George W Bush than to development issues, was pushed out of the institution, a flurry of excitement went around South Africa that Manuel might get the job. But despite the Commission for Africa's recommendations that the job be open to all, there was no sign that the United States would give up its traditional right to put an American in the post. The Commission for Africa published its report before Wolfowitz was even appointed: the principle was 'crystal clear', as Stern put it. 'In my view he (Manuel) would make a wonderful President of the World Bank ... He's probably the only minister of finance in a developing country who can pick up the phone and get through to a minister of finance in the rich world ... Mostly because of who he is and what he does. There's a respect for his wisdom and integrity and experience. He has enormous influence from where he is and he uses that influence behind the scenes. In moments of crisis that's particularly important because he has a cool head and sees the long-term consequences of any moment.'

But the moment for the IMF and World Bank may well have passed. Rustomjee believes that because developing countries are borrowing less from those institutions, they are losing their leverage: 'One of the reasons is how they treated the emerging markets earlier.' And their ability to influence their members is also waning: 'They can't tell industrial countries to open up trade because industrial countries won't listen to them.'

The debt issue offered a unique opportunity 'to mobilise electorates in favour of an outcome that can help low-income countries; it was a nice moral and financial issue', said Rustomjee. The question is where the 'real issues' are now, those that can help developing countries to grow in a sustainable way.

IN 2002, MANUEL TOPPED THE POLLS in the NEC elections at the ANC's 51st National Conference at the University of Stellenbosch, coming in just ahead of the perennially popular Cyril Ramaphosa. Everyone was a little surprised, including Manuel himself. He was moved almost to the point of tears. It was, writes political analyst, Richard Calland, 'his reward not just for his stewardship of the economy, a stable backdrop for the growing number of black businessmen in the ANC, but also his willingness to accept invitations by branches and where necessary imbibe the odd late-night whisky or two'.[29]

The conference was not without an acerbic tone. The 'Strategy and Tactics' document that preceded it had defined both 'neo-liberalism' and 'ultra-leftism', and eschewed both. 'Neo-liberalism' was defined as a system in which formal democracy should be underpinned by 'market forces to which all should kneel in prayer; everyone for himself and the devil takes the hindmost'.[30] 'Ultra-leftism' was defined as confusion between 'what is desirable and what is possible' or, as Gill Marcus had described it, the idea that the ANC government had a 'blank slate'. The words trickled around the conference like a mild toxin.

Soon after the NEC results were announced, I bumped into Maria Ramos on the sunny campus. She had heard the news on her car radio while driving there, and was both disbelieving and delighted. As she walked towards the caravan which housed a radio studio where Manuel was being interviewed, she came across Blade Nzimande, general secretary of the South African Communist Party, and Zwelinzima Vavi of COSATU, leaning against an outside wall. 'Ultra-left!' they grumbled. 'How can we be called "ultra-left"?' 'It hurts, doesn't it?' teased Ramos. 'Like being called "neo-liberal".'

The truth is the debate had moved beyond those labels by the end of 2002, which is partly why Manuel scored so well in the NEC elections. 'From 2000 onwards,' explained Joel Netshitenzhe, the principal author of the Strategy and Tactics document, 'we were already in a post-GEAR period. The stabilisation of the economy had been achieved. By 2002, 'the real fruits of GEAR are beginning to manifest themselves in terms of real exponential growth in social expenditure'. But there were other reasons for Manuel's victory. 'You see, there is also the element of being least controversial in the politics of the

ANC, not part of the fights and factions that might be there in the Western Cape or any part of the country,' Netshitenzhe told me. 'Almost everyone in the ANC would know a Trevor Manuel so if someone decided not to vote for him it would be a conscious decision … and I don't think anyone would have said I'm not voting for Trevor Manuel.'

Certainly the fact that he topped the polls meant that almost all of the COSATU or SACP-aligned delegates at the conference voted for him. And that Manuel himself was so overwhelmed at the show of support was a sign of the rough journey he'd travelled when he'd endured freedom songs at union conferences denouncing both him and GEAR.

Netshitenzhe thinks it was a sign that there was nothing 'negative' about Manuel. But ironically one of Manuel's fiercest critics, COSATU's Vavi, interprets his victory as an endorsement. 'It was pride,' Vavi told me, at having a black minister in charge who had not only shown that he could run a difficult economy, but who had made his mark internationally. 'Everybody has pride about that fact. And he's likeable. And he has a track record. And he has *not*, at least from the public point of view, taken an entrenched position of bashing a faction. And even in the worst period in 2001/2002, when I knew he was quite critical of COSATU, he didn't go out to enthusiastically bash COSATU in the general meetings of the ANC. No, he didn't do that. So even though people didn't like the economic policy, there was some recognition that 2002 was a turning point, government expenditure rose for the first time in real terms, and that was making a difference. I guess that he got lots of votes for that.'

'Manuel has become a world leader,' said Nick Stern, one of his closest international allies, 'only because he has a firm base, and that is recognised, it gives him the attention.'

But political popularity, as Manuel had learned, and was to discover again, is sometimes transitory for those who hold the public purse.

CHAPTER 29

'If I were the weatherman'

W ATERING CANS. THAT'S WHAT Trevor Manuel's aide Shahid Khan suggests he hand out in Parliament on Budget Day 2005. The year before, Manuel had handed out trees in pots. 'Now you need the tools to make them grow.'

But instead Manuel decides on music: two South African productions have just won international awards, Ladysmith Black Mambazo, whose album 'Lift Your Spirit Higher' won a Grammy, and a film of a Xhosa rendition of Bizet's opera *Carmen*, 'Carmen e-Khayelitsha', won the Golden Bear Award at the Berlin Film Festival.

'Can we play Ladysmith Black Mambazo in Parliament?' asks Kuben Naidoo.

Khan is sent to find out. He is an old hand in Parliament. He was Manuel's parliamentary liaison officer before becoming head of the minister's office. He knows every rule, every committee member, and every way around both.

But this time he is stumped.

'What do you mean there is no precedent?' he says over the phone to the assistant of the Speaker of Parliament, Baleka Mbete. 'Well, then we'll create one ... No, it's not a ridiculous request ... tell the Speaker we'll teach her how to dance.'

He is evidently unpersuasive. The Speaker declines the request ('only because you advised her wrongly', he tells her assistant crossly). The music idea is stymied, but in the end the company that produced the opera agrees to hand out CDs of 'Carmen e-Khayelitsha' to the legislators on Budget Day.

'Madam Speaker,' Manuel begins his speech. He is practising in the little waiting room in his ministerial offices in Cape Town in front of a teleprompter. 'We have recently celebrated the international success of Ladysmith Black Mambazo's new album, *Lift Your Spirit Higher*. This past weekend, the world acclaimed the production of the popular opera *Carmen*, sung in isiXhosa and filmed here in Khayelitsha. And if Madam Speaker had lifted *her* spirit higher we could have heard this CD here this afternoon ...'

The words are not in the speech. It is characteristic of the way the mood in the Treasury offices undulates between humour and tension, between frivolity and rigour in the build-up to Budget Day.

The Budget is compiled over months; the speech over several weeks; the final crafting over days. On the weekend before the Budget, the Treasury's senior officials gather in Cape Town and meet in Manuel's Cape Town house in the government estate that nestles under the most wooded part of the Newlands mountain. They go through the speech line by line. They go through the Tips for Trevor, the messages that come from South Africans before the Budget, handy advice that reflects what citizens are thinking. They range from pleas on tax on pensions ('For two years I've been begging you to do something about my tax on my pension. Mine will not even be half of what it is today if they deduct tax ...') to those that encapsulate South Africa's peculiar cusp in history, between traditionalism and modernity. In 2006 one man asked that *lobola* – bride price – be tax deductible. Another asked for a tax deduction on dating expenditure: 'It's really difficult lately to find a woman without first dating her and such expenditure is sometimes beyond our budgets. We either date or forever remain bachelors ...'

Tips for Trevor, initiated in 1999, had become an institution by the mid-2000s – a way that the public could make direct contact with Manuel. They come in their hundreds – each year between two and three thousand people write in with tips. They range from religious tidings ('God advises us that when we pay our tithes, He shall rebuke the devourer. And surely the taxman is a devourer,' wrote Mrs Lebo Manyatsi in 2008), to direct supplications. ('I suggest, Comrade, that in your Budget speech this year, you'll find provision to help the poor and me,' wrote a hard-pressed citizen in 2003.)

Some touch on the deep racial divisions that still pain the country; 'The way BEE (Black Economic Empowerment) is increasing you should tax them more,' wrote a bank manager in 2005. '*Them*,' said Gordhan with a contemptuous grunt, as it was read out during a discussion. 'Still the old *them.*'

Others provide insight into the real deprivation many still face. In 2005, fortuitously in the year that Manuel announced a R3 billion increase in expenditure on transport infrastructure, Luthendo Nethononda wrote from 'a remote rural village': 'It has become necessary that we shift our priorities to infrastructural development. This is important because even the old lady of Maliboho requires a taxi or bus to move from the mountains to the nearest shop to buy mielie meal. Infrastructural development will create jobs, improve the rural economy, improve accessibility and alleviate poverty.'[1]

But the tips perform another function for Manuel, as well. They allow him to use the skills he honed in the 1980s. He learned then how to make people feel as though he's talking to *them*, addressing *their* concerns, hearing *their* voice. It's something he's well aware of: 'For me, it's always been exceedingly important that in a big event like a Budget you focus on the communication. Not a hell of a lot of your life is a stage, but at least on that occasion when you step up to the lectern in Parliament, and South Africans want to know what you're saying, you've got to know who you're talking to. You've got to take this stuff out of the arcane language of the economists, out of the numbers, talk to people about themselves and the Budget and their lives.'

It is why he learned early on to use a teleprompter in Parliament 'because I want to look into a TV camera. Somebody sitting at home must feel I'm talking to them.' And even after 11 Budget Speeches, he will spend hours in the days preceding the Budget practising in front of the teleprompter with one of his assistants – the 'jockey', Manuel calls him – scrolling down the script on screen. There can be few finance ministers anywhere else who turn an annual accounting exercise into theatre.

Certainly there are few other South African politicians who do so. As president, Thabo Mbeki used a teleprompter for pre-recorded messages on television, but rarely, if ever, in live speeches. At the 2002 ANC conference in Stellenbosch, one of Manuel's aides tried to coax Mbeki into using a teleprompter, but the president felt lost without being able to look at his notes. This lack of eye-contact with an audience, particularly an audience watching on TV may be one of the reasons why his critics called him 'aloof' after he lost the race for ANC president in 2007. When he engaged with ordinary people on the many provincial imbizos he conducted throughout his presidency, he came across as engaged and interested; anything but aloof. But the millions who rely on television to hear what he is saying do not experience him like that, and his party rivals were quick to turn the word 'aloof' into a pejorative.

Manuel has been described by his critics as foul-tempered, belligerent, intolerant, but never aloof. In fact he is so familiar to the South African public that many feel they know him personally. He is often called 'Trevor' by strangers, from schoolboys to secretaries. This makes him foul-tempered, belligerent and intolerant. 'Do I know you?' he'll ask coldly. 'Did we play marbles together?'

The central message of each Budget is sharpened in the days before. 'What story are we telling here,' Pravin Gordhan will ask throughout the rehearsals. 'What is our message here?' Manuel will ask as he peruses each page.

In 2005 the message was that this was a 'season of hope'. Two South African musical productions had won international acclaim. The economy had grown 3,2 per cent for the past four years, inflation was within its target range of 3 to 6 per cent, spending on the poorest 40 per cent of households had gone up by 25 per cent in five years – things were looking up; South Africans could make it happen.

There are other messages, too, sometimes implicit in what is not said in the speech. In the 2005 Budget, new infrastructure projects were spelled out in detail, but a handful of state enterprises were not mentioned. One was Denel, the government-owned arms manufacturer, which falls under the Public Enterprises Department, headed by Alec Erwin from 2004 to late 2008. 'We haven't mentioned Denel,' says Ismail Momoniat two days before the Budget.

The key officials – Momoniat, Naidoo, Donaldson, Kganyago, as well as Jabu Moleketi, who became deputy finance minister in 2004, and Gordhan, are gathered around the long wooden table that spans the western wall in Manuel's Cape Town office.

'Yes,' replies Kganyago. 'I asked Alec what does it do for infrastructure. And he said, "you should see the interlinkages".' Kganyago rises from his seat and waves his arms through the air in an imaginary sketch of a complicated railway junction. Then he walks out to get himself tea.

The following year, 2006, the Treasury allocated R2 billion to Denel. Kganyago's passing comment was a reflection of an underlying policy tension within government, but specifically between Manuel and Erwin over the role that the state-owned enterprises play in economic development. That tension cascades down the ranks: Treasury officials bristled at some of Erwin's projects. Erwin, for his part, referred to the Treasury as the 'Dark Side of the Moon'. Sometimes he admitted that the role of the finance minister is to ensure maximum value for rand spent. Yet he insisted that 'the secret of changing economies is to take some bold and big decisions'.[2]

The French Marxists, such as Bettelheim, Erwin told me, had a name for it – the *filière* – a chain of value. 'A simplification of that would be if I start with iron ore, I can move from that to crude pig iron or I can put it into rough steel or stainless steel, or I can then make it into a motor car, or I can then make it into a ship, or maybe I can make it into an aeroplane. So by the time I get to a space rocket I'm right at the extremes of this *filière*. But at each stage there are other industries that are associated with it, so if I ship the iron ore, yes, I help shipping but I won't make those ships. If I start smelting I will have a whole lot of other inputs that will come into the smelting process; if I make a motor car, I've got to have components.' So government's role is to create clusters of industries that can be internationally competitive.

The debate has been crudified by the term 'picking winners' – giving state support to particular industries that can carve a successful export niche. The Taiwanese government, for instance, made a concerted attempt to promote the semiconductor industry, carrying it to a position where Taiwan became the fifth largest semiconductor producer in the world by the mid-1990s.[3]

But the perception exists that that's what Erwin did. 'Alec is an extremely smart person,' one of Manuel's senior officials told me. 'He is extremely articulate. I have a lot of respect for him. I just wish he would back some *winners*! We're giving Alcan a huge subsidy to build a smelter that's going to employ 834 people when it's finished. We're giving them R2 billion of direct tax investments and R25 billion of electricity concessions over a 25-year period. To employ 834 people! You need your head read to think that's a good idea.'

But the idea that he picks 'winners' is a 'slight distortion', Erwin told me. 'Basically what we were saying is that you've got to make interventions in key areas that will have knock-on effects on the economy. And I still would be opposed to the idea that says let us build a factory making a widget because we think that's a winner ... What we'd rather say is we'd like to strengthen the steel value chain because we've got big competitive advantages in this.'

Alcan is a global aluminium company headquartered in Canada that was envisaged as an 'anchor tenant' for the Coega industrial development zone around the port of Ngqura in the Eastern Cape. Its planned investment was about $2,7 billion; it signed a 25-year deal with Eskom, South Africa's electricity supply company under a special pricing programme to attract big investors; the company said that by 2014 it would produce 720 000 tons of aluminium a year, making it one of the largest smelters in the world.

Coega will be the deepest harbour on the South African coastline when it is complete, and will be able to accommodate what Erwin calls 'Cape-size' ships – those that are too large to go through the Suez Canal. Some of the new container ships are too large to dock in any of South Africa's extant ports.

Coega was the brainchild of Manuel's adviser in Trade and Industry, Paul Jourdan. Jourdan is a man of big ideas. One was the establishment of Industrial Development Zones. Many seemed so complicated that when Manuel was Trade and Industry minister he said to him one Friday: 'Listen, buddy, no more mega-projects.'

On the Monday, Jourdan came to Manuel and said: 'Chief, true to my word, no more mega-projects. But here's a giga-project!'

It was Coega. Manuel and he argued about its viability for a while but then Manuel left Trade and Industry, Erwin took over 'and bought Coega hook, line and sinker'.

'Paul's thinking on this matter had always been fantastic,' Erwin told me. 'I've always found him to be correct. So when he proposed the Coega project to me I immediately supported it, and the logic was clear, you've got to make an intervention because Coega was informed by things that have been correct. One is that world ships are getting bigger. If you want to improve your exports of ore you need bigger ships.'

Alcan was envisaged as the anchor tenant – the whale, to use Jourdan's discourse, around which the pilot fish could swim. But in early 2008, as a result of Eskom's power crisis, the Alcan project seemed to be in jeopardy. 'Alcan made total sense while we still had a surplus (of electricity),' said Jourdan. (The media rounded on Erwin when Eskom ran into its supply problems of electricity in early 2008, but Jourdan blamed the previous State Enterprises minister, the late Stella Sigcau, who, he says, ignored pleas 10 years before to build more power stations.)

The big industrial projects that he and Erwin pushed were based on 'comparative advantage'. 'We've got everything against us,' Jourdan told me. 'We've inherited a fuck-up. We don't have a dynamic comparative advantage because we didn't train our people, so short-term strategy has to be based on our natural comparative advantage, and our natural comparative advantage is natural resources, whether mineral or agricultural. But we're stronger on minerals because we're two-thirds desert or semi-desert.' And anyway, the first world 'cheats' on agricultural products but not on mineral resources because they have less of them – 'except steel, they cheat on steel'.

In Erwin's view, the big industrial projects that work are linked to the government programmes known as the Spatial Development Initiatives, or SDIs. The Maputo Development Corridor, centred around a new highway that runs from Pretoria to Maputo, is one that he describes as a success. The plan is for Coega to be part of an integrated SDI. When I spoke to Erwin in 2006 he said he had 'no doubt' that Coega would be a successful industrial development. Its aim was to encourage the beneficiation of steel, which would build the 'value chain'.

'So, yes, there were differences, the difference being that this was very expensive. Why are you spending on expensive stuff, why are you so capital intensive? And the debate that Trevor and I have had – certainly it's an unresolved debate – is that you don't create large employment by trying to introduce labour-intensive industries. A good example is, yes, I can have a clothing or textile industry, and yes, I can employ quite a lot of people because the labour output ratio is quite high – I can do that – but if I concentrate only on that, all the much larger magnitudes of employment that are created by producing machinery for your clothing industry (is lost). The way you create employment in the economy as a whole is not to focus on labour-intensive industries. It's to focus on the whole ambit of the value chain.' And anyway, he told me, the market is 'weak' when it comes to big investments: the state has to make the intervention.

The debate has led to strident arguments between Manuel and Erwin. Erwin's advantage is that he was close to (then) President Thabo Mbeki's thinking on the matter: his big projects – Coega, the Pebble Bed Modular Reactor, indeed the arms deal offsets – found ready presidential support. Erwin's supporters, such as Jourdan, charge that the Treasury has used delaying tactics to stymie industrial policy plans. 'Cabinet thinks they make the decisions but Treasury makes the decisions,' Jourdan told me. Treasury has to finalise decisions such as tax incentives for the industrial projects and, in his view, it deliberately delayed signing off on projects. 'So we're the only SEZs (Special Economic Zones) in the world that have no fiscal advantage: there's no tax break, no nothing.' With Treasury, he said, 'like those Californian depression dances, you just keep dancing, dancing, dancing. There's never any finalisation.'

At one point in the late 1990s, Mbeki instituted what were called the 'Stoep Discussions' for the economics ministers to discuss policy. They have probably been romanticised. They were not regular and did not last long. The basic difference between him and Manuel, Erwin told me, is that 'our economic base is a bit different. Mine is basically Marxist and Trev's not a Marxist economist. Not because he's opposed to it, just that he's never studied it.'

Perhaps this comment was designed to pinpoint what Manuel's critics perceive as his vulnerability: a lack of formal education in economics. But actually Manuel, in the youthful revolutionary mode of so many of his peers, devoured Marxist literature, including Karl Marx himself, to the point where, during his tenure as finance minister, he has been able to quote chapter and verse of Marx, who writes in *Capital* Volume 3 of the dangers of piling up too much public debt.

Manuel's view is this: 'There's always a risk of *dirigisme* for its own sake. I believe that in a country that has scarce capital you've got to measure what the money buys. And you've got to try to ensure that the money buys that which deals with your major contradictions. Unemployment is a major contradiction, so I tend to favour a labour/capital ratio that is higher.'

It is not a 'binary' debate. 'It's not correct to cast this as (an argument) about intervention and non-intervention; it being able to think through policy issues and come to rational conclusions. Very little happens automatically; you have to make things happen.'

Soon after he became finance minister, Manuel spoke at a conference about developing small and medium businesses. A Mozambican man came to him and said: 'Before we can talk about a small business like a corner shop, you need to build two roads to create the corner.'

'So I accept that sometimes you need to do things before you can get there … (But) if we only get capital-intensive investment, then we fail the poor in this country. That will probably be the lifelong debate between Alec Erwin and me ... I don't think either of us will convince the other.'

Ironically, in a time of relative fiscal plenty, the debate intensified. For the first time in decades, there was a Budget surplus at the end of the 2006/2007 fiscal year. It was a small surplus, and unplanned; it arose from a rollover of R5 billion that the Correctional Services Department failed to spend. In the Budget of 2007, Manuel announced a moderate budgeted surplus of 0,6 per cent of GDP for the next fiscal year.

The government was nervous of the political implications of such a surplus, and it was argued intensively in cabinet. But one of the problems – which cabinet accepted – was that government departments had to show they could effectively use the money. Most could not. Erwin, however, thought he could: 'The structures that can use that money effectively would be your big state enterprises.'

'He's a socialist who's gone to heaven,' said Kuben Naidoo. 'Socialists love these big state-owned enterprises. And he's gone to heaven. He's got a fiscal manager who's given him a budget surplus and he's got these big toys to play with.'

At Manuel's house the Sunday before the 2007 Budget, there is much discussion about the surplus. 'We shouldn't hammer it,' says Brian Molefe, the CEO of the Public Investment Corporation, who cut his teeth in the Treasury. But Kganyago replies: 'We're doing this thing because it is right and we're doing it to protect space. We cannot continue in an environment where the biggest actor in the economy is continuing to be in a dissaving position year after year.'

Savings in a country where savings have been traditionally low become an important theme. This is the first year the Treasury is to introduce the idea of a new social security tax to boost people's pensions after retirement. About half of those who retire do so with a pension that is less than one third of their final salary, and more than two-thirds of people are dependent on the state old age pension.[4] 'There's a tip that says we must prevent the recipients of pensions spending it on alcohol,' says Manuel.

There's a hard message in this Budget – the necessity of saving. And a softer one, too, based on the extension of social services: 'Human life has equal worth.'

Manuel wants translations of the phrase into all 11 languages. Molefe phones his grandmother in the rural province of Limpopo to find an idiom in

Sepedi. He comes back with a saying that people are not like cows – each one of us is different: 'When we die, none of us will be turned into biltong!'

Then he remembers an old Sotho saying about teeth. People are like teeth; they are not equal. Or is it, people are not like teeth, they are equal?

'Listen to how you're talking to my tribe,' retorts Manuel. 'Remember they pull their front teeth.'

Eventually the saying is pared down in Sepedi: *Motho ke Motho, ga a na bosehlana* ('a human being is a human being, there is no lesser human being').

The two-hour discussion, where the Treasury officials go through the speech line by line, paragraph by paragraph, is a steady mix of earnestness and banter.

'Human life has equal worth' refers to tackling the legacy of history. 'Sperm lottery' becomes 'accident of birth', and later 'shadow of history'. An attack on 'some' teachers who do not prepare their lessons properly 'and are unfit to be in a position where they nurture children', becomes an attack on a 'minority' of teachers. 'How do you know it's a minority?' asks Donaldson. Naidoo manages to include a snide reference to Denel, the arms manufacturer, being most successful in producing Tupperware (he'd told me earlier that the moulding equipment bought to make the heads on shells had been converted to make Tupperware). But it doesn't make the final version.

This is an unambiguously expansionary budget. In the following three years the planned expenditure on social services and infrastructure is to be R2 trillion ('that's a two followed by twelve zeros', Manuel is to tell Parliament). There is tax relief of R8,4 billion. But the Treasury is aware its budgeted surplus may be the most unpopular decision it has taken since GEAR.

On closer examination, the economic reasons for running a surplus are compelling. For one thing, much of the 5 per cent growth of the past year has been due to the boom in commodity prices, and to a substantial rise in consumption expenditure. Revenues have overrun their target once more. And the current account deficit has grown. This is a double-edged sword. On the one hand it is a reflection of rapid economic growth because of the imports of capital goods. On the other, it leaves the country vulnerable to trade shocks, such as the rising price of oil. 'We need to re-emphasise the importance of more rapid and diversified economic growth and improving our export performance, rather than reliance on uncertain portfolio inflows,' Manuel will say in his speech.

The next day, the speech is tweaked further in Manuel's office. 'On the current account deficit,' asks Gordhan, 'do you want to say that you're not perturbed by it?'

'We *are* perturbed by it but we don't want to say so,' replies Kganyago.

'Which is not the same as not being perturbed,' says Manuel.

But the Treasury successfully masks any signs of perturbance and the entire Budget of 2007 is upbeat, almost triumphalist. 'If you want the definition of fiscal space, here it is,' Manuel tells the press conference before he delivers the Budget Speech. 'I mean it's pretty heavy, it weighs a lot but if you want the definition here it is. Because firstly, whether we could deliver a fiscal surplus has been a question, and then, could we do it in a way that is entirely concomitant with the policy views we hold? We've answered that question. We say to you that here is a surplus (but) with real (expenditure) growth of 7,7 per cent per year over the MTEF (Medium Term Expenditure Framework).'

'What would have been the alternative scenario,' asks one journalist, 'if the decisions you took in 1996 hadn't been taken?'

'In 1996 we had to choose between a dependence on borrowing to finance what we needed to do and therefore fairly high deficits, and a lower deficit which would then impact on the balance of payments, and then a hard slog. And it was a difficult set of choices, partly because there still is an attachment in some quarters to high levels of borrowing.'

Then he told the story of Zimbabwe again: 'It's told in a number of different chapters but the first of those chapters would be the period 81 to 91 where by all accounts investments in people, in social services ... was truly unprecedented. The problem however is that it was financed with borrowings, and when the chips were called in and the first structural adjustment bit in 1991, you saw the cutbacks on those services. Clearly, it's something that policy makers need to understand everywhere.'

Today in South Africa, he told journalists, there is not a single government department 'that has plans that are reasonable, rational and motivated' that is not accommodated.

In fact Treasury officials knew – but didn't say so then – that at least one department received more than its minister asked for: the health department was allocated an extra R1,7 billion to roll out treatment for people with Aids. By 2009/10, this was expected to reach R5 billion. The minister of health, Manto Tshabala-Msimang, was already controversial for her pursuit of offbeat remedies for people with Aids. She was notorious for the tardiness in rolling out sites for the distribution of antiretrovirals. More than that, the basic functioning of her department in many respects failed the poorer citizens of South Africa who depend on public health facilities.

It was fortuitous that she herself was ill for much of the final period when the Budget was put together so her officials and those from the Treasury could shape a budget that would deliver better treatment to more people. The number of people who have used ARVs grew from about 100 000 in January 2006 to over 200 000 by the end of that year.[5] 'So from a fiscal policy perspective when you are having a successful programme, you ramp it up. You really make it successful. So we had to put more money into the grant,' said Kganyago.

Even in cold economic terms, it pays to treat people with Aids. In-house research by the Treasury shows that the debilitation and death that result from leaving the disease untreated – and the consequences of losing breadwinners, and leaving behind orphans – can dent economic growth by as much as one quarter to 0,3 per cent.[6] 'Most of the people who are Aids sufferers are people who still have a lot of productive life ahead of them,' Kganyago said. 'And to the extent that these people are in a work environment you see the impact through absenteeism and those kinds of things. And so, besides the humanitarian and social welfare and health cases, there was also a very strong economic case for the roll-out of the ARVs.'

The Health Department gives credence to the argument that the problem in the delivery of services in South Africa is not about money but about management and commitment. In the winter of 2006, four babies died in Cecilia Makiwane Hospital, which services the township of Mdantsane on the periphery of the seaboard town of East London. The babies died in their incubators in the intensive care unit after a generator failed to spring into action during a power failure. They died, one by one, over a period of five hours in the late afternoon.

The problem, according to a government source, was not that the generator didn't work but that a trip switch supposed to activate the generator failed to do its job. It was broken. And how much would it have cost to repair? A few hundred rands, is all. The management had not done its job. And, one should ask, as did the bereaved parents, what of the nurses, who in an ICU, are supposed to check their patients regularly? How did four babies die over such a prolonged period?

In 2006, soon after this incident, Manuel experienced the state of public hospitals first-hand when a government employee on his staff took seriously ill with Aids.

SYLVIA 'NOMIMI' NOSIPHIWO ZIQU has worked in the Public Works Department, which maintains the houses of cabinet ministers, almost since the start of the new government in 1994. At first she worked for Govan Mbeki ('the father of Thabo'), she told me. When he left government in 1997, the department assigned her to be the housekeeper in Manuel's Cape Town house on the Newlands estate soon after he became finance minister.

She was born in Idutywa in the Eastern Cape and came to Cape Town in 1991 in search of work. In the winter of 2001, her husband became ill. As the months passed, he got sicker. He was admitted to G F Jooste Hospital in Manenberg, where he languished for a few weeks. The doctors there advised Sylvia that he should be tested for HIV, but he refused. 'And then the doctor says they can't do anything for him, because they already tried a lot of tablets and medicines, and they didn't work.' The doctors then told her 'to come and take your husband because we can't do otherwise'. So Sylvia took him home. He died three days later on 27 October of that year, aged 38.

Sylvia's third child, a girl, had been born just six weeks before. She has two older daughters, then aged 11 and 15. She returned to work in mourning clothes after burying her husband in early 2002, by which time she was sick herself.

The sickness then was a persistent flu. Some weeks later she tested for HIV. The test came back positive. She was terrified. 'Who is going to look after my daughters? They are so young,' she thought.

She confided in Reg Moodley, one of the two police officers assigned as Manuel's bodyguards in Cape Town. Moodley urged her to tell Manuel. She could not bear to tell him face-to-face, so she telephoned him in Stellenbosch where he was in the middle of a conference.

'Minister was very, very shocked,' she recalled. 'But he said to me, "Look Sylvia, it's not the end of the world. There are many people who are HIV positive who are alive today. I'm coming back soon then we can talk."'

When he returned, Manuel took her to a clinic in Wynberg for counselling. Her CD4 count was normal, so she focused on living healthily and using vitamins through the winter to stave off colds. 'Minister and Maria', as the ministerial staff call the couple, bought her immune boosters and vitamins. She was fine through the winter of 2001, and through the next four winters.

Then in 2006, she caught a cold, which turned into flu, which turned into bronchitis, then pneumonia, and before long tuberculosis. 'It was just vertical,' said Manuel whistling through his teeth and plunging his hand downward. She had been off ill for a few weeks when, at Manuel's urging, Moodley went to her small house in Khayelitsha to see her.

Moodley was shocked when he found her. She had not eaten for days, and had hardly drunk anything. 'I was very, very concerned because she was looking in a very, very bad and poor state. So I spoke to her; she was speaking in a language that not even her family could understand. She was talking like gibberish, and she was disorientated, completely, and she was sort of frothing at the mouth. And she'd lost a lot of weight. She was really very thin.'

At dawn the next morning, with rain pelting from the skies, Moodley drove to her house, carried her to his car 'like a little baby', and took her to the local clinic in Khayelitsha. Scores of people were already there. He carried her through the crowds, down the corridors until his arms hurt. There was no wheelchair available. Eventually he got her CD-4 count results from the nurses (her daughters had to give permission), and he took her to private specialists, first in Mowbray, then in Kenilworth, middle-class suburbs of Cape Town, for which he had to pay. The Kenilworth doctor immediately admitted her to G F Jooste Hospital in Manenberg. It was dark by the time she was admitted even though Moodley had arrived there in the early afternoon with the barely conscious woman and her three daughters in tow.

For several months, Sylvia lay in the Jooste Hospital ward. Because she had lost all feeling in her feet and legs, the nursing staff assumed she was on her way out. 'The message we got from the nursing staff is that it's a hopeless case, a hopeless case! They say if she has lost movement in her feet, then it means she is slowly going, her body's giving in. And to add to the woes, she had TB. And so it was a huge battle.' Moodley took her daughters to see her daily, and made sure they had food in the house; he also brought her elderly mother to visit her from the Eastern Cape. 'Minister and Maria' went to visit her, but she was so ill that she cannot recall it. Moodley and Manuel arranged that the specialist from Kenilworth see her regularly. Moodley paid the medical bills and Manuel and Ramos reimbursed him. Without this treatment, she would surely have died, Moodley told me. The specialist said it was important first to stabilise her, then to treat her TB, then to start treating her with ARVs. But those months she lay in Jooste, said Moodley, her family lost hope. 'The conditions were pathetic.'

But then she began to make a little progress. She started to speak again. The Kenilworth doctor transferred her to Tygerberg Hospital 'where conditions were much better', and then to the Brooklyn Chest Clinic, a hospital in the northern suburbs of Cape Town where she was treated for TB. Brooklyn was better than Jooste, but Manuel was not impressed. When he went to visit her, he was appalled at the dirt in the corridors and grass in the garden that was 'knee-high'. He phoned Ebrahim Rasool, then premier of the Western Cape to tell him. Hospitals fall under the provincial administration although they are funded from the national budget. 'I said, go and see! Why don't you pull a surprise visit to the place? Go and see!' He also called the provincial MEC for Health, Pierre Uys. 'Go and see!' he urged after Sylvia had told him there was never any meat in the food. 'Because if you've paid for meat and someone says there's no meat in the food, then somebody is taking that meat. This is an elementary management problem.'

But it was at Brooklyn that Sylvia began to recover. There she began a course of ARVs, and had physiotherapy to teach her how to walk again. She had not put her feet on the ground for nearly six months. Moodley visited her daughters daily and brought them food, and 'every day', Sylvia told me, '*every day* Reg came to the hospital', sometimes with Manuel.

'Here is a living example,' Manuel told me, 'of someone who because of one or two interventions that demonstrated a marginally higher level of care is alive today. Left to her own devices, left in the G F Jooste Hospital where the nurses are overstretched, the view would be, she's here, she has Aids, leave her. Now it's very important to ask whether our health system has sufficient of the caring to deal with this.'

'It's difficult to find love in that hospital,' Moodley said. 'You know when you do something ... you've got to have love as well. Because you're caring for people who are poor – because those are *poor* people who are there – and they're people who really need help. They are desperate people. And you've got to combine it with love. And I saw nothing of that. What I did see was patients being spoken to rudely, being handled badly and it's like, you know – "Oh! We'll do what we're asked to do and that's it." '

'Part of it,' said Manuel, 'is that health workers don't care, part of it results from them being overstretched, and part of it is just poor management in the system.'

I met Sylvia Ziqu in April 2008. Her skin was glowing, her hair in braids. She is trim, but not skeletal, a pretty and thoughtful woman who has no doubt that had it not been for the intervention of Moodley and 'Minister and Maria', she would no longer be on this earth. 'Tjoe! If they didn't love me, if they didn't love me they wouldn't have done that; it's because they loved me. And because the Minister, he didn't say, and Maria also, she didn't say, Sylvia you are HIV positive and also you've got TB, don't use our cups, don't eat with our dishes.'

Sylvia had been taking ARVs for 18 months when I met her. Her two older daughters, instead of being orphaned, are studying accountancy and marketing at the Peninsula Technikon. Her youngest daughter attends school in Claremont. When she was discharged from hospital in December 2006 she went back to the Eastern Cape to see her elderly mother (who has since died). 'Here is Nomimi,' shouted the children in her village. Her mother could not believe her eyes. The last time she had seen her she was delirious and paralysed, on a hospital bed in a dirty ward, so sick that she did not even recognise her.

I asked Sylvia if I could use her name in this book. She said I should not only use her name, but her address too. She was proud of her recovery, but prouder still of the fact that there were people in her life who cared whether she lived or died, and had the energy to do something about it.[7]

That attitude cannot be taken for granted in the public health system in South Africa. It is not only a question about whether ARVs are made available or not – Manuel believes there are many steps between testing HIV positive and going on to ARVs. 'But that means our health system must be able to give the best to people; that means testing, it means counselling, it means trying to extend the period where the CD-4 count will be above the 200 mark,' usually the point where ARVs are administered.

In the Ashley Kriel lecture, Manuel had lambasted the state of education. 'But I wasn't picking on teachers. If I took the health workers and used examples like these ... the system breaks down.' Some of the facilities are bad, but not all; health workers get salaries every month; money is there to buy pharmaceuticals although the logistical systems to prevent them being stolen may not be.

In some of the private hospitals there is technology that allows doctors to check on a hand-held computer that the drugs they are prescribing for a patient will not clash with medication the patient may already be on. It is something that could well be introduced in South Africa's public hospitals. 'It's worth striving for, but you need the people and the systems to drive those kind of changes.' It's called getting value for money.

IF SERVICE DELIVERY IS a headache for Manuel, unemployment is a bigger one. It is the single most serious challenge to the South African economy and to the social fabric.

'Amazingly few people work in South Africa,' Ricardo Hausmann told an audience in Johannesburg in June 2008. The audience laughed as though he had touched on an embarrassing family truth.

Hausmann is a Harvard professor of economics. He's also had some of the roughening experience of real governance in a developing economy, having been an economics minister in Venezuela, his homeland, in the early 1990s.

Hausmann headed the 'Harvard group' as it became known, which was commissioned by the National Treasury to investigate ways of growing the economy that would dent the large numbers of jobless people. The Harvard group grew together over a period of about four years. In 2004, Manuel met Dani Rodrik, a renowned trade economist of Turkish origin who teaches at the Kennedy School of Government at Harvard University and who was also head of research for a group of developing countries within the IMF known as the G24. 'I've always been fascinated by his take on globalisation,' said Manuel. 'He was able to argue very forcefully against the notion of the Washington Consensus, and why endogenous economics is so very important, why countries need to be informed by economic realities but must actually take decisions about their own situation.'

Manuel had already begun to float new economic policy ideas to cabinet. The macroeconomic stabilisation policy had gone so far, but clearly was unable to push the country into growing employment. He outlined some ideas to cabinet in early 2005, the genesis of what became the Accelerated and Shared Growth Initiative for South Africa (AGSI-SA), which was later run out of the president's office. He mentioned these ideas to Gobind Nankani, a Ghanaian who was the World Bank's vice-president for Africa (he left in 2006 after Wolfowitz was appointed by George W Bush to head the World Bank), and Nankani suggested that a group of international developmental economists run a workshop on the proposals.

By early 2006, a group had formed that included Hausmann, Rodrik, Robert Lawrence, a native South African and naturalised American who had worked as President Bill Clinton's economic adviser, an Indian economist, Abhijit Banerjee, based at the Massachusetts Institute of Technology (MIT) and an expert on poverty, and Philippe Aghion, a French economist who had 'grown up in the Communist Party', now also at Harvard. Eventually the 'Harvard group' comprised 24 international economists and six South Africans. That year they made an initial presentation to the cabinet. Over the next two years, they visited the country four times, and by the end of 2007, a series of papers was ready.

They were not released immediately, partly because the Medium Term Budget Policy Statement was imminent 'and we didn't want too much noise', as Manuel put it, and then the ANC conference at Polokwane was on the doorstep. With the high emotions surrounding that conference, the Treasury decided to delay the release of the papers for fear of setting up 'all of this work as a kind of straw man to attack'.

There were also intense discussions in cabinet about who 'owned' the research and whether the government had editorial rights as it had commissioned the research. But at Mbeki's insistence, the authors retained editorial rights over their research. 'He said this work is exceedingly useful ... because these people have done work that has academic rigour. Their work must be able to stand up to the rigour that good quality academics need,' said Manuel.

In 2008, South African politics had moved far from the rational discussions of 1993, or even 1996. Emotion ruled the day in the wake of Thabo Mbeki's defeat at Polokwane as president of the ANC. 'We're not going to let a bunch of Harvard economists tell us what to do,' harrumphed COSATU's Vavi to reporters. In mid-2008, the unions did not even turn up to a 'Harvard group' presentation at NEDLAC, the economic council that they had always insisted be the place where new economic policy and ideas be debated. A boycott? I asked Manuel. 'They were playing silly buggers,' he replied.

But the research is not silly: it is a far-reaching examination of an economy that has grown, that is stable, whose governance is transparent, but has failed to deliver jobs.

When Hausmann first arrived in the country in 2005, the economic prospects seemed promising. For four years after GEAR was introduced, growth was steady but hardly spectacular, interest rates went up in the late 1990s, and the rate of unemployment increased. Now, by 2005, growth had accelerated to over 5 per cent; unemployment had come down (to 23 per cent in 2008); inflation, which reached 30 per cent at the end of the apartheid era, was now in single digits. 'So maybe you know this is your pay-off; this is the cheque in the mail that has finally arrived.'[8]

But Hausmann and his colleagues noticed that the growth was happening at the same time as a rapidly widening current account deficit – the same deficit that Manuel and Kganyago had hidden their 'perturbance' about during the 2007 Budget. It was also boosted by a commodity boom, so what they call 'trend-line' growth, or sustainable real growth, was only about 3,5 per cent, not the 5 per cent recorded in the figures and certainly not enough to reach the 6 per cent required for the 'shared growth' goals to lift most South Africans out of poverty.

The widening current account deficit was funding investment, but the investment was going into what Hausmann called the 'non-tradeable sector' – real estate, construction, retail. The growth was largely consumption growth. There was not enough investment in the 'tradeable' sector – manufactured goods that could be exported, for example. 'So how are you going pay for the additional debt?'[9] In 2000, the current account was almost balanced. By 2007 it had grown to 7 per cent. Worse, there had been little growth in South African exports – only 34 per cent in 44 years from 1960 to 2004. Compare this with 169 per cent in Argentina (the country that Treasury officials most like to think of as a basket case), 238 per cent in Australia, 1 887 per cent in neighbouring Botswana and an astonishing 4 392 per cent in Malaysia.[10]

So the growth that South Africa had seen was like a car accelerating beyond the speed limit. Manuel explained: 'The road is designed to travel at 80 kilometres an hour, but you don't want to go at 80. You want to go at 120. The problem is then that you must widen the road and flatten the curve so you minimise the risk.' The risk of accident is great and it comes in the form of 'trade shocks', particularly for a country still heavily dependent on imports such as oil. So how do you minimise risk? One solution is to increase the level of savings in the country, which the government has done in the form of a budget surplus. Another is to maintain the currency at a steady, but lower level to boost exports.

What does all this have to do with unemployment? It is this: the economic growth has largely been in the 'non-tradeable' sector which, the Harvard Group argues, employs relatively few unskilled people (with the notable exception of construction). The 'tradeable' sector – mining, agriculture, manufacturing – employs much greater numbers of unskilled people, proportional to the skilled workforce. And South Africa's large army of the unemployed comprises overwhelmingly unskilled people.

The more educated a South African is, the higher the chances of being employed. The converse is also true. So while 85 per cent of those with university degrees are working, fewer than 35 per cent of those without matric (the highest school grade) have jobs. The same pattern runs across age. The younger you are, the more likely it is that you'll be unemployed. And across race and gender. So the unemployed are predominantly the lesser educated, young black women. And there are many of them. In 2007, about 13 million South Africans were working – that's less than half of the working age population. Very few countries, Hausmann said, have lower workforce participation rates. If South Africa had the rate of employment of some comparator countries, for instance those in Latin America, about 6,6 million *more* people would have jobs.

But South Africa has another problem in its labour market too – as much as it suffers from a surfeit of unskilled labour, there is also too little skilled labour. 'The tradeable sector tends to be less skill intensive than (the non-tradeable sector),' explained Hausmann. 'This is going to be a slightly important problem – it's going to explain the issue at hand … You're trying to grow in the sector that is skill intensive and you're shedding jobs in the sector that is skill unintensive.'[11] And if you want shared growth, you have to share it with the millions who were victims of an entirely inadequate education system.

Their suggestions about how to transform the economy tread on some very powerful political toes. One set belongs to organised labour. The Harvard group suggests a wage subsidy for youthful workers, those who often don't get a look-in on the labour market. It would be a targeted subsidy that would 'accelerate the transition between school and work' for a group that experiences 'amazingly high' unemployment rates. Hausmann is confident the unions can be won over on this one – 'everybody goes through being 18 years old, even the children of union workers'.

The second may offend left-wing constituencies within the ANC. Abandon Keynesian policies, the Harvard group suggested. Keynesian policies focus on increasing domestic demand, but the demand for 'tradeables' will be supplied by imports. The demand for 'non-tradeables' may be met by the local economy but that will lead to growth in the very sector that is already battling for skills. That sector will poach skills from the 'tradeable' sector, exacerbating the structural cause of unemployment.

The skills constraint needs to be addressed by more flexible immigration polices. The relation of skilled to unskilled workers in manufacturing – part of the 'tradeable' sector' – is not like coffee and tea, said Hausmann, but rather like coffee and milk. Complements, not substitutes. The greater the number of skilled workers in the tradeable sector, the greater the number of jobs created for unskilled workers.

And here, thirdly, is where the recommendations are likely to unsettle another powerful domestic constituency – the rapidly emerging educated black middle class who have benefited significantly from affirmative action and Black Economic Empowerment (BEE) policies. It's tricky because on the one hand BEE has spread economic benefits and increased a sense of fairness in society. But there are elements that are anathema to shared growth. For instance, the BEE requirements for start-up firms discourage new investment, and the demand for senior black managers can actually add to a skills flight of those who feel there are limited career prospects for them in the country. 'Some of the BEE provisions, the equity provisions, in principle can be satisfied by having just one person owning 50 per cent of the stock, or (the requirement of) having directors that are black can be satisfied with one person sitting on 45 boards ... So somehow these things, equity participation and directorships can be satisfied by having very few people benefiting.'[12]

And, fourthly, the Harvard group's recommendation that the Reserve Bank adopt a policy that will lower the value of the currency – to encourage exports – may disadvantage a middle class, both black and white, used to the luxury of relatively cheap imports and travel.

Hausmann's criticism has echoed a long-standing exchange of ideas that Moeletsi Mbeki has had with Manuel and others in government. In a letter to Manuel, he wrote about the dangers of what he called the 'consumer revolution' driven by black nationalism. 'The Consumer Revolution is founded on paying high salaries by the State to the upper echelons of the civil service, parastatal management, and to serving politicians. The private sector is similarly compelled to employ the Black elite and pay them extravagant salaries on pain of exclusion from lucrative Government contracts.'[13] The equity provisions of BEE stifle entrepreneurship and productivity, Mbeki has argued. Moreover, the spending spree it has sparked is not sustainable 'because it is not based on an expanding productive base as is the case in, for example, China and India. In fact the Consumer Revolution is happening to the detriment of our country's productive sector in that it is diverting potential investment funds into private consumption much of which is consumption of foreign-made products. In the longer term therefore only China, South

Korea, India and other newly industrialising Asian countries benefit from South Africa's Consumer Revolution.'[14]

For Manuel, the Harvard group's research provoked deep thought about the economic policies necessary to free South Africa from poverty. Poverty is widely associated with unemployment,[15] and even though the social grants have made a considerable dent in it, they are not sufficient to allow new generations to grow more prosperous.

'Some of the stuff that Moeletsi says about BEE, you have to sit up and take notice,' Manuel told me in mid-2008. 'But then, the very real difficulty is that you can't have wealth appear to be a white thing and poverty a black thing. If you want your omelettes, you are going to have to break your eggs somehow.'

We were talking in his kitchen again, but in a different house in Johannesburg which he and Ramos had bought and were now living in. He was not breaking eggs as he spoke, but making soup on this winter's evening, reflecting on where South Africa's economic policy had taken the country in the past decade.

The country was in its seventh year of an expansionary budget. Yet unemployment, still, 'is the most intractable difficulty that confronts us'.

For the first time, he admitted that the name for the macro-stabilisation policy – Growth, Employment and Redistribution – was a 'terrible misnomer'.

'What we tried to do in 1996 with GEAR was to look at the macro but perhaps in its very name (we) thought that this policy would be so broad and encompassing that it would deal with every aspect.'

GEAR successfully dealt with a huge structural barrier to growth engendered by the economy's isolation as a result of apartheid – the fact that any growth over three per cent would have run into a balance of payments constraint. And there were no savings to speak of. In fact, government had run up a huge debt that would have escalated exponentially had it not been dealt with.

There was a surprising congruity between Manuel's thoughts in the winter of 2008, and those expressed by Jeremy Cronin when I spoke to him five months earlier: Cronin conceded that a macro-stabilisation plan was necessary. But to have stifled debate about the other issues – critically job creation and growth – was wrong. Manuel's argument – and it has been consistent – that if the country did not reduce its dependence on debt it risked losing sovereignty, was 'absolutely correct and to that extent I think some of the measures undertaken *were* right and have helped us'.

Cronin's insights run against a crude narrative that has put Manuel at odds with the left of the ANC. But if Manuel has one consistent trait it is this: he is flexible. Keynes's comment lives with him: 'When the facts change, I change my mind. What do you do, sir?'

'You don't take policy decisions and hang on to them with white knuckles and fend off all the hooligans who try to attack your policy; there (must be) a constancy of discussion and debate and it's the only way to do it.'

As he spoke he moved coffee cups and papers around his kitchen table to illustrate: 'You place (the unemployment problem) at the centre. Leave aside for the moment, the proposal on the wage subsidy. The central issue is that you must give young people a chance.'

Manuel was in the same situation once, looking for a job with a future. His letters went unanswered, phone calls unreturned: the first job he got was through his mother and sisters who were already working in a clothing factory. Through tenacity he managed to secure a spot in a civil engineering firm that gave him the possibility of broadening his horizons. In the South Africa of the early twenty-first century, there are tens of thousands of young people who look, often in vain, for that first important break into the job market.

'Ricardo puts it very nicely,' said Manuel. 'When you make policy you must make policy for the labour market you *have*, and not for the one you *wished* you had. And, secondly, markets function as *markets*. If you're running a fish market, you have fish, and that's supply, and you have people wanting fish and that's demand. And your interest is to try to get that market cleared. So if one day your market clears with the fish at R100, that's what the market clears at. If the next day, the market clears with fish at R50 that's what the market clears at. The problem in South Africa is that your labour market doesn't clear. And that's what you need to resolve.'

The Treasury began to incorporate some of the Harvard group's advice into the 2008 Budget. For instance, it stripped cyclical revenues (a reflection of the commodity boom) out of its calculations, so although the Budget reflected a fiscal surplus, there is actually a small structural deficit.

Manuel was disappointed that COSATU did not come to the NEDLAC discussion on the Harvard group recommendations. 'I'd like to sit down with Vavi and say, the biggest problem we have is the unemployment problem.

Leave aside all your other prejudices; let's talk about how we deal with this problem. COSATU must understand that you can only have development if the trade unions are (among) your actors for development.'

You can't, he said, 'build an economy on slogans'.

A FEW DAYS LATER, MANUEL did in fact meet with a delegation from the unions and the top ANC leadership elected at Polokwane, including Vavi and Gwede Mantashe, a former trade unionist who was elected the ANC's secretary general. The defeat of Thabo Mbeki as party president was widely seen as a left-wing coup, but in fact the coalition that supported Mbeki's rival, Jacob Zuma, was broad and ranged from communists to those who, like Zuma, had been in trouble with the law, to democrats who considered Mbeki too dictatorial. All of them had reason to dislike Mbeki who, in spite of his intellectual foresight, drove a wedge through the organisation in his last four years as president and who had profoundly misread internal party political dynamics.

Mantashe in particular has been a bridge between the old and new leadership. Manuel had appointed him to the Development Bank as an executive director, and he was also head of the technical task team of the Joint Initiative for the Priority Skills Acquisition (Jipsa), a project of the programme for shared growth (AGSI-SA). He has also been the national chair of the Communist Party and the general secretary of the same National Union of Mineworkers that spawned Vavi. He has shown, according to those in government who know him, an ability to listen and engage about some of South Africa's more pressing problems.[16]

After he and Vavi met with Manuel and Treasury officials, Mantashe spoke to fund managers about economic policy. He displayed an acute awareness of the potential looming economic traps, principally in the form of the widening current account deficit, and committed a new ANC government to 'investment rather than inflationary consumption spending'.[17]

About a week before the Polokwane conference, Manuel tried to meet with Mantashe, Vavi and Blade Nzimande, general secretary of the Communist Party. Manuel suggested a dinner because he wanted to discuss the 'perils of indebtedness' with them before the high emotion of what threatened to be a riven ANC conference engulfed them. The three tentatively agreed, but then Nzimande baulked, saying that any policy matter could be discussed at Polokwane. Mantashe, who was open to the meeting, phoned Manuel to say he could not persuade the other two.

Manuel was disappointed but not ready to give up. Although he had been schooled in economic policy, to a large extent, by Mbeki, who was now cast as chief rival number one, he was not seen as what became crudely known as an 'Mbeki-ite'.

'I still feel I have access (to Mantashe, Nzimande and Vavi), I don't have the same level of enmity with them. I can talk to them. I can disagree with them. I can argue with them.'

Manuel was in a peculiar position, though. He was steeped in an internal resistance tradition, and understood an internal political dynamic better than most of the former exiles who supported Mbeki. At times the left-wing coalition that had adopted Zuma as their man, made economic policy a major platform, and Manuel was the politician who had shepherded it for the past 12 years.

Yet the economic policy resolutions that emerged from the Polokwane conference were not substantially different from those adopted at either Mafikeng or Stellenbosch. There was more emphasis on the role of the 'developmental state', and more on the importance of creating an expanded public works programme. At the policy conference six months before Polokwane, the ANC called – somewhat idealistically – for the state to start its own mining company, but this was watered down at Polokwane. The final resolution called for the 'developmental state (to) ensure that our natural resources endowment including land, water, mineral and marine resources are exploited to effectively maximise the growth, development, and employment potential embedded in such national assets, and not purely for profit maximisation.'[18]

But the idea of a 'mixed economy' was endorsed and the 'substantial economic transformation' in the country was hailed, with poverty, unemployment and inequality being marked as priorities for fixing.

The main differences are not substantial policy ones – after all Jacob Zuma was, throughout his years in exile and in government, a close ally of Mbeki – but differences over governance. These manifested in the form of a resolution to disband the National Prosecuting Authority (NPA) which works independently of the police and had been at the forefront of prosecuting cases of corruption and organised crime even when these cases touched ANC potentates. It also manifested later from some Zuma supporters in vituperative attacks on the judiciary and on other independent institutions.

The signs of a major split on governance were there before the conference in an extraordinary interview with one of Zuma's closest comrades, Mo Shaik. Mo Shaik is the brother of Shabir Shaik, who was convicted of corruption and fraud in 2005. He worked with Zuma in Vula and was renowned for his courage and acuity during his days in the underground. In the post-apartheid administration, he was, variously, a senior intelligence official, an adviser to the minister of Foreign Affairs, and a diplomat. But he has not held elected position in either the ANC or government. This is what he said when a journalist asked him if Manuel should stay on as finance minister under a Zuma administration: 'It would be great to have Manuel stay on as finance minister but the challenge is this: when you have been part of the macroeconomic stabilisation programme do you have the right mindset for a period of heightened implementation? Would he have the flexibility of mind? If he has the flexibility, the next administration will have a role for him in some capacity.'[19]

Manuel was in Namibia on the day the paper came out. Somebody sent one of his officials a text message with a summary of the story. Manuel read the interview the moment he returned that evening. 'I was quite struck. People have said that Mo has said these kind of things in private. But to arrogate to himself the right to be able to say *this* in public is really serious.'

Strangely, Manuel wasn't angry. He saw it as a perfect opportunity to spell out a few political lessons. 'You led with your jaw,' he thought, 'let me crack it for you.'

The next morning he rose before dawn and wrote an open letter to Shaik, timed for the Sunday newspapers.

I suppose it is incumbent on me to say, 'thank you, bwana, for the mention.' But of course I will not.

Mo, like you, I have the ANC in my entire being. The privilege of serving this movement in any capacity has always been a part of that commitment. Being elected to serve as part of the collective of its National Executive Committee since 1991 has been a tremendous opportunity for learning and for my political development. And, the joy of being called by its two successive presidents in state, Mandela and Mbeki, to serve as South Africa's Finance Minister is unsurpassed.

The emphasis, Mo, is on service. Service to my country and people becomes an act of love – it is clearly not a job, nor could it ever be an undertaking for notional power or the salary. And yes, the assignment as Finance Minister is one that I draw great pleasure from. But be assured that the opportunity I speak of is not something I will grovel for, nor do I ever wish to be beholden.

So I may not have the qualities of flexibility that you are looking for – I am sorry that I fail you so. I also see that you see a great role for me – that is wonderful. But who asked you? You would know that your comments are exceedingly arrogant and gratuitous – but how do you claim this right?

And then, to the kernel of his complaint:

I thought that I had missed a trick. I then checked the published list of nominees to the NEC (National Executive Committee of the ANC) – your name should have been in position 139, between Shabangu and Shiceka – but it was not there. So what is the source of your raw power? …

My plea to you is simple … It has taken 96 years of the most unimaginable toil and sacrifice to build the ANC into this formidable movement, it could be destroyed in five days at Polokwane – don't do it! … Do not destroy the only vehicle capable of building democracy.[20]

Nor do I ever wish to be beholden. It is a statement that goes to the heart of the question of governance. There is a major difference between being accountable and being beholden. 'Beholden' is to patrons who dispense power and wealth in return for loyalty. 'Accountable' is to an electorate or a party constituency, which Mo Shaik was clearly not.

When I spoke to Manuel a week before Polokwane, Zuma was not the enemy for him. Having emerged from the Western Cape, a region infamous for its internecine battles, Manuel had developed 'an aversion to factionalism'. He had known what it was like to be labelled – sneeringly – the 'High Command' by political rivals in the resistance movement. He had known, too, what it was like to be assumed to be part of a 'coloured cabal' by Africanists up north. Now there was danger again of his being put into a camp. 'Yes, I'm close enough to Thabo Mbeki,' he told me, 'and I've been able to benefit immensely from his insights … to depend on his backing for some very tough decisions … Yet I'm not seen as part of his inner circle.'

He had worked with Zuma when he came into the country illegally before the official negotiations started and before he had been granted indemnity. He believed Zuma wanted 'nothing more' than to be a successful president. So there was genuineness, Manuel believed, when Zuma said there would be no significant change in policies. The great danger was his 'indebtedness to people who don't approach life like that ... It means that there's likely to be a stand-off about some issues big enough to cause great fissures.'

Mbeki lost the presidency at Polokwane, to his own surprise but not so much to Manuel's. It had been clear from 2005 that there were dynamics in the ANC that portended his defeat which he had not recognised. After he dismissed Zuma as deputy president in June 2005, the ANC National General Council insisted Zuma remain as deputy president of the organisation. At Polokwane, many of his supporters were voted off the NEC. Manuel himself made it on to the NEC but came in at number 57, a far cry from the first place he occupied in Stellenbosch five years before.

Still, it was significant because it meant that although he was not on the official Zuma 'list', Zuma supporters nonetheless voted for him, a finance minister who had piloted economic policies that many in that camp claimed were anathema.

The press, in particular, expected Manuel to be rattled by the signs of Zuma victory, and the narrative was played out in an altercation he had with photographers as he walked towards makeshift TV studios set up in a marquee. Rain poured from the skies, as it did for most of the conference. One photographer, a young woman, claimed he shoved her out of the way as she put up her lens to take a picture of him. Then, said news reports, he pushed his umbrella in the faces of other photographers. Manuel said he was on his way to talk to TV stations at the request of the ANC. 'I was walking with the brolly ... then suddenly this horde of photographers descended on me like complete paparazzi. Why they were sticking lenses in my face I don't know. I was walking with the brolly and I shielded myself. One journalist stuck a lens close to my face, and I covered the lens with my hand and continued walking.' She walked sideways next to him and Manuel said she must have 'tripped over her own feet'.

Of all cabinet ministers, Manuel has been one of the most engaging with the press. But the stories the next day were far from sympathetic. They reported he had just come from voting. 'He seems like a calm sort of guy, but then he came at me with an umbrella! I didn't know he could so aggressive! He must have been under a lot of stress,' said Felix Dlangamandla, a photographer for *Beeld*. But Manuel said he was not trying to escape the press; on the contrary he was heading for a TV interview 'down in the rain in that funny marquee'.

Yet there was an element of the old street fighter that emerged as he relived the tale: 'I didn't run at them (the photographers) or try to beat them up. You don't beat people up with an open brolly, in any event. If you want to beat them you close the brolly and you set on them!'

COCKTAIL UMBRELLAS. This is what Thoraya Pandy, Manuel's communications chief suggests he distribute to parliamentarians when he presents his 2008 Budget. Pandy is spunky and energetic. A former radio producer, with a good grasp of what makes news, she retains the irreverence of a journalist.

Her suggestion of cocktail umbrellas is only partly a reference to Manuel's run-in with journalists at Polokwane two months before. It also picks up the major theme of his speech. Not a time for fruit or trees or music this year. The global economic weather is distinctly chilly and South Africans have to weather the storm.

The Budget has come at a gloomy, if not stormy, time. Business is nervous. The entire country has spent most of January suffering regular power outages – euphemistically called 'load-shedding' – a result of Eskom's* inability to maintain a steady supply of power in the face of increasing demand. The power shortage has hurt small businesses and large ones. The mines, one of the biggest employers and exporters in the country, had to go on short time because of the outages, and for two weeks undertook to use just enough electricity to keep their shafts ventilated. There was no production.

Markets, as Phakamani Hadebe showed me in his graphs, are not amorphous at all. They are spiky animals. A graph showing how South Africa compared with other emerging markets in terms of credit ratings showed the country coasting along a gentle wave, significantly above other emerging markets. But in January 2008 it prickled and plunged so that the difference between South Africa and its emerging market cousins was now uncomfortably close. The downward spike was not due to Zuma's victory but to Eskom's defeat.[21]

But at the annual pre-Budget rehearsal at Manuel's Cape Town house, the mood is relaxed if focused. 'Please use half the 2008 budget to build 800 new power stations,' reads Pandy from one of the 2 400 Tips for Trevor. It is a tip that sends Manuel and his officials into a flurry of Eskom jokes doing the rounds, and soon they begin to refer to the power utility by the epithet it has earned itself: *Eishkom*. ('*Eish*' is South African slang used to express awe or horror, or a mixture of the two.)

---

* Eskom is the public utility company responsible for generating and distributing electricity.

Pandy reminds him that if he uses any Tips in his speech they ask permission from the senders. The '*lobola* guy' – the man who'd asked for a tax deduction on *lobola* payments – had demanded payment but he was mollified when Pandy gave him a signed copy of the Minister's speech. Later, when there is talk of a 'war room analogy' to spell out a 'war on poverty', Momoniat asks: 'Is it going to focus on performance so we can get rid of some of the non-performing soldiers?'

'It's not the soldiers,' says Kganyago. 'It's the officers in charge.'

They trawl through the issues of rising food prices. Kuben Naidoo reports that his domestic worker had asked him what the government is going to do about them; there is silence around the table until Kganyago says: 'She was talking about the government in the house.' And then, more seriously, Manuel refers to a news story that details what a state pension buys for a family: '50 kilograms of mielie meal at R238, five kilos of sugar beans at R49, five litres of cooking oil at R42 and a bag of potatoes for R32. School fees are R60 a year, a pair of Trafford school shoes costs R120 for each child, then there are shorts, dresses, shirts, jerseys and a few other items. After that there's not much left. I mean it's the ongoing problem: the problem is that the pension is not designed to keep children at school.'

'But that's the reality,' says Pandy.

'But you can't fix it through the pension. You can't fix unemployment through the pension scheme.'

All the time they are searching for the one message to convey. It's not the 'war-room' in the end. 'The messages are the weather forecast,' says Naidoo, 'riding the storm, acting differently, focusing on growth for the future.'

And Manuel decides to cast himself in the 2008 Budget as a weatherman.

Two days before the Budget, Manuel asks Pandy if she can get him into a TV studio before the Budget Speech so that he can record the part of his speech that deals with the global economy in front of a world weather map. Then he wants to play the TV tape on to the screens in Parliament (with no sound, just his lips moving) while he is speaking. The speech refers to the turbulence in the North American housing market, the lower growth prospects in Europe and Japan due to high oil prices, and the effect of lowered demand for exports on China's booming economy. To do this, they have to go to the parliamentary studio of the national broadcaster, the South African Broadcasting Corporation, set up a weather map with graphics of cold fronts and storm clouds, get him to speak the relevant words, and then play it into Parliament at precisely the right moment. Pandy is doubtful about the broadcaster's capacity to pull it off, says so, and hopes she has persuaded him to forget the idea.

But two hours later she runs down a corridor in the Treasury, breathless. 'He's really serious about this,' she says. 'Our Minister, Milli Vanilli.* I'm out of my *mind* here!'

Mostly, Manuel gets what he wants. On the afternoon before the Budget he and Pandy go to the SABC studio in Parliament, his bodyguard carrying the jacket and tie he is to wear on Budget Day. They find a young man in SARS, an artist with dreadlocks, who can do reasonable computer graphics depicting cold fronts, storm clouds and sunshine. Pandy is relieved that the two men in charge of the studio, Pieter and Rudi, are old hands, experienced cameramen and technicians.

Manuel stands in front of a green board wearing tomorrow's jacket and tie with today's trousers. There is no map behind him: it is projected on to a screen while he, like real weather presenters, has to conjure the world on to a blank board. One camera focuses on him, the other on the map. Pieter sits in the control room; two cameramen, Rudi and Lucky, go into the studio with Manuel and Pandy.

'Madam Speaker,' begins Manuel before rolling out the long list of salutations required by protocol. 'Zoom in slightly,' says Pieter. 'Right, we're at 'ladies and gentlemen,' says Manuel. 'The global economy grew ...'

'More, more,' says Pieter to Rudi.

'Where is the cue?' asks Rudi.

'If I were the weatherman. In North America ...'

'Zoom in, zoom in, yes!' says Pieter.

'Because the US is so big, it will have an impact everywhere ... China's economy, in contrast ... now I can't see where China is.'

'Don't pan, Lucky,' says Pieter. 'Knock it off the top.'

'China's expansion impacted on the price of all major commodities including oil ... the cross-currents of commodity prices remain supportive of economic growth in many parts of Africa. For South Africa and Australia ...'

'You didn't go to South Africa,' says Rudi.

'Aaah!'

The cameramen complain about a glow from Manuel's balding pate. One

---

* The pop group who made lip-synching famous.

scurries off to fetch make-up.

He starts again. 'Higher prices benefit commodity-rich economies like South Africa and Australia.' When he reaches for Australia his hand lands slap in the middle of the Indian Ocean.

By the third take, Manuel knows where Australia is. Pandy is flustered and worries about the timing: the tape must be played in at the precise moment in Parliament when he says, 'If I were the weatherman.'

'You just need a one-second break after, "If I were the Madam".'

Manuel takes a moment to notice, then says: 'If I were the Madam, I'd whip some butt.'

The cameramen crack up.

Manuel starts again: 'If I were the ... WEATHERMAN.'

Everyone stifles giggles and the take goes perfectly. The next day, during the Budget Speech, the technicians play it over the parliamentary TV screens a few seconds too early, but hardly anyone notices.

IF ANYONE WAS EXPECTING post-Polokwane depression at the pre-Budget press conference on Budget Day, they didn't get it. 'We can come back to all South Africans with an incredibly strong Budget,' Manuel says. 'Strong in every sense of the word. Its strength lies in the fact that we haven't been afraid to spend in areas that matter.' Non-interest public spending is to grow by 6 per cent over the next three years. Education takes the lion's share – R121 billion, 'rightly signifying that investing in capabilities on which dignity, self-reliance and social progress are built is the centre of our development strategy'.[22] Then social grants, then health – a 10,6 per cent increase, including a hefty allocation to programmes dealing with HIV and Aids. The criminal justice system and infrastructure get a significant increase. 'Eishkom' gets a R60 billion loan over five years to build new infrastructure.

This Budget quietly incorporates some of the Harvard group proposals. Cyclical revenues are separated, and the idea of a wage subsidy for young people is introduced.

Tax is cut – for corporates from 29 per cent to 28 per cent, and for small businesses, and adjusted for inflation for individuals. The Budget surplus is one per cent of GDP: 'Madam Speaker, what this means in practice is that we will weather the present storm and continue to invest for growth,' Manuel will say in Parliament.

He also tells the press why the Treasury is relaxing exchange control:

'We do this because we're confident; we can be confident about the choices we make now because we took the correct decisions early. We built the windmills before the storm, and now we will harvest this … we're not in this environment where so many people are so negative about prospects for growth around the world; we're focusing not on the storm, we're focused on what comes hereafter.'

A journalist says: 'This strikes me as a sunny, conspicuously happy Budget.' He means it as a criticism.

Has the 'newly elected leadership of the ANC' put pressure on the Treasury to produce a different kind of Budget, asks another. 'These newly elected leaders of the ANC,' replies Manuel, 'of which I am one, put a lot of pressure on these ones here (he gestures to his officials). I've never had any concerns about whether there'll be difficulty in these matters. We can look at the resolutions adopted at the 52nd national conference in Polokwane and look at the Budget and find there isn't a contradiction. But I can also say that by the time we went to Polokwane the Budget was effectively made, done, and dusted; it's not as though we are a group of people sitting in the Treasury or SARS getting our instructions from Mars. I'm a Member of Parliament. I represent the African National Congress.'

He is also asked whether this will be the last Budget he tables. 'I don't know. The president can get fed up with me this afternoon and fire me after I deliver the Budget. But I must thank the ANC for allowing me the wonderful set of opportunities that history has afforded me.'

'ROOTEDNESS' IS THE WORD Kader Asmal used to describe Manuel, his friend and erstwhile housemate and cabinet colleague. It is a rootedness not only in the streets of Kensington where he cut his political teeth, and where his mother and three sisters still live. It is a rootedness in the ANC, an organisation that gave him direction as a rebellious youngster and then hope, first as a prisoner, later as an embattled finance minister.

In mid-2008, the pall of uncertainty that had descended on the country in the early part of the year had not lifted. Nobody knew whether a new ANC administration would keep him on as finance minister, which ministers would return to Cabinet, or indeed, even if Cabinet would remain the same size. Manuel thinks that both the national and provincial cabinets are too large. But he was concerned about the apparent lack of succession planning.

'If you assume that only half of your cabinet returns, how do you run this thing? I mean there's only a year left to an election. Broadly, where are those other people [who could be leaders]? Somebody must be saying somewhere, we may not like Trevor Manuel but he's been kind of OK as a finance minister, but it's an eternity he's been there and this is not a lifetime job. We need to replace him now, quietly. Where do you find someone to replace him? When you replace him, what approach would he take if you send somebody to him?'

I ask him how it is possible that those discussions could take place without a whisper getting to him: 'I've never been part of those kinds of discussions,' he replies. Then: 'I suppose I'm pleading for rationality. I'm saying you don't put someone in a position for ever because each year that passes makes it more difficult for somebody else to take over. And here I am, having been in the job as long as I have. I can pick up the phone and call a finance minister anywhere in the world.'

By the end of 2007, after Gordon Brown became prime minister of Britain and when Peter Costello's Australian Liberal Party lost the election, Manuel became the longest serving finance minister in the world.

Would he take a job as head of the World Bank if the reformers won and changed the rules?

'I'd be very hard-pressed to leave the country.' He thinks for a moment then repeats: 'I'd be *very* hard-pressed to leave the country.' Anyway some of those jobs, such as World Bank president are 'trophy jobs', and the environments are 'exceedingly hard because you don't ever forget what the power imbalances are. But apart from that I'd be very hard-pressed. I suppose I'm so deeply passionate about South Africa, which is why I am so outspoken, why I don't think we should accept any mediocrity. I think the country's capable of greater things. You've got to keep raising the bar, keep pushing.'

Mbeki had told him once that if you want to push back the boundaries of poverty 'you must focus on excellence. Anything else is a complete sell-out.'

The Treasury staff knows this ethos. 'Everybody's on time … people dress professionally. You are not going to saunter in at 10am in your jeans. It's just not going to be tolerated.'

Manuel, and Ramos when she headed the Treasury, are 'irritating to work for because they are such perfectionists', Naidoo told me. 'But if you look at it from a country perspective, the guy in the street wants the highest standards from his government and nothing less. Trevor and Maria embody that. They don't say, ah, you know he's an affirmative action appointee, it's

OK if he makes a spelling error, they don't say, ah, you know he was from the struggle, or ah you know, he worked hard last night, he spent 14 hours here at the office, he's entitled to a mistake. Trevor and Maria never do that. They don't care who you are, they don't care what your position is, they don't care how hard you've worked the previous day. They expect standards that are absolutely at the top. And that's refreshing.'

Part of Manuel's struggle within the ANC in the interregnum between the Polokwane conference and the 2009 elections was not only to encourage 'rationality' in the debate on the economy, but also to press for a return to some of the values and self-assertion that drove the anti-apartheid struggle. Much of the jostling for power at the top in the post-Mandela era is about access to wealth and influence, whether it be through the state, business, or the public corporations. Some of the new black elite have accumulated significant wealth, and although the poor have not got poorer (in fact they are substantially better off than they were in 1994), the income gap has widened. It is not a South African phenomenon – inequality is growing in communist China as its economy grows. But the bitter fights that have, at times, descended into anti-constitutionalism have betrayed some of the values that drove the anti-apartheid movement.

In the *Ready to Govern* conference in 1992, the emphasis was on *governance* – on democracy, on anti-corruption, on transparency. 'We didn't know where we'd end up as individuals, but we knew that democracy meant focusing on issues of governance. You need people who understand that, who are hungry to make a difference and will push themselves.' What the ANC – and particularly Mandela – did for Manuel and his generation 'was to rapidly prepare us without ever anointing us as individuals'.

On one of his visits to India, Manuel visited Gandhi's tomb where the Mahatma's seven social sins are inscribed:

Politics without principle
Wealth without work
Pleasure without conscience
Knowledge without character
Commerce without morality
Science without humanity
Worship without sacrifice

'I've never understood that you can get rich without working for it,' he said. Nor does he understand why the new nation is not quite yet born. There has been a failure 'to communicate that change is a process that actually involves people themselves. This idea of a victim syndrome – crime happens; people can't do anything about it. Societies aren't built like that. Our whole struggle against apartheid was largely premised on the idea that we had to do something for ourselves and we actually did amazing things.

'And now we pretend we don't know how.'

Sometimes he longs to return to community work – a measure of 'ploughing back, an opportunity to teach, an opportunity to work with people in communities, not as an activist but trying to work against that victim syndrome'.

WHENEVER I HAVE VISITED Manuel's mother in his childhood home, I am struck by the values that envelop it. It is still modestly furnished and adorned mainly by pictures of her children and grandchildren, apart from a poster-size photograph of herself with Mandela, signed by the former president, presented to her on her eightieth birthday in June 2006. Hope, prayer, and hard work have got her through the crises in her life: her two mothers' deaths, the loss of her husband, the loss of family homes, her son's near fatal accident on a building site, and then his long detentions.

The years of apartheid made her first afraid – of the African people living in shacks in Kensington, of the banned political activist Taufie Bardien, who was her neighbour, of the security police who hunted her son – then ashamed of her fear, then angry.

But she never described herself as a victim.

Manuel's home imbued him with a sense of values that he now returns. When the Public Works Department replaced the furniture in his Cape Town house, his mother joked that she could use the old furniture. 'I can't do that, Mom,' he responded. 'It's not my furniture. It's the taxpayers' furniture.' It was a value she understood. 'Not our money.'

The challenge ahead for Manuel is not about money. 'Somebody needs to drive an agenda of state that says, ours is no longer a money problem, ours is an efficiency problem. Let's turn around the public service, put it at the service of the people, put the people as the key object of what (we're) doing, and drive that agenda. You step out of line, you take money that doesn't belong to you, we deal with you hard! We build an exemplary public service.

That challenge, I think, is the biggest challenge of our time.'

In 2002, Manuel received an honorary doctorate from the University of the Western Cape, the institution that had been the site of such bitter protests and violence during apartheid. It's within sight of the technical college where he'd trained as an engineer. He tracked his own past. 'I chose, you see, a practical and sensible line of work, in which the relevant calculus translates tidily into angles of elevation and appropriate stress factors and loading constraints, and drawings on a page convert after a few months ... into a three-storey building or an extra lane on a highway or a sewerage processing plant.

'Economics is not like that. It makes use of much of the same mathematics but the meaning is surrounded with so much more mystery ...'

The course in economic policy since 1994 had been difficult 'because the social challenges we face are so immense, the economic environment is ruthless and unkind, and we have faced undue scepticism from many quarters'.[23]

He chose, again, a poem by Ben Okri to explain how he felt. He did not say so, but it summed up his journey, incomplete as it is:

You can't remake the world
Without remaking yourself
Each new era begins within
It is an inward event
With unsuspected possibilities
For inner liberation.[24]

Postscript

How to put a full stop to a life still being lived, to work as yet unfinished?

I was asked this question by a radio interviewer as I finished writing this book shortly before the country was rocked by the political drama of September 2008.

The full stop is only on the narrative, not on the lived experience of a subject, or a people, or a country. I have changed the full stop into a semi-colon because of the apparent momentousness of the bitter fall-outs in the party that Manuel joined three decades ago.

On 20 September, the National Executive Committee of the African National Congress, after a long and bitter meeting, 'recalled' President Thabo Mbeki. The decision, said the ANC, was taken in the wake of a court judgment which ruled that the charges against Jacob Zuma, the president of the ANC elected at the Polokwane conference, were incorrectly brought. The judgment, by Judge Chris Nicholson of the Pietermaritzburg High Court, also found there to be 'plausible inference' that there was 'baleful' political influence in the decision by the National Prosecuting Authority to bring fresh charges against Zuma after he had won the ANC presidency in Polokwane.

Thabo Mbeki himself, against whom the 'inference' of political influence was made, was not party to the court proceedings and his side was not heard. But the judgment was the spark that allowed angry Zuma supporters on the NEC to successfully expel Mbeki from office just six months before his term was due to end.

Thabo Mbeki announced his decision to resign on Sunday, 21 September 2008, in a speech on national television that was mostly interpreted as being dignified and moving. The decision caused great anxiety around the country and in the ANC. But, and in spite of a worsening financial crisis in the markets of the developed world, the local South African markets remained steady. On the Tuesday, though, they began to plummet. The Johannesburg stock exchange lost 4 per cent of its value; the currency dropped by 2,5 per cent. In all, R220 billion worth of wealth was lost that day on the stock exchange. The reason? A statement was released to the media on Tuesday, 23 September by the Presidency's spokesman announcing the resignation of 11 cabinet ministers, including Trevor Manuel.

Some of Manuel's senior aides were as shocked as the markets when they heard the news that Tuesday morning. It went against all they expected. For the next few days newspaper commentators used words such as 'spiteful', 'mischievous' and 'malicious' to describe his move. 'Was it a shot across the bows,' asked a talk show host, 'to show how indispensable he is?' Barney Mtombothi of the *Financial Mail* described its effect rather than trying to guess the intention: 'It was a sobering introduction to the realities of global markets for the left-wing neophytes still giddy at an improbable victory achieved so swiftly and unexpectedly; a reminder, if one was required, that, in a modern globalised world, political power has its limits.'[1]

Others exonerated Manuel and blamed the former president for announcing the privately submitted resignation. 'If there are any South Africans who still think that the departure of Thabo Mbeki from the Union Buildings is a tragedy, they need only to look at the events of last Tuesday to see how callow, petty and vindictive the man's administration was,' wrote *The Times* columnist Justice Malala.[2]

Truth is hard to exact in a crisis of hurt egos and wounded feelings, but here is an attempt: Manuel wrote his resignation letter on the Saturday after the president was 'recalled'. He then left for New York and Washington, apparently with the blessing of both Mbeki and Zuma. He had tried to persuade all other cabinet ministers to resign on the principle that a new president should be able to appoint the cabinet he wanted. He had indicated, privately, that he was prepared to serve in a new administration. He expected the letters to be tabled in Parliament later the following week when the new president, Kgalema Motlanthe, was sworn in. While he was away in the United States, and before the letter was released, his office assured the public that he had not resigned. And he hadn't: the resignation was only supposed to take effect on the Thursday, immediately before the new cabinet was announced.

As the markets started to weaken on the Tuesday at the news of his resignation, he called a press conference from the IMF headquarters in Washington, spelling this out. It was clear that he had not been successful in persuading all of his fellow cabinet ministers to resign. In fact many of the less than stellar performers in the Mbeki government had not done so.

---

[1] Mthombothi, Barney: 'A smooth transition', *Financial Mail*, 10 October 2008.
[2] Malala, Justice: 'Mbeki's vindictive legacy', *The Times*, 29 September 2008.

At the Washington press conference he reiterated his willingness to serve in a new administration. Two days later he was indeed reappointed, now by new President Kgalema Motlanthe, with no effective break in his tenure. Motlanthe, Zuma's deputy president in the ANC, had been put forward by the ANC as president for the period up to the elections due in mid-2009.

Some close to the process of the resignations believe that the decision to release the letter earlier than agreed was not made by the president, but by one of his senior aides. The spokesman in whose name it was released was too junior a functionary, nor had he ever been a particularly proactive communications man, and was unlikely to have made the call himself. The motivation may well have been vengeful, but it was not a coordinated vengeance. It reflected the hurt that began to tear apart the oldest liberation movement in Africa.

People whom readers will have encountered in these pages are on opposite sides of this divide. Terror Lekota, the heroic 'battering ram' of the UDF, who spent long years in jail, resigned from his cabinet post and called a press conference to say that the new ANC leadership had broken faith with the values in the Freedom Charter. The principles of equality before the law had been abandoned in the search for a 'political solution' to Zuma's legal problems. Tribalism, anathema to the old ANC, was being fomented in the culture and slogans of Zuma supporters. Lekota had criticised pro-Zuma T-shirts proclaiming the wearer '100% Zulu boy'. Lekota indicated when he resigned from cabinet that he was not available for selection to the new ANC cabinet.

Yet those who have been equally committed to the values of democracy found themselves in new positions of power as a result of the shift in leadership. Barbara Hogan, for one, who had been marginalised by the Mbeki administration, was appointed the new minister of health, eliciting huge sighs of relief from the Aids lobbies and many others exasperated with the unhelpful style of the old minister.

There was no simple policy or ideological divide. Personal feelings of pain ran deep. Some cabinet ministers who had resigned and meant it, were angry about Manuel's apparent reluctance to defend Mbeki publicly before the Polokwane conference. Manuel was 'everything he was' only due to Mbeki. So the divide was also about personal loyalties. One realist in government said the change in leadership was merely the 'circulation of elites'.

Manuel's office, and the sequence of events, suggest that Manuel did not intend to rock confidence in the country with his purported resignation. Yet there was a deep irony in the fact that the financial markets reacted to his 'resignation', as he put it to a BBC interviewer a few days later, with the same panic as 'when Nelson Mandela appointed me as finance minister'. And the fall came at a time when markets the world over were 'very jittery, and there were exchange rate adjustments around the world'.[3]

It was a 'bit of a shock', he conceded, that Mbeki had been unseated in the manner in which he had been. It was clear 'there was lots of anger, and unresolved issues'. But then, he noted, South Africa is not unique. These things happen in politics, he said; they had happened in Great Britain when Gordon Brown succeeded Tony Blair.

He held a line. When asked whether Mbeki's Aids policy was not 'deeply flawed', he replied that South Africa had the largest treatment programme in the world. 'We've got more people on ARVs than any other country.' When the interviewer asked him whether policies would remain the same, quoting Mo Shaik's letter that had promised him a position in government if he showed 'flexibility of mind', he replied that Shaik had apologised to him for his 'outlandish' behaviour. By the time the interviewer asked him about a '40 per cent' unemployment rate, Manuel was in his stride: 'You must have seen those figures on a bubble-gum wrapper,' he said.

It was vintage Manuel: he not only put his interrogator on the back foot, he spelled out a message to some in the broad alliance of Zuma supporters who, he believes, have a less than realistic grasp on the world. Yet, as he had done in the Cape Town days of old, he avoided being trapped into any obvious faction in an ANC more riven than ever before.

What will become of him? The events of late September 2008 showed more clearly than ever the urgent need for a succession plan for the Finance Ministry. But his role in governance, in government, may not yet be done.

'I don't look at life as forward and backward movements,' he'd said to me shortly before the fracas that led to Mbeki's departure. He didn't see himself as a 'unifier' who could unite factions because 'I don't like factions and unifiers must tolerate factions'.

'But what do you do? What gets you up every morning? The opportunity to do things quite differently from the way they've been done.'

---

[3] BBC, Hard Talk interview, 29 September 2008.

Endnotes

A note on the references contained in the endnotes:
All outside sources have been referenced. Those quotes or facts not referenced in the text come directly from the author's own reporting or interviews.

PART ONE: Origins

CHAPTER 1: Shattered Cape

1. 'Black' in this context refers to both the African and coloured townships. Many of the areas set aside for blacks also spread to the east on the sandy dunes of the most windswept part of False Bay
2. Bickford-Smith, V, Van Heyningen, E & Worden, N: *Cape Town in the Twentieth Century*, David Philip, Cape Town, 1999
3. 'Rex Trueform, Clothing Company Limited', from Shorten, P: *Golden Jubilee Cape Town*, 1963
4. Ibid
5. Nicol, Martin: 'The Garment Workers' Union of the Cape Peninsula and the Garment Workers' National Unity Movement, 1927-1955', unpublished Honours thesis, University of Cape Town, 1977, p30
6. Ibid
7. Nicol op cit, p90
8. Hester Seale interview by Bill Nasson, 10 December 1985, African Studies Library, District Six oral history interviews, University of Cape Town. All quotations from Hester Seale are from this interview
9. Field, Sean: 'The Power of Exclusion: Moving Memories from Windermere to the Cape Flats 1920s-1990s', PhD thesis, Dept of Sociology, University of Essex, 1996
10. *Cape Times*, 15 May 1943, quoted in Field op cit, p156
11. Interview, Mrs C.S., quoted in Field op cit, p160
12. Interview, Mr H.B., quoted in Field op cit, p157
13. *Cape Argus*, 16 June 1944, quoted in Field op cit, p158
14. *Cape Times*, 23 June 1944, quoted in Field op cit, p172
15. Quoted in Field op cit, p154
16. Interview, Mr I.Z., quoted in Field op cit, p128
17. Mr I.Z., quoted in Field op cit, p178
18. Goldin, I: *Making Race: The Politics and Economics of Coloured Identity in South Africa*, Maskew, Miller, Longman, 1987, p115

CHAPTER 2: People of the world

1. Uys, Pieter-Dirk: *Evita for President* (play), 2007. The author is grateful to Pieter-Dirk Uys for sending her the relevant parts of his script, email correspondence with author, 18 April 2007
2. The Population Registration Act of 1950 was a cornerstone of apartheid laws; initially it defined coloured as those not 'generally accepted' as white or black; it was amended a number of times to make it stricter
3. See Adhikari, M: *Not White Enough, Not Black Enough: Racial identity in the South African*

Coloured Community (Ohio University Press, 2005) for a thorough exploration of this phenomenon of racism and self-hate

4. According to Joel Netshitenzhe, head of the Policy Unit in the Presidency, this was once hotly debated among exiles. Reg September, the ANC representative in the UK and Europe at the time, was opposed to the use of inverted commas (interview with author, 14 March 2007)

5. Adhikari op cit, p20

6. Quoted in Adhikari op cit, p23

7. Sampson, A: *Mandela: The Authorized Biography*, Harper Collins, 1999, p211

8. Adhikari op cit, p22

9. Fredrickson, George M: *White Supremacy: A Comparative Study in American and South African History*, Oxford University Press, 1981, p65

10. Mountain, Alan: *An Unsung Heritage: Perspectives on Slavery*, David Philip, Cape Town, 2004, p21

11. Ibid, p22

12. Adhikari, M: ' "The Sons of Ham": slavery and the making of coloured identity'. Paper presented at the Cape Slavery and After Conference, Univeristy of Cape Town, 10-11 August 1989. Adhikari argues that the 'Khoisan would often either kill escapees or turn them in'.

13. According to Mountain op cit, p32, there were 714 men to every 100 women among Cape slaves, compared with 150 men to 100 women in the Atlantic trade

14. Mountain op cit, p63. Mountain dates this incident as taking place in 1688

15. Ibid

16. See Shell, Robert: 'The Family and Slavery in the Cape, 1680-1808', *in* James, Wilmot G & Simons, Mary (eds), *Class, Caste and Colour: A Social and Economic History of the South African Western Cape*, Transaction Publishers, New Brunswick and London, 1992

17. Mountain op cit, p97

18. Ibid, p33

19. Adhikari op cit, p214 and Fredrickson op cit, p110

20. Ibid, p68

21. Quoted in Fredrickson op cit, p267

22. Fredrickson op cit, p271

23. Worden, N: 'Adjusting to Emancipation: Freed slaves and farmers in mid-nineteenth century South Western Cape', *in* James & Simons op cit, p32

24. Interview, David Manuel, Cape Town, 22 August 2005

25. Mountain op cit, p178

26. See Goldin, I: *Making Race: The Politics and Economics of Coloured Identity in South Africa*, (Maskew, Miller, Longman, 1987) and Lewis, G: *Between the Wire and the Wall: A History of South African 'Coloured' Politics* (David Philip, Cape Town, 1987), for excellent histories of the effects of segregation and apartheid on the coloured people

27. Goldin op cit, p41

28. Ibid

29. Lewis op cit, p161; Davenport, T R H: *South Africa: A Modern History*, Macmillan, 1987, p338

30. According to Professor Robert Edgar, professor of African Studies at Howard University in Washington, hundreds of African-Americans and West Indians came to the Cape, mainly in the post-Civil War period in the late nineteenth and early twentieth centuries. Most settled in the Cape. The earliest had come in the eighteenth century on whaling ships. Missionaries who established the AME church came in the 1890s, and mostly settled in District Six (personal communication with the author, March 2007)

31. Giliomee, H L: 'Die Groei van 'n Gemeenskap', unpublished manuscript, p30

32. Hofmeyr, A M: *in* Francois Smuts (ed.), *Stellenbosch Three Centuries*, Official Commemorative Volume, Stellenbosch Town Council with the Oude Meester Group, October 1979

33. Giliomee op cit, p31

34. From *In Ons Bloed* compiled by Hilton Biscombe, Sun Press 2006
35. Giliomee op cit, p3
36. *Cape Times*, 30 July 1940, quoted in Giliomee, H L: 'Die Slag van Andringastraat: Studente Onluste op Stellenbosch', unpublished manuscript, 1940
37. Ibid
38. Goode, Richard: 'A History of the Food and Canning Workers' Union, 1941-1975', MA thesis, University of Cape Town, 1986, p67
39. Ibid

CHAPTER 3: History unhooked

1.   The third is Livingstone, in Lansdowne
2.   Goldin, I: *Making Race: The Politics and Economics of Coloured Identity in South Africa*, Maskew, Miller, Longman, 1987, p79
3.   Interview, Hermann Giliomee, Stellenbosch, 29 September 2005
4.   Goldin op cit, p93
5.   Ibid
6.   West, Martin: 'Confusing Categories: Population groups, national states and citizenships', *in* Boonzaier, E & Sharp, J (eds), *South African Keywords: The Uses and Abuses of Political   Concepts*, David Philip, Cape Town, 1988, p102
7.   Valentine, S *in Sunday Times*, '100 Years of Stories', 2006
8.   Quoted in Goldin op cit, p80
9.   Interview, Reg September, Cape Town, 8 September 2006
10. James, C L R: *Beyond a Boundary*, Duke University Press, 1993, p50
11. Lewis, G: *Between the Wire and the Wall: A History of South African 'Coloured' Politics*, David Philip, Cape Town, 1987, p 192
12. See Pinnock, D: 'Ideology and Urban Planning: Blueprints of a garrison city', *in* James, Wilmot G & Simons, Mary (eds), *Class, Caste and Colour: A Social and Economic History of the South African Western Cape*, Transaction Publishers, New Brunswick and London, 1992, p164. Some 90 per cent of District Six was landlord-owned
13. Quoted in Pinnock op cit, p164
14. Alex La Guma's *A Walk in the Night* (Africasouth Paperbacks, 1991) represents a much darker side of the District not often recalled in oral history accounts
15. Quoted in Pinnock op cit, p164
16. Race Relations Survey 1947, quoted in Pinnock op cit, p164
17. Barrow, B: *in* Breytenbach, C, *The Spirit of District Six*, C Struik Publishers, 1987, p2
18. Quoted in Pinnock op cit, p152
19. Quoted in Swanson, F & Harries J: '"Ja! So was District Six! But it was a beautiful place": Oral Histories, Memory and Identity', *in* Field, S (ed.), *Lost Communities, Living Memories: Remembering Forced Removals in Cape Town*, David Philip, Cape Town, 2001, p64
20. Goldin op cit, p134
21. Pinnock op cit, p167
22. Some coloured people were still on the municipal voters' roll but this dwindled as the Group Areas Act took its toll and moved people to outlying areas. In 1972 they were removed altogether from the voters' roll. See Todes, A, Watson, V & Wilkinson, P, 'Local Government Restructuring in Greater Cape Town', *in* James & Simons (eds), op cit
23. See Omar, Abdul Rashid, 'The impact of the death in detention of Imam Abdullah Haroun on Cape Muslim attitudes', History Honours thesis, University of Cape Town, 1982. Ten days after Haroun's detention the *Muslim News*, of which he was the editor, had carried no news articles about his arrest, but wrote in an editorial (6 June 1969): 'The reason for his detention is not known to *Muslim News*. But it is safe to assume that Imam Haroun is not being detained for spreading the doctrine of Islam. If Imam Haroun is

being held for his political views, then there is nothing *Muslim News* can do about the situation, as Imam Haroun's position as editor was to express the religious aspects of the community.'

24. Goldin op cit, p154. By the 1975 election, the percentage poll was 37 per cent, and in a number of constituencies in the densely populated Peninsula, fewer than 10 per cent voted

PART TWO: An Education 1970-1975

CHAPTER 4: 'Let us live for our children'

1. Apartheid made education strictly segregated and strictly unequal. In 1953 the government passed the Bantu Education Act and, in 1965, the Indian Education Act
2. Lewis, G: *Between the Wire and the Wall: A History of South African 'Coloured' Politics,* David Philip, Cape Town, 1987, p 276
3. Finnegan, W: *Crossing the Line: A Year in the Land of Apartheid,* Harper and Row, 1986
4. Bundy, C: ' "Action, comrades, action!" The politics of youth resistance in the Western Cape, 1985', *in* James, Wilmot G & Simons, Mary (eds), *Class, Caste and Colour: A Social and Economic History of the South African Western Cape,* Transaction Publishers, New Brunswick and London, 1992
5. Adhikari, M: 'Let us Live for our Children: Teachers League of South Africa, 1913-1940', unpublished MA thesis, University of Cape Town, 1986, p16
6. Ibid, p27
7. Adhikari, M: *Not White Enough, Not Black Enough: Racial identity in the South African Coloured Community,* Ohio University Press, 2005, p71
8. Cited in Finnegan op cit, p26
9. Weider, Alan: *Voices from Cape Town Classrooms: Oral Histories of Teachers who Fought Apartheid,* Peter Lang Publishing Inc, New York, 2003, p7
10. Ibid, p20
11. Quoted in Weider op cit, p16

CHAPTER 5: The politics of withdrawal

1. Lewis, G: *Between the Wire and the Wall: A History of South African 'Coloured' Politics,* David Philip, Cape Town, 1987, p 17
2. Goldin, I: *Making Race: The Politics and Economics of Coloured Identity in South Africa,* Maskew, Miller, Longman, 1987, p30
3. Bickford-Smith, V, Van Heyningen, E & Worden, N: *Cape Town in the Twentieth Century,* David Philip, Cape Town, 1999, p27
4. See Goldin op cit, p33; Lewis op cit, p21
5. See Lewis op cit, p54
6. Ibid, p48
7. Ibid, p63
8. Adhikari, M: 'Let us live for our Children: Teachers' League of South Africa, 1913-1940', unpublished MA thesis, University of Cape Town, 1986, p22
9. Quoted in Goldin op cit, p38
10. Lewis op cit, p162
11. Goldin op cit, p43
12. Cited in Goldin op cit, p44. The commission was formally known as the 'Commission of Inquiry regarding the Coloured Population of the Union' and reported in 1937
13. Lewis op cit, p170

14. Quoted in Lewis op cit, p181
15. Alexander, Neville: 'Non-collaboration in the Western Cape, 1943-1963', *in* James, Wilmot G & Simons, Mary (eds), *Class, Caste and Colour: A Social and Economic History of the South African Western Cape*, Transaction Publishers, New Brunswick and London, 1992, p183
16. Quoted in Lewis op cit, p214
17. Alexander op cit, p183
18. Interview, Jakes Gerwel, 27 October 2005
19. Security police report to minister of justice on M T Bardien, undated, probably 1961. I am grateful to Aziz Bardien for giving me access to his father's security police file
20. Interview, Virginia Engel, 12 December 2005
21. Alexander op cit, p187
22. Ibid
23. Lewis op cit, p231
24. Alexander op cit, p187
25. Interview, Reg September, 8 September 2006
26. Unity Movement, Anniversary Bulletin, *50th Year of Struggle*, 1994

CHAPTER 6: Lessons from Taufie

1. The surname Domingo was adapted from a first name, according to Soda Bardien, apparently not to embarrass his family, who had Calvinist roots, when Bardien's grandfather had converted to Islam. Likewise, Mrs Bardien's maiden name, Hashim, was also adapted from a first name
2. Interview, Soda Bardien, 20 September 2005
3. A security police report on Bardien dated 1971 says he joined the CPC in 1957
4. 'Naturelle' in Afrikaans, the apartheid government's term for Africans in those days before they switched to 'Bantu'
5. Security police report to the minister of justice, 8 September 1961
6. Lelyveld, Joseph: *Move Your Shadow: South Africa Black and White*, Jonathan Ball, 1986, p320
7. Security police report, op cit, 8 September 1961
8. Bardien, M T: Letter to Minister of Justice B J Vorster, 22 October 1961
9. *Cape Argus*, 18 December 1961
10. Security police report to minister of justice, 17 January 1966
11. Bardien, M T: Letter to Cape Town magistrates, quoted in Compol report (security police), 18 April 1966

PART THREE: Building 1976-1985

CHAPTER 8: 'Like tides, like stars'

1. Quoted in Hopkins, Pat & Grange, Helen: *The Rocky Rioter Teargas Show: The Inside Story of the 1976 Soweto Uprising*, Zebra Press, 2001, p84
2. Quoted in Hopkins & Grange op cit, p120
3. Friedman, Steven: *Building Tomorrow Today: African Workers in Trade Unions, 1970-1984*, Ravan Press, Johannesburg, 1987, p37
4. Ibid, p39
5. See Friedman op cit, pp40-44, for a good account of this period
6. Jaffer, Zubeida: *Our Generation*, Kwela Books, 2003, p20
7. Friedman op cit, p43

CHAPTER 9: A new mission

1.   Unibel was flanked by two adjoining informal, and illegal, settlements, Werkgenot and Modderdam. All three were destroyed by the end of the 1970s
2.   Tressell's real name was Noonan, but he wrote under a pseudonym because he thought his strong socialist views would dim his job prospects. He was born into a middle-class English family and lived in both Cape Town and Johannesburg for about 15 years at the end of the nineteenth century where he was involved in the early builders' trade unions
3.   Todes, A & Watson, V: Local Government Reorganisation: Government's Proposals and Alternatives in Cape Town, UPRU Working Paper Number 34, UCT, January 1986, p11
4.   Ibid, p14
5.   Piet Koornhof was often a figure of parody for anti-apartheid critics. A cabinet minister notable for his large ears and distinctive drawl, he once famously declared in the United States that 'apartheid is dead' about 15 years before the funeral, as one columnist wrote. He then went on to preside over nearly three million forced removals. In the post-apartheid years he made news by leaving his wife for a coloured woman and joining the ANC
6.   Mandela, Nelson: *Long Walk to Freedom*, MacDonald Purnell, 1994, pp447-8
7.   McGregor, Liz: 'The Fatti's and Moni's Dispute', *South African Labour Bulletin*, vol.5, nos 6&7, March 1980
8.   *Cape Times*, 28 June 1979
9.   McGregor op cit, p127
10.   Interview, Virginia Engel, Cape Town, 12 December 2005
11.   Quoted in McGregor, op cit

CHAPTER 10: A network of networks

1.   Maulvi Cachalia was part of the second generation of the Cachalia family, each generation well known in South Africa and India for their active participation in the struggle for human rights and freedom. He was a member of the Transvaal Indian Congress and an early comrade of Mandela. He left the country in 1964 after being banned and heavily restricted
2.   For interesting elaboration on this point, see Suttner, Raymond: 'The African National Congress underground between Rivonia and 1976'. Paper presented at ICS/SOAS conference 'Looking at South Africa Ten Years On', London, September 2004
3.   Marcus Solomon was part of the Yu Chi Chan Club led by the academic, linguist and prolific writer Neville Alexander. The group was named after Mao's term for guerrilla warfare and was essentially an activist breakaway from the Unity Movement. Alexander and Solomon were sentenced with two others to lengthy terms of imprisonment in 1964 even though they had not actually committed any act of sabotage
4.   Jeanette Curtis and her six-year-old daughter Katryn were killed by a parcel bomb in southern Angola in 1984. The bomb was sent by the spy Craig Williamson

CHAPTER 11: What was to be done?

1.   Steinberg, J: *Nongoloza's Children: Western Cape prison gangs during and after apartheid*, Monograph, Centre for the Study of Violence and Reconciliation, July 2004
2.   High Court Judgment, Cape Provincial Division, Mr Justice D H van Zyl, 12 September 2003
3.   Adhikari, M: *Not White Enough, Not Black Enough: Racial Identity in the South African*

          Coloured Community, Double Storey Books, 2005, p147
4.   Leila Patel took over from him as *Grassroots* organiser after Issel was banned
5.   The Federation of South African Trade Unions (FOSATU), which organised industrial unions of mainly African workers in the Transvaal and Natal, decided to register
6.   Quoted in Friedman, Steven: *Building Tomorrow Today: African Workers in Trade Unions, 1970-1984*, Ravan Press, Johannesburg, 1987, p206
7.   *Argus*, 20 May 1980
8.   *Cape Times*, 21 May 1980
9.   Goldin, I: *Making Race: The Politics and Economics of Coloured Identity in South Africa*, Maskew, Miller, Longman, 1987, p209
10.   Quoted in Goldin, ibid
11.   *Cape Times*, 3 June 1980
12.   One exception was the Black Sash, composed of mainly white women, who monitored the pass laws and forced removals closely and set up Advice Offices across the country to help the many thousands who fell foul of the law
13.   *Cape Times*, 19 June 1980
14.   *Cape Times*, 25 August 1980
15.   WPGWU: 'The Cape Meat Strike', *South African Labour Bulletin*, vol.6, no.5, 1980
16.   Maseko, Sipho: 'Civic Movement and Non-Violent Action: The Case of the Cape Areas Housing Action Committee', *African Affairs*, 96: 356, 1997
17.   Ibid, p360
18.   Cape Areas Housing Action Committee, Minutes, First AGM, 11 July 1982
19.   Goldin op cit, p214 and Maseko op cit, p358
20.   CAHAC AGM Minutes, 1982
21.   *Argus*, 15 January 1982
22.   Various reports put the number at between 33 000 and 41 000. CAHAC's eventual claim was 41 000. The *Argus* estimated 33 000; Maseko 40 000. The number, in any event, was impressive for such a young organisation
23.   Maseko op cit, p361
24.   CAHAC: Report on CAHAC Delegation to the Minister of Community Development, Pen Kotze, 1 March 1982
25.   Ibid
26.   Ibid
27.   Manuel, T: 'Beyond Reform: The Challenge of Change', NUSAS July Festival, 1983, quoted in Maseko op cit, p362
28.   *Grassroots*, vol.3, no.3, April 1982.
29.   *Rand Daily Mail*, 30 December 1980, Saspu National 4/81 (from Karis-Gerhard Collection, *From Protest to Challenge: 1964-1990*)
30.   Seekings, Jeremy: *The UDF: A History of the United Democratic Front in South Africa, 1983-1991*, David Philip, Cape Town, 2000, p37
31.   *Sunday Times*, 3 May 1981
32.   Mandela, Nelson: Letter to Mrs Ferrus, 14 May 1981. Karis-Gerhard Collection, *From Protest to Challenge: 1964-1990*
33.   Saspu National 4/1981
34.   Cole, Josette: *Crossroads: The Politics of Reform and Repression, 1976-1986*, Ravan Press, Johannesburg, 1987, p12. Section 10 of the Black Urban Areas Act stipulated that no African could stay in an urban area longer than 72 hours unless he/she met certain conditions. Section 10 1(a) and (b) referred to the exception – if an African had lived legally in an urban area for at least 15 years or worked continuously for one employer for 10 years, then he/she could stay in an urban area permanently. The Coloured Labour Preference Policy in the Western Cape made these stringent conditions even more difficult to comply with
35.   Ibid, p21

CHAPTER 12: All, here, now

1.   Green, Pippa: 'A Church and its Apartheid History', *Christianity and Crisis* (New York), vol.49, no.8, 22 May 1989
2.   Genesis 11, verses 1-8 (King James Bible)
3.   'The influence of my mother was that truth was indispensable in a person's life. People like us who were poor and had no power ... had to find inspiration and comfort through the Bible which taught us that God was the father of the widows and orphans.' Quoted in Steenbok, A A, 'Gereformeerde wees in die NGSK/VGK (1976-2005): 'n Kerkhistorie en Outobiografiese Verhaal', p9. Thesis submitted for the degree of Master of Divinity, University of Pretoria, 2005, p9
4.   Allem, Alexandra & Merret, Nicholas: 'Strength in Unity; the 1976 Cape Town Uprisings'. Video produced for History Honours thesis, University of Cape Town, 2004
5.   Steenbok op cit, p44
6.   Boesak, A, quoted in Steenbok op cit, p53
7.   Pityana, Barney: 'Reflections of 30 years since the death of Steve Biko: A Legacy Revisited', *Sowetan*, 20 September 2007
8.   Ibid
9.   Labour Party: 'A Constitutional Design?' *Work in Progress*, Issue 25, February 1983
10.   Quoted in *WIP* op cit
11.   Ibid
12.   Ibid
13.   Ibid
14.   Quoted in Seekings, Jeremy, *The UDF: A History of the United Democratic Front in South Africa, 1983-1991*, David Philip, Cape Town, 2000, p49
15.   *Cape Herald*, 29 January 1983
16.   *EYE*, vol.3, no.1, February 1983. This small community newspaper based in Pretoria was the only paper at the time to report on the words that would later become synonymous with the UDF when it was launched in August 1983
17.   Harber, A: 'United – in the politics of refusal', *Rand Daily Mail*, 8 June 1983
18.   Ibid
19.   Tambo, O R: 8 January statement, 1983. ANC documents
20.   Lodge, T: 'The Politics of Refusal', *Leadership*, vol.5, no.1, 1986
21.   Seekings op cit p47
22.   'GWU and the UDF', *Work in Progress*, Issue 29, 1983
23.   Ibid
24.   Njikelana, S: 'Unions and the UDF', *Work in Progress*, Issue 32, 1984
25.   Sonn became a prosecutor in the Directorate of Special Operations after apartheid, and was the first cricket administrator from Africa to serve as President of the International Cricket Council. He died in 2007, aged 58
26.   United Democratic Front Conference, 20 August 1983. Transcript from tape recordings, William Cullen Library, University of the Witwatersrand. This account of the UDF launch is taken largely from this transcript and from interviews with various participants
27.   Based on the author's own reporting at the time

CHAPTER 13: 'I beg you, please be ungovernable'

1.   Quoted in Seekings, Jeremy, *The UDF: A History of the United Democratic Front in South Africa, 1983-1991*, David Philip, Cape Town, 2000, p94
2.   This account reconstructed from interviews with Manuel and Wort
3.   Labour Monitoring Group: 'The November Stayaway', *South African Labour Bulletin*, vol.10, no.6, May 1985
4.   Ibid
5.   *Financial Mail*, 19 October 1984

6. Seekings op cit, p118
7. *Financial Mail* op cit
8. Ibid
9. Quoted in Seekings op cit, p125
10. Fosatu Worker News, no. 32, 1984
11. Labour Monitoring Group op cit
12. Quoted in LMG report op cit
13. *Grassroots*, vol. 6, no.1, February 1985
14. Curnick Ndlovu, keynote address, Azaadville, quoted in Seekings op cit, p138
15. Curnick Ndlovu became national chair, and Azhar Cachalia treasurer
16. *Argus*, 18 March 1985
17. So, at that stage, had a young student activist, Siphiwe Mtimkulu. He had been poisoned while in detention and was suing the minister of law and order. He disappeared from the hospital where he had gone to get treatment in 1982. The TRC later established that he and his friend Topsy Madaka had been abducted by police on their way to the hospital, given spiked drinks, and shot in the head. Their remains were thrown into the Fish River
18. Dirk Coetzee, a former security policeman, later admitted to having led a band of apartheid agents to murder her
19. Quoted in Seekings op cit, p149
20. Nash, Margaret: 'Unrest spreads to the Cape Peninsula', *Sash*, vol.28, no.3, November 1985

CHAPTER 14: 'Say not the struggle naught availeth'

1. Nash, Margaret: 'Unrest spreads to the Cape Peninsula', *Sash*, vol.28, no.3, November 1985
2. Ibid
3. *Grassroots*, vol.6, no.8, October 1985
4. Most of the incidents were reported on by the author, filing dispatches for Inter Press Services under the pseudonym Zayne Fredericks, or the *Argus* newspaper (under the author's own name)
5. Green, Pippa (writing as Zayne Fredericks), IPS dispatch, 24 September 1985
6. This account is reconstructed from the Human Rights Violation hearings of the Truth and Reconciliation Commission in May 1997 (www.doj.gov.za/trc) and Gunn, Shirley: *If Trees Could Speak: The Trojan Horse Story*, Human Rights Media Centre, Cape Town, 2007, and the author's own interviews with witnesses and family in Thornton Road, 16 October 1985. The day after the Athlone incident, there was a similar incident in Crossroads where police ambushed and shot several youths and children, killing two
7. *Cape Times*, 18 October 1985
8. *Argus*, 12 October 1985
9. *Argus*, 19 October 1985
10. Manuel, T: Speech to launch Ahmed Kathrada's *Memoirs* (published by Zebra, 2004), 1 September 2004
11. Kathrada, Ahmed: email correspondence with the author, 7 August 2008
12. Clough, Arthur Hugh: 'Say Not The Struggle Naught Availeth', in *Selected Poems*, ed. Shirley Chew, Routledge, 2003

PART FOUR: Emergency 1986-1989

CHAPTER 15: 'The enemy faints not nor faileth'

1. Apartheid Barometer, *Weekly Mail*, 13 December 1985
2. Green, Pippa: 'A place to work: Sarmcol Worker Co-ops', *South African Labour Bulletin*,

vol.11, no.4, February-March 1986

3.   Inkatha set up its own union UWUSA in 1986 to counter COSATU. This was later found to have been financed by the South African security police. In 1986, too, I did a lengthy interview with a leader from the Metal Workers' Union of South Africa (MWASA), Jeffrey Vilane, a worker at ALUSAF and fervent COSATU supporter whose house in Esikawini in Northern Natal had been attacked by men with machine guns. His appeal was for tolerance between Inkatha and COSATU because at one stage he had been sympathetic to Inkatha but was now dismayed at its divisive role in union organisation. Maxwell Xulu, then still under cover, threatened the *Labour Bulletin* that if the interview was used he would canvass unions not to talk to the *Bulletin* any more. It became clearer in retrospect why he would oppose an appeal for tolerance. The editors of the *Bulletin* decided, unfortunately, to acquiesce to his request

4.   Testimony to the Truth and Reconciliation Commission, Chris Bateman, Cape Town, 27 November 1996

5.   Testimony to the Truth and Reconciliation Commission, Cynthia Nomvuyo Ngewu, Cape Town, 23 April 1996

6.   Quoted in Cole, Josette, *Crossroads: The Politics of Reform and Repression, 1976-1986*, Ravan Press, Johannesburg, 1987, p119

7.   Quoted in Cole op cit, p120

8.   Cole op cit, p121

9.   Quoted in Cole op cit, p124

10.   Cole op cit, p134

11.   Eminent Persons Group: Mission to South Africa: The Commonwealth Report, 1986

12.   Ibid

CHAPTER 16: 'Unnecessary noise'

1.   Eminent Persons Group: Mission to South Africa: The Commonwealth Report, 1986

2.   Ibid

3.   Ibid

4.   See Bizos, G: *Odyssey to Freedom*, Random House, Johannesburg, 2007, pp442-469, for an excellent account of this trial

5.   See Chubb, Karin & van Dijk, Lutz: *Between Anger and Hope: South Africa's Youth and the Truth and Reconciliation Commission*, Witwatersrand University Press, 2001; Yazir Henry's story, pp57-67

6.   Achmat, Z: Ashley Kriel Memorial Lecture, 2004

7.   Jaffer, Z: *Our Generation*, Kwela Books, 2003, p45

8.   Ibid, p46

9.   Seekings, Jeremy: *The UDF: A History of the United Democratic Front in South Africa, 1983-1991*, David Philip, Cape Town, 2000, p196

10.   Government Gazette, 26 October 1985

11.   Patel, Ebrahim: Ashley Kriel Memorial Lecture, 2005

12.   Branaman, Brenda A: South Africa: A Chronology, Foreign Affairs and National Defense Division, Congressional Research Service Report 1B86115, 1987

13.   *Rapport*, 8 June 1986

14.   Green, Pippa: 'Trade Unions and the State of Emergency', *South African Labour Bulletin*, vol.11, no.7, August 1986

15.   *Natal Witness*, 16 August 1986

CHAPTER 17: 'You're supposed to be smiling'

1.   Green, Pippa: 'Starving for Freedom', *In These Times*, March 22-29, 1989

2.   Davis, G: 'Surprise: Top UDF Leader Walks Free', *Weekly Mail*, 8 July 1988

CHAPTER 18: 'Forcing the sun to rise ...'

1. Application brought by Trevor Andrew Manuel, Cape Supreme Court, case no. 88/10416
2. Ibid
3. Allen, John: *Rabble-rouser for Peace*, Random House, 2006, p301
4. *Argus*, 19 February 1989
5. Ibid
6. Toms, a founding member of the End Conscription Campaign, and in the democratic era the director of health in the city of Cape Town, died of meningitis in March 2008
7. Quoted in Seekings, Jeremy, *The UDF: A History of the United Democratic Front in South Africa, 1983-1991*, David Philip, Cape Town, 2000, p239
8. There are several excellent accounts of this process, among them: Callinicos, Luli: *Oliver Tambo: Beyond the Engeli Mountains*, David Philip, Cape Town, 2004; Sparks, Allister: *Tomorrow is Another Country: The Inside Story of South Africa's Negotiated Revolution*, Struik, 1994; Slabbert, Frederik Van Zyl: *The Other Side of History*, Jonathan Ball, 2006; and Waldmeir, Patti: *The Anatomy of a Miracle: The end of apartheid and the birth of a new South Africa*, Viking, 1997
9. Waldmeir, Patti op cit, p56
10. Hirsch, Alan: *Season of Hope: Economic Reform under Mandela and Mbeki*, University of KZN Press, 2005, p24
11. Ibid, p23
12. *Financial Mail*, 26 July 1985
13. *Argus*, 19 June 1989
14. Quoted in Callinicos op cit, p574
15. Callinicos op cit, p596
16. Sampson, Anthony: *Mandela: The Authorised Biography*, Jonathan Ball, 1999, p391
17. O'Malley, Padraig: *Shades of Difference: Mac Maharaj and the Struggle for South Africa*, Viking, 2007, p300
18. Ibid, p306
19. Harare Declaration, ANC documents, www.anc.org.za
20. Interview, Trevor Manuel, 17 January 2006
21. Green, Pippa: 'New Waves of Defiance in South Africa', *The Nation* (New York), 18 September 1989
22. Seekings op cit, p252
23. Ibid
24. Bonner, Raymond: 'A reporter at large: Choices', *The New Yorker*, 25 December 1989
25. Green op cit
26. Ibid
27. Quoted in Allen op cit, p302
28. Quoted in Bonner op cit, p53
29. Ibid
30. Bonner op cit
31. Quoted in Bonner op cit
32. Green op cit
33. Quoted in Bonner op cit
34. Ibid
35. Green op cit
36. Quoted in Bonner op cit
37. See article by Mafolo, Titus, *The Weekly Mail*, 28 July 1989
38. Manuel, Trevor: Speech, St George's Cathedral, 20 August 1989. African Studies Library, University of Cape Town
39. Thurman, Judith: 'The Fast Lane: You Are What You Don't Eat', *The New Yorker*, 3 and 10 September 2007
40. *Argus*, 28 September 1989
41. Green op cit

42.   Quoted in Allen op cit, p307
43.   Ibid, p308
44.   Ibid, p309
45.   Ibid, p310
46.   Waldmeir op cit, p138
47.   *The Weekly Mail*, 15-21 September 1989
48.   *Cape Times*, 14 September 1989
49.   *The Weekly Mail*, 15-21 September 1989
50.   Quoted in Allen op cit, p311
51.   Slabbert op cit, p32
52.   Erwin, Alec: email correspondence with the author, 7 August 2008

CHAPTER 19: The narrative of freedom

1.   See Braam, Connie: Operation Vula (Jacana, 2004), and O'Malley, Padraig: *Shades of Difference: Mac Maharaj and the Struggle for South Africa* (Viking, 2007) for insightful and well-written accounts of Operation Vula
2.   *New Nation* (Johannesburg), 2-8 June 1989
3.   Mbeki, Moeletsi: email correspondence with the author, 20 September 2008
4.   Seekings, Jeremy: *The UDF: A History of the United Democratic Front in South Africa, 1983-1991*, David Philip, Cape Town, 2000, p255
5.   Ibid, p256
6.   Quoted in Seekings op cit, p257
7.   Ibid
8.   Sparks, Allister: *Tomorrow is Another Country: The Inside Story of South Africa's Negotiated Revolution*, Struik, p106
9.   Quoted in Sparks op cit, p107
10.   Johnson, Shaun & Evans, Gavin: 'Youths Run Amok as 50 000 Wait for Missing Mandela', *The Weekly Mail*, 12 February 1990
11.   Manuel, Trevor: Talk to Council of Humanities, Princeton University, 24 April 2006
12.   Press conference, Bishopscourt, Cape Town, 12 February 1990

PART FIVE: Transition 1990-1995

CHAPTER 20: 'Corner boy'

1.   Quoted in Sampson, Anthony: *Mandela: The Authorized Biography*, Jonathan Ball, Johannesburg, 1999, p413
2.   Winnie Mandela had suffered a major fall-out with the Mass Democratic Movement at the time as a result of her involvement in the abduction and assault of young men who had been taking refuge in Paul Verryn's Methodist Church shelter in Soweto
3.   Mandela, Nelson: *Long Walk to Freedom*, Macdonald Purnell, Johannesburg, 1994, p564
4.   Shabir Shaik was to fall foul of the post-apartheid law. He was convicted and sentenced to 15 years in jail in 2005 for paying bribes to Jacob Zuma to 'protect' one of the companies involved in South Africa's arms purchases
5.   O'Malley, Padraig: *Shades of Difference: Mac Maharaj and the Struggle for South Africa*, Viking, 2007, p366
6.   See Amnesty Hearings, August 1997 (AM7560/97), at doj/trc.gov.za for chilling testimony about how the two men were taken, handcuffed and blindfolded, to the mouth of the Tugela River, shot at point blank range, bound with wire to concrete and sunk in the river. The police provided a rather far-fetched story about how Ndaba had been their informant, but logic tells us that the alacrity with which the police got the

information that was to lead to the arrests of Gordhan, Nyanda and the others suggests the two men were severely tortured before being 'disposed of'

7. Waldmeir, Patti: *Anatomy of a Miracle*, Viking, 1997, p162
8. *Cape Times*, 15 August 1990
9. *Vrye Weekblad*, March 1990
10. Sparks, Allister: *Tomorrow is Another Country: The inside story of South Africa's negotiated revolution*, Struik, 1994, p121
11. Ibid, p122
12. Waldmeir op cit, p160
13. The charges against Yengeni and his co-accused were dropped in 1990 and they were released. He went on to become Chief Whip in the first democratic parliament. In 2002 he was convicted and sentenced to four years in jail for accepting kick-backs – in the form of a huge discount on a luxury car – from one of the bidders in the arms deal

CHAPTER 21: The 'guru with matric'

1. See Gevisser, Mark: *Thabo Mbeki: The Dream Deferred*, Jonathan Ball, 2007, who describes it as a 'palace coup' (p603), and Butler, Anthony: *Cyril Ramaphosa*, Jacana, 2007, who describes it as a 'putsch' against the exiled leadership (p261)
2. West, Norman: 'How a guru with matric plans to fix the economy', *Sunday Times*, 15 September 1991
3. Hirsch, Alan: *Season of Hope: Economic Reform under Mandela and Mbeki*, University of KZN Press, 2005, p49
4. Green, Pippa: 'Reunion', *Leadership*, vol.9, no.4, May 1990
5. Slovo, Joe: 'Has Socialism Failed?' SACP, January 1990
6. Hirsch op cit, p40
7. Freedom Charter, ANC, 1955
8. *Cape Times*, 19 February 1990
9. *Argus*, 23 February 1990
10. Gelb, S: *Business Day*, 21 February 1990
11. Quoted in Lewis, D: 'The silver's sold off so the state's happy to chat', Economy Review, *Weekly Mail*, 1990
12. See Hirsch, A: 'After 42 stale years, a rush of new ideas', Economy Review, *Weekly Mail*, 1990
13. Hirsch, Alan: *Season of Hope: Economic Reform under Mandela and Mbeki*, University of KZN Press, 2005, p47
14. Ibid
15. *Forward to a Democratic Economy*, ANC, Harare, 1990
16. Ibid
17. Fabricius, Peter: 'Swiss hothouse breeds truce', *The Star*, 6 February 1992
18. Robertson, Mike: 'SA leaders put their views to world body', *Sunday Times*, 2 February 1992
19. Interview, Tito Mboweni, 5 December 2006
20. Fabricius Peter: 'FW, Mandela in Harmony', *The Star*, 3 February 1992
21. It had not, and still has not, reached political renewal. The Davos conference took place just wo years after the Tiananmen Square clampdown.
22. The author is grateful to Professor Bruce Scott of the Harvard Business School for several of the points in this section. The quotes were originally used in draft chapters he gave his class in the Harvard Business School where he taught a course called 'Economic Strategies of Nations' and which the author attended as a Nieman Fellow at Harvard in 1998/99. Professor Scott has confirmed these quotes as appearing in his forthcoming book, *Capitalism, Democracy and Development* (Springer Verlag, Germany, 2008)
23. Scott, B: email correspondence with the author, 16 March 2008

24. Scott op cit. Hamilton was killed in a duel over a supposed insult by Aaron Burr, the third vice-president of the United States, on the banks of the Hudson River in1804. When Manuel visited Princeton in 2006, he delivered a lecture at the Aaron Burr Hall, named after Burr's father, the second president of Princeton. Noting that the first Secretary of the Treasury had been killed by the man whose name the hall bore, he quipped that he hoped it would not portend anything similar for South Africa's finance minister.

25. Reischauer, Edwin, quoted in Scott, op cit

26. Cardoso, Fernando Henrique: *The Accidental President of Brazil: A Memoir* (with Brian Winter), Public Affairs, New York, 2006, p184

27. Ibid, pp185-88

28. Quoted in Cardoso op cit, p240

29. Ibid, p199

30. World Bank: *The East Asian Miracle: Economic Growth and Public Policy*, Oxford University Press, 1993

31. *Argus*, 13 August 1991, ' "Cape Town is in my heart," says Jo'burg-bound Manuel'

32. Hirsch op cit, p51

33. Mandela, Nelson: Opening Address at the launch of MERG, November 1991, ANC policy documents, www.anc.org.za

34. Ibid

35. *City Press*, 29 November 1991

36. Figures from World Bank Report, 2000, quoted in Hirsch op cit, p2

37. Quoted in Sethi, S Prakash & Williams, Oliver F: *Economic Imperatives and Ethical Values in Global Business*, Kluwer Academic Publishers, 2000, p303

38. Minter, William: 'An Unfinished Journey' *in* Minter, William, Hovey, Gail & Cobb, Charles jr, *No Easy Victories: African Liberation and American Activists over a Half Century, 1950-2000*, Africa World Press Inc, 2008, p43

39. Goodman, David: 'The 1980s: The Anti-Apartheid Convergence', *in* Minter et al op cit, p156

40. Sethi & Williams op cit, p302

41. Quoted in Sethi & Williams op cit p364

42. Interview, Stephen Gelb, Johannesburg, 8 March 2008

43. Quoted in Sethi & Williams op cit, p365

44. Ibid, p364

45. Ibid, p365

46. Ibid

47. *Ready to Govern*, May 1992, www.anc.org.za

48. Patel, Ebrahim: 'New Institutions of Decision Making' *in* Patel, E (ed.), *Engine of Development: South Africa's National Economic Forum*, Juta, 1993, p2

49. Manuel, Trevor: 'Is there a future for the National Economic Forum?' *in* Patel, E (ed.), op cit, p23

50. Ibid, p26

51. *Ready to Govern*, op cit

52. Kalyan, Khoosum: 'The Mont Fleur Scenarios', Supplement to the *Weekly Mail & Guardian*, 1992

53. Kahane, Adam: *Solving Tough Problems: An Open Way of Talking, Listening and Creating New Realities*, Berrett-Koehler, San Francisco, 2004, p20

54. Kalyan op cit

55. Kahane op cit, p25

56. One of the more articulate and consistent proponents of this view is Patrick Bond. See Bond, Patrick: *Against Global Apartheid, South Africa meets the World Bank, the IMF, and International Finance*, Zed Press, 2004

57. Bond, Patrick op cit p68

58. Noble, Kenneth B: 'Zaire is in Turmoil as Currency Collapses', *The New York Times*, 12 December 1993

CHAPTER 22: What is G?

1. Hirsch, A: *Season of Hope: Economic Reform under Mandela and Mbeki*, University of KZN Press, 2005, p21
2. Ibid, p23
3. Ibid
4. The source was an international banker who did not want to be named
5. Hirsch op cit, p24
6. Rustomjee, Z, quoted in Hirsch op cit, p24
7. Interview, Rudolf Gouws, Johannesburg, 2 December 2006
8. Lunsche, Sven: 'Government Spending to Soar Above Budget', *The Star*, 13 October 1988
9. Perlman, John: 'Money Down the Drain Again', *The Star*, 20 March 1993
10. *Financial Mail*: 'Borrowing into Oblivion', 22 January 1993
11. Ibid
12. *The Star*, 6 February 1992
13. Waldmeir, Patti & Gawith, Philip: 'Vision and Sense go well together', *The Star*, 22 April 1993
14. *Mail & Guardian*, 16 August 1996
15. Davie, Kevin: 'The good, the bad, and the filthy', *Sunday Times*, 7 February 1993
16. Quoted in Davie, Kevin: 'The maladies linger on', *Sunday Times*, 28 March 1993
17. Ibid
18. *Cape Times*: 'Manuel Spells Out Tough Plan', 5 April 1993

CHAPTER 23: Losing home

1. Green, Pippa & Wilhelm, Peter: 'A Beacon for the World', *Leadership* 13 (2), 1994
2. Morris, Michael: 'Mandela reaches out to whites', *Argus*, 18 May 1991
3. Jeppie, Shamiel: 'The Western Cape: Between History and Change', www.ceri-sciences.po.org, October 1999
4. Fabricius, Peter: 'How I put a smile back on South Africa's face, by election guru', *Argus*, 16 June 1994
5. Interview, Willie Hofmeyr, 24 September 2006, Pretoria. Greenberg himself said support for the ANC in the Western Cape was 15 per cent among the coloured population at the start of the election (see *Argus*, 16 June 1994)
6. According to Hofmeyr in the interview with the author, Greenberg would not be quoted on the results of focus groups
7. Green, Pippa: 'Boundaries of the Possible', *Leadership* 12 (3), 1993
8. Green, Pippa: 'Who would have Dreamed?' *Leadership* 13 (2), 1994
9. Finnegan, William: 'The Silent Majority of Cape Town', in *Africa*, Granta, Autumn 1994
10. See Adhikari, Mohamed: *Not White Enough, Not Black Enough* (Ohio University Press, 2005), for a more detailed explanation of the community's acute 'interstitial' status
11. Miller, Eric, photograph, *Leadership* 13 (2), 1994
12. Finnegan op cit
13. Quoted in Adhikari, Mohamed: *Not White Enough, Not Black Enough*, Double Storey Books, Cape Town, 2005, p174

CHAPTER 24: New world

1. See Butler, Anthony: *Cyril Ramaphosa*, Jacana, 2007, pp313-5
2. Towards a Ten Year Review: Synthesis Report on Implementation of Government Programmes, The Presidency, October 2003; Manuel, Trevor: Farewell Speech to Kader Asmal, National Assembly, 26 February 2008. The Ten Year Review reports that 3,7 million

more households were provided with piped water between 1996 and 2001. Asmal's term as Water Affairs minister ended in 1999, but he was responsible for driving the initial programme.

3. Gevisser, Mark: *Portraits of Power, Profiles in a Changing South Africa*, David Philip, Cape Town, 1996, p116
4. Douglas, Colin: 'Learn to Compete, Manuel Blasts Business', *Argus*, 6 March 1995
5. Hirsch, A: *Season of Hope: Economic Reform under Mandela and Mbeki*, University of KZN Press, 2005, p156
6. Ibid, p207
7. Ibid, p209
8. *Cape Times*, 8 March 1995
9. Edwards, Lawrence & Lawrence, Robert Z: SACU Tariffs: 'Where should they go from here?', unpublished paper, 2007
10. Ibid
11. For more, see Hirsch op cit, p131
12. *Financial Mail*: 'No bouquets – just brickbats', 20 October 1995
13. *Argus*, 6 March 1995
14. Hartley, Ray: 'Minister who means business', *Sunday Times*, 23 April 1995
15. Ibid
16. Green, Pippa: 'PE Auto Industry: The End of an Era', *South African Labour Bulletin*, vol.11, no.6, 1986
17. Ibid
18. High import tariffs go back to the 1930s, but were substantially increased by the apartheid government
19. *Financial Mail*: 'No bouquets – just brickbats', 20 October 1995
20. *Sunday Times*, 23 April 1995
21. Quoted in UCT News, Monday Paper, 10 December 2007
22. There are some economists who argue that continued protection, albeit limited, is bad for the consumer and retards competitiveness. See Flatters, Frank: 'The Economics of MISP and the South African Motor Industry'. Paper prepared for TIPS/NEDLAC South Africa Trade and Poverty Programme Policy Dialogue Workshop, Johannesburg, 2005
23. Rautenbach, a Zimbabwean citizen, was at the time of writing the subject of an extradition request from South Africa. Reportedly an enthusiastic supporter of Zimbabwean president Robert Mugabe, he is also alleged to have paid the South African Commissioner of Police, Jackie Selebi, the sum of between $30 000 and $40 000 to cancel the extradition order, according to an indictment drawn up against Selebi by the National Prosecuting Authority. The indictment indicates that Selebi displayed a strong sense of the theatrical when he accepted the money from an intermediary in a Pretoria hotel in full police uniform
24. Interview, Zav Rustomjee, 6 October 2006, and telephonic interview with Willie Hofmeyr, Head of the Asset Forfeiture Unit, 5 March 2008. See also NPA vs Muller Conrad Rautenbach and Wessel Hendrik Moolman Rautenbach, Supreme Court of Appeal, case no. 146/2003
25. Interview, Zav Rustomjee, 6 October 2006
26. Manuel, T: Address to SACTWU Fashion Imbizo, Cape Town, 25 November 2004
27. Save Rex Trueform, Alternative Information and Development Centre, 18 March 2005. The pamphlet is signed by, among others, Tony Eihenreich, Western Cape COSATU general secretary; Wayne van Rheese, SACTWU national organising secretary; the Reverend Keith Vermeulen of the South African Council of Churches; and Zackie Achmat, director of the Treatment Action Campaign
28. Dominique, Herman: 'Import quotas beginning to bear fruit', *Cape Times*, 24 April 2007
29. Save Rex Trueform, op cit
30. Ebrahim Patel: Address to NEDLAC, 27 August 2005
31. Ibid
32. Manuel, T: Address to SACTWU Fashion Imbizo, Cape Town, 25 November 2004

PART SIX: Power 1995-2007

CHAPTER 25: Amorphous markets

1. Donaldson, Andrew: Deputy Director-General, National Treasury, email correspondence, 11 April 2008
2. In an amnesty hearing, Williamson said he could not 'recollect' this but did not deny it. He said if he had done it, the sending of such a card would be 'the type of psychological strategy that could well have been employed'. (TRC, Craig Williamson amnesty hearing, 16 September 1998) www.doj/trc.gov.za
3. Interview, Jakes Gerwel, 27 October 2005
4. Proceedings of the National Assembly, Hansards, 28 March 1996, p941
5. Ibid
6. Hansards op cit, p949
7. South African Reserve Bank, Quarterly Economic Review, June 1996
8. Mbeki, T M: Speech at the banquet to celebrate the 120th anniversary of the *Cape Times*, 3 April 1996
9. Barber, Simon: 'Govt must declare firm policy to bring rand back to health', *Business Day*, 30 April 1996
10. Ibid
11. Manuel, Trevor: Letter to Chris Liebenberg, 24 April 1996

CHAPTER 26: The outsider

1. Barber, Simon: 'Govt must declare firm policy to bring rand back to health', *Business Day*, 30 April 1996
2. Cronin, Jeremy: 'SA Foundation's document is a case of selective amnesia', *Sunday Times*, 24 April 1996
3. Ibid
4. Paton, Carol: 'The yawning chasm beween organised labour and business', *Sunday Times*, 7   April 1996
5. *Cape Times*, 31 October 1994
6. Cameron, Bruce: 'Liebenberg faces juggling act in a growing economy', *Business Report*, 16 March 1995
7. Cohen, Tim: 'ANC document calls for one macro-economic body', *Business Day*, 16 October 1995
8. *Cape Times*, 17 November 1994
9. Cohen, Tim: 'Mbeki takes over major economic policy functions', *Business Day*, 15 April 1996
10. Interview, Andre Roux, 13 November 2006
11. Ibid
12. Department of Finance: Growth, Employment and Redistribution: A Macroeconomic Strategy, 1996
13. Ibid
14. Between mid-February and early May 1996, the rand lost about 20 per cent of its value (figures quoted in Hirsch, Alan: *Season of Hope: Economic Reform under Mandela and Mbeki*, University of KZN Press, 2005, p96)
15. Proceedings of the National Assembly, Hansards, 14 June 1996, pp3041-42
16. Ibid, p3050
17. Ibid, p3089
18. Streek, Barry: 'Borrow now to jump start the economy', *Cape Times*, 10 November 1994
19. D'Angelo, Audrey: 'SA urged to borrow heavily', *Cape Times*, 15 August 1994
20. Interview, Kim Jaycox, Washington, 23 March 2006

21. Manuel recalls Jeremy Cronin being present, but Cronin says he attended a later meeting at Shell House. Vavi recalls that Blade Nzimande, general secretary of the SACP, was there
22. Department of Finance: GEAR, Appendix 5, 1996
23. Butler, Anthony: *Cyril Ramaphosa*, Jacana, Johannesburg, 2007, p146
24. Rabkin was jailed for seven years, and his heavily pregnant wife Sue for a month. He later died in exile. Sue Rabkin is the partner of ANC leader Pallo Jordan. She returned to South Africa in 1990.
25. Manuel, T A: National Budget Speech, 12 March 1997
26. This was sparked by the Mexican peso crisis in December 1994; money flowed out of emerging markets in early 1995. Recovery was uneven, with the Asian countries rallying first
27. In fact, Naidoo's political pedigree goes back to his great-grandfather, known as Thambi Naidoo, who worked closely with Mahatma Gandhi and was arrested 14 times for his part in passive resistance campaigns. Four of Thambi Naidoo's 14 children were adopted by Gandhi and went to India for their education, where they studied under the poet Rabindranath Tagore. One was Kuben Naidoo's grandfather, Roy Naransamy Naidoo. He returned to South Africa and became a trade unionist and leader of bakery workers on the Rand. Both Roy and his wife Ama were active supporters of Congress
28. Tabling of the Appropriation Bill, Hansards, 12 March 1997, p587
29. Gevisser, Mark: *The Dream Deferred: Thabo Mbeki*, Jonathan Ball, 2007, p671
30. Ibid, p672
31. Ibid, p673
32. Ibid, p672. Gevisser comments that it outlined a 'classically liberal agenda for cutting back government'
33. ANC: State and Social Transformation, November 1996
34. Interview, Trevor Manuel, Pretoria, 7 December 2006
35. Resolution on Economic Transformation, ANC 50th Conference, Mafikeng, December 1997
36. Mandela, Nelson: State of the Nation Address, Parliament, 24 May 1994

CHAPTER 27: 'Good luck being in charge'

1. National Treasury: Presentation to Zambian delegation, 2008
2. National Treasury: IMF Case Study on Debt Management, South Africa, 2002
3. Kganyago, Lesetja: 'Tough as Train Wheels', in *Maria*, National Treasury, 2003
4. Manuel, T A: Budget Speech, 1999; Constitution of the Republic of South Africa, 1996
5. Naidoo, Kuben, Head of Budget Office, National Treasury: email correspondence, 25 September 2008
6. Manuel, T A: Budget Speech 1999
7. Manuel, T A: Budget Speech, 1998
8. Manuel, T A: Budget Speech 1999
9. As this book was about to go to press, the ANC's National Executive Committee voted to 'recall' Mbeki as president and install Kgalema Motlanthe as acting president until the 2009 election
10. After several lengthy court battles, mainly over procedural matters, the Pietermaritzburg High Court ruled in September 2008 that the charges against Zuma were incorrectly brought. It did not make a finding about his guilt or innocence. Zuma's supporters in the ANC moved quickly to unseat Mbeki after the court finding. It is important to note, though, that only some of the charges Zuma faced related to the arms deal
11. Trewhela, Paul: Joe Modise Obituary, *Independent*, 30 November 2001
12. Gevisser, Mark: *The Dream Deferred: Thabo Mbeki*, Jonathan Ball, 2007, p684
13. Swarns, Rachel: 'Joe Modise, 72, Fighter Against Apartheid', *New York Times*, 29

November 2001
14.   Gevisser op cit, p681. Kuben Naidoo, in an interview in 2006, told the author that no fewer than 10 000 jobs had materialised
15.   Naidoo, Kuben: email correspondence, 25 September 2008
16.   Gevisser op cit, p677
17.   Ibid. BAE made a donation of some R5 million to the MK Veterans Association which Modise chaired, and after he left politics in 1999 he became chair of an electronics company which stood to benefit from the offset agreements entered into by BAE
18.   Gevisser op cit, p676; Feinstein, Andrew: *After the Party: A Personal and Political Journey inside the ANC*, Jonathan Ball, 2007, p164
19.   Crawford-Browne, Terry: Affidavit in case no. 5811/05 in the High Court of South Africa (Cape Provincial Division)
20.   Ibid
21.   Ibid
22.   Richard Young, the head of a bidding firm called Ci2i, has been one of the most proactive litigants against the government decisions on the successful contractors in the arms deal
23.   The Katz Commission was appointed in 1994 by Derek Keys; it produced nine reports on aspects of tax administration in the ensuing five years, working with successive finance ministers
24.   Green, Pippa: 'An industry where guns still help the wheels go round', *Mail & Guardian*, 26-30 January 1997
25.   Lamberti, Taryn: 'Crackdown Targets Import-Export Fraud', *Business Day*, 1 February 2001
26.   Joffe, Hilary: 'Revenue revamp raises money for budget generosity', *Business Day*, 22 February 1999
27.   Manuel, T A: Budget Speech, 2008
28.   Medium Term Budget Policy Statement, October 2008
29.   Interview, Mark Orkin, 6 December 2007
30.   Loxton, Linda: 'New Three-Year Plan Ready for Approval', *Business Report*, 31 October 1997
31.   Act 1 of 1999
32.   Open Budget Index, 2006: Center on Budget and Policy Priorities, Washington
33.   Correspondence between Ashlin Anderson and Manuel, 2004. I am grateful to Patti Smith for providing me with these letters

CHAPTER 28: Choice, not fate

1.   National Treasury: *Maria*, 2003
2.   Diop, David: 'Afrique'/'Africa', quoted in Manuel, T A, Budget Speech, 21 February 2001
3.   Manuel, T A: Budget Speech, 21 February 2001
4.   Donaldson, Andrew: *The Times of Trevor*, National Treasury, 4 April 2006
5.   Manuel, T A: Budget Speech, 21 February 2001
6.   Development Indicators: Mid Term Review, The Presidency, Republic of South Africa, 2007
7.   South African Reserve Bank: Announcement by T T Mboweni, Governor of the South African Reserve Bank, regarding the squaring-off of the oversold foreign exchange forward book and the introduction of a new publication format for the monthly report on official gold and foreign exchange reserves, 1 March 2004
8.   Development Indicators: Mid Term Review, op cit. By the broad definition, unemployment rose to 42 per cent that year
9.   Institute of Justice and Reconciliation: Transformation Audit, 2006
10.   Manuel, Trevor A: Ashley Kriel Memorial Lecture, University of the Western Cape, 20 July 2007

11. Registrar of Banks: Report to the Minister of Finance, 2000
12. Joffe, Hilary: 'Sector not Banking on a National Champion', *Business Day*, 23 June 2000
13. Mnyanda, Lukhanyo: 'Saambou share "sales" affected confidence', *Business Day*, 28 February 2002
14. Rose, Rob: 'Echoes of Saambou debacle in Wiese's odd departure', *Business Day*, 25 July 2003
15. Ibid
16. Joffe, Hilary: 'Back in 2002, SA avoided a rockslide', *Business Day*, 25 September 2007
17. Ibid
18. Manuel, Trevor Andrew: Opening Addess to the Board of Governors, IMF, 2000 Annual Meetings, Prague
19. Report of the Africa Commission, 2005, p25
20. Ibid
21. Kahn, Joseph: 'Protests Distract Global Finance Meeting', *New York Times*, 27 September 2000
22. Ibid
23. Interview, Cyrus Rustomjee, 25 June 2008
24. *New York Times*, 27 September 2000
25. Manuel, T A: 'Balancing Society and Market, Public Policy and Growth for Africa', Ditchley Park Lecture, 7 July 2006
26. Ibid
27. Brown, Gordon: Speaking Notes, Spring Meetings, 2006. Email correspondence from UK Treasury to author, June 2007
28. Ibid
29. Calland, Richard: *Anatomy of South Africa: Who Holds the Power?*, Zebra Press, 2006, p122
30. Molebeledi, Pule: 'ANC "finally" defines its opposition', *Business Day*, 19 December 2002

CHAPTER 29: 'If I were the weatherman'

1. Manuel, T A: Budget Speech, 2005
2. As this book was going to press, President Thabo Mbeki was 'recalled' by the ANC's National Executive Committee on 20 September 2008. A number of cabinet ministers, including Erwin, resigned with him on 25 September. Erwin played a crucial role in the making of economic policy since the late 1980s, and represents an important viewpoint about the role of the state in the economy; the debates between him and Manuel are likely to continue in government even though they may take place between different players
3. Mathews, John A: ' "A Silicon Valley of the East": Creating Taiwan's Semiconductor Industry', *California Management Review*, vol.39, no.4, Summer 1997
4. Manuel, T A: Budget Speech, 2007
5. National Treasury: Budget Review, 2007, p127
6. Interview, Lesetja Kganyago, 22 August 2007
7. Less than a year after Sylvia got out of hospital Anthony Butler, who writes a weekly column in a daily newspaper, quoted Manuel as saying: 'It does not make sense to spend money on people dying anyway, who are not even productive in the first place.' (Butler, Anthony: Holes in Rich Portraits of Mbeki, *Business Day*, 19 November 2007.) The quote was sourced to the book by Andrew Feinstein (*After the Party: A Personal and Political Journey inside the ANC*, Jonathan Ball, 2007). Feinstein sourced the quote to a *Business Day* article (*Business Day*, 19 March 2003). But the quote does not appear in that article. The article did, however, quote Manuel as saying that claims about the effectiveness of ARVs in the treatment of HIV/Aids were 'a lot of voodoo'. However, a few days later (*Business Day*, 26 March 2003), the editor of *Business Day* apologised for the report, saying Manuel had not said that. The Hansard report of the day shows that Manuel said, in his reply to the 2003/2004 Budget debate in response to an IFP

member, Mr Peter Smith, that 'he was speaking a lot of voodoo … this notion that it's antiretrovirals or bust is bunkum … there is no need to polarise society on this issue.' Where Feinstein (or Butler) got the quote about it 'not making sense to spend money on people dying anyway' is a mystery. However, William Mervin Gumede in his book quotes Manuel as saying 'It does not make financial sense to spend money on people dying anyway, who are not even productive in the first place' (Gumede, William Mervin: *Thabo Mbeki and the Battle for the Soul of the ANC*, Zebra, 2005, p163). He sources the quote to unnamed parliamentarians who attended a closed committee meeting on the Basic Income Grant. Closed committee meetings are rare in Parliament and Manuel says his diary bears no record of attending such a meeting. Manuel wrote a letter to *Business Day* pointing out the sentiments attributed to him by Butler showed laxity at best, mendacity at worst (*Business Day*, 21 November 2007). In December 2007 both Andrew Feinsten and his publishers Jonathan Ball wrote a letter of apology to Manuel. Feinstein said: 'I accept unequivocally that your overall view on HIV and Aids has been balanced and holistic' (Feinstein, Andrew: letter to Minister Trevor Manuel, 4 December 2007). However, Ross Harvey, who describes himself as a student of Butler's, accused Manuel of 'splitting hairs' (*Business Day*, 22 November 2007). A month earlier he wrote to the newspaper asking Manuel 'with all due respect … when he last witnessed a patient dying of Aids in a hospital corridor because the department couldn't give a damn about organising beds' (*Business Day*, 25 October 2007). It was ironic, given the timing, but a good example of how narratives take hold with few facts to support them.

8. Hausmann, Ricardo: Lecture, Gordon Instiute of Business Science, Johannesburg, 17 June 2008
9. Ibid
10. Hausmann, Ricardo et al: Final Recommendations on the International Panel on Growth. Paper presented to National Treasury, 2008
11. Hausmann, Lecture, op cit
12. Ibid
13. Mbeki, M: letter to Trevor Manuel, 29 August 2006; courtesy of Moeletsi Mbeki
14. Ibid
15. Hirsch, Alan: *Season of Hope: Economic Reform under Mandela and Mbeki*, University of KZN Press, 2005, p170
16. In July 2008 Mantashe was reported as saying that the Constitutional Court judges were 'counter-revolutionary', upsetting many within and without the ANC who were concerned   about creeping anti-constitutionalism among the ANC's new leaders. He later denied this, saying he had been 'misquoted'
17. Ensor, Linda: 'Mantashe vows ANC will keep inflation targeting', *Business Day*, 17 July 2008
18. Resolution on Economic Transformation, ANC 52nd National Conference, Polokwane, 2007
19. Hafajee, Ferial: 'We won't topple Mbeki', *Mail & Guardian*, 7-13 November 2007
20. Manuel, Trevor: Open letter to Mo Shaik, *Sunday Times*, 9 December 2007
21. Credit discrimination in volatile markets. RSA National Treasury. Paper prepared for the IMF, 2002
22. Manuel, T A: Budget Speech, 2008
23. Manuel, T A: Address to the University of the Western Cape on the occasion of the receipt of an honorary doctorate, 13 March 2002
24. Okri, Ben: 'Turn on your light', 1999, quoted in Manuel, Address to the Universiy of the Western Cape, 2002

≡ Bibliography ≡

INTERVIEWS

Interviews with the author
Goolam Aboobaker
Christine Amansure
Kader Asmal
Aziz Bardien
Soda Bardien
Pam Barron
Cheryl Carolus
Renecia Clayton
Jeremy Cronin
Jonathan de Vries
Andrew Donaldson
Ferdie Engel
Virginia Engel
Alec Erwin
Essie Esterhuyse
Judy Favish
Sean Field
Stephen Gelb
Jakes Gerwel
Hermann Giliomee
Ian Goldin
Pravin Gordhan
Rudolf Gouws
Phakamani Hadebe
Willie Hofmeyr
Barabara Hogan
Johnny Issel
Mkhuseli (Kusta) Jack
Edward V K Jaycox
Paul Jourdan
Derek Keys
Lesetja Kganyago
Helen Kies[1]
Daphne King
Chief Justice Pius Langa

Pali Lehola
Mosiuoa Patrick 'Terror' Lekota
David Lewis
Chris Liebenberg
Leslie Maasdorp
David Manuel
Philma Manuel
Trevor Manuel
Gill Marcus
Peter Matlare
Lynne Matthews
Moeletsi Mbeki
Tito Mboweni
Murray Michell
Ismail Momoniat
Reg Moodley
Mike Morris
Maxwell Moss
Kuben Naidoo
Wendy Nathan
Joel Netshitenzhe
Mark Orkin
Thoraya Pandy
Ebrahim Patel
Ivan Pillay
Sylmore Poggenpoel
Cyril Ramaphosa
Maria Ramos
Fred Robertson
Andre Roux
Cyrus Rustomjee
Zavereh Rustomjee
Reg September
Rashid Seria
Ashford Smith
Patti Smith
Michael Spicer
Sir Nicholas Stern

---

[1] Helen Kies did not grant me a formal interview but was generous with her provision of background knowledge and material from the Unity Movement.

Jan Theron
Franz Tomasek
Beryl Tungchun
Archbishop Desmond Tutu
Shaun Viljoen
Dawn von Söhnen
Ursula von Söhnen

Zwelinzima Vavi
Brian Williams
Moesgsien Williams
Father Oliver Williams
Logan Wort
Sylvia Ziqu

Non-author interviews
Johnny Issel, 2003, www.sahistory.org.za
Trevor Manuel, interview with Barry Streek, date unknown, circa 1985 (Streek
    Papers, Mayibuye Archive)
Trevor Manuel, interview with Julie Frederikse, Julie Frederikse Collection, William
    Cullen Libraries, May 1985
Hester Seale, interview with Bill Nasson, African Studies Library, District Six oral
    history interviews, 1985

WRITTEN CORRESPONDENCE WITH THE AUTHOR

John Allen
Gordon Brown
Andrew Donaldson
Aimie Dunckley
Professor Robert Edgar
Keryn House
Adam Kahane
Ahmed Kathrada

Chris Liebenberg
Moeletsi Mbeki
Ebrahim Mohamed
Kuben Naidoo
Martin Nicol
Professor Bruce Scott
Pieter-Dirk Uys

ARCHIVES/COLLECTIONS

African Studies Library, University of Cape Town:
    Collections:
    The Defiance Campaign
    District Six

Cape Archives, Cape Town
    Collections:
    Death Notices

Centre for Popular Memory, University of Cape Town
    Collections:
    Communities: Kensington

Communities: District Six
Communities: Windermere

The Deeds Office, Cape Town
Collections:
Title Deeds
Erf Register

Historical Papers, William Cullen Library, University of the Witwatersrand
Collections:
Julie Frederikse Collection
SA Political Material: Karis-Gerhard Collection:
File 316, Cahac
Folder 849: United Democratic Front: Transcript of UDF Launch
Folder 851: UDF launch
Folder 852: Minutes of UDF meeting, 10/11 September 1983, Phoenix Settlement
Folder 868: Memorandum on Constitution of UDF
Folder 870: Interview with Trevor Manuel in *Grassroots*, November, 1984
Folder 892: State of Emergency, clippings and documents

Manuscripts and Archives Department, University of Cape Town Libraries
Collections:
Gertrude Fester Papers
District Six Papers

South African Labour and Development Research Unit (Saldru) Clippings Collection

Truth and Reconciliation Commission
Human Rights Violations Committee Hearings
Amnesty Committee Hearings
www.doj.gov.za

UWC-Robben Island Mayibuye Archive
Collections:
Barry Streek Newspaper Clips
Karis-Gerhard Collection: From Protest to Challenge, 1964-1990: Hennie Ferrus
        Funeral collected documents and papers
Cahac
Trevor Manuel and Lynne Matthews papers
Graeme Bloch
Zora Ebrahim
Black Sash
Reg September
UDF
ERIP
Faiza Bardien

Neville Alexander
M T Bardien

NEWSPAPERS AND PERIODICALS

Argus
The Bulletin, the Official Journal of the New Unity Movement
Business Day (Mayibuye collection: Barry Streek collection in Mayibuye and
    www.businessday.co.za)
Business Report
Cape Herald
Cape Times
Christianity and Crisis
City Press
The Educational Journal, Official Journal of the Teachers' League of South Africa
Eikestad Nuus
Eye (www.disa.ukzn.ac.za)
Financial Mail
Fosatu Worker News (www.disa.ukzn.ac.za)
Grassroots (Mayibuye collection and at www.disa.ukzn.ac.za)
Independent
In These Times
Leadership SA
Mail & Guardian
Natal Witness (Streek collection, Mayibuye archives)
The Nation (New York)
The New Yorker
New York Times archives
Rand Daily Mail (Streek collection, Mayibuye archives)
Rapport (Saldru newclips)
Sash, Journal of the Black Sash (www.disa.ukzn.ac.za)
Social Review
South African Labour Bulletin
Sowetan
Sunday Times
Vrye Weekblad (Saldru news clips)
Weekly Mail
Work in Progress

OFFICIAL DOCUMENTATION

Of the Republic

Constitution of the Republic of South Africa, 1996

586

Government Gazettes (1985-1989)
High Court Judgment, Cape Provincial Division, Mr Justice D H van Zyl, 12 September
2003 No. 5811/05 in the High Court of SA (Cape Provincial Division)
Trevor Manuel vs The Minister of Law and Order and The Officer Commanding
Pollsmoor Prison, Case No. 88/10416
NPA vs Muller Conrad Rautenbach and Wessel Hendrik Moolman Rautenbach,
Supreme Court of Appeal, Case No. 146/2003
Proceeds of the National Assembly, Hansards (selected transcripts), 1990-2007
Statistics SA: General Household Survey, 2007

The Presidency
Towards a Ten Year Review: Synthesis Report on Implementation of Government
Programmes, October 2003
Development Indicators: Mid-Term Review, 2007
Development Indicators, The Presidency, 2008

Department of Finance/National Treasury
Growth, Employment and Redistribution: A Macro-Economic Policy, 1996
Registrar of Banks: Report to the Minister of Finance, 2000
Presentation to Zambian Delegation, 2008
IMF Case Study on Debt Management, South Africa
Credit discrimination in volatile markets, 2008
Global Economic and Financial Development, 5-6 November 2007
Presentation to Zambian Delegation: Asset and Liability Division, 24 August 2005
Maria, 2003
The Times of Trevor, 4 April 2006
Budget Reviews 1997-2008
National Estimates of Expenditure, 2001-2008

South African Reserve Bank
South Africa's National Accounts, 1946-2004
Quarterly Reviews, selected, 1996-2004

Of the African National Congress

January 8 Statements: Various
Cape UDF Struggle Legend Passes Away, 15 August 2002, www.anc.org.za/ancdocs/
pr/2002
Freedom Charter, ANC, 1955
Forward to a Democratic Economy, Harare, 1990
Ready to Govern, 1992
Resolution on Economic Transformation, ANC 50th National Conference, Mafikeng,
December 1997
Economic Transformation, ANC 51st Conference, Stellenbosch, December 2002
Strategy and Tactics, 1997, 2002
Resolution on Economic Transformation, ANC 52nd National Conference, Polokwane,
2007

The Core Values of the RDP, July 1997
State and Social Transformation, November, 1996
The Reconstruction and Development Programme: A Policy Framework, 1994
UDF Press Conference, Khotso House, Johannesburg, 1 August 1983 www.anc.org.
za/ancdocs/history

International

The Commonwealth Report, Eminent Persons Group Mission to South Africa, 1986
World Bank Reports (www.worldbank.org)
IMF Surveys (www.imf.org)
Africa Commission Report (www.commissionforafrica.org) 2005
Open Budget Index, 2006: Centre on Budget and Policy Priorities, Washington (www.
openbudgetindex.org)

LECTURES AND SPEECHES

TREVOR MANUEL
Trevor Manuel Speeches; various speeches, 1980-2008 (University of Cape Town
Library, African Studies Collection, Mayibuye archives, and www.treasury.gov.za)

This is not a comprehensive list but key speeches include:
Defiance Campaign speech, St George's Cathedral, August 1989
Balancing Society and Market: Public policy and growth for Africa, Ditchley Park
Lecture, 7 July 2006
Globalisation and the African State, Oxford Inaugural Lecture, 8 March 2004
Government Strategy on Economic Growth and Development, Hansards, 14 June
1996
Opening address to the IMF and World Bank Board of Governors by Chairman,
Prague, September 2000
Address to the University of the Western Cape on the occasion of the receipt of an
honorary doctorate, 13 March 2002
Ashley Kriel Memorial Lecture, University of the Western Cape, 20 July 2007
SACTWU Fashion Imbizo, Cape Town, 25 November 2004
Report to the Board and Governors of the Bank and Fund by the Honourable Trevor A
Manuel, Chairman of the Development Committee of the World Bank, at the Joint
Annual Discussion, 29 September 2002
Commission for Africa Seminar: Welcoming Remarks, Pretoria, 2 July 2004
Developing Partnership from Monterrey to Johannesburg: Statement of Governor
Trevor A Manuel at the Annual Meeting of the African Development Bank, 28 May
2002
Economic Policy in a Changing Global and Local Environment: Notes for a Speech to
the Department of Management at the University of the Western Cape, 13 October
2000
Budget speeches (1997-2008) www.treasury.gov.za
Medium Term Budget Policy Statement speeches; 2000-2007 www. treasury.gov.za
Budget Rehearsals attended by author: February, October 2000; February, October
2005; October 2006; February 2007; February 2008, courtesy of Trevor Manuel

OTHER LECTURES/SPEECHES

Boesak, Allan: Address at UDF Launch, 20 August 1983 (Mayibuye Archives)

Brown, Gordon: Speaking notes, Spring meetings 2006

De Klerk, F W: Address by the State President, Mr F W De Klerk, DMS, at the Opening of the Second Session of the Ninth Parliament of the Republic of South Africa, Cape Town, 2 February 1990 (www.info.gov.za/speeches)

Hausmann, Ricardo: Lecture, Gordon Institute of Business Science, Johannesburg, 17 June 2008

Mandela, Nelson: Opening Address at the launch of MERG, ANC Policy Documents, 1991 (www.anc.org.za)

Mandela, Nelson: State of the Nation Address, 24 May 1994 (www. gov.za/speeches)

Mandela, Nelson: Address to rally in Cape Town on his release from prison, 11 February, 1990 (www.anc.org.za)

Manuel, Trevor; Sen, Amatrya; Gordimer, Nadine: Panel Discussion, University of Witwatersrand Great Hall, Johannesburg, 20 April 2007

Mbeki, Thabo: Government Strategy on Economic Growth and Development, 14 June 1996, Hansards

Mbeki, Thabo: Speech to commemorate the 120th anniversary of the *Cape Times*, (www.anc.org.za)

Patel, Ebrahim: Ashley Kriel Memorial Lecture, University of the Western Cape, 18 August 2005

PAPERS, PAMPHLETS, LETTERS

Anderson, Ashlin, Letter to Trevor Manuel, 23 June, 2004 (courtesy of Patti Smith)

Anderson, Ashlin, Letter to Trevor Manuel, 2 November 2004 (courtesy of Patti Smith)

Branaman, Brenda A: 'South Africa: A Chronology', Congressional Research Service Report IB86115, Foreign Affairs and National Defense Division, 1987

Edwards, Lawrence & Lawrence, Robert Z: 'SACU Tariffs: Where Should They Go From Here?' Unpublished Paper, 2007

Flatters, Frank: 'The Economics of MIDP and the South African Motor Industry', paper prepared for TIPS/NEDLAC South Africa Trade and Poverty Programme Policy Dialogue Workshop, Johannesburg 2005

Giliomee, H L: 'Die Groei van 'n Gemeenskap', unpublished manuscript, p30

Giliomee, H L: 'Die Slag van Andringastraat: Studente Onluste op Stellenbosch', unpublished manuscript, 1940

Growth for All: An Economic Strategy for South Africa, South Africa Foundation, February 1996

Hausmann, Ricardo et al: Final Recommendations on the International Panel on Growth, paper presented to National Treasury, 2008

Institute of Justice and Reconciliation, Transformation Audit, 2006 (www.trans-formationaudit.org.za/scorecards/2006-scorecards/education-and-skills-development-scorecard3.pdf)

Manuel, Trevor: Letter to Chris Liebenberg, 24 April 1996 (courtesy of Chris Liebenberg)

Manuel, Trevor: Letter to Ashlin Anderson, 14 July 2004 (courtesy of Patti Smith)

Manuel, Trevor: Letter to Ashlin Anderson, 16 November 2004 (courtesy of Patti Smith)

Mbeki, M: Letter to Trevor Manuel, 29 August 2006 (courtesy of Moeletsi Mbeki)

Rex Trueform, Clothing Company Limited, from Shorten, P: *Golden Jubilee Cape Town*, 1963

'Save Rex Trueform', Alternative Information and Development Centre, 18 March 2005

Security Police Report on Taufik Bardien (circa 1961)

Slovo, Joe: 'Has Socialism Failed?' South African Communist Party, January 1990

Steinberg, Jonny: 'Nongoloza's Children: Western Cape Prison Gangs During and After Apartheid', Monograph, Centre for the Study of Violence and Reconciliation, July 2004

Social Equity and Job Creation, Congress of South African Trade Unions, 1996

Stellenbosch 300: 'Architecture Exhibition in the Art Gallery of the University of Stellenbosch', Study Group on Stellenbosch Architecture, 1979

Suttner, Raymond: 'The African National Congress Underground between Rivonia and 1976'. Paper prepared for ICS/SOAS conference 'Looking at South Africa Ten Years On', London, September 2004 (http://commonwealth.sas.ac.uk/resource/suttner.pdf)

Unity Movement, 'Anniversary Bulletin: 50th Year of Struggle', 1994

THESES

Adhikari, Mohamed: *Let Us Live for Our Children: The Teachers' League of South Africa, 1913-1940*, MA thesis, University of Cape Town, 1986

Allem, Alexandra & Merret, Nicholas: *Strength in Unity; the 1976 Cape Town Uprisings*, Honours thesis (documentary film), University of Cape Town, 2004

Cavernelis, Dennis Burt: *A Case Study of Aspects of the Political Life of Advocate Benjamin Mason Kies (1917-1979) and of* The Torch *Newspaper with which he was Closely Connected Showing how the Criminal Justice System in South Africa was Employed in an Attempt to Silence Political and Ideological Opposition to the Apartheid Regime*, MA thesis, University of Cape Town, 1993

Field, Sean: *The Power of Exclusion: Moving Memories from Windermere to the Cape Flats 1920s-1990s*, PhD thesis, University of Essex, 1996

Goode, Richard: *A History of the Food and Canning Workers' Union, 1941-1975*, MA thesis, University of Cape Town, 1986

Nicol, Martin: *The Garment Workers' Union of the Cape Peninsula and the Garment Workers' National Unity Movement, 1927-1955*, Honours thesis, University of Cape Town, 1977

Omar, Abdul Rashid: *The Impact of the Death in Detention of Imam Abdullah Haroun on Cape Muslim Attitudes*, Honours thesis, University of Cape Town, 1982

Steenbok, A A: *Gereformeerd Wees in die NGSK/VGK (1976-2005): 'n Kerkhistorie en Outobiografiese Verhaal*, MD thesis, University of Pretoria, 2005

BOOKS AND JOURNAL ARTICLES

Books

Adhikari, M: *Not White Enough, Not Black Enough: Racial identity in the South African Coloured Community*, Ohio University Press and Double Storey Books, 2005

Alexander, Neville, *Robben Island Dossier, 1964-1974*, UCT Press, 1994

Alexander, Neville: 'Non-collaboration in the Western Cape, 1943-1963', *in* James, Wilmot G & Simons, Mary (eds), *Class, Caste and Colour: A Social and Economic History of the South African Western Cape*, Transaction Publishers, New Brunswick and London, 1992

Allen, John: *Rabble-rouser for Peace*, Random House, 2006

Backscheider, Paula R: *Reflections on Biography*, Oxford University Press, 2001

Barrow, B: *in* Breytenbach, C, *The Spirit of District Six*, C Struik Publishers, 1987

Bickford-Smith, V, Van Heyningen, E & Worden, N: *Cape Town in the Twentieth Century*, David Philip, Cape Town, 1999

Biscombe, Hilton (compiler): *In Ons Bloed*, Sun Press 2006

Bizos, G: *Odyssey to Freedom*, Random House, Johannesburg, 2007

Bond, Patrick: *Against Global Apartheid, South Africa meets the World Bank, the IMF, and International Finance*, Zed Press, 2004

Braam, Connie: *Operation Vula*, Jacana, Johannesburg, 2004

Bundy, C: ' "Action, comrades, action!" The politics of youth resistance in the Western Cape, 1985', *in* James, Wilmot G & Simons, Mary (eds), *Class, Caste and Colour: A Social and Economic History of the South African Western Cape*, Transaction Publishers, New Brunswick and London, 1992

Butler, Anthony: *Cyril Ramaphosa*, Jacana, Johannesburg, 2007

Calland, Richard: *Anatomy of South Africa: Who Holds the Power?*, Zebra Press, Johannesburg, 2006

Callinicos, Luli: *Oliver Tambo: Beyond the Engeli Mountains*, David Philip, Cape Town, 2004

Cardoso, Fernando Henrique (with Brian Winter): *The Accidental President of Brazil: A Memoir*, Public Affairs, New York, 2006

Camus, Albert: *The Stranger*, Vintage Books, 1989

Chernow, Ron: *Alexander Hamilton*, Penguin, 2004

Chubb, Karin & Van Dijk, Lutz: *Between Anger and Hope: South Africa's Youth and the Truth and Reconciliation Commission*, Witwatersrand University Press, Johannesburg, 2001

Cole, Josette: *Crossroads: The Politics of Reform and Repression, 1976-1986*, Ravan Press, Johannesburg, 1987

Davenport, T R H: *South Africa: A Modern History*, Macmillan, 1987

Feinstein, Andrew: *After the Party: A Personal and Political Journey inside the ANC*, Jonathan Ball, 2007

Field Sean (ed.): *Lost Communities, Living Memories: Remembering Forced Removals in Cape Town*, David Philip, 2001

Finnegan, W: *Crossing the Line: A Year in the Land of Apartheid*, Harper and Row, 1986

Finnegan, W: The Silent Majority of Cape Town, *in Africa*, Granta 48, 1994

Fredrickson, George M: *White Supremacy: A Comparative Study in American and South African History*, Oxford University Press, 1981

Friedman, Steven: *Building Tomorrow Today: African Workers in Trade Unions, 1970-1984*, Ravan Press, Johannesburg, 1987

Friedman, Thomas L: *The Lexus and the Olive Tree*, Anchor Books, 2000

Gevisser, Mark: *Thabo Mbeki: The Dream Deferred*, Jonathan Ball, 2007

Gevisser, Mark: *Portraits of Power, Profiles in a Changing South Africa*, David Philip, Cape Town, 1996

Goldin, I: *Making Race: The Politics and Economics of Coloured Identity in South Africa*, Maskew, Miller, Longman, 1987

Goodman, David: 'The 1980s: The Anti-Apartheid Convergence', *in* Minter, William, Hovey, Gail & Cobb, Charles jr, *No Easy Victories: African Liberation and American Activists over a Half Century, 1950-2000*, Africa World Press Inc, 2008

Green, Lawrence G: *Cape Town: Tavern of the Seas*, Howard B Timmins, 1948

Gunn, Shirley: *If Trees Could Speak: The Trojan Horse Story*, Human Rights Media Centre, Cape Town, 2007

Hirsch, Alan: *Season of Hope: Economic Reform under Mandela and Mbeki*, University of KZN Press, 2005

Hofmeyr, A M: *in* Francois Smuts (ed.), *Stellenbosch Three Centuries*, Official Commemorative Volume, Stellenbosch Town Council with the Oude Meester Group, October 1979

Hopkins, Pat & Grange, Helen: *The Rocky Rioter Teargas Show: The Inside Story of the 1976 Soweto Uprising*, Zebra Press, Johannesburg, 2001

Jaffer, Zubeida: *Our Generation*, Kwela Books, 2003

James, C L R: *Beyond a Boundary*, Duke University Press, 1993

Kafka, Franz: *The Metamorphosis and Other Stories* (trans. Donna Freed), Barnes & Noble, New York, 1996

Kahane, Adam: *Solving Tough Problems: An Open Way of Talking, Listening and Creating New Realities*, Berrett-Koehler, San Francisco, 2004

Kathrada, Ahmed: *Memoirs*, Zebra Press, 2004

Keegan, Timothy: *Colonial South Africa and the Origins of the Racial Order*, University Press of Virginia, 1996

King James Bible

La Guma, Alex: *A Walk in the Night*, Africasouth Paperbacks, 1991

Lelyveld, Joseph: *Move Your Shadow: South Africa Black and White*, Jonathan Ball, 1986

Lenin, V I: *What is to be Done*, International Publishers, New York, 2005

Lewis, G: *Between the Wire and the Wall: A History of South African 'Coloured' Politics*, David Philip, Cape Town, 1987

Lodge, Tom: *Politics in South Africa: From Mandela to Mbeki*, David Philip, 2002

Malcolm, Janet: *Two Lives: Gertrude and Alice*, Yale University Press, 2007

Mandela, Nelson: *Long Walk to Freedom*, MacDonald Purnell, 1994

Manuel, Trevor: 'Is there a future for the National Economic Forum?' *in* Patel, E (ed.), *Engine of Development: South Africa's National Economic Forum*, Juta, 1993

Minter, William: 'An Unfinished Journey', *in* Minter, William, Hovey, Gail & Cobb, Charles jr, *No Easy Victories: African Liberation and American Activists over a Half Century, 1950-2000*, Africa World Press Inc, 2008

Mountain, Alan: *An Unsung Heritage: Perspectives on Slavery*, David Philip, Cape Town, 2004

O'Malley, Padraig: *Shades of Difference: Mac Maharaj and the Struggle for South Africa*, Viking, 2007

Patel, Ebrahim: 'New Institutions of Decision Making', in Patel, E (ed.), *Engine of Development: South Africa's National Economic Forum*, Juta, 1993

Pinnock, D: 'Ideology and Urban Planning: Blueprints of a garrison city', in James, Wilmot G & Simons, Mary (eds), *Class, Caste and Colour: A Social and Economic History of the South African Western Cape*, Transaction Publishers, New Brunswick and London, 1992

'Rex Trueform, Clothing Company Limited', in Shorten, P: *Golden Jubilee Cape Town*, 1963

Rassool, Ciraj & Proselandis, Sandra (eds): *Recalling Community in Cape Town: Creating and Curating the District Six Museum*, District Six Museum Foundation, 2001

Roberts, Ronald Suresh: *Fit to Govern: the Native Intelligence of Thabo Mbeki*, STE Publishers, 2007

Sampson, A: *Mandela: The Authorized Biography*, Harper Collins, 1999

Seekings, Jeremy: *The UDF: A History of the United Democratic Front in South Africa, 1983-1991*, David Philip, Cape Town, 2000

Seekings, J & Natrass, N: *Class, Race and Inequality in South Africa*, University of KZN Press, 2006

Shell, Robert: 'The Family and Slavery in the Cape, 1680-1808', in James, Wilmot G & Simons, Mary (eds), *Class, Caste and Colour: A Social and Economic History of the South African Western Cape*, Transaction Publishers, New Brunswick and London, 1992

Sethi, S Prakash & Williams, Oliver F: *Economic Imperatives and Ethical Values in Global Business*, Kluwer Academic Publishers, 2000

Slabbert, F Van Zyl: *The Other Side of History*, Jonathan Ball, 2006

Sparks, Allister: *Tomorrow is Another Country: The Inside Story of South Africa's Negotiated Revolution*, Struik Book Distributors, 1994

Swanson, F & Harries J: ' "Ja! So was District Six! But it was a beautiful place": Oral Histories, Memory and Identity', in Field, S (ed.), *Lost Communities, Living Memories: Remembering Forced Removals in Cape Town*, David Philip, Cape Town, 2001

Switzer, Les & Adhikari, Mohamed (eds): *South Africa's Resistance Press*, Ohio University Center for International Studies, 2000

Todes, A, Watson, V & Wilkinson, P: 'Local Government Restructuring in Greater Cape Town', in James, Wilmot G & Simons, Mary (eds), *Class, Caste and Colour: A Social and Economic History of the South African Western Cape*, Transaction Publishers, New Brunswick and London, 1992

Tressell, Robert: *The Ragged Trousered Philanthropists*, Flamingo Modern Classics, 1914

Unity Movement, Anniversary Bulletin: *50th Year of Struggle*, 1994

Van Heyningen, Elizabeth (ed): *Studies in the History of Cape Town*, volume 7, Cape Town History Project, University of Cape Town, 1994

Waldmeir, Patti: *The Anatomy of a Miracle: The end of apartheid and the birth of a new South Africa*, Viking, 1997

Walker, Michael: *Kalk Bay: A Place of Character*, self-published, 2002

Weider, Alan: *Voices from Cape Town Classrooms: Oral Histories of Teachers who Fought*

Apartheid, Peter Lang Publishing Inc, New York, 2003

West, Martin: 'Confusing Categories: Population groups, national states and citizenships', *in* Boonzaier, E & Sharp, J (eds), *South African Keywords: The Uses and Abuses of Political Concepts*, David Philip, Cape Town, 1988, p102

Worden, N: 'Adjusting to Emancipation: Freed slaves and farmers in mid-nineteenth century South Western Cape', *in* James, Wilmot G & Simons, Mary (eds), *Class, Caste and Colour: A Social and Economic History of the South African Western Cape*, Transaction Publishers, New Brunswick and London, 1992

World Bank: *The East Asian Miracle: Economic Growth and Public Policy*, Oxford University Press, 1993

Journals

Adhikari, Mohamed: 'Fiercely Non-Racial? Discourses and Politics of Race in the Non-European Unity Movement, 1943-70', *Journal of Southern African Studies*, vol.31, no.2, 403-18, 2005

Adhikari, Mohamed: ' "The Sons of Ham". Slavery and the Making of Coloured Identity', South African Historial Journal, vol. 27, pp95-112, November 1992

Bickford-Smith, Vivian: 'South African Urban History, Racial Segregation and the Unique Case of Cape Town', *Journal of Southern African Studies*, vol.21, no.1, 63-78, 1995

Field, Sean: 'Interpreting Memory: Life Stories from Windermere', *African Studies*, vol.60, no.1, 119-33, 2001

Lodge, T : 'The politics of refusal', *Leadership*, vol 5, no.1, 1986

Lodge, T: 'The Cape Town Troubles', *Journal of Southern African Studies*, vol.4, no.2, 216-39, 1978

Maseko, Sipho S: 'Civic Movement and Non-Violent Action: The Cape Areas Housing Action Committee', *African Affairs* , vol.96, no.384, 353-69, 1997

Nasson, Bill: 'The Unity Movement: Its Legacy in Historical Consciousness', *Radical History Review* vol.46, no.7, 189-211, 1990

Suttner, Raymond: 'The UDF Period and its Meaning for Contemporary South Africa', *Journal of African Studies*, vol.30, no.3, 691-701, 2004

Selected index

envoy (development financing) (2008) 517; becomes acting general secretary of national UDF 211-2; becomes full-time activist (1981) 151; birth of first son Govan 253; birth of second son Pallo 279; birth of third son Jaimé 360; elected chair, IMF development committee 515,517; elected general secretary, CAHAC 156; elected joint general secretary, Western Cape UDF 193; elected publicity secretary, Western Cape ANC (1991) 330; elected to ANC National Executive Committee 330; elected to ANC National Working Committee 331; elected to Pentech SRC 114; introduced Medium Term Expenditure Framework 492; joined Murray & Stewart 68; joint chair, G20 (2007) 515; meets Reg September in Botswana 129; offered Finance Ministry 423; reappointed minister of finance 560; relationship with Taufie Bardien 89-91; relationship with trade unions 364-5; released from Victor Verster prison (1988) 273; resigns as minister of finance 559;speech, St George's Cathedral 292

Maphai, Vincent 365

Marais, J S 19

Marais, Peter 209-11

Marawu, Sikolakhe 109

Marcus, Gill 379,421-2,425,439,440,441,442, 455,456,479-82,491,492,499,500,506,507,519

Marcus, Molly 421

Marcus, Nathan 421

Marrakech Agreement 405

Masekela, Barbara 301

Masondo, Amos 180

Mass Democratic Movement 283

Matlare, Peter 395-7

Matthews, Lynne 114-5,116,130,159,168,169, 184,194,217,224,225,233,243,245,250,253, 254,269-70,279,280,295,394,494,497

Mazwembe, Storey, 110,111,112,142

Mbeki, Govan 300

Mbeki, Moeletsi 332,339,351,363,441,541-2

Mbeki, Thabo 238,282,301,304,327,328,329, 333,341,357-8,359,369,372,392,393,417,419, 423,424,427,434,436,438,439,440,443,444, 445,454,455,471,475,476,489,523-4,527,528, 538,544,545,547,548,558,559,561

Mboweni, Tito 334-5,336,341,345-6,350,353, 354-5,361,364,365,368,372,377,392-3,395, 417,420,436,439,440-1,446,457,463,499,500, 506

McMenamin, Viv 334

Mdluli, Joseph 141-2

Meat workers' strike 152-5,307

Meer, Fatima 190

Meer, Ismail 190

Mehlomakulu, Zora 109-10,112,155

Messenheimer, Leonard 413

Meyer, Peter 64

Meyer, Roelf 394

Mhlauli, Sicelo 220

Michell, Murray 135-7,174,214,249,303,323-4

Miranda, Michael 229

Mitterand, Francois 417

Mji, Diliza 304

Mkalipi, Kwedi 184

Mkanda, Gibson 327

Mkapa, Benjamin 516

Mkhonto, Sparrow 220

Mlambo-Ngcuka, Phumzile 295

Modise, Joe 319,333,472-3,475,476,477,479

Mohamed, Ebi 223,255,259,273,279,295,326

Mohammed, Sheik Nazeem 299

Mohapi, Mapetla 142

Mokaba, Peter 285

Molefe, Brian 464,529,530

Molefe, Popo 197,207,211,215,217,218,219,248

Moleketi, Jabu 457,524

Molobi, Eric 180

Molteno, Donald 12

Momoniat, Ismail 169,180,283,335,353-4,490, 524,550

Monterrey Consensus 516

Mont Fleur Scenarios 365-8,380

Moodley, Reg 533-5

Moosa, Essa 223,245

Moosa, Valli 169,180,221,280,283,312,338

Morgenthau, Henry 509

Morobe, Murphy 180,217,221,280,304-5,310, 338-9

Morris, Mike 190,191

Mosala, Itumeleng 306

Mososoli, Tsili 294,295

Moss, Maxwell 206-7,264-5,266,268,271,272, 326,390

Motlanthe, Kgalema 559,560

Motor Industries Development Programme 407

Mpetha, Oscar 121,122,125,168-9,171,193, 197,199,218

Mpukumpa, Johnson 191

Mtombothi, Barney 559

Mufamadi, Sydney 283

Mugabe, Robert 319-20

Murray, Hugh 282

Mxenge, Griffiths 196,221

Mxenge, Victoria 196,221,222

Mzimela, Sipho 35,358,395

Rustomjee, Zavareh 398,399,400,403,404,409, 411
Rutgers, Leslie 98,99
Ryklief, Zainab 228,229

Sachs, Solly 6-7
SACTU. *See* South African Congress of Trade Unions
Salojee, Cassiem 197
Sampson, Anthony 320
Sands, Bobby 279,294
Schoon, Marius 139
Schroll, George 356
Seale, Ernest 29
Seale, Hester (née Manuel) 9,26,27,28,29,30, 39,43,46
Seekings, Jeremy 165,306
September, Dulcie 301
September, Reg 24-25,28,40,76-7,80-1,84,88,90, 91,93,129,130,131,132-3,136,331
Seria, Rashid 148,149
Shabalala, Mbuso, 324,325
Shade, Chris 468
Shaik, Chippy 476,479
Shaik, Mo 324,476,546-7
Shaik, Shabir, 324,476,546
Shilowa, Mbhazima 404,446,454,457
Shub, Bernard 6
Sibaca, General 239
Sibiya, Phineas 238
Sidina, Wilson 110,135
Simmers, Veronica 166,167
Simons, Jack 34,340
Sims, Ian 299
Sisulu, Albertina 169,170,197,199,217,291,335-6
Sisulu, Max 335-6,338,342
Sisulu, Walter 132,189,190,204,306,336,356
Sisulu, Zwelakhe 149
Skweyiya, Zola 392
Slabbert, Frederik Van Zyl 282,300,342
Slovo, Joe 319,322,323,327,328,339-40,451
Small Business Development Corporation 402-3
Smit, Basie 295
Smith, Ashford 397
Smith, Patti 398
Smuts, Jan 31,43,44
Sobukwe, Robert 85
Solomon, Marcus 134,150,151
Solomon, Theresa 134,210,278
Sonn, Franklin 275,287,309,388,430
Sonn, Percy 194
Sonto, Roseberry 267
South Africa Foundation 434

South African Allied Workers' Union 187
South African Coloured People's Congress 51,80,84,85
South African Communist Party 80
South African Congress of Trade Unions 121
South African Council of Churches 178
South African Indian Council 168
South African National Native Congress. *See* African National Congress
South African Students' Organisation 189
Soweto uprising (16 June 1976) 105
Spence, Michael 493
Spicer, Michael 401
Stals, Chris 355,463,466,499
Stansfield, Colin 145-7
Statistics SA 490. *See also* Central Statistics Service
Stern Nicholas 493,510,514,515,518,520
Stott, Eulalie 156,195
Strijdom, J G 38
Sullivan Principles 356-7
Suzman, Helen 88
Swartz, Derek 221-2
Swartz, Tom 51,55

Tabata, I B 76
Tahane, Tim 355
Tambo, Oliver 183,215,282,284,305,320-1,323, 330
Teachers and Educational Professional Association 51
Teachers' League of South Africa 51,61,63,65,69,74,77-9
Thatcher, Margaret 213,242,291,298,304
Theron Commission, 60
Theron, Jan 120-3,126,127,134,140,170,171,187, 188
Theron, M E 120
Thornton, Amy 277
Tinto, Christmas 135,166,184,255,261,261,265, 266,286,287
'Tips for Trevor' 397,522-3,549-50
Tobin, John 73,74
Tom, Godfrey 258,259
Trade Union Council of South Africa 109,121
Train Apartheid Resistance Committee 79
Transvaal Indian Congress 80,175,180
'Trojan horse' incident 228-30
Truter, Christopher 106
Truth and Reconciliation Commission 281
Tshwete, Steve 203,222,386
Tungcheun, Beryl (née Manuel) 4,14,29,53, 62,67,225,253-4
Tungcheun, Roy 253
Turok, Ben 511

Tutu, Desmond 178,185,216,221,278-9,285-6, 290-1,294,296-8,299-300,310,311,478
Tutu, Leah 296

Umbrella Rentals Committee 156
Umkhonto we Sizwe 131,183,249,472
Umsombomvu 484
Union of Black Journalists 148
United Democratic Front: 54,181; meeting with Eminent Persons Group 243; national launch 195-201
United Women's Organisation 134
Unity Movement 81,84,90,99,128,169,171-2
Uys, Pieter-Dirk 18

Van der Heyden, Elizabeth 151
Van der Merwe, Johan 295
Van der Merwe, Sue 365
Van der Ross, Richard 51
Van der Walt, Ronnie 39
Van Eck, Jan 229
Van Heerden, Trevor 479,480
Vavi, Zwelinzima 446,447-9,451,455,519,520, 544,545
Verwoerd, H F 38
Viljoen, Gerrit 299
Viljoen, Shaun 63,65,66,69,70,95,106,107,108, 114
Villa-Vicencio, Charles 297
Vlok, Adriaan 278-9,294,295,298,300
Von Söhnen, Anne 4-5,15,30,33-4,35,49,50
Von Söhnen, Dawn 31,32,119
Von Söhnen, Leonard 31,32,33,48,119,329
Von Söhnen, Maximillian 5,30,31-2,33,329
Von Söhnen, Paulina (née Daniels) 30-31
Vorster, B J 86
Vosloo, Ton 282

Waldmeir, Patti 299
Waterwitch, Robbie 249,285
Watson, Vanessa 312
Western Cape Garment Workers' Union 7
Wiehahn Commission 127,152,186
Wiese, Christo 506
Wilcox Commission 76
Willemse, Johan 309
Williams, Brian 52,53,70,98,99,100,101,114,118
Williams, Coline 249,285
Williams, Daphne. See King, Daphne
Williams, Davie 99,100
Williams, Moegsien 148,149
Williams, Noel 243,245,267,268
Williams, Oliver 356-60,399
Williamson, Craig 111,343,421-2
Witdoeke 241-2
Wolfowitz, Paul 518
Woods, Gavin 478
Workers' Advice Bureau 110-11,112
World Alliance of Reformed Churches 178
World Economic Forum 345-6,354
Wort, Logan 210,254,255,263,265-6

Xulu, Maxwell, 239
Xuma A B 79

Yacoob, Zac 169
Yengeni, Tony 330,451,472
Young Christian Workers 70,94,109

Zabow, Dr T 276
Zenawi, Meles 514
Ziqu, Sylvia 533-6
Zuma, Jacob 163,327,329,471,472,476,478,544, 545-6,547-8,558,559,560,561

602